People of the Earth

• • •

Carolina Algonquin Indians around a fire, painted by English artist John White in the late sixteenth century. His colleague Thomas Hariot wrote of these people: "They are verye sober in their eating and trinkinge, and consequently verye longe lived because they doe not oppress nature. . . . I would to God we would followe their exemple."

◆ ◆ ◆

PEOPLE OF THE EARTH

An Introduction to World Prehistory

Eighth Edition

BRIAN M. FAGAN

University of California, Santa Barbara

HarperCollins*CollegePublishers*

Acquisitions Editor: Alan McClare
Developmental Editor: Robert Westbook
Project Editor: Thomas R. Farrell
Text Designer and Art Manager: Alice Fernandes-Brown
Cover Designer: Kay Petronio
Art Studio: Academy ArtWorks, Inc.
Table Design and Layout: Paul Lacy
Photo Researcher: Mira Schachne
Electronic Production Manager: Angel Gonzalez Jr.
Desktop Administrator: LaToya Wigfall
Manufacturing Administrator: Alexandra Odulak
Electronic Page Makeup: RR Donnelley Barbados
Printer and Binder: RR Donnelley & Sons Company
Cover Printer: Coral Graphics Services, Inc.

Cover photograph by Christopher Donnan and Donald McClelland. Fowler Museum of Cultural History, UCLA / Museo Nacional Bruning de Lambayeque, Péru.

People of the Earth, Eighth Edition

Library of Congress Cataloging-in-Publication Data
Fagan, Brian M.
    People of the earth : an introduction to world prehistory / Brian
M. Fagan. — 8th ed.
        p.   cm.
    Includes bibliographical references and index.
    ISBN 0-673-52394-2
    1. Man, Prehistoric.   2. Civilization, Ancient.   I. Title.
GN740.F3   1995
930—dc20   94-8780
                                                                CIP

94 95 96 97   9 8 7 6 5 4 3 2 1

To all the dozens of archaeologists and students who have read and used this book in its various editions and sent me their comments and criticisms. This is the only way I can thank them all and expose them for what they are—honest and unmerciful critics. I am deeply grateful.

And as usual to our cats, who disapprove of authors in general and my writing efforts in particular. Their contribution was to tread on the manuscript—with muddy paws, of course.

Brief Contents

• • •

• PART V OLD WORLD CIVILIZATIONS 341
(c. 3000 b.c. TO MODERN TIMES)

• PART VI STATE-ORGANIZED SOCIETIES IN THE AMERICAS 477
(2000 b.c. TO a.d. 1532)

DETAILED CONTENTS

• • •

PART II   THE FIRST HUMANS   37
(c. 4 MILLION TO 40,000 YEARS AGO)

PART VI STATE-ORGANIZED SOCIETIES IN THE AMERICAS   477

(2000 B.C. TO A.D. 1532)

PREFACE

. . .

People of the Earth is an attempt at a straightforward narrative of human history from the origins of humankind to the beginnings of literate civilization. To make the book accessible to those who have not previously studied archaeology, I keep technical terms to a minimum and define them where they do occur.

World prehistory is an enormous subject, so, inevitably, I have had to gloss over many heated academic controversies and sometimes to give only one side of an academic argument. But the Bibliography of World Prehistory at the back of the book is designed to lead you into the more technical literature and the morass of agreement and disagreement that characterizes the subject. Much of what we know about prehistoric times is still based on very inadequate data. The important thing about archaeology, as with any other science, is that it deals not with absolute truth but with successive approximations of the truth.

The structure of *People of the Earth* is comparatively straightforward. Part I consists of one chapter, which covers the general principles of archaeology and some of the ways in which archaeologists try to explain the past. The remainder of the book is devoted to the story of human prehistory. Chronological tables appear at the beginning of most chapters, while the table on the front endpaper acts as a guide to the major developments of prehistoric times cross-referenced to individual chapters of the book. Key dates and terms appear in the margins to give you a sense of chronological directions throughout the text.

This is the eighth edition of a book first published in 1975. The intervening years have seen momentous changes in our understanding of world prehistory, reflected in major changes in each edition. This one is no exception. At a detailed level, I have rewritten, updated, expanded, and culled to reflect recent advances in our knowledge and new theoretical approaches. At the request of many users, Part I has been cut back to a single chapter, which focuses on the absolute basics of method and theory for the purposes of understanding the narrative in later chapters. The African sections of the text have been completely rewritten, I have incorporated new advances resulting from the accelerating decipherment of Maya glyphs, and I have revised several controversial sections, including that on the first Americans. The chronological tables have been changed completely throughout, and the illustrations have been expanded and improved. The past five years have been ones of unspectacular consolidation rather than dramatic new insights, and this edition reflects numerous minor changes in the narrative rather than complete revisions. To some degree, this is a reflection of a science that is becoming ever more specialized, one that generates important discoveries as much in the laboratory as on-site.

I hope that you enjoy your adventures in archaeology.

ACKNOWLEDGMENTS

Edition eight has benefitted greatly from the willing comments of many colleagues, especially Gina Barnes, Robert Foley, David Freidel, Patrick Kirch, and Chris Scarre.

I would like to thank the following archaeologists for their help in revising the eighth edition of *People of the Earth*. I appreciate their frank comments.

Marc Bermann, University of Pittsburgh
Jim Boylan, Montclair State College
Barbara Hall, Riverside Community College
Julia A. King, St. Mary's College
Edward M. Luby, San Francisco State University
Charles H. McNutt, Memphis State University
Sue Moore, Georgia Southern University
Donald A. Proulx, University of Massachusetts at Amherst
Barbara Thiel, Northern Kentucky University
Richard W. Yerkes, The Ohio State University

Lastly, my thanks to Alan McClare, Mira Schachne, Rob Westbrook, Tom Farrell, and all the editorial and production staff at HarperCollins. Without them, this book would never have seen the light of day, and I would have even more gray hairs.

BRIAN M. FAGAN

MEASUREMENTS NOTE

All measurements are given in feet and inches, with metric equivalents. Dates cited in the text before 40,000 years ago are normally given in years before present (B.P.), while later readings are in B.C./A.D. format, as this seems to reflect current usage. "Present" by scientific convention is A.D. 1950. When using radiocarbon chronologies, it should be noted that each date carries a statistical error (see Chapter 1), which is omitted in the text for clarity. For calibration of radiocarbon dates, see *Radiocarbon,* 1993.

PEOPLE OF THE EARTH

• • •

PREHISTORY

Thus the sum of things is ever being renewed, and mortals live dependent one upon another. Some races increase, others diminish, and in a short space, the generations of living creatures are changed and like runners hand on the torch of life.

LUCRETIUS, *DE RERUM NATURA*, II (FIRST CENTURY B.C.)

art I contains the essential background about the study of archaeology needed for any examination of human prehistory. We present some of the high points and basic principles behind archaeologists' excavations and laboratory research. My narrative is, in the final analysis, based on the systematic application of these principles.

C H A P T E R # ARCHAEOLOGY

• • •

INTRODUCTION

• • •

The two men paused in front of the doorway bearing the seals of the long-dead pharaoh. They had waited six long years, from 1917 to 1922, for this moment. Silently, Howard Carter pried a hole through the ancient plaster. Hot air rushed out of the small cavity and massaged his face. Carter shone a flashlight through the hole and peered into the tomb. Gold objects swam in front of his eyes, and he was struck dumb with amazement.

Lord Carnarvon moved impatiently behind him as Carter remained silent.

"What do you see?" he asked, hoarse with excitement.

"Wonderful things," whispered Carter as he stepped back from the doorway.

The door was soon broken down. In a daze of wonderment, the discoverers wandered through the antechamber of Tutankhamun's tomb. They fingered golden funerary beds, admired beautifully inlaid chests, and examined the pharaoh's chariots stacked against the wall. Gold was everywhere—on wooden statues, inlaid on thrones and boxes, in jewelry, even on children's stools. Soon Tutankhamun was known as the golden pharaoh, and archaeology as the domain of buried treasure and royal sepulchers (Figure 1.1).

Gold, silver, lost civilizations, unsolved mysteries, grinning skeletons . . . all are part of the romantic world of archaeology in most people's minds. Archaeologists seem like adventurers, digging into pyramids and finding long-forgotten inscriptions in remote places. Like Indiana Jones of movie fame, we seem to be students of sunken continents and great migrations, experts on epic journeys and powerful civilizations. A century ago, many archaeologists were indeed adventurers. Today, however, archaeology has become a complex and demanding scientific pastime that studies over 2.5 million years of human existence. The fascination of great adventure has been replaced by all the excitement of the detective story. Fictional detectives take a handful of clues and solve apparently insoluble murders. Archaeologists take a multitude of small and apparently trivial archaeological finds and use them to answer basic questions about past human behavior.

Even as late as the 1870s, you could go out digging in the Near East and find a long-lost civilization. German businessman-turned-archaeologist Heinrich Schlie-

FIGURE 1.1 Howard Carter and his fellow excavators peer with bright lights into the inner shrines of pharaoh Tutankhamun's tomb.

mann was convinced that Homer's Troy had actually existed. Armed with a copy of the *Iliad*, he went to Turkey and cut great trenches into the ancient mounds at Hissarlik. Schliemann found the remains of nine cities stratified one above the other and announced that the seventh was Homer's Troy (Ceram, 1953; Fagan, 1985). His discoveries caused an international sensation. So did Frenchman Emil de Sarzec when he unearthed Sumer in desolate southern Mesopotamia, a civilization that soon turned out to be one of the earliest in the world and the society where the Flood legend in Genesis probably originated (Fagan, 1979) (Figure 1.2).

The twentieth century has seen archaeology turn from a casual treasure hunt into a science. There have been dramatic discoveries by the dozens—Tutankhamun's tomb in 1922; the royal cemetery at Ur in Iraq in 1928; the spectacular early human fossils discovered by the Leakey family in East Africa during the last quarter century; and in the 1980s, magnificent royal burials in China, Guatemala, and Peru. Although these finds have stirred the popular imagination, archaeologists have been engaged in a less conspicuous but just as fascinating adventure of discovery—through 2.5 million years of prehistoric time.

Right. An epigrapher studies the cuneiform script on a clay tablet from the archives at Tell Mardik, Syria.

Below. Excavations on the earliest European settlement at St. Mary's, Maryland. This type of horizontal excavation exposes features like buildings, wells, and storage pits.

Bottom left. An exemplary excavation of an eighteenth-century kitchen at Colonial Williamsburg, Virginia. Large tree roots had damaged the north foundation. Behind it lies the H-shaped foundation for the chimney.

Bottom right. Recording details of an archaeological excavation. The overhead lights are for photography. All archaeological excavation depends on precise recording of the context of features and artifacts found in the trenches of the dig.

Above. A student archaeologist doing laboratory work; she is sorting through midden debris for small bones and artifacts.
Upper right. A technician working in a radiocarbon laboratory; he is dating archaeological samples from 500 to 50,000 years old.
Below. Excavation in progress on an early Kodiak Eskimo settlement at Karluk, Alaska.
Lower right. Field crew at work measuring a prehistoric Easter Island statue for the Rock Art Archive of the Institute of Archaeology, Los Angeles, California.

FIGURE 1.2   The famous "Flood Tablet" from Assyrian King Assurbanipal's library at Nineveh. The tablet, found by epigrapher George Smith in 1873, records the story of a flood that bears a remarkable resemblance to that described in Genesis. This was a copy of a much earlier Sumerian legend, that dates to much earlier than the writing down of the Old Testament.

People of the Earth takes you on a journey through prehistory, from the very earliest times to the appearance of the first urban civilizations. However, we begin by explaining some of the basic principles, methods, and theories of archaeology.

WHY STUDY WORLD PREHISTORY?

• • •

Why study world prehistory at all? Some people believe that any form of archaeology is a harmless luxury, a low priority in a world beset by inflation, famine, and geopolitics. Why look to the past, they ask, when all our energies should be devoted to preparing for an uncertain future? How can one look at the future, though, without an understanding of the past and, above all, of our own behavior? Whether we like it or not, we live with the legacy of the recent and remote past. Our civilization derives many of its most cherished institutions from classical Greece, whereas city life developed between the Euphrates and Tigris rivers in Iraq before 3000 B.C. Famine, slavery, warfare, and poverty are nothing new; they were familiar phenomena to the ancient Egyptians, the Chinese, and the Sumerians. In reality, we live with the consequences of decisions and actions that were enacted centuries or even millennia ago. The study of prehistory gives us a balanced perspective on our behavior and on our responses to pressing problems that are not new, even though they threaten us on a larger scale.

Western civilization has a written chronicle that extends back to Sumerian times, to about 3000 B.C. However, many of the world's societies have very limited written historical records and are known to us only through scattered folk memories or archaeological excavations. The Aztec people of Mexico first came into contact with the Spanish in 1519. Within a few years their civilization was in ruins, their written chronicles burned by zealous missionaries. As a result, our knowledge of Aztec history is a patchwork of incomplete data from dozens of sources, yet a knowledge of this history is vital not only for fostering a sense of identity among the surviving Aztec people and for nation building in Mexico but also for understanding the ways in which ancient Mesoamericans solved the problems of living (Schele and Friedel, 1990). It is no coincidence that many African nations have active archaeological programs, designed to reconstruct a national history from a morass of obscure tribal histories and excavations at archaeological sites. Likewise, some American Indian groups have become involved in archaeological research, in a search for their remote cultural roots (Kirk, 1975). In prehistoric times, most societies focused on living in equilibrium with their environment, existing in a world that was assumed to have been the same in the past and that would remain unchanged in the future. Today industrial civilization, with its concern with cultural roots and cultural identity, dominates the world, so there are compelling reasons for every society to have at least some sense of its cultural origins. In many cases, archaeology provides the only way of gaining this insight.

We live in a biologically and culturally diverse world, a world that is shrinking rapidly in this age of the jetliner, the satellite, and instant communications. Even half a century ago the world was a large place. Today the world, in all its bewildering diversity, comes right into our living rooms. We can contact Peru within seconds and watch wars on the other side of the globe as they are being fought. Confronting this diversity is often an uncomfortable experience, especially since we tend to perceive the differences between various societies as much greater than they really are. By looking back over the long millennia of prehistory, we obtain a quite different perspective of a world in which people have worked out solutions to extremely challenging problems with brilliant success, problems such as food shortages, rapidly growing populations, and catastrophic environmental changes. Very often the solutions of various societies, although they are separated by thousands of miles, have been remarkably similar: the advent of writing, the development of cities, or the formation of a state-organized society. What is striking is not the diversity of humankind but the remarkably similar ways in which we respond to external challenges. Societies may wax and wane, civilizations rise and fall, but something new always arises in their place. To look back at prehistory is to acquire a faith in humanity's ability to innovate and respond to changing circumstances. We are surrounded by doomsday prophets, by people who forecast the imminent demise of civilization, of humanity itself. Any serious student of prehistory can have no doubt that humankind will rise to the challenges of the twentieth century. We shall survive.

The study of world prehistory gives us an objective assessment of the human past, of awesome ruins, which have survived the centuries and millennia to enlighten our age: Monk's Mound at Cahokia, Illinois, planned and constructed by Mississippian people by A.D. 1100; the magnificent pueblos of the Southwest; and the brooding stone circles of Stonehenge in southern Britain, to say nothing of the Pyramids of

Giza, erected in about 2500 B.C., and the vast plazas and temples of the ancient city of Teotihuacán, Mexico. Sometimes, by learning about these societies, we can adopt their innovations for the modern world, like the long forgotten raised field agriculture developed by the people of ancient Tiwanaku by Lake Titicaca now feeding thousands of Bolivian and Peruvian farmers (Chapter 22).

ANTHROPOLOGY AND ARCHAEOLOGY

● ● ●

Anthropology, the study of humanity, encompasses the whole range of human cultures, both Western and non-Western (M. Harris, 1968). As the study of humanity, anthropology is a holistic discipline that uses comparative methods to examine variations in every aspect of human society. Anthropologists are interested in comparisons between different cultures and in biological and cultural evolution. The comparative and evolutionary aspects of anthropology make it unique among the social sciences. While *cultural anthropologists* study living societies, *biological, or physical, anthropologists* study the emergence and subsequent evolution of humankind and why human populations vary from one another (Weiss and Mann, 1988). Early human evolution is documented by fossil human and prehuman remains found in archaeological sites and geological levels. Physical anthropologists are also deeply involved in modern human biology, trying to find out why different human populations have adapted physically to widely differing natural environments.

Archaeology as part of Anthropology is the study of the lives and cultures of ancient peoples. Archaeologists study and interpret the material evidence of past human activity. Archaeology has three main objectives: the study of culture history, the reconstruction of past lifeways, and the explaining of cultural process (for definitions, see below). There are many types of archaeologists, each having distinctive objectives, methods, techniques, and theoretical approaches. *Classical archaeologists* study Greek and Roman civilization; *historical archaeologists* study relatively recent sites such as colonial American towns or medieval cities. *Anthropological archaeologists (prehistorians)* are concerned with sites of all ages, but they tend to concentrate their research efforts primarily on prehistoric settlements. *Paleoanthropologists* study the earliest human cultures of all.

History is the study of our past through written records; such records extend back only 5000 years, and then only in Mesopotamia and Egypt. *Prehistory,* the millennia before documentary history, goes back at least 2.5 million years.

HUMAN CULTURE

● ● ●

Culture is a term we will use again and again in these pages. Anthropologists study human cultures, and all of us live within a culture. Most cultural descriptions can be qualified by one or more labels, such as *middle class, American, mountain-dwelling,* or *Masai.* This qualification often becomes associated in our minds with certain behavior patterns or features that are typical of the culture so labeled. One such attribute for "middle-class Americans," for example, might be the hamburger.

Culture is a concept developed by anthropologists to describe the distinctive adaptive system used by human beings (Jochim, 1981). Culture can be called a society's traditional systems of belief and behavior, as understood (or adapted) by individuals and the members of social groups, and manifest in individual or collective behavior. It is also part of our way of adapting to our environment. Our tools and dwellings are also part of our culture. Humans are the only animals to manufacture tools for this purpose.

Ordinarily, when animals die their experience dies with them. However, humans, once biological evolution had led to the development of speech, were able to communicate their feelings and experiences from one generation to the next. Human beings use the symbolic system of language to transmit ideas and their culture. Culture is learned by intentional teaching as well as trial and error and simple imitation. People could share ideas, which in turn became behavior patterns that were repeated again and again. We see abundant evidence of this development throughout prehistory when the same types of tools and sites are found, almost unchanged, over millennia. A good example of this continuity is the stone hand ax, a multipurpose tool that remained in use for more than 1 million years. Culture is an ongoing phenomenon that changes gradually over time.

Unlike biological adaptation, culture is nongenetic and provides a much quicker way to share ideas that enable people to cope with their environment. It is the adaptive nature of culture that allows archaeologists to assume that artifacts found in archaeological sites are patterned adaptations to the environment.

A culture is a complex system (called a *cultural system*), a set of interacting variables—tools, burial customs, ways of getting food, religious beliefs, social organization, and so on—that function to maintain a community in a state of equilibrium with its environment. When one element in the system changes, say hunting practices as a result of a prolonged drought, then reacting adjustments will occur in many other elements, so that the system stays in a state as closely approximating the original system as possible. It follows that no cultural system is ever static. It is always changing in big and small ways, some of which can be studied in archaeological sites.

Culture, then, can be viewed as either a blend of shared traits or a system that permits a society to interact with its environment. To accomplish more than merely working out chronological sequences, however, the archaeologist has to view culture as a complex set of interacting components. Unless the processes that actually operate the system are carefully defined, these components would remain static, which is why archaeologists are deeply concerned with what is called *cultural process,* the processes by which human societies changed in the past.

Cultural changes take place through time, most being gradual and cumulative. Inventions and design improvements result in dozens of minor alterations in the ways people live. Generally, cultural evolution was gradual in prehistoric times, although there are cases of sudden change, such as the Roman conquest of Gaul. Dramatic cultural modification can result from the diffusion from neighboring areas of a new idea or invention, such as the plow or maize agriculture.

The cumulative effects of long-term culture change are easily seen. A comparison of the simple flaked stone tools of the earliest humans and the sophisticated contents of the Egyptian pharaoh Tutankhamun's tomb will help one to understand the power of cumulative change over thousands of years.

Earlier archaeologists often were content to describe changing cultures but made no effort to explain *why* change took place and *what* changes meant. Today's archaeologist is concerned with explanation as well as description of ancient cultures, with processes of cultural change through time. The term *process* is used in archaeology to refer to mechanisms by which cultures change.

THE ARCHAEOLOGICAL RECORD

● ● ●

The *archaeological* record is the data amassed from survey and excavation: We might think of it as the archival raw materials of world prehistory. Archaeologists have to be content, for the most part, with the surviving, more durable evidence of prehistoric culture (Deetz, 1967; Fagan, 1994a). Any excavator is like a detective piecing together events from fragmentary clues.

What we can find out about the past is severely limited by soil conditions. Stone and baked clay are among the most lasting substances, surviving under almost all conditions. Wood, bone, leather, and metals are much less durable and seldom remain for the archaeologist to find. In the Arctic, however, whole sites have been found frozen, preserving highly perishable wooden tools or, in Siberia, complete carcasses of extinct mammoths (J. D. G. Clark, 1965). Water-logged bogs in Denmark have preserved long-dead victims of human sacrifice, and wooden tools survive well in such sites too. Everyone has heard of the remarkable tomb of the Egyptian pharaoh Tutankhamun, whose astonishing treasure survived almost intact in the dry climate of the Nile Valley for more than 3000 years (Reeves, 1990). Still, in most archaeological sites only a few durable materials survive, and reconstructing the past from these finds is often difficult.

Consider for a moment a newly abandoned hunter-gatherer campsite in the Illinois valley of the Midwest. The inhabitants leave collapsing houses, newly extinguished hearths, broken-up bones, acorn husks, and all manner of domestic debris as well as worn-out artifacts behind them. The years pass. Rain and wind destroy the houses, and they become a scatter of foundation stones and postholes. The acorn husks and bones decay and vanish. Soon the site is covered with dense woodland and grass, soils accumulate, and there are no surface traces of the site left. Once buried, the surviving structures, hearths, and artifacts undergo still further change as a result of processes resulting from the distinctive soil chemistry on the site. Hundreds, if not thousands, of years later some archaeologists come along and dig up the site. All that they will unearth are the surviving remnants of generations of decay processes. These processes vary from site to site and are little understood.

Archaeologists rely heavily not only on sites where preservation conditions are exceptional but also on the assistance of scholars from other disciplines. Botanists and zoologists can identify seeds and bone fragments from ancient living sites to reconstruct prehistoric diets. Geologists study lake beds, gravels, and caves, the geological contexts of the many tools from early millennia. Paleontologists and paleobotanists specialize in the evolution of mammals and plants, studying bones from extinct animals and pollens from long-vanished plants. They help reconstruct ancient climates, which have fluctuated greatly through our long history. Chemists and physicists employ radioactive methods of dating for volcanic rocks and organic substances such as bone and charcoal. Modern archaeology is truly a multidisciplinary team effort, depending on scientists from many fields of inquiry. In one afternoon, an excavator may call on a glass expert, an authority on seashells, an earthworm specialist, and a soil scientist. Each has a piece to fit into the archaeological puzzle.

The records of written history are preserved in manuscripts, in books, and on clay tablets or papyrus—archives of the past that can be photocopied, transcribed, and traced. The archives of world prehistory are the sites, artifacts, and other material remains of human behavior that make up the archaeological record. This record is finite, an intricate association of individual archaeological phenomena and geological or occupation layers, the context in time and space in which they occur. Every time someone picks up an artifact or excavates a site or constructs a highway through an ancient Indian village, the archives of the prehistoric past are destroyed, or at best modified. The archaeological record is quite different from a forest. Trees can regerminate; forests can be reseeded. But once disturbed, the archaeological record is gone forever. Prehistory is nonrenewable, which means all of us should treat the past with care and respect (Figure 1.3).

ARTIFACTS, SITES, AND CONTEXT

• • •

World prehistory is recorded in thousands of archaeological sites and artifacts, each of which has a precise context in space and time.

Archaeological context is the culturally significant location of a find spot of any object in an archaeological site (Fagan, 1994a). *Cultural context* is a subcategory that represents the position of an object; was it found in a pit, in a room, on a surface? Metric data are used to define the position of the object uniquely. The time component of the context is the date of the object in years or its position in the layers of an archaeological site relative to other artifacts and layers. The time and space context of an archaeological find provides the basis for building up long sequences of archaeological sites in time and space.

An *artifact* is anything which exhibits any physical attributes that can be assumed to be the results of human activity. The term *artifact* covers every form of

FIGURE 1.3   Destruction by pot hunters on a Native American site at Slack Farm, Kentucky, close to the Ohio River. A group of looters paid $10,000 for the right to "excavate" the site, which is of critical historical importance and dates to between A.D. 1450 and 1650, the time of first European contact. Two months passed before police stepped in, but all charges against the illegal excavators were dropped. The site looked like a battlefield, a morass of shovel holes and gaping trenches. Looting on the scale of Slack Farm is unfortunately commonplace in North America, from the Bering Strait to the Virgin Islands, meaning that there will be precious little archaeology for our grandchildren to study.

archaeological find—from stone axes to clay pots, butchered animal bones, and manifestations of human behavior found in archaeological sites.

Archaeological sites are places where traces of ancient human activity are to be found. The Great Pyramid of Giza is an archaeological site; so is a tiny scatter of hunter-gatherer artifacts found on the surface of the Utah desert. Sites are limited in number and variety only by preservation conditions, by modern destruction, and by the activities of the people who lived on them. Some, like the early bone caches at Olduvai Gorge, Tanzania, were used for only short periods of time (M. D. Leakey, 1971). Others, such as the great Mesopotamian city mounds or *tells,* like Ur, were occupied for thousands of years (Postgate, 1992). Archaeological sites are often classified according to the activities that took place on them—living sites, kill sites, burial sites, religious sites, art sites, and so on. Many archaeological sites contain evidence of different activities: those of individual households; of entire communities; or perhaps even of a single craftsperson like a potter, whose artifacts lie in a pattern as they were abandoned.

SPACE

●　●　●

The archaeological context of space can run from a simple spatial relationship between two artifacts to the distance between several households, or even to the relationships between an entire regional network of communities (Flannery, 1976). Context in space is closely tied to cultural behavior. Archaeologists infer behavior from artifacts and their associations, from the patterning (spatial arrangement) of tools around, say, an abandoned bison carcass. A single projectile point dug up out of context at this particular site would allow us nothing more than the reasonable inference that it was part of a weapon. However, the patterning of many such weapon points in association with the butchered remains of the bison can tell us much about how the animal was killed and cut up. The relationships between the carcass and the tools in the ground are our primary source of information on human behavior there.

The Law of Association is based on the principle that an object is contemporary with the other objects found in the precise archaeological level in which it is found (Figure 1.4). The study of space is the study of associations between artifacts within their archaeological cultures. It also involves the study of the distribution of human settlements against a background of the ancient environment in which they flourished.

TIME

●　●　●

Dating the 2.5 million years of prehistory—the context of time—has preoccupied archaeologists for more than a century.

Relative Chronology

At the end of the eighteenth century, people realized that the earth's rocks were stratified, or laid down in layers, one after another. The notion of geological stratification was soon applied to archaeological sites and is now a cornerstone of *relative*

(a)

(b)

(c)

(d)

FIGURE 1.4   The Law of Association. (a) A skeleton associated with a single dagger and level II; (b) a pot and a stone ax, separated by a stratigraphic break, not in association; (c) two contemporary household clusters associated with one another; (d) an association of two communities that are contemporary.

chronology, the correlation of prehistoric sites or cultures with one another by their relative age.

Stratification is based on the *Law of Superposition,* which says that the lowest occupation level on a site is older than those accumulated on top of it. Figure 1.5 illustrates the principle of superposition in archaeological practice.

Superpositions are established by careful excavation and observation of archaeological layers. These layers are excavated with great care, and the artifacts associated with them are carefully studied relative to the stratigraphy of the site. We have stated that artifact styles change slowly through time. Every artifact style, however elaborate or simple, has a period of maximum popularity. This can be a few short months in the case of a dress fashion or tens of thousands of years for a stone tool type. By careful study of artifacts such as pottery found in the successive layers of

FIGURE 1.5 Superposition and stratigraphy. (a) A farming village built on virgin sub-soil. After a time, the village is abandoned and the huts fall into disrepair. Their ruins are covered by accumulating soil and vegetation. (b) After an interval, a second village is built on the same site, with different architectural styles. This in turn is abandoned; the houses collapse into piles of rubble and are covered by accumulating soil. (c) Twentieth-century people park their cars on top of both village sites and drop litter and coins, which when uncovered reveal to the archaeologist that the top layer is modern.

An archaeologist digging this site would find that the modern layer is underlain by two prehistoric occupation levels; that square houses were in use in the upper of the two, which is the later (Law of Superposition); and that round huts are stratigraphically earlier than square ones here. Therefore, Village 1 is earlier than Village 2, but when either was occupied or how many years separate Village 1 from Village 2 cannot be known without further data.

several archaeological sites in a single region, it is possible to develop a relative chronology of changing artifact styles that is based on the assumption that the period of maximum popularity of a particular pottery type, or series, is the one in which it is most frequently found (Figure 1.6). By using these plots of artifact frequencies, we can develop a relative chronology that later can be used to place isolated sites into the sequence on the basis of their artifact content. This type of ordered or *seriated* relative chronology is not expressed in years unless it can be checked by some dating method that provides dates in years (Marquardt, 1978).

Chronometric (Absolute) Chronology

Chronometric dates are dates in calendar years. Prehistoric chronologies cover long periods of time, millennia or centuries as opposed to days or minutes. Some idea of the scale of prehistoric time can be gained by piling up 100 quarters. If the whole pile represents the entire time that humans and their culture have been on earth, the

FIGURE 1.6 Seriation. The changing styles of New England gravestones from Stoneham, Massachusetts, between 1720 and 1829, seriated in three different styles. Notice how each style rises to a peak of maximum popularity and then declines as another comes into fashion.

length of time covered by historical records would equal considerably less than the thickness of one quarter.

How do we date the past in years? Five major chronological methods date the two-and-a-half million years of prehistory (Table 1.1) (Michels, 1973; Aitken, 1990).

Historical Records (Present day to 3000 B.C.)

Historical records can be used to date the past only as far back as the beginnings of writing and written records. The Sumerian King Lists of Mesopotamia are some of the first attempts to record past events (Crawford, 1991). Many areas of the world, such as New Guinea or tropical Africa, entered the realms of recorded history only in the last century, and continual historical documentation began in the Americas with Christopher Columbus (Fagan, 1991).

TABLE 1.1
Dating methods commonly used in world prehistory.

DATE B.P.	METHOD	MAJOR EVENTS
Modern times (after A.D. 1)	Historical documents; dendrochronology; imported objects most useful	European settlement of New World; Roman Empire
4,500 B.P.		Origins of cities
		Origins of agriculture
	Radiocarbon dating (organic materials)	First Americans
70,000 B.P.		*Homo sapiens neanderthalensis*
		Homo sapiens sapiens
500,000 B.P.	Potassium argon dating (volcanic materials)	*Homo erectus*
		Homo
		Australopithecus
5,000,000 B.P.	Uranium series dating	

These conventions have been used in the tables throughout this book:

——— A continuous line means the chronology is firmly established.

——→ A line terminating in an arrow means the time span continues beond the arrow.

———⊣ A line terminating with a horizontal bar means the limit of chronology is firmly established.

- - - - - A broken line means the chronology is doubtful.

?Escale A question mark beside the name of a site means its date is not firmly established.

Dendrochronology

TIME SPAN: Present day to sites dating to 332 B.C. in the American Southwest, to earlier than 3000 B.C. in Europe.

PRINCIPLES: Many years ago Dr. A. E. Douglass of the University of Arizona used the annual growth rings of trees in the southwestern United States to develop a nonarchaeological chronology for this area that extends back 8200 years (Baillie, 1982). Douglass studied the sequoia and other slow-growing trees to develop a long master series of annual rings that he used to date fragments of wooden beams found in Indian pueblos. By analyzing cycles of rings from dry and wet series of years, he was able to set up an archaeological chronology for the Southwest that extends back to 322 B.C. Dendrochronology has been used in other areas of the world as well—in Alaska and the American Southeast and with great success in Greece, Ireland, and Germany. European experts have linked rings from living oak trees to prehistoric trunks found in bogs and archaeological sites. A tree-ring sequence in Germany goes back as far as 9494 B.C., the time when tree cover first spread across Europe at the end of the Ice Age.

APPLICATIONS: The chronology of Southwestern archaeology described in Chapter 14 is developed from dendrochronology. Tree-ring chronologies are used to calibrate radiocarbon dates from Europe as far back as 7500 B.C. and soon will extend as much as 2000 years earlier.

Radiocarbon Dating (C14)

TIME SPAN: Approximately 40,000 years ago to A.D. 1500.

PRINCIPLES: The radiocarbon (C14) dating method, developed by physicists J. R. Arnold and W. F. Libby in 1949, puts to use the knowledge that living organisms build up their own organic matter by photosynthesis and by using atmospheric carbon dioxide. The percentage of radiocarbon in the organism is equal to that in the atmosphere. When the organism dies, the carbon 14 (C14) atoms disintegrate at a known rate. It is possible then to calculate the age of an organic object by measuring the amount of C14 left in the sample. The initial quantity in a sample is low, so the limit of detectability is soon reached, although efforts are being made to extend the limit beyond 70,000 years.

Radiocarbon dating is most effective for sites dating between 40,000 and about 500 years before the present (B.P.). Dates can be taken from many types of organic material, including charcoal, shell, wood, or hair. When a date is received from a C14 dating laboratory, it bears a statistical plus or minus factor; for example, 3621 ± 180 years (180 years represents 1 standard deviation) means that chances are two out of three that the true radiocarbon age is between the span of 3441 and 3801. If we double the deviation, the chances are 19 out of 20 that the span (3261 to 3981) is correct. Most dates in this book are derived from C14 dated samples and should be recognized for what they are—statistical approximations (Fagan, 1994a; Sharer and Ashmore, 1992).

The conventional radiocarbon method depends on measurements of a beta-ray decay rate to date the sample. Accelerator mass spectrometry allows radiocarbon dating to be carried out by direct counting of carbon 14 atoms, rather than by counting radioactive disintegrations (Gowlett, 1987). This method has the advantage of allowing very tiny samples to be dated, especially for the time period between 8000 B.C. and 30,000 years ago. Accelerator dating distinguishes between carbon 14 and carbon 12 and other ions through its mass and energy characteristics. The samples required are so small that it is possible, for example, to date an individual tree ring or a small wood fragment preserved in the socket of a bronze ax. Accelerator dating is playing an important role in dating the first settlement of the Americas and late Ice Age sites in Europe.

CALIBRATION: Unfortunately, the rate at which C14 is produced in the atmosphere has fluctuated considerably because of changes in the strength of the earth's magnetic field and alterations in solar activity. By working with tree-ring chronologies from the long-lived California bristlecone pine and European oaks, a number of C14 laboratories have agreed on correction tables for C14 dates between approximately 5200 B.C. and A.D. 1950. The discrepancies between radiocarbon and calibrated dates differ widely, but a typical adjustment is that for 10 B.C. ± 30, which has a calibrated interval of 145 B.C. to A.D. 210. New calibration sets based on uranium thorium and carbon 14 dating of ocean corals have pushed calibration data back to nearly 22,000 calendar years (*Radiocarbon*, 1993), but the information is too new to have received widespread archaeological application. (For calibration tables, see *Radiocarbon*, 1993.)

APPLICATIONS: Radiocarbon dating has been used to establish most of the chronologies described in this book for sites dating to between about 40,000 years ago and A.D. 1500. It has been used to date early agriculture in both the New and Old Worlds, the beginnings of metallurgy, and the first settlement of the Americas. Without the C14 method, world prehistory would be almost entirely undated.

Uranium Thorium Dating

TIME SPAN: Earlier than 300,000 years ago, sometimes up to a million years ago.

PRINCIPLES: As uranium decays by alpha and beta emission to lead, it forms many elements. By studying different isotopic pairs in the uranium decay series, a scientist can measure the amount of time that has passed since they were disrupted. Most uranium-disequilibrium dating systems are used to date deep-sea cores, but they have occasionally been used to date terrestrial carbonates deposited in caves. Uranium thorium methods are very useful, for calcium carbonate excludes thorium from its structure during crystallization but includes significant parts of uranium. As time passes the amount of ^{230}Th increases because of the decay of both ^{234}U and ^{238}U in the sample. Uranium thorium samples have dated finds of early human fossils in southern European caves dating to between 100,000 and 300,000 years ago.

Potassium Argon Dating

TIME SPAN: From the origins of life down to approximately 250,000 years ago.

PRINCIPLES: Potassium (K) is an abundant element in the earth's crust and is present in nearly every mineral. Potassium in its natural form contains only a small proportion of radioactive ^{40}K atoms. For every one hundred ^{40}K atoms that decay, 11 percent become argon 40, an inert gas that can easily escape from its material by diffusion when lava and other igneous rocks are formed. As volcanic rock forms by crystallization, the argon 40 concentration drops to almost nothing, but the process of ^{40}K decay continues, and 11 percent of every 100 ^{40}K atoms will become argon 40. Thus it is possible, using a spectrometer, to measure the concentration of argon 40 that has accumulated since the volcanic rock formed.

APPLICATIONS: We are fortunate that many of the world's earliest archaeological sites occur in volcanically active areas. Human tools are found in direct association with cooled lava fragments or ash from contemporary eruptions. Potassium argon has been used to date Olduvai Gorge and other famous early sites (Chapter 2) (Aitken, 1990).

However effective and accurate a chronometric method, it is useless unless the dated sample—be it a fragment of a wooden beam, a handful of charcoal, or a lump of cooled lava—is interpreted correctly. For instance, a lump of lava associated with an early stone tool does not date the tool; it dates the moment at which the lava cooled. It is up to the archaeologist to establish that the tool is contemporary with the lava. Beams may be used years after their parent tree was cut down. All these factors have to be taken into account when interpreting chronometric dates. The most securely dated sites are those with a chronology derived from several methods, say a combination of tree rings, thermoluminescence, and carbon 14.

FINDING AND EXCAVATING ARCHAEOLOGICAL SITES

● ● ●

How do archaeologists find sites? Many large sites, such as the pyramids of Giza in Egypt or Teotihuacán in Mexico, have been known for centuries. Evidence for less-conspicuous sites may be accidentally exposed by water or wind erosion, earthquakes, and other natural phenomena. Burrowing animals may bring bones or stone tools to the surface on ancient settlements. Farmers plow up thousands of finds. Road makers and land developers move massive quantities of earth. In contrast to these chance discoveries, however, most archaeological sites are discovered as a result of careful field survey and thorough examination of the countryside for both conspicuous and inconspicuous traces of the past (Schiffer and House, 1977). A survey can cover a single city lot or an entire river basin, a reconnaissance that could extend over several years. The theoretical ideal is to locate all sites in the survey area, but this is impossible because many sites leave few traces above ground and the best that one can hope for is a sample of what is in the area. Surface artifacts from newly discovered sites can provide clues about the identity of the occupants, although even scientifically collected surface finds are no substitute for excavation.

Survey

The environmental context of a site is often as important as the settlement itself, so much so that regional surveys of prehistoric sites and their settlement patterns are as important as excavation. *Settlement patterns* are distributions of prehistoric occupation on the landscape. Establishing such patterns requires a large investment of time and money. It took William Sanders and his colleagues a decade to survey the evolving settlement pattern in the basin of Mexico over the millennia that preceded the emergence of Aztec civilization in the fifteenth century A.D. (Sanders, Parsons, and Santley, 1979). They relied heavily on aerial photography to give an overhead view of the research area.

The destruction of archaeological sites by industrial activity, mining, and looting proceeds at a breathtaking pace. Since the archaeological record is being destroyed faster than it can be conserved, archaeologists are more and more avoiding destructive excavation where at all possible and turning to side-scan radar, satellite imagery, and other sophisticated remote-sensing devices to study the past without digging (Colwell, 1983). Remote sensing enables us to look at ancient landscapes and peoples' imprints upon them, and through computerized databases to begin to predict densities of archaeological sites in different landscapes. As the number of undisturbed archaeological sites dwindles, we can expect all forms of remote sensing to assume much greater importance than conventional excavation.

Excavation

The fundamental premise of excavation is that all digging is destructive, even that done by the experts. The archaeologist's primary responsibility, therefore, is to record a site for posterity as it is dug because there are no second chances.

Every excavation is undertaken to answer specific questions, according to a formal research design that is worked out beforehand. The research design can ask questions about the chronology of the site, the layout of the settlement it contains, or changing artifact styles within the levels to be excavated (Binford, 1964; Mueller, 1975). By meticulous digging and careful sampling of the archaeological deposits, the excavator implements the research design and digs up and records the data that are used to test the hypotheses developed as part of that research design. Most archaeologists distinguish between two basic excavation methods (Figure 1.7) (P. Barker, 1983; Joukowsky, 1981; Wheeler, 1954):

1. *Area or horizontal excavation,* in which the objective is to uncover large areas of ground in search of houses or entire settlement layouts. This type of digging is on a relatively large scale and is designed to uncover household and other activities that are normally discoverable only by digging over an extensive area.
2. *Vertical excavation or trenching,* designed to uncover stratigraphic information or a sequence of occupation layers on a small scale. This type of excavation often is practiced when chronology or artifact samples are a primary concern.

Site Types

The numerous archaeological sites described in this book fall into several broad categories, each of which presents special excavation problems. The most common are *living sites,* the places where people have lived and carried out a multitude of activities.

FIGURE 1.7   Area (horizontal) and vertical excavations. Although archaeologists excavate in many ways and sometimes use sampling techniques, there is a basic distinction between area and vertical methods.

An area excavation of a stone circle at Strichen, Scotland, is designed to expose large segments of ground on a site so that buildings, all other structures, and even the layout of the entire settlement can be traced over a much larger area than would be uncovered in a vertical excavation. Area excavation is widely used when the budget is not a problem and the archaeologist is looking for settlement patterns.

A vertical excavation of Maiden Castle, Dorset, England, shows how a narrow trench is cut through successive layers of an earth rampart. Notice that only a small portion of the layers in the trench walls has been exposed. The objective of this excavation was to obtain information on the sequence of layers on the outer edge of the earthwork and in the ditch that originally lay on its exterior side. Only a narrow trench was needed to record layers, the finds from them, and the dating evidence.

Much of our knowledge of the earliest hunters and gatherers is found by excavating abandoned living sites. These people favored open-air lake- or riverside camps or convenient rock overhangs for protection from predators and the weather, availability of abundant water, and ready access to herds of game and vegetable foods. Fortunately for archaeologists, they abandoned food bones and tools where they were dropped. Crude windbreaks were left and might have been burned down by the next brushfire or blown away by the wind.

Caves already occupied more than half a million years ago were reoccupied again and again as people returned to preferred spots. Many natural caves and rock shelters contain deep occupation deposits that can be removed by meticulous excavation with a dental pick, trowel, and brush. The sequence of occupation layers can be uncovered almost undisturbed from the day of abandonment (Deacon, 1979; Movius, 1977).

In contrast, farmers usually live in larger settlements than hunters, for they are tied to their herds and gardens and move less often. Higher population densities and more lasting settlements left more-conspicuous archaeological sites from later millennia of human history. In the Near East and many parts of the New World, farming sites were occupied time after time over several thousand years, forming deep mounds of refuse, house foundations, and other occupation debris. These *tells* require large excavations and extensive earthmoving if anything is to be understood about how towns and settlements were laid out.

Kill sites are places where hunter-gatherers killed large mammals, then camped around the carcass for several days as they butchered their prey. The most famous kill sites are in the American Great Plains, at which entire bison herds have been found trapped in narrow gullies where they were driven to their death (see Figure 6.6) (Wheat, 1972). The stone projectile points, scraping tools, and butchering artifacts used by the hunters have been found around the carcasses. *Ceremonial sites* may or may not be part of a living site (Weaver, 1981). Mesopotamian temples formed the focus of a city, and the pyramids, temples, and plazas of the Maya city of Tikal were an integral part of a city that presided over a scattered settlement pattern of towns and villages in the countryside (Figure 21.11). Some structures, like the Great Serpent Mound in Ohio (Fagan, 1991) or Stonehenge in England (Figure 20.6) (Chippindale, 1983), were sites that served the religious needs of a wider community around them.

Burial sites can yield important data from periods later than 70,000 years ago, the time when the first deliberate burials were made (Brothwell, 1985). Skeletons and their accompanying grave goods give us a rather one-sided view of the past— funerary rites (Figure 16.5). Among the most famous prehistoric burials are those of the royal kings deposited at Ur in Mesopotamia during the second millennium B.C. (Chapter 16) (Woolley, 1934).

STUDYING THE FINDS

● ● ●

Archaeological finds take many forms. They may include fragmentary bones from game or domesticated animals (Davis, 1987). Vegetable foods such as edible nuts or cultivated seeds sometimes are found in archaeological sites where preservation conditions are good (Ford, 1985; Pearsell, 1989). Pottery, stone implements, iron artifacts, and occasionally bone and wooden tools all build up a picture of early technical achievements.

Archaeologists have developed elaborate classification systems that set down certain criteria for their finds. They also apply sophisticated analytic techniques for both classifying and comparing human artifacts (Watson, LeBlanc, and Redman, 1984). They use collections of stone tools, pottery, or other artifacts like swords and brooches for studying human culture and its development. Whatever the classificatory techniques used, however, the objective of analyzing bones, pottery, and other material remains is the study of prehistoric culture and of cultural change in the past. We classify the remains into arbitrary groups either by their shape or design or by their use, the latter a difficult task (Figure 1.8). We fit them together to form a picture of a human culture.

From time to time we shall refer to archaeological groupings like the Acheulian culture or the Magdalenian culture, which consist of the material remains of human culture preserved at a specific space and time at several sites; these finds are the concrete expressions of the common social traditions that bind a culture. When we speak of the Magdalenian culture, we mean the *archaeological culture representing a prehistoric social system, defined in a context of time and space, which has come down to us in the form of tools or other durable objects.* The description *Magdalenian* is quite arbitrary, derived from the cave site at La Madeleine, France, where the tools of the culture were first discovered. Such labels as Magdalenian are devised by archaeologists for their convenience.

How did our forebears live? What animals did they hunt? What plant foods did they collect, or did they plant cereal or root crops or herd cattle or llamas? We study ancient subsistence by examining the fragmentary animal bones that survive in archaeological sites, as well as the seeds, pollen grains, and other traces of plant foods. These studies often throw important light on the hunting and herding practices of ancient peoples. For example, at 'Ain Ghazal in Jordan, Stone Age farmers of 7000 B.C. herded and penned goats. We know this because the goat bones from the settlement show the characteristic marks of tethering (Chapter 9). Tiny seeds are collected by using sophisticated flotation methods that collect small organic fragments by passing the soil through water. This method was used at Koster, Illinois, where Archaic peoples of 2000 B.C. not only foraged intensively for wild plant foods but also grew some native plants to supplement the annual yields from wild harvests (Chapter 6).

INTERPRETING THE FINDS

• • •

Anthropological archaeology is much more than inference and induction from the archaeological record, for our ultimate aim is to explain the past, not simply to describe it. The archaeologists of the 1990s try to explain culture change and variation in the archaeological record by examining the behavioral context of the material remains of the past. The concern is with long-term changes in the ways people have adapted to their environments. Students of world prehistory have a major concern with interpreting the static data of past human behavior—stone artifacts, broken bones, and so on—in terms of what was once dynamic human behavior in prehistoric times. To acquire this information, archaeologists use several innovative approaches, including ethnographic analogy and controlled experimentation to bridge the gap between past and present.

Archaeological data are the results of behavior, not the behavior itself. This behavior can be observed only in a living cultural system. So in a sense, modern approaches to world prehistory can be called a form of behavioral code cracking.

FIGURE 1.8   Inference from an artifact. This Chumash Indian parching tray from southern California shows how inferences can be made from an archaeological find. Clearly, the
range of inferences that can be made from artifacts alone is limited, especially when the find
has no context in a site.

The archaeological context of the tray is defined by its position in a site and what it is
associated with, level, square, etc.; its relationship to other features, such as houses, is also
recorded. Unless this information is known, the tray is an isolated specimen devoid of a cultural context or even a date. Context cannot be inferred from an artifact alone.

The tray was made of reed, its red-brown color determined by the reed, and materials known
from modern observations to be the best material available. The steplike decoration on the
tray was dictated by sewing and weaving techniques of basketry. The diamond patterns were
probably added as a personal touch by the craftsperson who made it. The shape and decoration of the tray are repeated in many others that have been found and are evidently part of a
well-established Chumash basketry tradition. More information about an artifact's construction and materials can be learned than about any other category of inference.

The flat, round shape of the tray is determined by its function, for such trays were used to
roast seeds by tossing them with embers in the tray. The function of a tray normally cannot
be inferred from its shape, but identical modern versions have been found that are used for
parching. We employ the technique of analogy, inferring that the archaeological find had the
same function as the modern tray.

The parching tray reveals something about the cooking techniques of the Chumash, but
again only by analogy.

Ethnographic analogy, comparing prehistoric societies with living peoples, has
been a backbone of prehistoric archaeology for more than a century. Another form
of analogy became popular in North America, where prehistory was, and still is,
regarded as a form of anthropology in the past. This is the so-called *direct historical
approach,* in which the archaeologist starts with a historical baseline, then excavates
stratified sites that link the known, historical present with much earlier prehistoric
cultures. A. V. Kidder (1927) used this approach with great success at Pecos pueblo

in the Southwest in the 1920s, developing an outline chronology of pueblo occupation that extended back more than 2000 years. Given the long continuity of Indian culture in this area, the approach was fundamentally sound. Unfortunately, however, this direct and comprehensive way of comparing ancient and modern society is simply too elementary (Wylie, 1985).

The modern attitude toward analogy is far more rigorous. Archaeologists now approach it in the context of a carefully defined problem, such as the function of an artifact, ways in which garbage was discarded, and so on. Here again, though, there are problems because the earlier the site, the more likely it is that many complex variables have affected the patterning of artifacts, food remains, and other phenomena in the ground.

Many archaeologists have turned to highly specific *artifact analogies* and have made exact replicas of prehistoric tools and weapons that they then tested under controlled conditions. Nicholas Toth (Toth and Schick, 1993) has replicated early human artifact assemblages from East Turkana and Olduvai Gorge in East Africa, artifacts more than 1.75 million years old. His experiments have demonstrated that our earliest toolmaking ancestors were adept stone workers, who were primarily interested in sharp flakes for cutting, sawing, and butchery (Chapter 2). Toth has even been able to show that some of the earliest toolmakers were left-handed by studying the flake scars on discarded cores and flakes.

In recent years, archaeologists have turned increasingly to microscopic studies of edge wear on stone tools and to painstaking attempts to refit tools to the flakes and cores from which they came. In each case, they are looking behind the artifact for insights into the human behavior of long ago. These approaches, and other controlled experiments, are more precise forms of analogy that lead logically into broader attempts to use modern hunter-gatherers or farming societies as a way of interpreting the past. This form of ethnographic analogy is called ethnoarchaeology, or "living archaeology."

Ethnoarchaeology is the study of living cultures undertaken for the purposes of studying the archaeological record (R. A. Gould, 1978). Ethnoarchaeologists are concerned with observing dynamic human behavior as it unfolds, and recording the material traces of this behavior—in the form of abandoned campsites, artifact waste, food remains, and so on—as a way of interpreting similar patterns in the archaeological record. One famous ethnoarchaeological study was carried out among the San hunter-gatherers of the Kalahari Desert in southern Africa. The San research began when anthropologist Richard Lee (1979) undertook a long-term study of !Kung hunter-gatherers. An archaeologist accompanied the research team and made detailed studies of butchery techniques as well as plans of abandoned settlements of known, historical age. John Yellen's research (1977) yielded a treasure trove of data on house and camp arrangements, hearth locations, population densities, and bone refuse. For example, he points out that a San camp develops through conscious acts, such as the construction of windbreaks and hearths, as well as through such incidental deeds as the discarding of refuse and manufacturing debris. Yellen recognized communal areas, open spaces where dancing and distribution of food took place. Then there were family hearths for food processing and cooking. These and other activity areas leave different tracks in the archaeological record (Figure 1.9).

Understanding the causes of variation in modern hunter-gatherer adaptations gives us a potentially powerful foundation for predicting and investigating just as varied adaptations in the remote past. And understanding such ancient adaptations

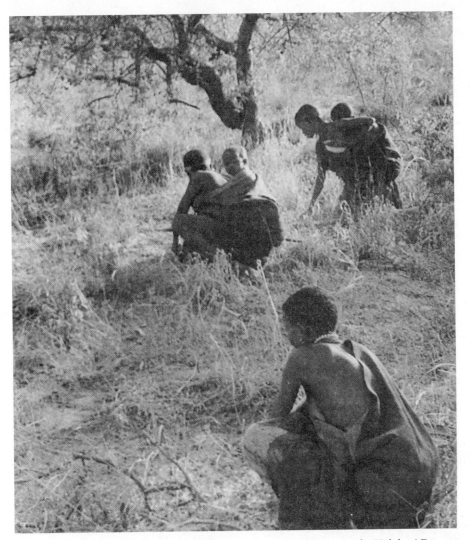

FIGURE 1.9 !Kung San women foraging for mongongo nuts in the Kalahari Desert, southern Africa. A wealth of information for archaeological interpretation has come from studies of living hunter-gatherer groups.

is a critical element in formulating explanations of the major developments of world prehistory.

EXPLAINING WORLD PREHISTORY

Two-million-year-old human remains, sequences of fossils and stone tools, early farming villages, great cities like Ur in Mesopotamia or Tikal in the Maya lowlands of Mesoamerica—these are the familiar landmarks of world prehistory, many of them easily described. As we have emphasized, it is one thing to describe the evidence of the past, quite another to explain what happened in prehistory. Why did human beings originate in tropical Africa and why did they spread into other continents a million years ago? How and why did our ancestors adapt to much colder environments during the later Ice Age? Why, eventually, did hunters and foragers start cultivating the soil and living in cities? Such questions are the hardest to answer, for they lie at the interface between theoretical explanations of the past and the myriad data from the archaeological record itself. We must now describe some of the major theoretical frameworks which seek to help explain prehistoric culture change.

Much of the prehistory recounted in these pages is fundamental culture history, based on hundreds of sites and cultural sequences and millions of individual artifacts (Figure 1.10). Culture history alone, however, does not explain culture change, nor does it provide information on the ways in which people have adapted to or exploited the natural environment. It is only in recent years that archaeologists have attacked the complex problems of reconstructing past lifeways and studying cultural process, with the aid of digital computers, sophisticated statistical methods, and enormous new bodies of excavated data from all over the world (Trigger, 1989).

PRIMARY CULTURAL PROCESSES: INVENTION, DIFFUSION, AND MIGRATION

• • •

How did cultural change occur? Archaeologists generally agree on three *primary cultural processes*—invention, diffusion, and migration, which figured importantly in world prehistory:

Invention involves creating a new idea and transforming it—in archaeological contexts—into an artifact or other tangible innovation that has survived. An invention implies either modifying an old idea or series of ideas or creating a completely new concept. It can be made by accident or by intentional research. Inventions are adopted by others if they are useful; if sufficiently important, they spread rapidly.

FIGURE 1.10   Nineteenth-century excavator Austen Henry Layard supervises the removal of a human-headed lion from the gates of an Assyrian palace at Nineveh, Iraq. Such large-scale excavations were unscientific, but they yielded spectacular discoveries.

The transistor, for example, is in almost universal use because it is an effective advance in electronic technology.

There is a tendency to think of inventions as dramatic discoveries, the products of a moment of inspiration. In practice, though, most inventions in prehistory were the result of prolonged experimentation, a logical extension of the use and refinement of an existing technology or a response to changes in the surrounding environment.

Diffusion is the label for those processes by which new ideas or cultural traits spread from one person to another or from one group to another, often over long distances. These ideas are socially transmitted from individual to individual and ultimately from group to group, but the physical movement of many people is not involved. Instances of diffusion are legion in prehistory, cases in which ideas or technologies have spread widely from their place of origin. A classic modern example is tobacco smoking, a favorite pleasure of the North American Indians that was adopted by Elizabethan colonists in the sixteenth century. Within a few generations, tens of thousands of Europeans were smoking pipes and enjoying the narcotic effect of American tobacco. Tobacco smoking soon reached every corner of the Old World, carried there not by thousands of people migrating from America to Europe but by small numbers of seamen and traveling merchants, by word of mouth, and through the human habit of adopting new, fashionable ideas. Smoking became socially acceptable and remains so to this day in many societies (although not necessarily in ours). There are numerous examples of the diffusion of religious beliefs in prehistory, transmitted through trading contacts and simply by the spread of ideas.

Migration involves the movement of a people and is based on a deliberate decision to enter new areas and leave the old. English settlers moved to North America, taking their own culture with them; the Spanish occupied Mexico. Such population movements result not only in the diffusion of ideas but also in mass shifts of people and in social and cultural changes over a wide front. Migration implies a complete, or at least an almost complete, transformation in culture. Perhaps the classic instance of migration in prehistory is that of the Polynesians; they settled the remote islands of the Pacific in consequence of deliberate explorations of the open ocean by their skilled navigators (Irwin, 1992). These superb seamen learned the lore of the heavens and made long-distance voyages of discovery, whereby they found such remote islands as Hawaii and Easter Island. In most cases, they returned safely to their homelands with detailed sailing directions that could be followed by later colonists.

CULTURE AS ADAPTATION

• • •

The classic mechanisms of cultural change form part of descriptive culture history. They answer the question "how?" but not the question "why?" The "culture as adaptation" approach to world prehistory attempts explanation by seeing human cultures as adaptations to the subsistence and ecological requirements of a locality. Culture is the result of human beings' unique ability to create and infuse events and objects with meaning that can be appreciated, decoded, and understood (Gamble, 1986b). To espouse this definition of culture as adaptation means that culture is *participated in* as well as *shared by* human beings. However, this participation and sharing differs greatly from place to place and from time to time, resulting in variations in prehistoric material culture—the data for studying prehistory. This viewpoint contrasts somewhat with that of culture historians, who tend to argue that all variability can be accounted for by a view of culture that explains patterning in the archaeological record as the result of shared ideas and cultural norms. (Note that this is a gross simplification of a complex issue.)

The culture as adaptation approach uses a much more complex, multidimensional model to investigate the significance of patterning and variation in archaeological finds (Binford, 1983; Gamble, 1986b). This model is based on two fundamental assumptions:

- First, since resources are not uniformly distributed within an environment, humans must expend energy in collecting and gathering them. They have to employ some form of adaptive strategy to minimize risk and make use of seasonal phenomena, such as availability of vegetable foods and game migrations. These seasonal strategies rely on the potential of available technology, food storage capacity, and so on. Among hunter-gatherers, for example, these strategies utilize the mobility of individual groups and their flexible social organization to divide them into bands of different sizes, membership, duration, and purpose (Jochim, 1976).
- Second, human activities and their cultural residues are distributed over the landscape through time and space. This scattering results from variations in the distribution and organization of energy. In other words, the archaeological record of world prehistory varies *over the landscape* as a result of past behavior related to adaptive strategies (Gamble, 1986b). Thus, no one site can be taken to represent an entire adaptation; the focus for studying world prehistory must be regional.

The fundamental point is that human behavior, both today and in the prehistoric past, is an adaptation not to a single site but to environmental regions. Thus, to understand individual sites and artifact patternings, the archaeologist has to study regions. The notion is that the archaeological record, certainly of hunter-gatherers, should be perceived not as a system of structured sites but as a continuous pattern of artifact distribution and density over the landscape. As individuals and groups hunt and forage their way across this landscape, they leave behind material remains of their presence, a record that reflects their continual behavior within the region.

MULTILINEAR CULTURAL EVOLUTION

• • •

Archaeologists seek to interpret cultural variation and adaptation on a regional basis, especially among highly mobile hunter-gatherer populations. The relationship between ecological and social systems is a critical part of this approach.

Early Victorian social scientists believed human societies evolved in a simple, linear fashion, slowly ascending an evolutionary ladder of human progress toward that ultimate pinnacle, Industrial Civilization. Such simplistic notions, with their assumptions of racial superiority, have long given way to much more sophisticated formulations. Today, the concept of *multilinear evolution* (multiple-lined evolution) is widely accepted as a general framework by students of world prehistory.

Multilinear evolutionary theory assumes that each human society pursues its own evolutionary course, determined by the long-term success of its adaptation, via technology and social institutions, to its natural environment (Sahlins and Service, 1960). The study of the total way in which human populations adapt to and transform their environments is called *cultural ecology*. Cultural ecology is at the core of multilinear evolutionary theory. Some societies achieve a broad measure of equilibrium with their environment, in which adaptive changes consist of little more than some refinements in technology and the fine tuning of organizational structures. Other societies become involved in cycles of growth that are triggered by environmental change or from within society. If these changes involve either greater food supplies or population growth, there can be accelerated growth resulting from the need to feed more people or the deployment of an enlarged food surplus. Continued growth can place additional strains on the society, triggering technological changes, adjustments to social organization, or alterations in the belief system that provides the society's integrative force.

Every society has its growth limits imposed by the environment and available technology, and some environments have more potential for growth than others. Certain types of sociopolitical organization, such as centralized control of specialized labor, are more efficient than others. The emergence of food production and the beginnings of urban civilization in Mesoamerica are both cases of societies entering on a major growth cycle after centuries of relatively slow cultural evolution. Adaptive changes have triggered technological innovation that has led to increased food supplies and higher population densities.

Multilinear cultural evolution combines the notion of cultural systems and cultural ecology into a closely knit, highly flexible way of studying and explaining cultural process (Sanders and Webster, 1978). For example, Kent Flannery (1968a) studied early agriculture in Mexico's southern highlands. He discovered that between 8000 and 2000 B.C. the highland peoples relied on five basic food sources— deer, rabbits, maguey, tree legumes, and prickly pears—for their sustenance. By careful prediction of the seasons of each food, they could schedule their hunting and gathering at periods of abundance and before animals gained access to the ripe plants. Flannery assumed that the southern highlands and their inhabitants were part of a large, open environmental system consisting of many subsystems—economic, botanical, social, and so on—that interacted with one another. Then something occurred to jolt the food procurement system toward the deliberate growing of wild grasses. Flannery's excavations at dry sites dating to between 5000 and 2000 B.C. showed wild maize cobs slowly increasing in size and other signs of genetic change. He suggested that the people began to experiment with the deliberate planting of maize and other grasses, intentionally expanding the areas where they would grow. After a long period of time, these intentional deviations in the food procurement system caused the importance of wild grass collecting to increase at the expense of other collecting activities until it became the dominant one (Figure 1.11). Eventually, the Indians created a self-perpetuating food procurement system—with its own vital scheduling demands of planting and harvesting—that competed with earlier systems and won out because it was more durable. By 2000 B.C., the highly nutritious bean and corn diet of the highland peoples was well established.

Flannery's Mexican research dramatizes the importance of looking at cultural change in the context of the interrelationships among many variables. There is no one prime agent of cultural evolution but rather a series of important variables, all with complex interrelationships. When we seek to explain the major and minor events of prehistory, we consider the ways in which change took place, the processes and mechanisms of change (cultural evolution, experimentation), and the socioeconomic stresses (population pressure, game scarcity, and so on) that trigger these mechanisms (Flannery, 1972).

Testing such multicausal models is a difficult task, involving rigorous methodologies for identification of the variables in the archaeological record and comparative studies of these variables in regions where a particular development (say, the emergence of civilization) occurred and where it did not, as well as in societies that flourished immediately before its development (Redman, 1978).

STAGES OF SOCIAL DEVELOPMENT

•   •   •

The sophisticated concept of multilinear evolution has led a number of anthropologists to talk of stages of social development in prehistory (Service, 1962). For convenience, many archaeologists think in terms of two broad groups: prestate societies and state-organized societies (for critiques, see Dunnell, 1980; Plog and Upham, 1983).

Prestate societies are societies on a small scale, based on the community, band, or village. They vary greatly in their degrees of political integration and are sometimes divided into three loosely defined categories (Figure 1.12):

1. *Bands* are associations of families that may not exceed 25 to 60 people. These bands are knit together by close social ties; they were the dominant form of social organization for most hunter-gatherers from the earliest times up to the origins of food production.

2. *Tribes* are clusters of bands that are linked by clans. A clan is a group of people linked by common ancestral ties, which serve as connections between widely scattered communities. Clans are important because they are a form of social linkage that gives people a sense of common identity with a wider world than their own immediate family and relatives. They are much more of a kin than a political unit and, as such, are not used as one of the major stages of social evolution in themselves.

FIGURE 1.11   Excavations at Guilá Naquitz, Valley of Oaxaca, Mexico.

	Band	Tribe	Chiefdom	State-Organized Societies
		Prestate		
Total Numbers	Less than 100	Up to few thousand	5,000 - 20,000+	Generally 20,000+

Social Organization	Egalitarian
	Informal leadership
		Segmentary society
		Pan-tribal associations
		Raids by small groups
			Kinship-based ranking
			   under hereditary leader
			High-ranking warriors
				Class-based hiearchy
				   under king of emperor
				Armies

Economic Organization	Mobile hunter-gathers	Settled farmers Pastoralist herders	Central accumulation and redistribution Some craft specialization	Centralized bureaucracy Tribute-based Taxation Laws
Settlement Pattern	Temporary camps	Permanent villages	Fortified centers Ritual centers	Urban: cities, towns Frontier defenses Roads

Religious Organization	Shamans	Religious elders
		Calendrical rituals
			Hereditary Chief with
			   religious duties
				Priestly class
				Pantheistic or monothiestic
				   religion

Architecture	Temporary shelters *Palaeolithic skin tents, Ukraine*	Permanent huts Burial mounds Shrines *Neolithic shrine Çatal Hüyük, Turkey*	Large scale monuments *Stonehenge England - final form*	Palaces, temples, and other public buildings *Pyramids at Giza* *Castillo Chichén Itzá, Mexico*

Archaeological Examples	All Palaeolithic societies, including Paleo-indians	All early farmers
		(Neolithic/Archaic)
			Many early metalworking
			   and Formative societies
			Mississippian, USA
			Smaller African kingdoms
				All ancient civilization e.g.
				   in Mesoamerica, Peru
				Near East, India and
				China, Greece and Rome

Modern Examples	Eskimos
	Kalahari San
	Australian Aborigines
		Pueblos, Southwest USA
		New Guinea Highlanders
		Nuer and Dinka in
		East Africa
			Northwest Coast Indians,
			   USA
			18th-century Polynesian
			   chiefdoms in Tonga,
			   Tahiti, Hawaii
				All modern states

FIGURE 1.12 General categories of prehistoric human societies. (Modified from Renfrew and Bahn, 1991.)

3. *Chiefdoms* are still kin-based but more hierarchical, with power concentrated in the hands of kin leaders responsible for the redistribution of resources. These leaders are usually individuals with unusual ritual, political, or entrepreneurial skills. Chiefdoms tend to have higher population densities (generally between 5000 and 20,000 people) and display clear signs of social ranking. Often there is local specialization in craft products. Frequently, surpluses of food and such products are paid to the chief, who redistributes them to his followers. Most chiefdoms have permanent ritual and ceremonial centers, which act as the central focus of the chiefdom, where the chief and his retainers live. Chiefdoms varied greatly in elaboration (Earle, 1978). For example, the Mississippian chiefdoms of the Midwest and South flourished during the early second millennium A.D., maintaining extensive trade networks and ritual contacts over long distances.

State-organized societies operate on a large scale with centralized political and social organization, class stratification, and intensive agriculture. They have complex political structures and many permanent government institutions, and they are based on notions of social inequality. Such societies are ruled by a tiny elite, who hold monopolies over strategic resources and use force to enforce authority. State-organized societies of the past were first ruled by priest-bureaucrats, then gradually came under the rule of secular kings, who sometimes became despotic monarchs, often with alleged divine powers. This type of social organization was typical of the early literate civilizations and was the forerunner of the classical civilizations of Greece and Rome.

POST-PROCESSUAL ARCHAEOLOGY

• • •

Under the culture as adaptation approach, the main emphasis is on identifying variations in ancient human cultures. This materialistic perspective, which, it must be confessed, is central to this book, focuses on the complicated relationships between cultural and environmental change, on the processes of culture change. Without question, evolutionary theory will continue to have a major impact on world prehistory, as scientists use comparative approaches to biological evolution to place human characteristics within a general framework of animal variability. In other words, they are analyzing human adaptation from a biological perspective, examining ecological and evolutionary adaptations between humans and other species which make up the biological community. Such evolutionary approaches have special relevance for the study of early prehistory, but the culture as adaptation approach tends to ignore people and their cultural traditions at the expense of process.

CONSTRAINTS

• • •

Cultural traditions provide guidance for coping with the environment, a force that can operate against innovation, and a body of intellectual information that changes constantly from one generation to the next. Ecological and other external factors can be culturally mediated, but they operate independently of human actions, which makes them susceptible to understanding in terms of evolutionary theory and other such generalizations. Cultural traditions are far more idiosyncratic, far more haphazard. This makes it difficult to impose evolutionary order on human history, for, despite external constraints, much cultural change is contingent on ever-changing circumstances and cultural traditions. Human culture's open-ended capacity for further elaboration creates a need for order to make its diversity understandable. By studying individual cultural traditions, archaeologists can explain the distinctive features of cultures in ways that evolutionists and cultural ecologists can never hope to. Thus, we should try and explain the past in terms of both external (environmental) and (internal) social constraints (Trigger, 1991).

Internal constraints include knowledge, beliefs, values, and other culturally conditioned habits, all of them different in each culture. Yet some of them are shared by cultures flourishing thousands of miles apart. For instance, two widely separated cultures may develop bronze metallurgy, which is based on a common body of technological know-how, but the cultural context of that knowledge is radically different, as it was, say, in the Shang civilization of China and Moche culture in coastal Peru. Some symbols, like the common practice of elevating chiefs or kings on a dais, or associations between rulers and the sun, have developed in many places. That does not mean that they are connected, but simply more-or-less uniform operations of the human mind.

According to this perspective, human cultures are historical phenomena shaped by both external and internal constraints. This counters the evolutionists' argument that new human concepts are like genes, the products of purely random processes that create the highly variable raw material upon which a cultural equivalent of natural selection operates. This somewhat biological view of culture change suggests that cultural selection automatically favors the most adaptive ideas, by ensuring that those cultures who adopt them survive. This ignores much anthropological evidence that the invention of new concepts is not a random process, like genetic mutations. Our ability to use our imaginations, to make calculated decisions, plays a significant part in streamlining any form of innovation. Our culture has a store of ideas and social values that channel and restrict innovation. Cultural traditions play a major role in constraining social change. Information transmitted from one generation to the next provides most of the knowledge an individual has available to deal with ecological and social realities. Each generation reworks this information and its accompanying cultural constraints to reflect the realities of their own circumstances, a process that, in time, transformed human societies and at times led to new social institutions.

THE MEANING OF THE ARCHAEOLOGICAL RECORD

● ● ●

Increased understanding of cultural forces and constraints has caused archaeologists to focus more attention on the meaning of the archaeological record, on ancient ideologies and religious beliefs, and on the symbolic context of prehistoric cultures. Some new research has tried to look beyond the material aspects of the archaeological record, to search for the intangible rules, as it were, which governed the ways in which prehistoric people went about their business. This approach, sometimes called post-processual archaeology, is an attempt to get at the ways in which the owners of ancient artifacts actually perceived them, at the wider symbolic meanings of material objects in their entire world of existence.

Post-processual archaeology is often concerned with ideology, with the complex, intangible ideas behind prehistoric societies. One of the few examples of such research is Linda Schele and David Freidel's remarkable work on Mayan iconography in ancient Mesoamerica, based on a combination of deciphered glyphs and archaeological data (Figure 1.13). Their work shows how ritual life, shrines, and temple structures help shape peoples' lives (Chapter 21). "The Maya believed in a past which always returned . . . in endless cycles repeating patterns already set into the fabric of time and space," they write in their book *A Forest of Kings* (p. 18). "Our challenge . . . is to interpret this history, recorded in their words, images, and ruins, in a manner comprehensible to the modern mind, yet true to the Mayas' perception of themselves."

INTERACTIONS BETWEEN PEOPLE

● ● ●

In the final analysis, it is people who share culture, groups and individuals who make decisions about daily life, about short- and long-term goals. Men interact with women, children with adults; a kin group quarrels within itself, pitting small faction against small faction; ethnic groups compete for access to wealth or political power—such dealings between individuals, between individuals and groups, and between groups are the forces which constrain or encourage cultural change over the short and long term. By its very nature, the archaeological record tends to be impersonal, its artifacts and food remains chronicling the dealings of blurred groups rather than individuals, or even categories of people, like, say, women at a given moment in time.

Only rarely can the archaeologist go beyond artifacts and food remains to study the roles of groups or individuals, the work they undertook, the subtle ways in which they influenced the course of events. For example, at the early farming village of Abu Hureyra in Syria, dating to 7000 B.C., biological anthropologist Theya Molleson (1989) observed malformations of the toes, knees, and lower vertebrae in

FIGURE 1.13 Victorian artist Frederick Catherwood's rendering of Stela C at the Maya center at Copán in Mesoamerica. More than a century was to pass before decipherment of Maya glyphs led to a scientific understanding of this society's complex ideology.

the skeletons of all the adult women, a condition due, almost certainly, to hours of grinding grain. Male skeletons did not display the same impairments. This is some of the earliest evidence for division of labor between men and women in human history.

Studying interactions between people requires extremely sophisticated research designs and the finest of fine-grained excavations and laboratory analyses. Such researches represent a new and exciting chapter in the study of human experience. They will result in major adjustments to the outline narrative of our long prehistory laid out in the chapters which follow.

CHAPTER SUMMARY

Chapter 1 describes the basic principles of archaeology, the best scientific way of studying the evolution of human biological and cultural diversity over long periods of time. Archaeology has three objectives: the study of culture history, the reconstruction of past lifeways, and the explanation of cultural change. Archaeological research focuses on the study of human culture change, the notion of "culture" being a theoretical concept formulated by anthropologists to define the unique adaptive systems by which we humans adapt to the challenges of the world's diverse environments. The narrative of world prehistory is based on the scientific study of the archaeological record in a context of time and space, using the Laws of Association and Superposition and a battery of sophisticated dating methods to date more than 2.5 million years of human experience. These dating methods include potassium argon dating, radiocarbon methods, tree ring dating, and dates based on historic documents. Archaeology is a sophisticated process of survey and controlled excavation, of scientific analyses that help us derive general theories about the relationship between human behavior and the surviving archaeological record. We describe the primary cultural processes of invention, diffusion, and migration that were developed to explain how cultures changed in different parts of the world. New theories are based on an approach that views culture as adaptation, culture change as humanity's way of adapting to ever-changing natural environments. Theories of multilinear evolution dominate the study of world prehistory today. We describe the differences between prestate and state-organized societies, and describe the current shift away from the study of general cultural processes to approaches that focus more clearly on individuals and on the constraints that operated on human societies in the past.

GUIDE TO FURTHER READING

Binford, Lewis R. 1983. *In Pursuit of the Past.* New York: Thames and Hudson.
A personal account of developing ideas in archaeology that is a marvelous introduction to archaeological reasoning. You may not agree with everything Binford says, but he makes you think.

Ceram, C. W. 1953. *Gods, Graves and Scholars.* New York: Knopf.
This probably is the best-known book on archaeology ever written. A classic account of early archaeologists and the discovery of the early civilizations written for a popular audience.

Fagan, Brian M. 1994. *Archaeology: A Brief Introduction*, 5th ed. New York: HarperCollins.
   A widely ranging brief introduction, with major coverage of subsistence and settlement patterns.

————. 1994. *In the Beginning*, 8th ed. New York: HarperCollins.
   A comprehensive survey of method and theory in archaeology that covers everything from stratigraphy to cultural resource management.

Renfrew, Colin, and Bahn, Paul. 1991. *Archaeology: A Handbook of Ideas and Methods.* New York: Thames and Hudson.
   A superbly illustrated textbook on archaeological methods most suitable for the more advanced reader.

Sharer, Robert, and Ashmore, Wendy. 1992. *Archaeology: Discovering the Past*, 2nd ed. Palo Alto, CA: Mayfield.
   Another detailed introduction to anthropological archaeology that is especially strong on American examples. Excellent bibliography.

Trigger, Bruce D. 1989. *A History of Archaeological Thought*. Cambridge, Eng.: Cambridge University Press.
   The definitive intellectual history of archaeology and the study of prehistory. Places archaeological research in stimulating perspective.

————. 1991. "Distinguished Lecture in Archaeology: Constraint and Freedom," *American Anthropologist* 93(3): 551–569.
   This important essay represents a balanced view on current theory.

Watson, Patty Jo, LeBlanc, Steven, and Redman, Charles L. 1984. *Archaeological Explanation: The Scientific Method in Archaeology.* New York: Columbia University Press.
   A description of the basic principles of processual archaeology, widely used by serious students.

PART

11

THE FIRST HUMANS

(C. 4 MILLION TO 40,000 YEARS AGO)

In each great region of the world the living mammals are closely related to the extinct species of the same region. It is, therefore, probable that Africa was formerly inhabited by extinct apes closely allied to the gorilla and the chimpanzee; and as these two species are now man's nearest allies, it is somewhat more probable that our early progenitors lived on the African continent than elsewhere.

CHARLES DARWIN, *THE DESCENT OF MAN* (1871)

We describe the origins of humankind and the early evolution of human culture from the first toolmakers to the emergence of modern humanity.

CHAPTER **HUMAN ORIGINS**

2

THE EMERGENCE OF EARLY HUMAN ANCESTORS

(4.0 MILLION TO 1.6 MILLION YEARS AGO)

• • •

I t was a blazing hot day at Olduvai Gorge in 1959. Back in camp, Louis Leakey lay in his tent, suffering from a bout of influenza. Meanwhile, Mary Leakey was excavating the small scatter of broken bones and crude artifacts deep in the gorge, sheltered by a beach umbrella. For hours she brushed and pried away dry soil. Suddenly, she unearthed part of an upper jaw with teeth so humanlike that she took a closer look. Moments later, she jumped into her Land Rover and sped up the track to camp. "Louis, Louis," she cried, as she burst into their tent, "I've found Dear Boy at last." Louis leapt out of bed, his flu forgotten. Together, they excavated the fragmentary remains of a magnificent, robust hominid skull. The Leakeys named it *Zinjanthropus boisei* ("African human of Boise"), a Mr. Boise being one of their benefactors. With this dramatic discovery, they changed the study of human evolution from a part-time science into an international detective story.

Not that the search for human origins began with the Leakeys. As long ago as 1863, the great Victorian zoologist Thomas Huxley called it the "question of questions," the nature of the exact relationship between humans and their closest living relatives such as the chimpanzee and the gorilla. Ever since his day, scientists have been locked in controversy, as they trace the complex evolutionary history of humanity back to its very beginnings (Table 2.1).

THE GREAT ICE AGE

• • •

The story of humanity begins deep in geological time, during the later part of the Cenozoic era—the age of mammals. For most of geological time, the world's climate was warmer and more homogeneous than it is today. As long ago as the Miocene epoch (Table 2.2), land began to rise up in many places and mountains began to form, continuing through the Pliocene into recent times (Butzer, 1974). During the Oligocene epoch, some 35 million years ago, the first signs of glacial cooling appeared with the formation of a belt of pack ice around Antarctica. This development was followed by a major drop in world temperatures between 14 and 11 mil-

35 million years

FIGURE 2.1   Map showing archaeological sites mentioned in Chapter 2.

lion years ago. As temperatures lowered, glaciers formed on high ground in high latitudes. About 3.2 million years ago, large ice sheets formed on the northern continents, locking up enough water to lower world sea levels by about 130 feet (40 m). Then, about 2.5 million years ago, glaciation intensified still more, and the earth entered its present period of constantly fluctuating climate. These changes culminated during the Quaternary period, or Pleistocene epoch, the most recent interval of earth history, which began about 1.6 million years ago (Goudie, 1983). This period is sometimes called the *Age of Humanity,* for it was during that time that human beings first populated most of the globe (Table 2.3, p.42). The major climatic and environmental changes that took place during the Pleistocene were the climatic backdrop for some of the most important stages in human evolution.

2.5 million years

Pleistocene
1.6 million years

The Pleistocene period had constant fluctuations between warm and intensely cold global climates. For long stretches of time, the northern parts of both Europe and North America were mantled with great ice sheets, the last retreating only some 15,000 years ago. There were at least nine of these glacials during the last 700,000

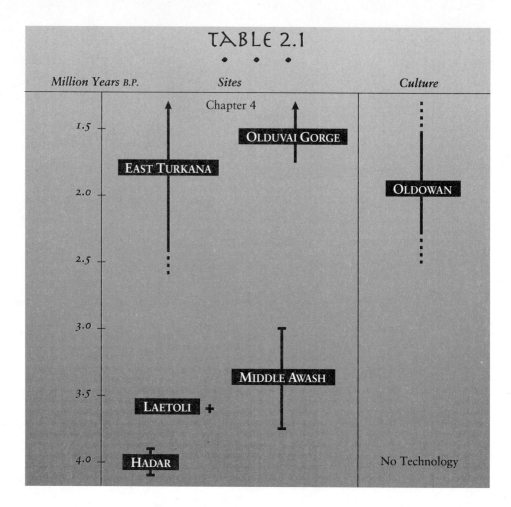

years, which is why the Pleistocene is sometimes called the Great Ice Age. Inter-glacials, with climates as warm as or warmer than that of today, were rare, and the constant changes repeatedly displaced plants and animals from their original habitats (Kurtén, 1968; Kurtén and Anderson, 1980). During colder cycles, plants and animals usually fared better at lower altitudes and in warmer latitudes. Populations of animals spread slowly toward more hospitable areas, mixing with populations that already lived there and creating new communities with new combinations of organisms. This repeated mixing surely affected the direction of evolution in many ways. No one knows how many mammal species emerged during the Pleistocene, although paleontologist Björn Kurtén once estimated that no fewer than 113 of the mammal species now living in Europe and adjacent Asia appeared during the past 3 million years.

Deep-sea cores lifted from the depths of the world's oceans have produced a complex picture of Pleistocene climate. These cores have shown that climatic fluctuations between warm and cold were relatively minor until about 800,000 years ago. Since then, periods of intense cold have reoccurred about every 90,000 years, with minor oscillations about 20,000 and 40,000 years apart. Many scientists believe that these changes are triggered by long-term astronomical changes, especially in the

TABLE 2.2

Geological epochs from more than 60 million years ago. The curve demonstrates lasting temperature changes on earth since the late Miocene. Notice that the general trend is toward cooler temperatures with more frequent fluctuations. (Pleistocene temperatures are shown in Table 2.3.)

MILLIONS OF YEARS B.P.	GEOLOGICAL EPOCHS	GLOBAL TEMPERATURES ← Lower Today Higher →		DEVELOPMENTS
2 3	Pleistocene Pliocene			Human evolution Hominoid radiation
10	Miocene			Many new mammal species
20				
30	Oligocene Eocene			Expansion of mammals
40				
50				
60	Paleocene			
70 75	Cretaceous			

(Left margin label: CENOZOIC)

earth's orbit around the sun (Covey, 1984), which affect the seasonal and north-south variations of solar radiation received by the earth.

The earliest chapter of human evolution unfolded during a period of relatively minor climatic change, indeed before the Pleistocene truly began. Between 4 and 2 million years ago, the world climate was somewhat warmer and more stable than it was in later times, and the African savanna, the probable homeland of humankind, contained many species of mammals large and small, including a great variety of the order of primates, of which we humans are part.*

Primates

*Specific details on later Pleistocene climatic change are to be found in Chapters 3, 4, and 5. Table 2.3 gives a general outline of the Great Ice Age for reference purposes.

TABLE 2.3

Geological events, climatic changes, and chronology during the Pleistocene (highly simplified), with approximate dates.

TEMPERATURE Lower Higher	DATES B.C.	EPOCHS	GLACIATIONS / INTERGLACIAL	DEVELOPMENTS IN PREHISTORY
		Holocene	Holocene	Origins of states First food production
	10,000			
	18,000		Weichsel Glaciation	First settlement of Americas Cro-Magnons in Europe
	40,000			First settlement of Australia Radiation of modern humans
	118,000	P L E I S T O C E N E	Eemian	Origins of *Homo sapiens sapiens*
	128,000		Saale Glaciation	
				Archaic *Homo sapiens*
Uncertain climatic detail			Uncertain climatic detail	
	730,000			
	1.6 Million			
		Pliocene		*Homo erectus* *Homo habilis* *Australopithecus*

THEORIES ON THE ORIGINS OF THE HUMAN LINE

• • •

All of us are members of the order primates, which includes most tree-living placental mammals. There are two suborders: anthropoids (apes, humans, and monkeys) and prosimians (lemurs, tarsiers, and other "premonkeys"). The research of more than a century has shown that the many similarities in behavior and physical characteristics between the hominids (primates of the family *Hominidae,* which includes modern humans, earlier human subspecies, and their direct ancestors) and the pongids (our closest living primate relatives) can be explained by identical charac-

Hominids

TABLE 2.4
Human development: 10 million to 5,000 years ago.

Date (B.P.)	Technology	Economy	Brain Changes	Body Changes
5,000	Writing, metals	Food production	↑	↑
10,000	Bows and arrows			
20,000				
31,000	Art in Europe			
37,000	Mounted tools		Fully developed brain and speech	Modern humanity
200,000				First *Homo sapiens* forms
250,000	Fire in use		Premodern speech	
500,000			Rapid brain expansion	
2,000,000	Stone toolmaking	Hunting and gathering	Reorganization of brain and slow expansion	Bipedalism is perfected—change in forelimbs Bipedalism begins (?)
10,000,000				

Note: The developments on this table began at the period indicated by the placement. They are assumed to continue until being either replaced or refined.

teristics that each group inherited millions of years ago from a common ancestor. (For an overview of human development covered in Part II, see Table 2.4.)

The question is, When did humankind separate from the nonhuman primates? Experts disagree vigorously about the answer (Klein, 1989).

Aegyptopithecus to *Sivapithecus*

Some 35 to 30 million years ago, large bands of small, fruit-eating primates known to paleontologists as *Aegyptopithecus* trooped through the lush, wet forests of the Nile Valley. These creatures were no larger than a fox and weighed no more than 9 to 10 pounds (4 to 4.5 kg). Elwyn Simons (1984) has found their jaws and skulls near the Fayum Depression west of the Nile. The bones bear some resemblance to those of later primates in East Africa dating to the Miocene epoch, which lasted from 23.5 to 5.2 million years ago. It was in Africa that apes and humans diverged from the monkeys, but no one knows when this divergence took place. Was *Aegyptopithecus* the basic primate stock from which the great apes and humans radiated, or did the separation occur during the Miocene?

Seventeen million years ago the world looked very different from what it is today. Continental drift linked Africa and Arabia with Europe and Asia. Hitherto they had been separated by sea. New mountain ranges like the Alps formed, and the climate became cooler as atmospheric and oceanic circulation patterns changed. As a result, previously separated animal species came into contact via the new land bridges, which led them into new habitats.

Several species of apes, some of which are now extinct, were already flourishing in Africa at the beginning of the Miocene, including a tree-dwelling, baboon-sized, hominoidlike primate named *Proconsul africanus* (Rose, 1984) (Figure 2.2) *(Hominoidea;* superfamily that includes apes and humans). *Proconsul* fossils may date to as early as 22 million to around 18 million years ago (Pilbeam, 1986). *Proconsul* was an unspecialized primate. Its successors in Africa are unknown, but other Miocene hominoids occur in Europe and Asia, including *Ouranopithecus* from Greece and a better known, quite different form from Turkey, India, and Pakistan known as *Sivapithecus,* ranging in age from about 12 to 7 million years ago. *Sivapithecus* resembles the modern orangutan in facial anatomy (see Figure 2.2) but otherwise is quite different. Its teeth and other features vary greatly from those of later hominoids, such as *Australopithecus* (see later). *Sivapithecus* is thought to have been an active climber and to have spent most of its time in the trees.

Let it be said at once that there is so little fossil evidence that any hypotheses are little more than intelligent guesswork. The basic anatomical pattern of the large hominoids appears in the Middle Miocene, 18 to 12 million years ago. One lineage of that first evolutionary radiation survives in modified form as the modern orang (Pilbeam, 1986). A second radiation begins in the Late Miocene, between 8 and 5 million years ago. This radiation eventually produces four lineages, at least one of

FIGURE 2.2   Side and top views of a reconstructed skull of *Proconsul africanus* (two-thirds actual size).

which, human beings, is known to have been considerably modified. These evolutionary patterns are monitoring changing climates and habitats—from warmer, less seasonal, more forested regimens to colder, more seasonal, and less forested conditions. Such changes occurred throughout the past 25 million years, but there were major, pulselike shifts between 17 and 14 million years ago and again between 8 and 5 million years ago. These reflected changes in the configuration of continents, mountain systems, and antarctic ice (Barry et al., 1985). Everyone agrees that the critical evolutionary radiation that produced the hominid line occurred in Africa.

Unfortunately, a vast chronological gap lies between *Ouranopithecus, Sivapithecus,* and the earliest hominidae, the australopithecines, which date to approximately 4 million years ago. The critical period was between 10 and 5 million years ago, when the segment of the African hominoid lineage radiated to produce gorillas, chimpanzees, and hominids. In the absence of key fossils, we can only speculate about the nature of the apelike animals that formed the hominoid segment during these millennia.

David Pilbeam (1986) has used existing fossils and evolutionary theory as well as molecular biology to guess—he can do no more—that these animals were mostly tree-living, like *Sivapithecus,* with long arms and legs and a broad chest. They would have used all four limbs in the trees, occasionally scrambling on the ground and even standing on their rear limbs at times. There was a marked difference in size between males and females, females perhaps weighing around 44 pounds (20 kg), males about double. At least one of the Late Miocene hominoid lineages led to the gorilla, a much larger, more terrestrial form.

Pilbeam goes on to speculate that a later hominoid lineage divided into western and eastern parts at least 5 million years ago (Figure 2.3). The western segment, the "proto-chimpanzee," remained dependent on fruit and other tree foods, scattered resources that required a flexible social organization. To the ancestors of modern chimpanzees, who enjoyed a specialized adaptation to the forest, tree-living behaviors remained essential. Knuckle walking (see Figure 2.4), which provides an excellent power thrust for jumping into a tree or a short sprint (think of a football lineman), was adaptive in the forest because long arms and hands as well as

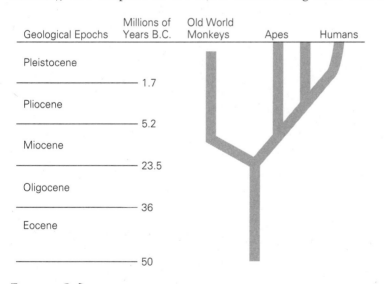

FIGURE 2.3 A much-simplified version of how Old World monkeys, apes, and humans evolved. For later human evolution, see Figure 2.12

(a)   (b)   (c)

FIGURE 2.4   Bipedalism and quadrupedalism. (a) Human bipedal posture. The center of gravity of the body lies just behind the midpoint of the hip joint and in front of the knee joint, so that both hip and knee are extended when standing, conserving energy. (b) A knuckle-walking chimpanzee. The body's center of gravity lies in the middle of the area bounded by legs and arms. When the ape walks bipedally, its center of gravity moves from side to side and up and down. The human center of gravity is displaced much less, making walking much more efficient. (After Zihlman.) (c) A baboon. Baboons are quadrupedal and adapted to living on the ground.

grasping feet were still vital for climbing. In contrast, today's humans are the descendants of the generalized common hominoid ancestor who underwent an adaptive shift to a different ecological zone, the savanna. Early hominids became bipedal, walking on two feet, over a long period of time, perhaps as a result of spending more and more time feeding on food resources on the ground. Bipedalism is a posture that is configured for endurance rather than power or speed. Walking is highly effective for wide-ranging foraging or running a marathon. It might have social advantages, too, allowing males to monitor females more efficiently when they were dispersed over larger areas (Pilbeam, 1986).

Molecular Biology and Human Evolution

Some years ago, two biochemists, Vincent Sarich and Alan Wilson, developed a means of dating primate evolution. They assumed that the albumin protein substances found in primate blood had evolved at a constant rate (Sarich, 1983). Thus the difference between the albumins of any pair of primates could be used to calculate the time that has elapsed since they separated. Sarich and Wilson showed that the albumins of apes and humans are more similar than those of monkeys and humans. Thus, they argue, apes and humans have a more recent common ancestry. They estimate that apes and Old World monkeys diverged approximately 23 million years ago, the gibbon and humankind only 8 million or so years ago, and that the chimpanzee, gorilla, and human last shared a common ancestor 6 to 7 million years ago. The apparent separation of apes and humans is so recent that statistically reliable numbers of differences have not yet accumulated.

Newer ways of comparing proteins and DNA are now refining the original "time clock" of evolutionary change and strongly imply some regular pattern of change along independent lineages. The new studies confirm that African apes and humans are similar, orangs roughly twice as distant, and gibbons a bit more dissimilar than orangs. The precise relationships between any genetic differences and the geological time scale are still uncertain and are the subject of much discussion (see Gingerich, 1985).

We are unlikely to achieve a greater understanding of very early human evolution unless we discover hominoid fossils dating to between 10 and 5 million years ago. These 5 million years were periods of major environmental change. As recently as 5.5 million years ago, the Mediterranean basin dried up when it became separated from the Atlantic. This development must have had major effects on the climate and ecology of Africa as well as the evolution of many species. That such evolution took place seems certain. During this critical period the African savanna, with its residual forests and extensive grassland plains, was densely populated by many mammal species as well as specialized tree-dwellers and other primates. Both the chimpanzee and the gorilla evolved in the forests, surviving from earlier times. On savanna plains other primates were flourishing in small bands, probably walking upright, and conceivably making tools. No fossil remains of these creatures have been found, so we do not know when primates first achieved the bipedal posture that is the outstanding human physical feature. We can, however, provide models of some of the ecological problems our earliest ancestors encountered.

THE ECOLOGICAL PROBLEMS FACED BY EARLY HOMINIDS

●　●　●

The evolutionary process is based on selection, which can be viewed in several ways (Foley, 1984b, 1987a). For example, one can consider the emergence of the first humans in terms of adaptive, evolutionary change. Organisms are mostly in balance with their environment. Mutations are the original source of variation in a population. They occur constantly and consistently, providing a reservoir of new variation. It is this variation, always present in a population, that occasionally provides significant advantage to some individuals, especially in cases of ecological transitions. Thus, a minority of the members of a population may increase their numbers through time because they have a selective advantage that may represent an improvement. As far as the behavioral evolution of the hominids is concerned, this process gives a model of terrestrial primates living in the increasingly dry environments of tropical Africa. Among one hominid group, mutations led to adaptive shifts—bipedalism, toolmaking, meat eating, and so on. These shifts put the group at an advantage over other terrestrial primates.

Selection

Another approach sees evolutionary changes arising as solutions to problems faced by the organism in its environment. New adaptations are selected if they solve problems effectively. The selective agent is the organism's environmental problems. Under this scenario, the characteristics of a hunter-gatherer adaptation would persist among hominids if they were solutions to problems faced in the environment.

Problem solving

One viewpoint sees a species' problems as the other species it eats, those with which it competes, and those that eat it. In other words, an evolutionary advance made by one species in an ecosystem can be seen as a deterioration of the environment for another. Thus, environmental problems are not inanimate forces but dynamic, evolving processes. An organism has to evolve as rapidly as possible just to maintain its current ecological adaptation. L. van Valen, the biologist who developed this

Red Queen model

approach, calls it the "Red Queen" model: "Now *here,*" the queen remarks in Lewis Carroll's *Alice Through the Looking-Glass,* "you see, it takes all the running *you* can do, to keep in the same place." The Red Queen model is one appropriate theoretical framework for studying the behavioral evolution of the earliest hominids (Foley, 1984c). These populations underwent adaptive changes through natural selection to solve environmental problems caused by the broader ecological community.

Adaptive Problems

Early hominids faced three major adaptive problems. They were large mammals; they were terrestrial primates; and they lived in an open, tropical savanna environment.

Large mammals

Human beings are large relative to the majority of warm-blooded animals. Hominids have become larger through their evolutionary history, a change that has led to additional food requirements because of higher metabolic rates. This means that every individual has to range efficiently over a larger area to obtain food. Population densities must fall because the carrying capacity of any territory is finite. There will be an increase in dietary breadth, for metabolic requirements will decrease relative to body size. It is interesting to observe that hunter-gatherers use a wider range of foods, many of lower quality, than do nonhuman primates. Larger

Range and mobility

mammals are more mobile than their smaller relatives. They cover more ground, which enables them to subsist off resources that are unevenly distributed not only in space but also at different seasons. Mobility allows larger-bodied animals to incorporate unpredictable, often seasonal resources in their diets. Larger mammals can also tolerate extremes of heat and cold, a capacity that may have contributed to the expansion of humans out of tropical latitudes later in prehistory. Bipedal humans have sweat glands and are heavily dependent on water supplies. These glands are a direct adjunct to bipedalism, for they enhance endurance for long-distance foraging. Efficient heat transfer aided early hominids because both large and small animals are at a disadvantage if attacked at high noon.

These and several other factors—such as increased longevity and brain enlargement— created adaptive problems for emerging humans. These problems resulted in a variety of solutions: wider territorial ranges, the need to schedule food gathering, broadening of diet, a high degree of mobility, and much greater behavioral flexibility. This flexibility included enhanced intelligence and learning capacity, parental care, and new levels of social interaction.

Being a Terrestrial Primate

An upright posture and bipedal gait are the most characteristic hominid physical features. Upright posture is vital because it frees the hands for other actions, like toolmaking. Knuckle walking, used, for instance, by chimpanzees, is a specialized way of walking in which the backs of the fingers are placed on the ground and act as main weight-bearing surfaces. Human arms are too short for us to be comfortable with this posture, used by football linemen and runners at the starting block. However, this posture is highly adaptive in forest environments, where apes jump into trees and need the power of a fast, short sprint. In contrast, bipedalism favors endurance and the covering of long distances, important considerations on the open savanna. Bipedalism was a critical antecedent of both hunting and gathering and toolmaking (Tuttle, 1972).

The fall in temperatures during the Late Miocene resulted in increasingly open environments in tropical latitudes. With this reduction in forested environments there probably came a trend toward terrestrially adapted species. The main constraint on arboreal primates is body size. Thus, to be part of the general trend toward larger body size among mammals, such primates would have to be at least partially terrestrial in their habits. Some 40 or more extinct and living primates, including the hominids, have adapted to a terrestrial existence. This secondary adaptation among tree-living forms may have occurred some time after 10 million years ago—expressed in the simplest terms, primates "came down from the trees" (Foley, 1987a). Coming down from the trees created three immediate problems:

Open environments

Coming down from the trees

- Locomotion difficulties arise for animals with limbs adapted to moving through forests, which are less efficient for moving on the ground. All terrestrial primates underwent some modification of their way of getting about—in the case of hominids a shift to bipedalism. We know that this selection was a powerful one. It was in existence at least 4 million years ago.

- Shelter becomes an acute problem in open country, where predators abound. Arboreal primates have special sleeping areas and are safe in the trees. Those adapted to living in open country return to trees at night or use cliff faces or caves, even if they have to disperse. Large hominids that are safer from predators make ground nests, where they sleep and also seek shade on hot days—"home bases." Exactly what forms these home bases take is a matter of constant scientific debate.

- Competition for food is another pressing problem for primates who require high-quality plant food, abundant in the forests. Such foods are dispersed widely in open country. There are two possible solutions—either specialize in a small spectrum of plant foods and become an effective competitor or maintain a broad dietary niche and expand the range of foods consumed. It is striking that such a broad-based niche is characteristic of later hunter-gatherers in tropical environments. And as part of human evolution, hominids expanded their food range to include meat.

Living in a Savanna Environment

Terrestrial primate populations can live in drier grasslands and woodlands, environments that present another set of challenging problems. Water supplies are certain to be restricted in distribution and by season, a critical environmental reality for hominids that need regular access to liquids. The distribution of water and hominid populations are closely connected. Further, plant foods in a savanna are of lower quality, and hominids had to compete for them with other animals. Most plant species were seasonal and of low productivity, so a great deal of time would have

Water supplies

been expended in searching for and processing the foods. A whole range of species would have been needed to ensure year-round food supplies.

Plant foods   Most plant species that do occur in the savanna are grasses, which are largely unsuitable for primates—but not for a diverse population of herbivores. This secondary biomass of animals could have been a valuable walking food source if the hominids found a way of tapping it. But there were competitors—a great diversity of predators, who would also have eaten an occasional hominid if the opportunity arose.

The long-term solutions to living in the savanna centered around an adaptation that involved exploiting a broad but patchy subsistence base. The lifeway was highly mobile, the range dependent on restricted water supplies. Meat became a larger part of the diet as a way of coping with long periods of plant scarcity. Among mammal species, these characteristics are associated with a trend toward larger brain size (Eisenberg, 1981). The earliest hominids lived at relatively low population densities. Their home ranges were larger than those of equivalent-sized mammals and primates. They were highly mobile and omniverous. This very general description coincides, in general terms, with that for human subsistence throughout most of prehistory. If the ecological model is on track in assuming that this lifeway evolved in response to selective pressures in the open savanna more than 2 million years ago, were the hominids of 2 million years ago true hunters and gatherers? Or were they far more apelike in behavior than their successors?

THE FOSSIL EVIDENCE FOR HUMAN EVOLUTION

● ● ●

Between 9 and 4 million years ago, the last common ancestral hominoid stock split into two main lineages, which evolved into apes and humans. The details of this split are still a complete mystery, largely because fossil beds dating to this critical period are very rare in Africa (Figure 2.1). The fossil record proliferates after about 5 million years ago but is still fragmentary and highly controversial. We can only navigate cautiously between the various schools of thought (Lewin, 1987).

Australopithecus and *Homo*

In 1925, an anatomist named Raymond Dart identified a fossil primate in South Africa that displayed both human and apelike features. He named his find *Australo-*

A. africanus   *pithecus africanus* (Latin for southern ape of Africa) (Figure 2.5). *A. africanus* was a gracile, small creature, in contrast to a second, more robust form that turned up among the dozens of australopithecine fragments found in later years. This has been

A. robustus   named *Australopithecus robustus,* a squat, massively built primate with a crested skull (Figure 2.6). None of the South African australopithecines could be dated by potassium argon methods, but they are estimated to be between 3 million and 800,000 years old (Dart, 1925; Rak, 1983).

For years, paleoanthropologists thought that *A. africanus* was the direct ancestor of humankind, that human evolution had proceeded in a relatively linear way through time. Then hominid fossils, not only gracile, but *robust,* australopithecines turned up in East Africa, finds that showed human evolution to be much more complicated. The many fossil finds are confusing, so we describe them in chronological order (see Table 2.3).

FIGURE 2.5 *Australopithecus africanus* from Sterkfontein, South Africa. *A. africanus* was probably 42 to 50 in. (107 to 127 cm) tall; the females, weighing 40 to 60 lbs (18 to 27 kg), were somewhat lighter than the males. The posture was fully upright, with the spinal curvature that places the trunk over the pelvis for balanced walking. (Apes do not have this curvature, nor are their legs proportionately as long as those of *Australopithecus*.) The foot was small, with a well-developed big toe. *Australopithecus* looked remarkably human but with a snout that was less prominent than the ape's. The canines were small, and the incisors were vertical in the jaw, whereas the ape's slope outward. A flat nose was combined with a well-developed forehead, and the brow ridges were much less prominent than those of modern tree-living relatives. The brain had a minimum size of about 450 cc, much smaller than that of a modern human male (1450 cc) and slightly larger than that of the chimpanzee (400 cc).

Awash and Hadar

The earliest australopithecines from East Africa are very fragmentary. The Middle Awash area of Ethiopia has yielded some skull fragments and a solitary thigh bone piece, found in deposits of potassium argon dated to between 4.1 and 3.9 million years ago. The skull fragments come from an australopithecine with almost no forehead and with brow ridges intermediate between those of apes and humans.

Middle Awash
4.1 to 3.9 million years ago (B.P.)

By far the most complete australopithecine finds earlier than 3 million years ago come from Hadar in northern Ethiopia (Johanson and Edey, 1981; Johanson and White, 1979). When Maurice Taieb and Donald Johanson discovered a remarkably complete skeleton of a small primate at Hadar on the Awash River, they named it Lucy. Lucy was only 3.5 to 4.0 feet (1.0–1.2 m) tall and 19 to 21 years old. Nearby, they found the remains of at least 13 males, females, and children. Lucy herself has recently been dated to 3.18 million years ago using a variant of potassium argon dating that employs computerized argon laser fusion. A nearly intact *A. afarensis* skull and arm bones from several other males have come from another Awash location about a mile upstream and date to about 3 million years ago, some 200,000 years later than Lucy (Kimbel et al. 1994). This important find confirms that all the

Hadar
3.18 to 2.9 million B.P.

FIGURE 2.6   A robust australopithecine from Olduvai Gorge, Tanzania. The robust australopithecine was both larger and heavier than the *africanus* forms, with a more barrel-like trunk. The biggest contrasts were in the facial appearance and the teeth. *Australopithecus robustus* had a low forehead and a prominent bony ridge on the crest of the skull, which supported massive chewing muscles. Its brain was slightly larger than that of *A. africanus,* and *A. robustus* had relatively well-developed cheek teeth as well as larger molars. There was considerable variation among the robust australopithecines (see text).

afarensis fragments found over the past 20 years are from a single australopithecine species. *A. afarensis* displays considerable size variation. Some individuals stood 5 feet (1.5m) tall and probably weighed approximately 150 lbs (68kg), a far cry from the small, slender Lucy. These creatures, however, were powerful, heavily muscled individuals, thought to be as strong as chimpanzees. *A. afarensis* was an anatomical mosaic, bipedal from the waist down, arboreal in the upper part of the body. All were fully bipedal, with the robust, curved arms associated with tree climbers. The arms were slightly longer for their size than the arms of humans. They had human-like hands, except that their fingers were slightly more curved. The Hadar hominids had brains approximating the size of chimpanzee brains, ape-shaped heads, and forward-thrusting jaws. There is no evidence that they made tools.

The Hadar finds are of great importance, for they demonstrate that the fundamental human adaptation of bipedalism *predates* the first evidence of toolmaking and the expansion of the brain beyond the level found in our nearest living relatives, the African apes. Bipedalism also implies that later hominids were preadapted to utilize their hands for toolmaking.

Many scientists believe *Australopithecus afarensis* was the common ancestor of the later hominids, including Raymond Dart's *Australopithecus africanus*. They consider *A. afarensis* a primitive form of the australopithecines, which displayed considerable anatomical variation yet was hardy enough to adapt to harsh, changing savanna environments and survive for nearly a million years.

FIGURE 2.7   The reconstructed male cranium of *Australopithecus afarensis*.

Bipedalism at Laetoli

Dramatic confirmation of hominid bipedalism by 3.75 million years ago comes from fossil-bearing beds at Laetoli in northern Tanzania, excavated by Mary Leakey and potassium argon dated to 3.75 to 3.59 million years ago. They have yielded not only the bones of extinct animals but also the incomplete jaws and teeth of at least 13 hominids (M. D. Leakey and Harris, 1990). The Laetoli hominids share many characteristics with those from Hadar, to the extent that Johanson believes they are the same species. The most remarkable finds came from the buried bed of a seasonal river, where thin layers of fine volcanic ash once formed a pathway for animals traveling to water holes. The hardened surface of the ash, dated to more than 3.59 million years ago, bore the footprints of elephants, rhinoceroses, giraffes, a saber-toothed tiger, and many species of antelope. Leakey also identified a trail of prints of two hominids (Figure 2.8). "The tracks," she wrote, "indicate a rolling and probably slow-moving gait, with the hips swiveling at each step, as opposed to the free-striding gait of modern man." The two hominid trails lay about 10 inches (25 cm) apart, probably laid down at different times. The feet display well defined arches, distinctive heel and toe prints made by upright-walking individuals about 4 feet 7 inches (1.4 m) and 4 feet 11 inches (1.49 m) tall. At least two hominids walked across the soft ash, along the same route.

Laetoli
3.6 million B.P.

Olduvai and Turkana

Olduvai Gorge is world-famous for *Zinjanthropus boisei* (Figure 2.6), potassium argon dated to 1.75 million years ago (L. S. B. Leakey, 1951; M. D. Leakey, 1971). The gorge is a spectacular rift in the great Serengeti Plain of northern Tanzania, a place where earth movements have exposed hundreds of yards of lake beds belonging to a long-dried-up Pleistocene lake (Table 2.5). Later, a more gracile hominid

Olduvai Gorge
1.75 million B.P.

FIGURE 2.8   Hominid footprints from Laetoli, Tanzania.

came from a level slightly lower than that of the original robust skull, a fossil Louis Leakey named *Homo habilis,* on the grounds that it was something quite different from the robust australopithecine nearby. The same levels yielded not only broken animal bones but also crude stone choppers and flakes that were more primitive than any previously discovered in the world.

The evolutionary picture was further complicated by discoveries of fossil-bearing beds on either shore of remote Lake Turkana in northern Kenya. The Leakey's son Richard and an international team of experts located hundreds of square miles of Pliocene and Lower Pleistocene fossil-bearing sediments. The hominids include both australopithecines and individuals with unmistakably larger brains, including the famous Skull 1470 (Figure 2.9), which dates to about 1.8 million years ago (Leakey and Lewin, 1977; Lewin, 1987).

Homo habilis

Even specialists are confused by the proliferation of hominids in East Africa by 2 million years ago, not only gracile and robust australopithecines but also other hominids with much larger brains. These hominids come from Koobi Fora and from Olduvai and have cranial capacities between 650 and 800 cc (Tobias, 1991). These larger-brained individuals are generally assumed to represent the appearance of the genus *Homo.* Louis Leakey was the first to identify one of these hominids at Oldu-

Koobi Fora
2.5 million B.P.

TABLE 2.5
Highly Schematic Chronology of Olduvai Gorge, Tanzania,
with positions of fossils and tools.

DATE (B.P.)	BED	FINDS	
	Bed IV	Acheulian hand axes	
Not less than 700,000			
	Bed III	Acheulian hand axes	
Not less than 1,000,000			
	Bed II[a]	Acheulian hand axes	
		Homo erectus	
		- - - - - - - - - - -	
		Homo habilis finds	
	Bed I	Oldowan chopper finds	
1,750,000		*Australopithecus boisei*	
		Homo habilis	
		Stone structure	
1,800,000		Volcanic lava	
c.2,200,000			

10 cm
0

[a] Broken line shows a possible break in the sequence.

vai, so his label *Homo habilis* has stood the test of time, even if there are suggestions that there were several forms.

If you had encountered *H. habilis* 2 million years ago, you would have seen little to distinguish the new hominid from *Australopithecus*. Both were of similar height and weight, about 4 feet 3 inches (1.3 m) tall and about 88 pounds (40 kg). Both were bipedal, but *H. habilis* would have looked less apelike around the face and skull. The head was higher and rounder, the face less protruding. Some of the most significant anatomical differences involve the teeth. The molars were narrower; the premolars smaller; and the incisors larger and more spadelike, as if they were used for slicing. However, microscopic wear studies of the teeth have shown that both *Australopithecus* and *H. habilis* were predominantly fruit eaters, so there does not seem to have been a major shift in diet between the two.

The first *Homo habilis* fragments, which came from Bed I at Olduvai Gorge in the early 1960s (Figure 2.10), consisted of some skull and postcranial fragments of a larger-brained hominid. Then Richard Leakey found the famous Skull 1470, a large-brained, round-headed cranium that confirmed the existence of *H. habilis* in no uncertain terms. Thigh and limb bones from Koobi Fora and from Olduvai con-

FIGURE 2.9   A tentative reconstruction of Skull 1470 from East Turkana. Provisionally identified as *Homo,* this cranium is remarkable for its large brain capacity and rounded back.

FIGURE 2.10   Olduvai Gorge, Tanzania.

firm that *H. habilis* walked upright. The hand bones are somewhat more curved and robust than those of modern humans. This was a powerful grasping hand, more like that of chimpanzees and gorillas than humans, a hand ideal for climbing trees. An opposable thumb allowed both powerful gripping and precise manipulation of fine objects. With the latter capacity, *H. habilis* could have made complex tools.

The discovery of 1.8-million-year-old *Homo habilis* skull and limb bones at Olduvai Gorge has shown that this was a tiny hominid, standing about 3 feet (1 m) tall, about the same size as Lucy from Hadar. There was probably considerable difference in size between males and females (the new Olduvai specimen, labeled OH 62, is thought to be female) (Johanson et al., 1987). This find throws important new light on hominid evolution between 4.0 and 1.5 million years ago; it shows that the small size of *Australopithecus afarensis* persisted for much longer than had been suspected.

Three major anatomical changes took place during the 2.5 million years between *Australopithecus afarensis* and the emergence of much larger and more advanced *Homo erectus* some 1.6 million years ago (see Chapter 3). Brain size increased from about 450 cc in *A. afarensis* to 1000 cc in *H. erectus*. There were further modifications to hips and limbs for bipedal locomotion and a reduction in sexual dimorphism (size difference due to sex). The latest Olduvai *Homo habilis* shows that the primitive body form and sexual dimorphism characteristic of earlier hominids vanished only with the emergence of the much more advanced *H. erectus*. These observations have important implications for deciding just how "human" *H. habilis* was.

The specimen OH 62 suggests that *Homo habilis* was distinctly less human than had been thought. Skeletal anatomy from many finds gives a mosaic picture of both primitive and more advanced features, of a hominid that both walked bipedally and retained the generalized hominoid ability to climb trees. A telling clue comes from OH 62's upper arm bones, which, like Lucy's, are within 95 percent of the length of the thigh bone. The chimpanzee has upper arm and leg bones of almost equal length, whereas modern human upper arms are only 70 percent of the length of the upper leg bones. Almost certainly *H. habilis* spent a great deal of time climbing trees, an adaptation that would make them much less human in their behavior, and presumably social structure, than had been assumed even a few years ago.

From Hominids to *Homo*

There is general consensus among the experts that *Homo habilis* in its various forms is the probable ancestor of the later human species *Homo erectus* and *Homo sapiens*. The sharp disagreement begins when one examines the evolutionary relationships between *Australopithecus afarensis* and later hominids and between *H. habilis* and the australopithecines. As British physical anthropologist Chris Stringer (1984) puts it, "The field is littered with abandoned ancestors and the theories that went with them."

Figure 2.11 and Table 2.6 summarize the fossil evidence and two major hypotheses for early human evolution. Hypothesis A argues that *Australopithecus afarensis* (Lucy) was the common stem from which came the eastern African "robust" australopithecine lineage and another lineage that led ultimately to the southern African "robust" form *(A. robustus)* and to *Homo* via a common ancestor in *A. africanus*, the gracile australopithecines. The *Homo* line led ultimately to *H. habilis* and *H. erectus*.

Hypothesis B argues that the robust australopithecines from eastern and southern Africa are a single evolutionary branch. *Australopithecus afarensis* is thought to be the last common ancestor of the robust australopithecine line and the lineage leading to humans. Under this theory, *A. africanus*, or a form like it, was the

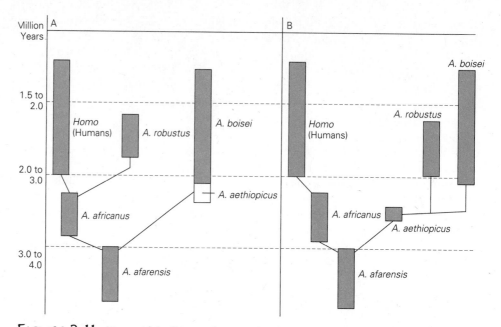

FIGURE 2.11   Two widely discussed, somewhat linear theories of early human evolution referred to in the text. Compare these with the "cladogram" in Figure 2.12, which reflects much current evolutionary thinking.

forebear of *Homo*. The robust taxa are grouped into a separate genus, *Paranthropus* (Delson, 1986). This scheme raises the possibility that the later australopithecines and *Homo* radiated rapidly and separately from a common ancestor. If such a rapid radiation took place, it was a unique event. Did hominids achieve some dramatic breakthrough in physiology or behavior? Was there a dramatic climatic change? We do not know.

In reality, the fossil hominid record compares poorly with that of many other mammalian groups, to the point that any theorizing about the relationships between the hominids of 4.0 to 1.5 million years ago is invalidated by the limitations of the field evidence. There have been great changes in the interpretation of human evolution in the past decade, resulting both from many new discoveries and from new theoretical advances. For example, some scientists believe there are grounds for creating no fewer than three robust australopithecine species alone, quite apart from at least two *Homo habilis* forms. Palaeoanthropologists now realize that hominid evolution involved a far greater level of species diversity than was previously thought (Foley, 1987b; 1989). Thus, human evolution is like a bush rather than the ladder that has been used as an analogy for so long.

Human evolution can be seen as one or more adaptive radiations rather than a simple, one-way evolution of successive species. This view stems from *cladistics,* an analytic system for reconstructing evolutionary relationships first proposed in the 1950s. Classical evolutionary analysis is based on morphological similarities between organisms. So is cladistics, but with a difference—cladistic analysis concentrates not only on features that identify common ancestry but also on those that are derived independently and are unique to specific lineages. Inevitably, cladistics tends to emphasize diversity over homogeneity.

The current view of human evolution begins with a widely accepted assumption that the sequence of hominid evolution began with the australopithecines, followed

TABLE 2.6

Four tentative groups of East and South African hominids, much simplified for this book

VARIABLES	HADAR/LAETOLI GROUP	GRACILE GROUP	ROBUST GROUP	HOMO GROUP
Brain size	Comparable to a Chimpanzee	450–550 cc	500–550 cc	650–775 cc
Teeth	Small back teeth; large front teeth	Large front and back teeth	Very large back teeth; relatively small front teeth	Variable; generally smaller than robust and gracile forms
Limbs	Bipedal; arms slightly longer than *Homo sapiens's*		Some elements of limb bones differ from those of modern humans	Bipedal, but lower limbs still partially adopted to arboreal life
Species and sites	*Australopithecus afarensis* East Africa: Hadar and Laetoli	*Australopithecus africanus* South Africa: Taung, Sterkfontein, Makapansgat East Africa: Omo?, East Turkana	*Australopithecus robustus* South Africa: Swarkrans, Kromdraai *Australopithecus boisei* East Africa: Olduvai, East Turkana, Omo *Australopithecus aethiopicus* East Turkana	*Homo* East Africa: Olduvai and East Turkana South Africa: Sterkfontein
Dates	East Africa: c. 4 million to c. 3 million B.P.	East Africa: c. 3 million to c. 1.5 million B.P. South Africa: no reliable dates	East Africa: c. 2.6 million to c. 1 million B.P. South Africa: no reliable dates	East Africa: c. 2 million to c. 1.5 million B.P.

by the emergence of *Homo habilis* through *H. erectus* to *H. sapiens*. But cladistics emphasizes considerable diversity at each stage, so much so that one cannot think of human evolution as simply a trend toward anatomically modern forms (Figure 2.12). As we have seen, the australopithecines were remarkably diverse, with the primitive A. *afarensis* form, the lightly built and later A. *africanus,* and the much more massive A. *robustus.* Between 5 and 1 million years ago, there was considerable adaptive radiation of australopithecines. The earliest members of the genus *Homo* were probably part of that radiation, *Australopithecus*-like forms with larger brains relative to body size. These forms are all classified as *H. habilis,* but it seems certain that there was considerable variability and that several subspecies will be identified in the future. *Homo erectus* appeared about 1.6 million years ago and may also have been part of this adaptive radiation. Thus, the pattern of human evolution based on the adaptive radiation seen with the australopithecines persisted into much later times.

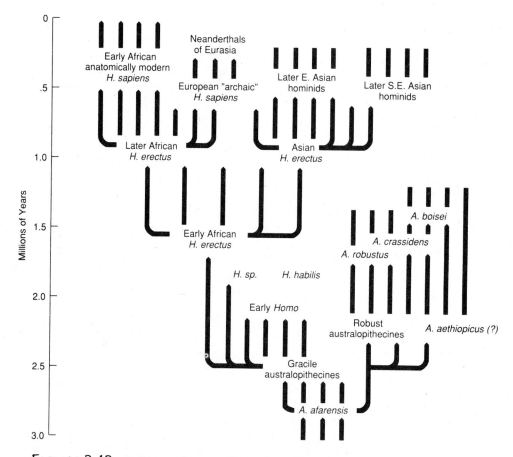

FIGURE 2.12   A diagram that sees the process of human evolution as a series of adaptive radiations. The basis for each radiation was a mixture of adaptations to local conditions and geographic isolation, isolation being especially important in later prehistory. The result was the evolution of diverse behavioral and ecological strategies and different species and subspecies. The model bears a much greater resemblance to models for other mammalian families, for it is a mistake to think of human evolution as different from that of other animals (after Foley, 1987).

ARCHAEOLOGICAL EVIDENCE FOR EARLY HUMAN BEHAVIOR

● ● ●

Studying early human behavior is complicated both by poor preservation conditions and by the vast time chasm that separates us from our remotest ancestors. In general terms, there are three lines of evidence that offer opportunities for testing hypotheses about early human behavior. One is scatters of artifacts and food remains that form the archaeological record for hominid activities, perhaps at predator kills, home bases, or meat caches. A second is manufactured artifacts; because of preservation conditions these are mainly objects made in stone. The transport of raw materials used to make these tools is also an important consideration. Finally, surviving food remains, almost entirely fragmentary animal bones, can reveal valuable information about our remote forebears.

Evidence for "Central Places"?

Later hunter-gatherers made habitual use of "central places," places where they returned to sleep, fabricate tools, cook food, and engage in a wide variety of social activities. Did the earliest humans have similar central places?

The only archaeological evidence comes from East Turkana and Olduvai Gorge, where a number of concentrations of bones and stone tools dating to around 2 million years ago and later have been excavated and studied with meticulous care. It is important to note that no such concentrations have been found with the earlier Laetoli or Hadar hominids.

For years, Louis Leakey and other pioneer paleoanthropologists believed that these scatters were "living floors," places where our ancestors slept, made tools, and butchered game. These were home bases, they argued, on the assumption that the hominids who created the artifact concentrations were hunters and gatherers behaving like primitive versions of living bands.

Recent thinking on the subject regards such assumptions as dangerous. First, the archaeological record is very ancient, so much so that the only way one can hope to interpret it is with a thorough knowledge of the geological and other processes that have affected the bone and tool scatter since it was abandoned by its makers. Second, we now know much more about living hunters and nonhuman primates, enough to undermine confidence that direct analogies from such populations have any validity when dealing with 2-million-year-old hominid behavior. Third, a whole new generation of research involving controlled experimentation, edge wear studies, and other sophisticated approaches has thrown doubt on the notion that *Homo habilis* was a hunter at all.

If the Koobi Fora and Olduvai scatters are not central places, what behavior do they represent? Some of the earliest manufactured tools in the world, some in association with animal bones, come from the Koobi Fora area of East Turkana (Isaac, 1981a; Isaac and Harris, 1978). Several localities have been excavated, among them a dry streambed where a group of hominids found the carcass of a hippopotamus about 1.8 million years ago. They gathered around and removed bones and meat from the dead animal with small stone flakes. The deposits in which the stones and flaked debris are found are so fine-grained that they contain natural pebbles no larger than a pea. Thus, every lump of rock at the site was carried in by the hominids to make tools at the carcass. Some of the cores came from nearly 9 miles (14 km) away, presumably so the people could strike off sharp flakes to butcher the carcass. This site provides clear evidence of toolmaking, raw material transport, and butchering. We simply do not know whether the hominids killed the hippopotamus. The site may represent a place where they paused briefly to scavenge meat from a predator kill or an animal that had died of natural causes. It was certainly not a central place.

Site FxJj50, also at Koobi Fora, is in an ancient watercourse, a place where the hominids could find shade from the blazing sun, located close to water and abundant supplies of stone for toolmaking (Figure 2.13) (Bunn et al., 1980). The site consists of a cluster of stone artifacts: choppers, crude scrapers, battered cobbles, and sharp-edged flakes. Approximately 2100 bones representing at least 20 vertebrates, mainly antelope, are associated with the tools, some of them bearing carnivore chewing marks. There are clear signs that the bones were smashed and cut by hominids, for reconstructed fragments show signs of hammer blows and fine linear grooves that can have resulted only from cutting bone with stoneworking edges. The excavators noted the lack of articular ends of bones, a characteristic of bone accumulations resulting from carnivore kills. Perhaps the hominids simply chased away lions and other predators, then moved in on a fresh kill; we cannot be sure. There is a strong possibility that successful hunting played a relatively limited role in hominid life at this early time.

Another site consists of a scatter of stone tools and broken animal bones, these from several antelope and larger mammals. The scatter lay on the surface of a dry streambed where water could still be easily obtained by digging in the sand. The banks of the watercourse were probably shaded by dense stands of trees that provided both shelter and plant foods. Perhaps the people who left the tools and bones climbed into these trees at night. The site was so sheltered that even minuscule stone chips were still in place, unaffected by the strong winds that sweep over the area; the leaves, too, left impressions in the deposits. The nearest source of toolmaking stone is 2 miles (3.2 km) from the site, so the inhabitants must have carried in their tools

FIGURE 2.13   Excavation at site FxJj50, Koobi Fora, Kenya.

and, in all probability, portions of the several animals whose bones accumulated at the site. This type of behavior—the carrying in of food to a fixed location—is fundamentally different from that of the nonhuman primates.

Much of our present knowledge about the lifeways of the earliest hominids comes from Olduvai Gorge, where Mary Leakey plotted and recorded sites in Bed I at the base of the gorge (M. D. Leakey, 1971). The *Zinjanthropus* floor at Olduvai was found to be 1239 square feet (115 m²), consisting of more than 4000 artifacts and bones. Many artifacts and bones were concentrated in an area some 15 feet (4.5 m) across. A pile of shattered bones and rocks lay a short distance away, the bones perhaps piled in heaps as the marrow was extracted. A barer, arc-shaped area between these bone heaps and the pile of more complete fragments remains unexplained. Leakey wonders whether it was the site of a crude windbreak of branches since the area lies in the path of today's prevailing winds.

Recent researches have approached the Olduvai locations from several angles (Bunn and Kroll, 1986; Potts, 1984a). Careful examination of the bones revealed that many of them had lain on the surface for considerable periods of time, perhaps as long as four to six, even ten, years, to judge from weathering patterns on modern East African bones. The bones of many different animals are found in the assemblages, and the remains of carcasses are from a very ecologically diverse set of animals. Limb bones predominate on the "floors," as if these isolated bones were repeatedly carried to the site. Furthermore, the stone tools found on the Olduvai surfaces were all imported from raw material sources some distance away.

What is one to make of this pattern of meat and marrow-rich bones concentrated in a small area with stone tools? The percentage of carnivore bones is somewhat higher than the natural environment would suggest, about 3 percent in the Olduvai assemblages, as opposed to 1 percent for the local environment today (in one case the figure was as high as 21 percent). Was there then intense ecological competition for game between hominids and other carnivores? It seems possible that the presence of carnivores restricted the activities of hominids at Olduvai. They may have grabbed meat-rich bones from carnivore kills, then taken them to a place where they had a collection of stone tools. There they could have hastily cut off meat and extracted marrow before abandoning the fresh bones to the carnivores hovering nearby. The Olduvai sites may not have been safe from carnivores, and without fire or domesticated dogs, *Homo habilis* probably had to rely on opportunistic foraging. As we have already noted, many of the Olduvai bones bear both carnivore teeth marks and stone tool cuts, perhaps a reflection of competition for game. It is also worth noting that one hominid bone found at Olduvai had been gnawed by carnivores.

Whatever their actual purpose, we can be sure that the Olduvai bone and artifact accumulations were places that were used only on a very transitory basis. Were they locations to which hominids returned to sleep, feed their dependents, and carry out other activities, or were they merely used occasionally for breaking up and eating meat? We know that the hominids transported toolmaking stone and portions of animal carcasses from one place to another. We cannot be sure that they actually lived at the places where these objects were abandoned, in the way that later hunter-gatherers did. Several experts believe that the accumulations were useful caches of stone artifacts to which bones and other food resources were taken for processing (Potts, 1984b). Perhaps these caches lay near water supplies or predictable food resources. Perhaps, too, they were maintained throughout a group's range, so the hominids did not have to carry meat or stone very far. However, a consistent pattern of caches spread throughout a territory requires a level of forethought, planning, and memory that may have been beyond the intellectual capacities of the Olduvai hominids.

All archaeology currently tells us is that the early Olduvai sites were places to which stone and food resources were carried. These may have been the predecessors to hunter-gatherer central places, which were to come into use in later prehistory, conceivably with the regular use of fire for heat and protection.

Hunting and Scavenging

Were our earliest ancestors fully fledged hunter-gatherers, or did they scavenge predator kills for meat? Or both? Therein lie some of the fundamental controversies of palaeoanthropology. Taphonomy, microwear studies, and other highly sophisticated approaches to the archaeological record of 2 million years ago have shown again and again the sheer folly of basing theories about early hominid behavior on crude analogies with contemporary hunting societies. Just for a start, the hominids belonged to a quite different species. Furthermore, their behaviors are not displayed by any living ape, nor indeed by all early hominids, some of whom never accumulated bones.

As we have seen, diverse carnivore and ungulate communities developed in eastern and southern Africa by 4 million years ago, with a wide diversity of hominids as part of the mammalian community. Some scientists believe that new ways of adapting to a heterogeneous environment like that of the East African savanna developed opportunistically. Under some ecological conditions, they argue, an opportunistic shift in the use of a food source such as meat could have led to a breakthrough in human behavior that had long-term significance.

With a wide diversity of predators in the savanna, hominids consuming meat would have to have competed successfully with carnivores to obtain it. This competitive ability was selected because meat eating became vital to survival and reproductive success, and the dangers of competing with carnivores were more than outweighed by the advantages of more available food supplies and increased reproductive success because of better nutrition and easily transportable meat for social feeding.

At present, it is difficult to choose between these very general ecological models.

The Olduvai sites contain bones of smaller animals for the most part, species that were less powerful than hominids. Rather than scavenging, hunters may have run down their quarry and thrown it to the ground before killing it. This is more of an apelike form of behavior, although apes have been observed scavenging meat from predator kills (Hasegawa et al., 1983).

Some microscopic evidence from very early archaeological sites at Olduvai Gorge suggests that scavenging may have been much more important. Pat Shipman (1984) and others have examined dozens of broken animal bones from Olduvai, peering at minute but distinctive cut marks resulting from such activities as butchery, disarticulation of carcasses, and skin removal. They made high-fidelity replicas of bone marks and then examined them under a scanning electron microscope, comparing the results with those obtained from a 2300-year-old agricultural settlement in Kenya, where the inhabitants were actively engaged in disarticulation, butchery, and other activities. They found that 90 percent of the 2300-year-old bones showed cut marks resulting from the disjointing of carcasses, but only 45 percent of those from Olduvai showed the same marks. This was also true with butchery marks, those made when removing meat from bones. In contrast, about 75 percent of both the Olduvai and the 2300-year-old bones show the characteristic marks left by skin and tendon removal, which are especially visible on the lower limb bones since they had little meat on them.

Both disarticulation and butchery were surprisingly uncommon at Olduvai, so it seems doubtful the hominids were butchering and disjointing large animals and carrying them back to base. They seem to have obtained meat without cutting up too many carcasses. It is possible that they scavenged it from predator kills. A tantalizing clue came from 13 Olduvai bones on which both carnivore and humanly made markings were present. In 8 instances, the human marks *overlay* carnivore tooth marks, as if the humans had scavenged the bones from carcasses that had already been killed by lions or other predators (see Potts, 1984a).

The diversity of animals, including nonmigratory species, represented in the Olduvai bone accumulations is striking. Richard Potts (1984b) believes that this represents the variety of animals found in a resident rather than a migratory ungulate population, where only a few species are represented. He argues that the hominids depended at least partially on resident animals in a situation in which the generalization about large carnivores being hunters *and* scavengers might apply. Thus, the Olduvai hominids were hunting resident mammals as well as competing with other carnivores in scavenging activity.

By studying body part frequencies in Olduvai accumulations, Potts (1984b) has shown that carnivore bone assemblages contain a high proportion of forelimbs, the body part usually removed first from a carcass by a scavenger. In accumulations where hominid activity had taken place, higher forelimbs are also common but hindlimbs are relatively abundant as well, as if the hominids were obtaining meat both early and later in the sequence of carcass disarticulation.

What do these new archaeological findings mean in behavioral terms? Robert Blumenschine has spent long field seasons studying animal predators on the game-rich Serengeti Plains of northern Tanzania (Blumenschine and Cavallo, 1992). This semi-arid, grassland environment, intersected by occasional water courses lined by trees, is the closest we can come to the open landscape exploited by our remotest ancestors. The Serengeti abounds in game animals of all kinds, and in predators that hunt them. It is an environment of plenty, yet of danger, where bipedal hominids would compete with lions and hyenas, and were potential prey themselves. The treeless savanna offered little refuge to hominids armed not with sharp teeth and claws but with sticks and stones, yet they acquired game meat successfully, either by being expert hunters or by opportunistic scavenging. Blumenschine observed dozens of predator kills and compared the surviving carcasses and shattered bones, comparing them to those from Olduvai and other hominid sites. At the same time, he identified two distinctive scavenging opportunities where hominids would have been at an advantage compared with their competitors.

The first lay in streamside woodlands, places where lions kill close to water in the dry season, feeding on a carcass lying under a canopy of trees, hidden from roaming vultures high above. In many cases, Blumenschine found that a day would elapse before even hyenas would find the abandoned kill, ample time for observant hominids to move in for their share. It is here, too, that leopards hide small antelope kills in trees, high above the ground. Two million years ago, sabre-toothed tigers may have killed much larger animals in similar riparian environments. During the dry months, large animals sometimes starved to death or died of disease near streams, another potentially important source of fresh meat.

Blumenschine believes that scavenging would have been most important in the dry season, when plant foods were in shortest supply. During these months, the best food-getting strategy was to scavenge from kills by many predators near permanent water supplies. The rainy season found the same predators ranging over the open plains, killing in places where hyenas and vultures would make quick work of the remaining carcass—far away from the trees that were so vital to puny hominids. But our ancestors then relied more heavily on plant foods, which came into season at different times. Thus, scavenging and foraging went hand in hand, each complementing the other at different times of the year.

The Blumenschine scavenging theory is highly plausible, for it is based on assumptions that hominids were subject to the same pressures as other animals, and on a rapidly growing body of scientific data from many sources. He observes that scavenging was not easy for slow-moving animals like humans. Careful observation was all important—the early morning, purposeful flights of vultures toward new kills, the telltale antelope fur tufts at the foot of a tree where a leopard has stashed its kill, the triumphant laughs of a feeding hyena at a fresh kill. Blumenschine theorizes that early hominids made what they call "mental maps" of their territories, which enabled them to predict where carcasses might be found, where clumps of fruit ripen in different months.

Archaeologist Glynn Isaac (1984) believes that opportunism is a hallmark of humankind—a restless process, like mutation and natural selection. The normal pressures of ecological competition were able to transform the versatile behavior of ancestral primates into the new and distinctive early hominid pattern. The change required feedback between cultural subsystems, such as hunting and sharing food. Weapons and tools made possible new ways of getting and processing foods, even with entirely new forms of diet, not only plant foods but meat as well. Foraging provided stability, making the savanna an ideal and vacant ecological niche for hominids, who lived on scavenging, hunting, and foraging combined. The microwear patterns on the tooth surfaces of *Australopithecus* and *H. habilis* show that both creatures flourished on a diet very similar to that of chimpanzees. But *H. habilis* had a much larger brain, a development that was probably associated with an increase in economic and social complexity, and perhaps food sharing as well.

Maybe our earliest ancestors shared food, dividing the labor of scavenging and foraging, of processing food, between males and females. Such social cooperation and advanced planning was necessary, especially since the stone used for flakes and hammers occurred in one place, animal carcasses often far away. To bring the two together required planning and social cooperation to the point where some groups carried stone as far as 6 miles (10 km) from source. And scavenging may have begun as a way of supplementing plant foraging as global cooling brought more open environments to tropical Africa. These environments were selected for scavenging behavior which was, to judge from modern observations, already a part of ape behavior. Thus, *Australopithecus* and *Homo habilis* with their flaked stone toolkits took not only marrow but fresh meat, using sharp-edged stones as the equivalent of hyena teeth.

Plant Foraging and the Early Hominids

Beyond some microscopic wear traces from plant tissues on early stone artifacts, there is as yet no archaeological evidence for plant foods being consumed by early hominids, because this kind of data does not preserve well. Yet a scanning electron microscope focused on tooth microwear has shown that some Lower Pleistocene hominids had diets very similar to those of modern nonhuman primates (Walker,

1981). The recent discovery of *Homo habilis* limb bones revealed an unexpected inconsistency, for their anatomy was far more arboreal than that previously assumed for a terrestrial, bipedal primate of 2 million years ago. Such adept tree climbers are certain to have relied on fruit and other plant foods, perhaps enjoying a diet closer to that of modern apes than to that of hunter-gatherers. Clearly, plant foods were a major element in a broadly based early hominid diet, even if the archaeological evidence tends to stress meat eating over foraging.

TOOLMAKING

● ● ●

Other animals, such as chimpanzees, make tools (Figure 2.14), but human beings manufacture tools regularly and habitually as well as in a much more complex fashion. In other words, we have gone much further in the toolmaking direction than other primates (Gowlett, 1984). One reason is that our brains allow us to plan our actions much more in advance. Prehistoric tools in all their simplicity and sometimes extraordinary complexity provide a record of ancient decision-making processes. By analyzing the ways in which prehistoric stone artifacts—the most enduring of all technologies—were made, we can gain insights into the mind processes of the people who created them.

All studies of stone artifacts are based on the assumption that a sequence of removing flakes ultimately produced a finished artifact, whether simple or complex,

FIGURE 2.14   Chimpanzee using a stick as a tool to fish for insects. Chimpanzees also use objects for play and display and carry them in their hands. Sometimes, they improve their sticks slightly with their teeth. They use leaves for cleaning the body and sipping water. Chimpanzees have inherited behavior patterns far closer to our own than to those of any monkey (Goodall, 1986).

(a)

(b)

FIGURE 2.15   Early stone technology. The principles of fracturing stone were fully understood by early stoneworkers, who used them to make simple but very effective artifacts. Certain types of flinty rock fracture in a distinctive way, as illustrated in (a). Early stoneworkers used a heavy hammerstone to remove edge flakes or struck lumps of rock against anvils to produce the same effect, as shown in (b). Oldowan tools were frequently made by removing a few flakes from lava lumps to form jagged working edges. Such flakes have been shown by modern experiments to be remarkably effective for dismembering and butchering game. Perhaps it is small wonder that this simple stone technology was so long-lasting. (a) When a blow is struck on flinty rock, a cone of percussion is formed by shock waves rippling through the stone *(left)*. A flake is formed *(right)* when the block (or core) is hit at the edge, and the stone fractures along the edge of the ripple. (b) Using a hammerstone *(left)* and anvil *(right)*.

to be used for a specific purpose (Figure 2.15). Many details of the world's earliest stone technology are debated, but there is no doubt that it was the work of individuals with an impressive knowledge of the properties of stone. They knew how to select the right rock, could visualize in three dimensions how to put it to use and flake it, had mastered the routine steps needed to create a tool, and were capable of passing this knowledge on to others.

The Oldowan Industry

Everyone has always assumed that the earliest stone technology would be very simple (Toth and Schick, 1986). When the Leakeys found crudely chipped stones in the long-buried lake beds at Olduvai Gorge, they were indeed nothing much to look at (Figure 2.16). (The Leakeys called their early tool assemblages Oldowan, after the gorge where they were first identified.) Most were broken cobbles and flakes, with flakes in the majority. Some Oldowan tools were so crude that only an expert can tell them from a naturally fractured rock, and the experts often disagree. All the

FIGURE 2.16   Oldowan technology. Many cobbles at Koobi Fora and Olduvai Gorge were used as cores to produce sharp-edged flakes. The technology was simple in the extreme. First, sharp blows were struck near the natural edge of a pebble to remove flakes. The pebble was then turned over and more blows struck on the ridges formed by the scars of the earlier flakes. A core with a jagged edge, perhaps sometimes used as a chopper, resulted. Many cores were "mined" for as many flakes as possible before being discarded. The figure shows two Oldowan cores from Olduvai Gorge. Arrows show flake edges. Front and side views (two-fifths actual size).

Oldowan choppers and flakes strike one as extremely practical implements; many are so individual in design that they seem haphazard artifacts, not standardized in the way later Stone Age tools were. Classifying them is very difficult, for they do not fall into distinct types. The tools cannot be described as primitive since many display a sophisticated understanding of stone's potential uses in toolmaking. We now know that the Olduvai hominids were adept stone toolmakers, using angular flakes and lumps of lava to make weapons, scrapers, and cutting tools. The tools themselves probably were used to cut meat and perhaps wood. In all probability, the hominids made extensive use of simple and untrimmed flakes for many purposes.

Oldowan industries have been found on several sites in East Africa dating to between about 2.5 and 1.5 million years ago. There appears to be relatively little variability between different toolkits, and the artifacts show certain common technological features. All of them were made from cobbles, often struck from lumps

Oldowan
2.5 to 1.2 million B.P.

with edges flaked from both sides (Figure 2.16). Some of these cores may have served as crude choppers, for the toolkit consisted of both heavy-and light-duty tool forms, some modified into crude scrapers. This seems like a very simple technology, but the artifacts show a skilled appreciation of basic stone-flaking techniques and flaking sequences that were envisaged in the mind's eye.

For years, archaeologists have thought of the Oldowan as a static technological stage without any perceptible change. As more sites come to light and analytic techniques are refined, though, the Oldowan appears in a different light—as a simple, highly effective technology that grew more complex over time, with the appearance of crude bifacial working, in which cores were flaked on both sides (Figure 2.17) (Gowlett, 1986).

Mary Leakey (1971) studied the Oldowan choppers and flakes from the early hominid levels at Olduvai and divided the artifacts into different morphological forms. Her classification remained unchallenged until Nicholas Toth and a new generation of scholars approached early stone technology from a more holistic perspective (Toth, 1985; Toth and Schick, 1993). The objective of their studies is to learn as much as possible about early hominid behavior from the stone artifacts left behind. Such research is founded on every aspect of technology, from raw material acquisition through artifact manufacture and use to discarding and incorporation of the tools into the geological record. As part of his work, Toth became an expert stone toolmaker and carried out edge wear and taphonomic studies on sites in East Turkana.

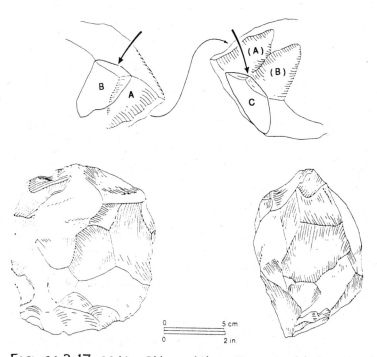

FIGURE 2.17   Making Oldowan bifaces. Top, a simplified picture of the process required for bifacial flaking. Bottom, a large Oldowan diskoidlike artifact from Chesowanja, East Africa, in plan and side views. The stoneworker used this bifacial technique but did not fashion the biface along a long axis, as later humans did (see Chapter 3). (After Gowlett, 1984.)

Toth emerged from his work with a very different view of the Oldowan. He points out that conventional approaches to the stone artifacts are based on the idea that the makers had premeditated artifact forms in mind. His experiments replicated thousands of Oldowan cores and flakes and led him to argue that much of the variety in Oldowan artifacts was, in fact, the result of flake production. Many of the choppers from Olduvai and Koobi Fora are actually "waste," cores discarded when as many flakes as possible had been removed from them. Toth also observes that the size of available raw material can profoundly affect the size and variety of choppers and flakes at an Oldowan site (Toth and Schick, 1986).

Toth's experiments with replicated tools revealed that sharp-edged flakes are far more effective for butchering animal carcasses, especially for slitting skin. Flakes, then, were of much greater importance than hitherto suspected—but this does not mean that all choppers were just waste. Some may have served as wood-chopping and adzing tools or for breaking open bones for their marrow. Microwear studies of the few Oldowan flakes made of fine-grained materials have hinted at three possible uses: butchery and meat cutting, sawing and scraping wood, and cutting soft plant matter.

What are the implications of Toth's studies for our knowledge of early hominid cognitive skills? Toth believes our earliest ancestors had a good sense of the mechanics of stone tool manufacture and of the geometry of core manipulation. They were able to find the correct acute angle needed to remove flakes by percussion. Not even modern beginners have this ability; it takes several hours of intensive practice to acquire the skill. Although chimpanzees use sticks and crack nuts with unflaked stones, they rarely carry their "artifacts" more than a few yards. In contrast, the Koobi Fora and Olduvai hominids carried flakes and cores over considerable distances, up to 8 miles (13 km). This behavior represents a simple form of *curation*, retaining tools for future use rather than just utilizing convenient stones, as chimpanzees do. Toth hypothesizes that the hominids tested materials in streambeds and other locations; transported the best pieces to activity areas; and sometimes dropped them there, carrying the rest off with them. He also points out that they must have relied heavily on other raw materials, like wood and bone, and that stone artifacts do not necessarily give an accurate picture of early hominid cognitive abilities.

The archaeologists' traditional view of the Oldowan considers it a "protohuman culture," with its simple stone artifacts a first step on the long evolutionary trail to modern humanity. Perhaps this view has been colored by analogies with modern hunter-gatherers and by overoptimistic interpretations claiming that early hominids aimed and threw stone missiles, shared food, and so on. Another viewpoint argues that the Oldowan hominids were at an apelike grade of behavior, on the grounds that all the conceptual abilities and perceptions needed to manufacture Oldowan tools also appear in ape-manufactured tools like termite-fishing tools and sleeping platforms (Wynn and McGrew, 1989). Furthermore, not only Oldowan hominids but also chimpanzees scavenge and hunt for game, chasing down small animals, carrying meat over considerable distances, and using "extractive technology" to break open animal bones and nuts. Chimpanzees, like early hominids, use the same places again and again, pounding nuts at the same locations and carrying food to their favorite eating sites. Even if the specifics vary in some instances and the natural environments are different, the behavioral pattern of Oldowan hominids is generally similar to that of apes. There are, however, two behavioral differences between apes and early hominids. First, hominids were at an advantage in that they were bipedal, a posture that is far more efficient for carrying objects than walking on four limbs. Second, the Oldowan humans were adapted to savanna living, where they had to organize and cover far larger territories in open country than their primate relatives in the forest. In the long term, this may have resulted in new concepts of space and spatial organization, concepts that were definitely reflected in more complex stone tool forms after a million years ago.

Early hominids with their larger brains probably would not have adapted or behaved the same way as modern apes. We can be certain that there were significant differences between nonhuman primates and hominids 2 million years ago, but these changes may not be reflected in stone artifacts. Without question, our ancestors became more and more dependent on technology. The opportunistic nature of primeval stone technology is in sharp contrast to the better designed, much more standardized stone artifacts of later humans.

THE DEVELOPMENT OF LANGUAGE

● ● ●

Cooperation, the ability to get together to solve problems of both subsistence and potential conflict, is a vital quality in human beings. We are unique in having a spoken, symbolic language that enables us to communicate our most intimate feelings to one another. One fundamental question about early prehistory surrounds this development: At what point did hominids acquire the ability to speak?

Our closest living relatives, the chimpanzees, communicate with gestures and many voice sounds in the wild, whereas other apes use sounds only to convey territorial information. However, chimpanzees seem to have a natural talent for learning symbolic language under controlled conditions. A famous chimpanzee named Washoe was trained to communicate with humans, using no fewer than 175 sign language gestures similar to those of American Sign Language (Gardner and Gardner, 1969). After more than a year, Washoe could associate particular signs with specific activities, such as eating and drinking. Another chimpanzee, named Sarah, was taught to read and write with plastic symbols and acquired a vocabulary of 130 words, to the extent that she obeyed sequences of written instructions given with the symbols (Premack and Premack, 1972). The research continues, but there is no evidence that chimpanzees can combine visual symbols to create new meanings or use syntax. Sequences of signs produced by trained chimpanzees may have a superficial resemblance to the first multiword sentences produced by children, but beyond the stage of learning isolated symbols, an ape's language learning is severely restricted (Terrace, Sanders, and Bever, 1979).

Clearly, articulate speech was an important threshold in human evolution because it opened up whole new vistas of cooperative behavior and unlimited potential for the enrichment of life. When did hominids abandon grunts for speech? There are only two potential lines of research. One uses *endocasts* (natural casts of the interior of the brain case). Dean Falk (1984) has studied the convolutions of early hominid endocasts and found that those of the early australopithecines are apelike. The brain cell of Skull 1470 (Figure 2.9) is about 300 cc larger, and the frontal lobe of its endocast is more humanlike, especially in the Broca's area, where speech control is located.

Endocast research is much more generalized than detailed anatomical studies of the position of the voice box, the larynx, using both comparative anatomy and actual fossils to study differences between apes and humans. Jeffrey Laitman (1984) and others studied the *position* of the larynx in a wide variety of mammals, including humans. They found that all mammals except adult humans have a larynx high in the neck, a position that enables the larynx to lock into the air space at the back of the nasal cavity. Although this position allows animals like monkeys and cats to breathe and swallow at the same time, it limits the sounds they can produce. The pharynx—the air cavity part of the food pathway—can produce sounds, but animals use their mouths to modify sounds since they are anatomically incapable of producing the range of sounds needed for articulate speech.

Until they are about 18 months to 2 years old, human children's larynxes are also situated high in the neck. Then the larynx begins to descend, ending up between the fourth and seventh neck vertebrae. How and why are still a mystery, but the change completely alters the way the infant breathes, speaks, and swallows. Adult humans cannot separate breathing and swallowing, so they can suffocate when food lodges in an airway. However, an enlarged pharyngeal chamber above the vocal cords enables them to modify the sounds they emit in an infinite variety of ways, which is the key to human speech.

Fortunately, the shape of the base of the skull is highly informative. Most mammals have flat-based skulls and high larynxes, but humans have an arched skull base associated with their low larynx. Using sophisticated statistical analyses, Laitman (1984) and his colleagues ran tests on as many complete fossil skulls as possible. They found that the australopithecines of 4.0 to 1.0 million years ago had flat skull bases and high larynxes, whereas those of *Homo erectus,* dating to about 1.5 million years and later, show somewhat more curvature, suggesting that the larynx was beginning to descend to its modern position. It was only about 300,000 years ago that the skull base finally assumed a modern curvature, which would allow for fully articulate speech to evolve.

Dutch anatomist Jan Wind believes that early humans were capable of making better associations between different senses like feeling, hearing, and vision than other primates. They also had larger storage capacity in their memories. Philip Tobias (in J. D. Clark, 1991), who studied the first *Homo habilis* fossil from Olduvai, believes that these earliest of humans were capable of some articulate speech, a means by which they taught their young much more complex patterns of behavior than those of apes and, indeed, *Australopithecus.* "This evolutionary accomplishment was announced neither in song, nor by manual signals, but by the spoken word," says Tobias. However, most paleoanthropologists believe that *Homo habilis* had very limited speaking abilities.

The real value of language, apart from the stimulation it gives brain development, is that with it we can convey feelings and nuances far beyond the power of grunts or gestures to communicate. We may assume that the first humans had more to communicate with than nonhuman primates, but it appears that modern articulate speech was a more recent stimulus to biological and cultural evolution.

SOCIAL ORGANIZATION

● ● ●

The few early sites that have been excavated show that the first phase of human evolution involved shifts in the basic patterns of subsistence and locomotion as well as new ingredients—food sharing and toolmaking. These led to enhanced communication, information exchange, and economic and social insight, as well as cunning and restraint. Human anatomy was augmented with tools. Culture became an inseparable part of humanity and social life acquired a new, and as yet little understood, complexity.

What sort of social organization did *Homo habilis* enjoy? However much we look at contemporary nonhuman primates, we cannot be sure. Most primates are intensely social and live in groups in which the mother-infant relationship forms a central bond. The period of infants' dependency on mothers found in, say, chimpanzees was probably lengthened considerably with *H. habilis*. The larger brain size would mean that infants were born with much smaller heads than adults, at an earlier stage of mental maturity. This biological reality would have had a major impact on social organization and daily habits.

Chimpanzees have flexible, matriarchal social groups. They occupy a relatively small territory, one with sufficient vegetable resources to support a considerable population density; this pattern contrasts sharply with the average hunter-gatherer band, typically a closely knit group of about 25 people of several families. The kind of systematic hunting such people engage in requires much larger territories and permits much lower densities per square mile. The few sites that have been excavated suggest that *Homo habilis* tended to live in bands that were somewhat more akin to those of modern hunter-gatherers. But in all probability their social organization resembled more closely that of chimpanzees and baboons, which are very different from those of humans.

Chimpanzees and baboons live in a world created in their brains by the integration of sight, sound, smell, and touch. The more complex the inputs and their neural processing, the more complex the inner world built by the brain. It may well be that this increase in complexity is what underlies the cumulative growth in brain size that is such a distinctive feature of mammalian evolution, from amphibians to reptiles, then through mammals to humans. The world of *Homo habilis* was much less predictable and more demanding than that of even *Australopithecus*. What was it that was more complex? Why do we have to be so intelligent? Not for hunting animals or gathering food but for our interactions with other people. The increased complexity of our social interactions is likely to have been a powerful force in the evolution of the human brain. For *H. habilis,* the adoption of a wider-based diet with a food-sharing social group would have placed much more acute demands on the ability to cope with the complex and unpredictable. And the brilliant technological, artistic, and expressive skills of humankind may well be a consequence of the fact that our early ancestors had to be more and more socially adept.

CHAPTER SUMMARY

The story of human evolution begins with the separation of the chimpanzee and human lines from a common ancestor about 6 to 7 million years ago. The first hominids were tree-living, with long arms and legs and broad chests, who eventually became bipedal, walking on two limbs. They adapted to more open country in Africa that resulted from global cooling over 4 million years ago, by broadening their diet to include meat, and achieving great mobility and behavioral flexibility. A small bipedal hominid named *Australopithecus afarensis* was ancestral to later hominids and flourished about 4 million years ago. By 2 million years ago, the hominid line had radiated into at least four forms, among them robust and gracile australopithecines and the larger-brained *Homo habilis*, the probable ancestor of later humans. *Homo habilis* was a forager, who also scavenged game meat, and perhaps hunted. Our earliest ancestors used a simple stone tool technology, had some ability at communication, and a very rudimentary social organization.

GUIDE TO FURTHER READING

Blumenschine, Robert, and Cavallo, John. 1992. "Scavenging and Human Evolution." *Scientific American* October:90–96.
> *An elegant discussion of a sophisticated scavenging hypothesis. Impressive for its multidisciplinary perspective and detailed field observations.*

Foley, Robert. 1987. *Another unique species: Patterns in human evolutionary ecology.* London: Longman.
> *A provocative book on the ecological background to the evolution of humankind. Crammed with thoughtful commentary and imaginative theorizing on the emergence of humanity. Essential for the serious student.*

Isaac, G. Ll. 1984. "The Archaeology of Human Origins." *Advances in World Archaeology* 3:1–87.
> *An authoritative account of the archaeological evidence from East Africa.*

Johanson, Donald C., and Edey, Maitland A. 1981. *Lucy: The Beginnings of Humankind.* New York: Simon & Schuster.
> *A well-written, racy account of the Hadar hominids that ranges widely over the major controversies of paleoanthropology. Superb descriptions of the research process and dating methods.*

Klein, Richard. 1989. *The Human Career.* Chicago: University of Chicago Press.
> *A summary of human biological and cultural evolution for more advanced students.*

Lewin, Roger. 1987. *Bones of Contention.* New York: Simon & Schuster.
> *An entertaining account of the major personalities and controversies surrounding paleoanthropology. Admirable for the general reader.*

———. 1988. *Human Evolution,* 2d ed. Oxford, Eng.: Blackwell Scientific Publications.
> *A lucid, multidisciplinary account of human origins; full of stimulating ideas.*

Toth, N., and Schick, K. D. 1986. "The First Million Years: The Archaeology of Protohuman Culture." *Advances in Archaeological Method and Theory* 9:1–96.
> *A synthesis of recent research into the archaeological record of early prehistory.*

CHAPTER 3
HOMO ERECTUS AND HOMO SAPIENS

(1.6 MILLION TO 40,000 YEARS AGO)

• • •

Eugene Dubois was a Dutchman obsessed with the Missing Link, the mythical human that was the evolutionary connection between apes and modern people. A surgeon by profession, young Dubois even wangled a posting as an army physician to distant Sumatra in southeast Asia in 1887, where, he was convinced, the Missing Link would be found. He remembered the words of the great biologist Alfred Russell Wallace, who had developed a theory of evolution parallel to Darwin's. "With what interest must every naturalist look forward to the time when the caves of the tropics be thoroughly examined," Wallace wrote, theorizing that the ancestors of humankind had originated in a "warm forest-clad land." Incredible though it may seem, Dubois actually found what he claimed was such an ancestor on nearby Java in 1891. Digging into fossil-rich ash and river sediments at Trinil on the Solo River in northeastern Java, he found not only the bones of extinct animals but a human tooth, a thick-walled skull, and a human thigh bone.

Dubois was ecstatic and named his fossil *Pithecanthropus erectus,* "ape-human which stood upright." This, he claimed, was the missing link between apes and humans, a very primitive human being. On his return to Europe in 1895, he was greeted with scepticism, then scorn. Dubois's reaction was to withdraw from the scientific arena. He is said to have kept his fossils under his bed, becoming increasingly convinced that they were the bones of an ancestor of the apes rather than human beings. Modern science has vindicated Eugene Dubois, for he was the first to discover what is now known as *Homo erectus,* a direct ancestor of modern humanity.

We must now describe this long-lived human ancestor and the evolution of modern humanity from these primordial roots. We shall see how the successors of the now-extinct australopithecines and those of *Homo* were humans capable of a far more complex and varied lifeway. These were hominids who used fire, made systematically manufactured rather than opportunistic tools, developed seasonal central places, and were the first to settle outside Africa.

PLEISTOCENE BACKGROUND

• • •

The evolutionary developments described in this chapter begin at the start of the Pleistocene and unfolded during a prolonged period of ever-changing Ice Age climate. These changes were the background both to an accelerating pace of human biological and cultural evolution and to the first peopling of the Old World outside Africa by human beings.

Lower Pleistocene (1.6 Million to c. 730,000 Years Ago)

As we mentioned in Chapter 2, the Pleistocene began about 1.6 million years ago, after an intensification of glaciation after 2.5 million years ago (Figure 3.1a) (Table 3.1). This arbitrary boundary coincides with a major geomagnetic reversal in the earth's magnetic field, which can be recognized on a worldwide basis. By this time, great mountain chains had formed in the Alps, Himalayas, and elsewhere.

1.6 million B.P.

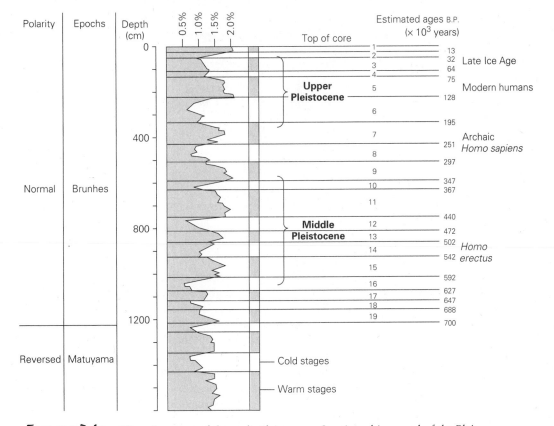

FIGURE 3.1A Climatic events of the early Pleistocene. Stratigraphic record of the Pleistocene from deep sea core V28-238, from the Solomon Plateau in the Pacific Ocean (Shackleton and Opdyke, 1983). The Matuyama/Brunhes boundary occurs at about 730,000 years ago, at a depth of 39.3 feet (1200 cm). Above it, a sawtoothlike curve records the relative size of the world's oceans and ice caps, and identifies eight complete glacial and interglacial cycles, a more complete record of the Middle and Upper Pleistocene than comes from land sediments.

FIGURE 3.1B Pleistocene glaciers in the northern hemisphere at their maximum extent. Shorelines caused by low sea levels are not known.

Landmasses had been uplifted; connection between these latitudes and southern areas was reduced, lessening their heat exchange and causing greater temperature differences between them. Three million years ago, northern latitudes were still warmer than today, but they were much cooler by the beginning of the Pleistocene.

The Lower Pleistocene is distinguished by surviving Pliocene animal forms and by the appearance of horses, cattle, elephants, and camels. Deep-sea cores tell us that climatic fluctuations between warmer and colder regimens were still relatively minor during this, the first million years of the Ice Age (Kurten, 1968). This was a critically important time, when *Homo erectus* evolved in Africa and moved out of the tropics into Asia and Europe.

Middle Pleistocene (c. 730,000 to 128,000 Years Ago)

730,000 B.P.   An abrupt reversal of the earth's magnetic field, back from reversed to normal, occurred about 730,000 years ago, an event that has been identified all over the world in both deep-sea cores and terrestrial deposits. This Matuyama/Brunhes

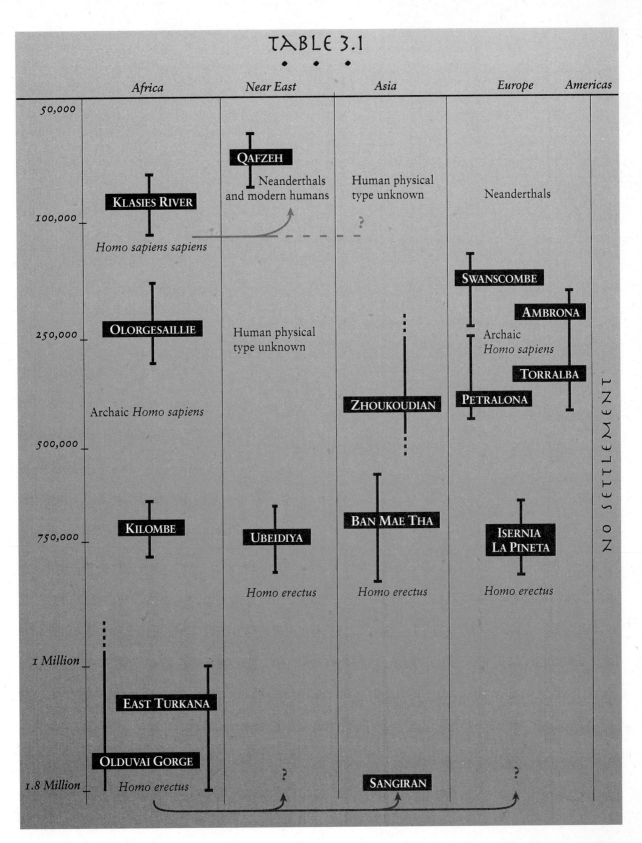

boundary, named after the geologists who first identified it, marks the arbitrary division between the Lower and Middle Pleistocene (Butzer and Isaac, 1975). The seesaw pattern of sea-core changes tells of constant climatic change from this point on. Consistently, the cores tell us, ice sheets formed gradually, but deglaciation took place with great rapidity, during phases that geologists call *terminations*. These correspond with major sea level rises that flooded low-lying coastal areas. Glaciers covered a full third of the earth's surface during glacial maxima. Great ice sheets mantled Scandinavia and the Alps, as well as much of northern North America (Figure 3.1b). The glaciers were about as extensive as they are today during interglacials (warmer periods). Thus, during interglacials, sea levels were within 18 to 20 feet (5.5 to 6 m) of present shorelines. Much less is known about changes in tropical regions. It is known that the southern fringes of the Sahara Desert expanded dramatically during cold periods.

**Elster
525,000 B.P.**

The outlines of Middle Pleistocene climatic change are still imperfectly known, but we know that there was a major glacial episode, known to European geologists as the Elster glaciation, about 525,000 years ago. At its height, there was ice as far south as Seattle, St. Louis, and New York in North America, and sea levels were about 650 feet (197 m) below modern levels. In contrast, there were periods of more temperate conditions between about 515,000 and 315,000 years ago, with colder incidents breaking up the warmer climate. It was during this interglacial that human settlement of temperate latitudes really took hold, as small bands of hunter-gatherers exploited the rich animal and plant resources of European and Asian river valleys and woodlands.

**Saale
180,000 to 128,000 B.P.**

The Middle Pleistocene ended with another intense glaciation, the Saale (known as the Illinoian in North America), that lasted from about 180,000 to 128,000 years ago. As we shall see, this colder cycle coincides in general terms with the period when anatomically modern humans were evolving in tropical Africa.

Both *Homo erectus* and *Homo sapiens* evolved during a period of constant climatic transition between warmer and colder regimens in northern latitudes. Experts believe that the world's climate has been in transition from one extreme to the other for over 75 percent of the past 730,000 years, with a predominance of colder climate over the entire period. These constant climatic changes played an important role in the spread of archaic humans throughout temperate and tropical latitudes (Gamble, 1986b).

The climatic events of the Upper Pleistocene are described at the beginning of Chapter 4.

HOMO ERECTUS

• • •

**Homo erectus
?2.0 million to ?200,000 B.P.**

Current estimates place the appearance of *Homo erectus* at about 2 million years ago or slightly later. *Homo erectus* fossils from Mojokerto and Sangiran on the Solo River in Indonesia have recently been dated to about 1.8 to 1.6 million years ago, comparable in age to the earliest *erectus* finds from East Africa (Swisher and others, 1994). The early East African specimens come from the Turkana area of northern Kenya. Skull KNM-ER 3733 from East Turkana dates to between 1.6 and 1.5 million years ago. This fossil, with its massive brow ridges, enlarged brain size, and high forehead, is morphologically very close to examples of *H. erectus* dating to a million years ago and earlier (Figure 3.2).

**Mojokerto
1.8 million B.P.**

**Sangiran
1.6 million B.P.**

**Lake Turkana
1.6 to 1.5 million B.P.**

FIGURE 3.2   Skull KNM-ER 3733, East Turkana, Kenya.

Richard Leakey and anatomist Alan Walker discovered the virtually complete skeleton of an 11-year-old *Homo erectus* boy on the western shores of the same lake, dating to about 1.6 million years ago. The footprints of hippopotamuses and other animals nearby suggest that the decomposing corpse was trampled to pieces. From the neck down, the boy's bones are remarkably modern looking. The skull and jawbone are more primitive, with brow ridges and a brain capacity perhaps as high as 700 to 800 cc, about half the modern size. The skeleton shows that the boy stood about 5 foot, 4 inches (1.6 m) tall, taller than many modern 12-year-olds. This Turkana find tends to confirm many scientists' view that different parts of the body evolved at different rates, the body achieving fully modern form long before the head.

Homo erectus is known to have lived over a wide area of the Old World. Apart from the early finds in East Africa and Indonesia, another early specimen is said to have come from Dmanisi in Georgia in the depths of Eurasia, a jaw claimed to date to earlier than 1.4 million years ago. There are important populations in China, notably from Zhoukoudian Cave near Beijing (Lewin, 1987) (Figure 3.3). These important fossils, found in a deep cave filled with animal bones, plant remains, and crude bone artifacts, are estimated to date between 500,000 and 350,000 years ago. Fossils fragments from Morocco, Algeria, central Europe, and Britain date to about 500,000 years ago. Further, although fossil remains of *H. erectus* are rarely encountered, their distinctive toolkit of stone axes and other artifacts

FIGURE 3.3   A plaster cast of *Homo erectus* from Zhoukoudian, China. The skull bones of *H. erectus* show that these hominids had a brain capacity between 775 and 1300 cc, showing much variation. It is probable that their vision was excellent and that they were capable of extensive thought. The *H. erectus* skull is more rounded than that of earlier hominids; it also has conspicuous brow ridges and a sloping forehead. With a massive jaw, much thicker skull bones, and teeth with cusp patterns somewhat similar to those of *Australopithecus africanus* and modern humans, *H. erectus* had limbs and hips fully adapted to an upright posture. It stood over 5 feet, 6 inches (1.8 m) and had hands fully capable of precision gripping and many kinds of toolmaking.

is relatively commonplace and tells us much about their distribution and adaptations.

During *Homo erectus*'s long history, humanity adapted to a far wider range of environments, ranging from tropical savannas in East Africa to forested Javanese valleys, temperate climates in North Africa and Europe, and the harsh winters of China and northern Europe. *Homo erectus* was certainly capable of a far more complex and varied lifeway than previous hominids, and with such a wide distribution, it is hardly surprising that some variations in populations appear. For example, some had more robust skulls than others, although it is said that the Zhoukoudian skulls display a gradual increase in brain capacity from about 900 cc in 600,000-year-old specimens to about 1100 cc in 200,000-year-old individuals. In any case, *H. erectus* was far more "human" than *H. habilis,* a habitual biped, who had probably lost the thick hair covering that is characteristic of nonhuman primates. Unfortunately, we are unlikely to know when we lost our dense facial hair because soft parts are never preserved. But it seems possible that this occurred when the dramatic enlargement of hominid brains recycled the developmental "clock"—perhaps with *H. habilis.* In any case, *H. erectus* certainly had abundant sweat glands and, presumably, in common with most tropical primates and humans, relatively dark skin (Rightmire, 1990).

FIRE

• • •

Fire caused by natural conflagrations was certainly part of the savanna environment in which our earlier ancestors lived. Great grass and brush fires swept across open and wooded country during the dry months, especially, perhaps, when markedly drier conditions were widespread in East Africa about 1.7 million years ago (Clark and Harris, 1985). This was a time when the faunal communities of East Africa adapted to drier, more open grassland conditions. It was also about the time that *Homo erectus* first emerged. From this point on, there are signs that human behavior changed. The first archaeological sites appear at higher East African elevations, and less densely vegetated areas are more intensively occupied. Butchery sites containing the remains of large animals are more common. Stone technology becomes more complex, for more elaborate hand ax-like artifacts and flake tools now appear.

The earliest traces of what may be humanly tamed fire come from Swartkrans in South Africa, dating to about 1.6 million years ago, and from Chesowanya in the Kenya Rift Valley. Both are assumed to be the work of *Homo erectus*. Chesowanya yielded evidence of hearthlike arrangements of stone artifacts, fragmentary bones, and baked clay that had been hardened in antiquity. Unfortunately, it has not proven possible to demonstrate that the inhabitants controlled the fire that hardened the clay. It is not until between 1 million and 700,000 years ago that fire is well documented in the archaeological record—significantly, in temperate China.

Swartkrans Chesowanya 1.6 million B.P.

It is not unreasonable to assume that the early hominids had learned to live with natural fires and were not afraid of them (Clark and Harris, 1985). Fire offers protection against predators and an easy way of hunting game, even insects and rodents, fleeing from a line of flames. The toxins from many common vegetable foods can be roasted or parched in hot ashes, allowing people to use a wider range of plants in their diet (Stahl, 1984). The prevalence of such toxins may be the reason chimpanzees eat so many insects—still an important protein source for many African peoples and perhaps for early hominids, too. Perhaps *Homo erectus* had the habit of conserving fire, taking advantage of long-smoldering tree stumps ignited by lightning strikes and other natural causes to kindle flames to light dry brush or simply scare off predators.

Hominid body size had increased dramatically with the appearance of *Homo erectus*. An ecological consequence of enlarged body size is extension of the home range, a fact well documented from animal behavior studies (Foley, 1984b). Larger quantities of food are needed because of higher metabolic rates. This may have been the time when hominids not only relied on smoldering tree stumps but also began to carry simple firebrands as protection against large predators. The new weapon would also allow them to move into more open country, where trees were much rarer, and to increase their home ranges into unfamiliar habitats.

Clark and Harris (1985) think it not unlikely that the conservation and taming of fire—as much as food sharing, meat eating, and new forms of sexual behavior—helped to forge close-knit family groups among hominid bands. The distribution of archaeological and hominid sites approximately 1.5 million years ago may reflect greatly increased home ranges and, perhaps, the time when humans domesticated fire. It may be no coincidence that the earliest human settlement of Europe and Asia, of more temperate latitudes, occurred after *Homo erectus* appeared in East Africa and, perhaps, mastered fire.

THE RADIATION OF HOMO ERECTUS

• • •

We know that the arliest hominids could adapt to a variety of climates and habitats. Both *Australopithecus* and *Homo habilis* adjusted to plunging global temperatures during a glacial episode between about 2.7 and 2.5 million years ago. The colder conditions turned much of Africa's moist woodlands into much drier, open savanna. The hominids thrived in these conditions, as tree-dwelling primates yielded to bipedal forms better able to survive in the open. This adaptability let hominids move into new environments, where their mixed diet of meat and plant foods caused them to move over large home territories. *Homo erectus* was just as adaptable and mobile, but was the first human to use fire, to fashion more elaborate tools, and to leave Africa.

Despite the apparent contemporaneity of the earliest *Homo erectus* fossils in both East Africa and southeast Asia, most scientists believe *erectus* originated in Africa. They point to the continuous record of human evolution in that continent, from *Australopithecus afarensis* to the australopithecines, then *Homo habilis* and *erectus*. However bushlike the evolutionary tree, and it was much more complex than we know today, the best and longest fossil record comes from tropical Africa. As we shall see later in this chapter, the same continent may have been the cradle of modern humans, *Homo sapiens sapiens*, also. But would a radiation of *erectus* populations from Africa to Asia occur within such a short time frame as 100,000 years? With *Homo erectus* covering large, open territories where food resources were scattered unevenly over the landscape, even an expansion of 20 to 30 milies (32 to 48 km) a year soon translates to hundreds, then thousands of miles within a few generations.

If we accept that *Homo erectus* evolved in Africa, then radiated quickly out of Africa into the Near East and Asia, why did this sudden movement occur? Around 2 million years ago, hominids were adjusting to cyclical alterations among savanna, forest, and desert as the Ice Age began. They did so by migrating with changing vegetational zones, as many mammals did, or by adapting to new environments, changing their dietary emphasis from meat to plant foods. Finally, they could move out of tropical latitudes altogether, into habitats that human beings had never occupied before.

Very likely *Homo erectus* adapted to changed circumstances in all these ways, radiating out of Africa by way of the Sahara, when the desert was capable of supporting human life. Neil Roberts (1984) has likened the Sahara to a pump, sucking in population during wetter savanna phases and forcing hunter-gatherers out northward to the margins of the desert during drier cycles. In radiating out of Africa, *H. erectus* behaved just like other mammals in its ecological community.

H. erectus was a carnivore and a plant eater, and thus linked ecologically with other predators. There was widespread interchange of mammals between Africa and more temperate latitudes during the Pliocene and Lower Pleistocene. For example, a major change in the mammalian populations of Europe took place about 700,000 years ago. Hippopotamuses, forest elephants, and other herbivores and carnivores such as the lion, leopard, and spotted hyena seem to have migrated northward from Africa at this time. Migrations by the lion, leopard, and hyena—the animals with which hominids shared many ecological characteristics—were in the same direction as that taken earlier by *Homo erectus*. That the first successful human settlement of

FIGURE 3.4   The radiation of *Homo erectus*. Map shows key sites mentioned in the text and the major technological provinces of *H. erectus*'s world. The radiating lines aim to give an impression of radiation outward from tropical Africa. Subsequent to this complex process of radiation, local populations diversified considerably.

tropical Asia, then, apparently later, of temperate Europe coincided with radiations of mammalian communities out of Africa seems plausible (Figure 3.4).

The radiation of *Homo erectus* remains one of the great mysteries of early prehistory, but it seems likely to have begun in tropical Africa and taken humans across to tropical Southeast Asia within a remarkably short time, perhaps as little as 100,000 years. Unfortunately, the archaeological and fossil evidence for this extraordinary radiation is tantalizingly incomplete.

Earliest Human Settlement in the Near East and Europe

The earliest recorded human settlement in the Near East comes from the Ubeidiya site, near the confluence of the Jordan and Yarmuk rivers in Israel. Some human and animal bones are associated with simple choppers and some crude hand axes at this lakeside site. Unfortunately, Ubeidiya's dating is somewhat controversial, but an estimate of about 700,000 years ago, close to the Matuyama/Brunhes boundary, seems likely (Bar-Yosef, 1975).

Ubeidiya
700,000 B.P.

The earliest dated human artifacts yet found in Europe come from lake beds at Isernia La Pineta, central Italy, stratified under volcanic deposits. They have

Isernia La Pineta
c. 500,000 B.P.

been dated on the basis of highly diagnostic vole (small rodent) teeth to soon after 500,000 years ago. The artifacts include flakes, scrapers, and choppers associated with bison, elephants, and other animals (Segre and Asconzi, 1986). A robust human thigh bone, perhaps of a *Homo erectus*, has come from Boxgrove in southern England, where, again, vole bones provide a date of about 524,000 to 478,000 years ago (Roberts et al., 1994). What is striking is that there are no widely accepted archaeological sites in Europe earlier than about 0.5 million years ago, as if this region was settled much later than Asia, and perhaps Eurasia, for reasons which still elude us. Certainly, human groups were living throughout western and central Europe and perhaps even further east by 350,000 years ago (Arsuaga et al., 1993).

*Boxgrove
c. 500,000 B.P.*

Homo erectus in Asia

Despite claims to the contrary, no australopithecines or *Homo habilis* fossils have come from tropical Southeast Asia. If the nearly 2-million-year old dates for *H. erectus* are correct, then humans settled in this heavily forested region soon after the first appearance of these archaic people in distant Africa.

Southeast Asia

The Mojokerto and Sangiran fossils are now dated to between 1.8 and 1.6 million years ago, dates acquired with a still, if sophisticated, experimental chronometric method (Swisher et al., 1994). Only time will tell if they stand further scientific scrutiny. The earliest traces of human settlement consist of three artifacts found in gravel deposits at Ban Mae Tha in northern Thailand. These split and flaked cobbles are dated through paleomagnetic and potassium argon studies to about 700,000 years ago (Pope et al., 1986). Given what we know about the earliest prehistory of Southeast Asia, it seems almost certain that these tools were made by *Homo erectus*. Dubois's *H. erectus* finds and other more recent discoveries from Indonesia are thought to date to no earlier than about 700,000 years ago (G. G. Pope, 1984), a point that appears to coincide with the appearance of similar hominids in Europe and perhaps in China as well. Five *H. erectus* specimens dating to about 500,000 years ago have recently come from Lang Trang Caves in Vietnam, the earliest securely dated human fossils in Southeast Asia.

*Mojokerto
1.8 million B.P.*

*Ban Mae Tha
c. 700,000 B.P.*

*Lang Trang
c. 500,000 B.P.*

Homo erectus may have reached east Asia in the very late Lower Pleistocene, perhaps via the so-called Sunda shelf, low-lying ground that joined many of the Southeast Asian islands during cooler cycles. This shelf appears to have acted as a faunal filter, preventing many tropical ungulate species from reaching the east. Southeast Asia was a tropical forest environment, with extensive patches of dense forest even during the driest periods of the Pleistocene. Geoffrey Pope (1984) believes that bamboo and other wood resources from these forests were of vital importance for the highly portable toolkit used by *H. erectus* in this environment. He also points out that fire, perhaps tamed by these people, is an important component in forest technology. Thus, the crude stone choppers and flakes that may have formed the simple stone technology of Asia for tens of thousands of years were only a limited part of forest material culture. Such implements are all that remain of a Stone Age lifeway that was based not on the pursuit of large savanna animals but on smaller game and forest resources, many concentrated around natural springs, sinkholes, and caves.

China

There are two or three artifact assemblages from China that are claimed to date to the Lower Pleistocene, but the dates of all of them are uncertain (Chang, 1986). The earliest widely accepted traces of human activity date to after 700,000 years ago, during the Middle Pleistocene. The Lan-t'ien and Q'en-Xia-wo sites in central China have yielded specimens of *Homo erectus* that probably date to the early Middle Pleistocene, before 600,000 years ago.

Lan-t'ien
Q'en-Xia-wo
600,000 B.P.

The most famous and largest Middle Pleistocene site in China is the Zhoukoudian Caves, 28.5 miles (46 km) west of Beijing (see Figure 3.5a). Zhoukoudian consists of many caverns and fissures, the most famous of which is Locality I, where both stone implements and human fossils have been found. These caverns were visited by *Homo erectus* over an immensely long period of time, from about 460,000 to 230,000 years ago (Chang, 1986). At least 40 *H. erectus* individuals have been found at Zhoukoudian, most of whom died before they were 14 years old. Many of them appear to have perished from injuries.

Zhoukoudian
460,000 to 230,000 B.P.

The Zhoukoudian people visited the caves when the climate was perhaps a trifle warmer and moister than today. They hunted deer and other animals; more than 60 species are represented in the deposits. Charcoal, burned bone fragments, and ash accumulations that formed hearths show that *Homo erectus* used fire.

About 100,000 stone implements come from Zhoukoudian, most of them made on flakes of rough-vein quartz. The people made choppers and scrapers, awls, crude points, and many multipurpose artifacts (Figure 3.5b). The toolkit evolved through the 100,000 years of occupation, with the earliest artifacts tending to be larger and made with simple percussion techniques. As time went on, the toolmakers produced smaller implements, many of them made of finer raw materials.

Taken together, the Asian fossils are remarkably homogeneous. They have broad-based skulls; low, receding foreheads; and prognathous faces. The upper skull bones are thick and show every sign that these humans had strong chewing muscles. These people were up to 5 feet, 6 inches (1.67 m) tall and had a brain capacity between 775 and 1300 cc. One has the impression of a biologically conservative human population that changed little over enormously long periods of time. The latest *Homo erectus* finds come from Java and Narmada in India and date to about 230,000 years ago.

Choppers and Chopping Tools

The early Asians took full advantage of the forest resources available to them. Instead of stone, they turned to wood, fiber, and bamboo, all of them organic materials that survive poorly in archaeological sites. In other words, our view of early Asia is biased simply because we lack evidence of the whole range of their forest cultures. Tropical forests are rich in animal and plant foods, but they are widely dispersed. Thus, human groups subsisting off forest foods must move constantly, carrying their artifacts with them. Under these circumstances, it is logical for people to use for their toolkits bamboo, wood, and other fibrous materials—the most convenient materials at hand. There was no need for the specialized, often complicated implements used in open country in the West, either for spear points or for the butchering tools used on bison or large antelope. The distribution of "chopper-chopping tool" sites coincides very closely with the natural distribution of bamboo, one of the most versatile materials known to humankind (Pope, 1989). Bamboo was efficient, durable, and portable. It could be used to manufacture containers, sharp

(a)

(b)

FIGURE 3.5   (a) Zhoukoudian Cave, China. (b) A crude chopping tool from Zhoukoudian, front and side views (one-half actual size).

FIGVRE 3.6 Bamboo scaffolding in use to build a modern highrise.

knives, spears, weapon tips, ropes, and dwellings. To this day, it is widely used in Asia as scaffolding for building skyscrapers (Figure 3.6). It is an ideal material for people subsisting not off large game but off smaller forest animals such as monkeys, rats, squirrels, lizards, and snakes as well as plant foods. Simple stone flakes and jagged-edged choppers would be ideal for working bamboo and may, indeed, have been used for this purpose over many millennia (Schick, 1994).

We still know little of the world of *Homo erectus,* beyond a certainty that humans had radiated far from their tropical homeland in Africa. By 700,000 years ago, *H. erectus* had settled in temperate Europe and the Near East, was probably living in India, and was certainly present in Southeast Asia and China. Human beings had now adapted to a far wider range of environments than ever before, where fire and efficient shelter were essential to survive dramatic contrasts in summer and winter climates. As far as is known, however, *H. erectus* did not settle in extreme arctic latitudes, in what is now the former Soviet Union and Siberia. Nor did they develop the watercraft needed to cross from island Southeast Asia to Australia, a landmass that remained isolated by the ocean throughout the Ice Age.

The Settlement of Temperate Latitudes

We must think of the first human settlement of temperate latitudes as part of a broader set of ecological processes, one of them the simultaneous radiation of modern grazing animals and new vegetational communities into Europe and other northern latitudes of the Old World. Humans were part of this vast animal community. Their long-term success resulted from their ability to adapt to the cyclical changes in the Ice Age environment, from temperate to much colder, then to full glacial conditions and an abrupt deglaciation as the climate warmed up again rapidly. These early human populations may have flourished in regions where dense, abundant, and predictable resources were to be found, isolated from other regions where similar conditions existed. The climatic changes of the Ice Age sometimes brought these isolated populations together, then separated them again, ensuring gene flow and genetic drift and continued biological and cultural evolution over the millennia (Butzer, 1982).

The first settlement of temperate latitudes was not simply a case of an opportunistic species seizing a set of favorable environmental circumstances (Gamble 1986b). By 500,000 years ago hominids had mastered the necessary hunting and foraging strategies to survive in much more diverse environments than tropical savanna. Most regions of the temperate world had the energy and resources for hominid settlement even when *Homo habilis* flourished. *H. habilis* had not evolved the long-term solutions, such as tailored clothing, for coping with cyclical climatic change and all the resource changes that resulted from it.

Most evidence for Middle Pleistocene settlement, between about 500,000 and 130,000 years ago, falls in periods when the climate was colder than today but not fully glacial, as it has been for most of the past 700,000 years, times when grazing animals formed the principal food resource in cooler latitudes. Plant and marine foods were much more costly to exploit and often sparse. The successful colonists of northern latitudes were those hominids who could exploit game animals distributed unevenly, at times very densely, over the landscape.

That is not to say, of course, that the hominids lived by hunting alone. They had to cope with long, sparse winter months, when their prey dispersed so widely that it was beyond human capacity to hunt them effectively. Perhaps people searched for frozen animal carcasses, a winter strategy that was adaptive for highly mobile predators like humans. This would have been a lower-risk strategy if a large group worked together, searching for the predictable refrigerated carcasses of large animals that died during the winter months (Gamble, 1986b).

During the spring and summer the people would concentrate on hunting migratory game, eating their kills quickly and stripping them of meat before other predators moved in. Many known sites are near lakes and streams, perhaps the places where the bands most commonly hunted and also where wood might have been found for tools and for the fires used to thaw frozen meat. The key to this entire adaptation was mobility; the bands could respond quickly to changes in resource distribution by moving into new areas. Gamble believes this was a primarily opportunistic adaptation based on knowledge of resource distribution rather than the result of deliberate planning.

THE TECHNOLOGY OF HOMO ERECTUS

• • •

Both Oldowan technology and the artifacts fashioned by *Homo erectus* remained in use in various forms for immensely long periods of time. Oldowan stoneworking lasted for as much as a million years, its more diverse successor for nearly half as long again. There is a tendency to think of both technologies as monolithic,

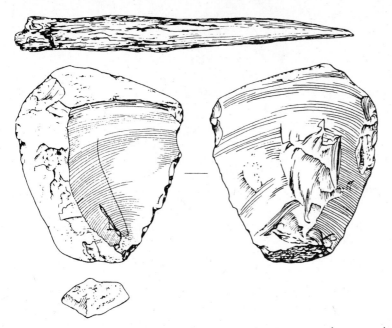

FIGURE 3.7 European wood and stone tools. *Top,* a wooden spear tip (perhaps a snow probe) from Clacton, England, dating to about 200,000 years ago (approximately one-eighth full size). *Bottom,* views of a flake from the same location. The upper surface is shown at left, the flake (lower) surface on the right. The striking platform is at the base (one-third actual size).

unchanging chronicles of human prehistory, fixed stages in human cultural evolution, partly because of the time scales involved and also because stone tools appear to have changed so little over hundreds of thousands of years. In fact, the technology of *H. erectus,* like that of *H. habilis,* displays considerable variability and development.

Homo erectus did not rely exclusively on stone, for we can say with confidence that our remote ancestors also made use of wood, one of the most versatile raw materials known to humanity. Unfortunately, timber rarely survives in the archaeological record. The earliest known wooden artifacts consist of a wooden spear tip (or possible snow probe) from Clacton in eastern England, dating to about 200,000 years ago (Figure 3.7), and a 150,000-year-old wooden spear from Lehringen in Germany. Most insights into the technology of *H. erectus* come from stone tools and the by-products associated with them, because wood and other organic materials are rarely preserved.

Hand Axes and Other Tools

In Africa, Europe, and some parts of Asia, *Homo erectus* is associated with a distinctive toolkit that includes not only a variety of flake tools and sometimes choppers but also bifacially flaked hand axes. These hand ax industries are grouped under the technological label *Acheulian,* after the town of St. Acheul in northern France, where many such artifacts have been found. Hand axes come in many sizes and shapes; they are sometimes artifacts of great refinement and beauty (Figure 3.8), so much so that people ignore all the other tools *H. erectus* made. In fact, human

(a)

(b)

5 cm

(c)

FIGURE 3.8   Acheulian technology. Hand axes were multipurpose artifacts that were shaped symmetrically around a long axis. (a) As the hand ax from Kilombe, Kenya, of 700,000 years ago shows, the stoneworker would sometimes use a minimum of blows to achieve the desired shape. Simple hammerstones were used to make many early hand axes and blanks for far more finished products. (b) Sometimes a hammer made of animal bone served to strike off the shallow flakes that adorn the margins of these tools.

Later hand axes assume many forms, among them the finely pointed shape in part (c), which shows front and side views of two early hand axes from Bed II, Olduvai Gorge, Tanzania (three-quarters actual size). Cleavers (Figure 3.10) are thought to have been butchering tools, artifacts with a single, unfinished edge that has proved effective in modern experiments for skinning and dismembering game. As time went on, the stoneworkers used carefully prepared cores to fashion large flakes that served as blanks for axes and other artifacts. They also produced flakes that were used as opportunistic artifacts, for woodworking, and for many other purposes.

technology between 1.5 million and 150,000 years ago shows considerable diversity, probably associated with local adaptations and the availability of suitable raw materials.

The hand ax has been found over a vast area of the Old World in all shapes and sizes, from crude tear-shaped forms to ovals, tongue-shaped axes, and occasional finely pointed specimens. Unlike the crude scrapers and choppers of the Oldowan, the Acheulian hand ax was an artifact with converging edges, which met at a point. The maker had to envisage the shape of the artifact, which was to be produced from a mere lump of stone, then fashion it not with opportunistic blows but with carefully directed hammer blows. Acheulian hand axes come in every size, from elegant oval types a few inches long to heavy axes more than a foot (0.3 m) long and weighing 5 pounds (2.3 kg) or more. They must have been a versatile, thoroughly practical artifact to have continued in use for so long.

Acheulian culture
1 million to 60,000 B.P.

What exactly were hand axes used for? Almost certainly they were held in the hand rather than being hafted on the end of a wooden shaft. They were simply too cumbersome, and in any case, hafted tools probably did not come into use until much later. Conventional wisdom has it that they were multipurpose artifacts, used for grubbing up roots, working wood, scraping skins, and especially skinning and butchering large and small game. There is no question that they were highly effective butchery tools. Many archaeologists have tried not only cutting up antelope carcasses but also slicing through hippopotamus and elephant hide—with great success. In some ways, the hand ax was ideal for this purpose because it could be sharpened again and again, and when it became a useless lump of stone, it could be recycled into flake tools. But you can achieve effective butchery with simple flakes as well, and a number of researchers have wondered whether the hand ax, which took longer to make, was not used for other purposes.

In contrast to the earlier Oldowan, the Lower Paleolithic technology of *Homo erectus* varied greatly throughout its duration, reaching considerable heights of delicate artistry (Figure 3.8). In addition to hand axes, the new technology resulted in scrapers and other artifacts for woodworking, skinning, and other purposes. But hand axes remain the most characteristic artifact of many *H. erectus* populations.

Hand axes have been found over an enormous area of the Old World (Figure 3.4). Fine specimens are scattered in the gravels of the Somme and Thames rivers in northern Europe, in North African quarries and ancient Saharan lake beds, and in sub-Saharan Africa from the Nile Valley to the Cape of Good Hope. Acheulian tools are common in some parts of India, as well as in Arabia and the Near East as far as the southern shores of the Caspian Sea and perhaps even farther north. They are rare east of the Rhine and in the Far East, where chopping tools were commonly used until comparatively recent times (Butzer and Isaac, 1975; Howell and Clark, 1963). No one has been able to explain why hand axes have this distribution. Were such multipurpose tools used only in big-game hunting camps? Was their use restricted by the availability of flint and other suitable raw materials? Did environmental conditions affect the hunters' choice of toolkits? Or were they used as projectiles in areas where big game abounded? We do not know.

Hand Axes and the Evolution of the Human Mind

While we recognize that *Homo erectus* made a wide variety of artifacts, the fact remains that the Acheulian hand ax is the most characteristic and one of the most widely distributed tools made between 1.5 million and 150,000 years ago. It also

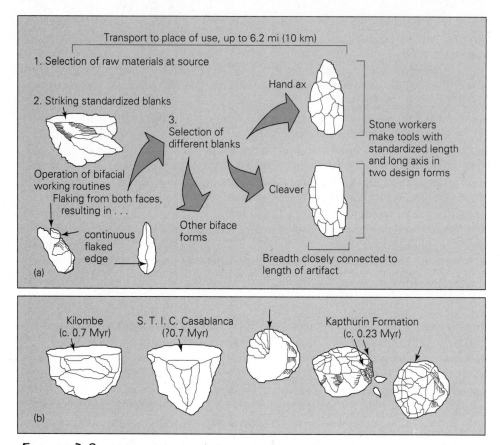

FIGURE 3.9   Making Acheulian bifaces. (a) The complex process used about a million years ago. (b) Early and late methods. The simple flaking process of 700,000 years ago (*left*), used in East and North Africa, compares with the expertise of the stoneworkers at Kapthurin, Kenya, 230,000 years ago (*right*). They prepared elaborately shaped cores to create flakes about 6 inches (16 cm) long as hand ax blanks. (After Foley, 1984b.)

provides us with an opportunity to consider the relationship between an artifact and the evolution of the mind.

Hand axes were the logical end result of long-used stone technology, made to a degree of standardization unimaginable in earlier times. The hand axes from Kilombe, Kenya, date to over 700,000 years ago. They display a very high statistical correlation among length, breadth, and thickness, standardization within a length of 3.14 to 9.40 inches (8–24 cm), which implies a well-defined mental image of the ideal end product shared by more than one person (Figure 3.9). *Homo erectus* had a geometrically accurate sense of proportion, which was imposed accurately on stone (Gowlett, 1978).

Acheulian technology was far from static. Another East African site, Kapthurin, near Kenya's Lake Baringo, contains hundreds of late Acheulian hand axes dating to about 230,000 years ago. The stoneworkers there used elaborately prepared cores, fashioned with perhaps 40 or more strokes, as the blanks for a single large flake, a dramatic contrast to the three or four flakes removed in earlier millennia (Figure 3.9). The large flake that resulted was then bifacially flaked into an elegant, versatile hand ax in a wide variety of useful shapes (Figure 3.10). Gowlett and others believe

Kilombe
700,000 B.P.

Kapthurin
230,000 B.P.

(a)

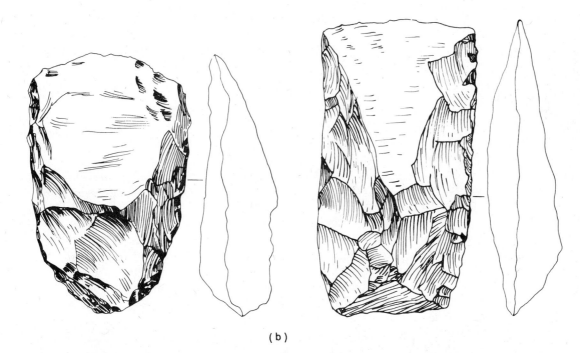

(b)

FIGURE 3.10   Hand ax technology. (a) Acheulian hand ax from Swanscombe, England (one-third actual size). (b) Two Acheulian cleavers, from Baia Farta, Angola (*left*), and Kalambo Falls, Zambia (*right*) (both one-half actual size).

that the problem-solving abilities needed to fashion Acheulian artifacts of all types were much more complex than has sometimes been assumed. One suspects that *Homo erectus* was capable of implementing elaborate hunting and foraging strategies and engaging in social interactions that were a quantum jump beyond those of much more apelike *H. habilis*.

Evidence for Behavior: Torralba and Terra Amata

What do we know of the behavior of these archaic tribes? Without question, *Homo erectus* hunted and foraged for food, probably in far more effective ways than *H. habilis*. Time and time again, hand axes and other butchering artifacts have been found in association with the bones of large game animals, which they were used to butcher. No one doubts that *H. erectus* butchered such animals. But did the hunters actually kill such formidable herbivores as the elephant and rhinoceros? To do so would require social mechanisms to foster cooperation and communication abilities far beyond those of *H. habilis*.

Torralba
400,000 or 200,000 B.P.

Evidence for butchery and perhaps big-game hunting comes from two remarkable Acheulian sites, at Torralba and Ambrona, northeast of Madrid in Spain (F. C. Howell, 1966). The Acheulians probably lived in this deep, swampy valley either 200,000 or 400,000 years ago (the date is disputed). Torralba yielded most of the left side of a large elephant that had been cut into small pieces, and Ambrona contained the remains of 30 to 35 dismembered elephants. Concentrations of broken food bones were found all over the site, and the skulls of the elephants had been broken open to get at the brains (Figure 3.11). Both kill sites were littered with crude hand axes, cleavers, scrapers, and cutting tools.

The elephant bones at both sites were buried in clays that were once treacherous marsh. The original scenario for the sites had hunters watching the valley floors where the elephants roamed. At a strategic moment several bands would gather quietly, set brushfires, and drive the unsuspecting beasts into the swamps, where they could be killed and butchered at leisure. Torralba and Ambrona were on important game trails between summer and winter grazing areas (Butzer, 1982). The hunters thus preyed on migrating elephants each spring and fall (Figure 3.12), dispersing into smaller groups during the other seasons. Other archaeologists believe that the hunters were actually scavenging meat from animals that perished when enmired (Shipman and Rose, 1983).

Terra Amata
300,000 B.P.

Terra Amata, excavated by Henry de Lumley, was occupied some 300,000 years ago (de Lumley, 1969). De Lumley excavated what he thought was a series of oval huts that consisted of shallow hollows 26 to 50 feet (8 to 15 m) long and 13 to 20 feet (4 to 6 m) wide, with an entrance at one end (Figure 3.13). When he cleared the hollows, he uncovered a series of posts approximately 3 inches (7 cm) in diameter that had once formed the walls. The bases of the posts were reinforced with lines of stones. The roofs were supported by center posts, and some huts had a hearth in the center. The excavators recovered the bones of wild oxen, stags, and elephants, as well as those of small rodents. There were even imprints of skins once laid on the floors. De Lumley records that the inhabitants never cleaned out their huts. They lived among butchered bones, discarded stone tools, and even their own feces. The feces yielded numerous fragments of nuts and seeds that had flourished in the late spring and early summer. De Lumley concluded that Terra Amata was a seasonal camp, occupied by a band of hunter-gatherers who returned to the same locale year after year in search of vegetable foods and shellfish, another common find at the site.

FIGURE 3.11   From Torralba, Spain, a remarkable linear arrangement of elephant tusks and leg bones that were probably laid out by those who butchered the animals.

Paola Villa (1983) threw serious doubt on this original interpretation when she tried refitting flakes from the site to one another in order to reconstruct stoneworking activity there. Over 40 percent of the refitted flakes came from different levels, implying that many specimens had been displaced vertically some 8 inches (21 cm). She believes that undetected natural phenomena such as soil creep, ice action, animal burrowing, and even earthworm tunneling transformed Terra Amata after its abandonment—to the point that de Lumley's houses of reeds and brush may not actually have existed. Terra Amata and many other sites of this age may have been disturbed so extensively since they were occupied that our interpretations of them will always be somewhat suspect.

Improvements in language and modes of communication are thought to have been a distinctive feature of *Homo erectus*'s style of life. With enhanced language skills and more advanced technology, it became possible for people to achieve better cooperation in gathering activities, in storage of food supplies, and in the chase. Unlike the nonhuman primates, who strongly emphasize individual economic success, Middle Pleistocene hunter-gatherers depended on cooperative activity by every individual in the band. The economic unit was the group; the secret of individual success was group success. Perhaps individual ownership of property was unimportant since neither individuals nor groups as a whole had tangible possessions of significance. People got along well as individuals, as families, and as entire groups.

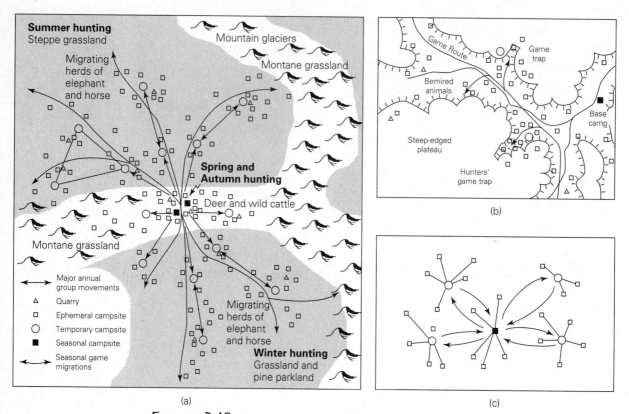

(a)

(b)

(c)

FIGURE 3.12 Reconstructed model for seasonal movement by Acheulian hunters at Torralba-Ambrona, Spain. (a) Interception of migrating animals in spring and fall. (b) Use of topography to secure game. (c) Schematic model of how the populations moved. The reconstructions were made by using information recovered from excavations (Butzer, 1982).

FIGURE 3.13 Henry de Lumley's controversial reconstruction of a hut at Terra Amata, France.

THE ORIGIN OF HOMO SAPIENS

● ● ●

For hundreds of thousands of years, *Homo erectus* flourished in the tropical and temperate regions of the Old World. Except for an overall increase in brain size, *H. erectus* remained remarkably stable in evolutionary terms for more than a million years, until less than 500,000 years ago. Eventually, *H. erectus* evolved into early *H. sapiens*, but we do not even know when the gradual transition began or how it took place. Some researchers believe it began as early as 400,000 years ago, others much later, some time around or after 200,000 years ago.

Homo sapiens sapiens means the "wise person," and the controversies surrounding the origins of modern humanity, of ourselves, rank among the most vigorous in archaeology. We are the clever people, the sage humans, animals capable of subtlety, of manipulation, of self-understanding. What is it that separates us from earlier humans, scientists wonder? First and foremost must be our ability to speak fluently and articulately. We communicate, we tell stories, we pass on knowledge and ideas all through the medium of language. Consciousness, cognition, self-awareness, foresight, and the ability to express oneself and one's emotions—these are direct consequences of fluent speech. They can be linked with another attribute of the fully fledged human psyche: the capacity for symbolic and spiritual thought, concerned not only with subsistence and technology but also with defining the boundaries of existence and the relationship among the individual, the group, and the universe. Fluent speech, the full flowering of human creativity expressed in art and religion, expert toolmaking—these are some of the hallmarks of anatomically modern humans. With these abilities humankind eventually colonized not just temperate and tropical environments but the entire globe. With the appearance of *H. sapiens sapiens* we begin the study of people biologically identical to ourselves, people with the same intellectual abilities and potential as ourselves. It is hardly surprising that controversy surrounds the appearance of our remote ancestors (Nitecki and Nitecki, 1994).

Continuity or Replacement?

Over generations of debate, two major, and diametrically opposed, hypotheses have developed to explain the origins of modern humans (Figure 3.14):

● The so-called candelabra model hypothesizes that *Homo erectus* populations throughout the Old World evolved independently, first to archaic *H. sapiens*, then to fully modern humans. This continuity model argues for multiple origins of *H. sapiens* and no migrations. Thus, modern geographic populations have been separated from one another for a long time, perhaps as long as a million years (Wolpoff, 1989).

● The Noah's ark model takes the diametrically opposite view. According to it, *Homo sapiens* evolved in one place, then spread to all other parts of the Old World. This replacement model implies that modern geographic populations have shallow roots and were derived from a single source in relatively recent times (Stringer and Gamble, 1993).

These two models represent extremes, which pit advocates of anatomical continuity against those who favor rapid replacement of primeval populations. Until fairly recently, most anthropologists strongly favored the candelabra model. They did so

(a)

(b)

FIGURE 3.14   Theories of the origins of modern humans, each of which interprets the fossil evidence in very different ways. (a) The Candelabra or multiregional model, which argues for the evolution of *Homo sapiens sapiens* in many regions of the Old World. The dotted lines between different columns represent gene flow between regions. (b) The Noah's Ark (Out of Africa) model, which has modern humanity evolving in Africa, then spreading to other parts of the world. (After Stringer and Gamble, 1992.)

because finds from western Europe and the Near East dominated academic discussion, largely because the largest numbers of fossils came from these areas. Furthermore, many deep, well-excavated caves and rock shelters appeared to document technological change from simple, relatively unsophisticated toolkits to the much more elaborate artifacts characteristic of *Homo sapiens*.

A torrent of new discoveries has turned our conception of Europe from one of the cradles of modern humans into somewhat of a backwater. The candelabra hypothesis was based in part on two famous 200,000- to 300,000-year-old European fossil skulls, from Swanscombe in England and Steinheim in Germany, thought to represent "Presapiens" humans with larger brains than *Homo erectus* and other modern features (Figure 3.15) (Stringer, 1984). Today, more sophisticated cranial analysis has shown that both skulls display many archaic features, which are shared by newer European finds, among them the Petralona skull from Greece (400,000 to 300,000 years ago) and the Arago skull and jaws from the French Pyrenees (about 200,000 years ago). These finds appear to represent not Presapiens populations but

Petralona
400,000 to 300,000 B.P.

Arago
200,000 B.P.

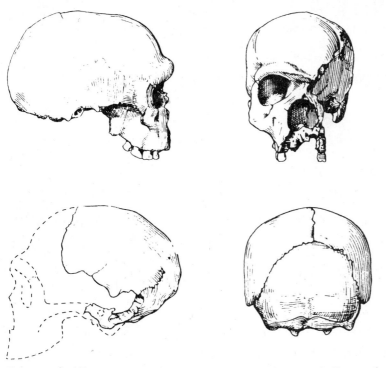

FIGURE 3.15   Steinheim (*top*) and Swanscombe (*bottom*) skulls (one-fourth actual size). The Swanscombe skull is shown with a tentative reconstruction of the missing parts.

Considerable controversy surrounds the classification of these and other European human fossils dating from about 300,000 to 120,000 years ago. Are they *Homo erectus* or archaic *Homo sapiens*? Chris Stringer and other paleoanthropologists have suggested that specimens like these and other well-known finds, such as the Petralona skull from Greece and the Arago specimens from France, be placed in "grades" of *H. sapiens*. Under this scheme, Steinheim and Swanscombe would be in *H. sapiens* Grade 1, modern *Homo sapiens* being in Grade 3 or 4, depending on the scheme. This system is coming into widespread use as a convenient way of classifying Middle Pleistocene human fossils. It does not necessarily imply any evolutionary relationship between different grades (for full discussion, see Stringer et al., 1979).

a very heterogeneous group of archaic humans whose descendants were the Neanderthals of the last interglacial and Weichsel glaciation.

Apart from the fossil evidence, basic principles of evolutionary biology make it appear unlikely that populations of *Homo sapiens* were living in central and western Europe for 200,000 years so isolated from one another that two different lineages could form.

Another important group of finds lent support to the candelabra model. These were the highly variable fossil populations found just before World War II in the Mt. Carmel Caves in what is now Israel (Garrod and Bate, 1937)—Neanderthals displaying startling anatomical variation compared with their European contemporaries.

Mt. Carmel
50,000 B.P. and earlier

Was the Near East a cradle of *Homo sapiens*? Many new discoveries from Southwest Asia and from sites like Qafzeh in Israel have confirmed that Near Eastern populations were very heterogeneous between 100,000 and 40,000 years ago. However, there is a considerable morphological gap between more archaic and only

Qafzeh
92,000 B.P. and later

slightly older fossils and those displaying more modern features, such as reduced brow ridges, more rounded crania, and larger limbs. Many experts believe that the differences between these individuals make local evolution of *H. sapiens* from Neanderthals unlikely (Trinkaus and Shipton, 1992).

Such an evolution would require an adequate amount of time for anatomical change to take place. This time frame does not appear to exist in Europe, for recent finds of Neanderthal-like individuals from Hahnofersand near Hamburg, Germany, and Saint-Césaire in the Charente (France) date to as late as 36,000 to 31,000 years ago. Anatomically modern humans were living in western Europe by this time. Very likely there was a period of coexistence and probably hybridization between the Neanderthals and the modern populations at about this time, when the latter had already replaced Neanderthals in the Near East (Stringer and Gamble, 1993).

Everything points not to anatomical continuity in Europe and the Near East but to replacement of primeval populations by *Homo sapiens*. Furthermore, Near Eastern excavations make it certain that *H. sapiens* populations were living there as early as 92,000 years ago, earlier than they were in Europe. This may indeed have been the area from which modern people—perhaps we can call them *proto-Cro-Magnons*—spread into the north and replaced the Neanderthals some time later. The Noah's ark model, then, seems to fit the available evidence better. But the central question remains unanswered. Where did the proto-Cro-Magnons come from? We know from distributions of Neanderthal finds that there were contacts and gene flow with North Africa. Might tropical Africa have been the ancestral homeland of modern human beings?

Hahnofersand Saint-Césaire 36,000 to 31,000 B.P.

Homo sapiens in Africa

Africa may have been the cradle of humankind, but for years it was regarded as a backwater in later prehistory, a place where modern humans arose very much later than they did in Europe. These ideas were formulated before radiocarbon chronologies and were based on a mere handful of fossil finds, among them the famous robust Broken Hill skull from Zambia, an archaic-looking cranium that seemed to epitomize a backward continent.

A new generation of research based on radiocarbon dates and sophisticated cave excavation has painted a radically different picture of African life after 200,000 years ago. We now know that Acheulian hand ax technology gave way to "Middle Stone Age" culture, with its more sophisticated flake tools and much more versatile toolkit, between 200,000 and 130,000 years ago in both eastern and southern Africa. The excavators of the Klasies River Mouth Caves in southeastern Africa were able to correlate Middle Stone Age occupation with deep-sea cores and date it to between 120,000 and 70,000 years ago. Numerous fragmentary human remains dating to between 125,000 and 95,000 years ago came from the Middle Stone Age levels, remains that displayed astoundingly modern features at a date far earlier than anything from the Near East or Europe (Deacon, 1992).

Klasies River 120,000 to 70,000 B.P.

In East Africa, Richard Leakey found a large, thick-boned human skull and limb bones at Omo Kibish in Ethiopia, dating to perhaps as early as 130,000 years ago. They come from a tall, well-built male, with a broad forehead and well-defined brow ridge that thinned at the edges (Stringer and Gamble, 1993). There are other sites in both eastern and southern Africa where skeletal fragments of ancient, modern-looking people have been reported, alas none of them well dated or complete.

At least three "grades" of *Homo sapiens* flourished in sub-Saharan Africa (Brauer, 1992). An "early archaic *Homo sapiens*" form was widely distributed from southern to northeast Africa some 200,000 years ago. These archaic populations had evolved from earlier *H. erectus* populations and had larger cranial vaults and many other anatomical features akin to those of anatomically modern humans. The Broken Hill skull from Zambia belongs in this group. A second group—"late archaic *Homo sapiens*"—includes fossils with mosaics of both archaic and modern features, with the latter tending to predominate. These specimens date to 100,000 years ago and earlier. The last group are anatomically modern individuals, with only a very few archaic features.

Very early anatomically modern *Homo sapiens* was widely distributed in eastern and southern Africa as far back as the early Upper Pleistocene, some 115,000 years ago, perhaps even earlier (Brauer, 1992). The developments that led to the emergence of *Homo sapiens* in eastern and southern Africa had run their course as early as between 100,000 and 70,000 years ago, far earlier than any equivalent developments in Europe or the Near East. At this time, the evolution of the classic and late Neanderthals had run its course in those areas.

In evolutionary terms, the transition from *Homo erectus* to archaic *Homo sapiens* seems to have occurred not quickly but relatively slowly and continuously. It is difficult to draw a line between the two species. In contrast, the "modernization" of the human skull into its present configuration took place considerably faster, some time at the very end of the Middle Pleistocene or the beginning of the Upper Pleistocene, by 100,000 years ago.

Molecular Biology and *Homo sapiens*

Molecular biology has played a significant role in dating earlier human evolution and is now yielding important clues to the origins of *Homo sapiens* (Cann et al., 1987). Researchers have zeroed in on mitochondrial DNA (mtDNA), a useful tool for calibrating mutation rates because it accumulates mutations much faster than nuclear DNA. Mitochondrial DNA is inherited only through the maternal line; it does not mix and become diluted with paternal DNA. Thus, it provides a potentially reliable link with ancestral populations. When genetic researchers analyzed the mtDNA of 147 women from Africa, Asia, Europe, Australia, and New Guinea, they found that the differences among them were very small. Therefore, they argued, the five populations were all of comparatively recent origin. There were some differences, sufficient to separate two groups within the sample—a set of African individuals and another comprising individuals from all groups. The biologists concluded that all modern humans derive from a 200,000-year-old African population, from which populations migrated to the rest of the Old World with little or no interbreeding with existing, more archaic human groups.

A storm of criticism has descended on the so-called Eve hypothesis, most of it directed against the calculations of the rate of genetic mutation. As Cann and others have pointed out, the methodology is very new and evolving rapidly. Nevertheless, with mitochondrial data from some 5,000 modern individuals, there is evidence that Africans display more diverse types of mitochondrial DNA than other present-day populations elsewhere in the world, which suggests they had more time to develop such mutations. An even larger database of normal (nuclear) DNA, also of its products (blood groups and enzymes), displays a hierarchy of clusters. There was a primary split between Africans and non-Africans, then a later one between Eurasians and southeast Asians. This also implies that modern humans originated in Africa, then dispersed from there to split again in Asia. It is thought that the ancestral population lived in Africa about 100,000 years ago. This also means that, assuming a constant rate of genetic diversification, all human variation could have arisen in the past 150,000 years.

At present, the earliest archaeological evidence for anatomically modern humans in Africa dates to between 130,000 and 100,000 years ago. With so few fossils to work with, all we can be sure of is that there was considerable anatomical variation in Africans between 200,000 and 100,000 years ago. It is also entirely possible that anatomically modern humans evolved in many locations south of the Sahara in highly varied and very isolated African populations.

Ecology and *Homo sapiens*

For generations, anthropologists have tended to treat the origin of *Homo sapiens* as a unique event that took place outside the processes of evolutionary biology. As Robert Foley (1984c) argues, one can understand this event only within a comparative ecological framework. Foley points out that modern humans were most likely to have originated within a single location. The savanna woodland of Africa around 100,000 years ago was an ideal environment for promoting the speciation of modern humans, he believes. Foley has studied monkey evolution in Africa and found that the widely dispersed populations had diverged; they did not continue on a single evolutionary course. Africa experienced considerable habitat fragmentation and re-formation during the alternating cold and warmth of the Pleistocene, fluctuations that enhanced the prospects of speciation among the continent's animals and plants. For example, Foley found that one monkey genus alone radiated into 16 species at about the same time that modern humans may have evolved on the continent. The tropical environments of Africa consisted of a constant mosaic of changing environmental patterns, a mosaic that tended to foster local evolution. This phenomenon contrasted with higher latitudes, where environmental changes were more marked and animal distributions changed significantly and rapidly over short periods of time.

Foley's monkey studies have convinced him that modern humans evolved in such a mosaic of tropical environments, developing distinctive characteristics that separated them from their archaic predecessors. Within tropical Africa's patchy environments were areas where food supplies were both predictable and of high quality. In response to such regions, some humans may have developed wide-ranging behavior, lived in larger social groups with considerable kin-based substructure, and been highly selective in their diet. As part of these responses, some groups may have developed exceptional hunting skills, a technology so effective that they could prey on animals from a distance with projectiles. With more efficient technology, more advance planning, and better organization of both hunting and foraging, our ancestors could have reduced the unpredictability of the environment in dramatic ways.

This ecological approach to modern human origins is still untested against archaeological evidence. Even at this stage in research there are unexplained anomalies between biology and archaeology. Once modern human beings had evolved, they manufactured a sophisticated tool technology, based on antler, bone, wood, and stone blade manufacture. In the long term, similar improved hunting and foraging technologies took hold throughout Africa, finally turning humans from expert scavengers and occasional hunters into super predators, capable of taking mammals large and small. The link between technology and anatomy is very loose, as if ideas and genes had moved at different rates. A number of lines of evidence strongly suggest that *Homo sapiens* originated in Africa and spread from there into other parts of the Old World.

The Spread of *Homo sapiens*

If tropical Africa was the cradle of modern humans, how and why did *Homo sapiens* spread into Europe and Asia (Brauer, 1992)? The critical period was between 100,000 and 45,000 years ago, the date by which *H. sapiens* is known to have been living in the Near East. The only major barrier to population movement between tropical Africa and the Mediterranean Basin is the Sahara, today some of the driest territory on earth. During the early Weichsel, the Sahara went through phases of relative aridity and greater rainfall. A cooler and wetter climate prevailed in the desert from before 100,000 until about 40,000 years ago and again between 32,000 and 24,000 years ago. For long periods, the country between East Africa and the Mediterranean was passable, supporting scattered game herds and open grassland. The Nile Valley was always habitable, even during periods of great aridity in the desert. Thus, anatomically modern *H. sapiens* may have hunted and foraged across the Sahara into the Nile Valley and the Near East in the early Weichsel. Then as the Near East became increasingly dry and less productive, the newcomers may have responded to population pressure and food shortages by moving across the wide land bridge that joined Turkey to southeastern Europe 45,000 years ago, spreading into the more productive steppe and tundra regions of Europe and western Asia (Fagan, 1990).

HOMO SAPIENS IN EASTERN ASIA

● ● ●

For hundreds of thousands of years, from over 750,000 years ago until perhaps later than 200,000 years ago, *Homo erectus* populations flourished in East and Southeast Asia. These archaic humans adapted to a wide range of environments, but the adaptations were conservative ones, especially in the tropical forests and woodlands of Southeast Asia, where bamboo may have been an important toolmaking material.

Although physical anthropologists argue over the anatomical differences between different Asian *Homo erectus* populations, no one doubts that there were gradual changes in human anatomy through time. Unfortunately, there is such a dearth of fossils and accurate dates for them that the experts can do little more than speculate intelligently about human fossils often separated in time by as much as 250,000 years. In China, there are scattered finds of what are said to be archaic forms of *Homo sapiens*, as opposed to anatomically modern people, dating to about 200,000 years ago from such sites as Dali and Maba. By this time, Chinese biologists believe they can recognize distinctive "Chinese" anatomical features, and there is general agreement that brain sizes were increasing by that date. Despite theories that anatomically modern people flourished in China as early as 70,000 years ago, there is a yawning fossil gap until finds in the 35,000-year-old range, much later in prehistory.

In Southeast Asia, where there is a similar chronological gap, physical anthropologists Milford Wolpoff and Alan Thorne (1984) compared a *Homo erectus* fossil from Sangiran in Java, estimated to be some 700,000 years ago, with a large sample of *Homo sapiens sapiens* skeletons from Kow Swamp in southern Australia (Chapter 7). On the basis of comparisons of selected anatomical features like the jutting forward of the face, they argued that there was strong evidence of anatomical continuity between *H. erectus* and more modern Asian populations. They and Chinese scholar Wu Zin Xhi (1984) believe that there was interbreeding of *H. sapiens sapiens* populations from centers of greater morphological variation like the Near East with archaic populations farther east (Groves, 1989; Hapgood, 1989). The farther one got from the "centers," they argue, the later the appearance of modern humans. One of the outer regions was mainland Southeast Asia, where *H. erectus* apparently survived far longer than in Africa and Europe.

Noah's ark critics of this candelabra form of hypothesis argue that Wolpoff and Thorne's research is based on a careful selection of a few anatomical features, some of which may be primitive retentions, and on fossils that are separated by hundreds of thousands of years of prehistoric time. It has to be admitted that if the Noah's ark hypothesis is correct, the date when anatomically modern humans spread into Asia and the processes by which they did it are a complete mystery.

The earliest well-documented *Homo sapiens sapiens* fossils date to long after modern people were living in the Near East. A poorly dated *H. sapiens sapiens* skull from the great cave at Niah in Borneo is believed to be about 40,000 years old, and an anatomically modern skull from Tabon Cave in the Philippines may date to about 23,000 years ago. Both of these specimens are said to display features that link them to gene flow from farther north in Asia. The earliest anatomically modern fossils in China date to somewhere between 50,000 and 35,000 years ago.

The earliest dated mainland site that might be attributed to *Homo sapiens sapiens* is the Long Rongrien cave on the west end of the Thai-Malay Peninsula in the thick rain forest (Anderson, 1990). The lowest occupation levels date to at least 37,000 years ago and are marked by small scrapers, some worked cobbles, and three antler or bone tools. We can only hypothesize about the inhabitants of mainland Southeast Asia between 100,000 and 40,000 years ago. In the forests, as Long Rongrien shows, there was no need for sophisticated stone artifacts when easily split and sharpened bamboo and various woods would suffice for weapons and knives.

In short, we do not know when anatomically modern people settled in Asia, but an intelligent guess would be after 100,000 years ago, by which time *Homo sapiens sapiens* was well established in the Near East and Africa.

Archaic Homo sapiens in Europe: The Neanderthals

● ● ●

We have hypothesized that anatomically modern humans moved into Europe during the last glaciation. It was there that they encountered the Neanderthals, indigenous inhabitants of Europe and Eurasia, who are still the subject of great controversy among physical anthropologists (Figure 3.16). Some people use the word *Neanderthal* to describe dim-witted, ugly people who are like apes, an insult aimed at those they consider dumb. This stereotype and that of the shambling cave people so beloved by cartoonists come from mistaken studies of Neanderthal skeletons in the early years of this century. In fact, the Neanderthals were strong, robustly built humans with some archaic features. Their skulls display retreating foreheads, projecting faces, and sometimes eyebrow ridges, when compared with modern people.

FIGURE 3.16   Distribution of the Neanderthals, their culture, and related technologies.

There is every reason to believe they were expert hunters and beings capable of considerable intellectual reasoning.

There are, of course, striking anatomical differences between Neanderthals and modern humans, both in the robust postcranial skeleton and in the more bun-shaped skull, sometimes with heavy brow ridges and a forward projecting face (Figure 3.17). These features are the reason this extinct hominid form is classified as *Homo sapiens neanderthalensis,* a subspecies of *Homo sapiens,* and not as *Homo sapiens sapiens,* a fully modern human.

In the century since the first Neanderthal skull from the German village of that name was unearthed, substantial numbers of Neanderthal individuals, most in western Europe, as well as contemporary human fossils from the Near East, Africa, and Asia have been unearthed. They first appeared during the Eem interglacial, well before 100,000 years ago, but they were apparently few in number. Large Neanderthal sites occur in the Dordogne area of southwest France, where deep river valleys and vast limestone cliffs offered abundant shelter during the Weichsel glaciation

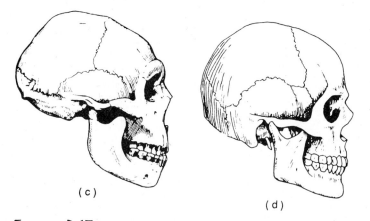

FIGURE 3.17   Comparisons of four fossil skulls and jaws. (a) The reconstructed *Homo erectus* skull has prominent brow ridges, a bun-shaped rear to the cranium, and a retreating chin. (b) A "classic" Neanderthal skull found at Monte Circeo, Italy, still has well-marked brow ridges and bun-shaped cranium but an increased brain capacity. The skull is lower and flatter than those of modern humans, and the jaw is chinless. (c) The Shanidar Neanderthal from Iraq is a less extreme example, with a higher forehead, somewhat reduced brow ridges, and a much more rounded skull. (d) Modern skull with well-rounded contours, no brow ridges, high forehead, and a well-marked chin.

(Bordes, 1968; Gamble, 1986b). The skeletons found in French caves look like anatomical anachronisms, with massive brow ridges and squat bodies. The Neanderthals walked upright and as nimbly as modern humans. They stood just over 5 feet tall (153 cm), and their forearms were relatively short compared with those of modern people. This "classic" variety of Neanderthal is confined to western Europe and is more noticeably different from *Homo sapiens* than its contemporary populations found elsewhere, especially around the shores of the Mediterranean and in Asia (Figure 3.16). We find much variability among nonclassic Neanderthals, who most often display less extreme features, particularly brow ridges and other cranial features, than the classic variety of western France. It is well demonstrated at the Mt. Carmel sites of et-Tabūn and es-Skhūl in Israel as well as at Krapina in central Europe (Stringer, 1988; Trinkaus and Howells, 1979).

The morphological differences apparent between many Neanderthals and modern *Homo sapiens* are startling. How do these heavily built, beetle-browed people fit into the picture of human evolution? The great French physical anthropologist Marcellin Boule believed, in the 1930s, that the classic Neanderthals were clumsy, shambling people, so specialized that they became extinct while other populations provided the evolutionary basis for modern humans (Boule and Vallois, 1957). Erik Trinkaus and William Howells (1979) reviewed Neanderthal populations from all over Europe and the Near East and point out that their anatomical pattern took approximately 50 millennia from 150,000 years ago to evolve, then stabilized for another 50 before changing rapidly to essentially modern human anatomy within a brief period of 5,000 years approximately 40,000 years ago. They indicate that Boule was mistaken, partly because his definitive studies were made on an elderly individual suffering from arthritis and partly because much more skeletal material is now available. The Neanderthals had the same posture, manual abilities, and range and characteristics of movement as modern people (Figure 3.18). They differed in having massive limb bones, often somewhat bowed in the thigh and forearm, features that reflect the Neanderthals' greater muscular power. For their height, the Neanderthals were bulky and heavily muscled, and their brain capacity was slightly larger than that of modern humans. Their antecedents may be chronicled by fragmentary human remains, including three skulls from a cave in the Sierra de Atapeurca, near Burgos in northern Spain, dating to more than 30,000 years ago. The more complete of these specimens display anatomical features closer to those of archaic *Homo sapiens* than *Homo erectus*, as if the evolutionary roots of the Neanderthals lie deep in earlier times (Arsuaga and others, 1993).

Morphological differences

EARLY HOMO SAPIENS ADAPTS

●   ●   ●

Although many details of the biological evolution of early *Homo sapiens* remain unresolved, we know a great deal about the many and diverse adaptations of these people. Their distinctive hunter-gatherer culture, which continued in the basic hominid tradition, is known from hundreds of sites in Africa, Asia, and Europe. The Neanderthals' *Mousterian* technology (named after the Le Moustier rock shelter in southwest France) was far more complex and sophisticated than its Acheulian predecessor, with many regional variations (Trinkaus, 1983a). Many of the Neanderthals' artifacts were made for specific purposes. Like their *erectus* predecessors, the early *Homo sapiens* bands occupied large territories, which they probably exploited on a seasonal round, returning to the same locations year after year when

Mousterian culture ?100,000 to 40,000 B.P. (Chapter 4)

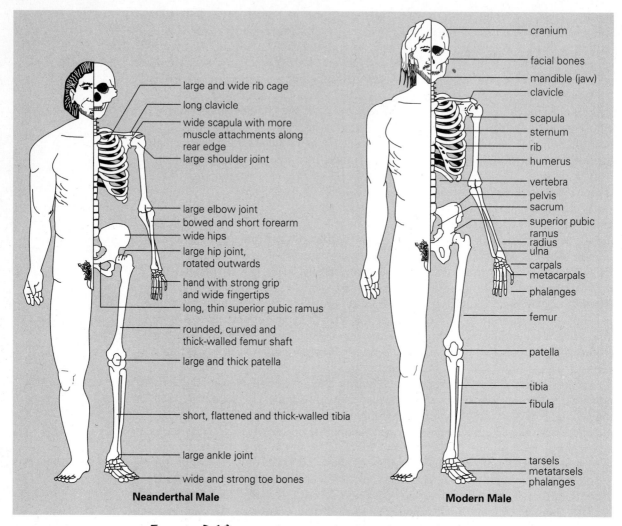

Neanderthal Male

- large and wide rib cage
- long clavicle
- wide scapula with more muscle attachments along rear edge
- large shoulder joint
- large elbow joint
- bowed and short forearm
- wide hips
- large hip joint, rotated outwards
- hand with strong grip and wide fingertips
- long, thin superior pubic ramus
- rounded, curved and thick-walled femur shaft
- large and thick patella
- short, flattened and thick-walled tibia
- large ankle joint
- wide and strong toe bones

Modern Male

- cranium
- facial bones
- mandible (jaw)
- clavicle
- scapula
- sternum
- rib
- humerus
- vertebra
- pelvis
- sacrum
- superior pubic ramus
- radius
- ulna
- carpals
- metacarpals
- phalanges
- femur
- patella
- tibia
- fibula
- tarsels
- metatarsels
- phalanges

FIGURE 3.18   The skeleton of a male Neanderthal (*left*) compared with that of a modern male. The Neanderthal is more robust and stockier than his modern counterpart. (After Stringer and Gamble, 1992.)

game migrated or vegetables came into season. The Neanderthals were skilled hunters who were not afraid to pursue large game animals like the mammoth as well as reindeer and wild horses. They also caught birds and fish. It appears that many western European bands lived in caves and rock shelters during much of the year as a protection against arctic cold. During the summer months they may have fanned out over the tundra plains, living in temporary tented encampments (for details, see Gamble, 1986b).

Clive Gamble (1986b) argues that the Neanderthal adaptation in Europe was significantly different from that of earlier human populations. He points to significant changes in human settlement patterns, that is, to a greater use of rock shelters and caves as well as repeated use of open sites as temporary stopping places for people away from the larger main group. This may have been a time when technology was more organized, when planning assumed greater importance—to reduce the risk of starvation. People were now developing hunting and foraging strategies

based on four main herd species—bison, horse, red deer, and reindeer. Gamble theorizes that storage assumed much greater importance for surviving winter shortages,
maximizing the meat culled from seasonally migrating animals. There may have
been higher population densities, greater population stability, and more adaptive
stability, with less risk of local populations dying out in times of stress.

For the new adaptive strategies, environmental knowledge was the key to effective planning. Factors such as herd size, migration seasons, and predictability of animal movements assumed vital importance. This pattern of adaptation resulted in
considerable interregional differences within the Neanderthal world. The southwestern areas of Europe, with their deep river valleys and large rock shelters, were
occupied constantly, whereas more open areas to the north and east were more
extensively exploited during periods of warmer climate and largely abandoned during glacial times. It is interesting to note that no Neanderthal sites have yet come to
light north of 56°N (see Figure 3.16).

STONE TOOL TECHNOLOGY

• • •

The stone technology used by the Neanderthals and other early *Homo sapiens* forms
has often been subsumed under the label Middle Paleolithic, on the grounds that the
techniques used were distinct from those of *Homo erectus*. In fact, the basic differences are much less radical than has often been assumed. There is a basic continuum
in stoneworking skills that begins in the Lower Paleolithic and continues through
the Middle into the Upper Paleolithic and even later in prehistory. Even the more
efficient technological changes associated with the spread of *Homo sapiens sapiens*
after 40,000 years ago have a strong basis in much earlier, simpler technologies (Figure 3.19).

Middle Paleolithic
technology

Levallois and Disk Core Reduction Strategies

At Kapthurin and other East African sites, Acheulian stoneworkers demonstrated a
remarkable skill at preshaping cores to produce large flakes for making axes and
other artifacts. With such prepared core techniques, which were to assume great
importance after 100,000 years ago, the core is shaped to predetermine the flake or
blade that is to be removed. The *Levallois technique,* named after the Paris suburb
where it was first found, produces broad, flat flakes, large blades, and triangular
points (Figure 3.20). The *disk core technique* is designed to produce as many flakes
of varying size as possible and results in residual cores with an approximate round
shape. The size of the raw material lumps available to the stoneworker probably
had a major effect on the flakes produced, for both techniques as well as simpler
flaking were widely used in Europe, Africa, and Asia.

Tool Forms and Variability

Mousterian and other Middle Paleolithic tools were made for the most part on
flakes, the most characteristic artifacts being points and scrapers (Figure 3.21).
Some of these were *composite tools,* artifacts made of more than one component—
for example, a point, a shaft, and the binding that secured the head to the shaft,

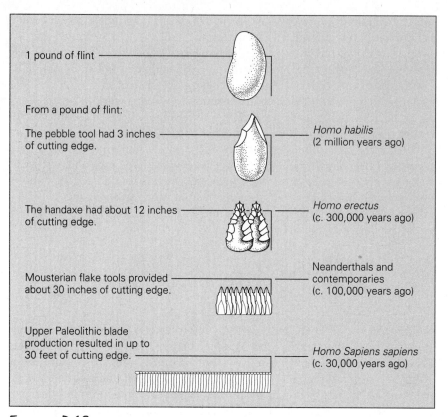

1 pound of flint

From a pound of flint:

The pebble tool had 3 inches of cutting edge.   Homo habilis
                                                                 (2 million years ago)

The handaxe had about 12 inches of cutting edge.   Homo erectus
                                                                 (c. 300,000 years ago)

Mousterian flake tools provided   Neanderthals and
about 30 inches of cutting edge.   contemporaries
                                             (c. 100,000 years ago)

Upper Paleolithic blade production resulted in up to 30 feet of cutting edge.   Homo Sapiens sapiens
                                                                                       (c. 30,000 years ago)

FIGURE 3.19   The growing efficiency of Stone Age technology is shown by the ability of ancient stoneworkers at producing ever larger numbers of cutting edges from a pound of flint or other fine grained rock. The Neanderthals were far more efficient stone artisans than their predecessors. By the same token, *Homo sapiens sapiens* used a blade technology (Figure 4.4), which produced up to 30 feet (9.1 m) per pound of flint.

making a spear. The edges of both points and scrapers were sharpened by fine trimming, the removal of small, steplike chips from the edge of the implement. These artifacts, almost universally distributed in Middle Paleolithic sites, were used in the chase, in woodworking, and in preparing skins. However, recent microwear researches have revealed that many untrimmed flakes were used for cutting, scraping, and other tasks; they were convenient working edges when needed at a moment's notice (Gamble, 1986b).

The complexity of Mousterian technology is striking. The French sites have yielded a great diversity of Mousterian artifacts and toolkits. Some levels include hand axes; others, notched flakes, perhaps used for stripping meat for drying or pressing fibrous plants. Subdivisions of Mousterian technology have been identified by the prevalence of specific tool types. The French archaeologist François Bordes (1968) excavated the Combe Grenal cave in the Perigord and studied a stratified series of intermittent Mousterian occupations between 90,000 and 40,000 years ago. Bordes identified no fewer than 60 different Mousterian tool types, made with a variety of toolmaking techniques, including the Levallois method, and with carefully prepared disk cores. He also identified four distinct

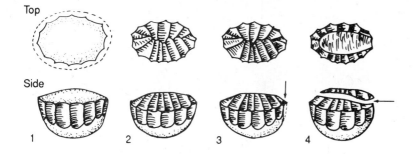

Top

Side

1   2   3   4

(a)

1

2

(b)

FIGURE 3.20 Prepared core techniques. Prepared cores were carefully flaked to enable the toolmaker to strike off large flakes of predetermined size.

The Levallois technique meant that the stoneworker would shape a lump of flint into an inverted bun-shaped core (often compared to an inverted tortoise shell). The flat upper surface would be struck at one end, the resulting flake forming the only product from the core. Another form was the disk core, a prepared core from which several flakes of predetermined size and shape were removed. The core gradually became smaller, until it resembled a flat disk. Disk cores were often used to produce points and scrapers. (a) Making a Levallois core: (1) The edges of a suitable stone are trimmed; (2) the top surface is trimmed; (3) a striking platform is made, the point where the flake will originate, by trimming to form a straight edge on the side; and (4) a flake is struck from the core and removed. (b) (1) A Levallois core from the Thames Valley, England, with the top of the core (*bottom*), shown from above and the end view (*top*). (2) A typical Levallois flake: upper surface (*center*), lower (flake) surface (*right*), and cross section (*left*). Both artifacts are one-third actual size.

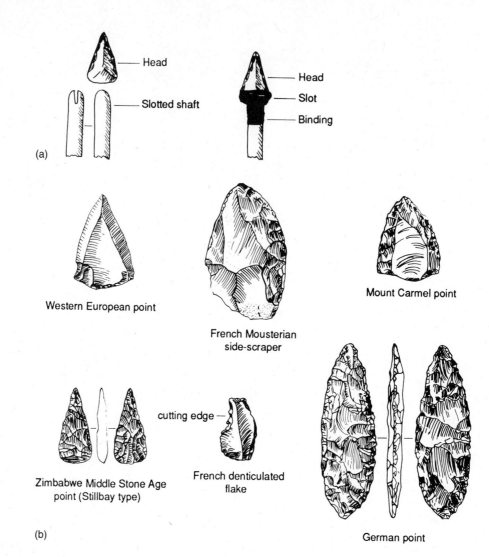

FIGURE 3.21 Middle Paleolithic tools and technology. This technology was based on simple stone techniques that were used for tens of thousands of years before the emergence of early *Homo sapiens*. By 100,000 years ago, artifacts of many types were of composite form—made from several different parts. A wooden spear might have a stone tip, a flint scraper, a bone handle. Unfortunately, we know almost nothing about the bone and wood tools used. (a) Stone-tipped Mousterian spear (a hypothetical example). The spear was made by attaching a pointed stone head to a wooden handle to form the projectile. The head probably fitted into a slot in the wooden shaft and was fixed to it with resin or beeswax; a binding was added to the end of the shaft. (b) Mousterian artifacts.

toolkits in the Combe Grenal levels: one associated with small hand axes, another with thousands of heavy-duty side scrapers, a third with a high proportion of saw-edged flakes, and some that contained an even balance of different tool types.

The Mousterian Debate

Such wide variation in Mousterian toolkits is found not only at Combe Grenal but also at other Neanderthal sites throughout Europe and the Near East and in North Africa where other archaic *Homo sapiens* made similar tools. Bordes (1968) believed that the Combe Grenal toolkits reflected four different Neanderthal groups who all visited the same location but who lived in almost complete isolation and rarely had any contact with one another. Others hypothesize that the variations in toolkits were the result of slow cultural change, with different tools, like the side scraper, in fashion at different times (Mellars, 1973). In contrast, Lewis and Sally Binford argue that Bordes's traditions reflect various distinct activities carried out within the same cultural system at different times of the year (Binford, 1983; Binford and Binford, 1966). Harold Dibble (1987) has studied Mousterian scraper technology, on the assumption that the various shapes of these artifacts represent a "reduction continuum," that is, a continuous process of flaking the edge of flake blanks. Thus, collections with more large side scrapers represent *less* intensive utilization of scrapers than those with greater variability in scraper forms. He argues that neither style nor function was the overriding factor in stone tool variability. Rather, the Neanderthals were using a fundamentally very simple stone technology, with both flaking techniques and reduction processes varying considerably in response to all kinds of external factors—availability of raw materials, size, climate, differing activities, and subsistence needs among them.

The Neanderthals and their contemporaries were developing tools for different activities far more quickly than ever before, perhaps at a time of growing human populations and slightly enhanced social complexity. Fundamentally Middle Paleolithic technology was simple, highly variable, and a logical development of technologies refined over many millennia.

THE ORIGINS OF BURIAL AND RELIGIOUS BELIEF

● ● ●

The Neanderthals were hunter-gatherers and the world's population was still small, but life was gradually becoming more complex. Some experts claim that they regularly buried their dead, the first signs of religious ideology, of a preoccupation with the life hereafter. Many Neanderthals were indeed buried by their companions, but all known burials have come from caves or rock shelters in Europe, the Near East, and Eurasia, often found under unscientific circumstances. Christopher Stringer and Clive Gamble point out (1993) that most complete Neanderthal bodies occur in caves where predator bones are rare, as if carnivores were not using such places for their dens. Thus, the abandoned corpses survived more or less intact, even if they were disposed of underground, for no hibernating bears dug them up or hyenas scattered the decaying bodies lying in their dens.

Neanderthal burials have been recovered from the deposits of rock shelters and caves as well as from open campsites. Single burials are the most common, normally accompanied by flint tools, food offerings, or even cooked game meat (evidenced by charred bones)—but many such associations are dubious, given unscientific excavation many years ago. One rock shelter, La Ferrassie near Les Eyzies in France, yielded the remains of two adult Neanderthals and four children buried close together in a campsite. One band of Siberian mountain goat hunters lived at Teshik-Tash in the western foothills of the Himalayas. They buried one of their children in a shallow pit, surrounding the body with six pairs of wild goat horns.

Burials at Teshik-Tash

Shanidar

Another remarkable single burial came from the Shanidar Cave in the Zagros Mountains of Iraq (Trinkaus, 1983b). There a 30-year-old man was crushed by a rockfall from the roof of the cave. He was buried in a shallow pit. Other single graves from France and central Europe were covered with red ocher powder.

No one can question that the Neanderthals buried some of their dead, but whether such burial was mere corpse disposal or associated with the appearance of beliefs in the afterlife is a matter for debate. What is striking, however, is that formal burials, sometimes with elaborate adornment, appear regularly with modern humans throughout the world.

CHAPTER SUMMARY

We described the climatic events of the Great Ice Age (the Pleistocene) between about 1.6 million years ago and 128,000 years before present. These complex fluctuations between glacial maxima and much shorter interglacial periods were the backdrop to the evolution not only of *Homo erectus*, but of modern humans, *Homo sapiens sapiens*, as well. *Homo erectus* evolved from earlier *Homo* in tropical Africa by 1.6 million years ago, at about the same time that fire was tamed, then radiated into Europe and Asia as part of a general radiation of mammalian species after about a million years ago. The new humans used a simple technology based on hand axes and basic flake technology in the west, relying heavily on bamboo and other forest products in southeast Asia. There was a gradual increase in brain size, perhaps beginning as early as about 0.4 million years ago, as archaic forms of *Homo sapiens* with enlarged brain capacities evolved in various parts of the Old World. The best known of these forms are the Neanderthals of Europe and Eurasia, who developed more sophisticated toolmaking technology, were more adept hunters and foragers, and were the first humans to bury some of their dead. Two competing theories account for the appearance of anatomically modern humans. The so-called Noah's ark hypothesis argues that modern humans evolved in tropical Africa before 100,000 years ago, then spread into other parts of the world from the Near East after 45,000 years ago (Chapter 4). The Multiregional (Candelabra) hypothesis has it that modern humans developed independently in Africa, Europe, and Asia, and that the biological diversity of contemporary humankind has very deep roots in prehistory. With the appearance of modern humans, the long prehistory of the archaic world ends.

GUIDE TO FURTHER READING

Bordes, François. 1968. *The Old Stone Age.* New York: McGraw Hill.
  A simple manual on the Paleolithic period that is out of date except for its simple descriptions of basic Stone Age technologies and European tool types. Ideal for beginners.

Fagan, Brian M. 1990. *The Journey from Eden*. New York: Thames and Hudson.
> *A synthesis of the controversies surrounding the origins of modern humans for laypeople. Written in nontechnical language. Recommended for beginning students.*

Gamble, Clive. 1986. *The Paleolithic Settlement of Europe*. Cambridge, Eng.: Cambridge University Press.
> *A full discussion of the fundamental issues surrounding the Middle Paleolithic adaptation in Europe. For advanced readers.*

Lieberman, Philip. 1991. *Uniquely Human: The Evolution of Speech, Thought, and Selfless Behavior*. Cambridge, MA: Harvard University Press.
> *An authoritative study of the evolution of language in humans.*

Mellars, Paul, and Stringer, Christopher, eds. 1989. *The Human Revolution,* vol. 1. Edinburgh: Edinburgh University Press.
> *A comprehensive series of essays on the origins of modern humans that summarizes not only biological and genetic evidence but archaeological as well. This is a comprehensively referenced, technical work.*

Stringer, Christopher, and Gamble, Clive. 1993. *The Search for the Neanderthals*. London: Thames and Hudson.
> *An up-to-date account of what we know about these archaic humans, aimed at the general reader.*

Trinkaus, Erik, and Shipman, Pat. 1992. *The Neanderthals: Changing the Image of Mankind*. New York: Alfred A. Knopf.
> *Another popular account of the Neanderthals, which is also authoritative.*

PART

III

THE SPREAD OF HOMO SAPIENS

(45,000 B.C. TO MODERN TIMES)

"I want you to remind yourself," he said, "that you have now spent 1 field season of excavation, 15 years of analyses, and thousands of dollars of taxpayers' money to find out no more than this: what a family of five did during the autumn, on six different occasions, scattered over a 2,000-year period. I earnestly hope that the thought will keep you humble."
"Would you believe 'deeply depressed'?"

KENT FLANNERY, *GUILA NAQUITZ*

This part recounts the rapid spread of *Homo sapiens sapiens* throughout the Old World and into the Americas and examines some of the many hunter-gatherer adaptations that developed after the Ice Age.

CHAPTER 4

EUROPEANS AND NORTHERN ASIANS

(c. 40,000 TO 6000 B.C.)*

• • •

Spanish landowner Marcellino de Sautuola had a casual interest in archaeology. He had visited an exhibit of some of the fine stone tools from French caves in Paris. In 1875, he decided to dig for some artifacts of his own in the caverns of Altamira on his estate. Sautuola's five-year-old daughter Maria begged for the chance to dig with him, so he good-naturedly agreed. Maria soon tired of the muddy work and wandered off with a flickering lantern into a low side chamber of the cave. Suddenly, he heard cries of ¡Toros! ¡Toros! ("Bulls, Bulls"). Maria pointed excitedly at brightly painted figures of bison and a charging boar on the low ceiling. Daughter and father marveled at the fresh paintings arranged so cleverly around bulges in the rock that they seemed to move in the flickering light.

Sautuola was convinced the paintings were executed by the same people who had dropped stone tools in the cave. But the experts laughed at him and accused the Marquis of smuggling an artist into Altamira to forge the bison. It was not until 1904 that the long-dead Spaniard was vindicated, when some paintings with strong stylistic links to Altamira came to light in a French cave that had been sealed since the prehistoric artists had worked there. Clearly, whoever had painted on the cave walls at Altamira was a far cry from *Homo habilis*—the earliest known toolmaker.

In the final analysis the long millennia of prehistory have seen humankind become ever more efficient at extracting energy from its environment (Table 4.1). The first hominids branched out into unfamiliar environments that took them away from an almost total dependence on forest fruits. *Homo habilis* was a scavenger as well as a collector, perhaps even an occasional hunter, a lifeway that further deepened the scope of our predecessors' lives. *Homo erectus* radiated into temperate latitudes, into the Near East, Europe, and Asia. These more advanced hominids were hunters as well as scavengers, who relied on enhanced cooperation for success in the chase. Once they became serious hunters, people could tap rich supplies of energy-rich meat, as well as vegetable foods. Hunters were, at first, yet another carnivore in a world well populated by successful carnivores. The transition to the new lifeway

*From this point on, dates are quoted not in years before present (B.P.) but as B.C./A.D., as this is more common usage.

TABLE 4.1

• • •

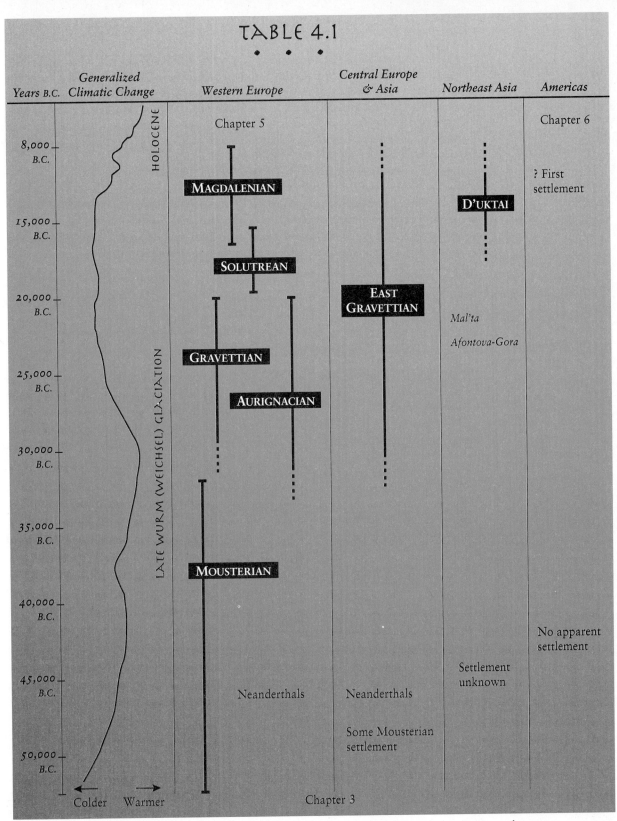

Years B.C.	Generalized Climatic Change	Western Europe	Central Europe & Asia	Northeast Asia	Americas
		Chapter 5			Chapter 6
8,000 B.C.					? First settlement
	HOLOCENE	MAGDALENIAN		D'UKTAI	
15,000 B.C.		SOLUTREAN			
20,000 B.C.			EAST GRAVETTIAN	Mal'ta	
	LATE WURM (WEICHSEL) GLACIATION	GRAVETTIAN		Afontova-Gora	
25,000 B.C.		AURIGNACIAN			
30,000 B.C.					
35,000 B.C.					
		MOUSTERIAN			No apparent settlement
40,000 B.C.					
45,000 B.C.		Neanderthals	Neanderthals	Settlement unknown	
50,000 B.C.			Some Mousterian settlement		
	← Colder Warmer →	Chapter 3			

There was considerable overlap between European cultures. Climatic changes are approximate, as they are subject to considerable controversy among experts.

must have been slow, at times painful, and may have occurred in several stages. There can be little doubt that increased efficiency as a carnivore played an important role in the emergence of both archaic *Homo sapiens* and anatomically modern *Homo sapiens sapiens*. In Chapter 3, we explored current thinking about the emergence of *H. sapiens sapiens* in tropical Africa and hypothesized that anatomically modern humans spread from the tropics into North Africa and the Near East in about 90,000 B.C. From there, *H. sapiens* may have entered Europe at a time of low sea level, crossing the land bridge that connected the Balkans with Turkey across the Bosphorus (for a full discussion, see Fagan, 1990; Stringer et al., 1984). This chapter chronicles the cultural changes that resulted from this replacement of European Neanderthals by anatomically modern humans and looks at the vigorous hunter-gatherer cultures that flourished in the northern parts of the Old World between 38,000 B.C. and postglacial times (Figure 4.1a and b shows sites in Chapters 5, 6, and 8).

THE UPPER PLEISTOCENE (C. 126,000 B.C. TO 8000 B.C.)

● ● ●

The Upper Pleistocene coincided with the last interglacial and glacial cycle of the Ice Age, which began in about 126,000 B.C. The detailed picture we have of this cycle gives us important clues to the general nature of the Ice Age climate—gradual glaciation and rapid deglaciation in cycles of cold, dry weather prevailing over northern latitudes for some 60 percent of the past 730,000 years. Full interglacial conditions, when the climate was warmer than today, brought forest and woodland to Europe (Figure 4.2a). The Upper Pleistocene began with the Eemian interglacial, which lasted only some 10,000 years. About 116,000 B.C., global temperatures started to cool gradually with the onset of the Weichsel (or Wurm) glaciation. By 113,000 B.C., North American and European ice sheets were expanding again, and sea levels had already fallen some 230 feet (70 m). Glacial conditions were intense about 73,000 B.C., when the Neanderthals were flourishing in Europe and the Americas were still uninhabited, and again after 27,000 B.C., reaching their height about 16,000 B.C., when sea levels fell to about 425 feet (130 m) below modern levels. This drop led to the exposure of huge continental shelves in Southeast Asia and elsewhere, and the Bering Strait was dry land.

At the height of the last glaciation, world temperatures fell by as much as 60°F (15.5°C) near the ice sheets, between 37° and 48°F (20.6° and 26.7°C) in the tropics. The world's vegetation was very different at the height of the Weichsel glaciation (Figure 4.2b). Treeless tundra vegetation extended south of the ice sheets, giving way to a wide belt of continental, cold steppe that extended from the Low Countries into China and from Siberia to the Mediterranean. The steppe was much narrower in North America, soon giving way to coniferous forest farther south. Huge zones of desert occupied more than half the earth's surface between latitudes 30°N and S, but some of today's desert areas—like the American Southwest, the northern Sahara, and the southern African deserts—were more hospitable, supporting scrub, grassland, and shallow lakes. The rain forests of tropical Africa and Asia gave way to open woodland and grassland; coral reefs and mangrove swamps contracted drastically as a result of cooler temperatures. However, despite the harsh world climate, humankind managed to survive and flourish in this very different world.

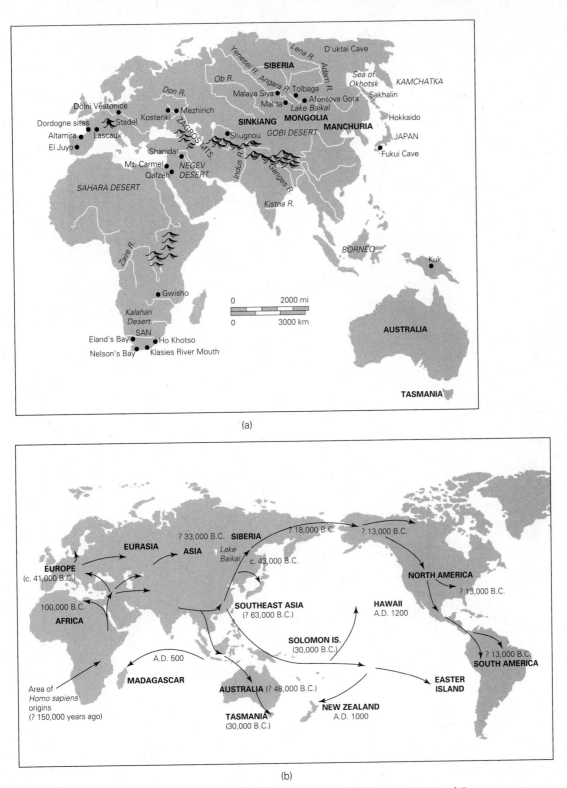

FIGURE 4.1   (a) Map showing archaeological sites mentioned in Chapters 4, 5, and 7.
(b) The spread of *Homo sapiens sapiens* in the late Ice Age and later.

FIGURE 4.2   (a) Generalized distribution of vegetation in Europe during the height of the Holstein interglacial. The succeeding Eemian interglacial was not quite as warm and was of shorter duration, but the same general vegetational patterns prevailed. (After Butzer, 1971.) (b) Generalized vegetation map of Europe at the height of the Weichsel glaciation, showing ice sheets. (After Butzer, 1971.)

NEANDERTHALS AND HOMO SAPIENS SAPIENS

•   •   •

If anatomically modern *Homo sapiens* spread from Africa into the Near East and Europe, the question immediately arises: What happened to the Neanderthals? Their sudden disappearance and replacement by modern humans has sparked some of the most vigorous controversies in archaeology and some scintillating, if speculative, popular novels. How did the Neanderthals become extinct? Were they attacked and killed by anatomically more advanced newcomers? Or did they interbreed with anatomically modern humans and adopt new cultural adaptations? It is hardly surprising that the fossil record gives no clues, for it is far too incomplete. Although some of the more pronounced facial features of the classic Neanderthals, like their brow ridges, did begin to recede in some later populations, this is far from a conclusive sign that the one population gave way to the other. The first *H. sapiens* populations, like the famous Cro-Magnon people of southwest France, although robustly built, show no anatomical signs that can be called transitional from the Neanderthals. It seems most likely that the *H. sapiens sapiens* replaced *H. sapiens neanderthalensis* rather than evolving from them (Stringer and Gamble, 1993).

If the Noah's ark hypothesis is correct, then *Homo sapiens sapiens* evolved from early *H. sapiens* in tropical Africa, and ultimately from *H. erectus,* by phyletic (evolution of different biological lines) change and by hybridization from earlier populations that displayed considerable variation (see Chapter 3). If this evolution took place in sub-Saharan Africa, did modern people evolve from the Neanderthals elsewhere? The most logical place to look is the Near East. There, *H. sapiens sapiens* was living at the Qafzeh Cave in Israel by at least 90,000 B.C., almost as early a date as modern humans are known to have flourished in southern Africa (Stringer and Gamble, 1993) (Figure 4.3). These fossils also imply that Neanderthals and anatomically modern people were living in the Near East at the same time and coexisted there without biological or cultural interaction for thousands of years, perhaps from before 90,000 until at least 43,000 B.C. Stone tools from Qafzeh, from caves on Mt. Carmel, and from the Negev Desert chart a slow evolution of human technology between about 100,000 and 40,000 B.C. Does this mean that Neanderthals evolved into anatomically modern people in the Near East, as the candelabra hypothesis implies (Chapter 3)? Alternatively, did Neanderthal groups move south from Europe to escape extreme cold, perhaps as late as 50,000 B.C., settling in a region where anatomically modern humans from Africa were already living? At present, we do not know. What is significant, however, is that after 43,000 B.C. new technologies based on fine stone blades and associated with *H. sapiens sapiens* become dominant in Near Eastern toolkits. Perhaps it was not until these new technologies developed that fully modern people had the competitive edge that enabled them to move northward into the new, challenging environments of late Ice Age Europe.

THE UPPER PALEOLITHIC TRANSITION

•   •   •

The biological transition from Neanderthals to *Homo sapiens sapiens* is still the subject of much debate; however, the replacement theory is most strongly favored. Can we, then, document the transition in technological and cultural terms (Hoffecker and Wolf, 1988)?

FIGURE 4.3   The early modern human skull Qafzeh 9 (cast) compared with a Neanderthal from et-Tabūn, Mount Carmel, both from Israel.

The final chapter of human biological evolution was accompanied by considerable technological changes, but these changes were far less dramatic than has sometimes been claimed. For generations, experts on the Stone Age assumed that the appearance of *Homo sapiens sapiens* was associated with the invention of radically new, much more advanced technologies that involved, among other things, the use of punches to produce fine, parallel-sided blades and a proliferation of specialized tools, not only in stone but in antler and bone as well. Although there is no doubt that such innovations did appear in the Upper Paleolithic, careful examination of earlier technological traditions shows that they were foreshadowed tens of thousands of years earlier.

Africa and the Near East

Rock shelters and caves in eastern and southern Africa have yielded large tools made on blades fabricated by skilled percussion from carefully prepared cores. The same peoples of 100,000 B.C. were using composite tools and a wider range of artifacts than many of their predecessors. In the Near East, great caves and rock shelters like et-Tabūn and Mugharet el-Wad at Mt. Carmel, Israel, and Shanidar, Iraq, document thousands of years of Neanderthal toolmaking. These sites were visited again and again by hunter-gatherer bands from more than 70,000 B.C. right into modern times.

The Mousterian levels in these caves contain tens of thousands of carefully retouched flakes and side scrapers, as well as the bones of large deer and wild cattle

(Marks, 1983). This technology was a very simple and conservative one that displayed considerable variability within fairly restricted limits. This variability included some horizons in which large, bladelike blanks were made with sophisticated percussion flaking. The Mousterian levels are covered by further occupation levels containing different toolkits that gradually replaced earlier artifact forms and technologies. In these, the long, parallel-sided blades that were the first stage in making stone tools were removed from cylindrical flint cores with a punch and a hammerstone (Figure 4.4). Some blades were up to 6 inches (15.2 cm) long. The tools made from them varied greatly; many were designed for specific tasks and, in later millennia, mounted in handles.

Anthony Marks (1983) studied hunter-gatherer camps in Israel's Negev Desert and found an interesting change in ancient settlement patterns. The climate was wetter and the hunting population tended to concentrate in more circumscribed areas by 43,000 B.C. As the climate dried up, the people were forced to become more mobile. Instead of camping close to convenient sources of toolmaking stone, they were forced to move around constantly, a reality that necessitated new ways of using precious fine-grained rock. Instead of using wasteful Levallois techniques (Figure 3.20), they experimented with more economical flaking methods, which evolved into the long, parallel-sided blades favored by Upper Paleolithic stoneworkers. So Upper Paleolithic blade technology was the logical result of millennia of gradual adjustment to more mobile lifeways, in which careful curation of toolmaking stone was essential.

MODERN HUMANS IN EUROPE

● ● ●

Why did it take *Homo sapiens sapiens* so long to move into Europe and Eurasia from the Near East? Environmental conditions may have militated against earlier settlement. From 100,000 to about 43,000 B.C., Europe was locked into extremely cold, full glacial conditions, with very long, severe winters. It may be no coincidence that *H. sapiens sapiens* first appears in continental Europe during a brief spell of more temperate climate after 50,000 B.C. Even then, climatic conditions and seasonal contrasts may have been severe enough to require new artifacts and more sophisticated hunting skills to exploit northern environments to the full.

Blade technology, with its highly portable cores and efficient small blanks, was highly adaptive for late Ice Age hunter-gatherers exploiting large periglacial hunting territories (periglacial: close to and around ice sheets). It has been likened to the Swiss Army knife, with its strong hinge and many blades. The knife is a foundation for many tool forms, as was the blade core (Figure 4.5). The stoneworker knocked off numerous blade blanks, which could be fashioned into a great variety of scrapers, awls, and knives, to say nothing of fine-edged graving tools, or burins, as archaeologists call them (Table 4.2, p. 130). This versatile stone technology produced the fine, sharp working edges necessary for grooving bone and antler, raw materials available in abundance in the periglacial north. The development of blade technology may well have enabled modern humans to move north from the Near East.

A scatter of radiocarbon dates and stone tools chronicles the spread of modern humans into late Ice Age Europe. Characteristic blade technology appears in Bulgaria as early as 41,000 B.C.; in Hungary by 38,000 B.C.; and in western Europe within a few millennia, perhaps as early as 38,000 B.C. There are clear signs that

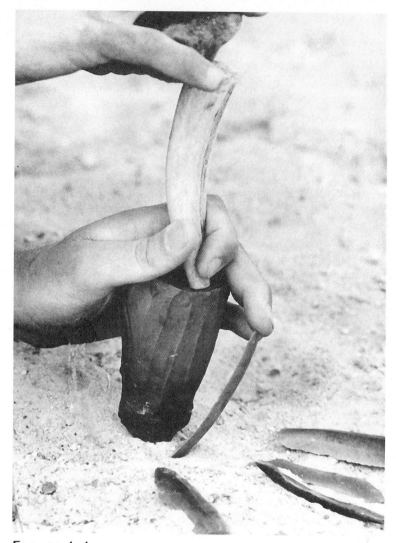

FIGURE 4.4 A modern stoneworker demonstrates blade manufacture with an antler punch. Various methods were used to strike off the blades, using a hand-held punch (as here), or a chest-impelled, longer punch. The punch allows intense pressure to be applied to a single point on the top of the core and channels the direction of the shock waves.

Neanderthals and newcomers lived alongside one another, for Mousterian occupation layers in some central European caves date to much later than 38,000, and there were Neanderthals making blade tools at Saint Césaire in France by 34,000 B.C. (Leveque and Vandermeersch, 1982). After 31,000 B.C., *Homo sapiens sapiens* was the only human form in Europe, and Upper Paleolithic blade technologies are universal.

Quite what form this population replacement took remains an enigma (Stringer and Gamble, 1993). There may have been interbreeding between Neanderthals and anatomically modern Cro-Magnons. The resulting gene flow would have produced mosaiclike changes, which may be reflected in a degree of variability in early Cro-Magnon populations. Alternatively, the Neanderthals may have been pushed aside,

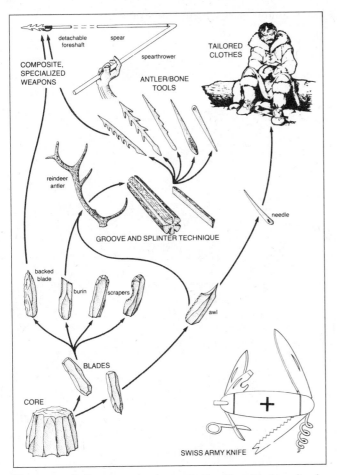

FIGURE 4.5   The Swiss Army Knife effect. Blade technology acted like the celebrated Swiss Army knife, producing blanks for making many specialized artifacts for working bone and antler.

forced to occupy hunting territories on the periphery, where they lived alongside the newcomers for some millennia. It was a long process of gene flow and small-scale population movement, and of cultural innovations also—new technologies and fresh strategies for the hunt. The flow of ideas may have been accelerated in situations in which hunters exploited large hunting territories and wandered far and wide in search of game and, perhaps, good toolmaking stone. Under such circumstances, technological innovation may have preceded gene flow and population movement, resulting in Neanderthals experimenting with more sophisticated artifacts, as apparently was the case at Saint Césaire.

The late Stone Age archaeology of Europe has been so well studied that we can discern a series of long-term trends that took hold in hunter-gatherer societies throughout the world after 33,000 B.C. The changes were by no means simultaneous, nor did they occur everywhere, but they were cumulative and led in the long term to major economic, social, and political changes everywhere, especially in areas such as southwestern France and parts of Australia, where food resources were abundant and seasonally predictable. Randall White (1982) lists the significant changes for late Ice Age Europe, many of which were mirrored elsewhere:

Upper Paleolithic trends
- A tendency toward higher population densities after 33,000 B.C.
- More regular social gatherings.
- Much more stylistic variation in stone artifacts that were patterned in time and space. Perhaps these represent different territorial or social boundaries.

TABLE 4.2
Much simplified outline of the Upper Paleolithic traditions of western Europe from 40,000 to 10,000 B.C.

The most commonly accepted scheme has two parallel cultural traditions: the Gravettian, characterized by backed knives, and the Aurignacian, favoring scrapers and sharpened blades (opposite, middle bottom). The Gravettian, with increasingly finer backed knives, became dominant after 30,000 years ago. Thereafter, there were considerable regional variations, reflected in different tool traditions.

The Solutrean, a culture that relied on sophisticated "cooking" of large pieces of flint so that it became porcelainlike in texture, flourished in France and Spain. The stoneworker could exert pressure on the flake edge to produce magnificent leaf-shaped spear points (opposite, right). Many variations of the Gravettian culture are found in central and eastern Europe. In the west, the Magdalenian tradition, which relied heavily on antler and bone (opposite, top), emerged about 18,000 years ago.

YEARS B.C.	CLIMATE	CULTURES	CHARACTERISTICS
	Temperate	Mesolithic cultures (Chapter 6)	Forest and coastal adaptations
10,000	warming up after 12,000 B.C.		Apogee of cave and antler art skillful bone and antler work
15,000		Magdalenian	
20,000	Very cold	Solutrean	Magnificent pressure-flaked stone spearheads
			Bas-relief sculpture
25,000	Cold	Gravettian Aurignacian	"Venus" figurines, some cave art Gradual elaboration of stone and bone technology
30,000	Somewhat temperate		Aurignacian—sharpened and etched woodworking tools Gravettian—backed stone knife blades
35,000			
	Cold	Arrival of *Homo sapiens sapiens*	Middle Paleolithic technology
40,000		Mousterian ↓ (Chapter 4)	

- Much greater emphasis on the working of bone and antler. Again, these tools display formal stylistic variation, perhaps with social significance.

- Some shift toward the hunting of herd animals that carry antlers for much of the year, especially in cold latitudes.

- Growing importance of personal ornamentation as a way of communicating corporate and personal identity.

- Acquisition of materials from distant sources, probably through structured exchange involving cooperation with other groups.

White believes there was a total restructuring of social relations during the critical transition period. It was then that corporate and individual identities became important and were enhanced by the skilled working of antler, bone, and stone, and by the use of ornaments. The Upper Paleolithic may have seen more structured relationships between the inhabitants of different geographic areas, expressed not only in trade but in better defined hunting territories and other social relationships. White believes that we should examine this transition on a very broad canvas. One of the most important questions is establishing whether *Homo sapiens sapiens* had to adapt to the close presence of other human groups as a matter of survival. In later prehistoric times, relationships with neighbors were to assume ever-increasing importance in adaptive strategies for long-term survival.

We cannot possibly describe the full diversity of hunter-gatherer peoples who flourished in all parts of the globe after 33,000 B.C., so our narrative concentrates on the following major developments:

- The hunter-gatherer cultures that flourished in southwest France and northern Spain between 33,000 and 6000 B.C. These cultures are of particular importance because of their adaptation to the last cold snap of the Weichsel glaciation and their remarkable artistic traditions.

- The big-game hunting cultures that developed on the west Russian plains and Siberia.

- The early settlement of the arctic latitudes of northeast Asia, from which the first settlement of the New World may have developed.

- The first human settlement of the Americas and the cultural traditions that stemmed from it.

- The early history of surviving hunter-gatherers in tropical latitudes, especially the Australians and the San peoples of southern Africa.

EUROPEAN HUNTER-GATHERERS (43,000 TO 6000 B.C.)

● ● ●

Central and western Europe was cold and dry during much of Upper Paleolithic times, with great ice sheets covering large expanses of northern latitudes. South of the ice sheets, thousands of square miles of steppe-grassland with occasional stands of trees covered much of the unglaciated land. There were many local variations, with extensive tree growth in deep river valleys and other sheltered areas. A rich mammalian community flourished in these diverse environments. It included bison, horses, reindeer, and mountain goats in more rugged areas; large herbivores like the mammoth, woolly rhinoceros, and wild ox were common on the open steppe. The human inhabitants could exploit not only a rich animal biomass but also a wide variety of plant foods, including blueberries, raspberries, acorns, and hazelnuts. The climate was changing constantly, so the people had to readapt by altering their diet, hunting and gathering strategies, and technology. Much of the great variability in Upper Paleolithic culture results from such readaptations.

The Upper Paleolithic of Europe began about 33,000 B.C. and witnessed constant changes in human behavior over the next 25,000 years (Knecht and others, 1992). These millennia have been subdivided into a series of cultural periods, each with its own technology and technological innovations (see Table 4.2; Figure 4.6). At first French archaeologists, who developed this cultural sequence from excavations in caves and rock shelters, thought of each period as a rigid "epoch," like a geological layer. Today the cultural phases are seen as changes stimulated by a variety of complex and little understood factors (Laville et al., 1980). Some of them may have been responses to practical needs, others purely dictates of fashion or small technological innovations.

As time went on, major regional differences emerged throughout central and western Europe (Gamble, 1986a). These can be identified from stone and antler tool types by contrasting stone technologies. As Randall White (1986) remarks, it is almost as if barriers to communication were arising, as if there were regional dialects in Europe for the first time.

Settlement Strategies and Lifeways

The Upper Paleolithic peoples of southwest France have long been thought of as one of the prehistoric models for the cave people so beloved of twentieth-century cartoonists. Although it is true that much of our knowledge of their cultures comes from French caves and rock shelters, these were by no means the only settlements occupied after 38,000 B.C. Southwest France is remarkable for its high density of Upper Paleolithic sites within a restricted area, sites that were sometimes intensively occupied over long periods of time.

Diverse food resources

Between 33,000 and 10,000 B.C., the climate of this region was strongly oceanic, with cool summers and mild winters by Ice Age standards. Summer temperatures may have been in the 53.6° to 59°F range, with winter readings around 32°F. The vegetation growing season was longer than on the open plains to the north and east, and snow cover was considerably less. Thus, food resources for large herbivores were more readily available, perhaps resulting in a much higher density of game animals as well as more plentiful edible foods. This was a region of diverse food resources, reflected not only in tree pollens in sheltered archaeological sites but also in the range of animals recovered from them. The people were mainly subsisting off reindeer, but they also took wild ox, red deer, bison, ibex, chamois, woolly rhinoceros, and mammoth. The sheer diversity of the environment gave the human inhabitants some economic security. In years when reindeer migrations were unpredictable, there were other sources of animal protein close at hand, to say nothing of plant foods.

Food resources

Many of these resources were relatively predictable. There were seasonal reindeer migrations, from the higher ground to the east in summer to the deep river valleys of the west in winter, where food resources could be found even in the coldest months (Figure 4.7). The hunters could intercept animals from a broad range of species, many of them migratory, from an ecological range extending perhaps some

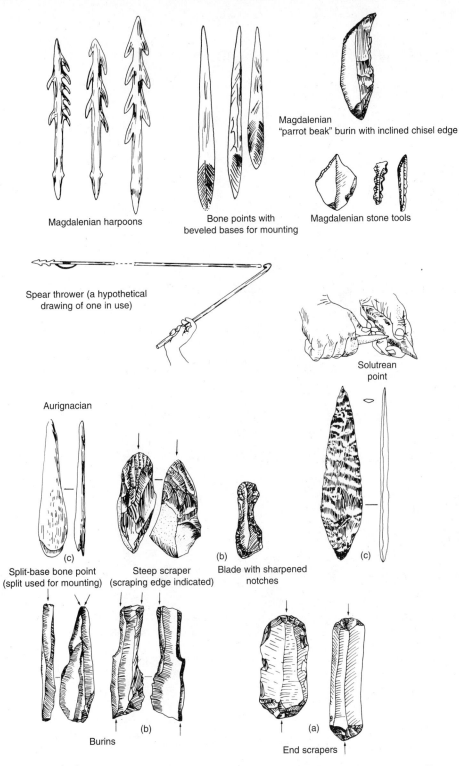

Magdalenian "parrot beak" burin with inclined chisel edge

Magdalenian harpoons

Bone points with beveled bases for mounting

Magdalenian stone tools

Spear thrower (a hypothetical drawing of one in use)

Solutrean point

Aurignacian

Split-base bone point (split used for mounting)

Steep scraper (scraping edge indicated)

Blade with sharpened notches

(c)

(b)

(c)

Burins

(b)

End scrapers

(a)

FIGURE 4.6 Characteristic artifacts used by Upper Paleolithic groups in western Europe. Every group relied heavily on scrapers (a), used for processing skins, working bone and antler, and for woodworking. The most important artifact was the chisel-ended burin (b), employed for grooving wood, bone, and especially reindeer antler, an important source of spear and harpoon points (c). Some Cro-Magnon artisans of 20,000 years ago fabricated magnificent leaf-shaped "Solutrean" points, named after the Solutré site in southwestern France.

FIGURE 4.7   A lion-headed anthropomorphic statuette, carved from a small mammoth tusk, reconstructed from fragments found in the Stadel Cave, South Germany. One of the earliest known human art works, this dates to about 30,000 B.C.

62 miles (100 km) on either side of their central places. Michael Jochim (1983) argues that large-scale salmon fishing during seasonal runs was a major factor in the evolution of complex hunter-gatherer societies in this region. The concentration of settlement along riverbanks, at places where the salmon runs were most prevalent, was a logical response to predictable food resources. Unfortunately, Jochim's argument has a serious weakness, for very few salmon bones have been found in the region's Upper Paleolithic sites (Mellars, 1985). Although fish hooks and harpoons, as well as fine engravings of salmon and seals, are known from many later Upper Paleolithic sites, it appears likely that hunting of large mammals was the predomi-

nant subsistence activity between 33,000 and about 8000 B.C. Fishing does seem to have assumed much greater importance at the very end of the Ice Age, perhaps as forests encroached on open grazing grounds and rising sea levels brought more fish to French rivers.

Whatever the precise makeup of Upper Paleolithic diet in southwest France, there were direct adaptive responses to these highly favorable ecological conditions. Population densities were locally much higher than in other parts of Europe, with groups living in the same locations for much of the year, close to seasonal concentrations of food resources. They exploited these resources with high efficiency, and some part of the population lived almost permanently in certain key locations. Smaller groups then exploited more distant resources in summer and according to need.

The people tended to choose many of their settlement sites with reference to plentiful water supplies and good views of the surrounding landscape, so they could observe game and perhaps their neighbors. More than 90 percent of all known sites are close to springs or riverbanks. The bands could live wherever they wanted, for they had the technology to survive hard winters in the open. Some of the largest cave and rock shelter sites lay close to river fords, places, perhaps, where migrating reindeer would cross each year. One such site is Laugerie Haute near Les Eyzies, where the skeletons of several reindeer lay between the great rock shelter and the river ford. When the people occupied a rock shelter or cave, it invariably faced south, so they could benefit from the sun's rays on cool days. They appear to have erected tents and hide curtains in the shelters for additional protection. Some overhangs lay near places where it was possible to stampede reindeer, horses, and other herd animals over precipitous cliffs. In the open, some groups laid out pavements of river cobbles as foundations for wood, skin, or sod structures. Sometimes they heated the pebbles first, perhaps so they could lay them over frozen ground to form a secure platform.

Settlement preferences

Social Life and Group Size

Many of the largest French Upper Paleolithic sites are close to places where seasonally abundant resources like reindeer could be exploited by large numbers of people. Other settlements were much smaller, little more than temporary camps occupied by a few families (Figure 4.7). Perhaps it is significant that the larger sites—like Laugerie Haute and Laugerie Basse or La Madeleine, the type site of the Magdalenian—contain many more art objects. The bands may have come together into larger social units at locations where abundant resources were available for a few months or weeks to cooperate in the food quest. Such aggregations could not have lasted year-round, partly because the environment would not support so many people in one place for long. If modern hunter-gatherers are any guide, the bands probably had no mechanisms for resolving disputes, except that practiced by modern San—walking away. This is what anthropologist Richard Lee (1979) calls "voting with your feet."

Social structure

The days, weeks, even months of aggregation are the high point of the year in living hunter-gatherer societies, as they must have been in Upper Paleolithic times. This was the time of marriage and initiation ceremonies, of highly intense rituals, in which the fine art objects of the people may have played important roles. This was when shamans told tales and wove spells, when the forces of the ancestors and the spirit world were invoked to ensure the continuity of life and the success of the hunt. It was also a time when men and women exchanged artifacts, ornaments, and exotic raw materials from near and far. Seashells from the English Channel and the Mediterranean, Baltic amber, and other exotica—items that were sometimes imbued with special magical, social, or prestige value—were apparently exchanged from hand to hand. Many of these may have been given and received as gestures of social obligation between individuals and groups.

The Upper Paleolithic societies of southwest France lived in relatively close juxtaposition, in a diverse environment with rich, predictable food resources. For at least part of the year, these societies may have lived a relatively sedentary existence and come together in much larger aggregations. Under these circumstances, it is reasonable to expect that their social organization would become more complex than was normal among egalitarian band societies.

Social complexity

Magdalenian culture was elaborate and sophisticated, to the point that we can predict that more sedentary living and larger group size might have resulted in social change, in more complex hunter-gatherer societies (Mellars, 1985) (for discussion, see Chapter 5). Certainly, the sometimes elaborate decorations of seashells, bracelets, even sewn clothing associated with the dead argue for complex spiritual beliefs, many involving abstract symbolic images of the Ice Age world that we will never be able to recover.

Upper Paleolithic Art

Nearly 200 caves bearing wall paintings and engravings are known from southwest Europe, mainly France and Spain. Some 10,000 sculpted and engraved art objects have come from Upper Paleolithic sites across Europe, far into Siberia, and in Africa. Upper Paleolithic people were brilliant artists in stone, antler, bone, clay, ivory, and wood. They used paint on rock walls, sculpted in bas-relief and the round, and made musical instruments (Bahn and Vertut, 1988). The artists created thousands of naturalistic images of animals, sometimes human and humanlike forms, and dozens of enigmatic signs. All this art conveys complex, long-forgotten ideas, a symbolic world of spirit animals and spirit humans, of forces benevolent and evil. Generations of archaeologists have grappled with the meaning of the art (Pfeiffer, 1982), so far with little success.

Cave art
30,000 B.C.

The earliest artworks date to perhaps as early as 30,000 B.C. (There are some earlier scratched bones from Mousterian sites, but these hardly constitute art.) The earliest Cro-Magnon artists carved some animals in the round in ivory and made simple paintings or engravings of animals and human sexual organs. British archaeologist Mark Newcomer has made an exact copy of a 32,000-year-old bone flute and played it, evidence that musical sounds were made early in the Upper Paleolithic (R. White, 1986).

c. 23,000 B.C.

Later artists executed incised engravings on walls and blew or brushed pigment against their hands to make imprints on cave walls. They also fashioned "Venus" figurines, sculptures and bas-reliefs of females, sometimes with pendulous breasts, sometimes pregnant, and with exaggerated sexual characteristics (Figure 4.8). Many scholars believe these were female fertility figurines. They have been found from Russia in the east to the Dordogne of France in the west, most in deposits dating to about 23,000 B.C. We have no means of knowing whether, in fact, these were fertility figures, but they seem to have been associated with a relatively short-lived set of beliefs that was in use over a wide area of Europe.

Bas-reliefs, friezes of animals like wild horses that adorn places where the people lived, came into fashion during the Solutrean. The Solutreans also painted ani-

FIGURE 4.8   Paleolithic art: Venus figurines from Brassempouy, France (*left*) and Dolní Vestonice, Moravia (*right*).

mals on cave walls, but 80 percent of all known Upper Paleolithic art comes from the Magdalenian, beginning around 16,000 B.C. The earlier Magdalenian saw some remarkable cave painting, from places like Lascaux, painted in about 15,000 B.C. Lascaux's walls were covered again and again with depictions of wild horses, bulls, reindeer, and many other animals. Many of the animals were painted with long, distorted necks and thick bodies, as if the artists were unaware of perspective (Figure 4.9). The paintings also include squiggles, spaghettilike patterns, and tentlike symbols (Windels, 1965). A Great Hall of the Bulls features four immense wild bulls, drawn in thick, black lines, with some of the body details filled in. Horses, deer, a small bear, and a strange unicornlike beast prance with the great bulls in a fantastic display of blacks, browns, reds, and yellows that truly brings the animals to life in a flickering light. It is hard to believe that the paintings are at least 17,000 years old.

The earliest tradition reached its height with an explosion of antler and bone work after 16,000 B.C. The hunters decorated their harpoons, spear points, spearthrowers, and other artifacts with naturalistic engravings, fine carvings of wild animals, and elaborate schematic patterns. Even fine eye details and hair texture were shown by delicate graving strokes (Figure 4.10). But the Magdalenians are most famous for their beautiful rock art, paintings and engravings deep in the caves of northern Spain and southwest France. At Altamira, in northern Spain, you walk Altamira deep into the hillside to enter a low-ceilinged chamber, where the painters left fine renderings of bison in red and black (Figure 4.11) (Breuil, 1908). By painting and

FIGURE 4.9   A giant stag painting from Lascaux, France.

FIGURE 4.10   A superb example of a Magdalenian carver's art: a spear thrower decorated with a wild horse.

engraving the animals around natural bulges in the rock, the artists conveyed a sense of relief and life. In cave after cave, the hunters left jumbled frenzies of large and small game and animals, hand impressions, dots, and signs, many of which must have had symbolic significance.

An enormous and highly speculative literature concerns the motives behind this remarkable art (Bahn and Vertut, 1988). Originally, Henri Breuil and other experts

FIGURE 4.11   A bison in a polychrome cave painting from Altamira, Spain.

(Breuil, 1952) argued that the caves were sacred places where the hunters gathered to perform rituals and sympathetic magic that would ensure the fertility of game and the success of the hunt. Even the signs on the cave walls were interpreted as snares and traps. Today we know a great deal more about symbolic behavior and the art that goes with it and much more about how hunter-gatherer societies function. The latest cave art research has concentrated not only on the art itself but also on the contexts in which it appears. French prehistorian André Leroi-Gourhan argued in 1965 that the art was not random but part of a system of meanings, an expression of a world view that organized Upper Paleolithic life. By counting the associations of subjects and clusters of motifs, Leroi-Gourhan found that certain themes, among them female figures, appeared in rock shelters and better lit locales, whereas others were in dark caverns. There are differences in the distribution of art, too. Bison, for instance, dominate northern Spanish cave walls, but they rarely occur on portable objects. Perhaps the social contexts of wall and portable art were different.

Alexander Marshack (1972, 1975) has carried out detailed microphotographic studies of Paleolithic art and shown that many of the visual forms are ecologically and seasonally related. Rather than concentrating on the naturalistic pictures of animals, he has studied the hundreds of nonnaturalistic pieces, with their patterns of lines, notches, dots, and groupings of marks (Figure 4.12). On some pieces, the marks were made with different tools at different times. These pieces, which Marshack named "time-factorial" objects, were used, he believes, as sequential notations of events and phenomena, predecessors of calendars. Marshack has examined hundreds of specimens stretching back as far as the Lower Paleolithic. He found duplicated designs, systematic groups of dots and notches that were either counting

Nonnaturalistic pieces

FIGURE 4.12   Engraved bone, 8.2 inches (21 cm) long from La Marche, France, which was intensively studied by Marshack. The close-up shot shows tiny marks in two groups, each engraved by a different point, with a different type of stroke. (© Alexander Marshack, 1972.)

tallies or the beginnings, he feels, of a writing system; but, he suggests, they differ from later, more formal writing systems that could be read by everyone: The Magdalenian and earlier notations were for the engraver alone to read, even if this person explained them to others on occasion. To formulate such a system required thought and theoretical abstractions far more advanced than those hitherto attributed to hunter-gatherers of this age. Marshack's ideas are highly controversial and not widely accepted, but they come out of the type of ground-breaking research that produces exciting new interpretations and insights into Stone Age life.

Today, we know that many hunter-gatherer groups use ritual and art, creating and manipulating visual forms to structure and give meaning to their existence. Many ethnographic studies have shown how symmetry and other artistic principles may underlie the designs of many art traditions and characterize every aspect of daily life, from social relationships to village planning. The people may use relatively few symbols to communicate meanings. Very often it is the context of the symbols that reveals the meaning. For the Upper Paleolithic artists, there were clearly continuities between animal and human life and with their social world. Thus, their art was a symbolic depiction of these continuities. The artists did not choose just any wall or piece of antler or bone for their drawings nor just any animal or geometric form to depict. Their selections were deliberate, symbolic acts that provide clues to the significance of the world's earliest artistic tradition (Bahn and Vertut, 1988).

Some archaeologists believe that the underground art, with its accurate depictions of reindeer and other animals at different times of the year, may have been a kind of storehouse of knowledge about the environment, passed from generation to generation. One such 14,000-year-old sanctuary comes from El Juyo Cave in northern Spain. Inside a large, stone-walled dugout, there are four trenches, topped by four layers between 30 inches (75 cm) and 3 feet (1 m) high. The mounds were made up of layers of burnt vegetation, containing red ocher and animal bones, accompanied by more than 40 bone spear points, alternating with packed lots of fill, turned out from cuplike containers to form rosettelike patterns. A foot- (30 cm-) tall stone carved into a half-human, half-feline face stood erect atop one mound facing the cave entry. The excavators believe this was a sanctuary (Freeman and Echegaray, 1981).

About 11,000 B.C., the Magdalenians seem to have stopped painting and engraving deep caves. Most art after that appears at cave entrances and in rock shelters, always exposed to the light of day. The paintings and engravings were no longer naturalistic, and they vanished altogether about 9000 B.C. By this time, much warmer climatic conditions had brought forest to the open plains, and the large arctic animals depicted in the earlier art were largely extinct. The brilliant efflorescence of Magdalenian culture had been replaced by new adaptations—to forests, rivers, and coasts. By this time, cave and antler art had given way to a complex symbol system, much of it painted on flat pebbles (Courand, 1985).

CENTRAL AND EASTERN EUROPE AND SIBERIA

● ● ●

The vast, undulating plains of western Russia and central Europe as far east as the Ural Mountains were a much less hospitable environment for Stone Age hunter-gatherers than the deep, well-watered valleys to the west. There were no convenient caves or rock shelters. For warmth and shelter the inhabitants of this area had to create artificial dwellings with their own tools and locally available raw materials. It may be no coincidence that few archaeological sites are found on these frigid plains, with their nine-month winters and short summers, until Upper Paleolithic times. The Neanderthals and early Upper Paleolithic populations may have ventured onto the steppe during the warmer summer months. It took some significant technological innovations, providing better cultural adaptations to bitter cold, to allow people to live there year-round. One important invention may have been the perforated bone needle, which enabled people to fabricate tailored layers of clothing, for layered garments provide the best protection against subzero temperatures. Advances in bone and antler technology may also have played a decisive role in Arctic adaptation, for they allowed not only more efficient hunting but also the development of such important artifacts as the spear-thrower, a highly effective weapon against large, gregarious animals.

Between about 28,000 and 8000 B.C., a series of Upper Paleolithic hunting and foraging societies known to archaeologists as the Eastern Gravettian complex flourished on the plains and varied terrain of central and eastern Europe (here the Gravettian flourished much later than in the west). There were many local groups within this large complex, people adapted to life on frigid, open plains (Soffer, 1993). Many of their camp sites contain mammoth bones, so much so that many earlier interpretations of these societies referred to them as "mammoth hunters." In fact, the Eastern Gravettians exploited a wide range of late Ice Age mammals, ranging in size from bison to arctic fox, the latter much prized for its soft fur. They may indeed have killed some mammoth, for such animals provided not only bones for constructing dwellings in treeless environments but also an abundance of meat and hide. Many of the bones may in fact have come from animals that died of natural causes, or even from mammoth "cemeteries," places where animals perished in large numbers in spring floods, such as are known from Siberia. At the famous Dolní Vestonice site in Moravia, for example, the nearby landscape is rich in calcite and other minerals that, when licked, provide vital magnesium and calcium for elephants in late spring and summer, at a time when fresh grass is high in potassium.

Dolní Vestonice was occupied again and again about 25,000 B.C., with campsites overlooking the Dyje River valley and a nearby swamp. Perhaps between 100 and 120 people dwelt at this spot, sometimes in summer, at other times in oval winter huts dug partially into the ground with bone and hide roofs. Vestonice is remarkable for its numerous burnt clay figures that were fired in a small, oval-shaped oven inside a winter house, the earliest fired clay objects in the world by at least 15,000 years (Figure 4.13). Here there is unequivocal evidence for deliberate burial. A recently discovered 27,000-year-old grave contained the body of an important individual of uncertain sex, flanked by two young males, both with ivory pendants encircling their skulls. A fire had been lit briefly over the bodies before the grave was filled in (Stringer and Gamble, 1993).

Moravia was the earliest center of Eastern Gravettian settlement between about 26,000 and 22,000 B.C. The groups concerned were highly mobile and habitually visited the Danube region of Austria, southern Poland, and northern Hungary. As the late Ice Age climate grew colder and resources scarcer, some of these people moved southward; others followed game herds onto the open steppe of the central Russian Plain. This west to east population movement took at least 4,000 years, with constant abandonment and resettlement of different regions in response to climate and resource changes (Soffer, 1993).

Only a few rivers dissect the Russian plains, among them the Don and the Dnieper. It is no coincidence that ancient river terraces were the most common locations for Stone Age hunting settlements. These were often promontories overlooking the river, where the hunters could spy on the movements of the herds of arctic elephant (mammoth), woolly rhinoceros, and wild horse that flourished in the valleys (Dolukhanov, 1982). At the height of the last glaciation, this area was a treeless periglacial landscape, a meadow steppe in warmer interstadials. It was a very inhospitable environment but one where hunter-gatherer societies flourished for thousands of years. Winter temperatures may have averaged −30° to −40°F, summer maxima rarely reaching 64°F.

FIGURE 4.13   Reconstruction of a 27,000-year-old house excavated at Dolní Vestonice, Moravia. The timber and bone structure supported a hide roof. This dwelling contained an oval oven used for baking clay figurines.

The earliest Upper Paleolithic sites, probably settlements of anatomically modern people, date to at least 33,000 B.C. (Hoffecker, 1988). The most intensive (Eastern Gravettian) occupation dates to the period between 16,000 and 12,000 B.C., when scattered hunter-gatherer bands lived in what were often spectacular mammoth bone structures (Soffer, 1985). The Mezhirich site overlooks the Dnieper River southeast of Kiev; it is a 15,000-year-old settlement of five houses, covering an area of some 110,000 square feet (10,219 m²) (Soffer, 1987). Each house was about 13 to 22 feet (4 to 7 m) across and up to 850 square feet (78.9 m²) in area (Figure 4.14). Foundation walls of massive mammoth bones supported an intricate framework of smaller limb bones, vertebrae, and other parts, sometimes arranged in fine herringbone patterns. The roof was supported by uprights that were stuck into holes broken through large mammoth bones, and the entire structure was almost certainly covered with elephant hide. Hearths and work areas lay inside the houses, which seem to have been occupied over long periods of time. More hearths and deep storage pits that kept meat refrigerated in the permafrost lay between the houses.

Mezhirich
13,000 B.C.

FIGURE 4.14   Excavation of dwelling 4 at Mezhirich, Ukraine.

The Mezhirich dwellings are thought to have housed about 50 people, each dwelling taking 10 men about five or six days to complete, a considerable investment of effort. Since mammoth bone dwellings found at other locations are less elaborate, it may be that this settlement was of unusual importance. The inhabitants hunted not only mammoth but also other large mammals, as well as river fish and birds. Judging by the evidence from several sites, they pursued mammoth in autumn and winter, reindeer in spring and early summer, fur-bearing animals in winter, and waterfowl in summer (Dolukhanov, 1982). So many mammoth bones were used in house construction that the people may have scavenged them from carcasses on the plains in addition to using their own kills. Russian archaeologists report that seashells from between 400 and 500 miles (643 and 804 km) away came from the Mezhirich houses, and amber, a stone thought by many prehistoric peoples to have magic qualities, was traded from 100 miles (160 km) away.

The famous Kostenki sites on the Don River were occupied about 2000 years after those to the west, between 22,000 and 21,000 B.C. (Grigor'ev, 1993). They contain large hollows filled with bones and other debris. Their plans are so irregular that it is difficult to be sure whether they were dwellings or storage pits. In some cases, several circular structures up to 15 feet (4.6 m) in diameter were built together in a huge depression with a row of hearths down the middle. Bands of considerable size must have congregated in these tented areas.

Central Asia

To the east of the western plains stretches central Asia, a vast area of continental territory that covers not only northern Afghanistan but also the arid Turan depression and the central Asian highlands. The archaeology of this area is still little known, although research has made rapid strides in recent years (Davis, 1987). There are numerous Mousterian sites dating to the early part of the Weichsel glaciation, as they do in the West, displaying different toolkit variations that probably reflect different seasonal activities. It is not yet known when the transition to the Upper Paleolithic took place, but one hunting camp at Malaya Siya on the White Iyus River west of Lake Baikal has been radiocarbon dated to about 32,500 B.C. (Larichev et al., 1988). Here people hunted mammoth, horse, reindeer, and other steppe animals, which they also engraved on bone, some of the earliest art in the world. Undoubtedly, however, the human population of this harsh country was very small.

Malaya Siya
32,500 B.C.

The Upper Paleolithic of central Asia is known from a late Weichsel culture that was widespread in caves, rock shelters, and open sites but is still not well-known. The Shugnou site southwest of the city of Samarkand lies at an altitude of 6700 feet (2000 m), one of the highest Upper Paleolithic sites in the world. Russian archaeologists found five occupation layers in a site above a mountain river, yielding evidence of big-game hunting, of horses, wild oxen, wild sheep, and goats, dating to at least 18,000 to 13,000 B.C. Pollen grains suggest that weather conditions were somewhat cooler and wetter than today. The hunter-gatherer population of central Asia may have been sparse for thousands of years, perhaps because of unfavorable climate conditions, but this is pure conjecture. Population densities rose at the end of the Pleistocene, and human settlement expanded into higher elevations.

Central Asia was subjected to cultural influences from both the flake and blade traditions of the West and the chopper-chopping tool traditions of the Far East. Consequently, stone tools here frequently were based on stone cobbles and were simple, highly effective artifacts that rarely achieved the sophistication or artistry of Western traditions. The same amalgam of cultural traditions filtered into Siberia in Far Eastern Asia (Larichev et al., 1987).

Remote from Atlantic and Pacific weather patterns, Siberia is dry country with harsh, dry winters and short, hot summers. Treeless plains predominate in the far north and extend to the shores of the Arctic Ocean. Rainfall was so sparse during the Weichsel glaciation that the great ice sheets of the West never formed here. Herds of gregarious mammoths grazed on the tundra and on the edges of the river valleys, where small bands of hunter-gatherers weathered the long winters. The archaeology of this enormous area and of northeast Asia is still little known, despite long-term excavation campaigns in recent years (Muller-Beck, 1982). Nonetheless, Siberia and northeast Asia are of vital importance, for they were the staging areas from which the first settlement of the Americas took place, across the Bering Strait. A number of key issues confront anyone working in this area:

Siberia

- What was the date of the first human settlement of the far northeast?

- Was there a pre-*sapiens* population in Siberia before 33,000 B.C.?

- What technological and cultural traits are found in the Far East that can be identified in the New World?

Local archaeologists claim that sites contemporary with Malaya Siya lie east of Lake Baikal, including one at Tolbaga, said to date to as early as 32,900 B.C., but few details of the site have been published (Larichev et al., 1988). All these settlements contain well-developed blade technology but also artifacts made by using Middle Paleolithic techniques. There is far less variation in tool forms than in later Stone Age cultures in the region.

Tolbaga
32,900 B.C.

By 20,000 B.C., two very different cultural traditions flourished in Siberia and into northeast Asia. The Mal'ta tradition is known from clusters of sites west of Lake Baikal and the Yenesei River Valley, many of them located in places sheltered from the prevailing northerly winds. The Mal'ta site itself, one of semisubterranean houses, covers more than 6458 square feet (600 m^2) and may have been reoccupied many times. Mal'ta was probably a winter base camp of houses framed with large animal bones covered with a lattice of reindeer antler to support a skin or sod covering. The hunters pursued mammoth, woolly rhinoceros, and reindeer, as well as small animals. The Mal'ta people were expert bone workers who carved female and bird figurines (Figure 4.15).

Mal'ta tradition
19,000 B.C.

The Afontova Gora-Oshurkovo tradition flourished over a much wider area, not only in the Yenesei River Valley but also over an enormous area of northern Asia, perhaps all the way from the Altai to the Amur River. The oldest sites, Afontova Gora itself on the Yenesei and Mogochino on the Ob' River, date to between 19,000 and 18,000 B.C. Again, the people hunted periglacial steppe mammals, making large tools fashioned on cobbles, blade artifacts, large cobble scrapers known locally as *skreblos,* and occasionally small blade artifacts fabricated on "microblades."

Afontova Gora-Oshurkovo tradition
19,000 B.C.

There are many general similarities between the Mal'ta and Afontova Gora-Oshurkovo traditions, which tend to transcend the local differences between them. Together, they reflect a varied adaptation by *Homo sapiens sapiens* to an enormous area of central Asia and southern Siberia from well west of Lake Baikal to the Pacific Ocean far to the east. Late Ice Age populations in this harsh area were never large and were concentrated for the most part in river valleys and near lakes. In general terms, their lifeway may have resembled that of plains big-game hunters on the steppe-tundra to the west, but it would be a mistake to argue that these Siberian

FIGURE 4.15   Figurines from Mal'ta, Siberia. (a) A bone figurine (actual size), two views. (b) An ivory bird (two-thirds actual size).

groups originated in western Eurasia. They may have moved north or northeast-ward onto the open steppe-tundra from more temperate environments, perhaps at about the same time as Cro-Magnons moved into Europe. Although Neanderthal settlements are known in the mountainous Altai region of central Asia, there are no signs of Middle Paleolithic sites on the steppe-tundra itself. Anatomically modern humans may have been the first to venture north into periglacial regions.

D'UKTAI AND THE FIRST SETTLEMENT OF FAR NORTHEAST ASIA

• • •

The first human settlement of periglacial northeast Asia appears between 38,000 and 28,000 B.C. and was well established just before the late glacial maximum of about 16,000 B.C. The Mal'ta and Afontova Gora-Oshurkovo traditions peter out as one moves north and east into the far frontiers of northeast Asia. The Ver-koy-ansk Mountains are thought to have been a major barrier to late Ice Age human set-tlement (Hoffecker et al., 1993). The western slopes of the range adjoin the Lena River Basin, which, we know, had been settled by humans by 20,000 to 13,000 B.C. Beyond the Ver-koy-ansk unfolds the vast landscape of extreme northeast Siberia, which ends at the shores of the Bering Strait. As we shall see in Chapter 6, this harsh and unforgiving region of periglacial steppe-tundra and occasional large river valleys was the homeland of the first Stone Age people to cross into the Americas, probably across a low-lying land bridge that connected Siberia and Alaska during the last glaciation.

Archaeologist Yuri Mochanov (1978) has identified a far-flung late Ice Age culture that once flourished in the Middle Aldan Valley, far north and east of Lake Baikal. He excavated D'uktai Cave, close to the river floodplain. There he found mammoth and musk-ox remains associated with large stone choppers, bifacially flaked stone points, burins, blades, and some "microblades." The cave deposits were much disturbed by freezing, thawing, and other natural phenomena, but Mochanov was able to date the occupation levels to between 16,000 and 10,000 B.C. Soon he found more D'uktai-like sites on the banks of the Aldan, sites that contained not only points and choppers but also highly distinctive "microblades" and the characteristic wedge-shaped cores from which they were formed (Figure 4.16). The dating of the D'uktai culture is very controversial, some scholars claiming that

D'uktai tradition
?16,000 to 10,000 B.C.

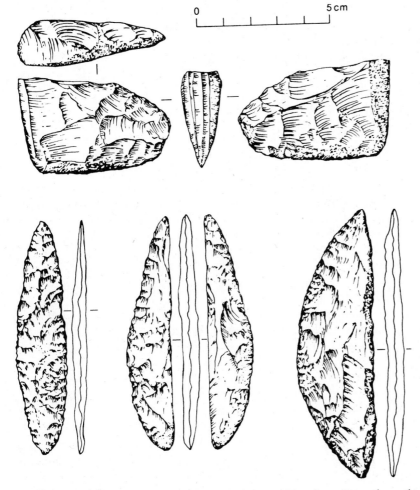

FIGURE 4.16 Artifacts of the D'uktai tradition. *Top,* four views of a wedge-shaped core, used to make tiny blades. *Bottom,* two bifacially flaked projectile points. The wedge-shaped core is a characteristic artifact found on both sides of the Bering Strait in contexts of about 10,000 years ago. It is, of course, a by-product of the production of fine microblades.

it was flourishing as early as 30,000 B.C. (Larichev and others, 1993). Many American experts believe that it originated no earlier than about 16,000 to 13,000 B.C.

Bifaces, Microblades, and the First Americans

Clearly the D'uktai tradition owes little to the well-defined plains big-game hunting traditions of central and western Eurasia. It is marked by "microblades," also by bifaces and some stone spear points. Since this is the only known late Ice Age culture from extreme northeast Asia, it may be one of the cultural traditions from which the culture of the first Americans came. Some of the D'uktai stone points recall those made by Clovis people in the New World, but without the distinctive "flute," a longitudinal thinning flake at the base of the head (Chapter 6). However, there are no signs of "microblades" in the earliest human cultures of the Americas, although these distinctive artifacts do appear later, in Alaska, by about 9000 B.C.

The most important artifacts used by the first Americans were stone-tipped spears and stone knives, made from flakes of fine-grained stone struck off large cores, often themselves fashioned into bifaces so they could be carried around from one camp to the next. Such artifacts must also have been important on the steppe-tundra of northeast Asia long before "microblades" came into use. Unfortunately, we know so little of D'uktai that we can only guess that it may represent more than one cultural tradition, one using bifaces and stone-tipped spears, a technology that spread early into the Americas, and, perhaps, a later version that relied more heavily on "microblades."

Microblades

The origins of "microblade" technology are somewhat better documented. We have put the word "microblade" in quotation marks up to this point, for this technology needs more precise definition. If there is one significant trend in human stoneworking technology during the late Ice Age, after 23,000 B.C., it is a progressive elaboration and diminution of stone tools. This trend is well documented in Africa, Europe, and southern Asia, and in the Far East as well. Chinese archaeologist Chen Chun (1989) believes that a primitive "microblade tradition" emerged in Asia quite soon after *Homo sapiens sapiens* appeared in the region. In time, microblade technologies were to dominate stone technology throughout northern China, Korea, Japan, and far to the northeast in Siberia and possibly extreme northwestern America as well.

Microblades are diminutive blades that were struck in the thousands off carefully prepared conical or wedge-shaped cores (Figure 4.16). By their very size, microblades were designed to be mounted in antler, bone, or wooden handles to serve as spear barbs, arrow points, or small knife or scraper blades. Microblade technology first appeared in northern China about 28,000 B.C. and soon spread over an enormous area, even into tropical environments far to the south (Chung and Pei, 1986; Olsen, 1987). They were widely used in China by 18,000 B.C., in Japan by about the same time (A. Anderson, 1987; Reynolds and Barnes, 1984), and in D'uktai country by at least 16,000 B.C. With its microblades and wedge-shaped cores, then, the D'uktai tradition has links with well-established cultural traditions in northern China that were flourishing by at least 28,000 B.C.

We can propose a scenario for what occurred. Perhaps microblade technology first developed in temperate Asia, in areas like the Gobi Desert and Mongolia, where people hunted over enormous areas. Here they needed a stone technology that was economical, easy to carry and manufacture, and yet capable of arming that was economical, easy to carry and manufacture, and yet capable of arming spears; and perhaps very late in the Ice Age, they needed bows and arrows with sharp, lethal points for taking game on the run in open country. In time, the same technology spread north and east into the harsh periglacial landscapes of Siberia, where small-scale and highly portable toolkits were highly adaptive, especially when used against such migratory periglacial animals as the reindeer. In time, small groups of microblade-using D'uktai people may have carried the same technology across the dry land of the Bering Strait into Alaska, perhaps after simpler biface and spear point toolkits had spread into the Americas (Fagan, 1990). This scenario receives some support from the dental researches of Christy Turner (1984). He has shown that the characteristic tooth features of Native Americans include specialized attributes, such as shovel-shaped incisors, that are mirrored on northern Chinese skeletons dating to about 18,000 B.C. He calls this group of features "Sinodonty," features that are never found on European Stone Age teeth. Turner believes that the first Americans originated in northern China, reaching their new homeland through eastern Mongolia and northeast Siberia. With that momentous development, *Homo sapiens sapiens* eventually reached the Americas.

CHAPTER SUMMARY

This chapter documents the spread of *Homo sapiens sapiens* into Europe and Eurasia from Africa and the Near East after 43,000 B.C., during the late Ice Age. By this time, there was increasing specialization and flexibility in human hunting and foraging, as anatomically modern humans replaced Neanderthal groups by 33,000 B.C. The sheer diversity of the late Ice Age environment gave the Cro-Magnon people of western Europe great flexibility. They developed more complex societies and developed elaborate bone and antler technology, also a complex symbolic life, reflected in intricate artistic traditions. These cultures reached their apogee in the Magdalenian culture, which flourished after 16,000 B.C., and for about 5,000 years. The Eastern Gravettian cultural complex was contemporary with Cro-Magnon societies in the west, and was based on exploitation of open plains and steppe. The many groups within this complex spread slowly eastward from Moravia onto the Russian plains, relying heavily on game of all kinds. Far to the northeast, western Siberia was settled at least as early as 28,000 B.C., but the extreme northeast was devoid of human settlement until the very late Ice Age, perhaps as late as 13,000 B.C. It was then that humans first crossed the Bering Land Bridge into the Americas.

GUIDE TO FURTHER READING

Bahn, Paul, and Vertut, J. 1988. *Images of the Ice Age.* New York: Viking.
   A superb general account of Paleolithic art, illustrated with magnificent photographs. Excellent on the motives behind the art.

Fagan, Brian M. 1990. *The Journey from Eden.* New York: Thames and Hudson.
   A synthesis of the spread of Homo sapiens sapiens *for the general reader. Recommended for the beginning reader.*

Provocative essay on the European Stone Age. Essential for all serious students of the subject.

————, ed. 1990. *The World in 18,000.* Cambridge, Eng.: Cambridge University Press.
Specialist essays that review the Stone Age cultures of the Old World at the height of the last glaciation.

Pfeiffer, John. 1982. *The Creative Explosion.* New York: Harper & Row.
A wide-ranging popular treatment of early cave art for the general reader.

Soffer, Olga. 1985. *The Upper Paleolithic of the Central Russian Plains.* New York: Academic Press.
An account of Mezhirich and other Upper Paleolithic sites. An exemplary essay on the Stone Age of the Ukraine.

———— and N. D. Prasov, eds. 1993. *From Kostenki to Clovis.* New York: Plenum Press.
A series of American and Russian essays on late Ice Age cultures in central and eastern Europe, related to the first prehistoric societies of the Americas. Up-to-date and well-written specialist accounts.

White, Randall. 1986. *Dark Caves, Bright Images.* New York: American Museum of Natural History.
Up-to-date, well-illustrated, and readable account of Cro-Magnons and their culture. Recommended for the general reader.

CHAPTER 5

INTENSIFICATION AND COMPLEXITY

(BEFORE 10,000 B.C. TO MODERN TIMES)

• • •

In about 7000 B.C., a small group of hunters and foragers camped in a sandy clearing near Meer in northern Belgium. They built a hearth and, presumably, erected brush or skin shelters, but no signs of these survive. After a while a right-handed artisan walked a short distance away from the settlement, sat down on a small boulder, and made some stone tools with prepared blanks he bought along with him. Among them were three borers for working wood or hide. Minute abrasions on the tips reveal he turned them clockwise, showing he was right-handed. Later a left-handed stoneworker came and sat down next to him, bringing a core with him. He proceeded to knock off some flakes, the scars from which showed clearly that he was a southpaw.

This remarkable, fine-grained research was the work of two Belgian archaeologists, David Cahen and Francis van Noten (1981). It demonstrates the level of detail, using refitting, edge wear analysis, and other analytical techniques that are needed to understand the new hunter-gatherer societies that developed after the Ice Age.

Despite the harshness of late Ice Age climates, especially in northern latitudes, *Homo sapiens sapiens* adapted successfully to a remarkable range of global environments. The last 50,000 years of the Ice Age saw human settlement of the globe reach its premodern limits, with two major exceptions. The subarctic lands and eastern Arctic regions of North America were mantled by ice and were uninhabitable until long after the Ice Age (Chapter 6). The far offshore islands of the Pacific were not to be settled until much later, after the development of the twin-hulled offshore canoe and new navigational techniques that allowed seafarers to voyage far out of sight of land during the closing 5000 years of prehistoric times (Chapter 12) (see Figure 4.1b).

All later developments in prehistory, including a new focus both on agriculture and on animal domestication and the establishment of much more complex human societies, which included the first civilizations, ultimately stem from the progressive settlement of the globe by *Homo sapiens sapiens* during the last glaciation (Fagan, 1990). The immediate consequences of the end of the Ice Age affected many hunter-gatherer societies scattered across the world when the great ice sheets finally retreated.

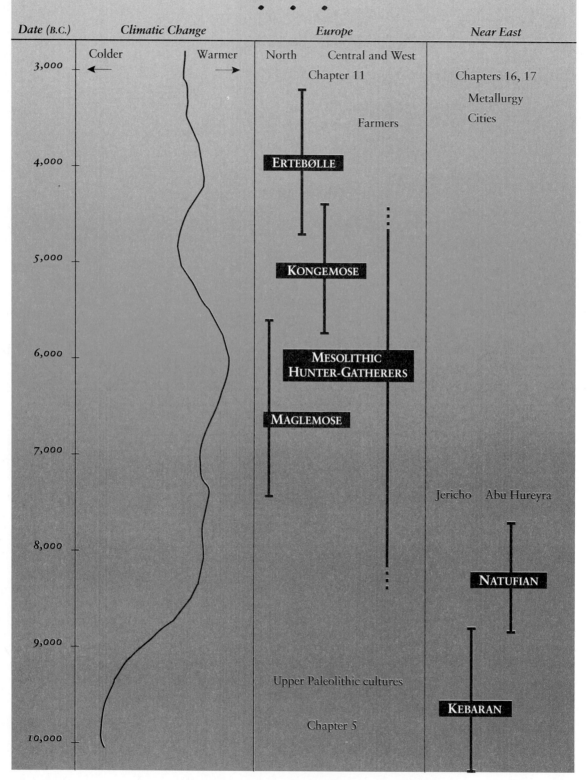

TABLE 5.1

Climatic and generalized archaeological sequence in the Old World after the Ice Age.

• • •

Date (B.C.)	Climatic Change		Europe		Near East
	Colder	Warmer	North	Central and West	
3,000	←	→		Chapter 11	Chapters 16, 17
					Metallurgy
				Farmers	Cities
4,000			ERTEBØLLE		
5,000				KONGEMOSE	
6,000			MESOLITHIC HUNTER-GATHERERS		
7,000			MAGLEMOSE		
8,000					Jericho Abu Hureyra
					NATUFIAN
9,000			Upper Paleolithic cultures		
					KEBARAN
			Chapter 5		
10,000					

THE HOLOCENE (AFTER 10,000 B.C.)

● ● ●

The world's climate remained extremely cold for about 4000 to 8000 years after the last maximum of the Weichsel glaciation around 18,000 B.C. Global warming began in earnest after about 13,000 B.C. (Table 5.1). Then the great ice sheets began to retreat, at times very rapidly, ushering in postglacial Holocene times (Greek: *Holos,* "recent"). Changes in ice distribution and sea levels were very irregular. Using core borings from coral beds off Barbados in the Caribbean, Richard Fairbanks (1988) has shown that sea levels at the glacial maximum were 396 feet (121 m) below modern levels. They rose by 66 feet (20 m) between about 15,000 and 10,500 B.C. Then there was an abrupt rise of 79 feet (24 m) in a mere 1000 years, a slight rise at about 9000 B.C., and another 92-foot (28-m) rise after 8500 B.C. that culminated at 7500 B.C. These new levels led to major changes in world geography. The Bering Strait was dry land as late as 13,000 B.C. and ocean again by 7000 B.C. By this time, sea levels were rising rapidly, especially in areas such as Scandinavia, where the earth's crust was depressed by the massive weight of retreating ice sheets. The North Sea was flooded, and Britain was separated from the continent by approximately 6000 B.C. Enormous areas of North America and northern Europe were exposed by retreating ice sheets and were available for human settlement for the first time in nearly 100,000 years.

We have hardly begun to understand the dramatic changes in temperature, rainfall, and vegetation that occurred during the early millennia of the Holocene, between about 13,000 and 5000 B.C. (N. Roberts, 1989) (Table 5.1). The most striking transformations took place in northern latitudes, in areas like western and central Europe, and in regions of North America contiguous to the great ice sheets. During the height of the Weichsel glaciation, for example, central Europe had been treeless periglacial tundra, and the Baltic Sea did not exist. Only 5000 years after the Scandinavian ice sheet began retreating, forests covered most of Europe and sparse human populations had settled on the shores of a newly exposed northern sea.

Throughout the world, game populations changed radically in the millennia after the Ice Age. By 10,000 B.C., the familiar mammoth and woolly rhinoceros hunted by the Cro-Magnons were extinct in central and western Europe, as were steppe bison and reindeer, all replaced by forest animals like the red and roe deer. In North America, mammoths, mastodons, camelids, and many other large animal species vanished abruptly about 9000 B.C. (Martin and Klein, 1984). Even in tropical Africa, the rich and diverse savanna faunas suffered losses at the end of the Ice Age. The extent to which humans were responsible for the rapid extinction of late Ice Age animals is a matter of great, and unresolved, controversy.

There were major and highly significant vegetational changes in warmer latitudes, too. For much of the Weichsel maximum, for example, the Sahara Desert had been as arid as it is today, but rainfall patterns changed at the end of the Ice Age, bringing large, shallow lakes and short grasslands to the desert. As late as 6000 B.C., hunter-gatherer populations flourished in the heart of the Sahara, in areas that are now arid wilderness. In the Near East, the late Ice Age climate of the Tauros and Zagros mountains was so cold and dry that no trees grew in the uplands. After about 9000 B.C., new plant assemblages immigrated into the now warmer highlands, among them wild cereal grasses that were to become the ancestors of domesticated crops. These cereals had long been native to the region, having survived the late Ice Age in sheltered locales. With the onset of warmer conditions, their distribution expanded greatly, making them accessible to many more hunter-gatherer bands distributed over a vast area. In Mexico, the climate of 18,000 B.C. was drier and colder than today. At the end of the Ice Age, temperatures rose, bringing a rich forest of cacti and legume trees to the mountain valleys of Puebla and Oaxaca. This thorn-scrub-cactus forest included many wild ancestors of domesticated plants, including the maguey; squash; bean; and teosinte, the wild grass that was the ancestor of domesticated maize.

These and other Holocene climatic changes had profound effects in hunter-gatherer societies throughout the world, especially on the intensity of the food quest and complexity of their societies. Why had such changes not occurred earlier in prehistory? There had been climatic changes of similar, if not even greater, magnitude in early millennia, say during the early part of the last interglacial, some 128,000 years ago. The reason may be population density. Then, human populations were much smaller and a great deal of the world was uninhabited. It was possible for human populations living in large hunting territories to move around freely, to adapt to new circumstances by shifting their homeland, even over large distances. This ability enabled them to develop highly flexible survival strategies that took account of the constant fluctuations in food availability. If, for example, an African band experienced two dry years in a row, it could move away or fall back on less nutritious edible foods, perhaps species that required more energy to harvest.

By 13,000 B.C., circumstances were very different. The world's hunter-gatherer population was probably approaching about 8.5 million people (Hassan, 1981). The carrying capacity of the world's many environments still exceeded that of the human population, largely because humans were becoming more efficient in their exploitation of a broad spectrum of food resources. After 13,000 B.C., the population curve approached that of carrying capacity (Figure 5.1). This development might have set off behavioral changes resulting from restricted mobility and greater competition. Notable among them would have been a necessity to solve problems locally rather than just moving away from them. People would have tended to exploit a wider range of local resources, both to avert starvation and to protect

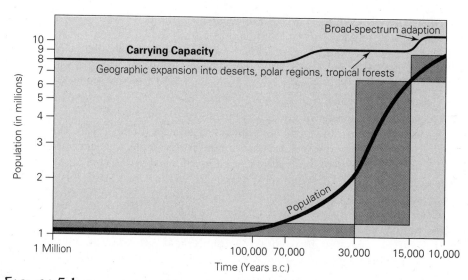

FIGURE 5.1   Increases in world population during the Ice Age matched against carrying capacity of the globe for humans.

themselves from food shortages caused by short-term droughts and other unpredictable changes.

In a sense, the world was full, or at least occupied sparsely by people who lived off its game, plant, and other food resources. *Homo sapiens sapiens* had settled in periglacial regions, in tropical rain forests, on offshore islands, and in the Americas. There were sparse hunter-gatherer populations throughout the world, many of them living in areas such as central Australia, for example, where carrying capacities of the land was very low indeed. Human populations had risen considerably, too, especially in areas with diverse and seasonally predictable food resources. Even in sparsely inhabited environments, hunting territories were more confined. There was less room to move around; there were often more mouths to feed; and new adaptive strategies were needed, strategies aimed at more efficient and productive exploitation of the environment. As a result of these new strategies, hunter-gatherer societies underwent profound changes and, in some areas, acquired much greater complexity (Price and Brown, 1985).

COPING WITH ENVIRONMENTAL VARIATION

●   ●   ●

Increasingly during the late Ice Age and more frequently in Holocene times, prehistoric hunter-gatherer populations were confronted with new challenges, challenges created both by major climatic changes at the end of the Pleistocene and by local population growth. Everywhere, much more circumscribed hunter-gatherers were forced to improve their strategies for coping with local environmental variations, both in predictable seasonal resources and in unpredictable shifts in such phenomena as rainfall patterns or game migration routes (Figure 5.2). This shift can be seen clearly in the Americas. As we shall see in Chapter 6, the Americans of 10,000 B.C. were small in numbers, highly mobile, and sparsely distributed on the ground. They subsisted in part off Ice Age big game, which became extinct very rapidly after 9000 B.C. The archaeological record now shows a much greater diversity of local adaptations over the millennia, as thousands of isolated hunter-gatherer groups became more and more restricted in their movements. The change is especially marked in areas of exceptional resource diversity like the Pacific Northwest coast, the southern California coast, and the fertile river valleys of the southern Midwest and southeastern United States. In all these areas, hunter-gatherer populations became more sedentary; developed often highly specialized technologies for hunting, foraging, or fishing; and in the process, developed some form of social ranking (Figure 5.3).

The intensification of hunting and gathering was marked by two long-term technological trends that went hand in hand. The first was the gradual downsizing of stone artifacts and the perishable antler, bone, and wood toolkit that went with them. The second was the development of highly efficient, often very specialized sets of hunting weapons or food-processing implements designed for intensive exploitation of specific food resources such as reindeer, sea mammals, birds, or acorns.

The trend toward diminution in stone technology began during the late Ice Age and coincides in general terms with the last glacial maximum of about 18,000 B.C. Spear barbs and knife blades became smaller, more lightweight, as if the hunters were relying more heavily on spear-throwers for propulsion velocity. It was sometime during the late Ice Age, too, that the bow and arrow came into use, a weapon with many advantages, among them greater accuracy, enhanced portability, and the ability to fire off several missiles within a very short space of time. The bow was also

FIGURE 5.2   San hunter with weapons from Ho Khotso, Lesotho, southern Africa. From a late Stone Age painting colored purple-red. The figure is approximately 8 inches (21 cm) high.

FIGURE 5.3   Salmon fishing in the Pacific Northwest. Nineteenth century painting by Paul Kane.

far more versatile than the spear, for the hunters could carry many more light-weight, lethal points with them in a small quiver, arrows that could be brought into use in a few moments. Under these circumstances, the chances of a kill were greatly enhanced (Figure 5.4).

FIGURE 5.4 Eskimo demonstrating a sinew-backed bow and ivory-tipped arrow at Chicago's Columbian Exposition in 1893.

We do not know exactly when the bow and arrow first came into use, but there is a good reason to believe that this versatile hunting weapon was in Europe by 13,000 B.C. and perhaps in Africa and the Near East at about the same time. In contrast, it reached the Americas very much later, in some areas as late as 200 B.C. As early as 28,000 B.C., and even more intensively after 13,000 B.C., stone tool technologies became more and more standardized and more and more oriented toward the production of parts of composite tools, especially small arrow and knife barbs, scrapers, and awls. In Europe and the Near East, this technology involved the production of thousands of small microliths, geometrically shaped barbs used on all manner of weapons (Figure 5.5). (The term *microlith* comes from the Greek *micros*, "small," and *lithos*, "stone.") These standardized artifacts were made by striking small bladelets off a conical core, then notching and snapping off the thicker end to form a small microlith. Microlith-tipped and barbed wooden arrows have been found intact in Danish swamps, environments where they were used to hunt forest game, rodents, and birds for many centuries.

A complete blade is notched on opposite sides or the same edge, depending on the shape of microlith required.

The blade is then snapped across the notch.

The middle segment forms the finished implement, here a parallelogram-shaped (left) or a trapezoidal (right) arrow barb.

Microliths (Actual size)

Mounted barbs
(hypothetical)
(Actual size)

FIGURE 5.5   Microliths. Stages in manufacturing a microlith, a small arrow barb, or similar implement made by notching a blade and snapping off its base after an implement is formed.

The diminution of stone technology reflected a much greater emphasis on specialized but versatile toolkits that were modified to reflect local needs. The early Holocene saw a much greater localization of artifacts of all kinds, a development reflected in a proliferation of new archaeological "cultures"; these, in fact, reflected a world in which movement was more circumscribed, in which thousands of small bands and occasionally larger population groups adapted to constant local environmental variation. This localization is well documented in areas like Europe, Australia, the Near East, and the North American Great Basin, as well as by Kent Flannery's important work on a microband who visited Guilá Naquitz cave, Mexico, between about 8750 and 6670 B.C. (Flannery et al., 1986) (see Figure 1.11). As Flannery has eloquently pointed out, the new local toolkits were part of a process whereby humans coped not only with long-term climatic change but also with the constant uncertainties of local climates. "Humans are well suited to the working out of resilient strategies for environmental variability," Flannery writes, "since they possess multigenerational memory and have unique methods for exchanging information and establishing cooperative relationships over long periods."

The new subsistence strategies often involved highly intensive exploitation of locally abundant and predictable resources such as salmon or nuts. Such intensive exploitation was adaptive in environments where seasonal phenomena such as salmon runs, caribou migrations, or hickory harvests required not only the harvesting of enormous quantities of food in a short time but also their processing and storage for later use. Storage technology now assumed a new and pressing importance; thousands of fish were dried on racks in the sun or in front of fires, and the nut and wild cereal harvest was placed in basket- or clay-lined pits for later consumption. There was nothing new in the notion of storage; much earlier in prehistory, big-game hunters, for example, dried meat and pounded it up to make food on the march. What was new, however, was the notion of large-scale storage in more sedentary settlements, where mobility was no longer a viable strategy. By using storage and by careful seasonal "mapping" of game, plant, and aquatic resources, early Holocene hunter-gatherers compensated for periodic food shortages caused by short-term climatic change and seasonal fluctuations. At the same time, they broadened their diet to include foods that were at a lower trophic level, another way of ensuring fallback in the diet in the event of staple shortages.

As early as 18,000 B.C., and more markedly after 13,000 B.C., human toolkits display much greater specialization and elaboration. We have already mentioned the development of the needle as a catalyst for layered, tailored clothing in periglacial environments, and both the Magdalenians and the Eastern Gravettian big-game hunters used a wide variety of specialized, and sometimes elaborate, antler and bone tools in the chase and in domestic life (Chapter 4). Holocene hunter-gatherer societies worldwide developed specialized toolkits for many purposes. Many North American societies relied heavily on seeds and nuts. They developed many forms of grinders and pestles to process such harvests (Figure 5.6), and the rich organic deposits of such sites as the Hoko River and Ozette on the Olympic Peninsula in the Pacific Northwest document a highly effective halibut-fishing and whale-hunting technology based on wood, bone, slate, and fiber (Figure 5.7) (Croes and Hackenberger, 1987). Canoes, bone-tipped fish spears, and wooden birding arrows were part of the specialized fishing and fowling toolkit of Holocene groups in northern Europe. Perhaps the ultimate in specialized hunting technology for sea mammals comes from the Bering Sea coasts of Alaska and the Thule culture of the Canadian Arctic (Chapter 6).

More circumscribed territories, less mobility, rising local population, and new strategies for dealing with seasonal and unpredictable environmental variations—these problems were common to postglacial hunter-gatherer societies throughout the world. A few of these societies, especially those living in areas with rich and diverse food resources that included fish or sea mammals, achieved a high degree of social complexity, with signs of some social ranking.

FIGURE 5.6   Pounders used for processing wild vegetable foods from the Gwisho late Stone Age cave site, Zambia, central Africa, c. 3500 years old. The peck marks served to hold the grains.

FIGURE 5.7   Replica of an ancient halibut fishhook used for fishing from Hoko River Site, Olympia Peninsula, Washington.

COPING WITH ENVIRONMENTAL UNCERTAINTY: MESOLITHIC HUNTER-GATHERERS IN EUROPE

● ● ●

An excellent example of how late Ice Age hunter-gatherers adapted to global warming comes from northwestern Europe, where Mesolithic forest and coastal hunter-gatherers replaced tundra reindeer hunters after 11,000 B.C. [*Mesolithic* refers to the period of postglacial times in Europe that preceded the introduction of farming (J. G. D. Clark, 1975, 1979).] The European Mesolithic spans about 4500 years, from about 8000 B.C. until the beginnings of farming in northwest Europe about 3500 B.C. (Figure 5.8).

    The environmental changes in Europe after 13,000 B.C. were so dramatic that the Magdalenian and other late Ice Age cultures vanished relatively quickly. The traditional view held that Europe was now populated by impoverished Mesolithic hunters and gatherers who had lost much of their capacity for economic and social relations. This notion of a cultural hiatus has crumbled in the face of recent sophisticated ecological researches. Instead of impoverished environments, each change in

European Mesolithic
8000 to 3500 B.C.

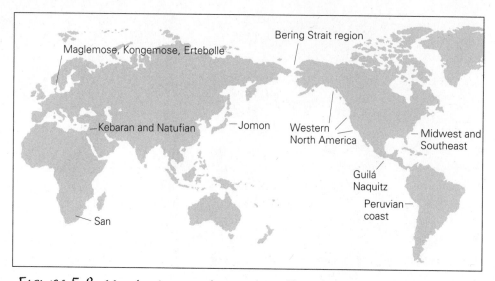

FIGURE 5.8   Map showing general areas where affluent hunter-gatherers mentioned in this book flourished.

postglacial forest composition probably brought greater ecological productivity. A range of forest ungulates such as red and roe deer replaced the migratory reindeer that were so important in Ice Age times. Plant foods such as nuts assumed much greater importance in Mesolithic life. These food sources may have contributed to an increase in Mesolithic populations. Coasts, estuaries, and lakes were highly productive, especially with such seasonal resources as salmon, water birds, and sea mammals, many of them relying on seasonal plankton production in the oceans. Many of these aquatic foods could be taken and stored, especially by people who occupied relatively permanent encampments nearby. Thus, larger populations were possible in some areas among people who relied on seasonal resources and used such nonseasonal foods as shellfish to "plug" the gaps (Rowley-Conwy, 1986). Some of these more sedentary groups enjoyed a bounty of food sources and a complexity of life that has been called "affluent foraging."

Were all European Mesolithic groups affluent foragers? The interplay of different resources varied dramatically throughout Europe, with its seasonal climates and productive environments. This was not a hostile environment peopled by only minimally complex hunter-gatherer bands but one where a great variety of adaptations was possible. At least two general models have been proposed for Mesolithic Europe:

- Lower latitudes supported somewhat generalized environments, where highly mobile bands exploited evenly dispersed animal and plant resources, shifting camp regularly as local resources were exhausted.
- Higher-latitude environments were more uneven in productivity and resource reliability, having few species in large numbers. These were specialized environments, where human groups moved less often and frequently directed their moves toward the exploitation of a single seasonal resource such as caribou. Larger numbers of people sometimes congregated for seasonal hunts.

These are, of course, by no means the only models for Mesolithic life that could be put forward, but they serve to remind us that this was a period when European populations enjoyed a wide range of adaptations, from peoples with highly mobile lifeways to permanently settled, "affluent" groups who dwelt in large villages or base camps, such as are found in northwest Europe and by the Iron Gates area of the Danube River. Without question, the Mesolithic was a period of broad variation in economic and social life, with some intensification of the food quest where uncertain environmental conditions dictated it.

Clive Gamble (1986a) points out that the adaptive trends seen in the European Mesolithic are not particularly innovative; indeed, most of them have their roots in a much earlier restructuring of the organization and use of resources with the arrival of modern humans in temperate latitudes some 35,000 years ago. The Upper Paleolithic saw much greater exploitation of regional resources and an enhanced ability to adapt to extremes of both glacial and fully interglacial climates. This restructuring gave Europeans the ability to solve the problems of exploiting not just a few resources but many different ones at once. This ability became vital at the end of the Ice Age, when food management strategies were able to cope with extremely varied combinations of food resources. These strategies included some elements that were of critical importance when people began to grow crops and tame animals: adaptations that were attuned to the scheduling of seasonal activities connected with growing and harvesting seasons and systems of information sharing. The Mesolithic hunters' schedule was comprehensive and flexible enough to cope with anything and could easily accommodate strategies that relied on deliberate cultivation of the soil or careful animal husbandry.

Efficient food management strategies involved more effective technology, too—more diverse toolkits for hunting forest animals and exploiting coastal resources such as sea mammals and shallow-water fish. The Mesolithic peoples who lived along the shores of the newly emerging Baltic Sea developed an astonishing range of fish spears, nets, harpoons, and traps, many of them preserved in waterlogged sites. Spears and arrows were tipped with tiny stone, bone, or antler barbs. Ground-edged tools were used for woodworking and processing forest plants. Large canoes, some of them dugouts hollowed from tree trunks, were in evidence. We know that Stone Age people were crossing open water as early as 10,000 B.C., for miners were visiting the island of Melos in the Mediterranean to collect obsidian that was traded far and wide (Torrance, 1986).

Many Mesolithic groups lived in larger, more permanent settlements, a number of them located on strategic bays or near lakes or rivers. Some locations were probably used year-round or certainly for many months, anchored by abundant aquatic resources nearby. There were smaller camps and specialist activity areas, too. Everything points to greater internal differentiation in society and to more intensive subsistence activities. Nuts and shellfish became far more important, and hunters took a far wider range of game than their Ice Age predecessors. It was not the dietary staples but merely the diversity of exploited food resources that changed.

Perhaps the most profound changes were those in population densities and social organization, both notoriously difficult phenomena to identify in the archaeological record. Grahame Clark (1979) has identified three major "social territories" at the end of the Upper Paleolithic, between the Netherlands, Poland, and southern Sweden. Three distinct cultures (Ahrensburgian, Swiderian, and Bromme) each covered territories of about 38,610 square miles (100,000 sq. km). As the postglacial wore on, these territories were rapidly reduced in size. By 6000 B.C., there were at least 15 territories in this same area, identified by different artifact styles or distributions of raw materials. Each of these zones was about 5791 to 7722 square miles (15,000 to 20,000 sq. km) in extent. This pattern may reflect major changes in the regional distribution, density, and social organization of Mesolithic populations. Douglas Price (1983) points out that as these changes were taking place, new artifact forms and presumably other innovations were spreading across wide areas of Europe. Among them was a characteristic trapeze-shaped microlith, widely used as an arrow barb by later Mesolithic peoples, that appeared all over the continent about 6000 B.C., perhaps somewhat earlier in southeast Europe (J. G. D. Clark, 1958). The Mesolithic ended with the rapid spread of agricultural economies into southeast Europe about 6000 B.C. From there they spread sporadically into central Europe by 4500 B.C. and to the northwest after 3500 B.C.

The European Mesolithic testifies to a continuity in human culture from Ice Age times, but this continuity was based on continuous adjustment to changing postglacial environments. In time, the same Mesolithic societies readapted to the warmest millennia of postglacial times not only by shifting their hunting and foraging methods but also by taking up new subsistence practices, often within the context of their existing society.

Mesolithic Complexity in Scandinavia

This continuity is well documented from waterlogged Mesolithic sites in Britain and Scandinavia, where three broad subdivisions of the northern Mesolithic are known (Price, 1985).

The Maglemose Period (7500 to 5700 B.C.)

Maglemose
7500 to 5700 B.C.

The Maglemose was a time of seasonal exploitation of rivers and lakes, combined with terrestrial hunting and foraging. Inland late spring and early summer settlements are represented by the Ulkestrup site in Denmark, where the people lived in large huts with bark and wood floors on a peat island in a swamp by a lake. One hut lay close to poles where canoes were once moored. A large wooden paddle lay nearby. The Maglemose people fished with bone and antler barbed points; trapped birds; and hunted such animals as red deer, wild ox, and pig. In fall, the bands foraged for hazelnuts and other edible plant foods, killing elk and other game in winter, when apparently fishing was less important.

The Kongemose Period (5700 to 4600 B.C.)

Kongemose
5700 to 4600 B.C.

Kongemose sites are mainly on Baltic Sea coasts, along bays and near lagoons, where the people exploited both marine and terrestrial resources. Many Kongemose sites are somewhat larger than Maglemose ones; among the better known is the now-submerged Segebro settlement in brackish water near the southwest Swedish coast. This settlement covered 164 by 82 feet (50 by 25 m) and was occupied year-round, but mainly in spring and summer. Carbon isotope analyses of human bones from Segebro show that fish and sea mammals constituted most of the diet, with no fewer than 66 species of animals found in the site. Not only freshwater and saltwater fish but also red deer, elk, boars, and seals were commonplace. Like the Maglemose people, Kongemose hunter-gatherers used small stone microlithic arrow barbs as well as artifacts and weapons of bone, antler, and wood.

The Ertebølle Period (4600 to 3200 B.C.)

Ertebølle was the culmination of Mesolithic culture in southern Scandinavia (Price, 1987). By this time, the Scandinavians were occupying many coastal settlements year-round, subsisting off a very wide range of food resources indeed. These included forest game and waterfowl, shellfish, sea mammals, and both shallow- and deepwater fish. There were smaller, seasonal coastal sites, too, many for specific activities such as deepwater fishing, sealing, or hunting of migratory birds. The Aggersund site in Denmark was occupied for a short period in the autumn, when the inhabitants collected oysters and hunted some game, especially migratory swans. Ertebølle technology was far more elaborate than that of its Mesolithic predecessors; a wide variety of antler, bone, and wood tools for specialized purposes such as fowling and sea mammal hunting were developed, including dugout canoes up to 32.8 feet (10 m) long.

With sedentary settlement comes evidence of greater social complexity. Some Ertebølle communities buried their dead in cemeteries, with the bodies placed in various positions and also with dog interments. The Vedbaek Bogebakken cemetery in Denmark dates to about 5000 B.C. and contains the graves of at least 22 people of different ages. Everyone was buried in an extended position, at least three people after injury or a violent death (Figure 5.9). Men and women were deposited with different grave goods, older people with red deer antlers. Other Ertebølle cemeteries from Denmark contain evidence of violent death; some people had projectile points in their ribs. There are also traces of cannibalism (Price, 1985).

The trend toward more sedentary settlement, the cemeteries, and occasional social differentiation revealed by elaborate burials are all reflections of an "intensification" among these relatively "affluent" hunter-gatherers of 3000 B.C. Mesolithic societies intensified the food quest by exploiting many more marine species, making productive use of migratory waterfowl and their breeding grounds, and collecting shellfish in enormous numbers. This intensification is also reflected in a much more elaborate and diverse technology, more exchange of goods and materials between neighbors, greater variety in settlement types, and a slowly rising population throughout southern Scandinavia. These phenomena may, in part, be a reflection of rising sea levels throughout the Mesolithic, inundations that flooded many cherished territories. There are signs, too, of regional variations in artifact forms and styles, of cultural differences between people living in carefully delineated territories and competing for resources.

Mesolithic cultures are much less well defined elsewhere in Europe, partly because the climatic changes were less extreme than in southern Scandinavia and because there were fewer opportunities for coastal adaptation. In many areas, settlement was confined to lakeside and riverside locations, widely separated from one another by dense forests. Many Mesolithic sites were located on ecotones (transitional zones between different environments) so that the inhabitants could return to a central base location, where for much of the year they lived close to predictable resources such as lake fish. However, they would exploit both forest game and other seasonal resources from satellite camps. In central Europe, for example, Michael Jochim (1976) believes that some groups lived during the winter in camps along the Danube, moving to summer encampments on the shores of neighboring lakes. In many areas like Spain, there appears to have been intensified exploitation of marine and forest resources. There was a trend nearly everywhere to greater variety in the

FIGURE 5.9   Burial of a man, a woman, and, between them, a small child from Ved-baek, Denmark, c. 5000 B.C. A bone point is embedded in the man's throat; the woman wears a string of animal teeth, which lies on her chest.

diet, with more attention being paid to less obvious foods and to those, like shell-fish, that require more complex processing methods than game and other such resources.

Thus, in parts of Europe, there was a long-term trend among hunter-gatherer societies toward more extensive exploitation of food resources, often within the context of a strategy that sought ways to minimize the impact of environmental uncertainty. In more favored areas such as southern Scandinavia, some such societies achieved a level of nascent social complexity that was to become commonplace among later farming peoples. When farming did come to Europe, this preadaptation was an important catalyst for rapid economic and social change (Chapter 10).

HUNTER-GATHERER COMPLEXITY

● ● ●

"Hunter-gatherers move around a lot and live in small groups." This statement has been a universal label for hunter-gatherer societies ancient and modern for a generation (Lee and DeVore, 1976). It paints a picture of hunter-gatherers in prefarming times who lived in small, temporary camps; were constantly on the move; and possessed a highly portable technology and flexible social system. These models were based in large part on anthropological researches among living societies like the !Kung San of the Kalahari Desert in southern Africa or the Inuit of the Canadian Arctic. Most of them are peoples living in areas of the world, like tropical rain forests, Arctic regions, or semideserts, where agriculture is an impossibility. Only a handful of hunter-gatherer societies, peoples like the Ainu of Japan or the Northwest coast Indians, enjoyed more complex adaptations at the time of European contact around the eighteenth century A.D. Generalizations about highly mobile, small-scale hunter-gatherer societies took little account of the great diversity among the many hunting and foraging societies that once existed on earth. This diversity, known almost entirely from archaeological researches, developed during the late Ice Age and Holocene. Above all, the archaeological record of the world of 13,000 to 4000 B.C. reveals a global trend toward great complexity in hunter-gatherer societies in well-defined regions as widely separated as northern Europe, southern Africa, Japan, the Midwest, and coastal Peru.

Conditions for Greater Complexity

Complex hunter-gatherer societies did not appear everywhere, but they occurred in a remarkable variety of environments, from fertile river valleys to coastal deserts. Whatever the environment, however, certain general conditions were necessary. First, population movements had to be limited by either geography or the presence of neighbors. Thus, one could not move away from resource shortages; solutions had to be found on the spot. Second, resources had to be abundant and predictable in their seasonal appearance. Small, numerous organisms with high reproductive rates played an especially important role in intensifying hunting and gathering. Such organisms include fish, shellfish, nuts, and seeds (Hayden, 1981), species that are available in abundance and seldom exhausted. Third, population growth might reach a point at which food shortages occur and there is an imbalance between people and their food supply. Again, a solution was to intensify the food quest, an intensification that might result in a more complex society.

Attributes of Greater Complexity

What features distinguish a more complex hunter-gatherer society from its less elaborate neighbors? The following appear to be of fundamental importance:

● Higher than normal population, concentrated in relatively small and restricted territories, such as individual river valleys, where movement is circumscribed by either geography or neighbors.

- A more intensive, more diversified, and more specialized food quest. Selected species such as nuts and seeds become more important, and foods that were not exploited previously because they required more effort are taken into the diet. In some cases, people will deliberately plant wild plants to ensure an adequate harvest.

- A system of food storage and preservation.

- Permanent and nearly permanent settlements, often base camps of much greater size than in earlier times. Settlements are often linear, distributed along, say, river banks; contain different forms of structures; and are often associated with burial grounds, which may serve as territorial boundaries.

- Highly developed hunting, fishing, or plant-processing equipment.

- Division of labor not only by sex and age but also by activity, such as whale hunting or a craft specialty like canoe building.

- Some form of simple social ranking, probably based on lineages or other kin groupings, marked by differences in wealth, diet, and burial customs.

- Often quite intensive exchange in exotic objects and raw materials with neighboring groups.

- More elaborate ritual beliefs and ceremonial life.

Debates About Social Complexity

We do not know when the first more complex hunter-gatherer societies appeared, but it seems likely that at least some late Ice Age societies enjoyed some level of complexity. Possible candidates may include the Magdalenians of southwestern France and northern Spain as well as the Eastern Gravettian plains hunters, with their mammoth-bone houses, who lived in the river valleys of the Ukraine in 16,000 B.C. (see Chapter 4). Complexity among hunter-gatherer societies became widespread after the Ice Age, especially in areas where freshwater or marine fish, shellfish, or sea mammals were available in abundance. Aquatic resources have the advantage of being both relatively plentiful and predictable, so much so that there are strong incentives for people to adopt sedentary lifeways along rivers and at lake and ocean shores. However, the full potential of marine and freshwater resources was only realized in a relatively few areas of the world, and then within the past 10,000 years.

The debates about social complexity among hunter-gatherers revolve around two opposing viewpoints. The first sees the oceans as a kind of "Garden of Eden" (Binford, 1983). Proponents of this theory point to the enormous abundance of shellfish in many areas of the world and to the great productivity of many estuaries and coastal waters easily exploited by shore-dwelling fisherfolk. This abundance allowed societies to become sedentary and to maintain population densities (Moseley, 1975a).

In contrast, another group of archaeologists, many of them studying post–Ice Age hunter-gatherers in Europe, argue that aquatic resources were a strategy of last resort, a response to population pressure and shortages of terrestrial resources such as game and plant foods (Gamble, 1986b). These authorities assume that marine and freshwater resources, no matter how productive, are more labor intensive to harvest and are less nutritionally valuable than food sources on land.

David Yesner (1987) has recently taken a somewhat different perspective. He argues that the shift to the exploitation of aquatic resources was the result of decisions made in periods of rapid environmental change, when population pressure was causing food shortages. The "optimal" strategy for people under these circumstances would be to turn to a resource that does involve more work and is, perhaps, as productive as big game.

All of these viewpoints assume, however, that maritime resources played a key role in the emergence of social complexity among Stone Age hunter-gatherers. The debate is unresolved, for we do not know exactly how decisive marine or riverine resources were in allowing dense populations and sedentary living, both essential prerequisites for social complexity. Nor do we know whether we can make comparisons between the elaborate and socially complex Northwest coast Indian cultures that flourished a few centuries ago and early Holocene hunter-gatherer groups living thousands of years earlier in prehistory.

HUNTER-GATHERER SOCIETIES IN THE LEVANT

● ● ●

The Near East has provided a fascinating picture of emerging social and cultural complexity among hunter-gatherers at the end of the Ice Age. Between 12,000 and 8000 B.C., the simple hunter-gatherer societies of the Levant, the coastal zone of Israel and Syria, gave way to more complex hunting and gathering societies and eventually to farmers (for a site map, see Figure 9.1). For years, scientists have discussed the origins of agriculture in the Near East, believing it to be a more radical transformation in human life than almost any other development in prehistory (see Chapter 8). In fact, recent researches have suggested that the earlier hunter-gatherer transition may have been much more profound.

In 12,000 B.C., the Levant was populated by small and highly mobile hunter-gatherer bands, subsumed under the general cultural name of Kebaran. Kebaran sites, marked by thousands of small, geometric microliths, occur not only in wooded country but also in the steppe and desert of the Negev and Sinai (Henry, 1989). The Kebarans are found in a wide variety of environments, which may account for the great variation in their toolkits (Figure 5.10). Everything points to the Kebarans having enjoyed a simple hunter-gatherer strategy, which placed a high premium on mobility (Bar-Yosef, 1987). In some areas, the people may have dispersed to the uplands in summer, moving into caves and rock shelters near lowland lakes in the winter. Apparently, plant foods were not overwhelmingly important, and the Kebaran toolkit lacks the specialized grinders and pounders found in later cultures, except at lower elevations, where some wild cereal grasses grew.

By about 9000 B.C., warming temperatures throughout the Near East brought significant environmental and vegetational changes. During the late Ice Age, warmth-loving plants like wild emmer wheat and barley, oaks, almonds, and pistachio trees were restricted to refuge areas lying below modern sea level. These sandy-soiled areas would have given only poor yields of wild cereals. As early Holocene temperatures rose, these plant and tree species colonized higher country, where clayey soils produced much higher yields (Henry, 1989). New, denser cereal stands were now much more resistant to short-term climatic change and also harvestable over a longer period of time each year. After 9000 B.C., many hunter-gatherer sites on higher ground contain ground stone tools—pestles and mortars, implements

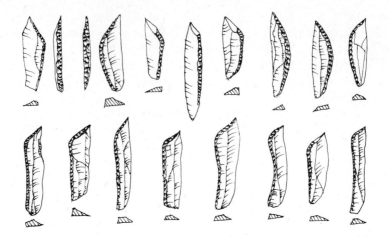

FIGURE 5.10   Geometric Kebaran microliths. Full size.

used to process seed harvests for storage, an essential in much more seasonal, and increasingly arid climates.

These abundant cereal and nut resources within the Mediterranean hill zone stimulated the development of more intensive foraging strategies, more sedentary settlement, and rapid territorial expansion until the most favored territories were filled. The emergence of these more plentiful plant resources coincided with the emergence of the Natufian culture from the earlier Kebaran, a culture that expanded rapidly to the edges of the Mediterranean zone within about 1500 years, during a brief cycle of wetter climate that ended about 9000 B.C.

The Natufians used a more complex hunting and foraging strategy than the Kebarans. They exploited wild emmer and barley intensively, as well as acorn, almond, and pistachio, all highly productive resources that were easily stored. The new subsistence strategies encouraged more sedentary lifeways and the development of much larger settlements, averaging about 7500 sq. feet (700 sq. m) in area. These villages, which contained semisubterranean houses, storage pits, and pavements, were associated with nearby small, transitory camps, where food was collected and processed (Figure 5.11). The Natufian toolkit contains all manner of specialized plant-processing tools, including querns, grinding slabs, pestles, mortars, and bone sickles with flint blades (Figure 5.12). These bear a characteristic "sickle gloss" caused by the silica in cereal grass stalks.

Natufian hamlets are confined to the Mediterranean hill zone, where wild cereals and nut-bearing trees had their natural habitat. The larger sites are close to the boundaries between the coastal plains or grassland valleys and the hill zone. Some were placed strategically to take advantage of good toolmaking stone. Such settlements enabled the Natufians to exploit spring cereal crops, fall nut harvests, and the game that flourished on the lowlands and on the rich nut mast on the forest floor in the hills above. Unlike their more mobile ancestors, the Natufians enjoyed many months of plentiful food by exploiting spring cereals and then following nut harvests up the slopes as they ripened at progressively higher elevations. Gazelle hunting assumed great importance at certain seasons of the year, with neighboring communities cooperating in game drives, ambushes, and other mass-hunting enterprises.

FIGURE 5.11 Natufian house foundations from Ain Mallaha, Jordan. There are mortars, pestles, and storage areas in structure 26, and a group of burials outside the hut.

By the end of Natufian times, about 8500 B.C., local populations were considerably higher than in earlier times. Natufian society offers intriguing glimpses at a new, more complex social order. The Natufians buried their dead in cemeteries, which have yielded a wealth of information on their society. There are clear signs of social ranking. One common and constantly recurring symbolic artifact, the dentalium seashell, is confined to a few burials, whereas elaborate grave furniture such as stone bowls with some individuals, including children, hints strongly at some form of social differences. Perhaps this social ranking was the result of a need for the redistribution of food surpluses and to maintain order within much larger, sedentary communities. Also, the stone slab grave covers and mortar markers associated with the cemeteries may have served as ritual markers of territorial boundaries, perhaps of lands vested in revered ancestors.

After 9000 B.C., the Natufians were faced with much drier climatic conditions at a time when their populations were expanding. The effect of increased aridity was to shrink the cereal habitats in the Mediterranean zone, causing the most productive stands to be found at higher altitudes. At the same time, the Natufians were forced to remain in sedentary settlements close to permanent water supplies, a fact of life that made the cost of harvesting cereals and nuts at remote locations much higher. How, then, could people living in a complex hunter-gatherer system solve the problem of declining staples? After nearly 2000 years' close involvement with cereal plants, they would have been well aware of what was needed to plant and grow

Sickle blades

Sickle handle

FIGURE 5.12   Natufian bone-handled sickle and flint blades.

cereal grasses deliberately. By deliberately planting cereals on a modest scale, the people tried to cope with uncertainty, to augment declining stands of wild wheat and barley with their own supplemental crops. As we shall see in Chapter 9, it was only a short time before full-time farming societies were flourishing over a wide area of the Near East. In a real sense, the development of a more complex hunter-gatherer society in this area preadapted the Natufians to plant crops.

The Natufian scenario from the Levant was mirrored under different circumstances in many parts of the world, where trajectories of cultural change followed many paths. In some areas, the new shape of the hunter-gatherer society preadapted people for the deliberate planting of cereal and root crops and for the domestication of animals. In other regions, such as southern California, that were marginal for subsistence farming, complex hunter-gatherer societies flourished until modern times. The chapters that follow describe the prehistory of hunter-gatherer societies from the arrival of *Homo sapiens sapiens* in all parts of the world.

CHAPTER SUMMARY

The Ice Age ended about 10,000 B.C., ushering in the beginning of the Holocene (recent) period. The Holocene was marked by dramatic climatic changes, including retreating ice sheets, major shifts in vegetational zones, and rises in sea level. Many large mammal species became extinct. Hunter-gatherer societies throughout the world developed highly localized adaptations to new, less predictable conditions, with more intensive exploitation of food resources and, in many areas, a trend toward more sedentism, use of storage technologies, and more complex hunter-gatherer societies. This increased social complexity is well documented in the Mesolithic cultures of Scandinavia, where groups exploited maritime resources and birds extensively. Such increases in social complexity were marked by higher population densities, more intensive food exploitation, more long distance exchange, and greater social ranking detected in burial ornaments. These shifts are well documented in the Levant region of the Near East, especially among the Natufian people, who were intensive foragers of wild cereals and nuts, and expert gazelle hunters. Such intensification of the food quest and greater sedentism preadapted many groups for adopting agriculture and animal domestication.

GUIDE TO FURTHER READING

Clark, J. G. D. 1952. *Prehistoric Europe: The Economic Basis*. Cambridge, Eng.: Cambridge University Press.
> *The classic essay on prehistoric European economies. Still of immense value on Mesolithic life.*

———. 1975. *The Earlier Stone Age Settlement of Scandinavia*. Cambridge, Eng.: Cambridge University Press.
> *A fundamental synthesis on Mesolithic northwest Europe.*

Henry, Donald O. 1989. *From Foraging to Agriculture*. Philadelphia: University of Pennsylvania Press.
> *This essay on the Near East is excellent on the Natufian.*

Price, T. D. 1985. "The Mesolithic of Western Europe." *Journal of World Prehistory* 1 (3):225–305.
> *A well-reasoned synthesis, which discusses complexity among hunter-gatherers.*

Price, T. D., and Brown, James A., eds. 1985. *Prehistoric Hunter-Gatherers: The Emergence of Cultural Complexity*. Orlando, FL: Academic Press.
> *Essays on emerging cultural complexity among hunter-gatherers in many parts of the world. A specialist volume.*

Roberts, Neil. 1989. *The Holocene: An Environmental History*. Oxford: Blackwell.
> *All you have ever wanted to know about the Holocene and more . . . rapidly becoming a classic work.*

THE FIRST AMERICANS

. . .

CONTROVERSIES OVER FIRST SETTLEMENT

. . .

One fine spring morning in 1908, a black cowboy named George McJunkin was riding slowly along the edge of a dry gully near Folsom, New Mexico. He was casting over the range in search of stray cattle. Suddenly, he saw some sun-bleached bones protruding from the side of the arroyo. He pried some out with his knife. As he did so, a sharp stone fragment came loose in his hands, a stone spear point like the ones he had seen lying on the surface elsewhere on the ranch. McJunkin took his finds back to the ranch house, where they lay around for seventeen years.

In 1925, someone was curious enough to send the bones to Jesse Figgins, the Director of the Colorado Museum of Natural History. He realized they were from an extinct form of plains bison, apparently from the same level as the stone point. The following year, he dug into the arroyo, found more stone tools and bison bones. He realized he had the proof that humans had lived in North America at the same time as long extinct animals. Soon experts flocked to Folsom, convinced that Figgins had finally found proof of the considerable antiquity of humankind in the Americas.

The controversies over the first Americans were raging long before the Folsom excavations, and they are still among the most vigorous of all debates in archaeology. How long ago did humans set foot in the Americas? What manner of people were they? By what route did they reach the New World? These questions have preoccupied scientists since soon after Columbus landed in the West Indies.

Almost all archaeologists agree that the first inhabitants of the Americas set foot in the New World by way of the Bering Land Bridge, at a time when the strait of that name was dry land. (See Figure 6.1 for sites mentioned in this chapter.) However, for all the agreement about the Siberian route, intense controversies surround the beginnings of human settlement in the Americas (Fagan, 1987; Dillehay and Meltzer, 1991; Meltzer, 1994) (Table 6.1). These controversies revolve around three fundamental questions:

- How long ago did humans first settle in the Americas?
- What toolkit did they bring with them, and what was their lifeway?
- What was the ultimate ancestry of the first native Americans?

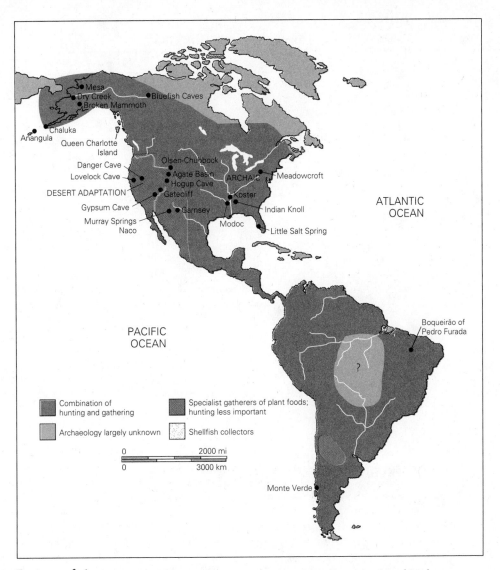

FIGURE 6.1 Prehistoric hunter-gatherers in the Americas. Sites mentioned in the text are indicated. (For the Bering Land Bridge, see Figure 6.2.) The diagonally hatched areas show the distribution of specialized hunter-gatherers after 7000 years ago.

Two competing hypotheses account for first settlement, each with passionate advocates:

- The *Pre-Clovis* hypothesis holds that the Americas were colonized by *Homo sapiens* some time during the Wisconsin glaciation, perhaps as early as 40,000 years ago or even earlier.
- The *Clovis* hypothesis argues that the first Americans crossed into the New World at the very end of the Wisconsin glaciation, perhaps as recently as about 13,000 B.C., and penetrated south of the Upper Pleistocene ice sheets as they retreated.

TABLE 6.1

• • •

	CLIMATE CHANGE	GENERAL CULTURAL DEVELOPMENTS IN THE AMERICAS		
Age B.C./A.D.	*Cooler Warmer*			*Developments elsewhere*
A.D. 1500	← →	Pueblo Cultures in Southwest	European contact	European Age of Discovery
A.D. 1000		Moundbuilder Cultures in East and Southwest	Maize and Bean cultivation in eastern North America and Midwest	
A.D. I		Woodland Cultures (Chapter 13)		Roman Empire
				Classical Greece
1,000 B.C.				
2,000 B.C.			Maize cultivation in Southwest	Shang Civilization in China
3,000 B.C.			Cultivation of native plants in eastern North America and Midwest	Sumerian and Ancient Egyptian Civilizations
4,000 B.C.		ARCHAIC CULTURES		
5,000 B.C.			Maize cultivation in Mexico (Chapter 13)	Rise of cities in Near East
6,000 B.C.				
7,000 B.C.				
8,000 B.C.		PALEO-INDIAN CULTURES THROUGHOUT THE AMERICAS		Farming in Near East
9,000 B.C.		Clovis	← Megafaunal extinctions	
10,000 B.C.		*Mesa* *Broken Mammoth*		
11,000 B.C.				
12,000 B.C.				
13,000 B.C.		*Monte Verde* *Meadowcroft*		Magdalenian Culture in Western Europe
14,000 B.C.		? First settlement		
15,000 B.C.				

Intense controversy surrounds not only the specific archaeological evidence for the first settlement but also the criteria that can be used to establish it. However, most archaeologists agree that securely radiocarbon dated, well-stratified cultural remains of undoubted human manufacture are the only acceptable evidence. So far, data whose quality is universally acceptable have eluded even persistent search, leaving one of the major mysteries of world prehistory still unsolved.

ICE SHEETS AND LAND BRIDGES

● ● ●

As we have seen in Chapter 4, human settlement in Siberia and far northeast Asia is documented as early as 16,000 B.C., perhaps somewhat earlier. These D'uktai people remain somewhat of an enigma, for dating Siberian sites situated in subarctic landscapes requires sophisticated geological and geomorphological fieldwork. However, judging from western and central Europe, human settlement of extreme Arctic environments expanded about 16,000 B.C., a date that coincides well with the apparent first appearance of hunter-gatherer culture in the far northeast. If we accept the notion that *Homo sapiens* was living near the shores of the Bering Strait after about 16,000 B.C., how did people cross into Alaska, only a short distance away?

At the time we are considering, world sea levels were as much as 330 feet (100 m) lower than today—so low that a land bridge stood where the Bering Strait now separates Asia and Alaska. (Sea levels drop when quantities of ocean water are frozen into continental ice sheets.) The strait formed part of a now almost submerged landmass known to geologists as Beringia. Only parts of west and east Beringia are dry land today—in Siberia and Alaska (Figure 6.2).

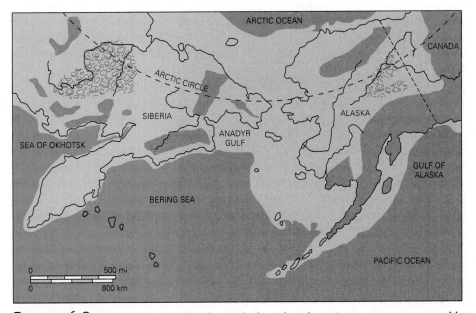

FIGURE 6.2 The Bering Land Bridge at the last glacial maximum, as reconstructed by the latest research.

Bering Land Bridge

Since modern *Homo sapiens* evolved, the Bering Land Bridge has always connected Siberia to America, a land connection of varying width. The low-lying land bridge was a continuation of the Siberian steppe-tundra, a landscape that extended like a peninsula from Asia eastward to the vast Wisconsin ice sheets that covered North America. We know from deep-sea cores that Beringia was a dry plain, with brief, warm summers; long, extremely cold winters; and continual winds. At first glance, the land bridge would seem like a most inhospitable place for human settlement, especially at the height of a glaciation. Its plains gave way to some marshy areas near rivers, which provided ample summer fodder for large grass-eating mammals like the mammoth, as well as for wild horses, musk-oxen, and other Arctic species. Judging from modern Arctic environments, the density of game may never have been high. This was no land teeming in milk and honey but a very savage climate indeed. Nevertheless, it may have been capable of supporting a human population of between 15 and 25 people per 386 square miles (1000 sq. km), a figure roughly equivalent to that for modern Eskimos living off the land and sea alone.

Could the first Americans have made their way across the strait by boat? We know that people colonized the remote landmass of Australia before 35,000 B.C. and that they could only have done so by crossing over some 55 miles (88.5 km) of open water even at the height of the glaciation, when sea levels were much lower than today. These were more benign tropical waters, where such hazards as floating ice, strong arctic winds, and the ever-present danger of hypothermia were unknown. The risks in the far north were much greater. Even in summer, fogs and rough seas make the strait a chancy place, and to cross winter pack ice is to invite disaster.

Unfortunately, we have no means of knowing whether early northeast Asians had skin boats, even kayaks, for their long-abandoned settlements lie under modern sea levels. We do know that the predominant dietary source for Stone Age hunters over an enormous area of Europe and Asia was big-game and land mammals of all sizes, with apparently much less concentration on seasonal vegetable foods, fish, and marine mammals. To venture onto the Bering Land Bridge required no new skills, merely the big-game hunting expertise that characterized generations of Ice Age hunters. That the first crossing into Alaska was by land rather than by boat seems likely, simply on deductive grounds. It may have been only later that Arctic peoples adapted to postglacial coasts and crossed freely from Asia to Alaska, maintaining social and cultural ties on both sides of the Bering Strait.

FIRST SETTLEMENT—ALASKA

• • •

Finding human occupation in Alaska is, as Richard Morlan says (1983), rather "like looking for a needle in a haystack (and a frozen one at that)." The first Alaskans are still a very shadowy entity, known only from a few stratified locations, but appear to date to just after 10,000 B.C., or perhaps slightly earlier, if the radiocarbon dates from Bluefish Caves in the Yukon date actual human occupation (Adovasio, 1993).

Mesa
9600 B.C.

The Mesa sites, transitory hunting camps in the southern foothills of the Brooks Range in northern Alaska, overlook a wide vista of treeless terrain. Archaeologist Michael Kunz has excavated a series of hearths, obtaining AMS radiocarbon dates between 7850 and 9600 B.C., making the Mesa camps among the oldest in Alaska. Kunz believes that only a single hunting group occupied the Mesa sites at intervals over about 2000 years. The visitors made lanceolate projectile points with carefully ground lower edges, presumably for mounting in a wooden shaft, just as many

ancient hunters did on the North American Plains far to the south. Then there is the
Broken Mammoth encampment in the Tanana Valley southeast of Fairbanks, on a
well-drained ridge overlooking marshy lowlands, where big game would have
grazed in summer. The earliest Broken Mammoth occupation dates to about 9700
B.C., exactly the same as that for the earliest Mesa hearth. These people hunted not
only bison and elk but also migratory geese and swans, which may have attracted
hunters to the area in spring. A second, later occupation zone dates to between 7350
and 9350 B.C.

Broken Mammoth
9700 B.C.

Dry Creek in the northern foothills of the Alaska Range is another 11,000-year-
old occupation site, containing cobbles, flakes, and thin bifacial knives. A later
occupation, dated to about 8700 B.C., does contain microblades and other small
artifacts.

Dry Creek
9100 B.C.

These three sites offer our only glimpse of the first Alaskans. Alaskan archaeologists have grappled with the problem of classifying these little-known cultures,
although they all agree that they may form part of a highly varied cultural tradition
that reflects adaptations to a complex mosaic of local environments at the end of the
Ice Age. The same hunting and foraging cultures may have been the ancestors of the
first human societies to flourish south of the ice sheets that mantled northern North
America during the Wisconsin glaciation.

Many experts still favor a late settlement of the Americas, one that coincided
with the general global warming between 12,000 and 10,000 B.C. that submerged
the Bering Land Bridge. As far as can be established, the predominant lifeway in
northern latitudes of Eurasia and northeast Asia during the last glacial climax was
based on big-game hunting (Gamble, 1986b). That this lifeway was pursued in
Beringia seems unquestionable. Once the ice sheets retreated, however, many Ice
Age big-game species became extinct, and big-game hunting bands had to adapt to a
far more diverse tundra and birch forest environment. This environmental diversity
is reflected in considerable toolkit variation within early Alaskan settlements.

A possible scenario for first settlement, then, has tiny groups of big-game
hunters crossing into Alaska either during the very late Ice Age or as climatic conditions improved dramatically. Some of these people, perhaps numbering only in the
dozens, were the first to move southward into the temperate latitudes that lay
beyond the great ice sheets covering much of Canada and the Rocky Mountains.

There remains one fundamental question: Why did humans settle in the New
World at all? Was it an inner urge that caused the first Americans to endure the
harsh climate of the Bering Land Bridge? Or was there some more prosaic reason?

Two great population dispersals occurred during prehistory, the first when
Homo erectus radiated from the tropics about a million years ago. The second took
place after the evolution of *Homo sapiens sapiens,* when the first human populations crossed from the Old World into the New and Australia was inhabited for the
first time. The exact dates of this later dispersal are still highly uncertain, but it
seems to have occurred soon after modern people appeared. The explanation for
these sudden radiations seems to lie mostly in the fact that humans tended to behave
as other animals did. Rather than responding to an inborn restlessness, the first
Americans were probably behaving in the same way as other animal predators. They
spent their days tracking the game herds, and perhaps sea mammls, that formed an
important part of their subsistence, and when Siberian game herds moved onto the
Bering Land Bridge during the coldest millennia of the last glaciation, their human
predators followed. The higher ground to the east—Alaska—formed part of the
same hunting grounds.

BIOLOGICAL EVIDENCE FOR THE FIRST AMERICANS

● ● ●

For more than a century, anthropologists have pointed to biological similarities between Siberians and North American Indians. Christy Turner (1984) of Arizona State University has studied the changing physical characteristics of Native American teeth, especially their crowns and roots, and compared them with those of Old World populations. These dental features are more stable than most evolutionary traits, with a high genetic component that minimizes the effects of environmental differences, sexual dimorphism, and age variations. After examining more than 4000 individuals, ancient and modern, Turner has developed a series of hypotheses about the first settlement of the Americas based on dental morphology (Figure 6.3).

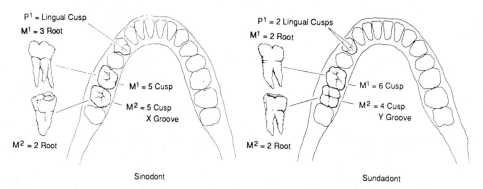

FIGURE 6.3   Dental morphology and the first Americans. Some of Christy Turner's theories about the peopling of America are based on differences between the teeth of the so-called Sinodonts (northern Asians and all Native Americans) and Sundadonts (eastern Asians). Sinodonts display, among other features, strong incisor shoveling (scooping out on one or both surfaces of the tooth), single-rooted upper first premolars, and triple-rooted lower first molars.

Turner points out that prehistoric Americans display many fewer variations in their dental morphology than do eastern Asians. He calls these characteristics "Sinodonty," a pattern of dental features that includes incisor shoveling, single-rooted upper first premolars, triple-rooted lower first molars, and other attributes. Sinodonty occurs only in northern Asia and the Americas. Turner's earliest evidence for Sinodonty comes from northern China in about 18,000 B.C., but he believes that it emerged much earlier, perhaps as early as 40,000 years ago. European Upper Paleolithic skeletons do not display Sinodonty. Turner believes that the Sinodont northern Chinese may have evolved from a primeval Southeast Asian *Homo sapiens* population, whom they resemble more closely than the northeast Asians and American Indians, who evolved from them.

Sinodonty

Using statistics to study evolutionary divergence, Turner has estimated the approximate dates at which Sinodont populations split off from ancestral Chinese groups. He hypothesizes that the first settlement of the Americas resulted from a population movement through east Siberia and across the now-submerged continental shelf around 12,000 B.C. Two subsequent population movements brought the present-day Athabaskan and Eskimo-Aleut populations into the Americas a few thousand years later. Neither of these groups penetrated deep into the continent.

If Turner is correct, there is some biological support for a late settlement date. His researches have been supported by studies of genetic marker distributions in modern American Indian populations. The research team found that more than 14,000 Central and South American Indians in their samples share the same Gm allotypes (variants in a protein found in the blood). Since interbreeding populations share sets of such variants, the genetic experts believe there was a single primeval migration of hunter-gatherers into the Americas, who evolved later by cultural differentiation (for discussion, see Fagan, 1987).

Dental morphology and genetic research hint strongly at a relatively late date for first settlement. So does the controversial linguistic work of Joseph Greenberg (1987). He has compiled a massive database on the vocabulary and grammar of American Indian languages, which leads him to believe that there were three basic Indian linguistic groups: Amerind, Aleut-Eskimo, and Na-Dene (Athabaskan). Most American Indian languages are in the Amerind group, whose speakers Greenberg believes arrived before 9000 B.C. It is only fair to point out, however, that some linguists consider Greenberg's classifications too broad.

THE CASE FOR EARLIER SETTLEMENT

● ● ●

Exactly the same problem—lack of sites—arises when we look for archaeological evidence of earlier settlement south of the great ice sheets. Decades of ardent search have produced only a handful of sites that *may* date to earlier than 13,000 B.C. (Dillehay and Meltzer, 1991; Fagan, 1987; Lynch, 1989).

The lack of evidence is depressing, to the point that many claims are based on emotionalism and specious argument from minimal data. There are numerous claims for early North American settlement based on poorly dated scatters of projectile heads and flaked tools from deep caves and open sites in many parts of the United States. Many of these have been disproved by later investigation, through improved dating methods or more sophisticated artifact analysis techniques.

ICE-FREE CORRIDORS AND SEA COASTS

• • •

If tiny bands of hunter-gatherers penetrated the fastnesses of Beringia during the late Wisconsin glaciation, how, then, did they reach the heart of the Americas? Again, the first settlement is fraught with controversies about hypothetical routes and the boundaries of ice sheets.

North America was very different during the Wisconsin glaciation. We know from deep-sea core studies that the Wisconsin began some 117,000 years ago, with an inexorable cooling of world temperatures. Great ice sheets covered much of northern North America during the early Wisconsin, until about 60,000 years ago. Between 60,000 and about 25,000 years ago, there was a prolonged period of glacial retreat and sea levels rose. With the possible exception of a much reduced ice sheet around Hudson Bay, most of North America was freed of glacial barriers. For these 35,000 years, any (hypothetical) human settlers would have encountered environments not very different from modern tundra and boreal forest.

Late Wisconsin 23,000 B.C. The Late Wisconsin, the earliest time period when human settlement seems possible, began about 23,000 B.C. The so-called Laurentide glaciers, centered on Labrador and the Keewatin areas of Canada, expanded south, west, and east, eventually fusing into a huge frozen wilderness. At its maximum in about 16,000 B.C., the Laurentide ice sheet extended from the Atlantic seaboard across the Great Lakes region into southeast Alberta. The mountain ranges of southern Alaska and British Columbia were heavily glaciated at the time, forming the Cordilleran glacier complex in the west. The Cordilleran extended about 30 miles (48 km) south of Seattle as recently as 12,500 B.C., apparently reaching its maximum extent after the Laurentide.

Clearly, these great Late Wisconsin ice barriers would have inhibited travel between Beringia and the southern latitudes of the New World. Did they stop human settlement altogether? In the 1950s, Canadian geologists reported that the Cordilleran ice flowed down the eastern flanks of the Rockies but apparently did not join the Laurentide ice sheet. The idea of an "ice-free corridor" soon took hold of archaeologists' imaginations. "Doubtless it was a formidable place," wrote Thomas Canby (1979) of the National Geographic Society, "an ice-walled valley of frigid winds, fierce snows, and clinging fogs . . . yet grazing animals would have entered, and behind them would have come a rivulet of human hunters." The picture is a compelling one—but was it reality?

The ice-free corridor has been mapped more thoroughly in recent years, to the point that we can be sure it was no superhighway for Stone Age hunters. In some places the ice sheets did merge. In others, especially in the far north and south, there was a corridor, but it twisted and turned through the roughest of terrain, country restricted by chill meltwater lakes, often with biologically sterile shores. At best the Late Wisconsin ice-free corridor was a barren and impoverished landscape. Even if it was passable, there is a good chance that there was no incentive to cross it between about 23,000 and 13,000 B.C., for much better food resources lay in Beringia. In any case, we lack evidence that human settlers had made Beringia their homeland earlier than 13,000 B.C.

If an interior route was used, chances are that it was traversed during a time of glacial retreat, sometime after 13,000 B.C., when the Laurentide glaciers shrank rapidly. If the ice-free corridor was a barrier to human settlement, could people have passed down ice-free coastal areas along the Alaskan and British Columbian coasts into temperate regions? Perhaps Late Wisconsin northwest coasts were relatively warmer and more productive than other areas, to the extent that they might have sustained human life. Unfortunately, however, we do not know whether these areas were accessible from mainland Beringia or, indeed, whether there were Late Wisconsin populations on the land bridge at all. If such people did exist, their sites are buried deep beneath modern sea levels. The earliest documented settlement occurs on the Queen Charlotte Islands of British Columbia, between 10,000 and 8000 B.C. Many archaeologists believe that much earlier coastal settlement is unlikely, on the (perhaps dangerous) assumption that everything we know about the earliest settlers suggests they were terrestrial hunters and gatherers, with a lifeway adapted in part to the pursuit of large Ice Age mammals.

Queen Charlotte Islands
10,000 to 8000 B.C.

ARCHAEOLOGICAL EVIDENCE FOR LATE WISCONSIN SETTLEMENT

● ● ●

A number of sites throughout the Americas have been claimed as evidence for Late Wisconsin settlement, mainly caves and rock shelters (Adovasio, 1993; Fagan, 1987). The most important are worth individual review.

Meadowcroft Rock Shelter

Meadowcroft Rock Shelter lies 30 miles (48.2 km) southwest of Pittsburgh, Pennsylvania, a sheltered location close to permanent water supplies. James Adovasio excavated and dated the 11 levels of the shelter with more than 70 radiocarbon dates. They show that it was occupied from about A.D. 1300 back to at least 10,000 and perhaps to 14,000 B.C. (Adovasio et al., 1981, 1990; Adovasio, 1993).

Meadowcroft
10,000 B.C. (perhaps as early as 17,000 B.C.) to A.D. 1300

Adovasio's meticulous excavations establish human occupation at 10,000 B.C. beyond any doubt. Controversy swirls over the lowest levels of the rock shelter, which were claimed to date to as early as 17,600 B.C. The earliest date of human occupation at Meadowcroft has now been estimated as being between 2000 and 3000 years before 9500 B.C., that is, perhaps as early as 12,500 B.C. (Adovasio et al., 1990).

No other claims of very early settlement in North America have stood meticulous scientific scrutiny.

Mesoamerica and Latin America

The evidence for Late Wisconsin human occupation is also sparse south of the Rio Grande. Supporters of earlier settlement reserve their greatest enthusiasm for two sites in Latin America.

Boqueirão of Pedro Furada

The Boqueirão of Pedro Furada rock shelter in northeast Brazil contains deep, sandy layers with pebbles and gravel beds (Guidon and Delibrias, 1986). Niede Guidon excavated 9.8 feet (3 m) into the cave and unearthed "traces of human occupation [that] succeed one another throughout the stratigraphic sequence." She believes the shelter was occupied again and again by a small human band, the earliest of whom

Boqueirão of Pedro Furada
?28,000 B.C.

left large circular hearths as well as stone pebble tools, mainly "pieces with blunt points obtained by . . . convergent flakings," along with a variety of other tools. Guidon claims occupation as early as 45,000 B.C., with continuing occupation between 28,000 and 10,000 B.C. She believes she has found a piece of rock with two painted lines—the first American rock art—in a hearth dated to 15,000 ± 400 B.C.

The Pedro Furada deposits are claimed to contain the remains of camps alongside a stream, and the layers may well be part of a streambed themselves. Are the "hearths" actually of human origin? Were the proposed artifacts, which look unconvincing to the dispassionate eye, actually humanly manufactured? Have chemical analyses of the red pigment from the 17,000-year-old "painting" been completed? Until definitive answers to these questions are forthcoming, Guidon's claims lack scientific authority, and the site must remain doubtful.

Monte Verde

**Monte Verde
11,000 to 10,500 B.C.**

Located in a small river valley in southern Chile, Monte Verde is a streamside settlement covered by a peat bog, so that not only stone and bone but also wooden artifacts survive. The site has been excavated very thoroughly and radiocarbon dated to between 11,000 and 10,500 B.C. (Dillehay, 1984). Thus far, only a portion of the site has been excavated, revealing two parallel rows of what are said to be rectangular houses, joined by connecting walls (Figure 6.4) (Dillehay, 1989). The skin-covered houses were 9 to 13 feet (3 to 4 m) square, with log and crude plank foundations and a wooden framework. Clay-lined hearths, wooden mortars, and large quantities of vegetable foods were found in the houses. A short distance away lay a wishbone-shaped structure associated with chewed bolo plant leaves (used today to make a form of medicinal tea), mastodon bones, and other work debris. This may have been a work area. The Monte Verde people exploited a very wide range of vegetable foods, including wild potatoes; they also hunted small game and

FIGURE 6.4   Excavations at Monte Verde, Chile.

perhaps mammals such as extinct camels and mastodons (it is possible that they scavenged such meat, however). Monte Verde was in a forest, with abundant vegetable foods year-round. The site was almost certainly a long-term campsite. What is fascinating is that 90 percent of the stone artifacts are crude river cobbles. It is clear that wood was the most important raw material. It was certainly used for spears and digging sticks and for hafting stone scrapers, three of which have survived in their wooden handles. Sites yielding simple flaked stone artifacts like those from Monte Verde have been found elsewhere in South America, as far south as Patagonia, but this is the first place that anyone has been able to make more complete discoveries.

The Monte Verde site shows just how scanty the archaeological record of the first Americans is and just how little we are likely to find out about them until more waterlogged sites come to light.

After more than a century of searching, the earliest archaeological sites in the Americas date to around 12,500 to 11,000 B.C., and even these occupations are poorly documented. As the years go on and the intensity of archaeological research throughout the New World picks up, the chances of finding indisputable evidence for Late Wisconsin or even earlier human settlement seem ever more remote. Add the realities of full glacial environments in the far north, the evidence from genetics and dental morphology, and the distribution of archaeological sites in northeast Asia as we know it, and a fairly compelling case can be made for late settlement. Under this scenario, the first Americans crossed into east Beringia (Alaska) from the Bering Land Bridge, perhaps at the very end of the last glaciation. Then, as the ice sheets retreated after 12,000 B.C., a mere handful of people hunted their way southward into the heart of a virgin continent. In the millennia that followed, human predators underwent a population explosion in the new lands, adapting to a great diversity of local environments everywhere between the ice sheets and Tierra del Fuego.

THE PALEO-INDIANS

• • •

About 9200 B.C., the highly distinctive Clovis culture appeared on the Great Plains of North America and much farther afield. These *Paleo-Indian* people are the first well-documented inhabitants of the New World, but many questions still remain about their ancestry and lifeway. What is certain, however, is that the Clovis culture was relatively short-lived. Judging from dated sites in the west, most sites were occupied during the three centuries after 9200 B.C. We now move onto solid prehistoric ground, for the archaeological record suddenly mushrooms from nothing to a well-documented scatter of locations from coast to coast in North America, with well-established Paleo-Indian occupation in Mesoamerica and Latin America as well.

Clovis

Although Paleo-Indian occupation is known from both eastern and western North America, the Clovis culture is best known from the Great Plains. At the end of the Wisconsin glaciation, the areas in the rain shadow of the western mountains of North America were dominated throughout the year by the dry mid-Pacific air mass. Most rain fell, and still falls, in spring and early summer, supporting short

Clovis
9200 to 8900 B.C.

grasses that keep much of their biomass beneath the soil. This structure helps retain moisture in the roots, providing mammoths, bison, and other ruminants with high-quality nutrients in the dry fall and into the winter. These grasslands expanded at the end of the Wisconsin and were colonized by herds of ruminants who were selective feeders. They were also the home of scattered bands of Clovis people. Within a few centuries, tiny hunter-gatherer bands had spread to both North American coasts and as far south as Guadalajara, Mexico, adapting to different environments they encountered.

The western plains of North America offer a highly diverse range of environments with a variety of protein-rich grasses and shrubs that once supported a browsing and grazing mammalian fauna, which in turn provided subsistence for a small number of hunter-gatherers (Frison, 1992). However, life was not easy for the bands, as they had to respond to different distributions of animals and plants each year, conditions that depended on rainfall, snowfall, runoff from the mountain peaks, and so on. The realities of the climate meant that the people had to collect dried meat and vegetable foods in the summer months and store them against the bitter winter. Each family group probably moved frequently, tending to visit the same campsites year after year, taking all their belongings with them. Archaeologically, they left very little behind, so the evidence for prehistoric occupation of the plains normally is limited to remains of large bison kills and scatters of broken flakes and projectile points.

The Clovis culture is known mainly from kill sites in the West. At Murray Springs, Arizona, for example, the people killed mammoth and bison, butchering them at separate locations, with a campsite nearby. Eleven bison died at Murray Springs, yielding enough meat to support up to 50 to 100 people, perhaps many fewer. Distinctive Clovis projectile points and other tools were found among the bones. At Naco, Arizona, no fewer than 8 points lay in one mammoth carcass. Perhaps between 4 and 8 hunters, a fifth of a band of about 20 to 40 people, killed the great beast. The hunters partially dismembered their quarry, sometimes making piles of the disarticulated bones. The Clovis people who camped in Blackwater Draw, New Mexico, a natural arroyo trap, could drive large animals into swampy ground. There they took mammoth, bison, horse, camel, and deer. Lehner, also in Arizona, is another well-known waterside site, where Clovis hunters may have killed 13 mammoth in one hunt.

Everyone agrees that the Clovis people hunted both big game and smaller animals, besides foraging for wild vegetable foods during spring, summer, and fall. Big-game hunting was probably the most important part of their subsistence. Large animals like the mammoth and bison could provide meat for weeks on end, as well as valuable byproducts for household possessions, tents, and even clothing. George Frison (1992) and others believe that Clovis hunters tended to concentrate on solitary mammoths, for their spear technology could not stop an elephant in its tracks, just wound it severely. They would stalk herds, concentrating on straying animals, sometimes perhaps driving them into swamps (for extended discussion, see Haynes, 1982). The hunters would wound an animal, then take their time to kill it with thrusting spears.

Clovis people, and other Paleo-Indian groups, used a portable toolkit that included bone, stone, and wood artifacts. Preservation conditions allow us to know most about their stone technology, often based on precious, fine-grained rock from widely separated outcrops. The hunters traveled great distances for their stone, trading it in core form for hundreds of miles. These cores were like a savings account, carried around so that flakes could be used to make finely pressure-flaked projectile points. The finished heads were mounted in wood or bone foreshafts set on the end of spear shafts (Figure 6.5). Once the spear penetrated an animal, the foreshaft would break off. The hunter could then rearm the spear with a new foreshaft in a few moments. Damaged points were resharpened and used again; some exceptionally large ones may even have been ceremonial artifacts.

Besides projectile points, the Clovis toolkit included butchering tools, scrapers, and dozens of untrimmed stone blades and flakes used as convenient knives. The people used bone, and presumably wood, for foreshafts, spears, and other artifacts. The origins of this technology are unknown but must lie in Upper Paleolithic big-game hunting traditions in the Old World. The fluted projectile point itself may have been an indigenous development in temperate North America (Haynes, 1982). Under this argument, big game and mammoths were to the Upper Paleolithic hunter what the reindeer is to the Laplander or the caribou to the inland Inuit. These authorities also believe that *general* similarities exist between Clovis stone and bone tools and those from classic mammoth-hunting sites in east Europe and the Ukraine. Thus, they speculate that the first settlement of North America was part of a primeval big-game hunting tradition that spread from northeast Asia into the New World. The descendants of these people wandered farther south, pursuing their favorite game, the mammoth. Eventually they reached the Canadian prairie, where

FIGURE 6.5   Clovis points found with a mammoth skeleton at Naco, Arizona.

they encountered new mammoth species and a greater bounty of other big game. Within a few centuries, Clovis people and their relatives were scattered all over the Americas.

This scenario for first settlement is almost as inadequately documented as those espousing earlier dates. However, the cumulative sum of the limited data tends to support rather than undermine it (Dillehay and Meltzer, 1991).

BIG-GAME EXTINCTIONS

• • •

The Clovis people flourished for about 300 years, and then, about 8900 B.C., they vanished abruptly, to be replaced by a multitude of hunting and gathering cultures. This sudden disappearance coincides with one of the great mysteries of modern science—the catastrophic extinction of Ice Age big-game animals in the Americas. Many large animals became extinct throughout the world at this time but nowhere as drastically as in the Americas. Three-quarters of the large mammalian genera there vanished abruptly at the end of the Pleistocene (Martin and Klein, 1984; Grayson, 1991).

Overkill

Speculations about this extinction have been long and lively. One theory that has long held on is that the large mammals were killed off by the Paleo-Indian bands' intensive hunting, as they preyed on large herds of animals that had formerly had relatively few predators to control their populations. This overkill hypothesis is weakened by the fact that many Pleistocene animals disappeared before the heyday of the Paleo-Indians. Besides, the Indians existed in very small numbers, and they had other subsistence activities as well. Surely the animals would have adapted to changed conditions and new dangers. Instead, the extinctions accelerated after the hunters had been around for a while; the modern bison, for example, never adapted to mounted hunters.

Climate change

Change in climate gives a second hypothesis for the cause of extinction. Changing environments, spreading aridity, and shrinking habitats for big game may have reduced the mammalian population drastically. Strong objections face this hypothesis too. The very animals that became extinct had already survived enormous fluctuations in Pleistocene climate without harm. If they had once migrated into more hospitable habitats, they could have done so again. Furthermore, the animals that became extinct were not just the browsers; they were selected from all types of habitat. This too-simple hypothesis is supported by the notion that desiccation leads to mass starvation in game populations, an idea refuted by ecological research in Africa. What actually occurs is that the smaller species and those with lower growth rates adapt to the less favorable conditions, leaving the population changed but not defunct.

Seasonal contrasts

A third hypothesis cites the great variation in mean temperatures at the end of the Pleistocene as a primary cause of extinction. In both the New and Old Worlds, the more pronounced seasonal contrasts in temperature climates would have been harder on the young of species that are born in small litters, after long gestation periods, and at fixed times of the year. These traits are characteristic of larger mammals, precisely those that became extinct. The less equable climate at the end of the Pleistocene, then, would have been a major cause of late Pleistocene extinctions in North America.

All three hypotheses contain some truth. Complex variables must have affected the steps that led to extinction, with intricate feedback among the effects of intensive big-game hunting, changing ecology, and the intolerance of some mammalian species to seasonal contrasts in weather. It may be that the hunters, being persistent predators, were the final variable, causing more drastic mammalian extinctions than might otherwise have occurred.

LATER HUNTERS AND GATHERERS

● ● ●

As the world climate warmed up rapidly at the end of the last glaciation, New World environments changed drastically. The great ice sheets of the north shrank, mountain snow lines and sea levels rose, and forest vegetation established itself in hitherto glaciated regions. If one word can be used to describe these momentous changes, it is *diversity*, a great diversity of local environments—lush river flood-plains, great deserts, grassy plains, miles upon miles of boreal and deciduous wood-land. The late Paleo-Indians and their successors adapted to this great diversity with brilliant success and ingenuity. In general, the West and Southwest United States became drier, but the East Coast and much of the Midwest grew densely forested. The large Pleistocene mammals became extinct, but the bison remained a major source of food. In the Southeast, the more favorable climate brought drier condi-tions, which meant less standing water, markedly seasonal rainfalls, and specializa-tion among humans for fishing or intensive gathering. Many areas had much economic diversity, as we see among the desert gatherer peoples of the Tehuacán Valley in Mexico. They flourished between 10,000 and 7000 B.C., at the same time hunter-gatherers in the Pacific Northwest were probably taking advantage of sea-sonal salmon runs in the fast-moving rivers.

North American climate and sea levels seem to have stabilized close to their modern configurations about 6000 B.C. Three thousand years later, human popula-tions started to grow more rapidly. Almost everywhere in temperate North America the number of archaeological sites mushroomed within a millennium. The stage was set for rapid cultural, economic, and social change in many areas, which was still cli-maxing as European explorers and colonists arrived in the New World.

In 6000 B.C., the human population of North America was still sparse, scattered in a myriad of isolated hunter-gatherer bands. Judging from sites in many areas, people spent most of the year living in small family groups, exploiting large hunting territories. They might have come together with their neighbors for a few weeks during the summer months at favored locations near rivers or nut groves. The bands would have held ceremonies, arranged marriages, and traded fine-grained rocks and other commodities. Then they would have gone their separate ways, following migrating game, trapping small animals, and foraging for wild vegetable foods.

At first there was plenty of vacant territory to go around, continues this hypo-thetical scenario. In time natural population growth and the low carrying capacity of the land combined to restrict mobility. Several long-term adaptive trends devel-oped.

First, the extinction of the Ice Age megafauna meant that hunters focused on smaller mammals, especially the white-tailed deer. Inevitably, people turned to alter-native food sources, including wild vegetable foods, birds, mollusks, and fish. Wild vegetable foods were a particularly favored dietary source, especially in areas like river valley bottoms and lakeshores, where they were seasonally abundant and diverse.

Second, there was a long-term trend toward less mobility, toward base camps that were occupied for many months of the year. These served as anchors for larger territories, which were exploited seasonally from outlying settlements. This settlement pattern was by no means universal, but it took hold in areas where there was an unusual diversity of food resources. Examples of base settlements are to be found in the desert West, in midwestern and southeastern river valleys, and in the Northeast.

Third, some areas witnessed a move toward sedentary settlement, occupation of the same settlement year-round or for most of the year. This type of settlement is different from a base camp used on a seasonal basis, even if the latter lasts for many months. It implies a permanent settlement within a highly restricted territory, a settlement lying within easy reach of sufficient game, vegetable, and aquatic resources to enable the occupants to stay through every season of the year. Sedentary settlement is hard to identify in the archaeological record, except through the presence of substantial dwellings or cemeteries. Such occupation was well established in some midwestern river valley bottoms by 2000 B.C. and perhaps in favored coastal areas, such as southern California and the Pacific Northwest, somewhat later.

These trends coincided with accelerating population growth in more favored areas after 2000 B.C.

Such was the diversity of North American environments in Holocene times that only a few relatively limited areas witnessed sedentary settlement and large-scale population growth. Perhaps it is no coincidence that it was in some of these areas, notably midwestern and southeastern river valleys and the Southwest, that people turned to the cultivation of domesticated plants.

Surviving Big-Game Hunters

In only one region—the arid grasslands from the frontiers of Alaska to the Gulf of Mexico—did big-game hunting survive. This was the "Great Bison Belt," which lay in the rain shadow of the western mountains. The short grass range of the plains was an ideal environment for the bison, one of the few Ice Age big-game species to adapt to Holocene conditions. The postglacial descendants of the Ice Age steppe bison have increased digestive efficiency to cope with the high-fiber, low-nutrient dead grass of winter. They can feed in deep snow and are less selective eaters than many of the Ice Age species that died out. By 8500 B.C., bison were the dominant species in all archaeological sites through the bison belt.

8500 B.C.

At first glance, the Great Plains appear homogeneous, even monotonous. Close examination reveals many subtle differences—stream courses and water holes where game congregated, places where longer grass and seasonal water favored larger bison herds. The late Paleo-Indians and their successors, who preyed on the herds right into historic times, could only survive by a careful, planned utilization of the plains' complex ecosystem (Frison, 1992).

8000 B.C.

After 8000 B.C., numerous variations of bison-hunting cultures appeared on the plains, all of them using portable toolkits that bear a strong resemblance to those of their Clovis ancestors. Stone-tipped projectile points with carefully thinned and ground bases made spear-throwers and spears effective weapons for bison hunting. At least seven major forms are known, with names like Eden, Folsom, Plainview, and Scottsbluff—to mention only a few (Frison, 1992; Haynes, 1982; Irwin and Wormington, 1970). Whether all these forms actually represent distinct cultural entities is a matter of controversy. The entire Paleo-Indian toolkit was highly portable and capable of being used for a wide variety of purposes, everything from woodworking to bison butchery.

Many plains sites are kill locations, strategic places where mass game drives could be organized. Such drives were far from daily events, perhaps taking place every couple of years or so. To pursue bison on foot means days of patient stalking and an intimate knowledge of the animals' habits. Perhaps several bands would cooperate in a game drive. They would encircle a few beasts or, more often, stampede a herd into a swamp or a narrow defile. In some cases, they would drive the frightened animals over a cliff or into dune areas. The archaeological evidence for such activities comes from a series of sites, among them the Agate Basin site in eastern Wyoming, where, judging from the age of the animals, the hunters apparently maneuvered 10 to 20 animals into an arroyo bottom in late February or early March (Frison, 1992). The hunters then drove them upstream until they reached a natural trap in the gully, where the confused bison could be killed with stone-tipped spears.

The Olsen-Chubbock site in Colorado is an example of a kill site, where approximately 200 bison of all ages were stampeded into a deep, narrow arroyo, probably during the summer or fall (Frison, 1992; Wheat, 1972). Because the skeletons of the prehistoric bison faced north, the excavators concluded that the wind was blowing from the south on the day of the hunt. The stampeding herd was driven into a gully and could not catch the scent of the people waiting for them at the arroyo. The hunters' artifacts were scattered around the carcasses of their quarry (Figure 6.6): scraping tools, stone knives, and flakes used for dismembering the bison.

Olsen-Chubbock
6000 B.C.

Smaller communal hunts were probably much more commonplace. John Speth's (1983) excavations at Garnsey, New Mexico, chronicle such a kill. About 400 years ago, a group of hunters visited a small gully where they knew bison would congregate in late March or early April. Instead of killing every animal on sight, they tended to concentrate on the males because, Speth believes, male bison are in better condition in the spring, when their bone marrow has a higher fat content. Fattier meat is an important source of energy and essential fatty acids and is difficult to come by after the lean winter months. So if Garnsey hunters killed a cow, they consumed only the choice, fatter parts.

Bison hunting was practiced on the plains right up until the advent of the horse and the repeating rifle, but Paleo-Indian peoples flourished throughout North America. Clovis-like projectile points are known from many locations in the East. Herds of caribou may have provided sustenance in northern sites around the Great Lakes and in the Northeast at locations such as Robert, Nova Scotia, where caribou hunters flourished (Meltzer, 1988). Paleo-Indian hunting and gathering economies may have varied a great deal from region to region, some bands specializing in big game, others in fishing or gathering, depending on the resources available in each territory. This variation is reflected in Paleo-Indian archaeological sites that can vary from kill locations to shell middens. That hunting was important in places where large game was abundant seems unquestionable, but this activity diminished rapidly in importance as the big game became extinct.

FIGURE 6.6   Olsen-Chubbock bone bed.

The Desert West

Economic emphasis shifted in the arid West and Southwest. As big game became scarce, many hunting bands relied more heavily on wild vegetable foods that required much more energy to collect and process than game meat. In the Great

Basin, smaller animals such as rabbits, squirrels, and deer became more common prey. At the same time, gathering of vegetable foods grew to dominate economic life, combined with some fishing and, in maritime areas, exploitation of shellfish. We are fortunate that arid climates in Utah, Nevada, and elsewhere have preserved many plant and vegetable foods eaten by these early hunter-gatherers. By 7000 B.C., a distinctive, desertlike form of Archaic culture had been developed over much of the western United States by small bands camping in caves, rock shelters, and temporary sites.

Excavations at later sites like Danger Cave in Utah and the Gypsum and Lovelock sites in Nevada reveal that the hunters were making nets, mats, and baskets, as well as rope (Figure 6.7) (D'Acevedo, 1986; Heizer and Berger, 1970; Jennings, 1957). Hogup Cave in Utah has yielded one of the world's most complete and longest archaeological culture sequences (Aikens, 1970). The site displays gradual adaptations at one settlement, changing it from a base camp to a short-stay camp that was associated with other base camps or with horticultural villages after people learned how to produce food. At all these sites the inhabitants used digging sticks to uproot edible tubers, and much of their toolkit consisted of grinding stones used in preparing vegetable foods. Most Great Basin peoples were obliged to be constantly on the move, searching for different vegetable foods as they came into season and camping near scanty water supplies. Only a few communities living near relatively permanent food sources or good fishing grounds could afford a more sedentary life.

The deposits at Gatecliff Rock Shelter near Austin, Nevada, are 40 feet (12.1 m) deep and span more than 8000 years of human occupation. The inhabitants lived by valleyside streams in the winter, then moved up to the shelter in the summer, gathering piñon nuts on the mountain slopes as well as hunting game, just as Shoshone Indians did in recent times (D. Thomas, 1973; Thomas and Bettinger, 1983).

Most western prehistoric societies continued to live by hunting and foraging right up to European contact. It was only in the most favored areas that people could stay in one place for months on end. One such location was Lovelock Cave in Nevada, where the base camp overlooked a lake rich in fish and waterfowl. The people hunted their prey with bows and arrows, using extremely lifelike reed duck decoys. Human feces show that over 90 percent of the Lovelock inhabitants' diet came from the lake area, including wetland grasses, such fish as chub, ducks, and mud hens (Heizer and Berger, 1970).

The southern California coast was another hospitable area, first exploited by small bands blending fishing with marine mammal hunting as early as 6000 B.C. The coastal population remained sparse except in favored areas, where much more elaborate societies evolved. For example, the historic Chumash people of the Santa Barbara Channel area congregated in large, more or less permanent villages ruled by local chiefs, who maintained trading contacts over extensive areas of the West (Moratto, 1985). Such sedentism was possible because of exceptional resource diversity. From November to March, the Chumash subsisted on dried meat and stored vegetable foods. They also collected shellfish and caught fish in the dense kelp beds close inshore. Come spring, they ranged far afield, collecting plants and tubers. Summer brought tuna and other warm-water fish to local waters. The people caught enormous quantities of fish from their canoes. Pine nuts and acorns were gathered in the fall and stored for the leaner months ahead. The Chumash hunted marine mammals and scavenged stranded whales whenever the opportunity arose. This maritime bounty resulted from upwelling that replenishes the surface layers of the Santa Barbara Channel with nutrients and zooplankton. At least 125 fish species

Desert tradition
7000 B.C. to modern times

Danger Cave
Gypsum Cave
Lovelock Cave

Hogup Cave

6000 B.C.

FIGURE 6.7 Artifacts from Danger Cave, Utah, preserved by the dry climate: (a and b) twined matting; (c) twined basketry; (d) coarse cloth; (e) coiled basketry; (f) hide moccasin; (g) wooden knife handle, 4.5 inches (7.4 cm) long; (h) dart shaft, 16 inches (41 cm) long; (i) arrow shaft with broken projectile point in place, 33 inches (84 cm) long; (j) bundle of gaming sticks, 11.5 inches (29 cm) long; (k) milling stone.

flourished in local waters, part of an incredibly diverse range of food resources that enabled not only relatively sedentary settlement but also higher population densities—as many as 15,000 people living near the shores of the channel and on the off-shore islands at European contact.

Eastern North America

Whereas the Great Plains are dominated by grasslands, eastern North America, the region from the Mississippi Valley eastward, is covered by deciduous woodlands and the Southeast by evergreen forest. Superficially, this could be considered a homogeneous natural environment with no sharp geographic barriers to interaction between different human groups, but in fact the area includes an almost bewildering array of microenvironments. As a result, it is almost impossible to generalize about cultural developments after first settlement in about 9000 B.C. (Stoltman and Barreis, 1983).

Paleo-Indian bands settled widely over the eastern woodlands from as far north as Nova Scotia to southern Florida (Meltzer, 1988) (Figure 6.8). They combined hunting with foraging, turning to the pursuit of the white-tailed deer and other smaller mammals as the Ice Age megafauna vanished. By 8000 B.C., a widespread shift to more generalized hunting and gathering was under way, as the peoples of the eastern woodlands exploited a broad variety of foods—forest resources, like gray squirrels and annual nut harvests, and pioneer seed-bearing grasses. It seems certain that small game, fish, mollusks, and vegetable foods assumed greater impor-

Archaic tradition **8500 to 1000 B.C. and modern times**

8000 B.C.

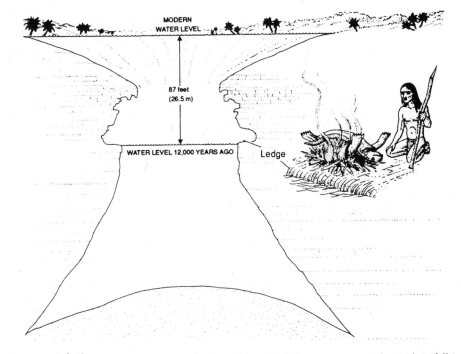

FIGURE 6.8   Little Salt Spring, Florida. About 12,000 years ago, a Paleo-Indian fell into a large sinkhole and swam to a dry ledge. There he found a turtle, thrust a wooden stake between shell and plastron, and cooked the animal in the shell. When the meat ran out, he starved to death.

Archaic

tance in the eastern diet after about 8500 B.C. Inhabitants were part of the broad-spectrum hunting and gathering tradition known as the *Archaic,* which lasted until about 1000 B.C. in many areas.

During the many millennia of the Archaic, there was a long-term trend toward increased efficiency and success in exploiting forest and river valley resources. The Archaic has been subdivided into early, middle, and late stages on the basis of stylistic changes in projectile points and the introduction of slate tools, copper artifacts, and other technological innovations (see Griffin, 1967, for details), but the basic patterns of Archaic life were established early on and are known to us from excavations and surveys in northeast Arkansas and the Little Tennessee River Valley (Chapman et al., 1982; B. Smith, 1986) (Figure 6.9).

Dalton
8500 to 7500 B.C.

The Dalton tradition flourished over a wide area of the Southeast and Midwest from about 8500 to 7500 B.C. Dan Morse and Phyllis Morse (1983) argue that in northeast Arkansas, Dalton band organization allowed a network of stable local family bands of 20 to 30 people who regularly used base camps centered on watershed territories. There they exploited easily accessible shallow-water fish, vegetable foods, seasonal nut harvests, and deer; the women married into neighboring bands in nearby river valleys, thereby maintaining trading links between each drainage, contacts that ensured ample supplies of fine-grained chert over large areas (see also Anderson and Hanson, 1988).

6000 B.C.

By about 6000 B.C., warmer and drier climates were developing in the East, culminating in the so-called Altithermal episode of 4500 to 4000 B.C. The major rivers of the Midwest and Southeast stabilized their courses, while prehistoric population

FIGURE 6.9   Artist's reconstruction of an Archaic camp on the Little Tennessee River, c. 8500 years ago.

densities were still low. The highest concentrations of population were in areas such as major river valley bottoms and lakeshores, which offered the greatest diversity of aquatic, game, and vegetable foods. In some favored areas, there was a slow trend toward living within more circumscribed territories and toward more sedentary settlement, made possible by an abundant constellation of seasonal foods.

The famous Koster site in the Illinois River Valley, with its 14 stratified occupation levels, provides an extraordinary chronicle of human exploitation of a midwestern river valley from about 7500 B.C. until A.D. 1200 (Struever and Holton, 1979). The first visitors to camp at Koster were Paleo-Indians, but about 6500 B.C., an early Archaic camp there covered about 0.75 acre (0.3 ha). An extended family group of about 25 people returned to the same location again and again, perhaps to exploit rich fall nut harvests in the area. Between 5600 and 5000 B.C., there were substantial settlements of rectangular, pole, brush, and clay houses that were occupied for most if not all the year, covering about 1.75 acres (0.7 ha). During spring and summer the inhabitants took thousands of fish, gathering freshwater mussels and hickory nuts in fall and migratory birds in spring. Perhaps the people moved to the nearby uplands to hunt deer. As long as this middle Archaic population remained stable, they could find most of their food resources within 3 miles (4.8 km) of their settlement. It was not until much later, after 2500 B.C., that the Koster people began exploiting a wider range of food resources.

A similar trend toward exploiting a relatively narrow range of wild foods is documented at other midwestern sites, among them the Modoc Rock Shelter near the Mississippi River (Brown and Phillips, 1983; M. L. Fowler, 1958). Modoc was occupied between about 8000 and 2000 B.C. As time went on, it became more and more of a base camp, where people lived for much of the year while they caught fish and exploited nut harvests. Both Koster and Modoc show that the middle Archaic adaptation was a conservative one, requiring at least a degree of careful scheduling to maximize the potential of nut harvests and to capitalize on the game that fed on the rich forest mast (undergrowth) each fall.

By about 2500 B.C., there had been a dramatic increase in the use of riverine resources over much of the Southeast and Midwest, perhaps coinciding with the onset of the Altithermal, when the stabilized river bottoms provided an abundance of oxbow lakes and swamps, where fish abounded and native grasses, shellfish, and other foods were to be found. Some of the river valleys lay on seasonal waterfowl migration routes, too, providing a bounty of food in spring and fall. This enhancement of aquatic habitats increased potential food supplies over long sections of river floodplains. In response, many groups adopted more sedentary lifeways, perhaps best described as a shift toward centrally based wandering, which involved a seasonally mobile lifeway and regular returning to the same base location for much of each year, especially during the summers (Figure 6.9).

Archaic populations in the East rose sharply after 4000 B.C., especially in favored areas. The Altithermal opened up vast areas of eastern Canada to caribou and human settlement. Rising sea levels and warming ocean temperatures allowed a steady northward expansion of fish and shellfish habitats. Flooded estuaries allowed more up-river fish runs in spring and fall. Nut-bearing forests spread farther north, into parts of the Great Lakes region, and river valley bottoms were exceptionally diverse and rich environments for Archaic hunter-gatherers (Yerkes, 1988).

In all probability, Archaic population growth was a response not only to environmental change but also to technological and subsistence advances, as well as new settlement patterns that took advantage of new riverine environments. The more

Koster
7500 B.C. to A.D. 1200

5600 to 5000 B.C.

Modoc
8000 to 2000 B.C.

2500 B.C.

sedentary living that accompanied the growth in many areas allowed people to store nuts and other winter foods on a much larger scale than if they were always on the move. This storage, in turn, created larger food surpluses, the ability to support higher population densities year-round, and opportunities for kin groups and individuals to play important roles in controlling labor and the redistribution of food and luxury goods. By the same token, people lived within more restricted territories, and there was far more local cultural variation.

There were also long-term changes in the ways people interacted with one another and their neighbors. The smaller territories inhabited by more people contained a diversity of food resources and raw materials, but there was always something lacking. Such items as obsidian for toolmaking had to be sought from elsewhere, by making a special journey or maintaining regular economic and social contacts with groups living nearer to the sources of what was needed. Over time, these trading connections assumed ever greater importance in the yearly round. They became a source not only of valued possessions and raw materials but also of social connections and prestige—a way of maintaining "diplomatic" relations with the outside world. These interactions also affected population densities, especially when demand for prestige items, such as copper objects or seashells, soared. More and more hands would be needed to increase the output of food and trade goods. The intensification of hunting and foraging to meet these demands would lead to population increases—and to the emergence of social ranks based on prestige and social and economic power within previously egalitarian societies.

Central Riverine Archaic 4000 B.C.

The late Archaic witnessed much greater regional variety in hunter-gatherer culture in the East (B. Smith, 1986; Snow, 1980). The so-called Central Riverine Archaic was the most elaborate and well developed of all eastern late Archaic traditions, for it was centered on midwestern and southeastern river valleys with a superabundance of aquatic, game, and vegetable foods. Between 3900 and 2800 B.C., a village covering 5 acres (2 ha) flourished at Koster, Illinois (Struever and Holton, 1979), housing perhaps 100 to 150 people in substantial homes. The inhabitants did not concentrate on faster-water fish like their predecessors. Instead they speared and netted thousands of shallow-water species such as bass and catfish. One Illinois fish biologist has estimated that the people could have taken between 300 and 600 pounds (136 and 272 kg) of fish flesh per acre from backwater lakes that covered hundreds of acres. The people still collected shellfish and exploited the fall hickory and acorn harvests, but they now collected many more seed plants, including marsh elder, a swamp-side grass, grinding the seeds with pestles and mortars. In spring and fall, they would also shoot and trap thousands of migrating waterfowl. Everything from this late Archaic settlement points to greater efficiency at food procurement, accompanied by exploitation of a broader spectrum of potential foods.

Koster 3900 to 2800 B.C.

Similar broad-spectrum exploitation is found at other midwestern sites, among them the celebrated Indian Knoll site in Kentucky (C. H. Webb, 1968), which has yielded more than 1000 burials. Judging from these graves, the people still lived in fairly egalitarian societies, even if a few individuals were buried with prized possessions, such as turtle-shell ornaments or copper ornaments from Lake Superior (for other middle and late Archaic sites, see Jeffries, 1987; Winters, 1967).

By 4000 B.C., the diverse hunter-gatherer populations of the East were living under very different social conditions than their remote ancestors; in territories with restricted boundaries, they cherished tenuous social and economic links that connected individual to individual, kin to kin, through valleys and entire drainages, over hundreds, even thousands of miles of North America. The long-distance exchange of materials associated with these networks first appeared about 4000 B.C. and escalated over the next 3000 years. Lake Superior native copper, hematite, Atlantic and Gulf Coast seashells, jasper from eastern Pennsylvania, chert and other fine-grained rocks—all these materials were exchanged between individuals just as obsidian was in the ancient Near East.

As studies of Lake Superior copper have shown, exotic artifacts and materials acquired greater prestige the farther they were traded (Figure 6.10). Within this context of regular social gatherings and exchanges, a greater degree of social differentiation based on reciprocity may have developed in late Archaic society. This may have been nothing more than a ranking between younger and older members of society or perhaps the emergence of one kin group as the "ranking" one. Judging from burial customs, both kin-based and individual social ranking took place within a context of increasingly elaborate ritual life. Perhaps some of the richly adorned burials from late Archaic cemeteries are those of individuals who achieved social rank not by force or through virtue of birth but because of their personal qualities as traders and diplomats, as people who helped break down the social, economic, and political isolation that came with restricted mobility (Yerkes, 1988).

More intensive exploitation of food resources (even some cultivation of native plants), greater sedentism, regular social interaction and long-distance exchange, increased ceremonialism—these were the culminating elements in late Archaic life that were to persist into the last few centuries before Christ, when new, much more elaborate burial customs appeared in the eastern woodlands (Chapter 13). In some areas of the Northeast and eastern Canada, much of the Archaic hunter-gatherer tradition survived until modern times, until people came into contact with European explorers.

FIGURE 6.10 Archaic copper artifacts from Lake Superior ore (approximately one-half actual size).

Specialized Hunter-Gatherers in Mesoamerica and Latin America

The hunter-gatherers of the central and southern portions of the New World enjoyed a wide variety of specialized adaptations after 7500 B.C. Sites of these specialized hunter-gatherer groups have been excavated from Mexico to Tierra del Fuego. One characteristic adaptation has been identified in the Andes, and another flourished on the uplands of eastern Brazil (Moseley, 1992; Rick, 1988). As in North America, intensified hunting and gathering concentrated the human population in favored localities such as lakeshores and seacoasts, where resources were unusually abundant.

Tehuacán

Sophisticated hunting and gathering strategies ensured food at all seasons. Kent Flannery (1968a) has shown, for instance, that the hunter-gatherers of the Tehuacán Valley in Mexico had a regular, almost scheduled, annual round of hunting and gathering activities that caused the population to gather in large camps during the plentiful season and scatter into small groups during the lean months. The people obtained a balanced diet by using different food procurement systems that varied in importance with the time of year.

Some of these specialized hunter-gatherers remained at the simple hunting and collecting level because of limitations in their environment and plentiful natural resources, making economic change unnecessary. However, in some areas of Mesoamerica and on the coast and highlands of Peru, hunter-gatherer bands began to experiment with the deliberate planting of vegetable foods, perhaps in attempts to expand the areas in which certain favored vegetable foods were found. These experiments became one of the vehicles of dynamic cultural change that resulted from the first development of agriculture in the New World (Chapter 13).

Fuegian Indians 4000 B.C. to modern times

The southernmost extremities of Latin America were inhabited until recent times by scattered bands of hunters and fisherfolk. The Ona, Yaghan, and Alacaluf peoples are vividly described by early missionaries who settled among them. They lived in small bands, using only the crudest shelters of skins or grass and driftwood, with nothing but skin for body covering during the height of the antarctic winter. Shellfish, some game, fruits, berries, and fish provided a simple diet, and for tools they had none of the more sophisticated weapons made by more northern hunters. Tierra del Fuego, however, was occupied remarkably early, and it is thought that the Fuegian tradition began as early as 4000 B.C., if not earlier. Many roots of these most southerly prehistoric humans lie in early hunting cultures that elsewhere were replaced thousands of years before by more advanced farming cultures.

ALEUTS AND INUIT

● ● ●

We started the story of the first Americans with Alaska, and we now end with a brief return to Arctic latitudes to trace the origins of the Aleuts and Inuit, whose remarkable hunter-gatherer cultures survived long beyond European contact into recent times. The origins of both the Aleut and the Inuit go back many thousands of years into prehistory, and their ultimate ancestry may lie both in Asian roots and in local cultural evolution. The differences between them are more cultural than physical and reflect varied adaptations to Arctic maritime environments. It is logical for us to end this chapter with the Arctic, for the Inuit were the first Native Americans to come into contact with Europeans, in Greenland and in the extreme continental Northeast (Dumond, 1987a,b).

By 9000 B.C., a small, but diverse population of tundra-dwelling hunter-gatherers flourished along the shores of the Bering Strait and throughout Alaska. Little is known of these "Paleoarctic" people, except for their diminutive stone microblades, which have some connections with contemporary cultures in Siberia. Nor is their relationship with earlier cultural traditions in Alaska understood. Paleoarctic people, culture, and language *may* be the ancestor of both Inuit and Aleut culture and language. It should be noted that both peoples are the most Asian of all indigenous Americans. By 7000 B.C., these two peoples had moved south as far as the Alaskan peninsula. Only a millennium later they had settled in the Aleutian Islands.

Paleoarctic tradition
9000 to 4000 B.C.

7000 B.C.

4000 B.C.

By 4000 B.C., there was more cultural diversity in the Arctic, as specialized adaptations developed on the coast and in the interior, and some American Indian groups moved northward into formerly glaciated regions in the interior. On the Pacific Coast and in the eastern Aleutians, the Aleutian tradition was among those that emerged.

Aleutian tradition
6700 B.C. to modern
times

The Aleuts have been in their island homeland twice as long as the Inuit have been in Greenland (Laughlin, Marsh, and Harper, 1979). Their ancestors entered the archipelago at a time when the sea level was lower than it is today. Their ancestry is perhaps in the Norton tradition (see later; Dumond, 1987a). The earliest occupation dates to approximately 6700 B.C. at Anangula, about a third of the way along the chain, at the terminus of the Bering Land Bridge. Anangula lies on a cliff 65.5 feet (20 m) above sea level and probably was occupied for at least 500 years by an estimated group of at least 100 (Aigner, 1970; Laughlin, 1980). The inhabitants lived by fishing, sea mammal hunting, and fowling, an ideal strategy for an isolated, stable marine environment. The nearby and later site of Chaluka carries the story of Aleutian occupation up to recent times. Radiocarbon dates suggest that the eastern and western ends of the Aleutian archipelago were occupied by approximately 1000 B.C., the people expanding outward from the Anangula area as the population density grew.

The origins of the Inuit (Eskimo) cultural tradition of modern times may lie in the Arctic Small-Tool tradition, a distinctive small-artifact technology that appeared in Alaska approximately 2300 B.C. The Arctic Small-Tool people may have had strong connections with Siberia and are thought to have been nomadic land mammal hunters who preyed on caribou and musk-ox. Some settled in Alaska; others wandered as far east as Greenland by 2000 B.C., becoming the first people to settle in the eastern Arctic. The eastern Small-Tool tradition eventually evolved into the long-lived Thule tradition, whose people were the first Native Americans to come into contact with Europeans (Maxwell, 1985; Schledermann, 1990).

Arctic Small-Tool
tradition
2300 to 1500 B.C.

The Arctic Small-Tool tradition began to disappear in Alaska in about 1500 B.C., to be replaced by cultures based on the intensive hunting of both sea mammals and land animals. This tradition, called the Norton tradition, in turn gave rise to the Thule tradition, which is thought to have originated among whale hunters in the Bering Strait. This tradition first emerged in the first millennium after Christ and developed into a highly distinctive sea mammal hunting culture with all the Inuit artifacts so well-known from popular publications—among them, the kayak, the umiak (open skin boat), and toggled harpoons, as well as fine ivory work (Figure 6.11). Many of the Inuit, especially those who hunted whales, lived by then in larger settlements. In approximately A.D. 900 the Thule people started to expand to the south and then to the east. Thule whale hunters appeared in the Arctic islands of the east in approximately A.D. 1000, where their open-water hunting techniques could be used with great effect. By the time the Thule reached northwest Greenland, the

Norton tradition (west)
1500 B.C. to A.D 500

Thule tradition
500 B.C. to modern times

FIGURE 6.11   Ornamental ivory object, perhaps a comb, from the Seward Peninsula in Alaska (Northern tradition and style). Length: 10.2 inches (26 cm).

Norsemen had been living in the southern parts of the island for some time (McGhee, 1984).

Inuit cultural traditions, like those of the Fuegians and other hunter-gatherer groups, continued to flourish after European contact, but within a few centuries, traditional lifeways were modified beyond recognition and exotic diseases decimated hunter-gatherer populations. Today, few of America's hunter-gatherers still practice their millennia-old lifeways; there are no longer the resources or the territory for them to do so.

CHAPTER SUMMARY

The first humans to settle the Americas crossed from northeast Asia, probably across the Bering Land Bridge, central Beringia. But the date of their arrival is highly controversial. Some scientists claim that archaeological evidence from South America proves that native Americans were flourishing in the Americas as early as 40,000 years ago. Most experts believe that first settlement occurred much later, perhaps at the very end of the Ice Age. There is evidence for human occupation in Alaska by 9700 B.C., while the Clovis people of North America flourished between 9200 and 8900 B.C.

After 9,000 B.C., many species of Ice Age animals large and small became extinct, so Native American hunter-gatherers diversified their economies to take full advantage of local resources. More complex hunter-gatherer societies arose in the Pacific Northwest and in Midwestern river valleys, as well as along the California coast, all cultures depending on abundant, seasonally predictable aquatic, animal, and plant resources. In other parts of the Americas, Archaic cultures based on hunting and foraging survived until the adoption of native plant cultivation or maize agriculture within the last 6000 years. In the arctic and extreme South America, hunter-gatherer societies flourished until historic times.

GUIDE TO FURTHER READING

The following references will guide you through the morass of books and articles on this complex subject:

Dillehay, Thomas, and Meltzer, David., eds. 1991. *The First Americans: Search and Research*. Boca Raton, FL: CRC Press.
> Excellent series of technical essays about the general problem of first settlement.

Fagan, Brian M. 1987. *The Great Journey*. New York: Thames and Hudson.
> A general, analytic discussion of the evidence for first settlement. For a popular audience.

———. 1995. *Ancient North America, 2nd ed.* New York: Thames and Hudson.
> A general summary of North American archaeology for beginning readers. Covers the entire spectrum from first settlement to historical archaeology.

Fiedel, Stuart J. 1992. *Prehistory of the Americas,* 2nd ed. Cambridge, Eng.: Cambridge University Press.
> A continent-wide survey of New World prehistory that focuses on general issues. Clearly written and a good introduction.

Hopkins, David M., et al., eds. 1982. *Paleoecology of Beringia*. New York: Academic Press.
> A fascinating and highly technical set of essays about the Bering Land Bridge that discusses everything from animal life to sea level changes.

Jennings, Jesse D. 1988. *The Prehistory of North America*. Mountain View, CA: Mayfield.
> A textbook for undergraduates, which summarizes basic culture history and artifact forms.

Moseley, Michael. 1992. *The Incas and their Ancestors*. London and New York: Thames and Hudson.
> The definitive general account of Andean archaeology for the general reader.

Phillips, J., and Brown, J., eds. 1983. *Archaic Hunter-Gatherers in the Midwest*. Orlando, FL: Academic Press.
> Essays on Archaic hunter-gatherers, some of which have broad application.

Smith, Bruce D. 1986. "The Archaeology of the Southeastern United States: From Dalton to de Soto, 10,500–500 B.P." *Advances in World Archaeology* 5: 1–92.
> A superb analytic synthesis of southeastern archaeology that has broad application elsewhere in the eastern woodlands. This is an excellent example of contemporary approaches to North American prehistory.

CHAPTER **AFRICANS AND AUSTRALIANS**

• • •

The wind blows strongly toward the open sea on a stormy day in 40,000 B.C., swishing through the dense mangrove swamps in sharp gusts. A man and a woman paddle their wooden raft across the shallow lagoon, poling their way to a shallow bank close offshore. They reach the shoal, drive wooden poles into the sea bed to hold the heavy raft against the wind. Oblivious to the wind, they set fishing lines where the bottom fish lie. A sudden squall descends on the raft, tearing it loose from the restraining poles. Frantically, the crew try and stop their craft over the shallows, but the wind carries them into deep water, ever farther from the low-lying coast. Ashore, their relatives watch helplessly as the raft vanishes over the horizon far downwind. They know that they will never see the man and woman again.

Perhaps it was by some such accident that a crude raft was blown far offshore, to drift helpless on the open ocean, and to ground days, even weeks later on an unknown, uninhabited land over the horizon. Or perhaps it was by deliberate waterborne voyage that human beings first came to offshore southeast Asia, to New Guinea, Australia, and the Pacific Islands during the late Ice Age. Having followed the complex population movements that took anatomically modern humans throughout Europe and Eurasia, and then into the Americas, we now examine cultural developments in southern latitudes (Table 7.1). Instead of attempting a detailed chronicle of dozens of local cultures in Africa and Asia, we focus on two adaptations of particular interest—those of the San peoples of southern Africa and on the first settlement of New Guinea, the southwestern Pacific, and Australia, population movements that involved the first open water voyages in human history.

AFRICAN HUNTER-GATHERERS: PAST AND PRESENT

• • •

As we saw in Chapter 4, *Homo sapiens sapiens*, anatomically modern humans, probably evolved in Africa, perhaps as early as 100,000 years ago. The long millennia of the Weichsel glaciation saw the peoples of Africa developing ever more

204

TABLE 7.1

• • •

Age B.C./A.D.	Climatic Change	Sub-Saharan Africa	Southeast Asia & Offshore	Developments Elsewhere
A.D. 1000	Colder ← → Warmer	Saharan gold trade		Maya Civilization
			Settlement of offshore islands in Pacific (Chapter 12)	
A.D. 1		Spread of farming and iron technology	Rise of states in Southeast Asia (Chapter 17)	Shang Civilization
				Sumerian Civilization
		Cattle herding in Sahara (Chapter 16)	Rice cultivation	Food production in the Near East
10,000				
				First settlement of Americas
		Late Stone Age cultures	Increasingly specialized hunter-gatherers	
20,000				Cro-Magnons in Europe
			Settlement in Solomon Islands	
			Hunter-gatherer settlement in Tasmania	
30,000				
		Middle Stone Age cultures		
40,000				Radiation of modern humans
			? First settlement of Australia	Neanderthals
50,000				

Chapter 3

efficient ways of hunting and foraging. Some fascinating indications come from coastal caves in South Africa, among them Klasies River Mouth and Nelson's Bay (Binford, 1984; R. Klein, 1979). Richard Klein found that the people who inhabited these caves lived not only off vegetable foods but off game and marine resources as well. Klasies River was occupied between about 120,000 and 70,000 years ago, then abandoned until about 3000 B.C. The early inhabitants collected limpets and also pursued seals and penguins. They took few fish; they preferred game on the hoof, especially such docile animals as the eland and bastard hartebeest. They did kill some more formidable beasts like the buffalo, black wildebeest, and roan antelope but in much smaller numbers, and some of the meat was perhaps scavenged. Interestingly, the bones of these individual species came from either very old or young individuals, which is the sort of age pattern found with predator kills. Only the eland and bastard hartebeest were taken at all ages. Klein concluded that they may have been driven into traps or over cliffs.

The Nelson's Bay Cave was occupied by modern *Homo sapiens* populations after 13,000 B.C. Again, eland and bastard hartebeest were common and taken at all ages, perhaps by game drives. The Nelson's Bay folk took bush pigs and warthogs, much fiercer and more formidable prey. Not only that, they used nets and fish hooks to catch a wide range of ocean fish. They also lived off flying sea birds such as cormorants. One could argue, of course, that the Klasies River people simply preferred game on the hoof, but the relative abundance of wild pigs strongly suggests that the Nelson's Bay hunters were much more expert and capable of exploiting a far wider range of game. They may have used the bow and arrow. Although the eland lives in widely dispersed herds, other antelope do not and would have been much more vulnerable to efficient hunting. Klein (1979) notes that several large mammal species became extinct between 10,000 and 8000 B.C.

We know very little about the climate of sub-Saharan Africa at the height of the last glaciation, but John Parkington (1987) and others believe that the human populations living at the southern tip of the continent were sparse. Parkington notes that larger animals appear to have been more common before about 7000 B.C.; small bands of hunter-gatherers may have roamed over large territories in search of large, gregarious animals. There is, however, almost no evidence to support this scenario, and much of the southern part of Africa may have been wet, cold, and windy during glacial times.

By about 7000 B.C., the world's southern oceans were warmer than today. It was not until 3000 years later, during the so-called postglacial climatic optimum, that the northern seas achieved higher temperatures. This delay is due to different land and water distributions in the two hemispheres, with Antarctica being much colder than the Arctic Ocean. Warmer, drier conditions in southern Africa led to more succulent vegetation at the expense of grassland and heath, with major changes in human subsistence. These changes are hard to document. John Parkington (1987) has chronicled one changing scenario at Eland's Bay Cave in the far south. In 11,000 B.C., the inhabitants hunted large and medium-sized antelope. But between 9000 and 7000 B.C., they turned their attention to smaller browsing animals, with estuarine and marine animals as well as limpets becoming ever more common. By 6000 B.C., the entire coastal plain was flooded, with only small browsing animals, mussels, and fish being taken. Then Eland's Bay Cave was abandoned suddenly, never to be reoccupied.

After 9000 B.C. the quantity of food bones increases dramatically, as does the variety of ostrich eggshell beads, water containers, bone tools, decorated bone work, and other artifacts (Figure 7.1). Parkington believes that this intensification in domestic activity was due to environmental change, to the dramatic encroachments of the postglacial ocean. Eland's Bay Cave was first visited, then lived in for long periods of time as the coastal plain shrank. Finally, the people moved into the interior or elsewhere along the shore when this stretch of coastline was no longer productive. It would be a mistake to describe the major changes in artifact inventories or subsistence as evolving culture change. Rather, they may reflect continuous adaptation to rapidly altering climatic conditions, changes that were reflected by

0 1 2 3 cm

FIGURE 7.1   An ostrich eggshell bead necklace from Gwisho, Zambia, central Africa, c. 3500 years old.

other adaptive shifts elsewhere on the coast, as at Nelson's Bay, and also in the warm interior.

The long-term trend over the past 15,000 years may have been toward smaller "food parcels" (Parkington, 1987). Many late Stone Age caves and rock shelters in southern Africa were used much more regularly in postglacial times, as if mountain and near-coastal locations were extremely favorable places to settle, places where smaller browsing animal herds would be concentrated. The warming trend in the earlier millennia of postglacial times may have led to increased aridity in many parts of the interior, with the densest human populations concentrated in areas of abundant water and diverse animal and plant resources. The result was probably a great diversity of hunter-gatherer societies throughout much of Africa.

Hilary Deacon (1979) has excavated several late Stone Age rock shelters and caves with exceptional care. He believes that there was a trend toward hunting smaller game and especially toward the exploitation of plant foods. Rabbits, tortoises, and both grasses and root plants became vital components in the hunter-gatherers' diet. Just when plant foods came to be of overwhelming importance is much debated, but they were especially significant after about A.D. 1, when herding peoples were settled in extreme southern Africa (Chapter 11), perhaps when the newcomers squeezed hunter-gatherers into more limited territories, away from cattle-grazing grounds.

The same general trend toward increasingly specialized subsistence strategies may also have developed in other parts of sub-Saharan Africa, just as in other parts of the world. The peoples of the open savanna lived off the abundant game populations and supplemented their diet with seasonal gathering of the rich vegetable resources of the woodland. Other bands settled on the shores of lakes and on riverbanks and lived by fishing. This valuable and reliable source of protein encouraged more lasting settlement and increased specialization. The rain forest peoples of the Zaire River Basin in central Africa were unable to hunt as wide a range of game as their savanna counterparts, so they relied heavily on vegetable foods and wild roots.

The later Stone Age hunter-gatherers of the eastern and southern African savanna are comparatively well documented not only from archaeological sites but also from their own rock paintings and engravings. Rock paintings are notoriously hard to date, but it is possible that Stone Age artists were at work in southern Africa as early as 18,000 B.C. They were certainly painting the walls of caves they visited by 6000 B.C. Modern ethnographic and historical records connect the San peoples who live today in the Kalahari Desert with this ancient artistic tradition. Their Stone Age lifeway survived into the twentieth century and appears to have changed relatively little for thousands of years.

Gwisho
1500 B.C.

The Gwisho hot springs in central Zambia provide evidence for a basically similar subsistence pattern by at least 1500 B.C. (Fagan and van Noten, 1971). Because the lower levels of the sites among the springs were waterlogged, many organic artifacts and food remains have survived, giving an exceptionally complete picture of Stone Age life in the region. The economy and material culture of the Gwisho people show a striking resemblance to those of modern San peoples in the Kalahari, although, of course, there are environmental differences (Lee, 1979). The Gwisho people hunted many species of antelope and caught fish in shallow pools of the nearby Kafue River. The waterlogged levels contained more than 10,000 plant remains, from only eight species, all of which were apparently collected to the exclusion of many other edible species. Nearby lay some fine arrowheads and some of the wooden artifacts made by the inhabitants, including some simple digging sticks used for uprooting tubers. These tools are identical to those used by Kalahari San today. There were traces of a grass and stick shelter, of hearths, and of layers of grass that may have served as bedding. Thirty-five burials were deposited in the soil of the campsites. The deposits were littered with hundreds of stone arrow barbs and tiny scraping tools that lay alongside pestles and grinding stones used to process the vegetable foods that were an important part of the Gwisho diet. So little have gathering habits changed in the past 3000 years that a San from the Kalahari was able to identify seeds from the excavations and tell archaeologists what they were used for.

The Gwisho hot springs are informative, for they confirm ethnographic observations made about the present-day San. Like that of their modern successors, the toolkit of the Gwisho people was highly portable, and much of it was disposable. Except for bows and arrows, the Kalahari San improvise many of their tools from the bush as they need them, making snares from vegetable fibers and clubs from convenient branches. The women use digging sticks like the Gwisho artifacts for digging tubers and a softened antelope hide, or kaross, as a garment and carrying bag. Their only other artifacts are a pair of pounding stones for breaking up nuts. The Gwisho site contained both digging sticks and pounders. We know from cave paintings that the San used karosses for thousands of years, and we can assume they were used at Gwisho and elsewhere.

Like those of the San, the Gwisho home bases were little more than small clusters of brush shelters. The average present-day !Kung San camp holds approximately 10 to 30 people. The small population of !Kung territory leads to a continuous turnover of the composition of camp populations. This constant change is a reality reflected in the !Kung's highly flexible kinship system. Every member of a band has not only close family ties but also kin connections with a much wider number of people living all over !Kung territory. The !Kung kinship system is based on an elaborate network of commonly possessed personal names, which are transmitted from grandparent to grandchild. People with similar names share kin ties even if they live some distance from one another. This network is such that individuals can move to a new camp and find a family with which they have kin ties to accept them. The resulting flexibility of movement prevents total social chaos. Presumably, the prehistoric San had a similar social organization to aid survival.

The vivid San paintings and engravings depict the game hunted, the chase, and life in camp (Lewis-Williams, 1981; Vinnecombe, 1976). The San drew running hunters, people fishing from boats, and scenes of gathering honey and vegetable foods (Figure 7.2). The hunters can be seen stalking game in disguise, hotly pursuing wounded quarry, and even raiding the cattle herds of their agricultural neighbors of later centuries. David Lewis-Williams, who has studied ethnographic records of San bands, has shown convincingly that many of the paintings depict complex metaphors that represent symbolic values in the San world. Each superimposition of paintings and each relationship between human figures and animals had profound meaning to the artists and the people. For instance, many of the paintings depict eland with dancers cavorting around them (Figure 7.3). Lewis-Williams believes that the dancers were acquiring the potency released by the death of the eland. The dancers go into trances so powerful that they become eland themselves (Figure 7.4). This symbolism survived into the nineteenth century. When Victorian anthropologist George Stow showed some rock painting pictures to an elderly San couple, the woman began to sing and dance. The man begged her to desist because the old songs made him sad. Eventually he joined in, and Stow watched the couple

FIGURE 7.2   San hunters depicted in a rock painting from Natal, South Africa.

FIGURE 7.3   A trance dance being executed by San shamans. Their elongated bodies convey the sense of being stretched out that is felt by people in altered states of consciousness. Dots along the spine of the central figure depict what the San describe as a "boiling" sensation as supernatural power rises up the spine and "explodes" in the head. The power is derived from certain animals, like the eland depicted to the right.

reliving the symbolism of past days. Only now, more than a century later, are archaeologists trying to probe this forgotten world.

A.D. 1   Prehistoric hunter-gatherers enjoyed the savanna woodlands of eastern and southern Africa undisturbed until approximately A.D. 1, when the first farming peo-

FIGURE 7.4 A curing dance among the San from the Nyae Nyae area of Namibia. Dances like this may have formed part of the ritual behind prehistoric rock paintings.

ples (other African folk) settled by the banks of the Zambezi and Limpopo rivers. The San placed second in the resulting competition for land: The farmers wanted grazing grass and prime land for cultivating, so they drove off the bands of San hunter-gatherers, who had to retreat into less favored areas. Some took up the new economies and married into farming communities. White settlement in South Africa increased the isolation of the San. As the pressure on their hunting grounds grew, the San moved into mountainous areas and desert regions. Even there they were harassed and hunted. Some of the white settlers made a sport of shooting them on Sunday afternoons. The doomed San of South Africa calmly continued to paint scenes of cattle raids and of European ships and wagons. They even depicted red-coated English soldiers on their expeditions into the mountains. By the end of the nineteenth century, there was no San painting in South Africa, and the art of stone toolmaking had all but died out. The last stoneworkers used glass bottle fragments to make their sharp arrowheads. They found this unusually pure "stone" vastly preferable to their usual quartz pebbles (A. Barnard, 1992).

A.D. 1800

A.D. 1890

SUNDA AND SAHUL: THE FIRST SETTLEMENT OF ISLAND SOUTHEAST ASIA

• • •

On the other side of the world, island Southeast Asia underwent far more profound change than tropical Africa after the Ice Age. Climatically, global warming brought generally drier conditions to the Australian interior and caused major changes in the distribution of tropical forests. Dramatic rises in post–Ice Age sea levels altered the geography of the off-lying parts of Southeast Asia beyond recognition. Therein lies one of the fascinating questions of world prehistory. The Australian Aborigines encountered by British navigator Captain James Cook and other early European explorers in the eighteenth century A.D. were still living in the Stone Age (Figure 7.5). For two centuries, anthropologists and historians have puzzled over the ancestry of these remarkable people. Where did the Australians come from and how long ago did people first settle on this remote continent (Allen, 1989; Lourandos, 1987)?

At the height of the last glaciation in about 18,000 B.C., sea levels were over 300 ft (100 m) below modern levels. Dry land joined Sumatra to Borneo, and great plains were exposed between many of the islands, which were connected to the Southeast Asian mainland. Great rivers dissected the now-sunken plains, known to geologists as Sunda (Figure 7.6). Farther offshore, nearly 19 miles (30 km) of open water separated Sunda from the island of Wallacea (modern Sulawesi and Timor); 62 miles (100 km) farther offshore lay a vast landmass, Sahul, a combination of Australia, New Guinea, and a low-lying shelf between them that is now the Arafura Sea. These are, of course, the coastlines of the glacial maximum, and sea levels were considerably higher for most of the last glaciation. For most of the period between about 100,000 and 13,000 B.C., people would have had to cross much wider stretches of ocean than those at the glacial maximum. Even at the height of the last glaciation, the colonization of Wallacea and Sahul would have required some form of watercraft and the technology to build them. This raises a fundamental and deeply interesting question: How long ago did people go offshore and cross wide tracts of ocean, perhaps paddling out of sight of land?

Despite intensive search, no traces of *Homo erectus* or archaic forms of *Homo sapiens* have come from the islands of Southeast Asia. Thus, it seems a reasonable assumption that anatomically modern people were the first to settle the off-lying landmasses. If *H. sapiens sapiens* had settled in Southeast Asia by about 75,000 years ago, as we hypothesized in Chapter 5, we can reasonably expect colonization to have occurred some time after that date. At the time, the plains of Sunda were relatively dry. Human settlement was probably concentrated in areas such as coasts, lakeshores, and rivers with more diverse and predictable food resources. As in the rain forests, easily split bamboo and other woods sufficed for many tasks. The coastlines that faced Wallacea and Sahul were lapped by relatively benign waters that probably offered a bounty of easily taken shallow-water fish and shellfish to supplement game and plant foods. Perhaps the people living along these shores fashioned simple rafts of bamboo and mangrove logs lashed together with forest vines (R. Jones, 1989). Such rafts would have served as stable platforms for fishing in sheltered, shallow water, for reaching offshore shell beds. Perhaps it was in such craft that some people crossed to Wallacea and Sahul well before the glacial maximum of 18,000 B.C.

Sunda
Wallacea
Sahul

FIGURE 7.5 An Australian Aborigine with his lightweight hunting kit. This somewhat romanticized portrait was drawn by François Peron, a naturalist attached to the Baudin expedition of 1802.

Two routes led offshore to Sahul. One led from southern Sunda to Wallacea, then across to the Australian shore. The other was from southern China, across the Philippines and Borneo, and into New Guinea via Sulawesi (Figure 7.6). Whichever route was used, the process of colonization involved both island hopping and open-water travel, the earliest instance of seafaring by human beings. As is always the case with ocean crossings, scholars debate endlessly about whether the first settlement was accidental or deliberate. In the case of Southeast Asia, with its strong northerly monsoon winds of summer, colonization was probably the result of dozens of accidental driftings offshore over thousands of years. Computer simulations have shown that there are moderate chances of a raft drifting from Timor to Australia in about seven days in front of strong monsoon winds. Undoubtedly many

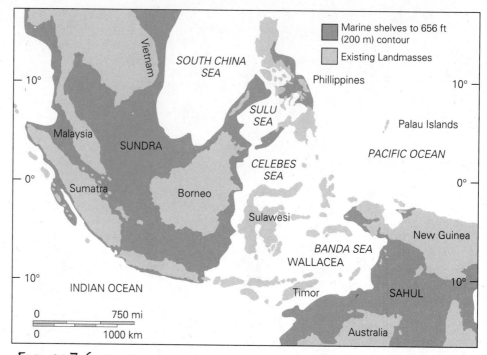

FIGURE 7.6   Late Ice Age, Southeast Asia. Low sea levels exposed dry land off main-land Asia and between Australia and New Guinea during the last glaciation, creating Sahul and Sunda.

of these strandings resulted in the group dying out, and computer simulations show that the chances of survival, even with men and women in the party, were very small. Eventually, however, a viable population (or populations) was established along the more than 1850-mile (3000-km) coastline of Sahul (Figure 7.7).

New Guinea

Much of Sahul was rolling, semiarid lowlands—what is now Australia, with New Guinea in the far north offering a quite different landscape of rugged mountains and highland valleys. The earliest evidence for human settlement in New Guinea comes from Bobongara on the Huon Peninsula, where archaeologist Les Groube found waisted ground axes and a single stone flake sealed under volcanic ash that dates to at least 38,000 B.C. (Figure 7.8). Groube believes these waisted axes were used to ring trees and clear forests, perhaps to encourage the growth of plants on the forest fringes—a form of deliberate manipulation of wild plants to enhance the growth of wild plant foods such as yams, sugarcane, and perhaps taro and fruit trees (Groube et al., 1986).

Bobongara
c. 38,000 B.C.

The Solomon Islands

The Huon Peninsula faces the Bismarck Strait, with the island of New Britain only a 30-mile (51-km) or so passage offshore. From there, it is only a short voyage to

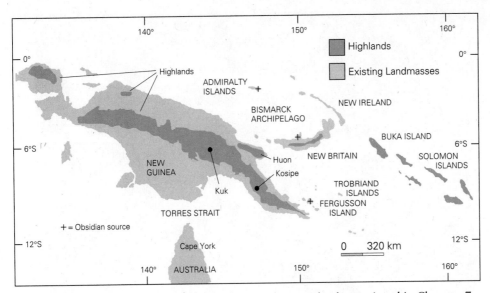

FIGURE 7.7 Map showing New Guinea and adjacent islands mentioned in Chapters 7 and 12.

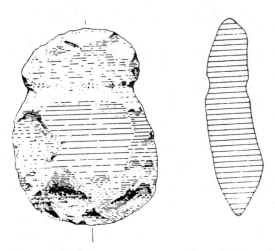

FIGURE 7.8 Waisted stone axe from the Huon Peninsula, New Guinea.

New Ireland. These two islands are visible from one another but are separated by deep water and were never joined during the last glaciation. Open-water voyages were needed to colonize them, and excavations in four limestone caves on New Ireland have yielded traces of human occupation by at least 30,000 B.C. (Allen et al., 1989). These were fisherfolk, who took shellfish and fish and hunted bats, reptiles, and birds. By 18,000 B.C., their successors were regularly trading obsidian for toolmaking across 19 miles (30 km) of open water from west New Britain, from a source 217 miles (350 km) in a straight line from their home.

Even farther offshore to the south, the Kilu Rock Shelter on Buka Island in the northern Solomons contains human occupation dating to between 26,000 and

30,000 B.C.

Kilu
26,000 B.C.

FIGURE 7.9   Excavations at Kilu Rock Shelter, northern Solomon Islands.

18,000 B.C. (Figure 7.9) (Wickler and Spriggs, 1988). Open-water crossings of at least 81 to 112 miles (130–180 km) would have been required to settle on Buka, depending on the route selected. Voyaging over this distance would certainly have required some form of open-water craft, as well as foods that could be preserved for use during longer voyages. Substantial water containers would also have been essential. From Buka, it would have been an easy matter to colonize the rest of the Solomon chain, for the islands are separated by short distances (Allen et al., 1989).

Farther offshore lay the limits of the late Ice Age world, for sea distances become much larger. More than 186 miles (300 km) lie between the Solomons and the environmentally impoverished Santa Cruz Islands, which were a much smaller target area even for expert navigators. The islands to the south and east lie within a region with no indigenous terrestrial mammals except bats and a progressively impoverished flora and fauna. Such remote oceanic environments were insufficient to support hunter-gatherers. It was not until much later that the development of larger offshore canoes, much more sophisticated navigational skills, and easily storable food crops enabled humans to colonize islands far offshore (Chapter 12).

Everything points to a relatively rapid spread of hunter-gatherer peoples with expert seagoing abilities through northern Sahul and contiguous islands at least as early as 38,000 B.C. This rapid colonization was aided by favorable climatic conditions, with generally good weather and predictable winds and currents that would carry people in small crafts from island to island without the necessity for elaborate technology. The Sunda-Sahul area was a superb "nursery" for seafaring expertise, and it is no coincidence that islanders in the western Pacific were venturing far offshore long before Westerners undertook ambitious voyages in the Mediterranean after 12,000 B.C. (Irwin et al., 1990; Irwin, 1992).

Australia

The first settlement of Australia, like that of the Americas, is an issue thwart with controversy (Allen, 1989; Frankel, 1991). The earliest absolutely indisputable evidence of human settlement dates to after 33,000 B.C., but there are finds of stone implements in river gravels and other sediments that are claimed to date back to 48,000 B.C., perhaps even earlier (Roberts et al., 1990) (Figure 7.10). It is, of course, possible that there was a long period of what archaeologist Jim Allen calls "invisible colonization" for thousands of years by peoples who are not represented in the archaeological record. Traces of human occupation immediately before and around 28,000 B.C. have accumulated rapidly in recent years. Some hunter-gatherers visited the Devil's Lair Cave near Perth in the southwest part of west Australia as early as 30,500 B.C. and used the site more regularly from 21,000 B.C. to the end of the Ice

48,000 B.C.

28,000 B.C.
Devil's Lair
30,500 B.C.

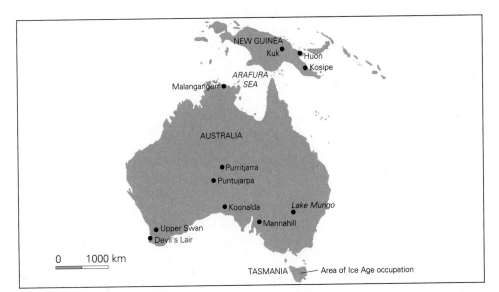

FIGURE 7.10 Archaeological sites in Australia and Tasmania.

Purritjarra
25,000 B.C.

Age (Dortch and Merrilees, 1973). The Purritjarra rock shelter in the arid center of Australia near the Northern Territory's Cleland Hills was occupied from at least 25,000 to about 4000 B.C.

Far to the east, in the Willandra Lakes region of western New South Wales, early sites cluster around long dried-up lakes. One group of sites includes shell middens located in dune systems dating to around 30,000 B.C., perhaps earlier. The

Lake Mungo
24,000 B.C.

Lake Mungo site of 24,000 B.C. comes from the same general area, a thin scatter of stone artifacts, hearths, fish bones, and other food remains (J. M. Bowdler, Jones, and Thorne, 1970). Humans were living in the arid zones of Australia, at places like

Koonalda
22,000 to 13,000 B.C.

Koonalda Cave on South Australia's Nullabor Plain, by 22,000 B.C. People lived there until 13,000 B.C., visiting the site to quarry stone and making patterned lines or "flutings" on the cave walls during their stays. Arnhem Land in the north was certainly occupied well before 18,000 B.C., with radiocarbon dated occupations of about 20,900 B.C. from Malangangerr Rock Shelter. Ocher pencils with traces of wear date to at least 17,000 and perhaps even to 28,000 B.C. It is possible that some of the earliest Arnhem Land paintings depict extinct animals, but the interpretation is much debated. Dates from coatings of "desert varnish" from engravings on rocky outcrops at Mannahill in South Australia are said to span a period from 29,000 to 14,000 B.C., but the dating method is still experimental (Dorn et al., 1988). There seems little reason to doubt, however, that prehistoric Australians were painting as early as artists in Europe and Africa (Figure 7.11).

Hunter-gatherers were living around the coast and on the fringes of the central Australian desert by 18,000 B.C. By 8000 B.C., they were exploiting every major environmental zone. As for the first settlement itself, scientists are deeply divided. Some believe that initial colonization was a slow and gradual process along coasts and then into the interior by people who had had to adapt not only to a new maritime environment but also to unfamiliar animal and plant foods (White and O'Connell, 1982). Others argue for a rapid colonization, with small groups expanding rapidly over the continent as a result of their highly mobile lifeway (Allen, 1989). Anthropologist Joseph Birdsell (1977) hypothesized that a mere doubling of the Australian population every 20 years after the first settlement would have resulted in natural population growth to eighteenth-century levels within only 2000 years. Recent, remarkable discoveries of late Ice Age wallaby hunters in Tasmania tend to support his hypothesis.

Ice Age Wallaby Hunters in Tasmania

Tasmania is now an island, but it was connected to mainland Australia by a land bridge from 35,000 to 27,000 B.C., at about the time of the first securely dated settlement of Sahul. During much of the last glaciation, climatic conditions throughout Tasmania were quite severe, with ice sheets on higher ground in the interior and

Bluff
ORS 7
29,000 B.C.

temperatures at the glacial maximum as much as 10.8°F (6°C) lower than today. Archaeologist Richard Cosgrove has excavated the Bluff and ORS 7 rock shelters in south-central Tasmania. The Bluff site was first occupied about 28,500 B.C., whereas ORS 7 was in use by 28,800 B.C. Both of these occupation levels contain emu eggs, which can be collected only during late winter and early spring, a bitterly cold time of year (Figure 7.12, p. 220) (Cosgrove et al., 1990).

FIGURE 7.11 Aboriginal bark painting from the Alligator River region, Northern Territory, Australia. Representation of the inner organs of man and kangaroo is characteristic of paintings from this region.

Both sites were occupied before the glacial maximum, but people continued to live in the rugged landscape of southwestern and central Tasmania through the coldest millennia of the last glaciation. The Kutikina Cave was occupied between 18,000 and 12,000 B.C., when what is now dense forest land was open tundra and grassland. The inhabitants hunted red wallabies, as did the people who lived in at least 20 other occupied caves nearby. Slightly to the east, another rugged area, now rain forest, is Bone Cave, occupied between 15,000 and 11,000 B.C. The groups in these areas appear to have been part of a common social system that flourished over a large area for many thousands of years. Some groups used Darwin glass, a natural glass from a meteorite crater a minimum distance of 28 miles (45 km) from Kutikina and over 62 straight-line miles (100 km) from the Bluff Cave area. Some of these people were painting hand stencils and other designs long before the end of the Ice Age.

These were the southernmost people living on earth during the last glaciation. With the severing of the land bridge, their successors remained isolated from the outside world for thousands of years until French explorer Marion du Fresne met some aboriginal Tasmanians face to face in A.D. 1772.

Kutikina
18,000 to 12,000 B.C.

Bone Cave
15,000 to 11,000 B.C.

FIGURE 7.12   Excavations at the Bluff Rock Shelter, Tasmania.

LATER AUSTRALIAN PREHISTORY

• • •

Between 23,000 and 8000 B.C., the population of Australia may have reached approximately modern levels, an estimated 300,000 people. Cultural change was gradual right into modern times. The same traditions of stoneworking and bone technology found in early sites survived almost unchanged for thousands of years (Mulvaney, 1975; R. V. S. Wright, 1977). For instance, flakes showing wear patterns characteristic of adz blades made by modern Aborigines date back as far as 18,000 B.C., and the same bone points used to fasten skin clothes in historic times have been found deep in the prehistoric levels of Devil's Lair. The Australian Aborigines were famous for their artistic traditions and elaborate ceremonial life. Abundant traces of ritual belief have been found in Australian sites. The Devil's Lair site yielded stone plaques, a deep pit, and human incisor teeth that had been knocked out with a sharp blow: Such evulsion of teeth was a long-lived Australian tradition.

Despite the essential conservatism of Australian stoneworking practices, some regional variations did appear over the millennia. Steep-edged scrapers, which were probably used as woodworking tools, were made over a wide area of Australia during much of the Upper Pleistocene. These and crude flake tools remained in use until recent times; they were joined after 4000 B.C. in some areas by stone points, set on shafts, and other microliths. There is good reason to believe that Aboriginal technology developed within Australia over a long period in response to local needs and without the benefit of cultural innovation from outside (Figure 7.13).

Some idea of the simple level of early Australian life can be obtained from the saga of the Tasmanians (Plomley, 1969). When the first European voyagers visited Tasmania in 1642, they found bands of hunter-gatherers living on the island. The Tasmanians lasted precisely 80 years after European settlement in 1802. They had no shafted tools (that is, tools made of stone heads or points with wooden shafts or handles) and relied instead on scrapers and choppers somewhat like those used by early hunter-gatherers on the mainland; they lacked the boomerangs, spear-throwers, shields, axes, adzes, and lightweight stone tools the Australians of the mainland had when they first entered written history. The result of Tasmania's isolation was that its populations, although forming part of the Australian cultural group, never received the later cultural innovations that spread through Australia after sea levels rose. Henry Lourandos (1987) and others have suggested that Tasmanian adapta-

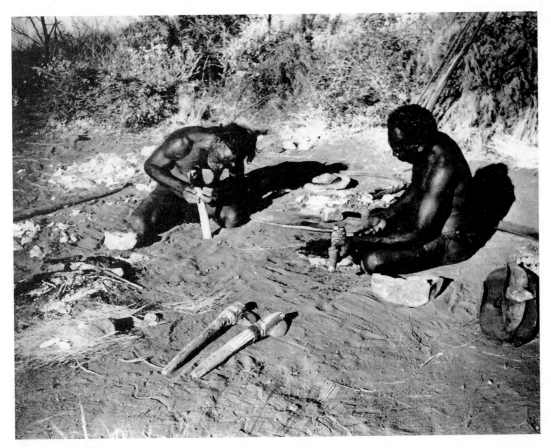

FIGURE 7.13 Australian Aborigines making stone tools.

tions preserved a rather specialized lifeway that was typical of much of Australia during the late Weichsel into modern times.

Fortunately for archaeology, at least some investigations of Aboriginal culture have been made that have important bearing on the interpretation of the archaeological record. Richard Gould (1977) spent many months among the Ngatatjara people of the Western Desert, carrying out ethnographic investigations that had objectives somewhat similar to those of Richard Lee among the San in Africa: He was interested in their cultural ecology and in the ways ethnographic observations could be used to interpret the archaeological record. His aboriginal informants took him to Puntutjarpa Rock Shelter, a site that they still visited regularly. Gould excavated the occupation levels in the shelter and found that people had lived there for more than 6800 years. The later stone implements were almost indistinguishable from modern Ngatatjara tools, to the extent that Gould was able to compare the wear patterns on both ancient and modern artifacts and decide which 5000-year-old tools had been mounted on shafts and which had not. He also compared modern living surfaces with equivalent features found in the rock shelter (Figure 7.14).

Puntutjarpa

FIGURE 7.14 Comparison of a prehistoric campsite at Puntutjarpa Rock Shelter, Australia, with a modern aboriginal campsite in the same area. Note that the modern encampment can be subdivided into living areas by using informants' data and anthropological observation, whereas the archaeological site is devoid of such information, consisting merely of artifact patterns.

The study of living Aborigine bands shows just how conservative Australian lifeways have been. There were few major technological innovations during Australian prehistory. Indeed, it was possible for the prehistoric Australians to maintain a thoroughly viable lifeway with minimal technology and only the simplest of artifacts. The Tasmanians, for instance, used only two dozen or so tools to hunt and forage. The great elaboration of Australian and Tasmanian culture was in social and ritual life, neither of which can readily be recovered by archaeological investigation. That much of this activity was designed to maintain the delicate balance between the Aborigines and the available resources in their environment was no coincidence. A belief in such balance lay at the very core of Australian life.

CHAPTER SUMMARY

As the Ice Age ended, hunter-gatherer groups living in Africa and Asia adopted increasingly diverse adaptations to local environments. In sub-Saharan Africa, people turned their attention to smaller browsing animals, continuously adapting to changing environmental conditions. The densest populations were probably concentrated in areas of abundant water and diverse animal and plant resources. It was from these diverse societies that modern-day African hunter-gatherer groups are descended.

During much of the Weichsel glaciation, New Guinea and Australia formed a single landmass, called Sahul. Sahul was settled perhaps as early as 50,000 to 70,000 years ago, but the earliest documented settlement is about 38,000 B.C. People using open-water craft had settled in the Solomon Islands of the southwestern Pacific by 26,000 B.C., while the first settlement of Australia dates to at least 33,000 B.C. Securely dated sites proliferate after 35,000 years ago, with late Ice Age hunters flourishing in Tasmania by 29,000 B.C. The later archaeological record shows that the Australian lifeway changed little over the millennia, except for some significant innovations in tool technology.

GUIDE TO FURTHER READING

Fagan, Brian M. 1990. *The Journey from Eden*. New York: Thames and Hudson.
   A synthesis of the first settlement of Sunda and Sahul for the general reader. Also some descriptions of late prehistoric hunter-gatherer life.

Frankel, David. 1991. *Remains to Be Seen: Archaeological Insights into Australian Prehistory*. Melbourne: Longman Cheshire.
   An attractive general account of the methods and approaches of Australian prehistory for the beginning student. Especially strong on the links between archaeology and anthropology. Well illustrated.

Lee, Richard B. 1979. *The !Kung San*. Cambridge, Eng.: Cambridge University Press.
   If there is one classic ethnographic study of hunter-gatherers, this account of the Kalahari San and their complex ecology is it. Strongly recommended to give the reader a clear understanding of hunter-gatherer lifeways.

Lewis-Williams, David. 1981. *Believing and Seeing: Symbolic Meanings in Southern San Rock Art*. New York: Academic Press.

 A superb, well-argued study of the meaning of prehistoric rock art in southern Africa that should be read by anyone interested in this subject.

White, J. Peter, and O'Connell, James. 1982. *A Prehistory of Australia, New Guinea, and Sahul*. New York: Academic Press.

 The definitive analytic synthesis of the prehistory of Australia. A superb, even masterly account but somewhat outdated.

FARMERS

(C. 10,000 B.C. T O MODERN TIMES)

Agriculture is not to be looked on as a difficult or out-of-the-way invention, for the rudest savage, skilled as he is in the habits of the food-plants he gathers, must know well enough that if seeds or roots are put in a proper place in the ground they will grow.

SIR EDWARD TYLOR, 1883

The beginning of food production—of agriculture and animal domestication—was one of the catalytic events of human prehistory. Part IV not only describes the sequence of farming cultures in all parts of the world but also analyzes some of the recent theories about the origins of farming. We will start with the theoretical background and then study farming in geographic areas. With the beginnings of food production we find the first signs of rapidly accelerating cultural evolution, of processes that are still operating at a record pace. However, our understanding of the early millennia of farming is incomplete. Future research is certain to modify drastically the story set forth in the following chapters.

CHAPTER 8 A PLENTEOUS HARVEST

THE ORIGINS

• • •

The men climb high above the ground, lopping off small branches with their stone-bladed axes. The women and children gather up the foliage and pile it around the bare tree trunks. It is hard, back-breaking work that goes on for days on end, as the farmers watch the brazen sky for thunder clouds and signs of rain. A few spits of rain and building clouds. The people fire the tinder-dry brush, which burns fiercely. The sky fills with dense brown smoke as far as the eye can see, as the women turn over the fresh ash into the cleared soil and plant their precious seed. Then everyone waits for the life-giving rains to conjure bright green shoots from the soil (Figure 8.1).

It is sometimes hard for us to imagine, buying our food from supermarkets, that for more than 99 percent of our existence as humans we were hunters and gatherers, tied to the seasons of plant foods, the movements of game, and the ebb and flow of aquatic resources. Food production, the deliberate cultivation of cereal grasses and edible root plants, is a phenomenon of the last 10,000 years of human existence. This relatively new human subsistence strategy is in large part responsible for the rapidly accelerating rates of population growth and cultural change in the past ten millennia. One of the major controversies in world prehistory surrounds the origins of food production: Why, when, and where did people first grow crops and domesticate wild animals?

THEORIES ABOUT THE ORIGINS OF FOOD PRODUCTION

• • •

As we saw in Chapter 5, changing environmental and demographic conditions at the end of the Ice Age, after 13,000 B.C., caused major long-term changes in hunter-gatherer societies. There was more localization, considerable technological innovation, and a trend toward sedentary settlement in areas with abundant and seasonally

FIGURE 8.1 Hoe cultivation.

predictable food resources. And as we saw with the Natufian culture of the Levant (Chapter 5), many of these societies were, in many respects, preadapted for food production. Why, then, did they choose to grow their own crops?

Early Hypotheses

Late Victorian archaeologists were the first to speculate about agricultural origins. They envisaged a solitary genius who suddenly had the brilliant idea of planting seed. Today, no one looks for a single genius or for the earliest maize cob. Rather, modern theory concentrates on the complex processes that caused gradual changes in human subsistence patterns (G. Wright, 1971).

The best known and longest lived of the early theories was Vere Gordon Childe's "Neolithic Revolution." He proposed a major economic revolution in pre-history, which took place in the Near East during a period of severe drought, a climatic crisis that caused a symbiotic relationship between humans and animals in fertile oases. The new economies ensured a richer and more reliable food source for people on the edge of starvation after the Ice Age (Childe, 1936, 1952). Childe's

Childe's Neolithic Revolution

simple theory was widely accepted, but it was based on inadequate archaeological and environmental data. It has long been surpassed by much more sophisticated formulations (H. Wright, 1993).

Systematic fieldwork into the origins of food production began only in the late 1940s, when Robert J. Braidwood of the University of Chicago mounted an expedition to the Kurdish foothills of Iran to test Childe's theory. He soon rejected any notion of catastrophic climatic change, arguing that economic change came from "ever increasing cultural differentiation and specialization of human communities" (Braidwood and Braidwood, 1983). Thus, people were culturally receptive to innovation and experimentation with the cultivation of wild grasses. Braidwood believed that Stone Age hunters had domesticated animals and plants in "nuclear zones," areas such as the hilly flanks of the Zagros Mountains in Iraq and upland areas overlooking the Mesopotamian lowlands. He was convinced that the human capacity and enthusiasm for experimentation made it possible for people to domesticate animals. All modern theories of food production have their beginnings in Braidwood's work, which focused attention on the notion that people were culturally receptive to new subsistence practices.

Braidwood's hilly flanks (margin note)

Multivariate Theories

Now that we can look at world prehistory on a far wider canvas than the pioneers, we know that agriculture appeared in widely distributed parts of the world at approximately the same time in the Near East, China, south and Southeast Asia, and the Americas. This development has led some scholars to think in terms of worldwide population pressure that caused many hunter-gatherer societies to abandon gathering because their growing populations had reached the limit that their food resources could support (for full arguments, see Cohen, 1977). No one denies that food production led to higher population densities and indeed ignited a population explosion (see Figure 8.2) (Lewin, 1988a). But there is no evidence for very high population densities in the Near East or Mesoamerica during the millennia when agriculture was taking hold, certainly not for the sorts of density that cause chronic food shortages (Flannery, 1983; Stark, 1986).

Cohen's population pressure (margin note)

Recent theorizing about the origins of food production revolves around complex, multivariate models that combine many factors (Flannery, 1965, 1968a). All these models take into account the emerging realization that many early Holocene hunter-gatherer societies were more complex and well preadapted to food production before anyone started planting wild cereal grasses or penning animals.

Barbara Bender (1985) argues for social factors. She theorizes that hunter-gatherer societies were becoming more complex, with far more elaborate, hierarchical social organizations. She points to the increasing abundance of trade objects and the appearance of richly decorated burials in preagricultural societies in the Near East, Europe, and elsewhere. Perhaps, she hypothesizes, an expansion of trade and of political alliances between neighboring groups created new social and economic pressures to produce more and more surplus goods, not only foodstuffs but other objects as well. This development, in turn, led to more sedentary lifeways. This social hypothesis tends to ignore the compelling factors of now well-documented environmental changes that were apparently one of the key elements in a move toward cultivation in areas like the Near East.

Bender's social theories (margin note)

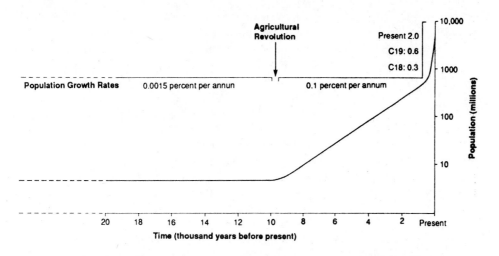

FIGURE 8.2 World population changes since the beginnings of food production. There has been an explosion in human population densities in the past 10,000 years.

Another category of theories is based on relationships between populations and resources. This category is an extension of a famous argument by economist Ester Boserup (1965), which points out that food production systems of any type are highly flexible. Thus, hunter-gatherers responded to favorable relationships between population densities and available resources by intensifying their hunting and gathering. Population growth in restricted areas with diverse resources can cause food shortages because there is less mobility and everyone has less territory to move around in, a situation that may have arisen in parts of the Near East (Chapter 9), northwestern Europe (Chapter 10), and the Americas (Chapter 13). These theories tend to concentrate on several interdependent factors: risk and population-resource imbalances. Apart from environmental change, all environments involve some form of risk for hunter-gatherer societies—drought cycles, long, cold winters, or unpredictable floods, to mention only a few possibilities discussed in earlier chapters. People respond to these risks by moving away, by developing new storage technologies for dried fish or plant foods, and by drying foods like powdered bison meat or salmon. A straightforward solution to rising populations, resulting food shortages, or risk factors may be to go one step further, to cultivate familiar plants and domesticate common prey so that people can draw on familiar "stored" resources in scarce months.

Population and resources

A third group of theorists focuses on ecological factors such as local variability in food resources and the interactive effects of human exploitation. Proponents of these ecological models talk of "opportunities" for the introduction of agriculture, of people turning to superior local resources when the moment arrived (Rindos, 1984). What happens is that some resources, say, wild wheat or barley or wild goats, are seen as attractive. People use them more and more, to the point that they are eventually domesticated. Kent Flannery (1968a) used this approach to examine the mechanisms by which Mesoamericans took up agriculture. The preagricultural

Ecological theories

peoples of the region adapted to a few animal genera and plants, whose range cut across several environments. These included deer, rabbits, cactus fruit, and wild grasses, including the wild ancestor of maize. They scheduled their annual round to be in the right place at the right time to harvest, say, cactus fruit. Over the centuries, genetic changes in the ancestor of corn made it more productive and progressively more important in the diet. As time went on, people spent more and more time cultivating it and rescheduled their annual round accordingly, thereby neglecting foods they once exploited in favor of cultivated crops.

The crux of ecological models is trying to identify the processes that caused people to make the shift to deliberate cultivation, again a very difficult task. For example, did cultivation enable people to widen their adaptive niches? Were these new cost-benefit realities that favored farming? What about such factors as the nutritive value and seasonal availability of foods? Did genetic changes in animals and plants play a role?

Most theories about the origins of food production are far from easy to test. It is difficult to link complex models with actual field data, largely because the models do not lend themselves to easy documentation. Such documentation will come from very meticulous excavations at single sites, which will be combined, eventually, into larger regional models (H. Wright, 1993). Such research has been conducted successfully at Abu Hureyra, Syria, and in the southern Levant (Chapter 9), also at Guilá Naquitz, Mexico. In the final analysis, however, no one theory of the origins of food production embraces all regions of the world (Gebauer and Price, 1992; Hayden, 1991).

GUILÁ NAQUITZ

● ● ●

Guilá Naquitz
8750 to 6670 B.C.

As part of a long-term archaeological project in the Oaxaca Valley of Mexico, Kent Flannery and his research team excavated Guilá Naquitz Cave, a small shelter used about six times over a 2000-year period between 8750 and 6670 B.C. (Flannery et al., 1986) (Figure 1.11). These sporadic occupations extend from the early Archaic, soon after the extinction of big game in the region, to a period when the occupants were using domesticated plants. The early Archaic occupants spent some of the year in large bands, splitting up to exploit larger areas of territory in much smaller groups, one of which used Guilá Naquitz upon occasion. The multidisciplinary research project revealed a wealth of information about the visitors to this shelter, identifying not only subsistence strategies but also the division of labor between women, who processed plant foods, and men, who did the hunting, through the distribution of artifacts and features in occupation levels. Most important of all, Flannery and his colleagues tried to answer two questions: What was the strategy that led to the choice of the wild plants eaten by the inhabitants, and how did this strategy change when they began planting?

Robert Reynolds (1986) developed a comprehensive and ingenious "adaptive computer simulation model" to approach these questions. He started with a hypothetical, and totally ignorant, band of five people who settle in the area. Over a long period of trial and error, they "learn" how to schedule 11 major food plants over the year, in an environment where the sequence of dry, wet, and "average" years is totally unpredictable. The collective memories of successive generations prove to be of vital importance, for past experience is the basis upon which they modify their strategies in future years that prove to be the same as already experienced ones. For example, a cycle of drought years may yield survival strategies that are remembered through the succeeding wet years, despite the passage of a generation or more, and are then used again. The strategies rank plants and vegetational zones in order of the size of the harvest, yielding collective decisions followed by the band. By the time the last preagricultural occupation occurs at Guilá Naquitz, the band is so efficient in all conditions that very few modifications improve the adaptation. Basically, there is a stable performance level.

The computer simulation produced a mix of plant species that matched the mix found in the occupation deposits very well. It also showed that the group used one set of strategies for wet years, when plant foods were available in abundance and a wide range of them was used, and another in dry years, when the people took fewer species and those with higher yields. Reynolds's simulation is based on the assumption that the first stages of agriculture were attempts to alter the densities of specific plants. The wet-year strategies were the ones that were the most flexible and most capable of incorporating experimentation without risk. At first, deliberate planting may have been a rarity, a strategy that was successful but only employed in wet years. It was a specialized strategy but one whose yields were seen eventually to have advantages, to the point that planting became more frequent, occurring not only in wet years but in dry ones as well, *once the experiment had been shown to work*. If the simulation is correct, the pace of experimentation was very slow, confined at first to wet years; at the same time, centuries-old foraging strategies continued. Reynolds's simulation suggests that bean cultivation near the cave itself allowed the people to collect more food and travel less, with ultimately a greater emphasis on foraging in the thorn forest near the site rather than farther afield. At the same time, traveling time decreased and collecting time increased—acorns from the thorn forest become much more common, for example. Less time is spent on lower-yielding, more marginal wild plants, as greater emphasis is placed on beans, squash, and maize. As the group gained experience with planting, yields rose, and the people placed ever more emphasis on cultivation as opposed to foraging.

Reynolds's (1986) simulation corresponds well with the shifts in plant species found in the six occupation levels at Guilá Naquitz. When he added climatic change and population growth to the equation, he found that two sources of uncertainty, unpredictable climate fluctuations and population shifts, were the factors that led to the most rapid increase in the density of high-yielding domesticated plants near the site. Reynolds believes that a high level of annual climatic variation—with its frequent wet years, for experimentation, and dry years, which put pressure on people to be efficient—was a major factor in the shift to food production in Oaxaca. So were short-term as opposed to long-term fluctuations in population densities, which also led to an accelerating reliance on cultivation not only on hill slopes but also on river plains in Oaxaca, the environments in which the first larger villages are found.

This sophisticated, hypothetical model is remarkable in that it corresponds well with excavated data. Reynolds demonstrates that these Oaxaca people were well preadapted to food production. There was no "trigger" that started cultivation. The people simply added gourds, beans, and a simple form of maize to a much earlier foraging adaptation, at first as a wet year innovation, which came into use in average and dry years once it proved reliable. As Flannery (1986) says, "Human hunting and gathering is, after all, economic behavior." Foragers make decisions about distances to travel and the plants and territory to exploit. When they shift to agriculture, they are changing the pattern of their decision making, not in an irreversible way but probably as one of several alternatives open to them. This change "has to be understood in terms of their previous decision-making pattern, the options open to them, and that new situation." At the same time, too, this culturally based explanation emerges from circumstances arising from larger processes, among them a worldwide climatic change at the end of the Ice Age and long-term evolutionary processes. In time, for example, early farmers anywhere acquired a selective advantage by virtue of their ability to disperse seeds from "a group of plants whose genetic program they had altered, in defiance of natural selection."

Probabilistic ecosystem model

The Guilá Naquitz research, with its sophisticated computer simulations, is an example of what future research into agricultural origins holds. In the final analysis, Flannery (1986) seems to prefer what he calls a "probabilistic ecosystem model." This model allows people to respond to changes in the ecosystem in several ways. The Guilá Naquitz people reduced their search area for wild plants, which may have led to protein deficiencies. Their solution was to grow beans, a protein-rich crop that allowed them to reduce their search area still more. In other parts of the world, like southern California or the Pacific Northwest, they intensified fishing and sea mammal hunting, and agriculture was never adopted on any scale, even if the people were well aware of it. Agriculture was not the only option. It was one of many, and one that achieved remarkable success in the regions where it did develop.

Once successful, food production spread rapidly, partly because population growth after the fact prevented people from reverting to hunting and gathering. There remains an interesting question. Why did food production not take hold much earlier in prehistory? Surely there were many previous occasions during the Ice Age when conditions were favorable for people to start cultivating plants. Here population models for prehistory offer some clues. We know there was gradual population growth during the Stone Age. The constant, cyclical changes of the past 700,000 years must have led to conditions in some areas that presented human societies with the challenge of constant environmental change and population shifts. However, as we saw in Chapter 5, it was not until the end of the Ice Age that global populations rose sufficiently to circumscribe mobility, and the easiest strategy for people faced with food shortages is to move away. It must be significant that there was initially a slow and then a rapidly accelerating intensification of hunter-gatherer lifeways during and after the last glacial maximum, especially during Holocene times. This intensification preadapted many societies for food production for the first time (McCorriston and Hole, 1991; Stark, 1986).

DIFFERING DATES FOR EARLY FOOD PRODUCTION

● ● ●

As we shall see in Chapters 9 to 13, food production began at very different times in various parts of the world, being well established in the Near East by 7000 B.C., in Mesoamerica by 3000 B.C., but in tropical Africa by about 1000 B.C., and then only in some locations. What were the local variations that accounted for this time lag?

David Harris (1980) argues that hunter-gatherers in subtropical zones such as the Near East and highland Mesoamerica were beginning to manipulate potential domesticates among wild grasses and root species at the end of the Ice Age. Dependence on such foods probably came earlier in these regions, where there were only a few forageable species. Such dependence was essential to long-term survival. In contrast, populations in more humid tropical regions, like the African and Amazonian rain forests, probably did little more than manipulate a few wild species to minimize risk in lean years; as a corollary, many African agricultural peoples turn to hunting and gathering in lean years to this day. The archaeological record shows that agriculture was established considerably earlier in the subtropical Near East, Middle and South America, Southeast Asia, and India than it was in humid, tropical zones, undoubtedly because that environment was rich in game and wild vegetable foods. Furthermore, domesticated crops and animals were more susceptible to irregular rainfall, locusts and other insect attacks, and endemic stock diseases. A strong and sustained incentive to obtain food must have been a prerequisite for a lasting shift from foraging to agriculture.

Harris points out that many variables must be understood before we can reconstruct the conditions under which agriculture was first regarded as a profitable activity. We are searching for a set of conditions in which population pressure, distribution of plants, the rate at which the environment is changing, and even techniques of harvesting wild grasses all play their part in making agriculture work. Then there are variations among the potentially domesticable plants and animals, some of which resist domestication because of their long life span or because parts of their lives take place outside human control. The seasonal distribution of wild vegetable foods or game could also have prevented experiments in domestication, when the seasons during which these wild foods were exploited coincided with the times of year when it was important that experimenting farmers stay near their growing crops. Under these circumstances, people would tend to pursue their traditional food-getting strategies rather than risk their lives for an uncertain outcome.

CONSEQUENCES OF FOOD PRODUCTION

● ● ●

The new food-producing economies proved dramatically successful. In 8000 B.C. virtually everybody in the world lived by hunting and gathering. By A.D. 1 most people were farmers or herders and only a minority were still hunter-gatherers. The spread of food production throughout the world took only about 8000 years. The problem for anthropologists is not only to account for why people took up agriculture but also to explain why so many populations adopted this new, and initially risky, economic transition in such a short time. Food production spread to all corners of the world except where an environment with extreme aridity or heat or cold rendered agriculture or herding impossible or where people chose to remain hunters and gatherers. In some places, food production was the economic base for urbanization and literate civilization; but most human societies did not go further than subsistence-level food production until the industrial power of nineteenth- and twentieth-century Europe led them into the machine age.

Food production resulted, ultimately, in much higher population densities in many locations, for the domestication of plants and animals can lead to an economic strategy that increases and stabilizes available food supplies, although more energy is used to produce them (Figure 8.2). Farmers use concentrated tracts of territory for agriculture and for grazing cattle and small stock if they practice mixed farming. Their territory is much smaller than that of hunter-gatherers (although pastoralists need huge areas of grazing land for seasonal pasture). Within a smaller area of farming land, property lines are carefully delineated as individual ownership and problems of inheritance arise. Shortages of land can lead to disputes and to the founding of new village settlements on previously uncultivated soil.

More enduring settlements brought other changes. The portable and lightweight material possessions of many hunter-gatherers were replaced by heavier toolkits and more lasting houses (Figure 8.3). Grindstones and ground-edged axes were even more essential to farming culture than they were to gathering societies. Hoes and other implements of tillage were vital for the planting and harvesting of crops. New social units came into being as more lasting home bases were developed; these social links reflected ownership and inheritance of land and led to much larger settlements that brought hitherto scattered populations into closer and more regular contact.

Food production led to changed attitudes toward the environment. Cereal crops were such that people could store their food for winter (Figure 8.3). The hunter-gatherers exploited game, fish, and vegetable foods, but the farmers did more; they *altered* the environment by the very nature of their exploitation. Expansion of agriculture meant felling trees and burning vegetation to clear the ground for planting. The same fields were then abandoned after a few years to lie fallow, and more woodland was cleared. The original vegetation began to regenerate, but it might have been cleared again before reaching its original state. This shifting pattern of

Slash-and-burn (swidden) agriculture

farming is called *slash-and-burn,* or *swidden, agriculture.* Voracious domesticated animals stripped pastures of their grass cover; then heavy rainfalls denuded the hills

FIGURE 8.3   A mud-and-pole hut typical of the Middle Zambezi Valley, central Africa (*left*). Such dwellings, often occupied 15 years or longer, are more lasting than the windbreak or tent of the hunter-gatherer or cattle herder. *Right* is a grain bin from an African village, used for cereal crops. Storing food is a critical activity of many hunters, foragers, and farmers.

of valuable soil, and the pastures were never the same again. However elementary the agricultural technology, the farmer changed the environment, if only with fires lit to clear scrub from gardens and to fertilize the soil with wood ash. Hunter-gatherers had deliberately set fires to encourage the growth of new grass for their grazing prey. In a sense, shifting slash-and-burn agriculture is merely an extension of the age-old use of fire to encourage regeneration of vegetation.

Food production resulted in high population densities, but growth was controlled by disease, available food supplies, water supplies, and particularly famine. Early agricultural methods depended heavily on careful selection of the soil. The technology of the first farmers was hardly potent enough for extensive clearing of the dense woodland under which many good soils lay, so potentially cultivable land could only be that which was accessible. Gardens probably were scattered over a much wider territory than is necessary today. One authority estimates that even with advanced shifting agriculture, only 40 percent of moderately fertile soil in Africa is available for such cultivation (Allan, 1965). This figure must have been lower in the early days of agriculture, with their simpler stone tools and fewer crops.

In regions of seasonal rainfall, such as the Near East, sub-Saharan Africa, and parts of Asia, periods of prolonged drought are common. Famine was a real possibility as population densities rose. Many early agriculturalists must have worriedly watched the sky and had frequent crop failures in times of drought. Their small stores of grain from the previous season would not have carried them through another year, especially if they had been careless with their surplus. Farmers were forced to shift their economic strategy in such times. We know that the earliest farmers availed themselves of game and vegetable foods to supplement their agriculture, just as today some farmers are obliged to rely heavily on wild vegetable foods and hunting to survive in bad years (Scudder, 1962, 1971). Many hunter-gatherer bands collect intensively just a few species of edible plants in their large territories. Aware of many other edible vegetables, they fall back on these only in times of stress; the less favored foods can carry a comparatively small population through to the next rains. A larger agricultural population is not so flexible and quickly exhausts wild vegetables and game in the much smaller territory used for farming and grazing. If the drought lasts for years, famine, death, and reduced population can follow.

NUTRITION AND EARLY FOOD PRODUCTION

●   ●   ●

Was food production a real improvement in human lifeways? For generations archaeologists have argued that human health improved dramatically as a result of agriculture, because people worked less and lived on more reliable food supplies (Butzer, 1982; Childe, 1952). In recent years, Ester Boserup (1965) and others have argued that in fact agriculture brought diminishing returns in relation to labor expended in the new systems that were adopted to feed many more people. Richard Lee's (1979) studies of the !Kung San of the Kalahari Desert tend to support her views. They show that these hunter-gatherers, and presumably others, had abundant leisure and worked less than farmers. Some nutritionists point out that foragers may have had better-balanced diets than many farmers, who relied heavily on root or cereal crops. Further, farmers, with their sedentary settlements and higher population densities, were much more vulnerable to famine than their hunter-gatherer predecessors. They would also have been more vulnerable to gastrointestinal infections and epidemics because of crowded village populations (Cohen, 1988).

While the theoretical controversies swirl, actual empirical data are still hard to come by. Some pioneer nutrition studies based on the skeletons of early farmers suggest some incidence of anemia and slow growth resulting from malnutrition. Signs of physical stress are even harder to come by. Ten regional studies of prehistoric populations have suggested a *decline* in mean age life expectancy in agricultural populations, which contradicts the commonly held perception. Taken as a whole, the paleopathological studies that have been published suggest a general decline in the quality, and perhaps the length, of human life with the advent of food production. It should be pointed out, however, that there are many unknowns involved, among them changes in fertility and population growth rates, which caused the world's population to rise even if general health standards and life expectancy fell.

What impact these studies will have on population pressure theories about the origins of agriculture is still uncertain. Certainly, any shift to food production caused by increasing population pressure could be reflected in a decline in the overall health and nutrition displayed by prehistoric skeletons. It is likely that the next generation of theories about early agriculture will be based on researches into the paleopathology of pioneer farming populations.

In the final analysis, some people probably turned to food production only when other alternatives were no longer practicable. The classic example is the Aborigines of extreme northern Australia, who were well aware that their neighbors in New Guinea were engaged in intensive agriculture. They, too, knew how to plant the top of the wild yam so that it regerminated, but they never adopted food production simply because they had no need to become dependent on a lifeway that would reduce their leisure time and produce more food than they required.

HERDING: DOMESTICATION OF ANIMALS

● ● ●

Potentially tamable species like the wild ox, goat, sheep, and dog were widely distributed in the Old World during the Upper Pleistocene. New World farmers domesticated only such animals as the llama, the guinea pig, and the turkey, and then only under special conditions and within narrow geographic limits. It is possible that the domesticated dog crossed into the New World with the first Americans before 13,000 B.C. or that it was domesticated elsewhere in the Americas, but the evidence is uncertain.

Having one's own herds of domesticated mammals ensured a regular meat supply. The advantages to having a major source of meat under one's control are obvious. Later, domesticated animals provided byproducts such as milk, cheese, and butter, as well as skins for clothes and tent coverings and materials for leather shields and armor. In later millennia, people learned how to breed animals for specialized tasks such as plowing, transportation, and traction (Clutton-Brock, 1981).

Domestication implies a genetic selection emphasizing special features of continuing use to the domesticator. Wild sheep have no wool, wild cows produce milk only for their offspring, and undomesticated chickens do not lay surplus eggs. Changes in wool bearing, lactation, or egg production could be achieved by isolating wild populations for selective breeding under human care. Isolating species from a larger gene pool produced domestic sheep with thick, woolly coats and domestic goats providing regular supplies of milk, which formed a staple in the diet of many human populations.

No one knows exactly how domestication of animals began. During the Upper Pleistocene, people already were beginning to concentrate heavily on some species of large mammals for their diet. The Magdalenians of southwest France directed much of their lives toward pursuing reindeer. At the end of the Pleistocene, hunters in the Near East were concentrating on gazelles and other steppe animals. Wild sheep and goats were intensively hunted on the southern shores of the Caspian Sea. Gregarious animals are those most easily domesticated; they follow the lead of a dominant herd member or all move together.

Hunters often fed off the same herd for a long time, sometimes deliberately sparing young females and immature beasts to keep the source of food alive. Young animals captured alive in the chase might be taken back to the camp and grow dependent on those who caged them, thus becoming partially tamed. A hunter could grasp the possibility of gaining control of the movements of a few key members of a herd, who would be followed by the others. Once the experience of keeping pets or of restricting game movements had suggested a new way of life, people might experiment with different species (Flannery, 1969). As part of domestication, animals and humans increased their mutual interdependence.

The archaeological evidence for early domestication is so fragile that nothing survives except the bones of the animals kept by the early farmers, and differences between wild and domestic animal bones are often so small initially that it is difficult to distinguish them unless very large collections are found. In the earliest centuries of domestication, corralled animals were nearly indistinguishable from wild species.

The process of animal domestication undoubtedly was prolonged, developing in several areas of the Near East at approximately the same time. Although animal bones are scarce and often unsatisfactory as evidence of early domestication, most authorities now agree that the first species to be domesticated in the Near East was the sheep, about 8500 B.C. Sheep are small animals living in herds, whose carcasses yield much meat for their size. They can readily be penned and isolated to develop a symbiotic relationship with people.

Cattle are much more formidable to domesticate, for their prototype was *Bos primigenius,* the wild ox much hunted by Stone Age people (Figure 8.4). Andrew

FIGURE 8.4 *Bos primigenius,* the aurochs or wild ox, as depicted by S. von Herbenstain in 1549. It became extinct in Europe in 1627, although recent breeding experiments have reconstructed this formidable beast.

Smith (1992) believes that the first domesticated animals came from better-disciplined wild herds in arid environments, where it was easier to control the movements of animals. Such conditions may have pertained over much of the Near East and Sahara Desert as the climate became drier after 7000 B.C.

It should be noted that some animals, such as sea mammals, resist domestication because much of their lives is spent out of range of human influence. Most early successes with domestication took place with gregarious animals. They can be thought of as a food reserve, as "grain on the hoof."

CULTIVATION: DOMESTICATION OF PLANTS

●   ●   ●

Many fewer wild vegetable foods were domesticated than foraged over the millennia. In the Old World, wheat, barley, and other cereals that grow wild over much of Asia and Europe became cultivated. In the New World, a different set of crops was tamed (D. Harris and Hillman, 1989; Zohary and Hopf, 1988). These included Indian corn *(Zea mays),* the only important wild grass to be domesticated. Root crops such as manioc and sweet potatoes, chili peppers, tobacco, and several types of bean were all grown. Common to both Old and New Worlds are gourds, cotton, and two or three other, minor crops (Ford, 1985).

In the Old World, tropical regions had many potential domesticates such as the yam and gourds. In Southeast Asia and sub-Saharan Africa, a long period of intensive gathering and experimenting with the deliberate planting of wild root crops probably preceded the beginnings of formal agriculture. Perhaps, however, the transition from gathering to cultivation of root crops was almost unconscious, for many tubers are easy to grow deliberately. The African yam, for example, can be germinated simply by cutting off its top and burying it in the ground. The hunter-gatherer bands who were familiar with this easy means of conserving their food supplies may simply have intensified their planting efforts to supplement shortages caused by changed circumstances. As with animals, however, certain heavily exploited species tended to resist domestication; among them were the long-lived trees like the oak and plants whose life spans were so long that they inhibited human selection. They also tended to cross-pollinate, a process that undoubtedly discouraged human efforts to trigger or control genetic variation.

In the Old World, the qualities of wild wheat, barley, and similar crops are quite different from those of their domestic equivalents (D. Harris and Hillman, 1989). In the wild, these grains occur in dense stands. They can be harvested by tapping the stem with the hands and gathering the seeds in a basket as they fall off or by uprooting the plant. The tapping technique is effective because the wild grain is attached to the stem by a brittle joint, or *rachis.* When the grass is tapped, the weak rachis breaks and the seed falls into the basket.

The first cultivated wheat and barley crops were of the wild, brittle-rachised type, and the resulting crops would probably have been large enough to generate domestic-type mutants in the first 2 to 5 years (Figure 8.5). Selection for the semitough rachised forms was, of necessity, an unconscious process during the earliest stages of domestication. Computer simulations have shown that domestic, semitough rachised forms may have been rare at first, but they would have been fully domesticated within 20 to 30 generations—for these cereals, between 20 and 30

Fragile, ineffective awns (often deciduous)

1mm

Poorly developed barbs on glumes

More rounded spikelet body (less arrow-like)

One segment of the semi-tough rachis

Rough breakage of rachis, leaving sharp corners which impede penetration

A single spikelet from a threshed ear, viewed from the adaxial face. The spikelet contains one plump grain.

Ripe spikelets remaining in ear

1cm

Ear shatters only when threshed

Dense ear due to shorter rachis segments

A fully ripe ear. The ear will shatter only when threshed.

Domestic einkon (*T. monococcum*) showing its semi-tough-rachised ear and its plumper spikelets which have lost some key features neccesary for self-implantation.

Long springey awns with backwards-pointing barbs:

Robust awn of fertile lower floret;

Smaller awn of the sterile upper floret

1mm

Pointed glume-tips facing backwards like arrow tangs

Backwards-pointing barbs on glume angles

Backwards-pointing hairs from rachis

One segment of the brittle rachis

Clean semi-circular disarticulation scar

Smooth rounded edge of rachis "point"

A single disarticulated spikelet viewed from its inside (adaxial) face. In this case, the spikelets contained a single grain.

Wild einkon (*Triticum boeoticum*) showing its brittle-rachised ear and arrow-shaped spikelets adapted for penetrating surface litter and cracks in the ground.

Ripe spikelets disarticulating (and falling to ground) as the ripening rachis breaks into its constituent segments

1cm

Near-ripe spikelets still attached in ear

The basal few spikelets which generally fail to disarticulate

A ± ripe ear in the process of shattering and thereby shedding its spikelets. The ear ripens from the top downwards.

FIGURE 8.5   The features affecting seed dispersal and spikelet implantation in wild and domesticated einkorn wheat.

years. Even with less intense selective pressures than those assumed in the experiment, domestication could have been achieved within 1 or 2 centuries (Figure 8.6) (Hillman and Davies, 1990).

Archaeobotanist Gordon Hillman believes that the farmers would have started conscious selection as soon as the domesticates became sufficiently common to be recognized, perhaps 1 to 5 percent of the crop. From then on, domestication would have been completed in 3 or 4 years.

Although the broad outlines of the process of domestication can be reconstructed through controlled experimentation and computer simulation, it is most unlikely that anyone will ever find "transitional" grains in Near Eastern sites that will document the actual process underway. The changeover from wild to domesticated strains was so rapid that we are more likely to find wild seeds in one level and domesticated ones in the next. This is precisely what has been found at Near Eastern sites such as Abu Hureyra, where farming appears abruptly about 7700 B.C. (see Chapter 9).

TECHNOLOGY AND DOMESTICATION

• • •

The technological consequences of food production were, in their way, as important as the new economies. A more settled way of life and some decline in hunting and gathering slowly led to long-term residences, lasting agricultural styles, and more substantial housing. As they had done for millennia, people built their permanent homes with the raw materials most abundant in their environment. The early farmers of the Near East worked and dried mud into small houses with flat roofs; these were cool in summer and warm in winter. At night during the hot season people may have slept on the flat roofs. Some less substantial houses had reed roofs. In the more temperate zones of Europe, with wetter climates, timber was used to build thatched-roof houses of various shapes and sizes. Early African farmers often built huts of grass, sticks, and anthill clay. Nomadic pastoralists of the northern steppes had no concern with a permanent and durable home, yet they, too, took advantage of the related benefits of having a domestic food supply: They used the skins to make clothing as well as tents to shelter them during the icy winters.

Agriculture is a seasonal activity, with long periods of the year in which the fields are lying fallow or are supporting growing crops. Any farmer is confronted with the problem of keeping food in ways the hunter-gatherer never has to ponder. Thus, a new technology of storage came into being. Grain bins, jars, or clay-lined pits became an essential part of the agricultural economy for stockpiling food for the lean months and against periods of famine. The bins might have been made of wattle and daub, clay, or timber (see Figure 8.3). Basket and clay-lined silos protected valuable grain against rodents.

Hunter-gatherers use skins, wood containers, gut pouches, and sometimes baskets for carrying vegetable foods back from the bush. Farmers face far more formidable transport problems: They must carry their harvest back to the village, keep ready-for-use supplies of foods in the house as opposed to storage bins, and store

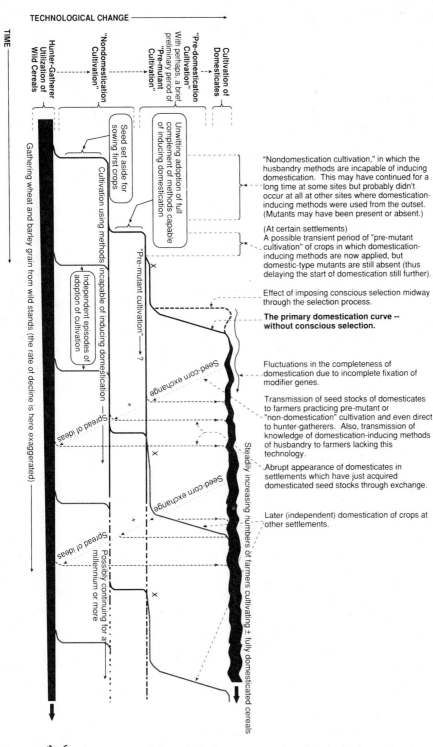

FIGURE 8.6   A summary of the principal events associated with the domestication of wheat and barley. For the sake of argument, this diagram assumes that domestication both of the wheats and barleys occurred at several settlements independently.

water. Early farmers began to use gourds as water carriers and to make clay vessels that were both waterproof and capable of carrying and cooking food (Figure 8.7) They made pots by coiling rolls of clay or building up the walls of vessels from a lump and firing them in simple hearths. Clay vessels were much more durable than skin or leather receptacles. Some pots were used for several decades before being broken and abandoned. Pottery did not appear simultaneously with agriculture. It came into use at different times in many widely separated places. For example, the Jomon hunter-gatherers of Japan were making simple clay pots by at least 8500 B.C. They lived a more or less sedentary life by their shell middens, using clay vessels long before agriculture became part of their way of life (Aikens and Higuchi, 1981). In the Near East, however, pottery was first used by farmers by approximately 6000 B.C. (Mellaart, 1975).

For tens of thousands of years, people dug up wild edible roots with simple wooden sticks, sometimes made more effective with the aid of a stone weight. The first farmers continued to use the digging stick to plant crops a few inches below the surface, probably on readily cultivable soils. They also used wooden or stone-bladed hoes (and much later, iron) to break up the soft soil. These they fitted with short or long handles, depending on cultural preference. European and Near Eastern farmers made use of the ox-drawn plow in later millennia, at first with a wooden-tipped blade, then bronze, and later iron (Chapter 15). The plow was an important innovation, for it enabled people to turn the soil over to a much greater depth than ever before. Every farmer has to clear wild vegetation and weeds from the fields, and it is hardly surprising to find a new emphasis on the ax and the adz. The simple axes of pioneer farmers were replaced by more elaborate forms in metal by 2500 B.C. in the Near East. Present-day experiments in Denmark and New Guinea have shown that the ground and polished edges of stone axes are remarkably effective in clearing woodland and felling trees (Figure 8.8). In later millennia, the alloying of copper and bronze and, later, the development of iron cutting edges made forest clearance even easier.

New tools meant new technologies to produce tougher working edges. At first the farmers used ground and polished stone, placing a high premium on suitable rocks, which were traded from quarry sites over enormous distances. Perhaps the most famous ax quarries are in western Europe, where ax blanks were traded the length of the British Isles and Grand Pressigny flint from France was prized over thousands of square miles. In the Near East and Mexico, one valuable toolmaking material, not for axes but for knives and sickles, was obsidian, a volcanic rock prized for its easy working properties, sharp edges, and its ornamental appearance. Early obsidian trade routes carried tools and ornaments hundreds of miles from their places of origin. By using spectrographic techniques, scientists have been able to trace obsidian over long distances to such places of origin as Lipari Island off Italy and Lake Van in Turkey (Renfrew and Dixon, 1976; Torrance, 1986).

All these developments in technology made people more and more dependent on exotic raw materials, many of which were unobtainable in their own territory. We see the beginnings of widespread long-distance trading networks, which were to burgeon even more rapidly with the emergence of the first urban civilizations.

We still know tantalizingly little about the ways humankind began to exercise control over food resources. We know that in the Near East there was a

FIGURE 8.7 Pottery manufacture. A common method of pot-making was to build up the walls from coils of clay (*top*). The pot was then smoothed and decorated (*left*) and fired, in either on an open hearth (*right*) or a kiln. These pictures illustrate Pueblo Indian pottery-manufacturing techniques from the Southwestern United States and are, of course, not necessarily typical of all potters.

FIGURE 8.8 Using a stone adze to fell a tree. A Tefalmin farmer at work in New Guinea in 1966.

dramatic shift in human subsistence patterns by 7000 B.C., in northern China by 5000 B.C., and in Mesoamerica about 3500 B.C. Some fascinating clues suggest that people were exercising some sort of control over their food supplies very much earlier. Perhaps Upper Paleolithic people who specialized in hunting reindeer or mountain goats made some attempts to manage their prey herds. Conceivably, too, hunter-gatherers living on the fringes of tropical rain forests could have engaged in deliberate opportunistic horticulture, planting yams and other food plants that could be regenerated for future use. The beginnings of the agricultural revolution may have taken hold many thousands of years before the explosion came. After all, we should never forget that humans have always been opportunistic, and the planting of food crops and the first taming of animals may have been the simple result.

CHAPTER SUMMARY

Many late Ice Age and early Holocene hunter-gatherer societies were pre-adapted for food production, as they were already exploiting some food resources intensively and living more sedentary lifeways. Most of these were in regions where food resources were diverse and seasonally predictable. In contrast to early theories that thought of food production as a revolutionary development, modern hypotheses invoke social causes, population growth, and ecological factors as multivariate causes of food production. The development of food production was a gradual process, one that saw increasing reliance on food crops, especially in areas with constant and unpredictable environmental change. Food production resulted in more sedentary human settlement, more substantial housing, elaborate storage technologies, and special implements for agricultural tasks. All these technological developments led to greater interdependence and to more long-distance exchange of raw materials, as well as increasing human social complexity.

GUIDE TO FURTHER READING

Childe, V. Gordon. 1936. *Man Makes Himself*. London: Watts.
> *Classic Childe arguments for a Neolithic Revolution that summarize all the evidence in favor of a revolutionary change in prehistory when food production began.*

Cohen, Mark. 1977. *The Food Crisis in Prehistory*. New Haven, CT: Yale University Press.
> *An original and thought-provoking essay on the origins of agriculture that advocates population as a major factor.*

———. 1989. *Health and the Rise of Civilization*. New Haven, CT: Yale University Press.
> *An essay on paleopathology and the origins of more complex societies that contains much original thinking.*

Flannery, Kent V. 1986. *Guilá Naquitz*. Orlando, FL: Academic Press.
> *A case study of a site occupied during the transition from hunting and gathering to food production, with excellent theoretical discussion.*

Gebauer, A. and Price, T.D., eds. 1992. *Transitions to Agriculture in Prehistory*. Madison, WI: Prehistory Press.
> *A useful series of essays on origins, addressed at more advanced readers.*

Harris, David, and Hillman, Gordon, eds. 1989. *Farming and Foraging*. Oxford: Clarendon Press.
> *Articles on the basics of agriculture and plant foraging crammed with useful background information. Somewhat specialized, but fascinating reading.*

Rindos, David. 1984. *The Origins of Agriculture: An Evolutionary Perspective.* New York: Academic Press.

> *A provocative discussion of the origins of agriculture that evaluates competing theories.*

Smith, Bruce D. 1994. *The Emergence of Agriculture.* New York: Scientific American Library.

> *A clear account of the origins of food production for the general reader. Smith uses AMS and other scientific advances to date major crops in the archaeological record.*

CHAPTER 9

THE ORIGINS OF FOOD PRODUCTION IN THE NEAR EAST

• • •

It was the final day of the 1953 excavation season at Jericho. For weeks, the top of a human skull had projected from the side of the trench dug deep into one of the earliest farming communities in the world. Excavator Kathleen Kenyon had given strict instructions that it was not to be disturbed until the stratigraphic layers in the trench wall had been drawn and photographed. Drawing completed, she somewhat unwillingly gave the site supervisor permission to remove the skull from the wall. That evening, he carried back to camp a complete cranium, carefully covered in clay, modeled in the human features, with the eyes inset with shells.

Next morning, Kenyon looked closely at the small hole in the wall. She could see two more plastered skulls within. They were removed. Three more now appeared behind them, then a final seventh head. It took five days to extract the nest of skulls from the wall, for the crushed bones were packed tightly with stones and hard earth. They formed the earliest portrait gallery in the world, each head modeled with individual features—nose, mouth, ears, and eyebrows molded with delicacy. Kenyon believed she had found the heads of revered ancestors, who were critical intermediaries between the living and the spiritual world. (Figure 9.4). They were symbols of a new spiritual order that linked people closely to the land that brought forth their crops.

Much of the theorizing about early food production has stemmed from archaeological research in the Near East, where many early farming settlements are found (Figure 9.1) (Table 9.1) (G. Wright, 1971). The time when food production began is called the *Neolithic,* the "period in which a pattern of village settlement based on subsistence farming and stockbreeding became the basis of existence for communities throughout the Near East" (Moore, 1985). The Neolithic of the Near East began about 8000 B.C. nearly everywhere and lasted until the sixth millennium B.C. in Mesopotamia and until as late as 4000 B.C. in the Levant (Henry, 1989).

Neolithic

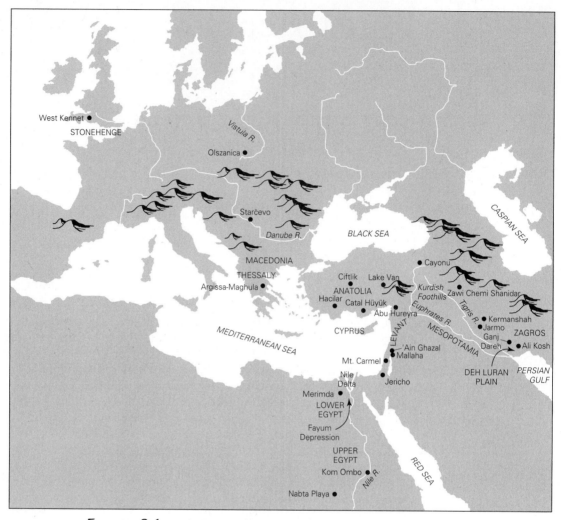

FIGURE 9.1   Early farming sites in the Near East, Europe, and the Nile Valley.

THE HOLOCENE ENVIRONMENT

• • •

Deep-sea cores and pollen studies tell us that the Near Eastern climate was cool and dry from about 18,000 to 13,000 B.C., during the late Weichsel (Moore, 1989). Sea levels dropped more than 300 feet (100 m); much of the interior was covered by dry steppe, with forest restricted to the Levant and Turkish coasts. Between 13,000 and 8000 B.C., climatic conditions warmed up considerably, reaching a maximum about 3000 B.C. Forests expanded rapidly at the end of the Ice Age, for the climate was still cooler than today and considerably wetter. Many areas of the Near East were richer in animal and plant species than they are now, making them highly favorable for human occupation.

TABLE 9.1

• • •

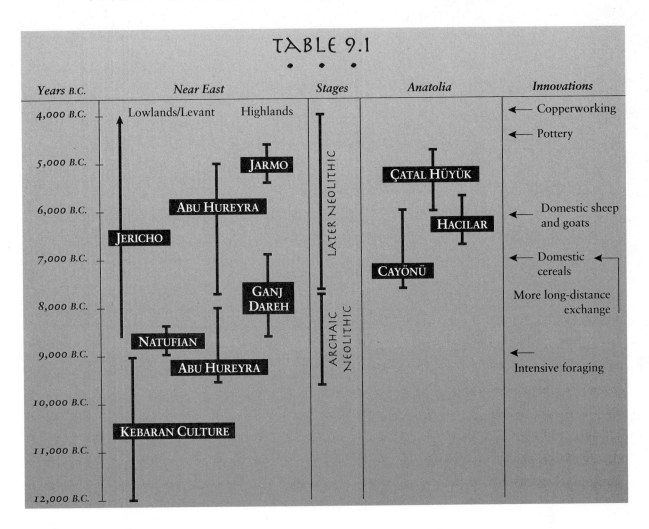

A SCENARIO FOR EARLY AGRICULTURE

• • •

The development and spread of agriculture took place in unusually favorable environmental conditions, probably in the southern Levant, specifically in the Jordan Valley region (Bar-Yosef and Belfer-Cohen, 1989; McCorriston and Hole, 1991; H. Wright, 1993). A widely accepted scenario for the first farming goes as follows: Southern Levant lies at the junction of mediterranean, continental, and monsoon-influenced climates and nurtured a unique and ever-changing set of ecotones. In the early Holocene, the climate shifted from a continental to a mediterranean regimen, with warmer temperatures, more forest cover, and increasing summer aridity. The vegetation became far more diverse, with a dramatic increase in annual cereal grasses that flower and produce seed in spring and become dormant through the long, dry summer months. These cereals appeared first in the south and spread northward. At the same time, hunter-gatherer groups may have disturbed and unconsciously diversified the vegetation by firing it in the dry season to encourage new grass growth, and the deer and other animals that fed upon it. The Jordan Valley was one such area, with an unstable climate. Only those hunter-gatherer groups with an ability to cope with such constant climatic change and marked seasonality, could flourish. They responded by developing storage technology, intensively exploiting cereals and grinding their seeds, and adopting much more sedentary lifeways. All this was not so much a shift toward broad spectrum hunting and foraging as an adjustment to climatic uncertainty. With scarcer surface water and months on end when plant foods and game were in short supply, people depleted their environments, unable to move, perhaps because other bands had territories nearby. Some groups converged around lakes like Lake Beisan, where they domesticated cereals and legumes as a way of amplifying available wild food supplies.

In Chapter 5, we recounted the dramatic changes in hunter-gatherer life throughout the Levant during the early Holocene. We described the simple Kebaran culture, which flourished over a wide area of the coastal zone and inland at a time of more severe climate than today. The Kebaran evolved into the much more sedentary and more complex Natufian culture. These people exploited the Mediterranean zone intensively, foraging on the slopes for cereal grasses and nuts, while exploiting gazelle and other game on the grassy lowlands. This same pattern of specialized hunting and gathering is documented elsewhere in the Near East in about 9000 B.C. The inhabitants of the Abu Hureyra site in Syria, for example, were hunting gazelle virtually to the exclusion of all other species. More than 80 percent of the mammal bones in this small settlement were from gazelle, while at the same time the people exploited only a few species of plants. To this extent, they were managing and tending their environment to a significant degree (Moore, 1989). At the same time, they, and the Natufians, were coping with increasingly dry seasonal climates, warmer than today. If the scenario outlined above is correct, these were the conditions that caused the Natufians, and soon afterward other peoples, to switch over to food production.

Natufian sites occur over much of the coastal strip from southern Turkey to the fringes of the Nile Valley and in parts of the interior (Bar-Yosef and Belfer-Cohen, 1989). They include not only small, temporary camps, but sizable villages of houses built partially into the ground, some settlements five to ten times the size of those of earlier times. The largest Natufian sites and cemeteries contain considerable evidence for social ranking and for a large volume of intercommunity exchange in such commodities as seashells, obsidian, and stone bowls. By 8500 B.C., favorable environmental conditions in the Mediterranean zone were giving way to much drier and more unpredictable conditions. It was at this point, specifically about 8300 B.C., that many Natufian communities turned to at least some deliberate cultivation of wild cereal grasses.

ABU HUREYRA, SYRIA

• • •

Andrew Moore's long-term excavations at the Abu Hureyra site near the Euphrates have led him to believe that agriculture and stock herding developed in this region of the Levant remarkably quickly, perhaps in no more than a few hundred years around 8500 B.C. The adoption of the new economy was accompanied by a major relocation of settlements, two related events brought about by population growth and environmental deterioration.

Under Moore's scenario, pre-Neolithic groups were, in many respects, preadapted to food production. They lived more sedentary lives than their predecessors, hunted a few game species intensively, perhaps even penning some, and probably deliberately planted some plants such as einkorn to supplement wild stands. Then, about 8500 B.C., agriculture and stockbreeding assumed much greater importance, although hunting and foraging continued to be important until about 6000 B.C.

Abu Hureyra began life as a small village settlement of pit dwellings with simple reed roofs supported by wooden uprights (Moore, 1979) (Figure 9.2). Using fine screens and flotation equipment, the excavators recovered thousands of wild vegetable foods, including wild einkorn, rye, and barley. Abu Hureyra lies outside the present-day range of these wild cereals. However, between 9500 and 8000 B.C., when the site was first occupied, the climate was somewhat warmer and damper than it is today. As a result, the village lay in a well-wooded steppe area where animals and wild cereals were abundant. At any rate, some hunter-gatherer groups such as the Hureyra people came together in more permanent settlements and harvested wild cereals as a deliberate subsistence strategy. The inhabitants also had access to a reliable meat source, Persian gazelles that arrived from the south each spring. The arrivals were apparently killed en masse each year and the meat stored. With such a favorable location, Abu Hureyra slowly increased in size to 300 to 400 people, until deteriorating climatic conditions, and perhaps deforestation due to heavy firewood consumption, caused them to leave. In its heyday, its people may have enjoyed a higher degree of social organization than that found in nomadic hunter-gatherer societies.

Just about half a millennium separated the first, gazelle-hunting settlement at Abu Hureyra and the subsequent, much larger farming settlement. About 7700 B.C., a new village, which grew to cover nearly 30 acres (12 ha), rose on the low mound. At first, the inhabitants still hunted gazelle intensively. Then, about 7000 B.C., within the space of a generation or two, they switched to herding domesticated sheep and goats and to growing einkorn, pulses, and other cereals. Visitors to the village would have found themselves wandering through a closely knit community of rectangular, one-story, mud-brick houses, joined by narrow lanes and courtyards. The multiroom dwellings had black polished plaster floors, sometimes decorated with red designs. Each was probably occupied by a single family. Abu Hureyra was finally abandoned in about 5000 B.C.

Abu Hureyra is not, of course, unique. Early Neolithic sites dating from about 8500 to 7600 B.C. are found in the Aleppo region of Syria as far south as the southern Sinai, but only as far east as the interior plateau, with just a few outliers in the Euphrates Valley. Most lie on low ground, near well-watered, easily cultivable land. Every settlement was considerably larger than earlier hunter-gatherer camps. The people lived for the most part in circular or oval one-room houses, often partially dug into the ground. These stone, mud, or mud-brick dwellings were between 13.0 and 19.6 feet (4 and 6 m) in diameter, densely clustered together in tightly knit communities.

Most Early Neolithic villages covered at most a couple of acres. In dramatic contrast, the settlement at Jericho extended over at least 9.8 acres (4 ha). A temporary Natufian camp had flourished at the bubbling Jericho spring at least 8500 B.C. (Kenyon, 1981), but a more lasting farming settlement quickly followed. Soon these people, whose technology did not include clay vessels, were building massive walls around their settlement. A rock-cut ditch more than 9 feet (2.7 m) deep and 10 feet (3.2 m) wide was bordered by a finely built stone wall complete with towers (Figure 9.3). The beehive-shaped huts of Jericho were clustered within the defenses. The

Abu Hureyra
c. 9500 to 8000 B.C.

c. 7700 to 5000 B.C.

Early Neolithic
8500 to 7600 B.C.

Jericho
8500 B.C.

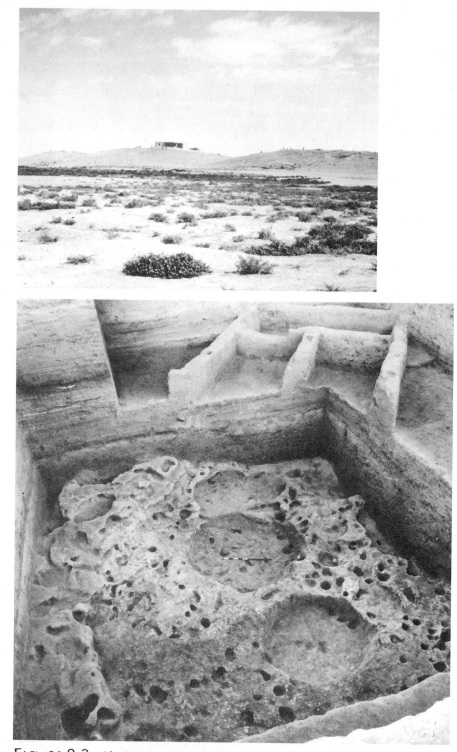

FIGURE 9.2   Abu Hureyra, Syria. *Top:* The mound of Abu Hureyra from the south-west. The site, which overlooks the Euphrates floodplain, consists of two superimposed settlements. *Bottom:* The earlier settlement consisted of a series of interconnecting pits dug into the natural subsoil. These were roofed with poles, branches, and reeds to form huts. Part of a later, rectilinear house can be seen near the top of the picture.

FIGURE 9.3   Excavated remains of the great tower in early Jericho.

communal labor of wall-building required both political and economic resources on a scale unheard of a few thousand years earlier. Why walls were needed remains a mystery, but they must have been for defense, resulting from group competition for scarce resources. Some recent geomorphological researches hint that the walls may have been flood-control works, but the theory is controversial (Bar-Yosef, 1986).

The population of the Levant increased considerably between 7600 and 6000 B.C. More than 140 sites are known, scattered throughout the Levant and far east onto the Syrian plateau. Many of them, like the later settlement at Abu Hureyra, are much larger than the earlier sedentary villages.

Types of houses similar to those at Abu Hureyra occur at Jericho and other contemporary settlements, where the dead were buried within the settlement, sometimes under house floors. At Jericho, 'Ain Ghazal in Jordan, and elsewhere, the people would sever the head and deposit it alone or with a cache of skulls. At both sites, they sometimes modeled the features of the deceased in painted plaster, perhaps in some form of ancestor cult (Figures 9.4 and 9.5). There are no signs of differences in individual status in society.

FIGURE 9.4   Plastered skull from Jericho, perhaps evidence for an early ancestor cult.

The farmers of 8000 B.C. hunted gazelles, wild cattle, pigs, goats, and other game species. None of the bones shows the characteristic morphological features of domesticated animals. Judging from the proportions of immature gazelles at some sites, the people were very efficient, selective hunters. This pattern of animal exploitation began millennia earlier, during the Upper Paleolithic. Sheep and goats very rapidly replaced gazelles as the principal meat supply at Abu Hureyra and else-where after about 7000 B.C. At the same time, there are signs that cattle and pigs were subject to increasing human control. By this time, the domestication of sheep and goats had proceeded to the point that their morphology is clearly that of domes-ticated animals. About 6500 B.C., it appears that the local gazelle herds were depleted: Sheep and goats now composed 60 percent of all meat consumed (Legge and Rowley-Conwy, 1987).

Emmer wheat, barley, lentils, and peas were grown in the Early Neolithic from as early as 8000 B.C. Even quite early on, agricultural methods were relatively sophisticated, cereals being rotated with pulses to ensure high crop yields and sus-tained soil fertility. An effective system of allowing fields to lie fallow also enabled larger sites. Abu Hureyra and Jericho were occupied continuously over many cen-turies as a result. Many settlements became trading centers, for the numbers of imported materials and exotic objects rise dramatically after 7000 B.C. The farmers were using obsidian from Anatolia, turquoise from Sinai, and seashells from the Mediterranean and Red Sea. The volume of trade was such that many villagers used

FIGURE 9.5   Plaster figurines from 'Ain Ghazal, Jordan.

small clay spheres, cones, and disks to keep track of commodities traded. These tokens are thought to have been a simple recording system that later evolved into written script (Schmandt-Besserat, 1992).

By 6000 B.C. there was considerable variation in farming culture throughout the Levant, caused by local cultural developments. But the farmers maintained fleeting contacts with communities many hundreds of miles away, even with peoples living in quite different culture areas in the Zagros and Anatolia.

THE ZAGROS AND MESOPOTAMIA

● ● ●

As in the Levant, the sequence of Neolithic cultures in the Zagros foothills and Mesopotamia can be divided into an earlier stage, from about 8000 to 6000 B.C., and later Neolithic, lasting until about 5000 B.C. There were sporadic contacts between these areas and the Levant, but cultural developments in this region were parallel to and independent of those at Abu Hureyra, Jericho, and other western locations.

Thanks to the pioneering work of Robert Braidwood (L. S. Braidwood, 1982), who looked for agricultural origins on the hilly flanks of Mesopotamia, we know more about the highlands, where agricultural conditions were less favorable, than we do about early food production on the lowlands, the undulating northern Mesopotamian steppe, where the Assyrian civilization flourished. To the south, the sandy Mesopotamian plain accumulated deep layers of silt throughout the

Holocene. Early farming settlement there is probably buried under several feet of alluvium. Only small farming villages preserved under great city mounds like those of Ur and Eridu tell us anything about early farming settlements in these regions, and they date to not much earlier than about 5000 B.C.

During the late Ice Age, human groups probably lived on the warmer lowlands. In the very early Holocene, the mountains were cool and dry, so agriculture probably began on the lowlands first, a natural habitat for wild cereals and pulses. As the climate warmed up, people moved into the mountain valleys of Zagros, open steppe country with seasonal resources spaced vertically up hill slopes. This was ideal country for herding sheep and goats, to the extent that herding may have developed earlier here than in other parts of the Near East (Moore, 1985).

Zawi Chemi Shanidar
9000 B.C.

About 9000 B.C., wild goats were a primary quarry for the hunters and gatherers exploiting the resources of the foothills. The people of a small encampment named Zawi Chemi Shanidar in the mountains of Kurdistan were hunting and gathering at this time, living in small, circular huts. The inhabitants were killing large numbers of immature sheep, as if they had fenced in their grazing grounds for efficient, intensive hunting. Zawi Chemi may have been a summer encampment on the steppe. Pollen studies show an increase in cereal grasses during the occupation, perhaps evidence of cultivation.

Ganj Dareh
8500 B.C.

High in a mountain valley near Kermanshah lies another early farming village named Ganj Dareh, first occupied about 8500 B.C. (P. E. L. Smith, 1978). The earliest settlement was probably a seasonal camp used by hunters and gatherers, but a later occupation, around 7000 B.C., consisted of a small village of rectangular mud-brick houses, some two stories high. The lower stories may have been used for storage because clay bins have been found there. Ganj Dareh represents the beginnings of permanent settlement in the Zagros, based on goat and cattle herding and possibly agriculture. Contemporary sites contain clear evidence for changes in goat bone morphology indicative of full domestication.

Jarmo
5000 B.C.

One of the best-known Zagros farming villages is Jarmo, a permanent hill village southeast of Zawi Chemi occupied in about 5000 B.C. (Braidwood and Braidwood, 1983). Jarmo was little more than a cluster of 25 houses built of mud bricks, forming an irregular huddle separated by small alleyways and courtyards. Storage bins and clay ovens were an integral part of the structures. The Jarmo deposits yielded abundant traces of agriculture: Seeds of barley, emmer wheat, and minor crops were found with the bones of sheep and goats. Hunting had declined in importance—only a few wild animal bones testify to such activity—but the toolkit still included Stone Age–type tools with sickle blades, grinding stones, and other implements of tillage. Jarmo contains exotic materials such as obsidian, seashells, and turquoise traded into the Zagros from afar. There are also numerous clay tokens, perhaps again evidence for a recording system connected with long-distance trade. Jarmo was a fully permanent, well-established village engaged in far more intensive agriculture than its predecessors. More than 80 percent of the villagers' food came from herds or crops.

Ali Kosh
8000 to 6000 B.C.

Below, on the lowlands, farming began along the eastern edge of the flat Mesopotamian plain at least as early as in the Levant. The well-known Ali Kosh site on the plains of Khuzistan, north of where the Tigris and Euphrates join waters, chronicles human occupation from as early as 8000 B.C. Ali Kosh began life as a small village of mud-brick rectangular houses with several rooms (Hole et al., 1969). As time went on, the houses became larger, separated from one another by lanes or courtyards. The people herded goats and sheep, which may have been driven to highland pastures in the mountains during the hot summer months. This transhumance pattern continues in the area to this day. Emmer, einkorn, barley, and lentils were cultivated from the earliest days of Ali Kosh. Hunting and gathering were important, as were fish and waterfowl from a nearby marsh. This well-excavated site documents more than 2000 years of farming and herding on the lowlands, a time span that saw the development of improved cereal strains and the first appearance of irrigation as a way of intensifying agricultural production.

Agriculture and herding were well established in the lowlands when Ali Kosh was founded in about 8000 B.C. As in the Levant, cereal cultivation and animal husbandry were probably developed by hunter-gatherer groups in the very early Holocene. (For details of the late Neolithic in the Levant and these areas, see Moore, 1985.)

ANATOLIA

• • •

Anatolia (Turkey) was a diverse, favorable highland and lowland environment for human settlement from early on in the Holocene. Sites like Hallan Çemi Tepesi in eastern Anatolia document sedentary settlement, pig domestication, and extensive obsidian trade as early as 8500 B.C. (Rosenberg and Davis, 1992).

Çayönü, about 62 miles (100 km) west of Hallan Çemi Tepesi, was occupied from about 7400 to 6000 B.C. (R. J. Braidwood and Cambel, 1980). The first phase of occupation lasted about 650 years, when the inhabitants lived in separate rectangular houses of various designs. The people cultivated cereals and pulses, collected wild vegetable foods, and relied increasingly on domesticated sheep for meat after 6700 B.C.

Çayönü
7400 to 6000 B.C.

Çayönü represents a relatively developed form of farming life, remarkable only for the sudden adoption of sheep herding, a phenomenon also found at Abu Hureyra in Syria. Perhaps the inhabitants of both sites started herding sheep as a result of contact with shepherd peoples from the highlands to the east, who had been herding small stock for a long time.

On the Anatolian plateau, James Mellaart (1975) excavated a remarkable early farming village at Hacilar, which was founded in approximately 6700 B.C. Seven phases of occupation took place at Hacilar before its inhabitants moved. They lived in small rectangular houses with courtyards, hearths, ovens, and plastered walls.

Hacilar
6700 B.C.

No pottery was used at Hacilar, but basketry and leather containers probably were. Barley and emmer wheat were cultivated, and some wild grass seeds were also eaten. The bones of sheep or goats and cattle and deer are present, but there is no evidence for the domestication of any animal except the dog. Hacilar was a simple and unsophisticated settlement, probably typical of many communities in the Near East in the early millennia of farming.

Most Neolithic sites in central and east Anatolia were within easy reach of the rich obsidian sources near Lake Van and elsewhere. Villages close to the volcanic flows where the fine stone came from used it almost exclusively for artifacts, trading a great deal of obsidian to communities near and far in the form of prepared blade cores. Small quantities of Anatolian obsidian traveled hundreds of miles into the Levant and as far as the Persian Gulf. Trace element analyses of artifacts from many sites show that the patterns of exchange were exceedingly complex, as different sources came into and went out of fashion.

The simplicity of many Anatolian farming villages contrasts dramatically with a more complex settlement engaged in widespread trading activity. The great mound

FIGURE 9.6   Schematic reconstruction of houses and shrines from Level VI at Çatal Hüyük, Anatolia, showing their flat roof architecture and roof entrances.

Çatal Hüyük
6000 to 5000 B.C.

of Çatal Hüyük covers 32 acres (13 ha); it was a town of numerous small houses built of sun-dried brick, which were designed to back onto one another, occasionally separated by small courtyards. Roofs were flat, and the outside walls of the houses provided a convenient defense wall (Figure 9.6). The town was rebuilt at least 12 times after approximately 6000 B.C., presumably when the houses began to crumble or the population swelled.

A most remarkable feature of Çatal Hüyük is its artistic tradition, preserved in paintings on carefully plastered walls and in sculptures, some of them parts of shrines (Figure 9.7). Most depict women or bulls. Some paintings show women giving birth to bulls. Much art was about fertility and the regeneration of life, and figurines of women in childbirth have been found.

Much of Çatal Hüyük's prosperity resulted from its monopoly on the obsidian volcanic glass trade from quarries in nearby mountains. Obsidian was only one of many materials traded by Near Eastern farmers after 8000 B.C. Marine shells, jadeite, serpentine, turquoise, and many other exotic commodities moved from village to village through a myriad of barter transactions. Perhaps these regular exchanges were used not only to obtain exotic materials but also to cement social relationships. Andrew Moore (1985) believes that this widespread exchange of raw materials accelerated the diffusion of all manner of innovations far and wide, among them sheep herding, the introduction of pottery, and eventually copper and bronze metallurgy.

Just how important the obsidian trade was in the area has been shown by spectrographic analyses of fragments of the volcanic glass in hundreds of sites between

FIGURE 9.7   Reconstruction of the east and south walls of Shrine VI.14 at
Çatal Hüyük, Anatolia, with sculpted ox heads, horns, benches, and relief models of bulls and rams. The shrine was entered by the ladder at right.

Turkey and Mesopotamia. The trace elements in obsidian are so distinctive that it is
possible to identify the natural source of the glass by this analysis and to reconstruct
the distribution of obsidian from dozens of localities. Colin Renfrew and others
were able to identify no fewer than 12 early farming villages that had obtained
obsidian from the Ciftlik area of central Turkey (Renfrew, Dixon, and Cann, 1966).
The study showed that 80 percent of the chipped stone in villages within 186 miles
(300 km) of Ciftlik was obsidian. Outside this "supply zone," the percentages of
obsidian dropped away sharply with distance, to 5 percent in a Syrian village, and
one-tenth of a percent in the Jordan Valley. Renfrew and his colleagues argue that
regularly spaced villages were passing approximately half the obsidian they received
to their more distant neighbors. Much early farming trade probably was a form of
"down-the-line" bartering that passed various commodities from one village to the
next.

Until about 5000 B.C., cultural development proceeded independently in each of
these three regions. In each, herding and agriculture emerged separately—not that
they were isolated one from another, far from it. There were no regular trading contacts between each area, contacts that may have led to the spread of cereal crops,
herding, pottery, and other innovations. In time, these well-established barter networks helped spread both economic and technological innovations throughout the
ancient Near East, and that is why similar developments and intensifications of agricultural production occur at about the same time in several places. Cereal agriculture and herding occurred much earlier than the Near Eastern Neolithic, among late
Ice Age hunter-gatherers. The Neolithic saw the culmination of these developments;
at this time the new economies became the foundations of human diet throughout
the Near East. Major changes in settlement patterns ensued. Sustained population
growth took hold some time after farming became commonplace and agriculture
sufficiently productive to feed many more people.

The development of the new food-producing economies took place in two
stages. The first saw some agriculture and control of animals, but most of the diet

came from game and wild vegetable foods. Then, about 6000 B.C., more productive cereal grains and the domestication of cattle, sheep, goats, and pigs created the fully agricultural and stock-raising economy that was to persist into historic times, albeit in elaborated forms.

This was a time of profound social change, when human societies developed new mechanisms for social control, settlement of disputes, and regulation of the cultivation and inheritance of land. Evidence for ranked societies appears in the form of richly adorned burials at Çatal Hüyük and, perhaps, the plastered skulls from Jericho; both were large, important settlements that were the focus of long-distance exchange and important religious rituals. Some scholars even refer to these large centers as towns, or "protocities," locations where new forms of ranked society first developed in the Near East. For the most part the new societies were still egalitarian, their economies based on the productive abilities of the household and the nuclear family. The plastered skulls from 'Ain Ghazal, Jericho, and other Neolithic sites (Figures 9.4 and 9.5) and complex rituals and ancestor cults show farmers already defining the relationship between living people and the spiritual world, the world of soil fertility, bountiful crops, and revered ancestors.

CHAPTER SUMMARY

The Near East was cool and dry immediately after the Ice Age, with dry steppe over much of the interior. Human populations were sparse and highly mobile under forests spread more widely throughout the region. The development and spread of food production took place under conditions of climatic uncertainty that favored wild annual cereal grasses. There was a general trend toward more sedentary lifeways and a greater emphasis on storage technology and seed grinding after 10,000 B.C., epitomized by the Natufian culture, groups who foraged intensively for wild cereals. Farming began in the southern Levant about 8300 B.C., and sheep and goats replaced gazelle abruptly at Abu Hureyra in Syria and other settlements after 7000 B.C. Herding was well established somewhat earlier in the Zagros highlands, while Anatolia was inhabited by farming communities linked by long-distance exchange routes by at least 7500 B.C. Cultural development then proceeded separately in each area of the Near East, but there were increasingly frequent trading connections between each region, which accelerated even more after 3000 B.C.

GUIDE TO FURTHER READING

Bar-Yosef, O. 1987. "Late Pleistocene Adaptations in the Levant." In Olga Soffer, ed., *The Pleistocene Old World: Regional Perspectives*, pp. 219–236. New York: Plenum.

An authoritative synthesis of late Upper Paleolithic cultures in the Near East designed for the serious reader.

Hole, Frank, Flannery, Kent V., and Neely, J. A. 1969. *The Prehistory and Human Ecology of the Deh Luran Plain.* Ann Arbor: Museum of Anthropology, University of Michigan.

An exemplary monograph on a lowland Mesopotamian excavation. Excellent discussion of subsistence changes after 8000 B.C.

Kenyon, Kathleen. 1981. *Excavations at Jericho*, vol. 3. Jerusalem: British School of Archaeology.
   The monograph on the early levels at Jericho. A fascinating specialist publication.

McCorriston, Joy, and Hole, Frank. 1991. "The Ecology of Seasonal Stress and the Origins of Agriculture in the Near East." *American Anthropologist* 93:46–69.
   A closely argued and persuasive scenario for the origins of food production in the southern Levant.

Moore, Andrew T. 1985. "The Development of Neolithic Societies in the Near East." *Advances in World Archaeology* 4:1–70.
   An excellent synthesis of the archaeological evidence for early agriculture in the Near East.

CHAPTER

EARLY EUROPEAN FARMERS

10

• • •

For many years, fishermen on the Swiss Lakes had spread rumors of sub-merged forests that snagged their nets. Then, a drought in the 1850s shrank the lakes dramatically and exposed veritable "forests" of wooden pilings set in the mud. Zurich archaeologist Ferdinand Keller dug around the piles at Ober-meilen on Lake Zurich. The mud had preserved all manner of objects large and small, not only prehistoric axe handles and weapons, but fruit and ripe hazelnuts, thousands of animal bones, and all the perishable debris from a long-abandoned farming settlement of "high antiquity," as Keller put it.

Keller's methods were rough and ready, for he merely dug into the mud around the pilings to recover as much as he could. He theorized that the "lake dwellings" were built on piles over the water, and that the inhabitants had dropped their arti-facts, food remains, and garbage into the lake. It was not until the 1920s that later, more meticulous excavators showed that the villages had flourished on dry land before being flooded by rising lake levels. But Obermeilen and other Swiss villages were the first evidence for early farming in Europe, sites that are now known to be relatively late in the history of European farming (Coles and Coles, 1989). In this chapter, we examine the evidence for the spread of food production through tem-perate Europe.

MESOLITHIC PRELUDE

• • •

In Chapter 5, we described the Mesolithic hunter-gatherers of central and western Europe, the indigenous peoples of these densely forested regions concentrated by seashores, lakes, and rivers and in forest clearings (Table 10.1). The Mesolithic lasted for about 4000 years, from about 8000 B.C. until the introduction of farming in northwest Europe about 4000 B.C. This temperate and boreal forest adaptation displayed considerable location variation. Except in areas of abundant aquatic resources and predictable food supplies, population densities were very low. In some areas, such as the Danube's Iron Gates region and the Baltic shores of Scandinavia,

8000 B.C.

TABLE 10.1
• • •

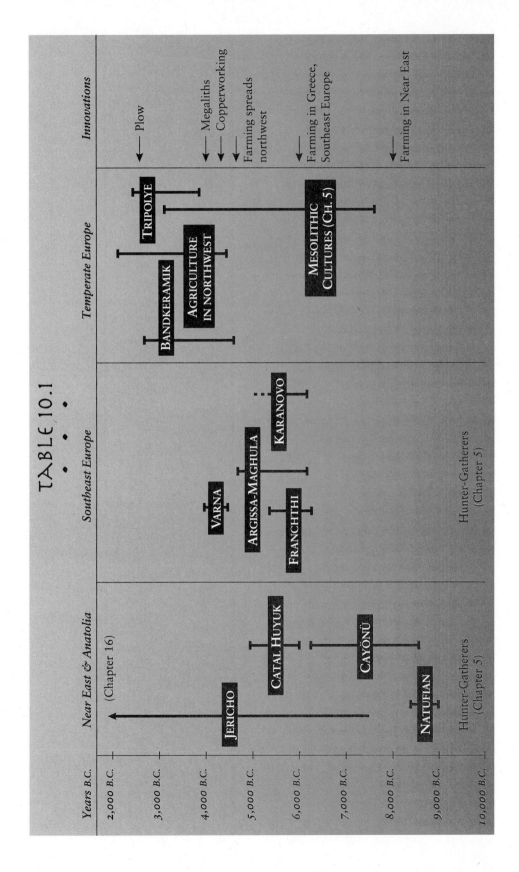

Years B.C.	Near East & Anatolia	Southeast Europe	Temperate Europe	Innovations

Near East & Anatolia (Chapter 16)

JERICHO

CATAL HUYUK

CAYÖNÜ

NATUFIAN

Hunter-Gatherers (Chapter 5)

VARNA

ARGISSA-MAGHULA

FRANCHTHI

KARANOVO

Hunter-Gatherers (Chapter 5)

TRIPOLYE

BANDKERAMIK

AGRICULTURE IN NORTHWEST

MESOLITHIC CULTURES (CH. 5)

→ Plow

→ Megaliths
→ Copperworking
→ Farming spreads northwest

→ Farming in Greece, Southeast Europe

→ Farming in Near East

2,000 B.C.
3,000 B.C.
4,000 B.C.
5,000 B.C.
6,000 B.C.
7,000 B.C.
8,000 B.C.
9,000 B.C.
10,000 B.C.

population densities were unusually high, and there are some signs of social ranking and great complexity in some late Mesolithic groups (Price, 1987).

6000 B.C.

These trends toward greater complexity, more sedentary lifeways, and more intensive hunting, foraging, and fishing took hold in Mesolithic societies throughout Europe at a time when Near Eastern societies were already experimenting with the deliberate cultivation and domestication of crops and animals. After about 6000 B.C., farming was well established in parts of the Aegean and in southeastern Europe. During the 2000 years that followed, European Mesolithic societies apparently embraced these new subsistence practices quite readily (G. Barker, 1975; Bogucki, 1993), abandoning the hunter-gatherer lifeways that had sustained their immediate and more remote ancestors for hundreds of thousands of years (Bonsall, 1989; Price, 1987). The details of this transition are still little understood, but it can be argued that the Mesolithic population was preadapted to cultivation and animal domestication, especially in areas where short-term population shifts and local environmental change may have required conservative subsistence strategies.

THE TRANSITION TO FARMING IN EUROPE

● ● ●

Did farming spread into Europe as a result of diffusion from the Near East, or did food production develop independently in the temperate zone? There are almost as many theories about this controversial subject as there are archaeologists; the theories pit diffusionists against those who argue that Europeans developed their own farming culture in southeast Europe before 6000 B.C.

Radiocarbon Dates and Prehistoric Europe

The conventional wisdom that agriculture and metallurgy had spread into temperate Europe from the Near East was overturned by radiocarbon chronologies, which have radically altered our view of European prehistory. V. Gordon Childe and his contemporaries worked before radiocarbon dates were available. All chronologies of epochs before approximately 3000 B.C., when civilization emerged in the Near East, were based on artifact typologies and inspired guesswork. The first radiocarbon dates showed that agriculture and metallurgy had begun in Europe much later than in the Near East, and there seemed nothing wrong with the traditional hypotheses.

When people started to calibrate radiocarbon dates against tree-ring chronologies, they found that European time scales between 1500 and 5000 B.C. had to be corrected several centuries backward (Fagan, 1994a; Klein et al., 1982; C. Renfrew, 1970; Suess, 1965). Egyptian historical (that is, from the written record) chronology from 2500 B.C. now agrees more closely with calibrated C14 dates rather than being several centuries too recent, as it was before.

British archaeologist Colin Renfrew (1973) has now moved the dates for temperate Europe back far enough to rupture the traditional diffusionist links between the Near East and Europe (Figure 10.1): That is, it is now apparent that events in Europe were contemporary with those in the Near East and not a later result of the spread of Near Eastern culture. Using historical dates for the Mediterranean has thrown what Renfrew aptly calls a "fault line" across the Mediterranean and south-

FIGURE 10.1   Chronology of Europe and calibration of C14 chronology. The calibrated chronology has hardly affected the dates after 3000 B.C. for the eastern Mediterranean and sites to the southeast of the fault line. The calibrated dates after 3000 B.C. for sites to the west and northwest of the fault line, however, have been pushed back several centuries, so that the old notion of innovation from the east is pushed back several centuries.

ern Europe. This line marks a chronological boundary, to the west of which radiocarbon (C14) dates after 3000 B.C. have been pushed back by calibration, making them older than the accurate, historically attested dates for the eastern Mediterranean and the Balkans, which are east of the fault. Of course, this fault line is a methodological boundary, but it serves to show that prehistoric Europeans were much less affected by cultural developments in the Near East than Childe had suggested. They adopted metallurgy and other innovations independently just when many such inventions were being brought into use in the Near East.

Greece and the Balkans

One reason that everyone assumed for so long that agriculture spread into Europe from the Near East was that they thought of Europe as one geographic entity and Turkey and the rest of the Near East just across the Dardanelles as another (Dennell, 1983). This artificial barrier combined with the assumption that rising population densities caused surplus farmers to spill over into Europe, bringing goats, sheep, and Near Eastern cereal crops with them. There is no evidence of uncomfortably high population densities anywhere in Anatolia at this time (although our knowledge is incomplete). Furthermore, the earliest farming sites in southeast Europe are situated in very favorable places, which could only have been familiar to people who had lived in the region for many generations. However, it is undeniable that food production began in the Near East about 8000 B.C. and some 2000 years later in southeast Europe. How, then, are we to account for the chronological gradient?

The assumption that the natural distributions of wild cereals and of potential animal domesticates have remained unchanged since the early Holocene is at best questionable (Dennell, 1983). As many authors have pointed out, human activity alone may have drastically reduced present-day ranges to the point that all we

6000 B.C.

record are residual distributions. Late glacial and early Holocene pollen diagrams from northern Greece demonstrate that barley and perhaps other cereals were present in southeast Europe long before farmers appeared, about 6000 B.C. Cereal grasses may have moved into temperate Europe ahead of woodlands in early Holocene times. Pulses may also have grown in Europe—the evidence is uncertain. As for potential animal domesticates, wild sheep are known to have flourished, albeit in scattered groups, in Upper Paleolithic Europe.

Robin Dennell (1983) argues that the development of food production in southeast Europe went through three phases: First, climatic conditions in the early Holocene favored more plant growth. Grasses like einkorn and barley became more abundant, growing in dense stands that could be harvested in sufficient quantities to support a family for a year (for a modern experiment, see Harlan, 1967). However, in reality, most groups probably relied on shorter-term supplies, as wild plant harvests were unpredictable. So they moved on and obtained much of their diet from hunting and other foraged foods.

A second stage began when trees colonized the areas previously occupied by grasses. This change would have scattered grass stands, decreasing the amount of grasses worth harvesting by human groups. The grasses were worth maintaining as a seasonally important food, so the people may have ring-barked tree trunks or burned the forest to clear space for wild grasses to grow. The harvested plots would gradually revert to woodland, where young shoots would attract deer, wild sheep, and other animals. Dennell (1983) believes that a simple interdependence between plant harvesting and animal exploitation developed in areas where woodlands were expanding at the expense of cereals. In such areas, human beings lived in small transitory settlements, many of them seasonal camps—just the kinds of sites found in the southern European Mesolithic (Zvelebil, 1986).

A third phase saw the establishment of permanent agricultural settlements. Through either local bartering or natural means, large-grained tough-rachis cereals were introduced into southeast Europe. These were Near Eastern cereals like emmer and bread wheat that were more predictable and productive than wild cereals. They required much more work to cultivate and careful sowing in specially prepared and selected fields. The farmers had to weed and protect their growing crops. All this extra effort involved creating special fields and gardens for crops, a mosaic of cultivated land based on carefully chosen soils and a rotation system that allowed exhausted soils to rest. Both domestic emmer and bread wheat extract large quantities of nutrients from the soil, which could be replaced by underplanting nitrogen-fixing legumes and using animal manure. This new farming habitat involved the integration of cultivation and animal husbandry into a closely knit subsistence strategy based on individual households supplying their own food needs.

This model envisages food production in southeast Europe as a largely indigenous development, stimulated in part by the immigration of some domestic plants and animals from across the Dardanelles. It also accounts for the chronological gradient, a time lag that resulted from the gradual "drift" of new crops and domesticated animals from the Near East.

Argissa-Maghula
6000 B.C.

Franchthi
6000 B.C.

The earliest known evidence of food production in Europe comes from the Argissa-Maghula village mound in Greek Thessaly (Figure 10.2). The inhabitants cultivated emmer wheat and barley. Domestic cattle, sheep, and pig bones in the lower levels of the site date to before 6000 B.C. The Franchthi Cave in southern Greece was occupied in Mesolithic times and continued in use for many thousands

FIGURE 10.2   Archaeological sites in temperate Europe and the distribution of Band-keramik (Danubian) pottery, Cardial ware, and western Neolithic cultures.

of years. Farming appeared there about 6000 B.C. These people had trading contacts with the Aegean islands (Jacobsen and Farrand, 1987; Perlès and C. Renfrew, 1992). Since domesticated crops appeared abruptly at Franchthi, it is reasonable to suppose that cereal agriculture had been developed somewhat earlier or elsewhere.

In the Balkans to the north, the earliest farmers settled on fertile agricultural soils on floodplains and elsewhere (Tringham, 1981; Whittle, 1985). Many of them lived in compact villages of one-room dwellings built of baked mud plastered on poles and wicker (Tringham et al., 1980). These Karanovo culture settlements were occupied over long periods. Farming villages were built on brown forest soils and alluvial river plains, and the economy was based on cultivated wheat and barley and domesticated sheep and goats. A number of culture traits, including *Spondylus* shells (a characteristic Mediterranean mussel much valued because it could be used for ornamentation), clay seals and figurines, and reaping knives, show continuing connections with the Mediterranean world. This is an area with great environmental variability and ranges in temperature. For example, there are fertile plains and spring areas where the soils are permanently moist. It was here that many farming communities settled in the same locations for centuries, just as Near Eastern and Anatolian farmers had done. The largest mounds are found where good arable soils are most widespread. It was in this area that metallurgy developed in approximately 3000 B.C. (see Chapter 19).

Karanovo culture

THE SPREAD OF FARMING INTO TEMPERATE EUROPE

• • •

The beginnings of farming in Europe have traditionally been explained as a process of colonization from the Near East (G. Barker, 1985). Under this theory, the newcomers spread across Europe from about 6000 B.C., ending with the introduction of farming to northwestern Europe in about 3500 B.C. The new economies effectively terminated hunter-gatherer societies in Europe. In fact, the process was much more complicated, a combination of both local and intrusive developments.

6000 B.C.

The adaptive processes and population movements involved are still little understood. These temperate zones have year-round rainfall and marked contrasts between winter and summer seasons. Timber and thatch replaced the mud-brick architecture used so effectively for houses in Near Eastern villages (Melisauskas, 1978). Agricultural techniques had to reflect the heavier soils and perennial rainfall of European latitudes, but the first introduction of farming coincided with a warm, moist phase, when midsummer temperatures were at least 2°C higher than today (Butzer, 1974). The forest cover was mainly mixed oak, shadier tree cover that reduced the grazing resources of large game animals such as deer and wild cattle. Much of the indigenous Mesolithic populations were settled by coasts, lakes, and rivers on ecotones, where they could exploit several ecological zones from summer and winter camps. The first European farmers settled on the mostly loess soils of central Europe, which were lightly wooded, fertile, and easily tilled with simple digging sticks and hoes (Starling, 1985).

No one questions that there was a directional movement of farming from the southeast to northwest (Ammerman and Cavalli-Sforza, 1984; J. G. D. Clark, 1952; Dennell, 1983). This is a far cry from thinking in terms of a wave of colonists, eager for new land, who poured into Europe. In fact, the first farming societies were thin on the ground, for the land had the potential to support far larger numbers of cultivators. Furthermore, there is good reason to believe that indigenous Mesolithic peoples were important players in the adoption of the new economies. Indeed, European farmers are remarkable for the ways in which they adapted to the challenging and varied environments of temperate Europe. Here, as in areas such as the Near East, China, and the Americas, early farming was a matter of trial and error, of success and sometimes failure.

Recent excavations have also raised the possibility that some animals and plants were actually domesticated in southeast Europe and not introduced from the Near East. The natural ranges of sheep and such plants as barley, einkorn, and some legumes may have once extended into southeast Europe (Dennell, 1983). Only emmer and bread wheat were certainly domesticated in the Near East. There is a real possibility, then, that hunter-gatherer societies in southeast Europe developed food production on their own, in response to such stresses as population pressure or environmental change—the exact stresses are still a mystery (G. Barker, 1985).

Graeme Barker (1985) proposes a general scenario: In Greece, farming villages were well established by 6000 B.C. and were based on sheep husbandry and the cultivation of crops sown each fall. North of Greece, the expansion of farming activity appears to coincide with a cycle of higher rainfall and warmer winters about 5500 B.C., which made Mediterranean styles of farming viable in the southern Balkans and somewhat different forms of agriculture possible to the north, in the Danube Basin.

About 5500 B.C., farming based on cattle herding combined with spring-sown crops developed during a period of wetter conditions over enormous areas of continental Europe, especially on optimum loess soils. This agricultural system was perfectly adapted to such conditions, whereas stock-herding assumed much greater importance in nearby, more low-lying regions. At the same time, hunter-gatherer societies continued to flourish for at least another millennium in areas that were marginal for cultivation or herding. Eventually, distinctive local farming adaptations replaced hunting and gathering in southern Scandinavia and lowland Britain as well as along the Atlantic Coast and at higher altitudes. Only in the farthest north did hunting, foraging, and fishing remain dominant subsistence strategies, areas that were vulnerable to minor climatic change.

5500 B.C.

Contrary to what Ammerman and Cavalli-Sforza (1984) claim, very complete radiocarbon chronologies characterize the spread of farming in Europe as a stop-and-start process. There were major expansions and then long pauses, not gradual waves of advance. Barker (1985) believes that the expansions coincided with climatic changes that affected local landscapes and made farming viable in new areas. In short, the spread of farming was a complex process that involved major cultural change over many centuries.

The best-known early European farming culture is called the Bandkeramik complex (or sometimes the Danubian), so named after its distinctive, linear-decorated pottery (Figure 10.3). Its first colonization of the Middle Danube was on a small scale about 5300 B.C. It appears that small groups of people migrated along river valleys, avoiding areas where Mesolithic folk lived. Their farming territories were widely spaced and apparently very small, perhaps on the order of about 500 acres (202 ha), of which about a third to a tenth was in cultivation at one time (Dennell, 1983; Howell, 1987). The people lived in hamlets made up of individual farmsteads, separated by about 100-yard (90-m) intervals. Individual houses were rectangular, from 18 to 46 feet (5.4 to 14.02 m) long, made of timber and thatch, presumably sheltering families, their grain, and their animals (Champion et al., 1984).

Bandkeramik
5300 B.C.

FIGURE 10.3   *Linearbandkeramik* pottery (linear pottery) from Sittard, Holland, with characteristic line decoration (one-fourth actual size).

Population estimates of between 40 and 60 people per village seem reasonable, with a new settlement being founded as the population expanded (F. Hammond, 1981).

The Bandkeramik people cultivated barley, einkorn, emmer wheat, and minor crops including flax. These they grew by using systems of crop rotation and fallowing, which enabled the farmers to remain in the same place for long periods of time, sometimes even growing hedges to delineate their field and to fence in their animals. Cattle were the most important animal in Bandkeramik life, indeed may have been domesticated from wild strains locally. The people also kept sheep, goats, and dogs. Population growth after first settlement was slow. As each settlement grew, companion villages were founded nearby, gradually filling in the gaps between widely spaced neighboring communities. Within four or five centuries, population densities in parts of Germany rose from 1 per 386 square miles (1000 sq. km) to 1 per 46 square miles (120 sq. km) (Milisauskas and Kruk, 1989).

4000 B.C.   By 4000 B.C., cereal crops and domesticated animals were widely used in southeast and central Europe, and perhaps also in southern France. These farming communities were surrounded by scattered hunter-gatherer societies.

The Bandkeramik people had spread far west to southern Holland, where they had settled by 4800 B.C., and east to the Vistula River and the Upper Dniester. In the prime agricultural areas, the people relied heavily on their cattle, sheep, and pigs. They may have moved their herds onto the northern European plain for part of the year. The Brzesc Kujawski site in southern Poland was inhabited by summer cattle herders, who also gathered wild vegetable foods and caught perch in northern streams (Grygiel and Bogucki, 1986; Bogucki, 1988). Eventually farmers settled on heavier soils. We find regional variations of Danubian culture in many parts of central Europe. Some farmers had to rely more on hunting and gathering because the soils of their gardens did not yield enough food to support their families. Defensive earthworks appeared later, as if vigorous competition for land had caused intertribal stress.

FRONTIERS AND TRANSITIONS

• • •

The Bandkeramik expansion created a "frontier" in many parts of Europe between farming communities and Mesolithic groups. It would be a mistake to think of this as a rigid boundary between different peoples, for both hunter-gatherer and farming societies have a tendency to stay within their own territories and to continue the way of life with which they are familiar (Dennell, 1983). By the same token, however, the peoples who lived on either side of the frontier inhabited a far from closed world. They knew of one another's presence, traded with one another, and interacted through an intricate web of contacts that were beneficial to both sides. There can be no doubt that Mesolithic people were well aware of cereal crops and domesticated animals. In many cases, they saw no advantage in adopting a new way of life that involved a great deal more work with few significant changes in the diet.

More likely, as Robin Dennell (1983) has argued, they incorporated some aspects of Neolithic culture into their lives, those that gave them immediate advantage. These could have included clay vessels for storage and cooking, perhaps status items acquired by trade that were soon copied by local women. Cereal crops and sheep may have been valuable simply because they solved problems of winter food supplies. Stored nuts, wild cereal grains, and dried deer meat or fish may have been Mesolithic winter staples. Sheep have lower feeding requirements than deer, have higher reproductive and growing rates, and can be used to keep woodland open for cereal growth. It would have been easy for Mesolithic people to graft sheep and domestic cereals onto their existing hunting and gathering practices. Dennell (1983) believes that these processes of assimilation caused farming to spread over much of temperate Europe after 6000 B.C. and continue until as late as 3500 B.C., when many Scandinavian groups finally adopted food production.

Marek Zvelebil and Peter Rowley-Conwy (1984) take the argument a stage further, distinguishing three transition phases from hunting and gathering to farming:

An "availability phase," when farming is known to Mesolithic peoples and there is some exchange of materials and information. Both farmers and hunter-gatherers are still independent units.

A "substitution phase" that has two forms: (1) Farmers move into and settle hunter-gatherer territory in competition with the indigenous residents, and (2) hunter-gatherers add cultivation or animal husbandry to their range of subsistence activities. During this phase, there is competition for land, food, and raw materials, and perhaps social competition as well.

A "consolidation phase," when food production becomes extensive and widespread, with hunting and gathering becoming subsistence strategies in emergencies. Farmers have now occupied the best soils and are using secondary areas with more intensive farming methods. By this time, the frontier has vanished.

The Zvelebil-Rowley-Conwy model serves as a descriptive device for analyzing the spread of food production into west and central Europe, but more data are needed to bolster it.

Social Changes, Lineages, and the Individual: 3500 to 2400 B.C.

● ● ●

Bandkeramik settlement was limited to very specific parts of the landscape—gravel river terraces overlooking medium-sized streams in areas of loess soils (Howell, 1987). These forest farmers deliberately selected places where damp lowland pasture coincided with tracts of light, friable upland soils. They were cultivating fertile soils, land where hoe-using farmers could grow emmer wheat and other crops year after year, fertilizing their fields with cattle dung and domestic waste. Cattle were an important element in Bandkeramik economy, pointing to a "pioneer" economy introduced from southeast Europe rather than an indigenous farming culture that made full use of local plants and game animals.

0   5 M   ⬭ Pits   ⊙ Small soil stain   ▨ Wall trench
                    ⊘ Postmold
                    ⊛ Postmold   ⧖ Large dark soil stain

FIGURE 10.4   Plan of a Bandkeramik house from Olszanica, Poland, with wall trenches, postholes, pits, and other features.

The Bandkeramik people built large, permanent timber houses, investments in time and labor that would have been totally uneconomic if they had been engaged in slash-and-burn agriculture and had shifted their villages regularly (Figure 10.4). Bandkeramik sites formed clusters of settlements, separated from one another by distances of 12.4 or 18.6 miles (20 or 30 km). The houses were apparently rebuilt in much the same place again and again. Bandkeramik settlements were occupied over long periods of time, so that a basic site, and the social structure within it, was maintained over many generations. There was continuity of residence location and inheritance from one generation to the next. In some areas, settlements were closely packed within small areas, each hamlet owning a territory of 37 acres (15 ha) or so—not because land was in short supply but because factors such as trade and local outcrops of flint and other materials may have played a role (Figure 10.5).

All of these characteristics point to farming societies that were producing food at the household level but with cooperation between different lineages at the settlement level—to build houses, erect enclosures, and herd cattle (J. Thomas, 1987). The first settlement in an area was, perhaps, the senior one, the place where the elder of the senior lineage lived. In burials, there were two general distinctions among grave goods: between graves of males and females and those of young and old. Many graves of Bandkeramik women are richly decorated, members of families who lived in long houses. Such dwellings are commonly associated in modern societies with matrilineage. Under these circumstances, women may have had high status in Bandkeramik society. Political power and social authority may have been in the hands of a group of older men, who controlled cattle ownership and the exchange of cattle and other exotic commodities with other settlements. In Bandkeramik society, then, a complex network of social relations controlled productiv-

FIGURE 10.5 Reconstruction of a Bandkeramik farming complex.

ity. Lineages within society formed the links between people and the lands of their ancestors.

About 4500 B.C., Bandkeramik settlements became more clustered and turned into villages. Many were protected by earthen enclosures. Divergent pottery styles hint that there were well-defined territories for different settlement clusters (J. Thomas, 1987). This was a time when more elaborate burial customs developed throughout Europe as ancestor cults became more complex.

In western Europe, communal tombs came into fashion, among them the celebrated megaliths, sepulchers fashioned from rough-hewn boulders and buried under earthen mounds (see Figure 10.8). Such corporate burial places may have had locations where revered kin leaders were buried; people with genealogical ties with the ancestors were of paramount and collective importance to a group of farming communities, where ancestors were guardians of the land. In time, communal tombs may have become important power symbols among local groups, linked with their neighbors and others by both lasting kin ties and burgeoning exchange networks that were expanding throughout Europe at this time (J. Thomas, 1987). It has been suggested, for example, that the communal burial mounds of northern Europe embody in earth and stone the notion of linearity, perhaps an ideology that came from Bandkeramik longhouses (Hodder, 1990).

Somewhat later, between about 2800 and 2400 B.C., another change in burial customs took hold in central and eastern Europe. For the first time, individual graves as well as communal sepulchers appeared. S. J. Shennan (1993) has argued that group-based ideologies were replaced by new beliefs that reinforced individual power and prestige. It would have been very hard for a single elder to preempt political and economic authority in Bandkeramik society. There were simply too many kin ties and reciprocal obligations to overcome, as well as the collective bond with the ancestors. By being buried separately, in a burial adorned with elaborate grave furniture, a prominent elder could take on the role of sole male ancestor, the fountain of authority over land ownership, a role now assumed by his successor. Inheritance of land and wealth was now legitimized.

2800 B.C.

This is, of course, a speculative scenario but one supported by telling clues. There are many cases in which men and women were buried together in a single grave. This practice, argue some archaeologists, indicates monogamous marriages rather than the polygamous ones of lineage-based Bandkeramik society. The dominance of male burials from this period suggests that men were of great importance in establishing descent and rights of inheritance. Many individual graves were dug into older communal monuments, perhaps to reinforce the idea that individual ancestors were more important than collective ones. The rich grave goods found in such burials reveal new emphases in society: Many weapons such as daggers and swords appear, as well as battle axes, fine copper ornaments, and drinking cups. Everything points to the emergence of individuals who thought of themselves as warriors. Personal achievement and prestige were associated with males, who were involved in expanding exchange networks that handled luxury goods such as amber, gold ornaments, and weapons. The beginnings of metallurgy in Europe may have been tied to a rising demand for shiny, prestigious ornaments. Luxury artifacts were the symbols of prestige, the means of cementing individual relationships, political links, and reciprocal obligations.

There are striking differences in the people buried, too. Bandkeramik farmers lavished their finest goods on older individuals. The later individual burials are those of men in their prime, indicating that personal achievement was the avenue to power and prestige.

THE INTRODUCTION OF THE PLOW

• • •

Andrew Sherratt (1981) believes that the introduction of plow agriculture was a seminal development in Europe. Plows are known to have been used as early as 3600 B.C., but Sherratt says they came into far more widespread and intensive use about 2600 B.C., when a number of other innovations or products reached Europe from the Near East. These included sheep shearing, milking, horse riding, and the use of oxen for traction. He goes so far as to argue for a "secondary products revolution," which transformed both settlement patterns and social organization throughout Europe.

Plow agriculture allows fewer people to work an acre of land; thus more land would be cleared, making an individual's fields more widely scattered, sometimes close to the outer limits of daily walking. The result was a much more dispersed settlement pattern, with a rapid expansion onto heavier soils and hitherto uncultivated areas around 2600 B.C. With much more acreage to clear and the technology to do it, the farmers of 2500 B.C. were less tied to ancestral lands and the realities of household production and the kin ties these imply. Fewer people worked in the field, creating "unproductive" individuals in greater numbers, and there were compelling needs for social change. So, in place of the kin-based society arose a new social order in which individual success, prestige, and inheritance of land were the norm—with momentous consequences for the Europeans.

RUSSIAN PLAINS FARMERS: TRIPOLYE

• • •

While the Bandkeramik complex was developing in central Europe, a mosaic of different subsistence patterns emerged on the Russian plains to the east between 6000 and 4500 B.C. (Zvelebil and Dolukhanov, 1991; Telegin, 1987). The areas best suited for farming, such as intermountain basins, were settled by agricultural peoples, while hunter-gatherers continued to exploit the river basins, such as those of the Bug and Dniester rivers. The farmers and foragers interacted with one another, living in complementary environments, where one did not threaten the other. By

4500 B.C.   4500 B.C., Bandkeramik peoples had moved as far east as the Ukraine, bringing a mixed farming economy with them. They settled on the higher terraces of major rivers, still interacting with Mesolithic folk in the valley bottoms. Both Mesolithic and Neolithic peoples maintained their own identities. Farming reached its greatest

Tripolye   extent in the forest-steppe regions of west Russia with the Tripolye culture in about
4000 B.C.   4000 B.C. Soon after this, the farmers finally submerged the Mesolithic foragers of the valleys, perhaps because they relied extensively on cattle, whose grazing demands may have competed with hunter-gatherers' foraging needs. In about 2800

2800 B.C.   B.C., the climate deteriorated, making cultivation less viable. At this point balanced economies emerged, relying on stockbreeding on the steppe and farming in the forest-steppe, a balanced dynamic that survived into recent times, with important historical consequences.

MEDITERRANEAN AND WESTERN EUROPE

• • •

New artifacts, such as pottery, and food sources, such as sheep, were added to hunter-gatherer adaptations as farming took hold in central Europe and farther afield. This transitional phase lasted for centuries throughout Europe. In many areas the new items added to existing practices, but they did little to change the fundamental structure of Mesolithic society or lifeways. The full-scale adoption of farming economies in areas such as west Russia took a long time to achieve, whereas in other areas, such as Britain, a full changeover occurred within five centuries or so.

In the Iron Gates region of the Danube Valley, coastal Yugoslavia, central Italy, and southern France, pottery, cereal crops, and sheep appeared, but there was little immediate change in daily life. Many sites where such artifacts occur are in the same type of setting as Mesolithic settlements, where hunting continued for centuries, even millennia. The shift to farming was only partial in many areas, for game and plant foods continued to be important, witness the well-preserved berries and nuts in waterlogged lakeside villages in Switzerland (Coles and Coles, 1989). In the Mediterranean Basin, the long-term changes were an expansion in the use of obsidian and much wider ranging trade in this material after 5000 B.C. Obsidian was found on three Mediterranean islands, including Sardinia, and was now regularly traded to neighboring islands and the mainland. This trade was part of a widespread network of contacts, linked partly by sea, that carried seashells, exotic rocks, and later copper ore the length and breadth of the Mediterranean.

This trade also coincided in general terms with the manufacture of distinctive pottery styles decorated with impressions of seashells, among them the cockleshell, *Cardium* (Figure 10.6). This motif has given rise to the term *Cardial ware* to describe a range of indigenously developed pottery styles that mark the first use of clay vessels by Western peoples. Like sheep and goats and perhaps cereal crops, pottery was selectively adopted, as were other elements of farming culture, by different groups long before full-time farming took hold.

The decisive shift from hunting and gathering in the West took place in the sixth millennium before Christ, with sheep and goats being acquired by trade, exchange, or theft considerably earlier, cereal crops arriving somewhat later.

By 4000 B.C., a series of fishing villages was thriving on the shores of the Swiss lakes (Coles and Coles, 1989). They were occupied by cattle and sheep farmers who cultivated barley and wheat as well as many minor crops, including cider apples and flax (to make linen cloth) (Figure 10.7). Their houses were built on the damp ground between the lake reed beds and the scrub brush of the valley behind. The first dwellings were small rectangular huts, but they eventually gave way to larger, two-room houses. Some villages grew to include between 24 and 75 houses clustered on the lakeshore, a density of population much the same as that of modern Swiss villages, which have approximately 30 households.

In the extreme northwest, food production was adopted comparatively late. From 6000 through 4000 B.C., the newly isolated Mesolithic peoples of Britain developed with little or no significant contact with the continent. The earliest traces of pottery and forest clearance appeared soon after 4000 B.C., with well-documented cereal agriculture by 4300 B.C. The same processes may have operated here as in west Europe. Robin Dennell (1983) theorizes that European farmers did not cross the channel and settle in Britain. Rather, Mesolithic peoples experienced

FIGURE 10.6   Cardium-shell-impressed pottery from southern France (one-fourth actual size).

FIGURE 10.7   Sample prehistoric stone axes mounted in deer antler handles from the Swiss lake dwellings, typical of those used by early farmers in Europe.

population pressure about 4000 B.C., perhaps as a result of forest expansion due to warmer climate and also because of population growth. Hunting became more difficult, so the people began clearing woodland to provide more animal forage and plant foods and to make hunting more predictable. The people also increased their exploitation of marine resources, and seafaring techniques developed, leading to contacts with other coastal communities in Britain and on the continent. Eventually, Mesolithic populations in Britain became aware of new food resources like domestic cereals and sheep and acquired them. Ample open grassland was available for herding and cultivation in southern Britain. Within five centuries or so, Mesolithic populations had transformed themselves into farmers with their own distinctive cultural traditions. Somewhat similar processes probably led to the adoption of agriculture and stock rearing among Mesolithic Scandinavians.

THE MEGALITHS

● ● ●

Early European farming societies were basically egalitarian, with the family as the basic productive unit at the center of a web of intricate kin ties and reciprocal social relationships that linked communities near and far and tied people to the land of their ancestors. There was probably equal access to resources, with sufficient food being produced to feed individual families. In a real sense, the subsistence farming economy *was* society (Champion et al., 1984). In general, early Neolithic burials in Europe do not reflect any social differentiation between individuals.

There are signs of variation, notably in the intensity of trading activities through barter networks and in burial customs. A slow process of social change can be documented throughout Europe after 4000 B.C., moving toward greater emphasis on craft specialization and burial ritual and the emergence of regional trading centers that controlled exchange networks, and perhaps ritual as well. The famous megalithic tombs of the Mediterranean and west Europe are one symbol of this trend toward social change.

As early as 4500 B.C., some French farmers were building large communal stone tombs, known to archaeologists as *megaliths* ("large stone" in Greek) (Figure 10.8). Megaliths are found as far north as Scandinavia, in Britain, Ireland, France, Spain, the western Mediterranean, Corsica, and Malta. For years, scholars thought that megaliths had originated in the eastern Mediterranean approximately 2500 B.C. and spread westward into Spain with colonists from the Aegean, who had carried a custom of collective burial and their religion with them. Megalithic tombs were believed to have then been built in west Europe, witnesses to a lost faith perhaps spread by pilgrims, missionaries, or merchants. With their massive stones and large burial chambers, megaliths remain one of the mysteries of European prehistory (Daniel, 1973; C. Renfrew, 1973).

This popular and widely accepted hypothesis was badly weakened by C14 dates from France that turned out to be earlier than others from west Europe. Furthermore, new calibrated dates have placed Spanish megalithic sites and their associated culture as early as approximately 4500 B.C., much earlier than their alleged prototypes in the Aegean. Thus, megaliths were being built in west Europe at least a millennium before massive funerary architecture became fashionable in the eastern Mediterranean. This remarkable freestanding architecture is a unique local European creation.

FIGURE 10.8   Interior of a megalithic chamber tome in West Kennet, England, C14 dated to approximately 3500 B.C. (Piggott, 1965).

What exactly were megaliths? Were they the surviving remains of a powerful religious cult that swept west Europe, or did they symbolize the emergence of new, more sophisticated political and social structures in the West? Colin Renfrew (1983) has argued that the tradition of communal burial developed in very early west European farming societies and that it is manifested by the famous long barrows of southern Britain (Figure 10.8), many of which had stone boulder, megalithic interiors. The long barrows were fairly small structures, requiring not more than about 5000 to 10,000 worker-hours to build (a figure equivalent to 20 men taking 50 days). Ian Hodder (1990) believes they may be a reflection of long-held ideologies surrounding long houses that were perpetuated in tomb design, on the grounds that ideology was a vital component in early European farming societies. Between 4000 and 3500 B.C., these barrows were associated with more elaborate monuments, among them enclosed earthworks (often called "causewayed camps"), which are known to have been protected by timber palisades. Recent excavations have shown that these camps were littered with human bones, many of them skeletons from which the flesh had weathered in the open. Perhaps these camps were places where the dead were exposed for months before their bones were deposited in nearby communal burials.

As time went on, the argument goes, burial ceremonies revolved around even larger monuments, the so-called henges, stone- and wood-built circles of which Stonehenge in southern Britain is the most famous (Figure 20.6). In this sense, megaliths of all types formed a kind of settlement hierarchy on the prehistoric landscape, a hierarchy that may have reflected profound changes in European society.

Another ingenious theory argues that megalithic monuments appeared in west Europe at just the moment when farming took hold all across Europe. This final colonization must have had a major impact on the stable Mesolithic societies that were exploiting coastal resources along the Atlantic Ocean and North Sea shores from the Bay of Biscay in France to the Baltic. Ian Kinnes (1982) believes that megaliths first appeared in the margins of Neolithic society, along the Atlantic Coast, where competition with Mesolithic groups may have been most acute. Perhaps, he believes, the megaliths served as territorial markers, signs of ancestral ownership of the surrounding land.

Colin Renfrew and others have called megaliths the "tombs of the living," lasting, humanly made symbols of the continuity of human life as well as symbols of the continuity of ownership of land from one generation to the next. The annual round of religious rituals at places like Stonehenge reinforced this continuity, and at a time when population densities were rising sharply, the megaliths associated with them became important symbols of political and social continuity. They also reinforced the political, economic, and spiritual power of those who supervised the building and worship at places such as Stonehenge (Figure 20.6). That such supervision was necessary is certain, for it has been estimated that Stonehenge required at least 30,000 worker-hours to complete. So the appearance of megaliths and the hierarchy of more elaborate stone and wooden monuments associated with them may have foreshadowed profound social changes in prehistoric Europe that came with the increasing use of bronze and other metals (Chippindale, 1983).

A complex set of processes governed the emergence of food production in temperate Europe, processes only rarely involving the movement of entire populations from one region to the next. Here, as in other parts of the world, one should think of agriculture not as a miracle invention or in terms of conquest but as yet another instance of how readily hunter-gatherers adapted to new opportunities and conditions. As is so often the case in prehistory, continuity was as important as change, but this continuity was born of inherent flexibility, an ability to adapt to new circumstances.

CHAPTER SUMMARY

Agriculture and animal husbandry developed in southeastern Europe as a result of a local shift to more intensive exploitation of cereals and wild sheep, also because of a "drift" of domestic animals and cereals across from the Near East. The widely distributed Bandkeramik complex documents the first settlement of southeastern European farmers in the Middle Danube Valley and on the light loess soils of central Europe around 5000 B.C. During the next millennium, food production spread widely throughout Europe, largely in the hands of indigenous Mesolithic peoples, who adopted sheep, pottery, and cereals, which they considered of immediate advantage to them. From about 4500 B.C., new religious ideologies spread widely in central and western Europe, reflected in the building of communal burial mounds and megalithic monuments. Some of these new beliefs reflected centuries-old ideologies connected with the long houses and communal ethics of the Bandkeramik farmers. Others, derived from central and eastern Europe, were beliefs that reflected the appearance of individual power and prestige as a potent factor in local life, power reflected in growing numbers of exotic artifacts and materials.

GUIDE TO FURTHER READING

Barker, Graeme. 1985. *Prehistoric Farming in Europe*. Cambridge, Eng.: Cambridge University Press.
> *An analysis, aimed at specialists, of the spread of farming into temperate Europe.*

Champion, T. G., et al. 1984. *Prehistoric Europe*. New York: Academic Press.
> *An up-to-date summary of European prehistory, with a major emphasis on trade, subsistence, and social organization.*

Clark, J. G. D. 1952. *Prehistoric Europe: The Economic Basis*. Palo Alto, CA: Stanford University Press.
> *The classic essay on prehistoric European economic life. Still of immense value to the general reader.*

Dennell, Robin C. 1983. *European Economic Prehistory: A New Approach*. New York: Academic Press.
> *An enjoyable essay on European prehistory that formed my ideas on this chapter. Strongly recommended for newcomers to the subject.*

Hodder, Ian. 1990. *The Domestication of Europe*. Oxford: Blackwell.
> *A provocative survey of later European prehistory that places heavy reliance on ideology and changing religious beliefs. An excellent counterpoint to much more traditional writing about Europe's prehistoric past.*

Renfrew, Colin. 1973. *Before Civilization*. New York: Knopf.
> *A well-written essay on recent advances in European prehistory that concentrates on the calibration of radiocarbon dating. Essential reading for any more-than-casual student of Old World archaeology.*

Trump, David. 1980. *The Prehistory of the Mediterranean*. New Haven, CT: Yale University Press.
> *A fundamental source on a key area of the world. For the informed reader.*

Whittle, Alastair. 1985. *Neolithic Europe: A Survey*. Cambridge, Eng.: Cambridge University Press.
> *A summary of the European Neolithic for the more advanced reader.*

Zvelebil, Marek, ed. 1986. *Hunters in Transition*. Cambridge, Eng.: Cambridge University Press.
> *A volume of articles that describes basic Mesolithic theory and analyzes the Neolithic transition in various parts of Europe.*

CHAPTER

EARLY FARMERS

OF AFRICA

• • •

O
ur finds caused quite a stir," 80-year-old Gertrude Caton-Thompson told me. "People didn't believe us when we showed them carbonized emmer and barley seeds from the baskets. They told us they were modern seeds that were mixed into the pits by accident." Caton-Thompson's memories of her late 1920s excavations in early farming settlements in Egypt's Fayyum were as vivid as if they had been from yesterday. She told me how she had worked almost alone, camping in the wilderness at the edge of a dried-up lake. It was there that she had uncovered the remains of small, oval-shaped pole-and-reed dwellings and small storage pits lined with baskets still containing domestic grains.

Caton-Thompson's finds were revolutionary in the late 1920s, for they pushed the origins of agriculture back to earlier than 4000 B.C. As she worked with almost no money and facilities, her research started a quest for the first farmers on the Nile that continues to this day (Caton-Thompson and Gardner, 1934).

The Nile slashes like a green arrow through the arid wastes of the eastern Sahara, rising high in the Ethiopian highlands and flowing northward more than 3000 miles (4828 km) to the Mediterranean. For most of its last 700 miles (1127 km), the Nile has cut a deep gorge through the desert, which it then filled with layer after layer of fertile river silt. This was a land of bounty, but an uncertain one dependent on rainfall far upstream. If there were good winter rains in the highlands, then the annual flood would inundate the fertile floodplain and replenish plant life. Poor rains would trigger but a meager flood, leaving the Nile Valley parched and baking under the summer sun. Occasionally, too, record rainfall in Ethiopia would bring catastrophic floods downstream, raging waters that swept everything before them. For all these uncertainties, the Nile Valley was always an isolated oasis, a strip of green, fertile land flowing between desert bastions. The valley floor itself consisted for the most part of seasonally flooded natural basins that supported grass and brushland. People lived on higher levees along the river, where trees grew and settlements escaped the annual inundation. For tens of thousands of years, this was a paradise for hunters and foragers (Table 11.1).

TABLE 11.1

• • •

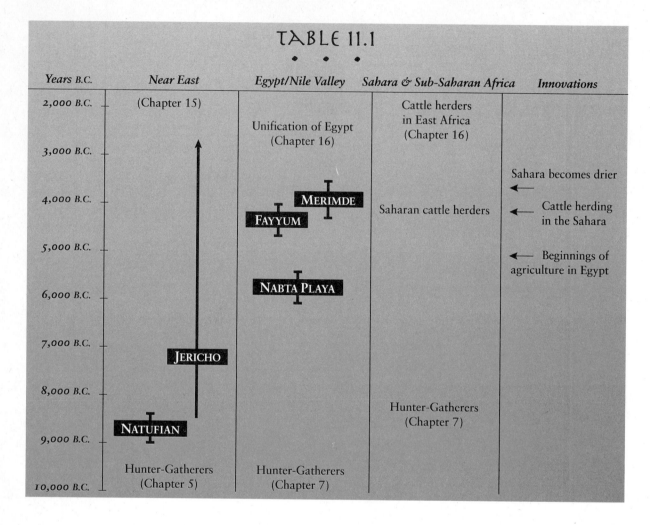

Years B.C.	Near East	Egypt/Nile Valley	Sahara & Sub-Saharan Africa	Innovations
2,000 B.C.	(Chapter 15)	Unification of Egypt (Chapter 16)	Cattle herders in East Africa (Chapter 16)	
3,000 B.C.				Sahara becomes drier ←
4,000 B.C.		MERIMDE FAYYUM	Saharan cattle herders	← Cattle herding in the Sahara
5,000 B.C.				← Beginnings of agriculture in Egypt
6,000 B.C.		NABTA PLAYA		
7,000 B.C.				
8,000 B.C.	JERICHO		Hunter-Gatherers (Chapter 7)	
9,000 B.C.	NATUFIAN			
10,000 B.C.	Hunter-Gatherers (Chapter 5)	Hunter-Gatherers (Chapter 7)		

HUNTER-GATHERERS ON THE NILE

• • •

During the last millennia of the Ice Age, the Nile Valley was a rich, diverse habitat, abounding in game of all sizes and in wild vegetable foods. Fish and waterfowl added to the bounty of resources. But those who lived there had to employ flexible and conservative ways of life to adjust to constant fluctuations in the flood levels.

Wadi Kubbaniya 17,000 to 15,000 B.C.

We know something of their lifeways from excavations at ancient camps in Wadi Kubbaniya dating to between 17,000 and 15,000 B.C. northwest of Aswan in upper Egypt (Wendorf et al., 1980). The tiny settlements, little more than scatters of stone tools, bones, and charcoal, lay atop sandy dunes about 1.9 miles (3 km) from the narrow Nile floodplain. Rising floodwaters inundated the dunes for some weeks each summer, but for the rest of the year the inhabitants looked out over a marshy floodplain. The annual cycle at Wadi Kubbaniya began with rising floodwaters in July, when vast numbers of catfish congregated in the shallows to spawn. After mating, they lay sluggish in the water for several hours. It was then that every member of the group would flock to the water's edge, catching fish with their hands, impaling them with spears, even trapping them with upturned containers. Hundreds of fish were gutted and laid out to dry in the sun during the precious few days of spawning.

When the floodwaters reached their height, flooding root plants in the wetlands, the people fished and foraged at water's edge, harvesting ripe dates and acacia seeds from trees at the edge of the desert. As the inundation receded, men and boys would comb the shallow pools left by the retreating water for trapped catfish. Meanwhile, the women armed with wooden digging sticks turned their attention to the ripe swards of nut-grass and club-rush tubers in the newly exposed wetlands. Even today, nut-grass is abundant along the Nile, yielding small, bitter-tasting tubers high in carbohydrates and fiber. But they are toxic, especially during later stages of growth, so the women would rub and grind them, then leach them before consumption. A family armed with digging sticks could have gathered enough carbohydrates for several days within a matter of hours.

As fall and winter came, the foragers would turn to water lilies, sedges, wild millets, and other wetland plants, while the hunters would take migratory coots, ducks, and geese. Come spring, the people would eat acacia seeds and dates, cattail and other wetland plants, relying on a broad spectrum of edible plant foods that were vital when staples were in short supply.

Not that the wadi people enjoyed a comfortable life, for the annual floods varied so much that they lived in a constant state of uncertainty. A high flood could delay plant harvests, low waters cause the marshlands to dry up for months on end. It was for this reason that they exploited a very broad range of food resources, seeking in any way possible to adapt to their demanding environment.

The same broad-based hunter-gatherer economies persisted for the remainder of the Ice Age and well into Holocene times, with, however, a trend toward more sedentary settlement and to more intensified exploitation of plants and fish. In all probability, numerous local groups lived in the valley, all the way from the Delta in the north into the Sudan (Nubia) in the far south, distinguishable in the archaeological record by minor differences in their toolkits. One such group was the so-called Qadan culture from central Egypt, best known from microlithic tools found on riverside campsites near the Nile (J. D. Clark, 1971). In the earlier stages of the Qadan, fishing and big-game hunting were important, but large numbers of grindstones and grinding equipment came from a few localities, which seems to show that gathering wild grains was significant to at least part of the economy. Some Qadan settlements were probably large and occupied for long periods. The dead were buried in cemeteries, in shallow pits covered with stone slabs. Some pits held two bodies. In six instances, small stone tools were embedded in the bones of these Qadan people, who must have met a violent end.

**Qadan culture
13,000 to 4500 B.C.**

These war casualties are a sign that life was not easy along the bountiful Nile, probably because of the sheer unpredictability of the annual flood, and because of constant drought, especially after 6000 B.C. Most groups settled close to permanent water supplies, relying on predictable seasonal foods to tide them through the lean months of the inundation.

The end of the Ice Age brought much higher rains to northern Africa. Raging floods cut through the Nile floodplain, sweeping away rich marshlands and fertile soils, until rising Holocene sea levels reduced the river gradient and the inundation again deposited rich silt on the valley floor. At the same time, higher rainfall brought semi-arid grassland and shallow lakes to much of the Sahara, making it possible for hunters and foragers to live in hitherto uninhabited lands. There was also regular movement between the desert and the Nile Valley. Perhaps about 1000 people lived in tiny family groups in this unpredictable, harsh environment between 8000 and 3000 B.C. Perhaps as much as 80 percent of their diet came from edible plants, also from gazelles, hares, and other small animals that flourished in stony terrain. Life became much harder in the Sahara after 6000 B.C., when drought cycles became longer and the lakes shrank rapidly. By this time, desert populations may have risen to the point where there were well-defined territorial boundaries and there were no unexploited lands. The Saharans responded to drier conditions by settling closer to permanent water, where they faced the same problem as the people of the Nile—seasonal food shortages and the constant threat of starvation.

AGRICULTURAL ORIGINS ON THE NILE

● ● ●

For years, people assumed that cereal crops and domesticated animals were introduced into the Nile Valley from southwest Asia sometime after 8000 B.C. (Childe, 1952). In recent years, this view has been challenged by those who believe that food production arose independently in Egypt, the Sudan, and even the Sahara (Hassan, 1986). The evidence for such a development is both fragmentary and controversial, for the deep alluvium of the Nile Valley has long buried the relevant settlements near the valley. Prevailing expert opinion seems to favor an outside introduction, perhaps as a result of drought throughout the region. This scenario goes as follows.

In about 6000 B.C., severe drought conditions prevailed over much of the Near East, decimating game populations and causing widespread crop failures among the tiny farming populations that flourished in what is now Israel and Syria. The farmers responded by moving from drier zones into the Mediterranean forest zone near the coast, one day to be the source of the famed "cedars of Lebanon" mentioned in the Scriptures. During these years of dislocation and resettlement, some nomadic groups with goats and sheep may have crossed the Sinai into Lower Egypt, bringing domesticated barley, emmer wheat, and other crops with them. The Nile Valley was also gripped by drought. Human populations moved closer to the shrinking river, the locations where animals still grazed and plant foods were still plentiful. Inevitably, group territories shrank, too, so people responded by turning to domesticated plants and animals as part of a complex safety net that protected them against a very unpredictable environment. Not that there was any drastic change in daily life, for initially the new economies were practiced on a very small scale. Early Nile agriculture may have been a form of insurance, practiced sporadically and on the smallest of scales when circumstances merited by people who were preadapted to the new life way (Hassan, 1986). Agricultural methods were probably of the simplest. Some villagers would plant some wheat on damp ground at the receding floodwater's edge, a crop timed to ripen when food was short. The plots were small and left to fend for themselves.

Thus, farming began along the Nile when people living in an unpredictable riverain environment wanted to amplify their food supplies. Within a remarkably short time, probably only a few centuries, domesticated forms of these same cereals became important staples. These new strains were much more demanding than their wild ancestors, needing constant attention, weeding and watering. Each village was now tied to its herds and gardens.

Archaeological evidence for early farming is virtually nonexistent. Domesticated barley is known from the Nabta Playa site in the Western Desert and dates to about 6000 B.C. These cultivators and their neighbors at Bir Kiseiba to the

Nabta Playa
6000 B.C.

west were living in large settlements with houses set in rows or in an arc. Perhaps as many as 14 families lived in these villages, dwelling in low pit houses sunk into the ground (Wendorf et al., 1984).

Farther north, in the Fayyum depression west of the Nile, small fishing camps flourished along the water's edge at the time of Bir Kiseiba and Nabta (Wenke et al., 1988). Unlike their relatives far to the south, they did not use cereals. For reasons that are still not understood, the Fayyum was abandoned after about 6000 B.C. Then, about 4350 B.C., the lakeshores were home to people living in short-term seasonal camps that moved as the lake level fluctuated. These people cultivated wheat and barley, locating their gardens on patches of fertile soil whose distribution changed as the lake did. They also herded cattle, sheep, and goats, but fish were overwhelmingly important in their diet. Unlike their contemporaries in the Near East, the Fayyum people never built permanent villages, for their environment was too unpredictable to allow complete dependence on agriculture. Considerable debate surrounds the Fayyum discoveries, which have long been hailed as evidence for the earliest farming in the Nile area (Caton-Thompson and Gardner, 1934). In fact, this lake-filled depression may have supported groups who only partially adopted the new lifeways because their environment was too unpredictable. In fact, dozens of farming villages may have flourished in the fertile Nile Valley as early as 5000 B.C. if not earlier, settlements that are now inaccessible beneath deep alluvial deposits laid down by thousands of years of river floods.

Fayyum
4350 B.C.

The earliest dated farming settlements from the Nile Valley, both from Egypt and the Sudan, date to between 4300 and 3300 B.C. Hassan believes that the nomadic peoples of the desert now included the fertile river valley in their wanderings, moving in and out of the desert as conditions warranted, as they do in the Sahel at the southern fringes of the Sahara today. These movements, he believes, were especially significant after 2500 B.C., when conditions became very arid indeed. This was also a time of exceptionally low Nile floods, so the sparse agricultural sites dating from early farming times are probably buried under many feet of later river alluvium. Hassan argues that irregular population movements involving small numbers of people continued for thousands of years and came into the valley from many desert regions. The result was considerable cultural diversity within the Nile Valley, caused by both immigration and fusion with existing populations.

4300 B.C.

Many of the new floodplain settlements may have been like the village of Merimda Beni Salama near the Nile Delta. There a cluster of oval houses and shelters was built half underground and roofed with mud and sticks (Hoffman, 1979). An occupation mound 7 feet (2 m) high accumulated over 600 years from approximately 3900 B.C. Farming at a subsistence level was characteristic of large areas of the Nile floodplain for thousands of years (Hassan, 1988).

Merimda
c. 3900 B.C.

Other farmers who flourished along the Upper Nile are known to us mainly from cemetery burials. Like their northern neighbors, they used bows and arrows in the chase, many tipped with finely flaked arrowheads. Emmer wheat and barley were cultivated, and cattle and small stock provided much of the meat. Settlements here were typified by mud-brick and transient architecture. The dead, however, were buried with some ceremony—in linen shrouds and covered with skins. The women wore ivory combs and plaited their hair. This culture, named the *Badarian* after a village where the first settlements were found, is thought to have been broadly contemporary with Merimda (Butzer, 1976; Hassan, 1988; Hays, 1984).

Badarian culture
3700 B.C.

The early farming communities of the Nile continued to use the forested riverbanks for settlement (Butzer, 1976). Animals grazed in the flat grasslands of the plain for most of the year, and crops were planted on wet basin soils as the waters receded. Game was still abundant in the Nile Valley in 4000 B.C.; even so, the people ventured to the edge of the deserts in search of gazelles and other small animals. They buried their dead in cemeteries overlooking the Nile, where the graves would not take up valuable agricultural land.

By 3500 B.C., the inhabitants of the Nile Valley were living almost entirely off agriculture, with hunting playing a negligible role in daily life. Four hundred years later, Egypt was unified into a single state. The density of population was probably low enough so that the people had no need of either government or government-regulated irrigation canals. They made use of natural floods and drainage basins to grow their crops, allowing early Egyptian farmers to harvest grain over perhaps two-thirds of the floodplain of the Nile. The first appearance of irrigation seems to have coincided with the unification of Egypt and is described in Chapter 16.

THE SAHARAN PASTORALISTS

● ● ●

Many people think of the Sahara as a vast sand sea, one of the most desolate places on earth. In fact the Sahara is a highly diverse, albeit dry, region that has undergone major climatic changes since 10,000 B.C. (McIntosh and McIntosh, 1988). As recently as 6000 B.C., the southern frontier of the desert was far to the north, while semi-arid grassland and shallow freshwater lakes covered much of what is now arid plains. This was a landscape where antelope of all kinds abounded—and *Bos primigenius,* the wild ox. The areas that are now desert were, like all arid regions, very susceptible to cycles of higher and lower rainfall, resulting in major, sudden changes in distributions of plants and animals. The people who preyed on the sparse desert fauna responded to drought by managing the wild resources they hunted and gathered, especially wild oxen, which must have regular water supplies to survive.

Even before the drought, the Sahara was never well watered. Both humans and animals were constantly on the move, in search of food and reliable water supplies. Under these circumstances, archaeologist Andrew Smith believes (1992), the small herds of *Bos primigenius* in the desert became closer knit, smaller breeding units. The beasts were more disciplined, making it easier for hunters to move among them, predict their habits, and cull animals at will. At the same time, both cattle and humans were more confined in their movements, staying much closer to permanent water supplies for long periods of time. It was under these conditions that cattle and humans came into close association. Smith believes that the hunters were well aware of the more disciplined ways in which their prey behaved. Instead of following them on their annual migrations, they prevented the herd from moving from one spot to another. They did this in such a way that they were no threat to the beasts, moving around and through the herd on its home range, never threatening it. At first, they controlled the movement of the herd, while still maintaining their all-important symbolic and ritual relationships with their prey and assuring continuance of their meat diet. But soon they also gained genetic control of the animals, which led to rapid physical changes in the herd. South African farmers who maintain herds of wild eland report that the offspring soon diminish in size, unless wild bulls are introduced constantly from outside. The same effects of inbreeding may have occurred in controlled cattle populations, with some additional, and perhaps unrecognized, advantages. The newly domesticated animals behaved better, were easier to control,

FIGURE 11.1   Cattle in a Saharan rock painting from Tassili n'Ajjer.

and may have enjoyed a higher calving rate, which in turn yielded greater milk supplies. Certainly, we know from rock paintings deep in the Sahara that the herders were soon selecting for different horn shapes and hide colors (Figure 11.1).

It is still unclear whether domesticated cattle were tamed independently in northern Africa or introduced into the continent from the Near East. Whatever the original source of the original tamed herds, it seems entirely likely that much the same process of control and juxtaposition occurred in both the Near East and northern Africa, even in Europe, among peoples who had an intimate knowledge of wild cattle behavior. The experiments with control, with domestication, probably occurred in many places, as people living in ever-drier environments cast around for alternative, more predictable food supplies.

If Andrew Smith is correct, it was a combination of drought, profound familiarity with prey, and human opportunism that domesticated one of the Ice Age's most intractable, curmudgeonly beasts. The very flexibility and mobility of hunter-gatherer life in Saharan lands probably made pastoralism adaptive. It is thought that some cattle bones found in the Egyptian part of the eastern Sahara are from domesticated beasts dating to between 8000 and 6000 B.C. After a short drying period around 5000 B.C., climatic conditions in the central and southern Sahara improved (Rognon, 1981). The lakes expanded and filled again. This time cattle herders camped by their shores. Some cattle bones from a cave in southwest Libya dated to about 3000 B.C., but they may be as early as 5000 B.C. Pastoralists were widespread in the central and southern Sahara during the fourth millennium B.C., and it seems certain that they were using wild cereal grasses and perhaps cultivating such tropical crops as sorghum.

The cattle herders had only a few possessions, unsophisticated round-based pots and flaked and polished adzes. They also hunted with bow and arrow. The Saharan people left a remarkable record of their lives on the walls of caves deep in the desert. Wild animals, cattle, goats, humans, and scenes of daily life are preserved in a complicated jumble of artistic endeavor extending back perhaps to 5000 B.C. (Lhote, 1959). The widespread distribution of pastoral sites of this period suggests that the Saharans were ranging their herds over widely separated summer and winter grazing grounds.

About 3500 B.C., climatic conditions again deteriorated. The Sahara slowly became drier and lakes vanished. Rainfall rose in the interior of west Africa, and the northern limit of the tsetse fly belt moved south (this insect is endemic to much of tropical Africa and is fatal to cattle). So the herders shifted south, following the major river systems into savanna regions. By this time, the Saharan people were probably using domestic crops, experimenting with such summer rainfall crops as sorghum and millet as they moved out of areas where they could grow wheat, barley, and other Mediterranean crops (J. D. Clark, 1984; McIntosh and McIntosh, 1988).

EARLY FOOD PRODUCTION IN SUB-SAHARAN AFRICA

● ● ●

At the end of Pleistocene times, the indigenous inhabitants of sub-Saharan Africa were already adapted to many kinds of specialized environment. Some lived by intensive fishing, others by gathering or hunting, depending on their environment. In a simple way the techniques of food production may have already been employed on the fringes of the rain forests of west and central Africa, where the common use of such root plants as the African yam led people to recognize the advantages of growing their own food (J. D. Clark, 1984). Certainly the yam can easily be germinated by replanting its top. This primitive form of "vegeculture" may have been the economic tradition onto which the cultivation of summer rainfall cereal crops was grafted as it came into use south of the grassland areas on the Sahara's southern borders (Harlan et al., 1976).

Vegeculture (plant manipulation)

As the Sahara dried up after 5000 B.C., pastoral peoples moved southward along major water courses into the savanna belt of West Africa and the Sudan. By 3000 B.C., just as ancient Egyptian civilization came into being along the Nile, they had settled in the heart of the East African highlands far to the south. The East African highlands are ideal cattle country and the home of such famous cattle-herding peoples as the Masai today. The highlands were inhabited by hunter-gatherers living around mountains near the plains until about 3300 B.C., when the first cattle herders appeared. These cattle people may have moved between fixed settlements during the wet and dry seasons, living off hunting in the dry months and their own livestock and agriculture during the rains (Ambrose, 1984; Bower, 1984).

As was the case elsewhere, cattle were demanding animals in Africa. They required water at least every 24 hours and large tracts of grazing grass if herds of any size were to be maintained. The secret was careful selection of grazing land, especially in environments where seasonal rainfall led to marked differences in graze quality throughout the year. Even modest cattle herds required plenty of land and considerable mobility. To acquire such land often required moving herds considerable distances, even from summer to winter pastures. At the same time, the cattle owners had to graze their stock in tsetse fly-free areas. The only protection against human and animal trypanosomiasis was to avoid settling or farming such areas—which severely limited the movements of cattle-owning farmers in eastern and central Africa. As a result, small cattle herds spread south rapidly in areas where they could be grazed. Some hunter-gatherer groups in the savanna woodlands of eastern and southern Africa may have acquired cattle, and perhaps other domesticated animals, by gift exchange or through raiding herding neighbors long before cereal agriculture took hold far south of the Sahara.

Contrary to popular belief, there is no such phenomenon as a "pure" pastoralist, a society that subsists of its herds alone. Almost certainly, the Saharan herders who moved southward to escape drought were also cultivating sorghum, millet, and other tropical rainfall crops. By 1500 B.C., cereal agriculture was widespread throughout the savanna belt south of the Sahara. Small farming communities dotted the grasslands and forest margins of eastern West Africa, all of them depending on shifting agriculture, the clearance and cultivation of woodland soils. This form of agriculture involves clearing woodland, burning the felled brush over the cleared plot, then mixing the ash into the soil. After a few years, the soil is exhausted, so the farmer moves on, exploiting new woodland and leaving the abandoned fields to lie fallow. Shifting cultivation, often called "slash-and-burn" agriculture, is highly adaptive for savanna farmers without plows, for it allows cereal farming with the minimal expenditure of energy. It is also wasteful of land.

The process of clearance and burning might have seemed haphazard to the uninformed eye, but it was not. Except in favored areas such as regularly inundated river floodplains, tropical Africa's soils are only of moderate to low fertility. One expert has estimated that only about 40 percent of such soils are cultivable, even with plows. Farmers using simple axes, digging sticks, and hoes would have been at an even greater disadvantage, especially on the heavily wooded, clayey soils so common on the African savanna. The art of farming was careful soil selection, knowing which soils were light and easily cultivable, readily turned with small hoes, and which would maintain their fertility over several years' planting, for cereal crops rapidly removed nitrogen and other nutrients from the soil.

It was iron technology, which appeared south of the Sahara about 700 B.C., which was one catalyst for the spread of farming throughout sub-Saharan Africa. Once it had taken hold, slash-and-burn agriculture expanded its frontiers rapidly, as village after village took up new lands, moving forward so rapidly that one expert has estimated that it took a mere two centuries to cover 1250 miles (2000 km) from East to southern Africa. By A.D. 1, farming villages flourished on the banks of the Zambezi River. Other farmers and cattle herders had crossed into what is now South Africa within a few centuries (Chapter 16).

CHAPTER SUMMARY

Food production was probably introduced into the Nile Valley at a time of drought by 6000 B.C. The hunter-gatherers of the Nile and of the then-inhabitable Sahara Desert were pre-adapted for the new economies, which they may have taken up as a means of staving off food shortages in drought years. By 4000 B.C., agriculture was well established along the Nile, while cattle were domesticated and herded in the depths of the Sahara. Nile valley communities soon became dependent on agriculture, but relied on natural flooding to water their gardens until about 3000 B.C. As the Sahara dried up after 3000 B.C., pastoralists with cereal crops moved south of the desert, introducing cattle herding as far south as the East African highlands.

Cereal agriculture, based on shifting cultivation, did not take hold in much of sub-Saharan Africa until the introduction of ironworking south of the desert in the first millennium B.C.

GUIDE TO FURTHER READING

Butzer, Karl. 1976. *Early Hydraulic Civilization in Egypt.* Chicago: University of Chicago Press.

> *A fundamental source on ancient Egyptian irrigation that has great relevance to this chapter.*

Clark, J. Desmond, and Brandt, Steven A., eds. 1984. *From Hunters to Farmers.* Berkeley: University of California Press.

> *A set of scholarly essays summarizing recent evidence for early agriculture in Africa. Excellent for specialists, and definitive.*

Hassan, Fekri. 1988. "The Predynastic of Egypt." *Journal of World Prehistory* 2 (2):135–186.

> *A definitive critical summary of early agricultural and later societies on the Nile. For the advanced reader.*

Hoffman, Michael A. 1979. *Egypt Before the Pharaohs.* New York: Knopf.

> *A fascinating study of prehistoric Egypt that not only recounts key discoveries but also recalls the archaeologists who made them. The first detailed account of this subject for many years, written for the general reader.*

Smith, Andrew B. 1992. *Pastoralism in Africa.* Johannesburg: Witwatersrand University Press.

> *A specialized monograph on pastoralism that has far wider application than merely African archaeology. A must for the serious student of the past.*

CHAPTER 12 · ASIA

RICE, ROOTS, AND OCEAN VOYAGERS

• • •

A high surf fell upon the shore . . . in the midst of these breakers 10 or 12 [people] were swimming. . . . With [the stern of an old canoe] before them they swam out as far as the outermost breach. Then one or two of them would get into it and opposing the blunt end to the breaking wave were hurried in with incredible swiftness. . . . We stood admiring this very wonderful scene for full half an hour. . . ." Scientist Joseph Banks visited Tahiti in 1769, one of the first Europeans to visit the island. He and his companions were astounded by Tahitian canoes, by the people's seamanship and by their sophisticated, apparently paradisial society. Ever since then, scientists have been fascinated by the origin of these remarkable seamen of the Polynesians. This chapter explores the origins of food production in Asia and the developments that led up to the settlement of the remotest landmasses of the Pacific Ocean.

In 13,000 B.C. much of Southeast Asia was inhabited by hunter-gatherers whose stone toolkits reveal remarkable uniformity over large areas of the mainland and islands (Bellwood, 1985; Higham, 1989) (Table 12.1). These stone assemblages do not necessarily reflect a stagnation of cultural innovation or a simple lifeway. Rather, it seems certain that the people were exploiting a broad range of game and vegetable foods.

Spirit Cave in northeast Thailand overlooks a small stream (Figure 12.1) and was first occupied before 9000 B.C. (Bellwood, 1985). The inhabitants exploited all manner of wild plants, including almonds, betel nuts, broad beans, gourds, water chestnuts, peppers, and cucumbers. The seeds found in Spirit Cave were from plants that can still be collected in the wild and have a variety of dietary, medicinal, and other uses. The large range of animal species found in the sites indicate a broadly based hunting economy that focused on deer, pigs, and arboreal creatures such as monkeys.

There was a wide variety of yams and other potential domesticates in Thailand and elsewhere in Southeast Asia that were exploited by hunter-gatherers at the end of the Pleistocene. As we have pointed out before, yam planting is very simple, and hunter-gatherers are well aware that deliberate cultivation is possible. The problem is to identify the factors that led people to deliberate experimentation with various plants. In the absence of firm archaeological evidence, we can speculate that primitive shifting agriculture, with a combination of diverse crops and some animal herding, may have had its origins in a broad spectrum of hunting and gathering, as it did

TABLE 12.1

• • •

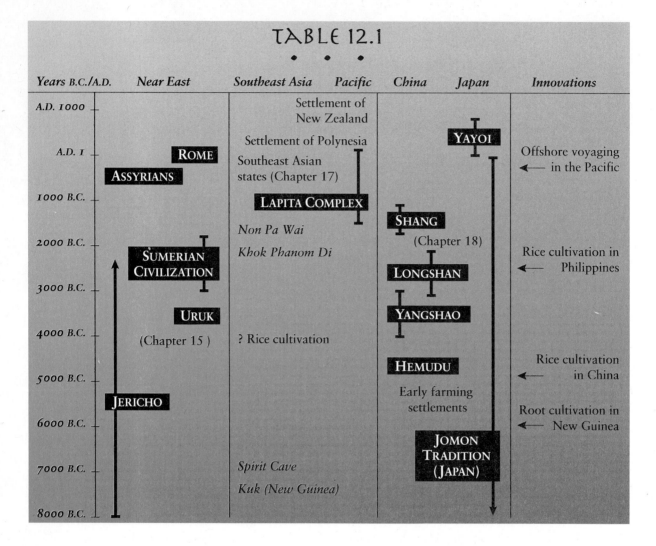

Years B.C./A.D.	Near East	Southeast Asia	Pacific	China	Japan	Innovations
A.D. 1000		Settlement of New Zealand			YAYOI	
A.D. I	ROME ASSYRIANS	Settlement of Polynesia Southeast Asian states (Chapter 17)				← Offshore voyaging in the Pacific
1000 B.C.		LAPITA COMPLEX		SHANG		
2000 B.C.	SUMERIAN CIVILIZATION	Non Pa Wai Khok Phanom Di		(Chapter 18)		← Rice cultivation in Philippines
3000 B.C.				LONGSHAN		
4000 B.C.	URUK (Chapter 15)	? Rice cultivation		YANGSHAO		
5000 B.C.				HEMUDU		← Rice cultivation in China
6000 B.C.	JERICHO			Early farming settlements		← Root cultivation in New Guinea
7000 B.C.		Spirit Cave		JOMON TRADITION (JAPAN)		
8000 B.C.		Kuk (New Guinea)				

in other regions of the world. In the final analysis, all that is needed for a culture to make the transition are some clearings at the edge of the forest and a simple digging stick, already used for gathering, to plant the crop. But, in the final analysis, it was rice, not root crops, that was the staple of Asian agriculture.

RICE CULTIVATION

• • •

Rice was certainly one of the earliest plants to be domesticated in the northern parts of Southeast Asia and southern China. Botanists believe that the rices and Asian millets ancestral to the present domesticated species radiated from perennial ancestors around the eastern borders of the Himalaya Mountains at the end of the Ice Age (R. White, 1982). There is fairly general agreement that the wild annual ancestor of modern cultivated rice was first domesticated in many places between northeast India, northern Southeast Asia, and southern China (Chang, 1986). The initial cultivation of rice is thought to have taken place in an alluvial swamp area, where there was plenty of water to stimulate cereal growth. Perhaps this cultivation occurred

FIGURE 12.1   Southeast Asian sites mentioned in this chapter. Shaded areas show the extent of low sea levels during the Weichsel glaciation.

under conditions in which seasonal flooding made field preparation a far from burdensome task (Bellwood, 1985). Such conditions could have been found on the Ganges Plain in India and along the rich coastal habitats of Southeast Asia and southern China with their dense mangrove swamps.

Peter Bellwood (1985) hypothesizes that a sedentary lifeway based on the gathering of wild rice developed in areas like this at the beginning of the Holocene, with systematic cultivation resulting from a response to population growth, climatic change, or some other stress. The Hemudu site just south of the Shanghai delta provides evidence of well established rice cultivation in southern China, where cooler weather and a shorter growing season exerted greater selection pressure on the early cultivated cereals and made them more dependent on human care. These ideas are based on the most inadequate of evidence, and we may learn that rice was domesticated in several different areas by 5000 B.C., perhaps considerably earlier.

Charles Higham (1989) has excavated an early rice farming community at Khok Phanom Di in Thailand, a settlement that was close to coastal mangrove swamps between 2000 and 1400 B.C. but is now over 12 miles (19.3 km) from the seashore (Figure 12.2). The site covers 12.3 acres (5 ha), is 39 feet (12 m) deep, and contains rice specimens and other evidence of agriculture. Higham hypothesizes that the inhabitants of the coastal plains took up wild rice cultivation as sea levels rose, inundating the game and woodland resources of the fertile shoreline.

Khok Phanom Di
2000 to 1400 B.C.

FIGURE 12.2   Excavations of Khok Phanom Di, Thailand.

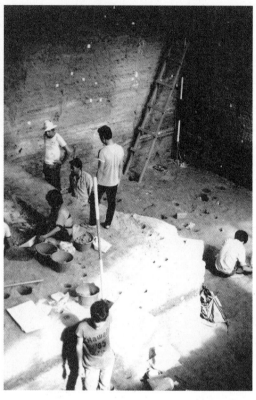

During the late third millennium B.C., there was a proliferation of new village communities with rice and domestic stock. Many of them, like the low mound of Non Nok Tha near the Mekong River, lie near tributary streams of the major rivers, in locations where they would escape major flooding. There was, in short, a dramatic expansion in farming activity, which was to affect societies living far from the coast in coming centuries. Southeast Asia did not suffer from the drastic climatic changes of northern latitudes, but its long dry season makes food storage essential, an important quality of domesticated rice. Only dramatic rises in low sea levels altered the geography and environment of Southeast Asia, creating islands from dry land and reducing the amount of coastal floodplain available to hunters and gatherers. Conceivably, these major changes in coastline and available land surface were among many factors that moved the inhabitants of Southeast Asia to experiment with plants and domestic animals.

EARLY FARMING IN CHINA

● ● ●

"In the wealth of its species and in the extent of the genus and species potential of its cultivated plants, China is conspicuous among other centers of origin of plant forms," wrote the great Russian botanist N. I. Vavilov many years ago (Vavilov, 1951). Early agriculture occurred in at least six different regions of China, three of them—the southern and eastern coastal areas and the north—of major importance (Keightley, 1983).

Southern and Eastern China

No one knows when agriculture first began in southern China, but Chang (1986) hypothesizes that it may have begun as early as 10,000 B.C. with the cultivation of roots and tubers. It is possible that the many ways of exploiting wild vegetable foods in Southeast Asia may have been practiced in southern China too.

The Holocene climate of China fluctuated markedly, just as it did elsewhere in the world. From about 8000 to 6500 B.C., there was a marked warming, resulting in higher lake levels, just as there was in the West. Then cooler conditions returned about 6500 B.C. before a longer warm-up began, culminating in the Holocene climatic optimum, punctuated by short cooler incidents. Apparently, it was during the cold snap after 6500 B.C. that rice cultivation began, just as cereal agriculture took hold in the Near East, during the drought conditions of precisely the same cooler interval (Higham, in press). Just as in the Near East, it may have been in local areas of rich animal and plant diversity such as the Yangtze Valley that experiments with food production began in response to climatic change, just as they did elsewhere in the world.

During the early Holocene, warmer conditions may have allowed wild rice to colonize the lakes and marshes of the middle and lower Yangtze Valley, at a time when hunter-gatherer societies throughout China were exploiting a broad spectrum of animal and plant resources. The Pengdoushan site in the Middle Yangtze Valley dates to between 6500 and 5800 B.C. This large settlement with substantial dwellings and 19 burials has been claimed as an early rice farming village, on the basis of grain impressions in clay vessels. Until actual rice grains come to light, a strong possibility remains that the Pengdoushan people were collecting wild rice on a large scale.

Pengdoushan 6500 to 5800 B.C.

The Lake Taihu region of the lower Yangtze Valley east of Shanghai is another potential area of early agriculture, a lacustrine environment with a wealth of plant and aquatic resources and abundant freshwater vegetation that could be exploited and deliberately cultivated as well. More than 100 early farming sites are known from this region, of which at least 20 have been excavated. Wang Tsun-kuo divides the Lake Taihu sites into three phases, the earliest two dating to between about 5000 and 3000 B.C. (Chang, 1986).

5000 to 3000 B.C.

The earliest Lake Taihu "Majiabang" sites occur on slightly higher ground or artificial mounds near rivers and ponds. The people lived in rectangular houses built of timber with carefully fashioned mortise and tenon joints and sand, shell, or clay floors. The people grew rice and a plant named the water caltrop as well as bottle gourds. They used domesticated dogs, water buffalo, and pigs, hunting a wide variety of mammals, birds, and fish. Wood, bamboo, antler, and bone served to manufacture arrowheads, trowels, needles, and many other artifacts. Stone-bladed adzes and axes were used for woodworking, and bone spades turned the soil. The people were skilled potters and expert farmers, whose economy depended heavily on raising annual crops of sun-loving aquatic plants that grow naturally in marshes and lakes. Later phases of this distinctive and well-established farming culture witnessed much greater sophistication in pottery forms and considerable elaboration of material culture.

Parallel farming cultures are known from other parts of southern China, where rice cultivation was well established by at least 5000 B.C. One such contemporary culture was the Hemudu, south of Shanghai, dating to about the same period as Majiabang. Hemudu itself lies in a marshy area and was once surrounded by forests

Hemudu c. 5000 to 3500 B.C.

and ponds and a great diversity of natural resources. Four cultural layers have been radiocarbon dated to between about 5000 and 3500 B.C. The lowest level of this remarkable site has yielded beautifully mortise-and-tenon-joined building planks, bone hoes, and coarse black pots decorated with cord impressions. This is ideal rice-growing country, and it was hardly surprising to find abundant rice in the site as well as the remains of bottle gourds and numerous wild vegetable foods. The Hemudu people were skilled hunters who kept water buffalo, pigs, and dogs.

Tapenkeng
5000 B.C.

Many other early farming traditions are known to have emerged in southern China after 5000 B.C. (Chang, 1986). Much of the earliest agricultural development may be associated with the widely distributed cord-decorated pottery traditions found in Hemudu and other mainland sites. Offshore, the Tapenkeng culture of Taiwan is one of the better known of early farming traditions, a culture of people who lived close to lakes and rivers. As early as 5000 B.C., the Tapenkeng people were engaged in intensive fishing and shellfish collecting, and hunting and foraging. Chang (1986) believes they may have been gardening as well. It is likely that this is only one of many cord-decorated cultural traditions that flourished over this vast area in the millennia after the first development of agriculture.

By 3000 B.C., much more sophisticated agricultural societies were flourishing on the Yangtze River and farther afield (Chang, 1986). The archaeology of these traditions is known primarily from cemetery excavations that show slow changes in grave goods. The earliest graves indicate few social differentiations, but later sepulchers show not only a much wider variety of artifacts—pottery, bone and stone tools, jade objects, and other ornaments—but also an increase in the number of elaborately adorned burials. Richard Pearson, who has analyzed several cemeteries, argues that they demonstrate an increase in the concentration of wealth, a trend toward ranked societies, and a shift in the relative importance of males at the expense of females; the last trend may be associated with the development of more intensive agriculture, an activity in which males are valued for their major roles in cultivation and production of food.

Northern China

The earliest farming traditions of the south are represented by the widespread cord-decorated pottery cultures that date to before 5000 B.C. Another set of early farming traditions emerged in the north, either independently or as a result of interaction with the south (Barnes, 1993; Chang, 1986).

Northern Chinese agriculture was based on millet, whereas the southern staple was rice. The first northern agricultural communities were sited in the central regions of the Yellow River Valley (Figure 12.3). The area is a small basin, forming a border between the wooded western highlands and the swampy lowlands to the east. As in the south, the early Holocene saw a warming trend, followed by a cooler interval, then a more prolonged period of climatic amelioration. It was during the colder period, dating to after 6500 B.C., that the first sedentary farming villages appear in the Huanghe Valley.

During the glaciations of the Pleistocene, loess soils were formed over a wide area of the north. The fine, soft-textured earth was both homogeneous and porous and could be tilled by simple digging sticks. Because of the concentrated summer rainfall, cereal crops, the key to agriculture in this region, could be grown successfully. The indigenous plants available for domestication included the wild ancestors of foxtail millet, broom-corn millet, sorghum, hemp, and the mulberry. Ancient

FIGURE 12.3   Early Chinese farming cultures, with names of three major local variants. Yangshao sites occur both within the northern shaded area and outside it. Southern sites of corded pottery are found in the Kwangtung, Fukien, and Taiwan areas.

Chinese farmers developed their own cultivation techniques, which persisted for thousands of years. Although irrigation gradually became the basis of the agricultural economies of Egypt, the Indus Valley, and Mesopotamia, it was not important in northern China until much later (Ho, 1969).

The earliest millennia of northern Chinese agriculture are still a blank on the archaeological map. Two hypotheses are possible. We can assume that the inhabitants of the Huanghe River region passed through a long phase of experimental cultivation and intensive exploitation of the indigenous flora before developing their own distinctive agricultural techniques, or we can assume that food production was developed farther south in China and adopted later in the north. Neither hypothesis can be tested with the available evidence. It is known that early farming villages were associated with coarse, cord-marked pottery found on the banks of the Huanghe River in western Henan province. Perhaps these vessels are related to the cord-decorated pottery traditions of southern China, Southeast Asia, and Taiwan.

The earliest farming villages in central and northern China date to as early as 5000 B.C. (see Figure 12.3) (Barnes, 1993). Many settlements consisted of semi-subterranean houses with large storage pits. Their owners grew foxtail millet and kept dogs and pigs. By far the best known of China's early farming cultures is the Yangshao, which flourished over much of the Huanghe River Basin, an area as large as the early centers of agriculture in Egypt or Mesopotamia, from before 5000 B.C. to about 3200 B.C.

Early farming
5000 B.C. and earlier

FIGURE 12.4   Reconstruction of Yangshao houses from Banpo, China.

Yangshao
5000 to 3200 B.C.

Each Yangshao village was a self-contained community, usually built on a terrace overlooking fertile river valleys, situated to avoid flooding or to allow maximal use of floodplain soils (Figure 12.4). Using hoes and digging sticks, the farmers cultivated foxtail millet as a staple, mainly in riverside gardens that were flooded every spring. Hunting, foraging, and fishing were still important, and the people moved their villages when local soils became exhausted. Yangshao culture evolved over many centuries. By 3000 B.C., it boasted of a characteristic, and thoroughly Chinese, culture, with its own naturalistic art style (Figure 12.5), and expert potters who made cooking pots for steaming food, the technique which forms the basis of much Chinese cuisine to this day. The Chinese language may have its roots in Yangshao as well.

Over the centuries, the distribution of Yangshao culture expanded as new villages split off from older communities and brought new land under cultivation. Yangshao and other settlements tended to follow a pattern of river valleys as many regional variations of peasant farming culture developed throughout China (Figure 12.6). Agriculture developed over wide areas at about the same time, with people adapting their crops and farming techniques to local conditions. In time, the success of the new economies led to local population increases, more complex cultures, and the concentration of wealth in privileged hands.

Longshanoid
3800 B.C.

By 3000 B.C., "Longshanoid" farming cultures flourished throughout much of northern China, based on larger, more permanent, and often earthen-walled settlements. Longshanoid cultures were based in part on irrigation and rice cultivation, for the new tropical crop had been introduced from the lush water meadows of the south, reducing dependence on dry agriculture. These much more elaborate, and wealthier, farming cultures were among the roots of Chinese civilization (Figure 12.7). (For Korea, see Nelson, 1993.)

FIGURE 12.5 Yangshao pottery from Banpo, China (approximately one-fourth actual size). The fish motifs often used to decorate Yang-shao pottery can be clearly seen (other motifs are drawn separately).

JOMON AND EARLY AGRICULTURE IN JAPAN

● ● ●

By 10,000 B.C., sea levels around Japan were rising and the landmass area available to hunter-gatherers shrank considerably. In postglacial times, many Asian groups settled by coastlines and lakeshores, just as they did in Europe. They began exploiting a wide range of land and maritime resources in many different climatic zones. In some areas where resources were concentrated, people began to adopt more sedentary settlement patterns and live in well-defined territories. In Japan, for example, shellfish collecting provided a relatively stable subsistence base for the Jomon people. As early as 10,500 B.C., they made clay vessels, which they used for steaming mollusks and making vegetable foods palatable (R. Pearson et al., 1986). These are some of the earliest clay pots ever made, but the same cultural development may have taken hold elsewhere as Stone Age people adapted to radically new environmental conditions and exploited an even wider resource base. As postglacial times continued, the people turned to another logical adaptive strategy, deliberate growing of crops and taming of animals to ensure more reliable food supplies (Reynolds and Barnes, 1984; Barnes, 1990).

More than 30,000 Jomon sites are known, most of them from Honshu in central Japan (Figure 12.8). All are linked by a common cultural tradition that lasted for thousands of years, but there were probably different ethnic groups, who perhaps spoke different languages and adapted to diverse environments. The Jomon

Jomon tradition
10,500 to 300 B.C.

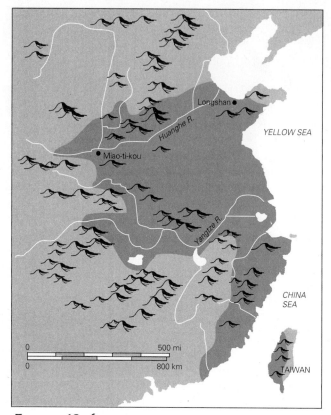

FIGURE 12.6   Approximate distribution of later farming cultures in China (cross-hatched area).

FIGURE 12.7   Some typical Longshanoid vessels used for cooking and other purposes, from Miaotiku, China (scale not recorded).

people hunted deer and other game with bows and arrows, collected thousands of shellfish, mainly in the spring, and fished much of the year. At first they caught all types of fish, but as time went on they concentrated on a few carefully selected species, inshore and lake fish as well as deepwater forms such as the bonito and

FIGURE 12.8   Jomon gray-bodied molded jar, of conical form with loop handles and decorated with combwork.

tuna. Above all their diet depended heavily on wild vegetable foods such as acorns, nuts, and edible seeds. They lived in relatively sedentary settlements, perhaps because of carefully scheduled seasonal hunting, gathering, and fishing activities. Some believe that they supplemented these activities with cultivation of root crops and cereals or simply by careful management of nut trees. The evidence for agriculture is still sketchy, but it seems possible that the Jomon people flourished by developing an elaborate technology for processing and storing huge stocks of nuts, an activity they may have combined with cultivation of milletlike plants (Crawford, 1992).

The Jomon tradition lasted from as early as 10,000 B.C. until as late as 300 B.C. During this period, the focus of settlement shifted from the coasts to central Honshu and to the northern shores of Japan. By 5000 B.C., the inhabitants of Honshu were enjoying an elaborate material culture, including finely made ritual clay pots adorned with intricate decorations. The people often lived not in the caves and simple pit houses of earlier times but in large clusters of wooden houses with elaborate hearths. After 3000 B.C., the climate became cooler, overpopulation may have strained the carrying capacity of arable land, and clearance of natural vegetation affected hunting activities. Hence, the population declined and the major centers of Jomon occupation moved toward the coasts. In the south, the inhabitants of Kyushu took up rice and barley cultivation after 1000 B.C. (Akazawa, 1982).

The basis for what was to become traditional Japanese society was formed during the Yayoi period, which began after 300 B.C., when new crops and technologies spread through the islands. Japan was unified into a single state in approximately A.D. 600, by which time complex, stratified societies were commonplace throughout the archipelago.

Yayoi
300 B.C.

Unification
A.D. 600

RICE AND ROOT CULTIVATION
IN ISLAND SOUTHEAST ASIA

● ● ●

Offshore from mainland Asia one enters what archaeologist Peter Bellwood (1985) has called "a totally different Neolithic world." He believes that swamp cultivation of rice was introduced from the north, where it took hold considerably earlier. Rice agriculture dates to around 3500 B.C. on Taiwan, perhaps earlier, and only dates back to about 1700 B.C. in the Philippines, although agriculture may be as early as 3000 B.C. there and on Sulawasi (Spriggs, 1989). Farmers were living on East Timor before 2100 B.C. and offshore in the Bismarck Archipelago by 1900 to 1500 B.C.

3000 B.C.

This initial farming settlement is marked by a relatively homogeneous Neolithic culture of farmers who settled mainly by coasts and rivers. Canoes played a major role in intervillage exchange, which persisted for 2000 years. These constant exchanges meant that such items as clay vessels, adzes, and axes were fairly standardized over large areas, and communities as far separated as Taiwan and Manus enjoyed the same general economy, material culture, and social organization. The same exchange networks carried New Britain obsidian and occasional metal objects over hundreds of miles.

2000 B.C.

This culture does not appear to have penetrated highland New Guinea, where agriculture developed quite independently. Here hunter-gatherers lived in damp, often densely forested environments, where the cultivation of root crops like taro and yams and fruit trees such as bananas required less forest clearance. Agricultural systems of this type, widespread in parts of Indonesia and in island Melanesia, spread widely after 2500 B.C.

Archaeologists Jack Golson, Peter White, and others have researched early horticulture in the New Guinea highlands, using both pollen analysis and the study of old irrigation channels to amplify the archaeological record (Allen, 1969; Golson, 1977). There are traces, at approximately 7000 B.C., of deliberate diversion of river water in the Kuk Basin, which have been interpreted to mean that the people were cultivating taro or yams at a very early date. The evidence is still uncertain, although signs of increased erosion in the area may be the result of forest clearance for taro or yam gardens or possibly for the deliberate growing of indigenous New Guinea plants (White and O'Connell, 1982).

Kuk Basin
7000 B.C.

By 4000 to 3500 B.C., much more organized horticultural works were found in the Kuk Basin. There is pollen evidence for quite extensive forest clearance in the general area. These works may have been created for yam and taro crops, while indigenous plants were grown on the better-drained soils between the channel banks. After 2000 B.C., the first highly developed drainage systems occurred in the area, a sign that people were farming much more intensively. After 500 B.C., the people depended more and more heavily on dry and wet agriculture, for the forest resources they had relied on were replaced by an environment that had been altered permanently by human activity. A slow population growth resulted eventually in the taking up of uncleared land. After that was exhausted, the only option was to shorten the fallow periods on cleared gardens—something that, if taro was the crop, would have resulted in lower crop yields.

4000 B.C.

2000 B.C.
500 B.C.

The archaeological investigations and pollen analysis of Golson (1977) and others have produced firm evidence for sedentism, forest clearance, stone agricultural tools, and water-control techniques in the New Guinea highlands by 4000 to 3000

B.C. What is uncertain, however, is the means by which food production began in New Guinea. Was it developed locally with introduced plants after the local hunter-gatherers had manipulated indigenous plants for centuries? Or did the people manipulate local plants as a result of adopting a few introduced crops first? Whatever the answer, it appears that the New Guinea highlands were an area where people created an artificial garden environment as a result of a long period of experimentation, in which they were raising plants *within* their natural environment. By exploiting a wide range of tropical animals and plants, the people became more sedentary and later started to plant small plots of root crops; ultimately, they would have intensified their food production until they modified their environment beyond recognition. This hypothetical model for early agriculture in New Guinea may serve as a possible model for other tropical areas in Asia as well.

AGRICULTURE IN THE PACIFIC ISLANDS

● ● ●

The origins of the peoples of the Pacific islands have fascinated scientists since the seventeenth century (Figure 12.9), but most authorities now look to Southeast Asia for the origins of the Melanesians, Micronesians, and Polynesians. They point out

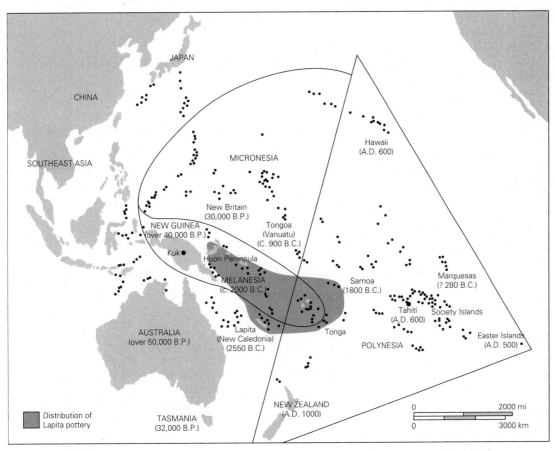

FIGURE 12.9   Map of Pacific sites. Cross-hatching shows distribution of Lapita cultural complex.

that settlement of the offshore islands depended on the successful cultivation of root crops such as taro and yam, as well as breadfruit, coconuts, and sugarcane. Chickens, dogs, and pigs were also valued as food and were domesticated in Asia before being introduced to the Pacific. Oceanic islands lack much in the way of wild food resources, so domesticated plants and animals were essential for successful colonization. Small animals such as pigs and chickens could readily have been carried from island to island in canoes, as could easily germinating root plants such as the yam. Both food sources allowed a sizable population to spread to many hundreds of small islands separated by miles of open water.

The settlement of the remoter Pacific islands is closely connected to the early cultivation of yams, and especially of taro. As we pointed out earlier in this chapter, taro and yams were probably domesticated in Southeast Asia before the development of rice cultivation, but exactly when and where they were first grown is unknown. In all probability, there were several centers of early domestication within Southeast Asia as early as 38,000 B.C., as early seafarers settled not only New Guinea but also close island chains like the Solomons and perhaps the Bismarck Archipelago as early as 29,000 B.C. (Chapter 7). Beyond the Solomons and farther offshore was a biologically more impoverished world that awaited domesticated crops and animals and more developed seafaring and navigational techniques before human colonization.

The Lapita Cultural Complex and the Settlement of Melanesia and Western Polynesia

•   •   •

The settlement of remoter, offshore Melanesia covered a distance of 3100 miles (5000 km) of island chains and open ocean during a period of six centuries from about 1600 to 1000 B.C. This was human settlement that followed on the domestication of plants and animals and the development of new maritime technologies, presumably including oceangoing, double-hulled sailing canoes. In archaeological terms, this development is associated with the highly distinctive Lapita Cultural Complex, named after a site on New Caledonia Island. Most experts agree that the Lapita people were Austronesian-speakers, who traded widely through the southwestern Pacific. Their settlements are marked by characteristic stamp-decorated pottery, often adorned with elaborate designs (Figure 12.10).

The original homeland of the Lapita people is a matter of considerable debate. One school of thought considers them to have originated in western Melanesia, whereas others believe they arrived in the islands from the Southeast Asian mainland (Kirch, 1988; White et al., 1988). The issue is unresolved, but it is clear that there was widespread trade in New Britain obsidian that traveled far and wide through the Southeast Asian islands, through exchange networks that carried the same toolmaking stone as far west as farming settlements on the eastern coast of Borneo (Bellwood and Koon, 1989). That is not to say, of course, that Lapita canoes traveled all the way to Borneo. Rather, there was what Peter Bellwood calls a "linked chain" of exchange networks over more than 5000 miles (8100 km) through the Southeast Asian islands deep into the central Pacific by 1000 B.C. People living in small island environments usually depend on their neighbors for many important commodities, an interdependency that was reflected in complex exchange

FIGURE 12.10   Lapita pottery from Melanesia.

networks spanning many miles of open ocean. The commodities carried in canoes ranged from foodstuffs to manufactured items and may have included ceremonial objects as well. The social and economic complexities of Melanesian trading systems have long excited anthropologists, starting with Bronislaw Malinowski's (1922) famous fieldwork on the celebrated *kula* ring of the Trobriand Islanders that circulated shell necklaces and bracelets from island to island in complex circles. The *kula* ring with its elaborate ceremonial is just one of many related exchange trading systems that linked all parts of coastal New Guinea and much of Melanesia. These networks are reciprocal and self-perpetuating and have their ancestry in much earlier exchange patterns that began, albeit in a more simple form, among Lapita peoples (Allen and White, 1989; Terrell, 1988).

The Lapita homeland is thought by some to have been in the Bismarck Archipelago area, which was inhabited during the late Ice Age (Chapter 7) as far back as about 35,000 B.C. (Gosden et al, 1989). There is clear evidence for open-water voyaging as far as Manus Island, an island where obsidian is to be found, some 124 straight-line miles (200 km) offshore by 2900 B.C. An Australian research team has identified widespread human occupation through the Bismarck Archipelago before Lapita pottery appeared about 1500 B.C., and it may be that some, if not most, elements of the Lapita Cultural Complex came from local roots. By identifying the sources of island obsidians and pottery clays, the Australians have been able to show that local trading patterns changed constantly during pre-Lapita times and throughout the Lapita occupation of the archipelago. Clearly, both these cultures were dynamic, ever-changing systems.

These excavations show that there is a very long history of human occupation indeed in the Bismarck Archipelago, one that stretches back far into the Ice Age. Throughout most of this long period, obsidian was moved through the islands and far beyond them toward Southeast Asia. The region was never isolated from the outside world, but its inhabitants were part of a vast network of interconnections that linked the entire western Pacific and island Southeast Asia over a period of at

Bismarck Archipelago
9400 to 1500 B.C.

least 1500 years. It was not until sometime after Christ that these broad links vanish, to be replaced by more local cultural developments.

Lapita
1600 to 1000 B.C.

The Lapita Cultural Complex was either a migration of new peoples from Southeast Asia into the islands, as was once thought, or a vast exchange system that linked island after island through reciprocal trading between kinspeople. Archaeologically, we know that Lapita pottery from the Santa Cruz Islands, decorated with stamped designs and made of clay tempered with shell, is found as far east as Vanuatu, Fiji, Tonga, and Samoa. We know it dates generally to the last thousand years before Christ but seems to have gone out of fashion by A.D. 200 (Kirch, 1982). To associate this pottery distribution with a migrating ethnic group is to oversimplify a very complex picture of long-distance exchange, ocean voyaging, and island settlement.

Clearly, one catalyst for this expansion was the development of the oceangoing, double-hulled canoe. This canoe was the means by which efficient exchange networks were maintained from island to island over distances up to 372 miles (600 km) far out into the Pacific, into western Polynesia. The rapid expansion from island to island that carried Lapita pottery far offshore developed among societies living in an island environment that extended from the Southeast Asian mainland far southwestward. The inhabitants of this vast archipelago lived on relatively benign coasts and maintained contacts with one another that extended over hundreds of miles. That there was some standardization of artifacts and culture among them after 2000 B.C. is hardly surprising. It is only when one reaches off-lying islands such as Fiji and Tonga that one can legitimately think in terms of Lapita "settlers," who were the first human settlers of the Pacific. Here, open-water distances are much longer, involving, for example, voyages of nearly 600 open-water miles (592 km). In Fiji, Samoa, and Tonga, the first settlers carried Lapita artifacts with them, but subsequent cultural development proceeded along local lines.

LONG-DISTANCE VOYAGING IN THE PACIFIC

● ● ●

From Melanesia, canoes voyaged through western Polynesia, taking the plants and domesticated animals of their homelands with them. As distances grew longer, so did the navigational challenges, challenges so formidable that many early scholars argued that the Polynesian islands were settled by accidental voyages. Some compelling studies of Polynesian navigation and voyaging by both anthropologists and small-boat sailors have dispelled any lingering doubts about the navigational abilities of the early Polynesians. Recently, Geoffrey Irwin (1992), himself an expert sailor, has used computer modeling and his own voyages to suggest that the exploration was rapid and deliberate, a systematic process that led to ever more improved navigational techniques. At the same time, he believes that rather than sailing randomly downwind, the early voyagers made their explorations upwind, against the prevailing winds, knowing that they could always turn downwind and return home with ease.

Nearly all the long trips attributed to the Polynesians were from north to south, which involved simple dead-reckoning calculations and an elementary way of measuring latitude from the stars. Several modern studies have collected navigators' lore from surviving practitioners of the art (Lewis, 1972). The pilots were a respected and close-knit group. Young apprentices learned their skills over many years of making passages and from orally transmitted knowledge about the stars and the oceans accumulated by generations of navigators. The navigational techniques used the angles of rising and setting stars, the trend of ocean swells, and the myriad inconspicuous phenomena that indicate the general direction and distance of small islands. The navigators were perfectly capable of voyaging over long stretches of open water, and their geographic knowledge was astonishing. They had no need for the compass or other modern aids, and their landfalls were accurate.

From Melanesia, canoes voyaged to Micronesia and eastern Polynesia, taking the plants and domestic animals of their home islands with them. The colonization of Micronesia and eastern Polynesia took place within the last 2000 years, some 1300 to 1600 years after first settlement of western Polynesia. The sudden, and apparently rapid, expansion may have resulted from population growth in already settled islands that sent voyagers farther eastward looking for new, pristine lands (Spriggs and Anderson, 1993). It is thought that the Polynesians originated in the Fiji area before the great elaboration of Melanesian culture after A.D. 1. After a lengthy period of adaptation in western Polynesia, small groups began to settle the more remote islands. The Marquesas were settled by A.D. 500 and the Society Islands and Tahiti by A.D. 800. The first canoes arrived in Hawaii in about A.D. 600 and on Easter Island by the late first millennium A.D. (Kirch, 1985). The human settlement of Polynesia seems to have taken approximately 2500 years from its beginnings by people who were still, technologically speaking, in the Stone Age. They relied heavily on stone axes and adzes and an elaborate array of bone and shell fishhooks (Figure 12.11). The crops the people planted varied from island to island, but

**Eastern Polynesia
150 B.C. to A.D. 800**

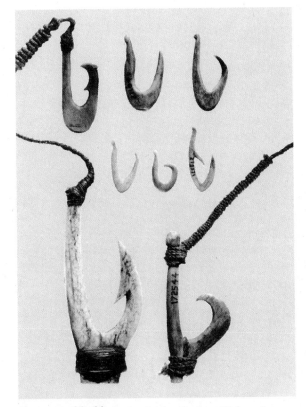

FIGURE 12.11   Bone fishhooks from Polynesia.

breadfruit, taro, coconut, yams, and bananas were the staples. Sweet potato, a South American plant, was a staple when Europeans first arrived. No one knows how this American crop reached eastern Polynesia, but it may have been the result of (as yet unidentified) Polynesian voyaging to the South American mainland (Hather and Kirch, 1991). The food surpluses generated on the larger islands were used as a form of wealth.

When the French and British visited Tahiti in the eighteenth century, they chanced upon the center of a vigorous eastern Polynesian society (Oliver, 1977). The islands were ruled by a powerful hierarchy of chiefs and nobles, many of them descendants of the canoe crews who had settled the archipelago. The chiefs acquired prestige by controlling and redistributing wealth and food supplies. Their formidable religious and social powers led them to warfare and to the undertaking of elaborate agricultural projects and the erection of monumental shrines and temples of stone: The famous *maraes* of Tahiti are typical examples (Figure 12.12). On remote Easter Island the people erected vast statues up to 32 feet (9.8 m) high. They are thought to be images of deified ancestors associated with different kin groups.

The full diversity of Polynesian culture is still imperfectly understood, for archaeological research has hardly begun in the South Seas, but it is certain that the Polynesians were making ocean voyages on a large scale at a time when the Greeks and Romans were little more than coastal navigators.

FIGURE 12.12   An eighteenth-century drawing of a *marae* on Tahiti.

The Settlement of New Zealand

New Zealand is the largest and among the most remote of all of the Pacific islands; it is actually two large islands. It has a temperate climate, not the tropical warmth enjoyed by most Polynesians. Despite this ecological difference, New Zealand was first settled by Polynesians who voyaged southward in comparatively recent times and settled on the North Island. Maori legends tell of a migration from Polynesia in the mid-fourteenth century A.D. Settlers including Toi Ete'hutai, who came to New Zealand in search of two grandsons blown away from Tahiti during a canoe race, may have arrived 400 years before. The earliest C14 dates for New Zealand archaeological sites are a matter of controversy, but a recent careful study places first settlement between A.D. 1000 and 1200 (A. Anderson, 1992).

First settlement ?
A.D. 1000 to 1200

The temperate climate of the North Island formed a southern frontier for most of the basic food plants of Polynesia. Taro, yams, and gourd can be grown only there, but the sweet potato can be cultivated in the northern part of the South Island if adequate winter storage pits are used. The Polynesian coconut never grew in New Zealand. The earliest settlers relied heavily on hunting, fishing, and gathering. Even later, though some peoples specialized in food production, others did not, especially on the South Island, where many settlements were close to abundant ocean resources (Davidson, 1985).

The first settlers found great flocks of flightless Moa birds, cumbersome and helpless in the face of systematic hunting. They hunted the Moa into extinction within a few centuries (Anderson and McGlone, 1991). Fish, fern roots, and shellfish were important throughout New Zealand's short prehistory. The introduction of the sweet potato made a dramatic difference to the New Zealanders, for the tubers, if carefully protected from cold, could be eaten in the winter months, and some could be kept for the next year's planting. Sweet potatoes have a large crop yield and are thought to have contributed to a rapid population buildup, especially on the North Island. This, in turn, led to competition among groups for suitable agricultural land to grow the new staple (Davidson, 1985).

When the Moa became extinct, the Maori had few meat supplies except birds, dogs, and rats. Their only other meat source was human flesh. The archaeological record of Maori culture from approximately A.D. 1400 onward shows not only population growth but also an increasing emphasis on warfare, evidenced by the appearance of numerous fortified encampments, or *pa,* protected with earthen banks. The distribution of *pa* coincides to a large extent with the best sweet potato lands (Bellwood, 1970). In the course of a few centuries, warfare became a key element in Maori culture, to the extent that it was institutionalized and an important factor in maintaining cohesion and leadership in Maori society. The booty of war was not only *kumara* (sweet potato) but also the flesh of captives, which became a limited part of the Maori diet.

Maori
A.D. 1400

Maori warfare, mainly confined to the North Island, where more than 5000 *pa* have been found, was seasonal and closely connected with the planting and harvest of sweet potatoes, when everyone was busy in the gardens. Military campaigns were short and intense, very often launched from the sea in war canoes up to 78.7 feet (24 m) or more in length (Figure 12.13). These elaborately carved vessels could hold as many as 150 men on a short expedition. So formidable was the reputation of the Maori that European ships avoided New Zealand ports for years before permanent white settlement was achieved. The last Maori war ended in 1872, by which time the indigenous population had been decimated by disease, warfare, and European contact.

FIGURE 12.13   Maori war canoe recorded by Captain James Cook in 1769.

CHAPTER SUMMARY

As in the Near East, food production began in Asia during the Holocene, perhaps in a cold interval that followed initial warming, around 6500 B.C. In Southeast Asia, the staple crop was rice, probably first cultivated along low-lying, swamp coasts. The new economies soon spread inland during the third millennium B.C., bringing village life to much of Southeast Asia. In southern China, wild rice was gathered as early as 6000 B.C., but it is not known exactly when it was first cultivated. Rice agriculture was well established by 5000 B.C. The staple in the Huanghe Valley of northern China was millet, cultivated at least as early as 5000 B.C. The Yangshao culture flourished over much of the Huanghe Basin, a society of self-contained villages, replaced by more elaborate Longshanoid cultures by 3000 B.C.

Island Southeast Asia was settled by hunters and foragers at least as early as 35,000 B.C., with simple root horticulture established in highland New Guinea by 7000 B.C. The people of the Lapita cultural complex traded widely through the southwestern Pacific after 1600 B.C., but it was not until the past 2000 years that offshore canoes settled Micronesia and Polynesia, with New Zealand being colonized between A.D. 1000 and 1200.

GUIDE TO FURTHER READING

Barnes, Gina L. 1993. *China, Korea, and Japan.* London, Eng., and New York: Thames and Hudson.

> *An up-to-date synthesis of recent research in eastern Asia by a scholar who commands the local literature. Strongly recommended as a starting point.*

Bellwood, Peter. 1986. *The Prehistory of the Indo-Malaysian Archipelago.* Sydney: Academic Press.

> *A valuable summary of Southeast Asian mainland prehistory.*

———. 1987. *The Polynesians.* London: Thames and Hudson.

> *A synthesis of what we know about Polynesian prehistory. Excellent illustrations.*

Davidson, Janet. 1985. "New Zealand Prehistory." *Advances in World Archaeology* 4:239–292.
   An exemplary article on general trends in New Zealand prehistory with a very complete bibliography.

Irwin, Geoffrey. 1992. *The Prehistoric Exploration and Colonisation of the Pacific.* Cambridge, Eng.: Cambridge University Press.
   Irwin is a practical sailor, which makes his sophisticated analysis of the offshore settlement of the Pacific doubly convincing. A truly fascinating work.

Kirch, Patrick V. 1984. *The Evolution of the Polynesian Kingdoms.* Cambridge, Eng.: Cambridge University Press.
   A splendid analysis of this important development in Polynesian prehistory.

Lewis, David. 1972. *We the Navigators.* Honolulu: University of Hawaii Press.
   An account of traditional Polynesian navigational methods based on both local lore and experiments navigating a yacht without a compass and sextant. What makes this book fascinating is that the author is a practical sailor himself.

CHAPTER 13

THE STORY OF MAIZE

EARLY FARMING SOCIETIES IN THE AMERICAS

• • •

When Harvard archaeologist Alfred Kidder dug into the complex layers of Pecos Pueblo, New Mexico in 1915, he was searching for the ancient roots of Pueblo Indian culture deep in the middens of this long occupied site. Kidder had visited archaeological sites in Egypt and Greece and had seen at first hand how careful stratigraphic observation had yielded rich chronological dividends. Over many field seasons, he sunk enormous trenches into the depths of the Pecos deposits, uncovering dozens of small occupation layers and dense concentrations of potsherds. Back in the laboratory, he pored over thousands of painted potsherds and turned them into a long cultural sequence that has been the foundation of all subsequent research in the Southwest. "It is safe enough to postulate the former presence in the Southwest or a more or less nomadic people, thinly scattered over the country, ignorant of agriculture and pottery making," he wrote (1927) of the earliest occupants. American archaeologists have searched for the first native American farmers not only in the Southwest, but throughout the New World ever since (B. Smith, 1994).

The American Indians domesticated an impressive range of native New World plants, some of which—like maize, potatoes, and tobacco—were rapidly adopted by farmers in other continents after European contact (Table 13.1)

The most important staple crop was Indian corn, properly called maize, the only significant wild grass in the New World to be fully domesticated. It remains the most important food crop in the Americas, being used in more than 150 varieties as both food and cattle fodder. Root crops formed another substantial food source, especially in South America, and included manioc, sweet potatoes, and white potatoes. Chili peppers were grown as hot seasoning; amaranth, sunflowers, cacao, peanuts, and several types of bean were also significant crops. Some crops, such as cotton and gourds, are common to both Old and New Worlds but were probably domesticated separately.

In contrast to Old World farmers, the Indians had few domesticated animals, including the llama of the Andes and alpacas, which provided wool. Dogs appeared in the Americas, and the raucous and unruly turkey and the muscovy duck were domesticated.

Most archaeologists now agree that there were two major centers of plant domestication in the Americas: Mesoamerica for maize, beans, squash, and sweet

TABLE 13.1
• • •

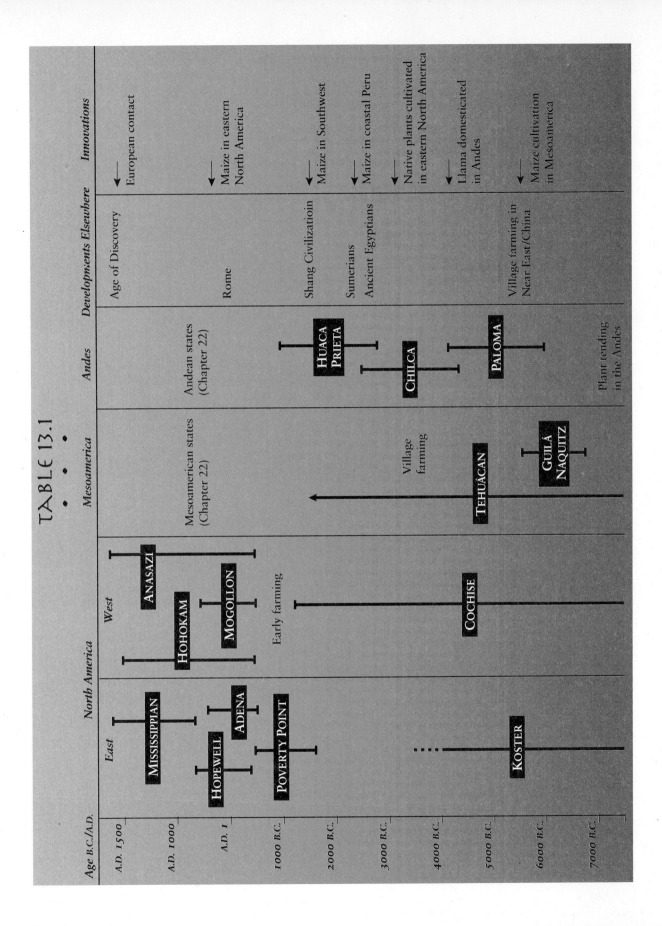

Age B.C./A.D.	North America		Mesoamerica	Andes	Developments Elsewhere	Innovations
	East	West				
A.D. 1500					Age of Discovery	← European contact
A.D. 1000	MISSISSIPPIAN	ANASAZI				
A.D. 1	HOPEWELL ADENA	HOHOKAM MOGOLLON	Mesoamerican states (Chapter 22)	Andean states (Chapter 22)	Rome	← Maize in eastern North America
1000 B.C.	POVERTY POINT	Early farming			Shang Civilizatioin	← Maize in Southwest
2000 B.C.			Village farming	HUACA PRIETA	Sumerians	← Maize in coastal Peru
3000 B.C.				CHILCA	Ancient Egyptians	← Native plants cultivated in eastern North America
4000 B.C.		COCHISE	TEHUACÁN	PALOMA		← Llama domesticated in Andes
5000 B.C.			GUILÁ NAQUITZ		Village farming in Near East/China	← Maize cultivation in Mesoamerica
6000 B.C.	KOSTER					
7000 B.C.				Plant tending in the Andes		

potatoes, and the highlands of the central Andes for root crops. There were also four major areas of later cultivation activity: tropical (northern) South America, the Andean area, Mesoamerica, and eastern North America (B. Smith, 1994).

THE ORIGINS OF PLANT DOMESTICATION IN MESOAMERICA

● ● ●

In Chapter 8, we described the sophisticated model, which chronicles the shift from hunting and foraging to agriculture in the valley of Oaxaca, a model derived from Kent Flannery's excavations at the Guilá Naquitz rock shelter (Flannery et al., 1986; R. Reynolds, 1986). Flannery established that the changeover took a very long time indeed, and he believes it was the result of strategies designed to cope with continuous short-term climatic fluctuations and constant population shifts. This model, based as it is on only one excavation, seems to agree well with what we know about the gradual adoption of agriculture elsewhere in the Tehuacán Valley (see later) and other locations. It provides a working scenario for the beginnings of farming over a wide area of Mesoamerica.

Flannery believes that the gourds, members of the Cucurbitaceae family, were the first plants domesticated in the Americas, not only pumpkins and squashes but also the bottle gourd, an invaluable container for holding liquids both before and after its domestication. The latter may be of African origin, where it is widely used as a fishing net float. Perhaps, argue some experts, it floated across the Atlantic and washed up on American shores, possibly even before European settlement. At any rate, the seeds would provide hunter-gatherers with an easy source of water containers, a preadaptation that might have led to the cultivation of wild squashes and other cucurbits. They were certainly in use in Mesoamerica as early as 5000 B.C.

Wild ancestors of beans occur in Mesoamerica, and small, wild runner beans were collected at Guilá Naquitz as early as 7000 to 5500 B.C. As is well known, maize, beans, and squash, which can be grown in the same garden, are a classic triumvirate of food crops in the Americas. Initially, this association probably occurred in the wild, for runner beans and squashes grow naturally around the stalks and bases of teosinte, thought to be the ancestor of maize. In the end, humans disturbed the land by clearing it, observed the association of teosinte, beans, and squash, and domesticated the three in combination.

Of these three crops, by far the most complex and most debated is *Zea mays*, maize.

MESOAMERICA: TEHUACÁN AND THE ORIGINS OF MAIZE AGRICULTURE

● ● ●

Maize was the staff of life for many Native Americans when Christopher Columbus landed in the New World. It was cultivated over an enormous area of the Americas, from Argentina and Chile northward to Canada, from sea level to high in the Andes, in low-lying swampy environments and in arid lands. Hundreds of races of domesticated maize evolved over the millennia, each a special adaptation to local environmental conditions.

The origins of domesticated maize are still the subject of great controversy, which centers on the relationship between a wild grass named teosinte *(Zea mexicana),* which grows over much of Mesoamerica, and early strains of domesticated maize (Galinat, 1985). The botanist George Beadle (1981) theorizes that a teosinte of about 6000 to 13,000 B.C. was the direct ancestor of modern corn and was transformed into a primitive corn through human selection. According to Beadle, there was a mutation in the tunicate gene in an ancestral form of teosinte that converted the hard fruit cases of the grass into shallow, softer cupules that carried elongated glumes, which enclosed and protected the kernels. This change made wild teosinte much easier to thresh. The transformation to a domesticated form of early maize may have taken place simultaneously in many areas and may have occurred within a very short time, perhaps only a century.

There are impressive grounds for considering teosinte the wild ancestor of maize. A perennial teosinte found in Mexico in recent years has been crossbred with maize. Experiments have shown that teosinte can be "popped" in a fire, on a hot rock, or on heated sand, just like the popcorn we consume at the movies. Dry teosinte seeds also can be cracked with even a simple grindstone, or softened before eating by being soaked in water.

The hypothetical scenario for maize domestication goes as follows (Figure 13.1). The process may have started as an unintentional byproduct of gathering wild teosinte, for gathering would lead to selective pressure for harvestable types of the grass, with their spikes condensed into fascicles. Such condensation made it harder for the seeds to scatter. In time, this form of teosinte would become established by campsites and in abandoned middens. These colonies would automatically diverge toward greater domestic kinds of variation, from which human beings could select the most useful types. In time, too, humans would remove weeds from these teosinte stands, then start deliberately planting the more useful types. Thus the female teosinte spike became canalized down a pathway leading toward maize. Cultivation and fertilization of semiwild grass populations were followed by attempts to sow selected seed from the most desirable types. At first the planted teosinte was no more productive than wild forms, but it was easier to harvest, a critical stage in the process of domestication. When people began selective harvesting and planting of transitional forms of teosinte, the grass's reproductive strategy changed to dependency on human intervention. A genetic revolution followed, in which attributes that made harvesting easier and favored teosinte's use as a human food had a selective advantage.

There is no archaeological evidence for transitional forms of teosinte, perhaps because the domestication process was very rapid. Some of the oldest maize cobs discovered in archaeological sites, as well as ancient teosinte grasses, do bear marks of earlier transformations. One maize cob from Tehuacán Valley in Mexico dating to about 5000 B.C. appears to show some intermediate features between teosinte and maize, but it may be a degenerate form. The earliest known archaeological occurrence of condensed teosinte comes from Tlapacoya in the valley of Mexico and dates to about the same time.

Traces of early experimentation with the deliberate cultivation of crops such as maize and squash have come from regions in Mexico, notably from Sierra Madre, Sierra de Tamaulipas, and the Tehuacán Valley (Figure 13.2). The dry, highland Tehuacán Valley in southern Mexico has many caves and open sites and is sufficiently arid to preserve seeds and organic finds in archaeological deposits. This was the valley that Richard MacNeish (1970, 1978) chose as a promising area in which

FIGURE 13.1   The various stages in an apparent transformation from teosinte to maize. The earliest teosinte form is (a), the stabilized maize phenotype (e). The harvesting process increased condensation of teosinte branches and led to the husks becoming the enclosures for corn ears. (After Galinat, 1985.)

to seek the origins of domesticated maize. MacNeish soon found domestic maize cobs dating back to approximately 3000 B.C., but not until he began digging in the small Coxcatlán rock shelter (Figure 13.3, p. 318) did he find maize that even vaguely resembled what at that time was considered the hypothetical ancestor of maize. Coxcatlán contains 28 occupation levels, the earliest of which dates to approximately 10,000 B.C.

MacNeish found that the earliest Tehuacán people lived mainly by hunting horses, deer, and other mammals and also by collecting wild vegetable foods. These hunters used stone-tipped lances in the chase. They also hunted large numbers of jackrabbits, probably in organized drives. MacNeish estimates that 50 to 60 percent of the people's food came from game in 10,000 B.C., and only 30 to 40 percent in 7000 B.C.

10,000 to 7000 B.C.

After 8000 B.C., the game population declined, and the people turned more and more to wild plant foods. Instead of hunting year-round, the Tehuacán bands scheduled their food gathering on a seasonal basis and were able to exploit the vegetable and other foods in their environment very intensively. The dietary scenario has been reconstructed by using carbon and nitrogen isotope ratios in bone collagen from

FIGURE 13.2 Archaeological sites and culture areas mentioned in this chapter.

people who lived in the Tehuacán Valley after 6000 B.C. (Farnsworth et al., 1985). By at least 4500 B.C., about 90 percent of the Tehuacano diet consisted of tropical grasses such as *Setaria,* and such plants as cacti and maguey. So much grain was necessary that cultivation or domestication may have been essential by this time.

Crop yields grew after 3000 B.C. People grew foods that when stored would tide them over lean months: beans, amaranth, gourds, and maize. They lived in larger and more permanent settlements, grinding their maize into quite well-made grindstones (metates). The maize itself was smaller than modern strains and probably much like teosinte (Figure 13.1). By this time, the scheduled gathering and nomadic settlement patterns of earlier times had been replaced by more sedentary villages. Their ample storage facilities helped the people live through the lean months.

The sequence of events at Tehuacán is by no means unique, for other peoples were also experimenting with cultivation (Killion, 1992). Different hybrid forms of maize are found in Tehuacán sites; these were not developed locally and can have been introduced only from outside. Dry caves elsewhere in northern Mesoamerica

FIGURE 13.3   Excavations at Coxcatlán Cave, Tehuacán Valley, Mexico.

show that other cultures paralleled the cultural events in Tehuacán. On the other hand, the highland lakes of the valley of Mexico and elsewhere may well have supported sedentary communities subsisting on fish and wild vegetable foods as well as experimenting with amaranth and other crops as early as the fourth millennium B.C.

If Kent Flannery's hypothesis is correct, plant domestication in Mesoamerica was not so much an invention in one small area as a shift in ecological adaptation deliberately chosen by peoples living where economic strategies necessitated intensive exploitation of plant foods. It appears that the evidence from both Tehuacán and Guilá Naquitz bears out this hypothesis.

Earlier theories of the origins of maize assumed that it was domesticated in many areas of the Americas from six or more presumed wild races. Modern pollen studies have shown convincingly that there was never a wild *Zea* with a wide range that extended outside southern Mexico and Guatemala. Apparently, a primitive form of domesticated eight-rowed maize *(Maíz de ocho)* with soft glumes represented at Tehuacán was the common ancestral corn that spread thousands of miles from its original homeland after 3000 B.C.

EARLY FOOD PRODUCTION IN THE ANDES

• • •

The Highlands

The great eighteenth-century German naturalist Alexander von Humboldt was the first European scientist to explore the high Andes. He marveled at the great variety of wild plants and animals that thrived in the harsh and varied landscape of high peaks and mountain valleys. Only a handful of these many species had been tamed by the farmers living in the foothills of the great mountains. They lived in horizontal environmental zones stacked one above the other on the sides of deep valleys. Humboldt observed how the ever-growing human populations moved upward and outward into much harsher and more marginal environments. As they did so, they tried to encourage animals and plants living in one zone to adapt to another, to extend their range into unoccupied land. By seeding beans and cereal and transplanting roots and fruit trees, they struggled constantly to maintain a foothold outside natural faunal and floral ranges. The same upward assault continues to this day in the Andes, a quiet battle waged with robust root crops and hardy cereal strains. It seems that much the same struggle went on in early prehistory, too (Moseley, 1992).

According to veteran archaeologist Richard MacNeish, the finds from Pikimachay Cave high in the Andes show that the few inhabitants of this and other sites at the end of the Ice Age had several subsistence options. They could hunt various sizes of mammal, including the giant sloth and varied small creatures, or concentrate on foraging for plant foods (Moseley, 1992). Their options were exercised by priority rather than by season, the idea being that one acquired food with the minimum effort. About 9000 B.C., however, the subsistence strategies changed. There is reason 9000 B.C. to believe that seasonal exploitation had replaced other options, with hunting, trapping, and plant collecting at high altitudes important in the dry season. During the wetter months, collecting and possibly penning small game, as well as seed collecting, were dominant activities.

About 10,000 B.C., small groups of hunter-gatherers began using Guitarrero Cave, 1.5 miles (2.5 km) above sea level in the Peruvian Andes (Lynch, 1980) (Figure 13.4). They relied on a technology that made heavy use of hemplike fibers and wood, the former to make cordage, nets, and simple textiles. In 8000 B.C. levels, Thomas Lynch, the excavator, recovered local wild fruit and tubers. It is possible that people living in these forests first domesticated the lima, and later, domesticated beans spread into drier terrain across the mountains.

FIGURE 13.4   Guitarrero Cave, Peru, looking toward the Andes.

Some form of early plant tending may have persisted in the Andes for many centuries. Gourds, potato, and ulluco were probably grown by 8000 to 7000 B.C. in the same area but, like beans, served as a supplementary food and as a means of expanding into hitherto marginal areas. It was many thousands of years before these plants became the economic staple.

5000 to 4500 B.C.   After 5000 to 4500 B.C., the archaeological evidence becomes more abundant. In the Ayacucho-Huanta region 25 dry- and wet-season camps have been found, which provide signs of continued exploitation of wild vegetables as well as game
Pikimachay   during the dry season. The Pikimachay Cave levels of this period yielded wet-season living floors. There, wild seeds are abundant, along with remains of gourds and seeds of domesticated quinoa and squash. Game remains are very rare, as if a vegetable diet, whether wild or domesticated, was of prime importance during the wet
Puente   months. Another wet-season locality, Puente Cave, yielded a few bones of tame guinea pigs as well as the remains of many small wild mammals. Grinding stones and other artifacts used for plant collecting, or perhaps incipient agriculture, are also common at Puente. Throughout this period, many wet-season camps became larger and more stable, with their use extending over longer periods of the year.

4000 B.C.   After 4000 B.C., the Ayacucho peoples relied more on food production. The potato was cultivated; hoes appeared, as well as domesticated corn, squashes, common beans, and other crops. Guinea pigs were certainly tamed, and llama were
3500 B.C.   domesticated in central Peru by at least 3500 B.C. By this time, too, there was more interaction between coast and interior, trade in raw materials, and some interchange of domesticates. Richard MacNeish believes corn spread from the north, ultimately from Mesoamerica, into Ayacucho. Root crop agriculture may have diffused from highland Peru into the lowlands, too.

The Ayacucho sequence is illustrative of the complex adaptive shifts that took place in many parts of South America after 5000 B.C. In both highlands and lowlands, the beginnings of agriculture were a gradual adjustment, with food production gradually supplanting gathering as the major subsistence activity.

The Coast

On the Peruvian coast, fishing and the gathering of vegetable foods were supplemented by irrigation farming as early as 3000 B.C., while the highland peoples were cultivating a variety of crops by the same time, crops that amplified the horizontally stacked natural resources of their mountain homeland.

Peruvian coast   The Peruvian coast forms a narrow shelf at the foot of the Andes, crossed by small river valleys descending from the mountains to the sea. These valleys are oases in the desert plain, with deep, rich soils, blooming vegetation, and plentiful water. For thousands of years Peruvians have cultivated these valley floors, building their settlements, pyramids, and palaces at the edges of their agricultural land. Because conditions for preservation in this arid country are exceptional, the archaeological record often is quite complete. The coast itself forms a series of related microenvironments, such as rocky bars where shellfish are abundant, places where seasonal vegetable foods nourished by damp fogs are common, and the floors or sides of river valleys flow into the Pacific. One would assume that a combination of these microenvironments would provide a rich and uniform constellation of food resources that could normally be exploited with ease from relatively sedentary base camps (Moseley, 1975b). However, the bountiful maritime environment occasionally is disrupted by a warm countercurrent known as El Niño, which can flow for as long as 12 months. El Niño occurs at highly irregular intervals, perhaps every 6 years and sometimes much longer. It reduces marine upwelling so much that the fish migrate elsewhere, and thus one of the coastal peoples' staple diet sources is greatly reduced. This phenomenon is so unpredictable that the people could not store food against its arrival; they also could not move from the coast, and they did not have the offshore vessels needed for deepwater fishing. Their only strategy, other than moving or starving, was to limit their population densities to the lowest levels of available natural resources until such time as they developed alternative food sources, such as maize grown by intensive irrigation agriculture (Raymond, 1981).

The archaeological evidence for the Peruvian coast is incomplete for the period immediately preceding early food production. During the dry winter months the inhabitants collected shellfish and other marine resources, and hunting and vegetable foods were more important in the summer. After 5000 B.C., however, more efficient collecting strategies came into use, with greater attention to exploiting maximally natural food sources. Fishing, in particular, became more important. Between approximately 4200 and 2500 B.C., Peruvian coastal peoples depended on marine resources—fish, sea birds, and mollusks—for much of their diet. During the warmest and driest period after the Pleistocene, the coastal peoples moved closer to the shore, dwelling in larger and more stable settlements. Along with the shift to more lasting coastal dwelling came the development of sophisticated equipment for deep-sea fishing.

As early as 5500 B.C., the coastal peoples were manipulating plants for their own purposes. The Paloma site on the central coast was occupied earlier than 5500 B.C.; it was a settled community with numerous simple huts and grass-lined pits where the inhabitants stored food for the occasional lean year. The people relied heavily on fishing and gathering but also manipulated some plant species, including tuberous begonias, gourds, squashes, and peppers. They may also have kept llamas, the same species used much later by the Incas for carrying loads in the Andes (Benfer, 1982).

A later coastal settlement that perpetuated the same subsistence pattern flourished at Chilca, 45 miles (72 km) south of present-day Lima. Frederic Engel excavated refuse heaps there and C14 dated the earlier Chilca occupation to between 3800 and 2650 B.C. When the site was in use, it probably lay near a reedy marsh, which provided both matting and building materials as well as sites for small gardens. The Chilca people lived on sea mollusks, fish, and sea lions; they apparently hunted few land mammals. They cultivated jack and lima beans, gourds, and squashes, probably relying on river floods as well as rainfall for their simple agriculture.

One remarkable Chilca house was uncovered: A circular structure, it had a domelike frame of canes bound with rope and covered with bundles of grass (Figure 13.5); the interior was braced with bones from stranded whales. Seven burials had been deposited in the house before it was intentionally collapsed on top of them. The skeletons were wrapped in mats and all buried at the same time, perhaps because of an epidemic.

The new emphasis on fish, increased use of flour ground from wild grass seed, and availability of cultivated squashes provided new sources of nutrition for some coastal groups. This supply may ultimately have set off a sustained period of population growth. Certainly the succeeding millennia saw many permanent settlements established near the ocean; the people combined agriculture with fishing and mollusk gathering. Domesticated cotton first appeared around 2500 B.C. Squashes, peppers, lima beans, and other crops remained staple foods until recent times. Maize

5000 B.C.

4200 to 2500 B.C.

Paloma
5500 to 2500 B.C.

Chilca
3800 to 2650 B.C.

2500 B.C.

FIGURE 13.5   Reconstruction of a Chilca house. (After Willey, 1971.)

and other basic foods were still unknown. Agriculture remained a secondary activity much later than it did in Mesoamerica.

Huaca Prieta
2500 to 1800 B.C.

One later site is Huaca Prieta, a sedentary village that housed several hundred people on the north coast of Peru between 2500 and 1800 B.C. (Hyslop et al., 1987). The vast refuse mound there contains small one- or two-room houses built partially into the ground and roofed with timber or whalebone beams. The inhabitants were remarkably skillful cotton weavers who devised a sophisticated art style with animal, human, and geometric designs.

Playa Culebras

Maize made its first appearance on the coast at Playa Culebras, another important and contemporary settlement south of Huaca Prieta (Moseley, 1992). The new crop was soon grown on a considerable scale in large irrigation systems in coastal river valleys. Irrigation required efficient organization and deployment of people to dig and maintain canals, communal work on a scale that could only be organized by a system of taxation by labor, such as was commonplace in the Andes in later millennia. Much higher crop yields resulted as the focus of coastal population moved inland and local kin leaders and priests assumed much more prominent roles in society. These social changes were reflected in more permanent housing and in large ceremonial pyramids and other public buildings. A complex of stone and mud mortar platforms lies at El Paraíso on the floodplain of the Chillón Valley, some distance from the sea. At least one mound had complexes of connected rooms built in successive stages. Settlements such as El Paraíso obviously depended more on agriculture than had earlier sites. By the time the temple complexes were built there, after

2300 to 1800 B.C.

1800 B.C., loom-woven textiles and pottery had come into widespread use (Figure 13.6). All the major food plants that formed the basis of later Peruvian civilization were employed.

EARLY FARMERS IN SOUTHWESTERN NORTH AMERICA

• • •

In 9000 B.C. the Southwest United States was populated by hunter-gatherers whose culture was adapted to desert living (Cordell, 1984a, b). A distinctive foraging culture, the Cochise, flourished in southeast Arizona and southwest New Mexico from about this time. The Cochise people gathered many plant foods, including yucca

Cochise
9000 to 1000 B.C.

FIGURE 13.6   A double-headed snakelike figure with appended rock crabs revealed by plotting the warp movements in a preceramic twined cotton fabric from Huaca Prieta, Peru. The original length was approximately 16 inches (40 cm). The shaded area indicates the surviving textile. Double-headed motifs persisted through more than 3000 years of Andean art. (Courtesy of Junius Bird.)

seeds, cacti, and sunflower seeds. They used small milling stones, basketry, cordage, nets, and spear-throwers. Many features of their material culture survived into later times, when cultivated plants were introduced into the Southwest.

The earliest Mesoamerican crops to cross the Rio Grande were maize, beans, and squash, which were probably cultivated for some time in northern Mexico before they reached the Southwest. The maize farmers of northern Mexico must have had sporadic contact with Archaic hunter-gatherers living in the deserts to the north, so it would have been easy for knowledge of plants, even gifts of seeds or seedlings, to pass from south to north. Probably, the opportunity for adopting crops was there long before anyone thought it worth doing so.

Between about 2500 and 100 B.C., the southwestern climate was relatively stable, perhaps somewhat wetter than today. However, it was an environment where hunting and gathering were high-risk occupations, mainly because rainfall patterns were always unpredictable. Despite generally low population densities, local populations may have occasionally risen to saturation point, causing food shortages. Domesticated plants like maize and beans had one major advantage: They might have low yields, but they were predictable. Cultivators of the new crops could control their location and their availability at different seasons by storing them carefully. Perhaps people living in the southern deserts of the Southwest began growing maize because it gave them food supplies to tide them over the lean months until spring. Farther north, in the uplands, growing crops would have enabled hunter-gatherer peoples to exercise more effective control over their environment. In the final analysis, it was probably a combination of rising populations and food shortages that caused the adoption of low-yielding forms of maize. One could argue, indeed, that the people accepted the new crops not because they wanted to become farmers but so they could be more effective foragers (Wills, 1989).

The hardy, low-yielding maize that first entered the Southwest was the so-called Chapalote form, a small popcorn of great genetic diversity. It may have arrived during a period of higher rainfall between 1500 and 1000 B.C. It was soon introgressed with the indigenous, wild teosinte, creating a highly varied, more productive hybrid maize with larger cobs and more kernel rows.

However, a radically different maize, Maize de Ocho, was the key to new cultural developments in the Southwest. Maize de Ocho, with its large, more productive, flowery kernels, may have evolved from earlier, highly variable Chapalote maize. It may have resulted from a selection for a large kerneled corn that was easier to grind and flowered earlier, both important attributes in the hot and arid Southwest. Here, growing seasons are often restricted by the irregular timing and distribution of rainfall, leaving little time for kernels to fill out. These characteristics of Maize de Ocho were highly adaptive in North America, with its short growing seasons and very diverse, temperate environments.

Archaeologists Steadman Upham and Richard MacNeish have found Maize de Ocho in rock shelters in southern New Mexico dating to about 1225 B.C. (Upham et al., 1987). It spread widely through the Southwest in later centuries, as did other maize forms. Southwestern farmers experimented with the new crop at many elevations. After 500 B.C., they combined maize with beans, for these legumes when underplanted with corn return vital nitrogen to the soil, nitrogen that is depleted by maize. By planting the two crops together, the southwestern farmer could maintain the fertility of the soil for longer periods of time.

In the Southwest, as in the Andes, the farmers were working close to the limits of corn's range. Maize is intolerant of too-short growing seasons, weak soil conditions, and such hazards as crop disease and strong winds. Most important were adequate soil moisture and water supplies. By careful seed selection, the farmers developed higher-elevation varieties with elongated cobs, distinctive root structures, and seeds that could be planted at considerable depths, where they could be nourished by retained ground moisture. The farmers became experts at soil selection, favoring those with good moisture-retaining properties in north- and east-facing slopes that receive little direct sunlight. They also favored floodplains and canyon mouths, where the soil was naturally irrigated. They would divert water from seasonal streams, springs, or rainfall runoff to irrigate their lands. As with hunting and foraging, risk management was vital, so the cultivators widely dispersed their gardens to minimize the danger of local drought or flood. Over the centuries, a great diversity of highly effective dry-climate agricultural techniques developed through-

out the Southwest. Between A.D. 300 and 500, another complex of domestic tropical plants, including pigweed, cotton, and several varieties of beans, arrived in the region. These tended to require more irrigation and were confined to the hot regions of the south, where the irrigation-experienced Hohokam adopted them.

The appearance of maize did not trigger a dramatic revolution in southwestern life. The earlier corns were not that productive and could be planted fairly casually. Under these circumstances, their yields were probably less than those of good piñon nut harvests. Eventually, however, they became of staple importance to many southwestern peoples, who were now living in more permanent villages and in more restricted territories. As life became more sedentary, the people invested more time and energy in their crops, which provided protection from shortages of wild plant foods in their smaller territories.

By 300 B.C., experimentation and new hybrid varieties of maize introduced from the south had led to sedentary villages and much greater dependence on farming. The cultural changes of the period culminated in the great southwestern archaeological traditions: Hohokam, Mogollon, and Anasazi (Cordell, 1984b).

300 B.C.

The Hohokam tradition has long been thought to have originated in the Cochise. No one knows exactly when the tradition emerged, but it was probably in the first five centuries of the Christian era. However, Emil Haury, who dug the important Snaketown site in the Gila River Valley, believes that the Hohokam people were immigrants from northern Mexico who brought their pottery and extensive irrigation agriculture with them (Haury, 1976) (Figure 13.7). Under this scenario, the newcomers soon influenced the lifeway of the local people, and a desert adaptation of Hohokam resulted. Recent research tends to discount the migration theory. Reexamination of the Snaketown data and further fieldwork suggest that the Hohokam enjoyed complex trading and ceremonial relationships with peoples living all over the Southwest and northern Mexico. As time went on, this trade expanded, perhaps within the context of a common ceremonial system centered on the ball courts and other ceremonial structures at Snaketown and other focal points.

Hohokam
?300 B.C. to A.D. 1500

FIGURE 13.7 The Hohokam settlement at Snaketown, Arizona, during 1965 excavations.

In all probability, the Hohokam was an indigenous culture, one that acquired much greater social complexity through time (Crown, 1990; Crown and Judge, 1991).

Hohokam subsistence was based on maize, beans, cucurbits, cotton, and other crops, as well as on gathering. The people planted their crops to coincide with the semiannual rainfall and flooding patterns. Where they could, they practiced irrigation from flowing streams; otherwise they cultivated floodplains and caught runoff from local storms with dams, terraces, and other devices. Hohokam people occupied much of what is now Arizona. Their cultural heirs are the Pima and Papago Indians of today (Figure 13.8). (For essays on recent Hohokam research, see Crown and Judge, 1991).

Hohokam culture evolved slowly over as long as 2000 years. There are at least five stages of the culture, culminating in a classic period from approximately A.D. 1100 to 1450, when large pueblos (communal villages) were built and canal irrigation was especially important. At this time and somewhat earlier, pre–Columbian Mexican influences can be detected. These include new varieties of maize, the appearance of platform mounds and ball or dance courts at Snaketown and elsewhere, and imports such as copper bells. Does this mean that Mexican immigrants transformed Hohokam culture, or were there internal factors that caused greater

FIGURE 13.8   A scheduled agricultural round. Diagram shows how the Pima Indians of the Southwest, descendants of the Hohokam, schedule their plantings and harvests around rainy seasons. The Hohokam probably relied on much the same round. The thickness of the shaded area reflects the relative plenty of food resources. (From Jesse D. Jennings, *Ancient North Americans,* New York: Freeman, 1978, p. 349.)

elaboration of local society at the same time as some ideas arrived from Mexico? Archaeologists remain divided on this point (Ericson and Baugh, 1993).

Originally, anthropologists believed the Mexican influence was transitory and weak, but excavations at a prehistoric town named Casas Grande in northern Chihuahua, Mexico, have changed their minds (Di Peso et al., 1974). (This site should not be confused with Casa Grande, Arizona.) At the height of its prosperity, around A.D. 1400, Casas Grande boasted approximately 1600 rooms and housed more than 2200 people. The dig showed that its inhabitants exchanged turquoise and painted pottery from the Southwest for marine shells and exotic bird feathers from Mexico. Local traditions connect Casas Grande with a settlement named Paquimé, which was more of a Mexican town than an Indian pueblo. The archaeologists argue that Paquimé was founded by Mexican traders from the south, possibly itinerant merchants known to the Aztec as *pochteca,* who often served as spies. Perhaps, too, contacts between the Hohokam and Mexican civilization were far more regular than once was suspected (see also Ravensloot, 1988).

The Mogollon tradition emerged from Archaic roots between 300 B.C. and A.D. 200 and disappeared as a separate entity between A.D. 850 and 1450, when it became part of Anasazi (Haury, 1936). The Mogollon is well-known from dry caves in New Mexico as an agricultural tradition in which hunting and gathering in the highlands were always important. Mogollon agriculture depended on direct rainfall, with only very limited use of irrigation. The people lived in small villages of pit dwellings with timber frames and mat or brush roofs. Their material culture was utilitarian and included milling stones, digging sticks, bows and arrows, fine baskets, and characteristic brown-and-red pottery.

Mogollon
300 B.C. to A.D. 200

At least six regional variants of Mogollon are known, and there were five chronological stages, the fifth ending approximately 500 years ago. Early Mogollon villages often were located on high promontories close to more fertile lands. The settlement pattern varied from area to area but had a tendency toward larger sites and increased populations throughout the life of the tradition. By A.D. 1500, pueblos of several hundred rooms had developed in some areas, but by this time Mogollon had become part of the western pueblo Anasazi tradition.

The Anasazi tradition is, in general terms, ancestral to the cultures of the modern Pueblo Indians—the Hopi, Zuni, and others (Cordell, 1984). Its emergence is conventionally dated to A.D. 1, but this is a purely arbitrary date, for Anasazi's roots lie in Archaic cultures that flourished for a long time before. The Anasazi people made heavy use of wild vegetable foods, even after they took up maize agriculture seriously, after A.D. 400. Most of their farming depended on dry agriculture and seasonal rainfall, although they, like the Hohokam, used irrigation techniques when practicable. They made use of flood areas, where the soil would remain damp for weeks after sudden storms. Moisture in the flooded soil could be used to germinate seeds in the spring and to bring ripening crops to fruition after later rains. However, this is a very high-risk type of agriculture, and the Anasazi relied on wild resources to carry them through lean years.

Anasazi
Last 2000 years

The Anasazi tradition is centered in the "Four Corners" area, where Utah, Arizona, Colorado, and New Mexico meet. Anasazi chronology is well established thanks to the use of dendrochronology on beams from abandoned pueblos. There are at least six Basketmaker and Pueblo subdivisions of Anasazi; each marked a gradual increase in the importance of agriculture and the emergence of some larger sites with *kivas,* ceremonial sweathouses. Pueblos, which are complexes of adjoining rooms, occurred more frequently after A.D. 900; the population congregated in fewer but larger pueblos after A.D. 1180. These were located in densely populated areas, some of them moved from the open to under cliff overhangs, the so-called cliff dwellings. Some of the features of these sites, such as turrets and loopholed walls, appear to be defensive (Crown and Judge, 1991).

At the same time that people concentrated in larger sites, there was depopulation of many areas of the northern Southwest. The reasons for these changes are imperfectly understood. In some areas, such as Chaco Canyon, New Mexico, the concentrated populations enjoyed roads, extensive irrigation systems, and more elaborate social and political organizations as well as trading connections with widespread areas of the Southwest, but most pueblos seem to have been more egalitarian in their organization and relatively self-sufficient. It may be that the changes generated by the developments in Chaco and elsewhere caused people to congregate more closely. Alternatively, it has been argued that some climatic and environmental changes, as yet little understood, may have caused major shifts in the settlement pattern. More likely, a combination of environmental, societal, and adaptive changes set in motion a period of turbulence and culture change (Sebastian, 1992).

By approximately A.D. 500, the basic Anasazi settlement pattern had evolved, and above-the-ground houses were being substituted for the pit dwellings of earlier centuries. The pit dwellings developed into kivas, subterranean ceremonial structures that existed in every large village. Large settlements of contiguous dwellings became the rule after A.D. 800, with clusters of "rooms" serving as homes for separate families or lineages. Large settlements such as Pueblo Bonito developed around A.D. 1100; this was a huge D-shaped complex of 800 rooms rising several stories around the rim of the arc (Figure 13.9). The room complexes surrounded courts, with the highest stories at the back. They formed a blank wall; a line of one-story rooms cut off the fourth side. Within the court lay the kivas, always one great kiva and usually several smaller ones. The great kivas were up to 60 feet (18.2 m) in diameter, with wide masonry benches encircling the interior. The roof was

FIGURE 13.9   Pueblo Bonito, Chaco Canyon, New Mexico, dated by dendrochronology to A.D. 919–1130. The round structures are kivas.

supported by four large pillars near the center, where a raised hearth lay. Two subterranean, masonry-lined rooms were situated on either side of the fireplace. A staircase leading from the floor of the kiva to the large room above it gave access to the sacred precinct.

The period between A.D. 1000 and 1300 was one of consolidation of population into a few more-congested settlements, where more elaborate social organizations may have developed. The pueblos were probably communities run for the collective good, with at least some ranking of society under a chieftain. In modern Hopi society, clan superiority and kinship lineages play an important role in the election of chieftains. Thrust into close intimacy by the nature of pueblo architecture, the people developed well-integrated religious and ceremonial structures to counteract the tensions of close living.

The Anasazi enjoyed a relatively elaborate material culture at the height of their prosperity; at this time they were making distinctive black-and-white pottery, well-formed baskets, and fine sandals. However, their architecture was neither very sophisticated nor particularly innovative. Rocks and baked mud were formed into boxlike rooms; a roof of mud rested on horizontal timbers. Room after room was added as the need arose, using local materials and a simple architectural style entirely appropriate for its environment.

The southwestern farmer won success by skillfully using scarce water resources and bringing together soil and water by means of dams, floodwater irrigation, and other systems for distributing runoff. Planting techniques were carefully adapted to desert conditions, and myriad tiny gardens supplied food for each family or lineage. This successful adaptation is also reflected in the architecture.

PREAGRICULTURAL AND AGRICULTURAL SOCIETIES IN EASTERN NORTH AMERICA

● ● ●

The Archaic hunter-gatherer traditions of eastern North America enjoyed many regional variations in material culture; these occurred because the people concentrated on different, locally abundant food sources (Fagan, 1991a; B. D. Smith, 1992; Yerkes, 1988). In general, however, the lifeway was similar among them: a seasonal one, based on a very broad spectrum of game and vegetable foods (Brose, 1980). As long as the population density was low, every band could react relatively easily to changes in local conditions. Since many of their favorite vegetable foods were subject to cycles of lean and abundant years, a flexibility in choice and movement was essential. However, as population grew slowly throughout the Archaic, this flexibility was increasingly restricted and the people tended to specialize in local resources that were available most of the year. They developed better storage techniques and fostered closer contacts with their neighbors through exchange networks that handled foodstuffs and other commodities. The development of these types of response may have required more complex social organization than the simple band structure of earlier times, and it is no coincidence that burial patterns during the late Archaic, in about 1700 B.C., reflect greater differentiation in social status. Cemeteries may also have served as territorial markers.

Under these circumstances, perhaps it was inevitable that late Archaic peoples in the eastern woodlands turned to the deliberate cultivation of food plants to supplement wild plant yields. They did so quite independently of other centers of plant

Transitional period
3000 to 100 B.C.

domestication (B. Smith, 1992). By 2000 B.C., marsh elder was being planted, soon followed by other native plants such as sumpweed and goosefoot. Sunflowers were probably domesticated by 2000 B.C. Most of these species flourished in river valleys, where there were many and diverse wild vegetable foods, and they may have first been cultivated to supplement natural stands. Sumpweed was widely cultivated in the Midwest in the first millennium B.C., and sunflowers were prized for their edible seeds and oil by the same period. Several species were grown outside their natural ranges, but it seems likely that domestication of these native plants first took hold in locations like the lower Mississippi River Delta, where wild ancestors of these species grow in abundance. It is significant that none of the domesticates required the kind of wholesale adaptive shift in year-round routine that maize cultivation demanded of its practitioners. Maize and bean agriculture did not flourish in the eastern woodlands until much later in prehistory.

2000 B.C.   After 2000 B.C., we find increasing signs of preoccupation with burial and with life after death, a new ideological foundation for local society in the East. These burial cults shared many practices, among them cremation, the deposition of exotic objects with the dead, and the custom of building burial mounds.

More intensive exploitation of food resources, greater sedentism, regular social interaction and exchange, a degree of social ranking, increased ceremonialism—these were the culminating elements in late Archaic life in eastern North America. While most groups still lived in temporary encampments or even sizable base camps used for most, if not all, of the year, the Poverty Point culture of the lower Missis-
Poverty Point   sippi Valley and adjacent Gulf Coast offers a dramatic contrast.
1450 to 1100 B.C.

The earliest Poverty Point sites date to about 1600 B.C., forming the oldest component in a cultural sequence that lasted for 1000 years. Poverty Point itself is the nexus of the culture and stands on Macon Ridge overlooking the Mississippi floodplain, near the confluence of six rivers (Figure 13.10). This was a strategic point from which to trade upstream and downstream, to receive and exchange raw materials and finished products. Some of the exotic materials at Poverty Point came from as far as 620 miles (997 km) away. The leaders of Poverty Point not only exchanged

FIGURE 13.10   Poverty Point, Louisiana. Aerial view of the site taken about 45 years ago, showing the concentric earth ridges. The ridges and intervening hollows (swales) show up as light and dark stripes in the fields.

materials with peoples who lived far away but also redistributed them to regional centers in their own culture area.

Poverty Point, with its great earthworks, is a remarkable contrast to the humble base camps elsewhere in the East. Six concentric semicircular earthen ridges are divided into segments. They average about 82.0 feet (25 m) wide and 9.8 feet (3 m) high and are set about 131 feet (40 m) apart. Their significance is a complete mystery, beyond a suspicion that they were connected with astronomical observations. To the west lies an artificial mound more than 66 feet (20 m) high and more than 660 feet (200 m) long. A person standing on this mound can sight the vernal and autumnal equinoxes directly across the center of the earthworks to the east. These are the points where the sun rises on the first days of spring and fall. Built between 1000 and 600 B.C., Poverty Point took more than 1,236,007 cubic feet (35,000 cu. m) of basket-loaded soil, a task that would have taken 1350 adults laboring 70 days a year 3 years to complete. Estimates of Poverty Point's population are hard to come by, but even a population of 1000 people makes the site unique for the period. At present, the significance of this extraordinary site and associated culture is little understood (C. H. Webb, 1968).

The Poverty Point culture went into decline in about 650 B.C., just as mound building reached new heights in the Ohio Valley, to the northeast (Otto, 1979).

Adena

By 700 B.C., the people of eastern North America enjoyed a tradition of long-distance trading that had flourished for centuries. The trade carried not only prosaic commodities such as stone ax blades but also large quantities of prestigious imports such as conch shells and copper artifacts, most of which were deposited in the graves of their owners. These exotic objects may have been status symbols, indicating some social differentiation within groups. As far as is known, these artifacts were buried with their owners at death, and the special status associated with them was not passed on from one generation to the next (Yerkes, 1988).

Adena
500 B.C. to A.D. 400

Between 500 B.C. and about A.D. 400, the Adena culture flourished in the Ohio Valley. The people lived in seasonal camps, relying not only on hunting and gathering but also on the cultivation of squash and local starchy and oily plants. Major camps lay close to ceremonial burial mounds. The construction of even the largest mounds involved relatively few people. This mound building and other earthwork construction may have reflected a strengthening of group identity and the establishment of social and territorial boundaries, which were often marked by cemeteries (Yerkes, 1988). At the same time, the Adena people developed large exchange networks that extended over enormous distances, the prototypes of even more elaborate trade routes in later centuries. It was powerful loyalties to local lineages that caused the people to commemorate their dead not only with imposing burial mounds but with extensive earthworks as well.

Adena earthworks follow the contours of flat-topped hills and form circles, squares, and other shapes, enclosing areas perhaps as much as 350 feet (105 m) in diameter. The earth used to make the enclosures came from just inside the walls, giving a false impression of an interior moat. These were probably ceremonial compounds rather than defensive earthworks. The Adena people built large burial mounds, some placed inside enclosures, others standing independently outside. Most are communal rather than individual graves. The most important people lie in log-lined tombs. Their corpses are smeared with red ocher or graphite. Nearby lie ceremonial soapstone pipes and tablets engraved with curving designs or birds of prey. Some prestigious individuals were buried inside enclosures or mortuary structures, which were burned down as part of the funeral rites. Occasionally, the burial chamber was left open so that bodies could be added later. Dozens of people from miles around piled basketfuls of earth to form an imposing burial mound for a single ruler. More often, the mounds were piled up gradually over the years, as layers of bodies were added. However, the vast majority of less important Adena people were cremated: Only their ashes were placed inside the burial mound.

Hopewell

Hopewell
c. 250 B.C. to c. A.D. 400

The Hopewell tradition, a later elaboration of Adena, first appeared in Illinois in about 200 B.C. (Figure 13.11). Its religious cults were such a success that they spread rapidly from their heartland as far as upper Wisconsin and Louisiana and deep into Ohio and New York State. For nearly 1000 years, the Midwest experienced a dramatic flowering of artistic traditions and of long-distance trade that brought copper from the upper Great Lakes region, obsidian from Yellowstone, and mica from the southern Appalachians. The Hopewell people themselves lived in relatively small settlements and used only stone artifacts to plant, hunt game, and fish. They wore leather and woven clothes of pliable fibers. Much wealth and creative skill were lavished on a few individuals and on their life after death. At first glance, the exotic artifacts and ritual traditions of the Hopewell seem completely alien to the indigenous culture of the area, but a closer look reveals the links between the underlying traditions and the magnificent art created by Hopewell artisans. Their manufactures

FIGURE 13.11   Great Serpent Mound, Ohio, a depiction of a serpent swallowing a burial mound.

were traded from hand to hand throughout Hopewell territory in a vast exchange network of prestige goods, which moved between local elites and were used in status-enhancing ceremonies, in life, and in burial rituals. Such exchanges also linked kin leaders with lasting obligations to one another (Prufer, 1964; Brose and Greber, 1979).

The cult objects associated with this trade are found in dozens of Hopewell burial mounds and tell us something of the rank and social roles of the people with whom they are buried. Some of the exotic grave goods, such as pipe bowls or axes, were buried as gifts from living clan members to a dead leader. Others were personal possessions, cherished weapons, or sometimes symbols of status or wealth. Hopewell graves contain soapstone pipe bowls in the form of beavers, frogs, birds, bears, and even humans. Skilled smiths fashioned thin copper sheets into head and breast ornaments that bear elaborate repoussé animal motifs (Figure 13.12). There were copper axes and arrowheads, trinkets, and beads. A few specialists cut mica sheets into striking lustrous silhouettes of human figures, bird talons, and abstract designs. Most of these artifacts were manufactured by a few artisans, perhaps produced in workshops within large earthwork complexes, themselves close to major sources of important raw materials. Some elaborate artifacts may also have been manufactured at special "mortuary camps" for use in the graves of high status individuals (Yerkes, 1988). The same prestigious objects may have been distributed via the trade networks that carried foodstuffs and tools throughout Hopewell territory. Many of them show surprisingly little wear, as if they were soon buried with their owners.

Hopewell burial mounds are much more elaborate than their Adena predecessors. For example, Cook's Mound in Louisiana rises 40 feet (12 m) and is more than 100 feet (30 m) across. Its builders followed the established custom when they buried 168 bodies within an extensive earthen platform. Then they placed a further

FIGURE 13.12 Hopewell artifacts: (a) raven or crow in beaten copper; (b) bird claw in mica; (c) soapstone frog.

214 corpses on the platform before covering the entire sepulcher with a large mound. Another Hopewell burial mound complex in Ohio, appropriately named Mound City, contains no fewer than 24 mounds inside an enclosure covering 13 acres (5.2 ha). The Newark, Ohio, Hopewell earthworks cover 4 square miles (1040 ha).

The decline of the Hopewell culture after A.D. 400 is still imperfectly understood, but it is possible that a rapid and dramatic population increase strained the limits of the economic system, causing competition between trading networks and rupturing long-established economic and political relationships. It is possible, too, that as agriculture became more efficient and spread to other groups there was an increase in population and in the number of settlements, so much so that there was greater competition for land. This in turn would have led to the development of local rule by chieftains who could have challenged the overbearing powers of those who controlled the centuries-old burial cults (Dragoo, 1976). In contrast, David Braun argues (1988) for much more regional integration, because of larger, more sedentary communities and changing settlement patterns and growing populations that dispersed people from major river valleys into outlying watersheds. We do not know why the center of religious and political power had spread southward from the Ohio Valley into the lower Mississippi bottomlands by A.D. 800, but the shift may be connected with the realization that maize offered great potential as a food staple.

Maize may have spread from the Southwest in forms preadapted to high altitudes and lower temperatures along riverine areas toward the Northeast. Midwestern twelve-row or Chapalote maize was known to southeastern populations by the late first millennium A.D., but it was some time before its dietary staple potential was realized in the Late Woodland and Mississippian cultures of the Midwest (B. D. Smith, 1992; Yerkes, 1988). The lush floodplain of the lower Mississippi was ideal for cultivating high-yielding maize strains and also for growing beans. Beans arrived after the full potential of maize agriculture was realized. They had not only the advantage of a high protein value but also the asset of compensating for the amino-acid deficiencies of corn.

Mississippian

A.D. 1 to 450

Between A.D. 1 and about 450, two important cultural developments emerged in the Southeast. First, mortuary customs became far more elaborate. Second, there are signs that some individuals had achieved greater social and political importance among what had been relatively egalitarian societies. These four and one-half centuries saw the construction of hundreds of low, oval, or circular burial mounds throughout much of the Southeast. The burials within them vary considerably in their elaborations, a reflection of the increased social complexity that accompanied accelerating population growth, intercommunity exchange, and more intensive cultivation of native plants and later maize between A.D. 450 and 800. These developments were to culminate in a series of remarkable riverine cultures after A.D. 900, in the great Mississippian tradition of the South and southern Midwest.

The Mississippian's ultimate roots lay in much earlier Archaic and woodland cultures that flourished long before maize agriculture became widespread in the great river valleys of eastern North America (Milanich et al., 1984; Steponaitis, 1986; Yerkes, 1988). But it was the widespread cultivation of maize and beans that helped foster higher population densities and the more complex social and political organization of the centuries immediately before European contact in the sixteenth century. Most likely, the shift to maize agriculture was the result of stress largely precipitated by population pressure or the demands of elites. Such stress could easily occur even if plenty of land was available because the start-up labor needed to create maize gardens was much larger than that for native plants. Begun initially to create more supplemental foods, the new agriculture transformed valley landscapes in such ways that hunting and foraging soon provided less food for energy expended than maize cultivation. Within a short time, an entirely new economic pattern came into being.

Between A.D. 800 and 1000, there were significant changes in subsistence, material culture, and settlement patterns over much of the South and Southeast. Maize and bean agriculture now transformed many valley landscapes. Many of the cultural changes of these centuries, including new pottery forms, platform mounds, and substantial rectangular houses, may reflect the adoption of maize not only as a crop to be eaten at once but also as one to be stored for use throughout the year. Settlements were sometimes palisaded, perhaps for defense, and more formal layouts included grouping houses around open plazas and mounds. Society itself was changing, perhaps becoming more hierarchical as a powerful elite gradually emerged, based on larger communities with burial mounds and other symbols of religious and political power. Regional Mississippian societies developed in river valleys large and small over a large area at about the same time and interacted with one another for several centuries. Many Mississippian societies flourished on river valley soils fertilized by water-borne nutrients. It has always been assumed that this distribution occurred because of the availability of easily tilled soils. In fact, we know now that this restricted distribution was the result of the complex adaptation that the people developed in an area with well-defined bands of arable soils fertilized by spring floods just before planting season. They lived in valleys with many lakes and swamps, where fish trapped by receding floods were plentiful and migrating waterfowl paused to rest in spring and fall. The Mississippian people not only grew maize, squashes, and beans, but they also relied heavily on seasonal crops of nuts, fruits, berries, and seed-bearing plants. They hunted deer, raccoon, and turkey and took thousands of migratory waterfowl in spring and fall. Fish and waterfowl may have constituted up to 50 percent of the diet of the villagers living within the meander zones of the floodplain. Bruce Smith (1978a) defines the Mississippian as a society that "had a ranked form of social organization, and had developed a specific complex adaptation to linear, environmentally circumscribed floodplain habitat zones" in the eastern deciduous woodlands. This definition reflects the great variation in social complexity, with great centers like Cahokia in the so-called American Bottom near St. Louis at one end of the spectrum (Figure 13.13a and b) and hundreds of small local centers and minor chiefdoms at the other. Mississippian populations lived under a variety of circumstances. Some groups flourished in small, dispersed homesteads, while others dwelt in compact villages often best described as towns; in locations like Cahokia, tens of thousands of people lived.

By A.D. 900, some Mississippian centers presided over what might even be described as forms of state-organized society, while complex chiefdom is probably a more appropriate description for others. Larger Mississippian communities housed thousands of people and were fortified with defensive palisades. The largest Mississippian center was Cahokia, on the east bank of the river at St. Louis (Figure 13.13) (M. D. Fowler, 1978; Stoltman, 1992). Cahokia once contained more than 100 earthen mounds and catered to a population of at least 30,000 to 35,000 people. It was a great ceremonial center; its mounds and plazas dominated the countryside for miles. Monk's Mound at the center of Cahokia rises 102 feet (32 m) above the floodplain and covers 16 acres (6.4 ha) (Figure 13.13b). This gigantic mound is as

Mississippian
A.D. 800 to 1580

Cahokia

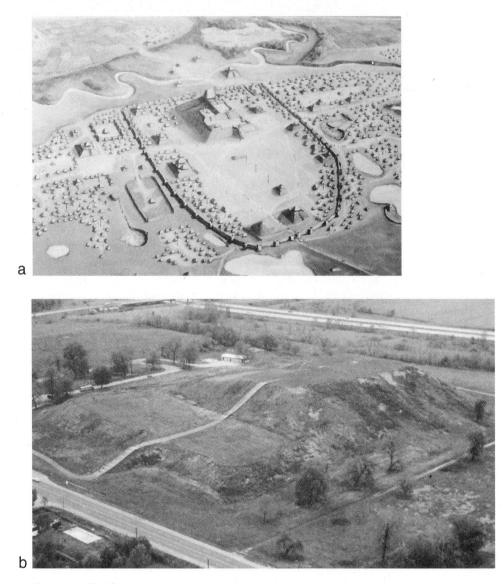

FIGURE 13.13   Cahokia, Illinois. (a) Central portion of Cahokia as it may have appeared around A.D. 1150, at its peak; (b) aerial view of Monk's Mound, Cahokia, Illinois, taken in 1983. (Courtesy Cahokia Mounds State Historic Site.)

tall as a ten-story building and was erected in at least four stages between the ninth and eleventh centuries A.D. Millions of basketloads of soil deposited by thousands of people went into this monumental earthwork. On the summit stood a thatched temple at the east end of an enormous central plaza. Around the plaza rose other mounds, temples, warehouses, administrative buildings, and the homes of nobles. The entire "downtown" area covered more than 200 acres (80.1 ha) and was fortified by a log fence with gates and watchtowers. Numerous mounds and lesser communities lay outside the walled interior core of Cahokia, each with its own plazas and burial mounds. The pole-and-thatch houses of the residential areas extended over 2000 acres (809 ha), the clusters of houses being separated by several acres of land. There is every reason to believe that Cahokia was planned and controlled by a powerful central authority and that there were many craft specialists.

Cahokia was by no means unique. It lay in the north of Mississippian territory, and its southern rival was Moundville in Alabama. Dozens of small centers and towns sprang up between the two. More than just sacred places for annual ceremonies of planting and harvest, the centers were markets and focal points of powerful chiefdoms. Cahokia owed some of its importance to the manufacture and trading of local salt and chert, a fine-grained rock used to make hoes and other tools (Perigrine, 1992). Above all, Cahokia and its neighbors were the places where the Mississippian leaders displayed their political and religious power.

The floodplain was ruled as a series of powerful chiefdoms, or even small states, by an elite group of priests and rulers who lived somewhat separated from the rest of the population. The chieftains controlled most long-distance trade and were the living intermediaries between the ancestors and the gods. As in the Hopewell culture, high-ranking individuals went to the next world in richly decorated graves, with clusters of ritual objects of different styles that symbolized various clans and tribes. Excavations at one burial mound revealed at least six different burial events that involved 261 people, including 4 mutilated men and 118 women, who were probably retainers sacrificed to accompany a chief in the afterlife. One such chief lay on a layer of thousands of shell beads, surrounded by grave offerings from as far afield as Wisconsin and Tennessee (Yerkes, 1988).

Cahokia and other, larger Mississippian communities enjoyed a more or less standardized layout. Their inhabitants built platformlike mounds and capped them with temples or the houses of important individuals. These mounds were grouped around an open plaza, while most people lived in humbler, thatched dwellings clustered nearby. Hardly surprisingly, many scholars have pointed to these large earthworks, the plazas, and the platform mounds, and assumed they were the result of cultural influence from Mexican civilizations far to the south. As we shall see in Chapter 21, Mesoamerican civilizations relied on an intricate, intensely symbolic, and highly complex religious cosmology, commemorated with elaborate public ceremonies centered around large pyramids and plazas.

Mississippian graves and mound centers contain finely made pottery and other artifacts that bear elaborate decoration and distinctive artistic motifs. These artifacts include axes with head and shaft carved from a single piece of stone, copper pendants adorned with circles and weeping eyes, shell disks engraved with woodpeckers and rattlesnakes, elaborately decorated clay pots, and engraved shell cups adorned with male figures in ceremonial dress. The themes and motifs on these objects have many common features throughout the South and Southeast, so much so that they have been thought to link a vast area as far inland as the borders of the Ohio Valley to a common set of ritual beliefs and an art style that has been called the "Southern Cult" or "Southeastern Ceremonial Complex" (Galloway, 1989). Some of these motifs, such as the persistent use of bird symbolism and a "weeping eye" theme, were thought to display Mexican influence.

The term *Southern Cult* was coined in the 1930s, when many fewer Mississippian ceremonial objects were known, and those from larger centers. Today, we know that only a few distinctive stylistic elements were widely used. These include striped poles and fringed aprons on some human figures. As Jon Muller (1989) has pointed out, there are so many differences and similarities among local Mississippian art traditions that it is more economical to attribute the varied regional art styles of the Southern Cult to centuries of intensive exchange among hundreds of different local communities. In time, there was a degree of standardization in art traditions over a wide area, reflecting also a complex, highly variable set of religious mechanisms that supported the authority of local leaders. Undoubtedly, some of the ceremonial artifacts associated with the cult served as badges of rank and status. Far from having Mexican ancestry, the religious beliefs behind Mississippian society had their roots in far earlier indigenous beliefs. Any Mexican connections with Mississippian culture are now discounted. It was an entirely local efflorescence, born of centuries of vigorous cultural evolution in an area of exceptional resource diversity and potential.

A.D. 1500   Cahokia, Moundville, and other great Mississippian centers were past the height of their powers by the time European traders and explorers reached the Mississippi Valley. Cahokia was abandoned by 1500, even if Moundville was still an important center. Numerous chiefdoms still flourished in the mid-South and Southeast right up to European contact and beyond, some of which, like the kingdom of Coosa, were visited by conquistador Hernando de Soto during his journey across the Southeast in 1540–1542 (M. Smith, 1987). There are grounds to suspect, however, that smallpox and other diseases had spread among the peoples of the interior before the arrival of the Spaniards, decimating and weakening Mississippian society (Ramenovsky, 1987).

A.D. 1720   In the year 1720, French explorer Le Page du Pratz spent some time among the Natchez people of the Mississippi Valley. He found himself in a rigidly stratified society, divided into nobles and commoners and headed by a chieftain known as the Great Sun, who lived in a village of nine houses and a temple built on the summit of an earthen mound. Pratz witnessed the funeral of the Great Sun. His wives, relatives, and servants were drugged, then clubbed to accompany him in death (Swanton, 1911). Pratz was the first and only European to witness a Mississippian funeral, for epidemics of smallpox and other exotic diseases had already caused the fabric of this most complex of North American societies to fall apart. Within two centuries of De Soto, the last vestiges of Mississippian society had been submerged.

CHAPTER SUMMARY

Native American agriculture was based on quite different crops from those in the Old World, root crops like manioc, potatoes, and sweet potatoes. Maize was the most important cereal. Since there were many fewer potential domesticates, domesticated animals were limited—the llama, turkey, and guinea fowl. The earliest agriculture developed among hunter-gatherer societies who were coping with constant environmental change and unpredictable population shifts. At locations like Guilá Naquitz, Mexico, wet-year subsistence strategies involving deliberate planting eventually became permanent shifts in subsistence activities. The staple of native American agriculture was maize, probably domesticated from a native grass named teosinte in central America as early as 3000 B.C. Maize agriculture spread from southern Mexico and Guatemala thousands of miles to the north and south. There were farmers in the highland Andes and in coastal Peru by 3000 B.C., but maize and cotton farming, two vital staples, did not become important until about a thousand years later.

Maize agriculture reached the North American Southwest by about 1200 B.C. By 300 B.C., sedentary villages and a much greater dependence on farming were characteristic of the Southwest, leading to the emergence of the Hohokam, Mogollon, and Anasazi cultural traditions, among which the ultimate ancestry of modern Southwestern peoples lie. Many groups in eastern North America turned to the deliberate planting of native plants as food supplements after 2000 B.C., but maize and bean agriculture did not arrive from the west until the first millennium B.C.

After 1000 B.C., a series of powerful chiefdoms arose in the Southeast and Midwest, peoples among whom elaborate burial customs and the building of burial mounds and earthworks were commonplace. The Adena tradition appeared in about 700 B.C., was overlapped by the Hopewell in approximately A.D. 200. About A.D. 800, the focus of economic, religious, and political power shifted to the Mississippi Valley and Southeast with the rise of the Mississippian tradition. This tradition, with its powerful religious and secular leaders, survived in a modified form until European contact in the sixteenth century A.D.

GUIDE TO FURTHER READING

Cordell, Linda S. 1984. *Prehistory of the Southwest.* Orlando, FL: Academic Press.
   A definitive, closely argued synthesis of southwestern archaeology.

Fagan, Brian M. 1995. *Ancient North America,* 2nd ed. New York: Thames and Hudson.
   A general account of North American archaeology with a long summary of southwestern and eastern woodlands prehistory. Heavily referenced and aimed at the beginning reader.

Fiedel, Stuart J. 1992. *Prehistory of the Americas,* 2nd ed. Cambridge, Eng.: Cambridge University Press.
   Discusses the major issues in New World prehistory for beginners. Well written, continent-wide account.

MacNeish, Richard. 1978. *The Science of Archaeology.* North Scituate, MA: Duxbury Press.
   An account of MacNeish's research in Mexico and Peru that summarizes the work and contains much common-sense advice about contemporary archaeology.

Moseley, Michael E. 1975. *The Incas and their Ancestors.* London and New York: Thames and Hudson.
   Comprehensive, critical synthesis that is fundamental to understanding Andean archaeology and early food production.

Smith, Bruce D. 1992. *Rivers of Change.* Washington, DC: Smithsonian Institution Press.
   Bruce Smith's monograph is fundamental to understanding early agriculture in eastern North America.

Wills, S. H. 1989. *Early Prehistoric Agriculture in the American Southwest.* Santa Fe, NM: School of American Research.
   An intelligent, closely argued study of early maize cultivation and its antecedents in the desertic environments of the Southwest.

Yerkes, Richard. 1988. "The Woodland and Mississippian Traditions in the Prehistory of Midwestern North America." *Journal of World Prehistory* 2(3): 307–358.
   A useful account of later cultural developments in the Midwest.

PART V

OLD WORLD CIVILIZATIONS

(C. 3000 B.C. TO MODERN TIMES)

The great tide of civilization has long since ebbed, leaving these scattered wrecks on the solitary shore. Are those waters to flow again, bringing back the seeds of knowledge and of wealth that they have wafted to the West? We wanderers were seeking what they had left behind, as children gather up the coloured shells on the deserted sands.

AUSTEN HENRY LAYARD

Part V deals with the beginnings of complex states and urban civilization, not only in the Near East, but also in lesser known parts of the world, such as Africa and Southeast Asia. Research in Africa and Asia has hardly begun; future excavations in these regions are likely to throw significant new light on such much-debated issues as the importance of ceremonial centers and long-distance trade in the emergence of complex societies. Once again, the reader is urged to start with the theoretical background embarking on the narrative cultural history.

CHAPTER 14

THE DEVELOPMENT OF CIVILIZATION

• • •

P aul Emile Botta was appointed the French consul in Mosul in northern Iraq in 1840, with one official objective alone—to dig the nearby mounds of Biblical Nineveh. Botta had no archaeological qualifications whatsoever, except that he was an experienced traveler who spoke several oriental languages. At first, he dug fruitlessly into Nineveh, finding nothing but inscribed bricks. Then one of his workers told him of similar bricks that formed the chimney of his house at a village named Khorsabad 14 miles (23 km) away. To get rid of the man, he sent two of his laborers to investigate. A week later, they returned with stories of richly carved walls adorned with strange animals. Botta leapt on his horse and rode to Khorsabad, where he gasped at the curious bas-reliefs in the walls of the small pit— bearded men in long gowns, winged animals, and wild beasts. He moved his excavations to Khorsabad. Within a few weeks, he had uncovered room after room of sculpted limestone slabs, the wall decorations of a magnificent, exotic royal palace. "I believe myself to be the first who had discovered sculptures which with some reason can be referred to the period when Nineveh was flourishing," he wrote excitedly of the palace.

We know now that Botta had uncovered not Nineveh but Assyrian King Sargon's palace, constructed at great expense in the eighth century B.C. Even so, his remarkable discoveries ushered in a classic era of nineteenth-century archaeological discovery—which revealed to an astonished world not only the Assyrians but, in addition, the Sumerians, Mayans, Minoans, Mycenaeans, and other hitherto unknown civilizations. Today, there are no more unknown civilizations to be unearthed, but archaeologists are still striving to understand the origins and workings of the world's earliest states (Figure 14.1). In this chapter, we review some of the ways in which they have attempted to explain their beginnings.

CIVILIZATION

• • •

Everyone who has studied the prehistory of human society agrees that the emergence of civilization in different parts of the world was a major event in human

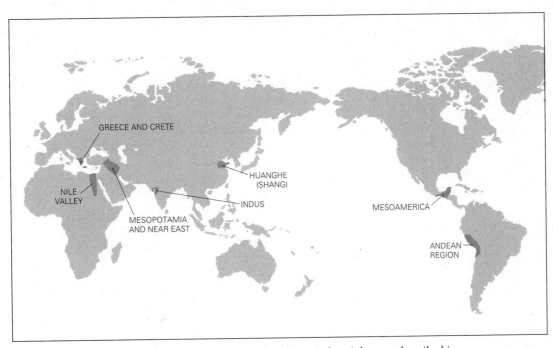

FIGURE 14.1   Map showing locations of major early preindustrial states described in this book.

adaptation. The word *civilization* has a ready, everyday meaning. It implies "civility," a measure of decency in the behavior of the individual in a civilization. Such definitions inevitably reflect ethnocentrism or value judgments because what is "civilized" behavior in one civilization might be antisocial or baffling in another. These simplistic understandings are of no use to students of prehistoric civilizations seeking basic definitions and cultural processes.

Civilization

Some special attributes that separate civilizations from other societies can be listed as follows:

- Urbanized societies, based on cities, with large, very complex social organizations. The early civilization was invariably based on a specific territory, such as the Nile Valley, as opposed to smaller areas owned by individual kin groups.

- Symbiotic economies based on the centralized accumulation of capital and social status through tribute and taxation. This type of economy allows the support of hundreds, often thousands, of nonfood producers such as smiths and priests. Long-distance trade and the division of labor, as well as craft specialization, are often characteristic of early civilizations.

- Advances toward record keeping, science and mathematics, and some form of written script.

- Impressive public buildings and monumental architecture.

These attributes are by no means common to all early civilizations, for they take different forms in each.

CITIES

• • •

Archaeological research into early civilization concentrates on the origin and development of the city. Today the city is the primary human settlement type throughout the world, and it has become so since the industrial revolution altered the economic face of the globe. The earliest cities assumed many forms, from the compact, walled settlement of Mesopotamia to the Mesoamerican ceremonial center, with a core population in its precincts and a scattered rural population in villages arranged over the surrounding landscape. The cities of the Harappan civilization of the Indus were carefully planned communities with regular streets and assigned quarters for different living groups. The palaces of the Minoans and Mycenaeans functioned as secular economic and trading centers for scattered village populations nearby.

City   A *city* is best defined by its population, which is generally larger and denser than that of a town or village. A good and generally used rule of thumb is a lower limit of 5000 people for a city. However, numbers are not a sufficient determinant: Many people can congregate in a limited area and still not possess the compact diversity of population that enables the economic and organizational complexity of a city to develop. It is this complexity that distinguishes the city from other settlement types. Most cities have a complexity in both organization and nonagricultural activities that is supported by large food surpluses. Further, the city is a functioning part of a complex system of different settlements that rely on its many services and facilities.

AN URBAN REVOLUTION?

• • •

Early scholars who debated the origins of civilization were concerned with the cultural evolution of humankind from a state of savagery toward the full realization of human potential. This, in their Victorian eyes, was civilization. They considered that their civilization had originated in ancient Egypt and that bold mariners had spread its ideas all over the globe. These simplistic hypotheses collapsed in the face of new archaeological discoveries in Mesopotamia and the Nile Valley in the early decades of this century. With the discovery of Sumerian sites and early Egyptian farming villages, scholars came to realize that early civilization had developed over a wide area and a considerable span of time.

Urban revolution   The first relatively sophisticated theories about the origins of urban civilization were formulated by European archaeologist V. Gordon Childe. Childe claimed that a "Neolithic Revolution" was followed by an Urban Revolution, when the development of metallurgy created a new class of full-time specialists and changed the rules of human social organization (Childe, 1936, 1952). He argued that the new specialists were fed by food surpluses raised by the peasant farmers. The products of the craftsworkers had to be distributed, and raw materials had to be obtained from outside sources. Both needs reduced the self-reliance of peasant societies. Agricultural techniques became more sophisticated as a higher yield of food per capita was needed to support the nonagricultural population. Irrigation increased productivity, leading to centralized control of food supplies, production, and distribution. Taxation and tribute led to the accumulation of capital. A new class-stratified society, based on economic classes rather than kin, came into being. Writing was essential for keeping records and for developing exact and predictive sciences. Transportation by water and land was part of the new order. A unifying religious force dominated urban life as priest-kings and despots rose to power. Monumental architecture testified to their activities.

The notion of an Urban Revolution dominated archaeological and historical literature for years, but this hypothesis has flaws as an all-embracing definition of civilization and a description of its development. Childe's criteria are far from universal. Some highly effective and lasting civilizations, such as those of the Minoans and the Mycenaeans, never had cities. The Maya built elaborate ceremonial and religious centers with semiurban populations concentrated around them, surrounded by a more scattered rural population clustered for the most part in small villages. Writing was absent from the Inca civilization of Peru. Some craft specialization and religious structure are typical of most civilizations, but it cannot be said that these form the basis for an overall definition of civilization (Claessen and Skalník, 1979).

LATER THEORIES ABOUT THE ORIGINS OF STATES

● ● ●

American archaeologist Robert Adams (1966) stresses the development of social organization and craft specialization during the urban revolution. He raises objections to the Childe hypothesis, arguing that the name implies undue emphasis on the city at the expense of social change, that is, the development of social classes and political institutions. Many of Childe's criteria, like the evolution of the mathematical sciences, have the disadvantage of not being readily preserved in the archaeological record. Furthermore, Childe's urban revolution was identified by lists of traits, although the name implies emphasis on the *processes* of culture change. Childe believed technological innovations and subsistence patterns were at the core of the urban revolution. Adams directed his work toward changes in social organization; he describes early Mesopotamia and central Mexico as following "a fundamental course of development in which corporate kin groups, originally preponderating in the control of land, were gradually supplemented by the growth of private estates in the hands of urban elites." The eventual result was a stratified form of social organization rigidly divided along class lines (Service, 1975).

Adams: social organization

By the time Adams was criticizing Childe's Urban Revolution, people were beginning to investigate the many interacting factors that led to the emergence of complex states. Everyone agreed that complex societies appeared during a period of major economic and social change, but different scholars emphasized various possible factors that contributed to the rise of civilization. These factors include ecology, population growth, technology, irrigation, trade, religious beliefs, and even warfare.

Ecology

Many have said that the exceptional fertility of the Mesopotamian floodplain and the Nile Valley was a primary reason for the emergence of the cities and states in these regions. The fertility and benign climate led to the food surpluses that were capable of supporting the craftsworkers and other specialists who formed the complex fabric of civilization. This notion was the foundation of what was known in the 1920s and 1930s as the Fertile Crescent theory.

Reality, of course, is much more complicated. The true surplus was probably one of capacities, a *social surplus,* which is one that consciously reallocates goods or services. A social surplus is created by a society's deliberate action through some

Social surplus

form of government force. In a sense this is a taxation authority, a person or organization that wrests surplus grain or other products from those who grow or produce them. Another problem with the Fertile Crescent theory is that the environments of all the major centers of early civilizations are far too diverse—in altitude above sea level, for example—for any assemblage of environmental conditions to be set forth as the requisites for civilization's start.

The earliest civilizations in Egypt and Mesopotamia were certainly based on complex subsistence patterns (Hassan, 1988), patterns that involved integrating several ecological zones. Complex subsistence patterns like these were almost certainly active in Mesoamerica and Southeast Asia, to say nothing of Egypt, although the evidence is very incomplete. Even in the best-documented areas, evidence comes from later, well-documented periods, and we can only surmise that complexities were similar in earlier times. Several ecological zones became integrated, each producing a different food as a main product. A localized center of power could control different ecological zones and the products from them, a more deliberate hedge against famine that was indispensable for planning food surpluses. This is not at all the same as saying that favorable ecological conditions caused trade and redistributive mechanisms, and therefore some form of centralized authority, to develop. Rather, ecology was only one component in a close network of the many changes that led to civilization.

Population Growth

Malthus and Boserup   Thomas Henry Malthus argued as long ago as 1798 that human reproductive capacity far exceeds the available food supply. Many people have argued that new and more intensive agricultural methods created food surpluses. These in turn led to population growth; more leisure time; and new social, political, and religious institutions, as well as the arts.

Ester Boserup, among others, has criticized this point of view. She feels that population growth provided the incentive for irrigation and intensive agriculture (Spooner, 1972). Her theories have convinced others that social evolution was caused by population growth. No one has explained, though, why the original populations should have started to grow. By no means do all farming populations, especially those using slash-and-burn cultivation, live at the maximum density that can be supported by the available agricultural land; population often is regulated artificially. Claiming that population growth explains how states were formed necessitates finding out why such decisions would have been made.

Slash-and-burn, or *swidden,* agriculture, with its shifting cultivation, is very delicately balanced with the rest of its ecosystem. Populations are dispersed and have relatively little flexibility in movement or growth because the land has low carrying capacity and relatively few ecological niches to carry edible crops. More lasting field agriculture, like that in Mesopotamia, is far more intensive and exploits much more of the environment in an ordered and systematic way. The more specialized ecosystem created by these efforts supports more concentrated populations. It creates conditions in which more settlements per square mile can exist on foods whose annual yields are at least roughly predictable.

Most significant concentrations of settlements that might be called prototypes for urban complexes developed in regions like Egypt and Mesopotamia where permanent field agriculture flourished. However, unlike the period immediately after food production began, there is no evidence for a major jump in population immediately before civilization appeared. Also, a dense population does not seem to have been a precondition for a complex society or redistribution centers for trade. We have no reason to believe that a critical population density was a prerequisite for urban life.

Technology

In Mesopotamia, again our best-documented area, agricultural technology did not advance until long after civilization began. The technological innovations that did appear (the wheel, for example) were of more benefit to transportation than to production. Copper and other exotic materials were at first used for small-scale production of cult objects and jewelry. Not until several centuries after civilization started were copper and bronze more abundant, with demand for transportation and military needs burgeoning. Then we see an advance in technology or an increase in craftspeople. Technology did evolve, but only in response to developing markets, new demands, and the expanded needs of the elite.

Irrigation

Most scholars now agree that three elements on Childe's list seem to have been of great importance in the growth of all the world's civilizations. The first was the creation of food surpluses, used to support new economic classes whose members were not directly engaged in food production. Agriculture as a way of life immediately necessitates storing crops to support the community during the lean times of the year. A surplus above this level of production was created by both increased agricultural efficiency and social and cultural changes. Specialist craftsworkers, priests, and traders were among the new classes of society that came into being as a result.

Second, agricultural economies may have tended to concentrate on fewer, more productive crops, but they remained diversified so that the ultimate subsistence base was still relatively wide. The ancient Egyptians relied on husbandry, especially in the Nile Delta. The diversity of food resources not only protected the people against the dangers of famine but also stimulated the development of trade and exchange mechanisms for food and other products and the growth of distributive organizations that encouraged centralized authority.

The third significant development was intensive land use, which probably increased agricultural output. Intensive agriculture usually implies irrigation, often hailed as one fundamental reason for a civilization's inception. Archaeologists have long debated how significant irrigation was in getting urban life started. Julian Steward and Karl Wittfogel argue that irrigation was connected with development of stratified societies (Steward et al., 1955; Wittfogel, 1957). The state bureaucracy had a monopoly on hydraulic facilities and created the hydraulic state; in other words, the social requirements of irrigation led to the development of states and urban societies. Robert Adams (1966) takes a contrary view. He feels that the introduction of great irrigation works was more a consequence of dynastic state organizations, however much the requirement of large-scale irrigation subsequently may have influenced the development of bureaucracies.

Irrigation and the hydraulic state

Early irrigation in Mesopotamia was conducted on a small scale (R. M. Adams, 1981; Adams and Nissen, 1972). Natural channels were periodically cleaned and straightened; only small artificial feeder canals were built. Maximum use was made of the natural hydrology of the rivers. Most settlement was confined to the immediate vicinity of major watercourses. Irrigation was organized by individual small communities. Large-scale artificial canalization did not take place until long after urban life appeared. The same is true of ancient Egypt, where construction of large artificial canals seems to have been the culmination of long evolution of intensive agriculture (Kemp, 1989).

Building and maintaining small canals requires neither elaborate social organization nor population resources larger than those of one or several communities. Large-scale irrigation requires technical and social resources of a quite different order. Huge labor forces must be mobilized, organized, and fed. Maintenance and supervision require constant attention, as do water distribution and resolution of disputes over water rights. Because those living downstream are at the mercy of those upstream, large irrigation works are viable only as long as all who enjoy them remain within the same political unit. A formal state structure with an administrative elite is essential.

Growth of Trade

The origins and evolution of complex societies in human prehistory have long been linked to burgeoning trade in essential raw materials such as copper and iron ore or in luxuries of all types. However, claiming that a dramatic increase in trading was a primary cause of civilization grossly oversimplifies a complicated proceeding. Trade is two things: a helpful indicator of new social developments and a factor in the rise of civilization. Many commodities and goods are preserved in the archaeological record, including gold and glass beads, seashells, and obsidian mirrors. These finds have enabled archaeologists to trace trade routes through the Near East, Europe, and other regions. With the many analytic methods for looking at the sources of obsidian, stone ax blanks, and metals, people now realize that prehistoric trade was much more than a few itinerant tradespeople passing objects from village to village (Sabloff and Lamberg-Karlovsky, 1975).

Trade and exchange networks

Trade as an institution could have begun when people sought to acquire goods from a distance for prestige and individual profit. The decision to acquire any commodity from afar depends both on how urgent the need for it is and on the difficulties in acquiring and transporting it. Much early trade was based on obtaining specific commodities, such as copper ore or salt, that had peculiar and characteristic problems of acquisition and transport. There was no such thing as trading in general. Trade in any one commodity was almost a special branch on its own. Clearly such items as cattle or slaves are more easily transported than tons of iron ore or cakes of salt; the former move on their own, but metals require human or animal carriers or wheeled carts. To ignore these differences is to oversimplify the study of prehistoric trade.

In more complex societies, the ruler and his immediate followers were generally entitled to trade and to initiate the steps leading to acquisition of goods from a distance. The king might employ merchants or traders to do the work for him, but the trade was in his name. The lower-class traders of Mesopotamian society were more menial and were often bound by guilds or castes. These were carriers, loan administrators, dealers—people who kept the machinery of trade going. Both the royal merchant and the lower-class trader were distinct from peoples such as the Phoenicians, who relied on trade as a continuous activity and a major form of livelihood.

Trade before markets were developed can never be looked at as the one cause of civilization or even as a unifying factor. It was far more than just a demand for obsidian or copper, for the causes of trading were infinitely varied and the policing of trade routes was a complex and unending task. It is significant that most early

Mesopotamian and Egyptian trade was based on rivers, where bulk transportation was easier. When the great caravan routes opened, the political and military issues—tribute, control of trade routes, and tolls—became paramount. The caravan predates the great empires, a form of organized trading that kept to carefully defined routes set up and armed by state authorities for their specific tasks. The travelers were bent only on delivering and exchanging imports and exports. These caravans were a far cry from the huge economic complex that accompanied Alexander the Great's army across Asia or the Grand Mogul's annual summer progress from the heat of Delhi in India to the mountains, moving half a million people including the entire Delhi bazaar.

Markets represent a more complex form of trading. The market encourages people to develop one place for trading at the relatively stable, almost fixed prices for staple commodities. This does not, however, mean regulated prices. The trade market is a network of market sites (marketplaces) at which the exchange of commodities, especially the *mechanisms* of the exchange relationship, from an area where supplies are abundant to one where demand for the same materials is high is regulated to some degree.

Such viewpoints require study of market networks and the mechanisms by which supplies are channeled along well-defined routes; how profits are regulated and fed back to the source, providing further incentive for more supplies; and so on. There may or may not be a marketplace; the focus of the trading system and the mechanisms by which trade interacts with other parts of the culture are formed by the state of affairs surrounding the trade. This means regarding archaeological finds as the material expressions of interdependent factors. These include the need for goods, which prompts a search for supplies, themselves the product of production above local needs, created to satisfy external demands. Other variables are the logistics of transportation and the extent of the trading network, as well as the social and political environments. With all these variables, no one aspect of trade is an overriding cause of culture change or of evolution in trading practices.

The reality is that long-distance trade was carefully melded with fluctuating demands and availabilities of supplies. It is not enough to think of trade in terms of the distribution of exports and imports (Kohl, 1978). Any study of prehistoric trade must consider also the production and consumption of the goods involved. Were they essential raw materials or exotic luxuries, finished manufactures or ax blanks that were completed at their destination? Was the trade continuous or seasonal, carried on by specialist traders, only by the wealthy, or by everyone? Changes in the volume and nature of trade can influence and modify not only production in a society but its social and economic structures as well. For example, we know that the Aztec merchant in highland Mexico could purchase the title *Lord*, presumably as a measure of his status as a successful trader. There was room for private dealing, specialist merchants, commodities markets, perhaps even smuggling and tax evasion. Archaeologists cannot understand a trading network without analyzing the social and economic structures of each society participating in the exchange, for in many cases they became interdependent, often without realizing that they were. Until there is much more systematic study of the data for early trade, no one will fully understand trade's influence on nascent civilization anywhere.

Warfare

Robert Carneiro (1970) has suggested a "coercive theory" of state origins. Based on the archaeology of Peruvian coastal valleys, it argues that areas such as these valleys,

Carneiro: "coercive theory"

where the amount of agricultural land is very limited and circumscribed by desert, are the ones where states may well form through a predictable series of events. Carneiro's scenario begins with autonomous farming villages scattered over the valley landscape. As the population grows and more land is taken up, the communities start fighting and raiding one another's fields as they compete for limited acreage. Soon some village leaders emerge as successful warlords, become chieftains, and preside over larger tribal politics. The valley population continues to grow and warfare continues to intensify until the entire region falls under the sway of one warrior-ruler, who presides over a single state centered within the valley. Then this ambitious ruler and his successors start raiding neighboring valleys. Eventually a powerful state emerges and rules over several valleys, which creates much larger civilizations.

The Carneiro hypothesis is difficult to test, but an attempt to do so in the Santa Valley, Peru, has produced an interesting picture of changing settlement patterns. Suffice it to say here that there are no signs of the kinds of dispersed, autonomous village that Carneiro's scenario begins with. The processes that shaped the emergence of state societies in the Santa Valley appear to have been much more complex and multifaceted than just tribal warfare. David Wilson (1983) points out that the only "coercive" processes came in about A.D. 400, when the Moche people carved out a multivalley state by military conquest of neighboring valleys. Their conquest took place long after complex, irrigation-based societies flourished in the Santa Valley. As with irrigation hypotheses, reality is much more complex than the straightforward scenario Carneiro developed.

There is an attractive simplicity to the idea that the early town or city was a mighty fortress to which the surrounding tribes could run in times of stress. This has been the argument for the massive stone walls and tower that protected early Jericho (Chapter 9), for example. Thus, goes the argument, the groups that flocked within the walls came to depend on one another and their city as a fundamental part of society. However, warfare can be rejected as a primary cause of civilization without much discussion since large military conflicts appear to have been a result of civilization, not a direct cause of it. For one thing, the earliest ceremonial centers apparently were not fortified. For another, in earlier times the diffuse social organization of village communities had not yet led to the institutional warfare that resulted from the concentration of wealth and power in monopolistic hands. Only when absolute and secular monarchs came to power did warfare become endemic, with raiding and military campaigns designed to gain control of important resources or to solve political questions. This type of warfare is a far cry from the tribal conflict common to many peasant societies. It presupposes authority.

THE CEREMONIAL CENTER

● ● ●

The nucleus of the first cities was a complex of public buildings that fulfilled both secular and religious functions (Eliade, 1959). These centers were either very compact, like the Mesopotamian *ziggurat*, or dispersed, like Mayan examples. Those of the Mesopotamians and Chinese were relatively compact, with a reasonably dense population around them. Many Maya centers, such as Tikal in Guatemala, were huge urban complexes, with dense city and rural populations (Coe, 1993). The priestly elite and rulers who lived at the center were surrounded by retainers and craftsworkers. The rural population in the environs was probably bound to the center both economically and by kinship ties. The ceremonial functions of the center were of fundamental importance in validating these links. As such a center became a focus for a group of independent settlements, it supplied reassurance, or what Chinese historian Paul Wheatley (1971) calls "cosmic certainty." It was "the sanctified terrain where [the common people were] guaranteed the seasonal renewal of cyclic time, and where the splendor, potency, and wealth of their rulers symbolized the well-being of the whole community." The rural population felt no alienation from those who lived at the center; the distinction was between the ruler and the ruled.

To this school of thought, the ceremonial center was not a prime mover of civilization but an instrument of religious power. The religious and moral models of society provided a sacred canon circumscribing economic institutions and laying out the social order. It ensured the continuity of cultural traditions and was recited in temples, where the word of the gods rang out in reassuring chants passed from generation to generation. The ceremonial center was a tangible expression of this continuity.

Eventually the ceremonial center was taken over by the rising secular kings, who were sometimes installed by force. As the kingship's power grew, the ceremonial center's political power declined, although its religious functions were faithfully retained. In Mesopotamia, church and state separated when the power of the temple ruler, or *en,* was restricted to religious matters after 3000 B.C. The *lugal,* or king, assumed the secular and often militaristic leadership of the state (Crawford, 1991).

We can detect secularization of the ceremonial center in the appearance of the palace, where the secular king resided. The king himself might have enthusiastically believed in the state faith, but his functions were almost entirely secular, even if he used religion to justify his actions. He might have assumed a divine role himself. When the palace appears, we find the royal tombs standing as garish and splendid monuments to the awesome political and social power behind them.

With the changeover from hunting and gathering to food production, the relationship between people and their land changed fundamentally. Complex issues of land ownership—of inheritance of field from one generation to the next or of field boundaries—changed political and social institutions and the religious beliefs associated with them. In many societies, the relationship between the living and the dead, the ancestors, played a major role in ceremonies that interceded with the spiritual world for fertile soils and good crops. There are clear signs of ancestor cults in early Jericho and other farming settlements at 'Ain Ghazal (Chapter 9), and shrines and sacred places occur at Jericho; Çatal Hüyük; and Las Haldas, Peru. These religious shrines were predecessors of the great ceremonial centers of Mesopotamia and Egypt, Mesoamerica, and Peru. In each part of the world where civilization appeared, ceremonial centers were preceded by inconspicuous prototypes tended by priests or cult leaders. These people must have been among the first to be freed of the burden of having to produce food, supported by the communities they served. In every region the ceremonial center was the initial focus of power, exchange, and authority, an authority vested in religious symbolism and organized priesthoods.

It is no coincidence that the Mesopotamians' earliest recorded gods were those of harvest and fertility, or that in Mexico Tlaloc was the god of rain and life itself. These preoccupations may have become the focus of new and communal belief systems. Those who served the deities of fertility thus became people of authority, the individuals who controlled economic surpluses, offerings, and the redistribution of goods. The temple became a new instrument for organizing fresh political, social, and religious structures.

As society grew more complex, more sophisticated ethics and beliefs provided a means for sanctioning the society's new goals. The temple was an instrument for disseminating these new beliefs, a means for the new leaders to justify their acts and develop coherent policies. Symbolic statements describing society served as models not only for behavior and belief but also for the ceremonial centers that perpetuated and formulated them.

SYSTEMS AND CIVILIZATIONS

• • •

Everyone seems to agree that urban life and civilization came into existence gradually during a period of major social and economic change. The earlier linear explanations invoking irrigation, trade, or religion as a major integrative force are inadequate for our purposes.

Adams: multiple causes

Robert Adams has been a pioneer in looking at multiple causes of state formation. In 1966 he argued that irrigation agriculture, increased warfare, and "local resource variability" were three factors vital in newly appearing civilizations. Each affected society and the other factors with positive feedback, helping to reinforce one another. The creation of food surpluses and the emergence of a stratified society were critical developments. Irrigation agriculture and more intensive horticulture could feed a bigger population. Larger populations and increased sedentariness, as well as trade with regular centers for redistributing goods, were all pressures for greater production and increased surpluses, actively fostered by dominant groups in society. The greatly enlarged surpluses enabled those who controlled them to employ large numbers of craftsworkers and other specialists who did not themselves grow crops.

Adams develops his thesis further by arguing that some societies were better able to transform themselves into states because of the favorable variety of resources on which they could draw. Higher production and increased populations led to monopolies over strategic resources. These communities eventually were more powerful than their neighbors, expanding their territories by military campaigns and efficiently exploiting their advantages over other peoples. Such cities became the early centers of religious activities, technological and artistic innovations, and the development of writing (Figure 14.2).

Flannery: systems

Kent V. Flannery (1972) has a more complex and somewhat abstract scheme, further explaining the state's origins. He and others see the state as a very complicated living system, the complexity of which can theoretically be measured by the internal differentiation and specialization of its subsystems, such as those for agriculture, technology, religious beliefs, and so on. The ways these subsystems are linked, as well as the controls that society imposes on the system as a whole, are vital. Archaeologists who think this way make a fundamental distinction among the following:

- The *processes* of culture change, the succession of changes by which the early states developed their new complexity.

- The *mechanisms,* the actual ways in which the processes of increasing complexity occurred.

- The socioenvironmental *stresses* that select for these mechanisms. Socioenvi-

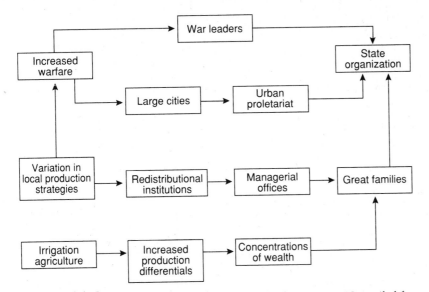

FIGURE 14.2   Hypothetical model of the state's beginnings. (Compiled from R. M. Adams, 1966.) Compare with Figure 14.3.

ronmental stresses can include food shortages, warfare, and population growth and are by no means common to all states.

"An explanation of the rise of the state then centers on the ways in which the processes . . . took place," writes Flannery.

A series of subsystems operate in human cultural systems, subsystems that interact with one another, just as the cultural system as a whole interacts with the natural environment. Each subsystem is regulated by a control apparatus that keeps all the variables in a system within bounds so that the survival of the system as a whole is not threatened. This apparatus of social control is vital, for it balances subsistence needs with religious, political, social, and other ideological values. There is a well-defined hierarchy of regulation and policy, ranging from those decisions under the control of individuals to institutions within society with specialized functions (such as the priesthood) on up to the basic, highest-order propositions, those of societal policy. These abstract standards or values lie at the heart of any society's regulation of its cultural system. Not only crops and domesticated animals but also all sorts of subtle relationships and regulatory measures make up the basis of a civilization (see Figure 14.3 for an example from Mesopotamia).

The management and regulation of a state is a far more elaborate and centralized undertaking than that of a hunter-gatherer band or a small chiefdom. Indeed, the most striking difference between states and less complicated societies is the degree of complexity in their ways of reaching decisions and their hierarchic organizations, not in their subsistence activities. Any living system is subjected to stress when one of its many variables exceeds the range of deviation that the system allows it. The stress may make the system evolve new institutions or policies. Such coping mechanisms may be triggered by warfare, population pressure, trade, environmental change, or other variables. These variables create what Flannery calls an "adaptive milieu" for evolutionary change. His specific mechanisms include "promotion" and "linearization," when an institution in a society may assume new powers or some

Control apparatus

FIGURE 14.3 A systems diagram showing the interrelationships between cultural and environmental variables that led to increased stratification of class structure in early Mesopotamian urban society. (Developed by Redman, 1978.)

aspect of life may become too complex for a few people to administer. Both mechanisms lead to greater centralization, caused by selective pressures on the variables that produced the coping mechanisms.

The ultimate objective of a systems analysis of how a civilization began could be the establishment of rules by which the origins could be simulated, but such rules are a goal for the future. Flannery lists 15 beginning rules that could affect the cultural evolution of a simple human population forming part of a regional ecosystem. These rules can lead to new models for understanding the cultural evolution of civilization. Such models are certain to be most complex. We now must be specific about the links between subsystems—distinguishing between the mechanisms and processes and the socioenvironmental pressures that are peculiar to each civilization and have, until now, been the means by which we have sought to explain the origins of civilization (Redman, 1978). Religion and control of information now appear to be key elements in the regulation of environmental and economic variables in early civilizations and, indeed, in any human society.

Flannery's ecologically based theories have enjoyed a relatively long life compared with some other hypotheses, but they face the objection that testing multicausal models is very difficult indeed. William Sanders and David Webster (1978) point out that Flannery's approach relies heavily on cultural evolution and invokes a number of universal processes that affected the formation of complex societies (see also Binford, 1983), when in fact the environment in Mexico and other centers of early state formation was much more complex and variable. In their classic study of the Basin of Mexico, Sanders and others (1979) show how the Aztec created and organized huge agricultural systems that spread over the shallow waters of the basin's lakes. The variability of the basin environment meant that the Aztecs had to exploit every environmental opportunity afforded them. Thus, Sanders argues, the state organized large-scale agriculture to support a population of up to 250,000 just in and close around the Aztec capital, Tenochtitlán.

ECOLOGICAL AND STRUCTURAL APPROACHES

● ● ●

Two theoretical approaches to the emergence of states have dominated archaeological thinking in recent years (Brumfiel, 1983). The first originates in the pioneer work of Julian Steward in the 1950s, relating state formation to the challenges offered by the local environment. Population growth and pressure are thought to be the dynamics that fuel the process of state formation. The initial stages of state formation are claimed to be accelerated by the ecological benefits the people accrue from a more centralized (state) organization. The second approach argues that states came into being as a result of certain social and cultural conditions. This "structural" approach, which owes much to Karl Marx and Friedrich Engels, argues that even societies with stable populations and balanced relationships with their environments possess an internal dynamic that fuels their progress toward greater social complexity. In other words, social components of society are more important than general conditions within a human population as a whole.

The ecological approach to state formation has focused attention on the effectiveness of centralized organization as a way of solving social and environmental problems. A powerful leader has the information about state-held resources at his or her disposal to make decisions along with the ability to command people's labor and to collect and redistribute the results of that labor. Thus, goes the argument, states arise in social and environmental contexts in which centralized management solves problems effectively.

Ecological approach

Centralized organization was at the core of Wittfogel's arguments for hydraulic civilizations, but as we have seen, his theories proved invalid when it was shown that large-scale irrigation developed in Egypt and Mesopotamia long after urban civilizations had emerged. Management has been the focus of many other theories, too—theories that invoke the need to distribute food within a region; to organize the procurement of metals, salt, or other essentials from outside; to maintain defense or conduct wars of conquest; or to perform a multitude of interlocking functions. Kent Flannery's systems approach to state formation epitomizes the management view, for it argues that effective leadership endowed emerging states in many parts of the world with the ability to deal with a great diversity of ecological and population problems.

Flannery's hypotheses have been elaborated even further because we must account for one unquestionable fact. States arose only in a few locations at certain moments; state formation is not a universal phenomenon. Those who espouse the ecological approach have focused on the complex interactions between population growth and the local environment. For example, William Sanders and Barbara Price

(1968) argue that, in the Valley of Mexico, rapid population growth caused serious problems for small-scale societies after centuries of relatively egalitarian political organization. States emerged because they were beneficial as a way of organizing both increased food supplies through intensified agriculture and trade and external relations with neighbors. Thus, states would emerge only in certain environmental settings, those with especially severe population problems or shortages of agricultural land. Effective, centralized management of food production, through state-organized irrigation systems and other means, and of trade could bring ecological imbalance under control within a short time.

The ecological approach has problems. How, for example, does one tell which environments would foster state formation? Fertile floodplains like Mesopotamia? Coastal river valleys like those in Peru? Or areas where land is in short supply (also coastal Peru)? States have arisen in regions where there are few geographic constraints, like the Maya lowlands of Mesoamerica, and in the Nile Valley. Further, civilizations have arisen without any sign of rapid population growth, in Iran and other parts of the Near East. Although agricultural intensification often accompanied state formation, it occurred in many forms—in the adoption of swamp garden agriculture (Maya lowlands), in the diversion of river water into flood basins (Egypt), and by exploitation of different ecological zones (Aegean). The classic models, like Flannery's, of the origins of state-organized societies rely on positive feedback between population growth and recurring population pressure to maintain the cultural system in a state of evolutionary change, or on some other device. These models result invariably in complex feedback diagrams, which are fine in general theory but very difficult to document with archaeological data (for a full critique, see Brumfiel, 1983; 1992).

Brumfiel: structural approach

Elizabeth Brumfiel (1983) names the "social" approach to the origins of the state the "structural approach." Under this rubric, the social structure of a society ultimately determines its transformation over time. Perhaps the most commonly invoked structure is that of social conflict, first espoused by Marx and Engels more than a century ago. They believed that new technological innovations like metallurgy led to new economic institutions like slavery that divided society into ranked classes. The state, with its special mechanisms for maintaining law and order, came into being as a way of reducing social conflict. Although Engels was obviously wrong in invoking technological innovation as a catalyst for civilization, some anthropologists believe that the state did develop as a means of suppressing conflict between social classes. However, Elman Service (1975) among others argues that Engels was entirely wrong. Social inequality, or social ranking, evolved as a result of the intensification of social institutions like tribute and taxation of goods and labor that were commonplace in chiefdoms, societies less developed than states. In other words, social inequality was already in existence.

Service (1975) also points out that there is no evidence for class conflict wars in early civilizations, as Engels would have had us believe. Service believes that there were political reasons for state formation. Many early chieftains, even if they were perceived as having divine powers, were in insecure positions. Thus, he argues, they secured permanent dominance by developing new political structures to bolster their authority. Brumfiel (1983) notes that "if, in certain types of political systems, threats to the leader's status are regularly generated," then one might be able to formulate an alternative to the Marxist social conflict theories, a theory "that explains the state as a consequence of conflicts resulting from political, rather than economic, structures."

We know that many historic chiefdoms were politically insecure, faced with constant rebellions and threats to their authority. Tahitian chiefs faced competition for power and prestige (D. Oliver, 1977), as did Hawaiian rulers. They achieved power by a combination of aggressive warfare, trading, and control of irrigated lands (Earle, 1978). Thus, argues Brumfiel (1983), the structure of societies where political systems involve weak, permanent leadership can lead to social conflict that has both a political and an economic basis. "The process of state formation might be nothing more (or less) than a series of effective strategies designed and implemented by beleaguered rulers to survive . . . challenges to power," she writes. At first, the strategies used to maintain power might vary greatly, encompassing everything from politically motivated marriage alliances with neighbors to regional trade or outright wars of conquest. As time goes on, the rulers' options would widen since they would be less constrained by the realities of their own insecurity and local conditions. However, in many cases the limited potential of the underlying agricultural system or the realities of the environment, which might limit communication or trade (as happened in Hawaii), may profoundly affect the prospects for state formation. Environmental factors play an important role in structural models of state formation, just as they do in ecological ones.

The crux of the Brumfiel argument is simple: that pressures for state formation are triggered in some social and cultural systems but not in others, hence the historical distribution of early states in the world. Thus, a search for the causes of state formation involves identifying the structures that lead to state formation and the conditions that determine their distribution in time and space. In particular, we need to focus on population ecology, on how "ecological variables present obstacles and opportunities to individuals pursuing their political goals in various structural contexts" (Brumfiel, 1983).

Brumfiel supports her structural model with an analysis of Aztec state formation in the Valley of Mexico. Aztec civilization (see Chapter 21) had roots in a millennium of earlier states, but the stages of its emergence are instructive. She hypothesizes that the Aztec state came into being in four "logically discrete" steps, each made possible by the structural changes that preceded it:

1. Competition intensified between petty kingdoms in the valley. This intensification crystallized in the famous Triple Alliance, formed in A.D. 1434 by the rulers of Aztec Tenochtitlán, Texcoco, and Tlacopán.

2. The emerging rulers centralized their power by organizational reforms that reduced the power of subordinate rulers and the nobility, thereby eliminating much of the competition for political leadership.

3. The Triple Alliance further consolidated its power by undertaking ambitious public works in the Valley of Mexico, not only wars of conquest but temple building, causeway and canal construction, and massive swamp agriculture.

4. The final development was the emergence of a complex bureaucracy that oversaw the affairs of state, with specialized administrative personnel and several levels of decision making.

By the time of the Spanish conquest, in 1519–1521, the population of the Valley of Mexico was about four times that of earlier periods; the state was performing many of the ecological functions that one might expect of powerful bureaucratic and political systems. This structural model directs attention away from purely ecological factors to the specific problem of what implications ecological variables have for prestate political orders. In other words, the question that still faces students of state formation is how ecological opportunity or necessity is translated into political change. What were the goals of the political actors, who were pursuing their individual goals while states were coming into being? Which ecological variables were obstacles? Which were opportunities (Brumfiel, 1992)? Until we have the answers to these questions, it will be difficult to develop any general theories of state formation.

THE COLLAPSE OF CIVILIZATIONS

● ● ●

The great British historian Arnold Toynbee (1962) is only one of many scholars who have written about cycles of history. Toynbee was referring to civilizations that rise to power, enjoy a period of prosperity, and then suddenly decline. Eventually, another civilization arises to take its place, which in turn goes through the same cycle of rise and fall. The cyclical view of history has recently enjoyed a new popularity in the hands of David Kennedy, whose *Rise and Fall of the Great Powers* (1987) has been required reading for policymakers in Washington, D.C. The record of early civilizations could easily be interpreted in cyclical terms, for states have risen and then collapsed with bewildering rapidity in all parts of the world within the last 5000 years. In Mesopotamia, for example, Sargon of Akkad used military force and trading acumen to establish his rule over Mesopotamia in about 2317 B.C. This empire lasted a mere two centuries before it collapsed in the face of widespread rebellion. Half a century later, the III Dynasty kings of Ur created an enormous bureaucratically controlled empire that extended far to the north and northwest of Mesopotamia. It, too, collapsed rapidly, with disastrous results (Chapter 15). Later, Assyrians, Persians, Parthans, and Islamic rulers all created empires that encompassed Mesopotamia. Finally, between the seventh and tenth centuries A.D., the agricultural economy in the early heartland of civilization collapsed. Within five centuries, the occupied area of the alluvial lowlands between the Tigris and Euphrates shrank to only 6 percent of its former size. The rest became desert.

A similar history of remarkable volatility can be found in Mesoamerica and Peru (Chapters 21 and 22). In the Mesoamerican highlands, for example, the great city of Teotihuacán flourished between about 200 B.C. and A.D. 700. In A.D. 600, it had a population of more than 125,000 people and was the sixth-largest city in the world. For 600 years or so, more than 85 percent of the population of the eastern and northern Valley of Mexico lived in or close to Teotihuacán. Then in about A.D. 700, the city collapsed. Within half a century, the population declined to a fourth of its former size. The lowland Maya, Monte Albán, and the Toltecs were other Mesoamerican civilizations that collapsed with extraordinary rapidity.

Few archaeologists, preoccupied as they are with the rise of civilizations, have ever paused to study their collapse. Only the collapse of the classic Maya has received serious attention (Chapter 21), yet "collapse is recurrent in human history, it is global in its occurrence, and it affects the spectrum of societies from simple foragers to great empires" (Tainter, 1988). When a complex society collapses, it suddenly becomes smaller, simpler, and often more egalitarian. Population densities fall; trade and economic activity dries up; information flow declines; and as Tainter puts it, "for those who are left the known world shrinks." What were the conditions under which early civilizations collapsed? Was it the result of food shortages, a catastrophic event, social conflict, or warfare?

Joseph Tainter, one of the few archaeologists to study collapse, points out that an initial investment in a society in growing complexity is a rational way of trying to solve the needs of the moment. At first the strategy works. Agricultural production increases through more intensive farming methods; an emerging bureaucracy works well; expanding trade networks bring wealth to the new elite, who use their authority and economic clout to undertake great public works, such as pyramids and temples, that validate their spiritual authority and divine associations. Maya civilization prospered greatly in the Mesoamerican lowlands for many centuries until a point of diminishing return was reached.

As the most costly solutions to society's needs are exhausted, so does it become more and more imperative that new organizational and economic answers be found, which may have much lower yields and cost a great deal more. As these stresses develop, argues Tainter, a complex society such as that of the Maya is increasingly vulnerable to collapse. There are few reserves to carry society through famines, floods, or other natural disasters. Eventually, collapse ensues, especially when important segments of the society perceive that centralization and social complexity simply do not work anymore and that they are better off on their own. The trend toward decentralization, toward collapse, becomes compelling. Tainter calls collapse not a catastrophe but a rational process that occurs when increasing stress requires some organizational change. The population declines and other catastrophic effects that either just preceded, accompanied, or followed collapse may have been traumatic at the time, but they can be looked at as part of what Tainter calls an "economizing process."

There is, of course, more to collapse than merely an "economizing process." Complete collapse can only occur in circumstances in which there is a power vacuum. In many cases, there may be a powerful neighbor waiting in the wings. The Ottoman Empire headed by the Sultan of Turkey was a dominant force in Near Eastern politics for centuries after the fifteenth century. The empire never collapsed; it simply declined, finally to vanish in the morass of World War I. Victorian statesmen called it "the sick man of Europe." Over many generations, the Ottomans lost territory to eager competitors. In earlier times, numerous small city-states or polities traded and competed with one another within a small area. Sumerian city-states in Mesopotamia, Mycenaean palace-kingdoms in Greece and the Aegean, the Maya in Mesoamerica—all lived in close interdependence, in a state that Colin Renfrew and Simon Shennan (1982) have called "peer-polity interaction." These situations are often competitive, maintained by trade, warfare, and constant diplomacy. Under these circumstances, to collapse is an invitation to be dominated by one's competitors. It is interesting to note that both Mayan and Mycenaean states existed as peer polities for centuries, then all collapsed within a brief time of one another. There is only loss of complexity when every polity in the interacting cluster collapses at the same time. As Colin Renfrew puts it, "The specific state is legitimized in the eyes of its citizens by the existence of other states which patently do function along comparable lines."

The collapse of early civilizations may, then, be closely connected to declining returns from social complexity.

CHAPTER SUMMARY

V. Gordon Childe's pioneer definition of the urban revolution was widely accepted in the 1930s; it centered on the development of the city, metallurgy, food surpluses, writing, and a unifying religious force. Unfortunately, his criteria are not universal enough to be generally applicable. We summarize the major potential causes for civilization: ecological stress, population pressure, technological change, irrigation agriculture, and the notion of the "hydraulic civilization." Exchange networks, religion, ceremony, and warfare have all been espoused as potential factors and have been approached both structurally and ecologically. Kent Flannery has used an ecologically based systems approach to early civilization, arguing that the emergence of complex societies was a gradual process caused by many interacting factors. One must look at the processes and mechanisms by which the necessary changes took place. Religious and informational factors seem to have been key elements in the regulation of environmental and economic variables in early civilization. Elizabeth Brumfiel argues for a social or "structural" approach to the origins of states. She believes that the social structure of a society ultimately determines its transformation over time. Pressures for state formation are triggered in some social and cultural systems but not in others. The search for causes therefore involves identifying the structures that lead to state formation and the conditions that determine their distribution in time and space. This process means focusing on ecological variables and the obstacles and opportunities they present to individuals pursuing political goals in different societies. In other words, how is ecological opportunity or necessity translated into political change?

GUIDE TO FURTHER READING

Adams, Robert M. 1966. *The Evolution of Urban Society.* Chicago: Aldine.
> *An essay on the origins of civilization that stresses social and economic change, based on the author's fieldwork in Mesopotamia and comparative data from the New World.*

Brumfiel, Elizabeth. 1983. "Aztec State Making: Ecology, Structure, and the Origin of the State." *American Anthropologist* 85 (2):261–284.
> *A lucid and provocative analysis of the origins of states that uses the Aztec as a model. Represents much current thinking on the subject.*

Flannery, Kent V. 1972. "The Cultural Evolution of Civilizations." *Annual Review of Ecology and Systematics.* Palo Alto, CA: Annual Reviews, pp. 399–426.
> *A masterly summary of the systems approach to early civilization that demonstrates the complexities of explaining the past.*

Redman, Charles L. 1978. *The Rise of Civilization: From Early Farmers to Urban Society in the Ancient Near East.* San Francisco: Freeman.
> *A book that covers all the theories of the 1960s and 1970s about the origins of civilization and the key sites and concepts for the advanced student. Strongly recommended as a follow-up to this volume.*

Sanders, William T., Parsons, Jeffrey R., and Santley, Robert S. 1979. *The Basin of Mexico: Ecological Processes in the Evolution of a Civilization.* New York: Academic Press.
> *An exemplary area study of highland Mesoamerican civilization that is crammed with wisdom about the study of complex societies. Also an unusually thorough archaeological study. Technical, but strongly recommended.*

CHAPTER 15

MESOPOTAMIA AND THE FIRST CITIES

• • •

I n 1872, an earnest banknote engraver turned clay tablet expert named George Smith was sorting through the dusty fragments of Assyrian King Assurbanipal's royal library in the British Museum. Suddenly, he came across a tablet bearing a reference to a large ship grounded on a mountain. Immediately, he realized he had found an account of a flood that bore a remarkable resemblance to the biblical story of the Flood in Genesis. A prophet named Hasisadra is warned of the gods' intention to destroy all of sinful humankind. He builds a large ship, loads her with his family, "the beast of the field, the animal of the field. . . ." The flood destroys "all life from the face of the earth." The ship goes aground on a mountain. Hasisadra sends out a dove, which returns. Eventually a raven is dispatched and never returns. Hasisadra releases the animals, becomes a god, and lives happily ever after.

George Smith's discovery caused a public sensation at a time when people believed in the literal historical truth of the Scriptures. Seventeen lines of the story were missing, so the London *Daily Telegraph* paid for him to go to Nineveh to find the missing fragments. Incredible although it may seem, Smith found them within five days. The tablets can be seen on display in the British Museum, duly labeled "DT"—"Daily Telegraph" (Figure 1.2).

The Victorians thought of Mesopotamia (Greek for "land between the rivers") as the location of the biblical Garden of Eden. Today, it is a far from paradisial place, for the delta regions and floodplain (Table 15.1) between the Tigris and Euphrates rivers form a hot, low-lying environment, much of it inhospitable sand, swamp, and dry mud flats. Yet this now-inhospitable region was the cradle of the world's earliest urban civilization (Lloyd, 1983; Postgate, 1993). From north to south, Mesopotamia is approximately 600 miles (965 km) long and 250 miles (402 km) wide. (Figure 15.1 shows its location.) The plains are subject to long, intensely hot summers and harsh, cold winters. There are few permanent water supplies away from the great rivers and their tributaries. However, once watered, the soils of Mesopotamia proved both fertile and potentially highly productive. The agricultural potential of the areas close to rivers and streams could be realized for the first time. By 5000 B.C. and perhaps earlier, village farmers were diverting the waters of

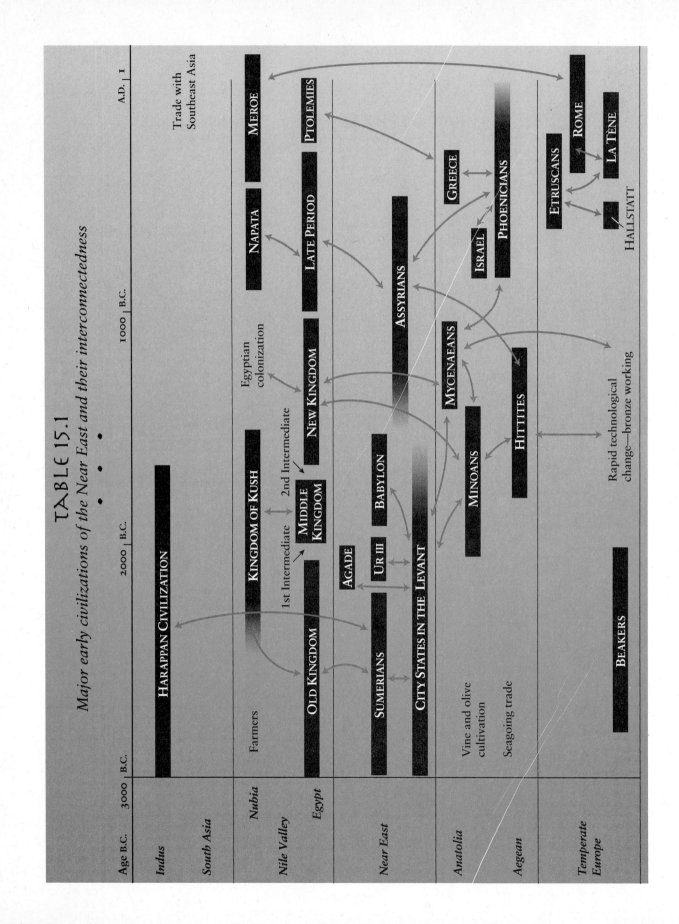

TABLE 15.1

Major early civilizations of the Near East and their interconnectedness

Age B.C.	3000 B.C.		2000 B.C.	1000 B.C.	A.D. I
Indus					
South Asia	HARAPPAN CIVILIZATION				Trade with Southeast Asia
Nile Valley *Nubia*	Farmers	KINGDOM OF KUSH		NAPATA	MEROE
Egypt	OLD KINGDOM	1st Intermediate	MIDDLE KINGDOM — 2nd Intermediate	NEW KINGDOM — LATE PERIOD — Egyptian colonization	PTOLEMIES
Near East	SUMERIANS — AGADE — UR III — BABYLON			ASSYRIANS	
	CITY STATES IN THE LEVANT			ISRAEL — PHOENICIANS	
Anatolia	Vine and olive cultivation		MINOANS — HITTITES	GREECE	
Aegean	Seagoing trade		MYCENAEANS		ROME
Temperate Europe	BEAKERS		Rapid technological change—bronze working	ETRUSCANS — HALLSTATT	LA TÈNE

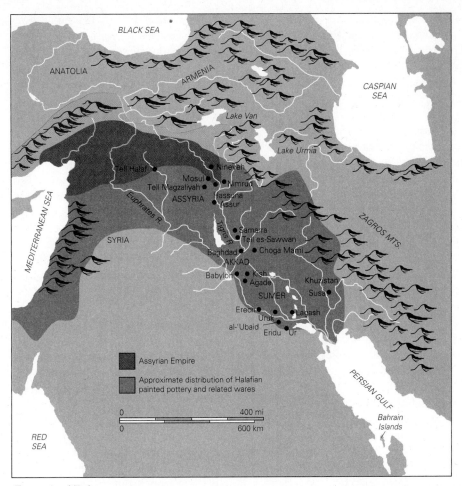

FIGURE 15.1   Sites and culture distributions mentioned in this chapter. (Tepe Yahya and Shari-i-shokhta lie to the east of the map.)

the rivers. Within 2000 years the urban civilization of the Sumerians was flourishing in Mesopotamia (Maisels, 1993).

UPLAND VILLAGES

● ● ●

With continued improvement in the effectiveness of agriculture and development of such technological innovations as pottery, the village communities of the Zagros foothills, east of Mesopotamia, achieved a more efficient subsistence base, which fed a gradually increasing farming population. These technological and economic changes were far from spectacular: By at least 6000 B.C., farmers were living on the Assyrian plains, at first in areas where they could rely on seasonal rainfall to water their crops; later they settled by the rivers, with animals and crops that could tolerate the climate of the lowlands. There they developed simple irrigation methods to bring water to their fields.

The first farmers to settle in Assyria were scattered over the undulating plains in compact village settlements like Tell Magzaliyah. The successive occupation layers of these sites are filled with handmade pottery of coarse clay painted or incised with

Hassuna
6000 B.C.

dots, circles, and other designs (Figure 15.2). Such wares—named Hassunan pottery, after Hassuna, the first village of this type excavated—are found over a wide area of the north, from the upper Tigris Valley to the plains west of the modern city of Mosul.

Samarra
5500 B.C.

The regions between Mosul in the north and Baghdad in the south were inhabited by irrigation farmers by at least 5500 B.C. We know this from discoveries of villages in the region of Samarra, on the fringes of the Mesopotamian delta. Samarran culture painted pottery (Figure 15.2), which comes from such sites as Choga Mami, reveals early farming villages situated in areas where irrigation agriculture was the only viable means of food production (Oates, 1973). The Samarran sites near Choga Mami are situated along low ridges parallel to nearby hills, where irrigation could be practiced with the least effort. Traces of canals are found at Choga Mami, as are wheat, barley, and linseed, a crop that can be grown in this area only when irrigation is used. Choga Mami itself lies between two rivers, where floodwaters could be diverted across the fields and then drained away to prevent salt buildup. This is a relatively easy form of irrigation to adopt. Presumably, later refinements in technology enabled other farming settlements to move away from naturally flooded areas into regions where more extensive irrigation was necessary. There is every indication that the Samarrans were advanced farmers who lived in substantial villages which, in the case of Choga Mami, may have covered up to 14.8 acres (6 ha) and housed more than 1000 souls.

The Samarrans occupied relatively low-lying territory between the arid delta of the south and the dry agriculture areas of the Hassunans to the north. Their newly developed irrigation techniques and heat-tolerant strains of wheat and barley enabled them to settle in areas that were hitherto inaccessible. Their sedentary and permanent settlements and great reliance on agriculture allowed them to forge community and external social and economic bonds that provided a catalyst for more complex societies to develop in future millennia.

Halafian
5500 B.C.

In about 5500 B.C., many village farmers in the Near East began to make a characteristic style of painted pottery, abandoning the monochrome wares they had made before. The new fashion spread from southwest Turkey around the shores of Lake Van, famous for its obsidian, and as far east as the Zagros Mountains. The most brilliantly painted pottery was made in northern Iraq by the inhabitants of Tell Halaf, whose enormous kilns produced bowls, dishes, and flasks adorned with elaborate, stylized patterns and representations of people and animals (Figure 15.3). The Halafian cultural tradition flourished in what had once been Hassunan territory, and the people maintained regular contact with the Samarrans to the south.

The Halafians still lived in much the same ways as their predecessors and made no startling agricultural or technological innovations. They developed new contacts between villages hundreds of miles apart, trading such commodities as obsidian, semiprecious stones, and other luxury items including painted pots with motifs that are standardized over large distances. Neutron activation and other chemical studies of pottery clays have shown that Halafian painted pots made at a so-far unidentified location were traded to settlements like Mersin and Choga Mami, about 600 miles (965 km) apart. In some areas, most of the fine pottery found in the villages of the surrounding hinterland were produced in the main settlement. It is as if production and distribution of some items favored by elite members of society were concentrated at key trade centers along water routes. In the Khabur area, the same clay studies hint that both major and minor Halafian settlements produced the goods consumed in their own hinterlands, while restricting access of nearby subordinate villages to this higher-level trade. This may be a sign that important chiefdoms had

(a)

(b)

FIGURE 15.2 Early Mesopotamian painted pottery: (a) vessels from Hassuna;
(b) Samarra-type vessels from Hassuna. An eighth full-size.

evolved among Halafian communities in the region. As with the Hopewell in North
America, these new elite groups required greater communication and the sharing of
status goods such as painted pottery to reinforce their authority (Redman, 1978).

FIGURE 15.3   Halafian vessel from Iraq.

SETTLEMENT OF THE LOWLANDS

Environmental Change

In about 15,000 B.C., during the late Ice Age, the Persian Gulf was dry land, so the Tigris and Euphrates Rivers flowed into the Gulf of Oman 500 miles (800 km) south of their present mouths. After 12,000 B.C., sea levels rose rapidly, as they did in other parts of the world, rising from about −66 feet (−20 m) in 6000 B.C. to 7 feet (2 m) above modern levels between 4000 and 3000 B.C. As sea levels rose, so river-borne alluvium filled the Gulf, building a vast delta that advanced gradually to the south, leaving freshwater lakes and marshes in its wake (Sanlaville, 1989). These thick layers of alluvium mask the archaeological record of any late Ice Age or early Holocene occupation of the lowlands. Almost certainly, however, both hunter-gatherers and farmers lived off fish and other resources in these low-lying areas for many thousands of years.

Douglas and James Kennett (1994) believe that the dramatic environmental changes at the end of the Ice Age were important factors in the development of city states in southern Mesopotamia. They hypothesize that hunter-gatherer populations in the region lived within very circumscribed territories as a result of rapid sea level rise, close to rivers and their floodplains, surrounded by arid country. As conditions became drier during the Holocene, their movements became even more limited. These major environmental changes triggered intense competition between different groups at a time of population growth. This same competition concentrated people into areas of much denser population for, among other things, defensive purposes. This development in turn stimulated technological innovation and accelerated cultural development. By 4000 B.C., sea levels had stabilized, creating much more extensive floodplains and a relatively high water table. This provided the first opportunity for floodplain agriculture and irrigation works, developments that led, in turn, to much more complex social hierarchies and to cities located strategically where fresh- and seawater met, and where trade routes connected with one another. Thus, it was no coincidence that the first cities in southern Mesopotamia formed between 3500 and 3000 B.C., soon after local sea levels stabilized.

The Kennetts' hypothesis provides a possible scenario for the emergence of civilization in southern Mesopotamia, a development that took hold somewhat earlier here than in the Nile Valley, where environmental changes were less dramatic. Unfortunately, the archaeological sites that would document the early stages of their theory are buried under deep layers of silt, for it is not until the sixth millennium B.C. that the first sites appear in the archaeological record. What, then, do we know from archaeology?

Archaeological Evidence

The first known farming communities date to around 5700 B.C., small communities located in clusters along the Euphrates channels. The largest of these clusters consisted of small rural communities located around a larger town that covered about 28 acres (10 ha) and housed perhaps between 2500 and 4000 people. The fields around these settlements were watered by small canals up to 3 miles (5 km) long. The farmers grew barley and dates and herded cattle, sheep, and goats (Wright and Pollack, 1986). These clusters of settlements are subsumed under the term 'Ubaid, after a small site of that name near Ur (Huot, 1989).

We do not know anything about how the first inhabitants of the Mesopotamian floodplain acquired or developed the skills needed to survive in their harsh environment. Interdependence among members of the community was essential because raw materials suitable for building houses had to be improvised from the plentiful sand, clay, palm trees, and reeds between the rivers. Digging even the smallest canal required at least a little political and social leadership. The annual backbreaking task of clearing silt from clogged river courses and canals can have been achieved only by communal effort. As both Robert Adams (1966) and Kent Flannery (1972) point out, the relationship between developing a stratified society and creating food surpluses is close. Distinctive social changes came from the more efficient systems for producing food that were essential in the delta. As food surpluses grew and the specialized agricultural economies of these 'Ubaid villages became successful, the trend toward sedentary settlement and higher population densities increased. Expanded trade networks and the redistribution of surpluses and trade goods also affected society, with dominant groups of 'Ubaid people becoming more active in producing surpluses, which eventually supported more and more people who were not farmers.

'Ubaid settlements display considerable variation. The earliest known community is Tell al 'Ouelli, near Larsa, which dates to before 5300 B.C. (Forest, 1986). Some of the larger settlements had substantial buildings, alleyways, and courtyards, but rural settlements like al-'Ubaid itself consisted of mud brick and reed huts with roofs formed of bent sticks (R. M. Adams, 1981; Adams and Nissen, 1972). Al-'Ubaid and similar small clusters of hamlets shared ceremonial centers and were linked by kin and clan ties, with one clan authority overseeing the villagers' affairs and, probably, the irrigation schemes that connected them. In time, the small village ceremonial centers grew, as did the one at Eridu (first settled around 4750 B.C., when the Tell Halaf peoples were still making their painted pottery in the north). Except at the very end of 'Ubaid times, there are no signs of social ranking in cemeteries or of any great differences in wealth between different individuals.

'Ubaid Period
?6000 to 3700 B.C.

Eridu consisted of a mud-brick temple with fairly substantial mud-brick houses around it, often with a rectangular floor plan. The craftsworkers lived a short distance from the elite clustered around the temple, and still farther away were the dwellings of the farmers, who grew the crops that supported everyone. By 4500 B.C., the Eridu temple had grown large, containing altars and offering places and a central room bounded by rows of smaller compartments. It has been estimated that the population of Eridu was as high as 5000 at this time, but exact computations are impossible.

4500 B.C.

URUK—THE MESOPOTAMIAN CITY

● ● ●

Uruk
3600 to 2800 B.C.

As Mesopotamian society grew in complexity, so did the need for social, political, and religious institutions that would provide an integrative function for everyone (Nissen, 1988). The ancient city of Uruk epitomizes cultural developments just before and during the early stages of Sumerian civilization (Algaze, 1989; Crawford, 1991). Archaeologically, we know most, of course, about the later stages of the city. During early Dynastic times, in about 2800 B.C., the city core covered an estimated 617 acres (250 ha), with more people living in the hinterland. Anyone approaching Uruk in those days could see the great ziggurat, the stepped temple pyramid, for miles (Figure 15.4). Built with enormous expenditure of work as a community project, the ziggurat complex and its satellite temples were the center of Uruk life. The temples were not only storehouses and places of worship but also redistribution centers for surplus food. Hundreds of craftsworkers labored for the temple as stonemasons, copper workers, weavers, and dozens of other specialized tasks. None of these people tilled the ground or worked on irrigation; they formed a distinctive class in a well-stratified society (Lloyd, 1983). In its earliest manifestations, between 3600 and 3000 B.C., Uruk was a nascent city on a much smaller scale but a settlement that was growing rapidly, many surrounding villages becoming part of the dense urban landscape. An earlier and smaller ziggurat towered over the city, which formed the core for the later monumental structure of early Dynastic times.

Even as early as 3000 B.C., the entire life of Uruk and its connections with cities, towns, merchants, and mines hundreds of miles away revolved around the temple. The ruler of Uruk and the keeper of the temple was the *en,* both the secular and religious leader. In its heyday, Uruk was far more than a city. Satellite villages extended out at least 6 miles (10 km), each with its own irrigation system, but population densities around the city were lower than they were in earlier times. All provided food for those in the city, whether grain, fish, or meat. Each settlement depended on the others for survival, at first because each provided things essential for a well-balanced existence; later they needed protection from outsiders who would have plundered their goods. The Mesopotamian city had developed an elaborate system of management with a well-defined hierarchy of rulers and priests, landowners and bureaucrats, traders and peasants. This system organized and regulated society, meted out reward and punishment, and made policy decisions for the thousands of people who lived under it.

The city was a hallmark of early Mesopotamian civilization, but each urban center had different settlement characteristics and histories. Archaeological surveys record the remarkable fact that over 80 percent of the Sumerian population lived in settlements covering at least 25 acres (10 ha), in a form of "hyperurbanism" in the

FIGURE 15.4   *Above:* Reconstruction of an Uruk temple at Eridu. Notice the great platform supporting the temple and the drainage pipes in the walls. *Below:* A photograph of the
great ziggurat (temple mound) of Ur, built in approximately 2300 B.C.

third millennium B.C., a figure that declined steadily to just over 50 percent by 2000
B.C. (Adams, 1981).

By 3400 B.C., the first signs of writing appear. One theory has it that the Sumerians' commercial transactions were so complex that the possibilities for thievery
and accounting mistakes were endless. It was impossible to keep all the details in
one's head. Many people used marked clay tokens, which they carried around on
strings. Eventually some clever officials made small clay tablets and scratched them
with incised signs that depicted familiar objects such as pots or animals (Schmandt-
Besserat, 1992). From there it was a short step to more simplified, conventionalized,
wedge-shaped (cuneiform) signs that were modeled closer and closer to phonetic

syllables and spoken language (Figure 15.5). In fact, the earliest economic texts deal with internal administrative matters, usually small numbers and inventories, not with external trade. The new script was also commonly used for compiling lists of all kinds—of occupations, places, things in the world, and so on—a common application of writing systems all over the globe, for example, as among the Mycenaeans of Greece (Chapter 19).

At first, specially trained scribes used cuneiform to record inventories and administrative and commercial transactions. Over more than 1000 years, they gradually began to explore the limitless opportunities afforded by the ability to express oneself in writing. Kings used tablets to trumpet their victories and political triumphs. Fathers chided errant sons, and lawyers recorded complicated land transactions. Sumerian poetry includes love stories, great epics, hymns to the gods, and tragic laments bemoaning the destruction of city after city (Kramer, 1963). Temple records and accounts tell us much not only of economic and social organization but also of Mesopotamian folklore and religion.

On the plateau to the north, copper tools and ornaments had been in use for centuries, first appearing as early as the fifth or sixth millennium B.C. (Hassan, 1987). Although many peasant societies were aware of the properties of native copper, and both the early Egyptians and American Indians made hammered ornaments from it, the softness of the metal limits the uses to which it can be put. Eventually, though, people familiar with the kiln firing of pottery developed techniques for smelting copper ore. Copper is fine and lustrous and makes admirable ornaments. At first, it was a high-status metal, valued for its prestige. Copper was in widespread use for ornamentation in Iran during the fourth millennium and was imported into southern Mesopotamia as early as 3500 B.C., perhaps earlier. It enjoyed high status, for utilitarian implements like stone-bladed sickles remained in use throughout the third millennium. Eventually, during the early second millennium, alloying with lead or tin came into widespread use, as metalsmiths learned how to produce bronze and other forms of tougher metal. Once alloying was understood, copper assumed a more important place in agriculture and warfare (Moorey, 1982). The later development of bronze weapons can be linked to the rise of warfare as a method of attaining political ends, for cities like Eridu and Uruk were not isolated from other centers. Indeed they were only too aware of their neighbors. The city-states of Lagash and Umma were uneasy neighbors and engaged in a tendentious border dispute that dragged on for three or four centuries (Cooper, 1983). Cities soon had walls, a sure sign that they needed protection against marauders. Earlier cylinder seals bear scenes with prisoners of war.

By this time, too, there were southern Mesopotamian "colonies" in what is now northern Iraq, at Susa across the Tigris, in the Zagros, and elsewhere on the northern and northeastern peripheries of the lowlands. Some of these colonies were entire transplanted communities; others are represented by characteristic Uruk-style artifacts far from their homelands. Artifacts and artistic styles characteristic of Uruk and also Susa have come from the Nile Delta during the centuries when long-distance caravan trade was expanding rapidly in Egypt and across the Sinai.

SUMERIAN TRADE

• • •

With the emergence of the Sumerian civilization in about 3200 B.C., we have entered a new era in human experience, one in which the economic, political, and social

Earliest pictographs (3000 B.C.)	Denotation of pictographs	Pictographs in rotated position	Cuneiform signs c. 1900 B.C.	Basic logographic values	
				Reading	Meaning
	Head and body of man			lu	Man
	Head with mouth indicated			ka	Mouth
	Bowl of food			ninda	Food, bread
	Mouth + food			kú	To eat
	Stream of water			a	Water
	Mouth + water			nag	To drink
	Fish			kua	Fish
	Bird			mušen	Bird
	Head of an ass			anše	Ass
	Ear of barley				še	Barley

FIGURE 15.5 Development of Sumerian writing, from a pictographic script to a cuneiform script and then to a phonetic system. The word *cuneiform* is derived from the Latin word *cuneus,* meaning "a wedge," after the characteristic impression of the script.

mechanisms created by humans begin to affect the lives of cities, towns, and villages located hundreds, if not thousands, of miles apart. No human society created by *Homo sapiens sapiens* has ever flourished in complete isolation, and as we saw in Chapter 5, regular interaction and exchange between neighboring hunter-gatherer groups assumed ever-greater importance in the late Ice Age and early Holocene. In the Near East, after 8000 B.C., long-distance exchanges in such vital commodities as obsidian, to say nothing of luxury goods like seashells, reached considerable proportions and extended over much of Anatolia and the Levant and even farther afield (Algaze, 1993). The real launching point in long-distance exchange and organized trade took place during the fourth millennium B.C., the first millennium in prehistory when the history of an individual society can only be understood against a background of much broader regional developments. In a real sense, a rapidly evolving "world system" linked hundreds of Near Eastern societies all the way from eastern Iran and the Indus Valley in Pakistan to Mesopotamia, the Levant, Anatolia, and the Nile Valley with ever-changing cultural tentacles. In the third millennium B.C. this system not only embraced the Near East but also extended to Cyprus, the Aegean, and mainland Greece.

This nascent world system developed as a result of insatiable demands for non-local raw materials in different ecological regions where societies were developing along very similar general evolutionary tracks toward greater complexity. The broad, and apparently linear, cultural sequence in southern Mesopotamia just described can be matched by equivalent developments in northern Mesopotamia and east of the Tigris. In each area, these developments and many technological innovations were triggered not only by basic economic needs but also by the competitive instincts of newly urbanized elites, who used lavish display and exotic luxuries to reaffirm their social prestige and authority.

Sumerian civilization is a mirror of this developing regional interdependence. The Sumerians lived in a treeless, lowland environment with fertile soils but no metal, little timber, and no semiprecious stones. They obtained these commodities by trading with areas where such items were in abundance, perhaps initially on a village-by-village basis and later in far more organized fashions. Much of this trade was in the hands of temple organizations, for the temples served as centralized storehouses, and many luxury goods were used to embellish public buildings. Trading was an integral part of Sumerian life, a multifaceted activity absorbing the energies of many people. Food and many basic commodities were redistributed by different institutions for specific purposes. For example, temples would distribute food rations to those who labored for them. Petty officials were allocated land for their services. Raw materials were obtained from the highlands and the Iranian Plateau to the east for the manufacture of weapons, ornaments, and prestigious luxuries.

The increased tempo of interregional exchange is reflected in increased wealth in archaeological sites both within Sumer and outside its boundaries. Metal tools became much more common, and domestic tools as well as weapons proliferated Metallurgy benefited from important technological innovations carried along trade routes, among them the development of alloying copper with tin to make bronze. This produced tougher-edged, more durable artifacts that could be used for more arduous, day-to-day tasks. One resulting innovation was the metal- and wood-tipped plow, an implement dragged by oxen that was capable of digging a far deeper furrow than the simple hoes and digging sticks of earlier times. The plow, which incidentally was never developed in the Americas, was developed as irrigation agriculture assumed greater importance in Sumer, and the combined innovations increased agricultural yields dramatically. These yields not only supported larger urban and rural populations but also provided a means for the rulers of city-states both in Sumer and farther afield to exercise more control over food surpluses and over the wealth obtained by long-distance exchange. Soon, Sumerian rulers became more despotic, controlling their subjects by military strength, religious acumen, and economic incentive (Crawford, 1991).

Lowland Mesopotamia lacked the mineral and stone resources that were plentiful in distant, more highland environments in Anatolia to the northwest and on the Iranian Plateau to the east. By the same token, the Sumerians controlled not only large surpluses of grain that could be moved in ships but also a flourishing industry in textiles and other luxuries. Demand rose steadily for raw materials, which arrived in Sumerian cities along southern Mesopotamian waterways, especially up the placid Euphrates, easily navigable for long distances. This great river transmitted raw materials from the north and trade goods from the Persian Gulf to the Mediterranean. From the rivers and cities, intricate, centuries-old exchange networks and sometimes formal caravan routes carried metals, timber, skins, ivory, and precious stones over enormous distances and often rugged terrain. Even as early as Sumerian times, caravans of pack animals (in later times, often black asses) joined Anatolia to the Euphrates, the Levant to Mesopotamia, and Mesopotamia to isolated towns on the Iranian Plateau. An intricate and ever-changing system of political alliances and individual obligations of friendship linked community with community and city-state with city-state. In time, financial and logistical checks and balances were maintained by an administrative system based in the temples to bring order to what had begun as informal bartering. Specialized merchants began to handle such commodites as copper and lapis lazuli. There was wholesaling and contracting, loans were floated, and individual profit was a prime motivation. Increasingly, every city-state, and indeed entire civilizations, came to depend on what we have called a nascent world system, not so much for political stability but for survival. Reliable, long-term interdependency became a vital factor in the history of Near Eastern states by 3000 B.C. (Algaze, 1993; Edens, 1992).

EXCHANGE ON THE IRANIAN PLATEAU

● ● ●

The rise of urbanization in Sumer was by no means a unique phenomenon, for cities came into being upstream of the lowlands by 3500 B.C. in areas where only dry farming was possible (Weiss, 1986). Cultural developments remarkably parallel to those in Sumer unfolded in the area between the Zagros foothills and the Tigris and Euphrates (Lamberg-Karlovsky, 1978; Wright and Johnson, 1978). These developments did not occur in isolation, for even as early as 3000 B.C. there was regular interaction between the two regions.

3500 B.C.

During the sixth and early fifth millennia B.C., small farming villages flourished in the heart of Khuzistan. The people were irrigation farmers who herded goats, sheep, and cattle as well. So many of their sites are known that it seems certain that areas such as the Deh Luran Plain were intensively settled by this time. During the next thousand years or so, Khuzistan was still densely populated, and village settlements grew larger and larger. It was about this time that the famous archaeological site of Susa began to achieve special prominence.

6000 B.C.

The earliest occupation levels at Susa are broadly contemporary with the late 'Ubaid occupation of Mesopotamia. The first village on the site was 61.7 to 74.0 acres (25 to 30 ha) in area and was inhabited by metal-using farmers. Strong Mesopotamian influence can be detected in slightly later levels at Susa, as if there was at least some colonization of Khuzistan by Uruk people from the delta toward the end of the fourth millennium B.C.

Susa

**Proto-Elamites
3200 B.C.**

By 3200 B.C., a distinctive cultural tradition known as the *Proto-Elamite* (Elamite is a language) appeared at Susa and elsewhere in Khuzistan. The Proto-Elamite state seems to have evolved in what is now southwest Iran, but within a short time its distinctive tablets, seals, and ceramic types came to be found in widely scattered sites on the Iranian highlands. Their clay tablets have turned up in settlements in every corner of the Iranian Plateau, in central Iran, and on the borders of Afghanistan. Susa itself grew into a great city, where the trade routes between Mesopotamia and the east converged. The Elamite state emerged in all its complexity after 3000 B.C. and came under the rule of Akkadian kings from central Mesopotamia for a while, but by 2000 B.C. the Elamites were strong enough to attack and destroy Ur in Sumer. The Elamites' power and importance depended on their geographic position at the center of a network of trade routes that led to the Iranian Plateau, to the Persian Gulf, and to most city-states in the lowlands.

**Elamites
3000 B.C.**

From as early as 5000 B.C., raw materials from the Iranian Plateau were traded to the lowlands. As the volume of the plateau trade increased, Susa was in an increasingly strategic position to control access routes. Proto-Elamite developments at Susa followed on the Uruk episode at the site and can be seen as a local response to the Uruk domination of lowland Khuzistan, even if the same administrative devices such as writing and cylinder seals were retained in local forms.

On the resource-rich Iranian Plateau, long-distance exchange joined widely separated communities in what has been called an "interaction sphere," which linked most of the southern part of the region for many centuries. These long-lived networks are little studied but may have linked major centers near key sources of such commodities as lapis lazuli, turquoise, chlorite, and other materials. Each center became a locus for the manufacture and exchange of prestigious objects made of these commodities, maintaining contacts with remote areas such as Sumer and Elam.

**Tepe Yahya
3400 to 3200 B.C.**

One such center was Tepe Yahya, which was a prosperous rural community between 3400 and 3200 B.C. (Lamberg-Karlovsky, 1973, 1978). The inhabitants exploited local sources of chlorite (steatite). After 3200 B.C., Tepe Yahya grew and was engaged in much more intensive trading activities. Eventually, it became an important political and administrative center that manufactured and traded carved chlorite bowls. The bowls produced at Tepe Yahya and elsewhere were definitely luxury items, so highly prized in Mesopotamia that they may have caused keen competition among those rich enough to afford them (Kohl, 1975). Chlorite tools and ornaments were so popular that they occur over a very wide area of the Iranian Plateau as well as on islands in the Persian Gulf and at Mohenjo-daro, one of the major cities of the Harappan civilization of the Indus Valley (Chapter 17).

The plateau trading networks also extended to the important settlement of Shari-i-Shokhta, which stood by the shores of Lake Helmand south of the Hindu Kush in east Iran. An extensive trade in turquoise and lapis lazuli flourished there after 2800 B.C. The lapis came from the distant Hindu Kush embedded in limestone. Shari-i-Shokhta's artisans chipped away the limestone and turned the semiprecious stone into beads. The beads and lumps of raw lapis were then traded across the desert to Mesopotamia and also north into southern Turkmenia, probably in exchange for textiles (Tosi, 1983).

The plateau trade handled the work of local artisans but was ultimately founded on the movement of a number of vital, staple commodities, among them textiles and timber (Possehl, 1986). The nature of this trade is the subject of some controversy. Some scholars believe that the commerce was based on markets and in the hands of traders controlled by Sumer and Elam, who could affect the trade by simple application of the laws of supply and demand (Kohl, 1978). Another viewpoint suggests that the trade itself may have been in the hands of entrepreneurs, but the areas of high demand for its products were both local and at a distance in Mesopotamia and Elam. Although some of the commodities found on the Iranian Plateau may have been transported in large quantities, much exchange proceeded in more informal ways, through occasional purchases, gift exchanges, tribute, booty-taking, and individual initiative. It was not until the third millennium that much larger-scale, highly organized trade became the rule rather than the exception. The Iranian Plateau trade may have developed as an indigenous exchange system, which later spilled over to the west in response to demands from the lowlands. However, this latter trade was a question of people getting what they could get rather than a high degree of organization. In other words, supplies were irregular rather than predictable, in sharp contrast to the much more highly organized regional trade organizations that evolved after 2000 B.C. (Possehl, 1986).

Whatever the mechanisms of the Iranian trade, it is clear that an extensive network of interdependence was linking widely separated city-states and polities all over the Near East by 2500 B.C. This network of interdependence and interaction was highly flexible but continued to develop over many centuries, as different city-states and larger states vied with one another to control and administer ever-larger kingdoms.

THE WIDENING OF POLITICAL AUTHORITY

● ● ●

By 2800 B.C., Mesopotamia held several important city-states, each headed by rulers who vied with the others for status and prestige. The Sumerians were in contact with other states and urban centers in northern Mesopotamia and across the rivers in Elam and farther afield to the east. They maintained regular contacts with Anatolia, the Levant, and sporadically with the Nile Valley. Political authority was still most effective at the city level, with temple priests as the primary controllers of trade, economic life, and political matters. Inevitably, as society became more complex, so city rulers became more secular. At the same time, the volume of long-distance trade rose dramatically, to the point, some experts believe, that Sumerian rulers made a conscious decision to develop a formal maritime trade through the Persian Gulf with areas to the east such as the Indus Valley (Possehl, 1986) (Chapter 17).

In political terms, the population shifts of the third millennium B.C. may also reflect a much greater concern with defense, for both Sumerian tablets and the archaeological record tell of warfare and constant bickering between neighbors. Competition over natural resources intensified as each state raised an army to defend its water rights, trade routes, and city walls. The onerous tasks of defense and military organization passed to despotic secular kings supposedly appointed by the gods. As the wealth and power of the cities increased, so did internecine strife. Such states as Erech, Kish, and Ur had periods of political strength and prosperity when they dominated their neighbors. Then, just as swiftly, the tide of their fortunes would change and they would sink into obscurity. There was a constant threat from nomadic peoples of the surrounding mountains and deserts, who encroached constantly on settled Sumerian lands. At times, they disrupted city life so completely that any form of travel became an impossibility.

Some Sumerian cities nurtured powerful and wealthy leaders. When Sir Leonard Woolley (1934) excavated a royal cemetery in Ur (Figure 15.6), he found a series of kings and queens who had been buried in huge graves with their entire retinue of followers. One tomb contained the remains of 59 people who were poisoned to accompany the king, even courtiers and soldiers as well as serving women. Each wore his or her official dress and insignia and had lain down to die in the correct order of precedence, having taken poison.

Inevitably, the ambitions of some of these powerful and proud Sumerian rulers led them to entertain bolder visions than merely the control of a few city-states in the lowlands (Postgate, 1992). They were well aware that they lived in a wider world of prosperous and not-so-prosperous neighbors, in a world in which control of lucrative sources of raw materials and trade routes was the secret of vast political power. The first recorded success at such an endeavor was that of Lugalzagesi (c. 2360–2335 B.C.). Not content with the control of Uruk, Ur, Lagash, and several other cities, he boasted of overseeing the entire area from the Persian Gulf to the Mediterranean. The god Enlil, king of the lands, "made the people lie down in peaceful pastures like cattle and supplied Sumer with water bringing joyful abundance" (Kramer, 1963). Lugalzagesi's boasts must be taken with a large pinch of historical salt and must be judged not in terms of conquering armies but in the context of a nascent world system of interaction and trading, which carried Sumerian political and religious ideas as far as the shores of the Mediterranean. The tenuous and sometimes more regular contacts maintained by Mesopotamia with dozens of city-states in Anatolia and the Levant foreshadow the constant political and economic rivalry that was to dominate Near Eastern history during the second millennium B.C., rivalry over control of the Levant. Here two oceans and three continents meet. The Levant had no natural harbors, so the control of its overland routes was the key to dominating a vast area of the known world, resource-rich Anatolia and grain-rich Egypt. As we shall see in Chapter 19, the history of this region was bound inextricably to the fortunes of the larger powers that surrounded it.

Lugalzagesi 2360 to 2335 B.C.

AKKADIANS AND ASSYRIANS

● ● ●

While Sumerian civilization prospered, urban centers waxed and waned in neighboring areas. In these regions, too, lived rulers with wider ambitions, who had a vision of a larger role. By 2500 B.C., Akkadian cities to the north of Sumer were competing with lowland cities for trade and prestige. Approximately 2370 B.C., a Semitic-speaking leader, Sargon, founded a ruling dynasty at the town of Agade, south of Babylon. By skillful commercial ventures and judicious military campaigns, his northern dynasty soon established its rule over a much larger kingdom that included both Sumer and northern Mesopotamia. After a short period of economic prosperity, northern Mesopotamia went through a catastrophic drought that lasted some 300 years. Starving farmers thronged to the rich southern cities. Violent clashes ensued and the Akkadian kingdom collapsed. Fifty years of political instability ensued before the powerful III Dynasty kings of Ur took control of Sumer and Akkad and created an empire that extended far to the north. Sargon had forged an

Sargon 2370 B.C.

2317 to 2191 B.C.

FIGURE 15.6   A famous ornament from the Royal Cemetery at Ur, titled *Ram in the Thicket*. The wood figure was covered with gold leaf and lapis lazuli, the belly in silver leaf, and the fleece in shell.

empire by military conquest but had never followed up his victories with proper administrative governance. The kings of Ur were a new breed of ruler, who placed great emphasis on consolidating their new empire into a powerful and well-organized bureaucracy. We know much of this kingdom from thousands of administrative tablets from III Dynasty levels at Ur (Steinkeller, 1989). With the Akkadian and Ur empires was forged a persistent tradition of Mesopotamian civilization—the combination of trade, conquest, ruthless administration, and tribute to forge large, poorly integrated, and highly volatile empires that sought to rule an enormous territory between the Mediterranean and the Persian Gulf.

Babylon

Hammurabi 1792 B.C.

Ur in turn gave way to Babylon and its Semitic rulers by 1990 B.C. Babylon's early greatness culminated in the reign of the great king Hammurabi in 1792 B.C. He integrated the smaller kingdoms of Mesopotamia for a short period, but his empire declined after his death as Babylonian trade to the Persian Gulf collapsed and trade ties to Assur in the north and for Mediterranean copper in the west were strengthened.

The Assyrians

By this time, the various masters of Mesopotamia were major players in a much wider eastern Mediterranean world (Chapter 19). They vied with the Hittites of Anatolia, with Mitanni on the Euphrates, and with the Egyptians for control of the Levant. Perhaps the most successful of them were the Assyrians, who rose to prominence in the mid-fourteenth-century B.C. as Babylon declined.

Assur on the Tigris had been a major force in Near Eastern trade since Sumerian times (Postgate, 1992). The merchants of Assur traded far to the east and west and controlled the trade down the Tigris to Babylon and beyond. The city came into great prominence during the reign of King Assur-uballit (1365–1330 B.C.). He created a great state through ruthless and efficient conquest and political maneuvering that maintained diplomatic relations with the pharaohs of Egypt, with the Hittite and Mitanni kingdoms of Anatolia (Chapter 19), and with Babylonia. His power was based on control of trade routes and the rich cereal-growing lands of northern Iraq, as well as on military prowess. His armies swept everything before them and occupied Babylonia for a while. The empire collapsed soon after the king's death.

Assyrian Empire c. 1350 to 612 B.C.

A second imperial expansion occurred in the ninth century B.C. under Assyrian monarchs based in northern Iraq, who expanded their domains with annual campaigns of military conquest. These were absolute despots, vain and grandiloquent men, who boasted of their conquests on their palace walls. When King Assurnasirpal completed his palace at Nimrud he threw a party for the 16,000 inhabitants of the city, 1500 royal officials, "47,074 men and women from the length of my country," and 5000 foreign envoys (Postgate, 1993). The king fed this throng of more than 69,000 people for ten days, during which time his guests ate 14,000 sheep and consumed more than 10,000 skins of wine. Following a succession crisis, the Assyrian Empire collapsed but was revived in a more bureaucratically efficient form by King Tiglathpileser III. The last of the great Assyrian kings was Assurbanipal, who died in approximately 630 B.C. When he died, the Assyrian Empire entered a period of political chaos. The Babylonians achieved independence, and Assyrian power finally was broken in 612 B.C., when Nineveh was sacked by the Persians and Babylonians. For 43 years, the mighty King Nebuchadnezzar of Babylon ruled over Mesopotamia and turned his capital into one of the showpieces of the ancient world. His double-walled city was adorned by magnificent mud-brick palaces with elaborate hanging gardens, a great processional way, and a huge ziggurat. It was to Babylon that a large contingent of Jews were taken as captives after Nebuchadnezzar's armies sacked Jerusalem, an exile immortalized by the lament "By the waters of Babylon we sat down and wept" (Psalm 137:1).

The Babylonian Empire did not long survive the death of Nebuchadnezzar in 556 B.C. His successors were weak men who were unable to resist the external forces that now pressed on Mesopotamia. The armies of Cyrus the Great of Persia took Babylon virtually without resistance in 539 B.C., and Mesopotamia became part of an empire even larger than that of the Assyrians. By this time, the effects of constant political instability and bad agricultural management were beginning to make themselves felt. The Mesopotamian delta was a totally artificial environment by 2000 B.C., and poor drainage and badly maintained irrigation works in later centuries led to inexorable rises in the salt content of the soil and to drastic falls in crop yields in some areas. Nothing could be done to reverse this trend until modern soil science and irrigation techniques could be imported to the delta at vast expense.

Cyrus
539 B.C.

CHAPTER SUMMARY

By 6000 B.C. highland peoples settled in northern Mesopotamia in areas where agriculture was possible through the use of seasonal rainfall. These Hassuna people lived in close contact with other societies downstream that developed irrigation agriculture. Then, in about 5500 B.C., Halafian painted wares appeared over a wide area of upland northern Mesopotamia and Anatolia; they are thought to have coincided with the emergence of chiefdoms in this area. The delta lowlands may have supported farmers before 6000 B.C., but the first traces of them appear in the 'Ubaid culture of the sixth millennium. They practiced small-scale irrigation and lived in groups of communities linked by trade networks. In time, some, like Eridu, became ceremonial centers and towns. A rapid evolution to urban life ensued—marked by fast population growth, congregation of people in small cities, and development of long-distance trade. This new urban society was organized in distinctive, stratified social classes. Copper metallurgy developed at about the same time on the highlands and soon came into widespread use.

By 2900 B.C., Sumerian civilization was in full swing. As such, it did not flourish in isolation, for it was part of what we call a "nascent world system," which linked polities as far afield as the Iranian Plateau and the Indus in the east with the Mediterranean and the Nile Valley in the west. Mesopotamia never achieved political unification under the Sumerians. Rather, dozens of city-states vied for political and economic supremacy and competed with other societies in northern Mesopotamia and close to the Zagros Mountains. Sumerian civilization flourished until about 2000 B.C., when it was eclipsed by Akkadian and then Babylonian power. In the late second millennium B.C., the city of Assur in the north nurtured the Assyrian Empire, which was extended by vigorous and despotic kings during the first half of the succeeding millennium. The Assyrian Empire at one time stretched from the Mediterranean to the Persian Gulf. The Assyrian Empire fell in 612 B.C., and the power vacuum was filled by the Babylonians under the rule of Nebuchadnezzar. Babylon fell to Cyrus of Persia in 539 B.C., and Mesopotamia became part of the Persian Empire.

Guide to Further Reading

Crawford, Harriet. 1991. *Sumer and the Sumerians*. Cambridge, Eng.: Cambridge University Press.

> *An up-to-date summary of Sumerian civilization from a multidisciplinary perspective. Read in conjunction with Kramer (1963).*

Kramer, Samuel. 1963. *The Sumerians*. Chicago: University of Chicago Press.

> *The classic account of Sumerian civilization, written by one of the foremost experts on Sumerian cuneiform tablets and literature. A model of what such books should be.*

Lloyd, Seton. 1983. *The Archaeology of Mesopotamia*, 2nd ed. 1983. London: Thames and Hudson.

> *A synthesis of Iraqi archaeology that concentrates mainly on the early civilizations. Strong on archaeological data, well illustrated, and informative on architecture.*

Nissen, Hans J. 1988. *The Early History of the Ancient Near East, 9000 to 2000 B.C.* Chicago: University of Chicago Press.

> *An up-to-date, useful introduction to Mesopotamian history and archaeology for beginning students.*

Postgate, Nicholas. 1993. *Early Mesopotamia: Economy and Society at the Dawn of History*. London: Kegan Paul.

> *Postgate gives us an authoritative, articulate summary of early Mesopotamian civilization. Amplifies the issues discussed in this chapter.*

CHAPTER

16 ANCIENT EGYPT, NUBIA, AND SUB-SAHARAN AFRICA

• • •

N early overcome, I . . . contrived to sit; but when my weight bore on the body of an Egyptian, it crushed it like a band-box . . . I sank altogether among the broken mummies, with a crash of bones, rags, and wooden cases, which raised such a dust as kept me motionless for a quarter of an hour, waiting till it subsided again." Thus did the notorious Giovanni Belzoni, circus performer turned tomb robber, explore ancient Egypt in 1817. Belzoni and his ilk thought nothing of using gunpowder, even of going after rivals with a gun, for everyone was out for spectacular finds and all the loot they could gather. Yet the modern science of Egyptology sprang from these adventurous roots. Belzoni was followed by a gentler breed of patient scientists and hieroglyph experts, who have spent more than a century piecing together the portrait of ancient Egyptian civilization we enjoy today (Fagan, 1992). We must now examine this most remarkable of early civilizations.

By 3600 B.C., the average Egyptian probably lived much as Upper Nile villagers do today (Wenke, 1991b) (Table 16.1). Wheat and barley were cultivated in riverside gardens and supplemented by intensive gathering of wild vegetable foods. Cattle, goats, sheep, and pigs were herded. The meat from the herds was supplemented by the rich Nile game population and by fishing. The human population of the valley was growing slowly, and there was some cultural fusion and increased interaction between more closely spaced settlements along the river, a natural highway for hundreds of miles. Pottery was still being made, but elegant stone vessels in alabaster and basalt also were used, probably shaped by specialist craftsworkers and traded widely throughout the valley. A gradual enrichment of pre-Dynastic culture can be discerned over the centuries, resulting in part from the introduction of coppersmithing from Asia. Soon metalworkers were making pins, flat axes, and daggers of the new material. The Egyptians now imported copper from Sinai, and lead and silver came from Asia. The proportion of luxury goods to functional goods rose steadily; one of the locally manufactured items was *faience*, a form of glass widely traded in prehistoric times. Nile settlements slowly became larger, and social structure became more elaborate (Figure 16.1).

TABLE 16.1

The web of interconnectedness: Relationships between Asia, Africa, and other regions after 500 B.C.

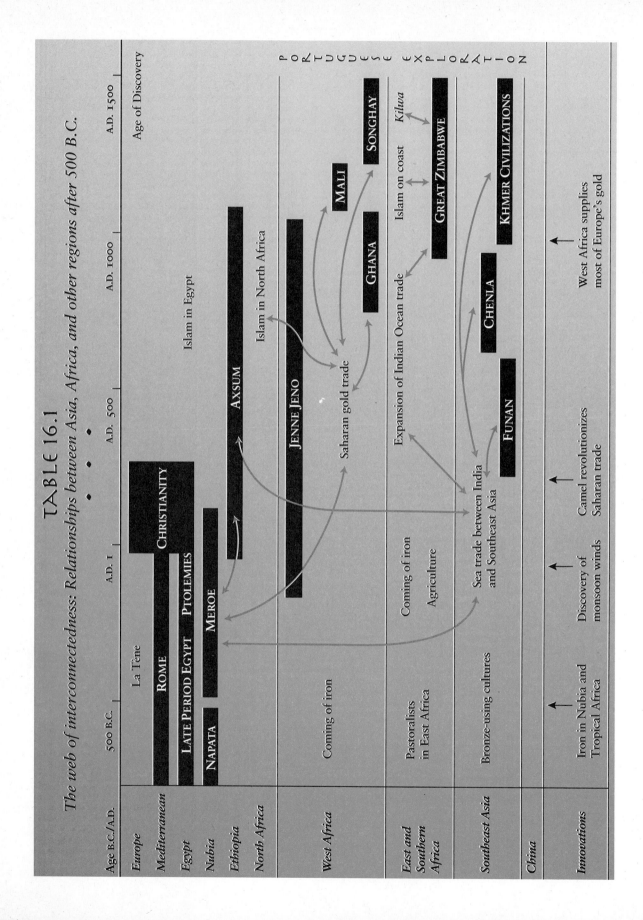

Age B.C./A.D.	500 B.C.	A.D. I	A.D. 500	A.D. 1000	A.D. 1500
Europe	La Tène				Age of Discovery
Mediterranean	ROME				
Egypt	LATE PERIOD EGYPT PTOLEMIES		Islam in Egypt		
Nubia	NAPATA MEROE				
Ethiopia		CHRISTIANITY AXSUM			
North Africa			Islam in North Africa		
West Africa	Coming of iron	JENNE JENO	Saharan gold trade	GHANA MALI GHANA	SONGHAY
East and Southern Africa	Pastoralists in East Africa	Coming of iron Agriculture	Expansion of Indian Ocean trade	Islam on coast GREAT ZIMBABWE	Kilwa
Southeast Asia	Bronze-using cultures	Sea trade between India and Southeast Asia	FUNAN	CHENLA KHMER CIVILIZATIONS	
China					
Innovations	Iron in Nubia and Tropical Africa	Discovery of monsoon winds	Camel revolutionizes Saharan trade	West Africa supplies most of Europe's gold	

PORTUGUESE EXPLORATION

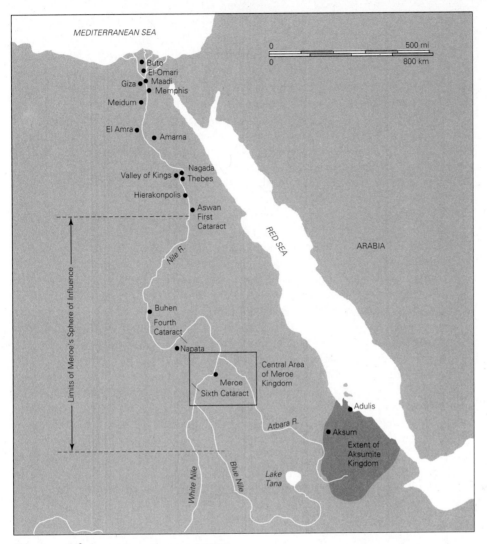

FIGURE 16.1   Ancient Egypt and Nubia.

EL-OMARI AND MAADI: TRADE ON THE NILE

• • •

There are signs to show that the earlier barter networks that linked Nile communities may have given way by about 3200 B.C. to more formalized trade (Hassan, 1988). This change was linked with not only increasing craft specialization but also major social and political changes in the valley. At the El-Omari sites near Helwan in the Nile Delta, one location contains more than 100 dwellings, as well as the burial of a chief or ruler holding a well-made wooden staff or scepter. This remarkable object, pointed at one end and flat at the other, foreshadows the ceremonial staffs carried by later Egyptian pharaohs and gods. There are many imports in the El-Omari settlements, among them seashells, ostrich eggshells, mother of pearl, and necklaces and pendants fabricated from Red Sea gastropods.

In contrast to simpler burials of earlier centuries, the El-Omari dead were buried in cemeteries outside the settlement, the body wrapped in a mat or coarse

El-Omari
3200 B.C.

fabric and placed on its left side, facing south. One cemetery associated with a small village contained the burials of higher-status individuals, graves covered with stone mounds. Interestingly, the village contained many cellarlike storage areas that held large numbers of stone tools and roughs for such implements as knife blades and arrowheads. The settlement may have belonged to traders, who apparently maintained contacts with the Levant (Rizkana and Seeher, 1985).

Maadi
3650 B.C.

The Maadi site on the outskirts of Cairo was an important trading center in about 3650 B.C., a place with large, roofed oval or rectangular cellars up to 13 feet (4 m) long and 3 to 7 feet (1 to 2.1 m) deep. They contained jars, grains, animal and fish bones, stone vases, beads, and lumps of imported asphalt. Rows of large clay storage pots held grain, cooked meat, dried fish, flint tools, spindle whorls, and other objects. Maadi was an important link in a major trade network that brought commodities from the Levant and perhaps even from Mesopotamia to the Nile, probably by donkey caravan (Caneva et al., 1987). The port of Buto in the Delta may have served as a terminus for ships carrying commodities from the Levant, already a meeting point for trade routes from distant Mesopotamia (Wenke, 1991b).

At this time, many Egyptians still lived in dispersed settlements, with the occasional larger community housing up to 2500 people. Only a few of these small towns were of more than local importance, and then only for their sacred shrines and important deities. These settlements probably contained many farmers as well as nonfood producers, for the configuration of the narrow floodplain probably inhibited the formation of large cities. By about 3600 B.C., a network of larger, sedentary settlements, with a subsistence based firmly on cereal agriculture and more formal trade networks, were the foundation for the rise of a powerful elite and a funerary cult that was an integral part of a symbolic transformation at the center of Egyptian kingship (Hassan, 1988). The elite lived in great splendor and were buried with an elaborate panoply of worldly goods, which served to legitimize their authority.

WRITING

• • •

The increased volume of trade during late pre-Dynastic times is reflected in the importation of not only copper but also other exotic items that occur in profusion in sites of about 3500 B.C. Some of these objects are of unmistakable west Asian or Mesopotamian origin. The Nagada site, for example, yielded a cylinder seal of Mesopotamian form. Some pots bear depictions of Mesopotamian boat designs and of fabulous animals and creatures with intertwined necks and other motifs that derive from Asia.

Writing

The same trade brought another innovation: the art of writing, which became fully developed in Egypt. Hieroglyphs (Greek for "sacred carving") are commonly thought to be a form of picture writing. In fact they constitute a combination of pictographic (picture) and phonetic (representing vocal sounds) script, which was not only written on papyrus but also carved on public buildings or painted on clay or wood. It seems likely that writing was first developed in Mesopotamia and that Egyptian priests developed their own script, which was easier to produce with papyrus reed paper and ink rather than on clay. Doubtless, early hieroglyphs played an important role in trade and record keeping, but they may also have evolved as a way of conveying the meanings of funerary rituals on painted pots deposited with the dead (Hassan, 1988).

Ultimately, Egyptian scribes developed a cursive (running-on) hieroglyphic script that was a form of handwriting and was much easier to use on documents and other, less formal communications. Only the consonants were written in all forms of hieroglyphs; the vowel sounds were omitted, although both were pronounced. With practice, reading this form of script is easy enough, and a smpl tst 'f ths srt shld shw ths qt wll (Figure 16.2) (Diringer, 1962; Pope, 1973).

UNIFICATION AND THE RISE OF THE EGYPTIAN STATE

● ● ●

The acquisition of writing, with all its organizational possibilities, was one of the catalysts for the unification of all Egypt into a single political entity. This moment of unification cannot be pinned to a precise date. As we saw in Chapter 14, many causes contributed to the rise of state-organized societies. Fekri Hassan (1988) hypothesizes that the social ecology of Nile agriculture played an important role in the initial stages of the process. Neighboring communities pooled their efforts to minimize the effects of catastrophic fluctuations in the annual Nile flood. In time, local chiefs emerged as key players in these cooperative ventures. As the economic unit grew larger over the generations, regional political structures came into being. These leaders sought to legitimize their positions with fine possessions and elaborate funerary rites. Unification was the culmination of local social and political developments that resulted from centuries of gradual change in economic and social life. Pre-Dynastic villages were autonomous units, each with its local deities. During the fourth millennium B.C., the more important villages became the focal points of different territories, which in Dynastic times became the *nomes,* or provinces, through which the pharaohs administered Egypt. The nomarchs (provincial leaders) were responsible for the gradual coalescence of Egypt into larger political and social units. Their deeds are recorded on ceremonial palettes that were used for moistening eye powder. Some of these palettes show alliances of local leaders dismantling conquered villages. Others commemorate the administrative skills of leaders who brought their villages through drought years by skillful management. The unification of Egypt was a gradual process of both voluntary and involuntary amalgamation. Voluntary unification resulted from common needs and economic advantage.

Hieroglyphs				
Cursive hand (hieratic script)				
Shorthand				
Translation	Amon	rŏemt mankind	per-'o Pharaoh	hru day

FIGURE 16.2 Egyptian writing is referred to as hieroglyphs, the familiar symbols that appear in formal inscriptions and on tomb walls. In fact, Egyptian scribes developed cursive hands used in everyday life. These examples show formal hieroglyphic script (*top line*) and below it both the cursive script and the scribe's shorthand, which was used for rapid writing.

Perhaps it was only in the final stages of unification that military force came into play to bring larger and larger political units under single rulers (Hoffman, 1979).

Nekhen

There is little archaeological evidence that documents the long process of unification. Michael Hoffman and a team of Egyptologists (1982) have investigated ancient Nekhen, a city called Hierakonpolis, "City of the Falcon," by the Greeks. Pre-Dynastic settlements and cemeteries surround the town. In 3800 B.C., Nekhen was a village inhabited by a few hundred people. During the next three centuries the population mushroomed to perhaps as many as 10,500. People lived in closely clustered mud-brick and plaster dwellings, the more important artisans and traders in larger houses with separate compounds. For the first time, there are signs of social differentiation in Egyptian society. The Abu Suffian cemetery near Nekhen housed important citizens, many of them prosperous traders who had profited from locally made, fine-quality "Plum Red" pottery, which was used to adorn tombs up and down the river. These people became powerful members of the community, with widespread contacts with settlements near and far.

3500 B.C.

About 3500 B.C., the fragile ecological balance of desert and grassland collapsed, perhaps as a result of overgrazing by goats and sheep and intensive pottery firing by local artisans. Hoffman believes that some of the local leaders profited from the disaster by using their wealth to foster irrigation agriculture and settlement closer to the Nile. Their venture was successful and yielded large grain surpluses under the control of the new elite. They used their wealth to increase trade, erect public buildings like temples, and invest in imposing sepulchers. The ambitious leaders of Nekhen were buried in the same Abu Suffian cemetery, which straddled a dry gulch, their graves laid out on either side of the wadi in what Hoffman believes is a symbolic map of a unified Upper and Lower Egypt.

2900 B.C.

Egypt was finally unified under the pharaoh Narmer at Hierakonpolis in about 2900 B.C. In economic terms, the unification may have involved some intensification of agriculture as population densities rose; but as Karl Butzer (1976) has pointed out, the technology for lifting water was so rudimentary that the early rulers of Egypt were unable to organize any elaborate forms of irrigation. In all probability, most ancient Egyptian agriculture involved irrigation schemes on a modest scale that merely extended the distribution of seasonal floodwaters from natural flood basins. Still, even these efforts must have required a considerable degree of administrative organization. Also, with a centralized form of administration, the divine leader, the pharaoh himself, was responsible for the success of the harvest. Since the Nile flood fluctuated considerably in cycles of abundant and lean years, and the pharaohs could do little to control the success or failure of irrigation without much more elaborate technology than they possessed, their political position could, theoretically at any rate, be threatened by famine years. If the divine leader could not provide, who could? Perhaps a different leader. Small wonder that some periods of political instability, which may have coincided with poor flood years, saw rapid successions of ineffective pharaohs.

Karl Butzer (1981) has pointed out that civilizations can be regarded as ecosystems that emerge in response to sets of ecological opportunities. Over time, a variety of social and environmental adjustments are inevitable, some of them successful, leading to population growth, and others unsuccessful, so that the population shrinks. These demographic adjustments are commonly associated with ups and downs of political power. The political structures of, say, ancient Egyptian civilization are not nearly as durable as the basic adaptive system they purport to control or the cultural identity of which they were once part. Butzer draws an analogy with the ecological concept of trophic levels among biotic communities, in which organisms with similar feeding habits, such as herbivores and carnivores, define successive tiers interlinked in a vertical chain. Likewise, he hypothesizes, an efficient social hierarchy comprises several levels arranged in what he calls a "low-angle pyramid, supported by a broad base of farmers and linked to the peak of the pyramid by a middle-level bureaucracy. The vertical structures channel food and information through the system, and an efficient energy flow allows each trophic level to flourish in a steady state." In this model, a flatter pyramid with little vertical structure would provide less information flow and limit the potential productivity of the lower levels. Butzer's pyramid would allow growth at the lower levels, with new technologies or organizational devices favoring expanded energy generation. A steep, top-heavy pyramid laden with nobles and bureaucrats places excessive burdens on the lowest levels, so much so that external and internal forces can undermine the stability of society.

This model, when applied to the long history of ancient Egyptian civilization, shows how the Egyptians persisted in adjusting to a floodplain environment for thousands of years. They overcame external and internal crises by reorganizing their state and economic structure. The key variables were the fluctuations of the Nile itself, occasional foreign intervention, the character of the pharaohs' leadership, and a progressively pathological society of elite nonproducers who persisted in exploiting the common farmer, a process that led to eventual social collapse. However, through all these variables the essential components of the sociopolitical system survived more or less intact, right up to the nineteenth century A.D. Indeed, the visitor to rural Egypt can still see farming villages functioning much as they did in ancient Egyptian times.

PYRAMIDS AND THE ARCHAIC AND OLD KINGDOMS: 2920 TO 2134 B.C.

● ● ●

Egyptologists conventionally divide ancient Egyptian civilization into four broad periods, separated by at least two intermediate periods that were intervals of political change and instability (Table 16.2). The most striking feature of ancient Egyptian civilization is its conservatism. Many of the artistic, religious, and technological features of early Egyptian civilization survived intact into Roman times. The political and religious powers of the pharaohs changed somewhat through time, as later rulers became more imperialistic in their ambitions or different gods assumed political supremacy, but the essential continuity was there in the form of a civilization whose life was governed by the unchanging environment of the Nile Valley, with its annual floods, narrow floodplain, and surrounding desert.

Archaic and Old
Kingdoms
2920 to 2134 B.C.

After four and a half centuries of consolidation during the Archaic (or Early Dynastic) period, the Old Kingdom (c. 2575 to 2134 B.C.) saw four dynasties of pharaohs governing Egypt from a royal capital at Memphis near Cairo. Apparently the country's resources were well organized and controlled by a centralized government, for the state survived a catastrophic drought cycle between 3000 and 2800 B.C. Some of the pharaohs had reputations as cruel despots, notably Khufu and Khephren, who built the pyramids of Giza. The building of pyramids is regarded as the mark of the Old Kingdom pharaohs (Lehner, 1994; Mendelssohn, 1974). The first royal pyramid was built by Djoser in approximately 2680 B.C.; it was a six-step

TABLE 16.2
Major Subdivisions and Developments of Ancient Egyptian Civilizations

YEARS B.C.	PERIOD	CHARACTERISTICS
30 B.C.	Roman occupation	Egypt an imperial province of Rome
332 to 30 B.C.	Ptolemaic period	The Ptolemies bring Greek influence to Egypt, beginning with conquest of Egypt by Alexander the Great in 332 B.C.
1070 to 332 B.C.	Late period	Gradual decline in pharaonic authority, culminating in Persian rule (525 to 404 and 343 to 332 B.C.)
1530 to 1070 B.C.	New Kingdom	Great imperial period of Egyptian history, with pharaohs buried in Valley of Kings; pharaohs include Rameses II, Seti I, and Tutankhamun, as well as Akhenaten, the heretic ruler
1640 to 1530 B.C.	Second Intermediate period	Hyksos rulers in the delta
2040 to 1640 B.C.	Middle Kingdom	Thebes achieves prominence, also the priesthood of Amun
2134 to 2040 B.C.	First Intermediate Period	Political chaos and disunity
2575 to 2134 B.C.	Old Kingdom	Despotic pharaohs build the pyramids and favor conspicuous funerary monuments; institutions, economic strategies, and artistic traditions of Ancient Egypt established
2920 to 2575 B.C.	Archaic period	Consolidation of state (treated as part of Old Kingdom in this book)
2920 B.C.	Unification of Egypt under Narmer-Menes	

pyramid that was surrounded by a veritable town of buildings and shrines. The step pyramid is a somewhat hesitant structure, its architectural roots in earlier stone-built tombs, but the great pyramids built over the next century show increasing confidence, culminating in the brilliant assurance of the pyramids of Giza, with their perfect pyramid shape (Figure 16.3). The largest of these, the Great Pyramid, covers 13.1 acres (5.3 ha) and is 481 feet (146 m) high. It dates to the IV Dynasty reign of Khufu, approximately 2550 B.C. Just under two centuries later, the pharaohs stopped building huge pyramids and diverted their organizational talents to other public works.

The pyramids reflect the culmination of centuries of gradual evolution of the Egyptian state, during which the complexity of the state, religious institutions, and the authority of the bureaucracy grew hand in hand. Symbolic depictions in stone of the sun's rays bursting through the clouds, they were a stairway for the king to ascend to heaven, to take his place alongside the sun god on his journey across the heavens. They reflect the importance that the Egyptians placed on the life of the pharaoh in the afterlife and in the notion of resurrection, a central belief in their religion for thousands of years.

FIGURE 16.3   The Pyramids of Giza.

Kurt Mendelssohn (1974) has argued controversially that the pyramids were built over a relatively short period of time, during which the architects experimented with the pyramid shape. At least one pyramid collapsed during construction, before the builders mastered the correct 52° angles of the Great Pyramid. Every flood season, when agriculture was at a standstill, the pharaohs organized thousands of peasants into construction teams who quarried, transported, and laid the dressed stones of the pyramids. The permanent (year-round) labor force comprised relatively few, mainly skilled artisans, the fruit of whose work was placed in position on the main structure once a year. As far as is known, the peasants were paid volunteers, fed by the state bureaucracy, whose loyalty to the divine pharaoh provided the motivation for the work. Mendelssohn feels the construction of the pyramids was a practical administrative device designed to organize and institutionalize the state by trading redistributed food for labor. As construction proceeded from one generation to the next, the villagers became dependent on the central administration for food for three months a year, food obtained from surpluses contributed by the villages themselves in the form of taxation. After a while the pyramids fulfilled their purpose, and the state-directed labor forces could be diverted to other, less conspicuous state works. A new form of state organization had been created, one that both fostered and exploited the interdependence of Egyptian villages (for a discussion, see Wenke, 1991b).

THE EGYPTIAN STATE

• • •

Egypt was the first state of its size in history (Kemp, 1989). The pharaohs ruled by their own word, following no written laws, unlike the legislators of Mesopotamian city-states. The pharaoh had power over the Nile flood, rainfall, and all people, including foreigners. He was a god in his own right, respected by all people as a tangible divinity whose being was the personification of *Ma'at,* or "rightness." *Ma'at* was far more than just rightness; it was a "right order" and stood for order and justice. The pharaoh embodied *ma'at* and dispensed justice. *Ma'at* was pharaonic status and eternity itself—the very embodiment of the Egyptian state.

The pharaoh's pronouncements were law, regulated by a massive background of precedent set by earlier pharaohs. Egyptian rulers lived a strictly ordered life. As one Greek writer tells us, "For there was a set time not only for his holding audience or rendering judgment, but even for his taking a walk, bathing, and sleeping with his wife; in short, every act of his life" (Aldred, 1986).

A massive, hereditary bureaucracy effectively ruled the kingdom, with rows of officials forming veritable dynasties. Their records tell us that much official energy was devoted to tax collection, harvest yields, and administration of irrigation (Figure 16.4). An army of 20,000 men, many of them mercenaries, was maintained at the height of Egypt's prosperity. The Egyptian Empire was a literate one; that is, trained scribes who could read and write were an integral part of the state government. Special schools trained writers for careers in the army, the palace, the treasury, and numerous other callings (Aldred, 1986; Kemp, 1989).

Despite the number of scribes and minor clerics, a vast gulf separated one who could read and write from the uneducated peasant worker. The life of an Egyptian peasant, given good harvests, was easier than that of a Greek or a Syrian farmer, although the state required occasional bouts of forced labor to clear irrigation canals or to haul stone, both tasks being essential to maintain Egyptian agriculture. Minor craftsworkers and unskilled laborers lived more regimented lives, working on temples and pharaohs' tombs. Many were organized in shifts under foremen. There were strikes, and absenteeism was common. A scale of rations and daily work was imposed. Like many early states, however, the Egyptians depended on slave labor for some public works and much domestic service, but foreign serfs and war prisoners could wield much influence in public affairs. They were allowed to rent and cultivate land.

THE FIRST INTERMEDIATE PERIOD AND MIDDLE KINGDOM: 2134 TO 1640 B.C.

• • •

The Old Kingdom effectively ended with the death of Pepi II in 2152 B.C. His death coincided with another catastrophic drought cycle that brought repeated famines to the Nile for more than three centuries. Since the pharaohs were the guardians of fertility, of the land, their political and religious power fell into disrepute. A period of political instability now known as the First Intermediate ensued, during which there

First Intermediate period
2134 to 2040 B.C.

FIGURE 16.4   A tomb painting from the tomb of Menena at Thebes showing the harvesting and measurement of fields near the Nile.

were Asian incursions into the fertile delta country and Egypt was ruled by local rulers, even though there was nominal allegiance to a central government.

In about 2134 B.C., the city of Thebes in Upper Egypt became the center of rebel movements that eventually took over the country under pharaoh Mentuhotep II in 2040 B.C. The Middle Kingdom pharaohs who followed were mostly energetic rulers who extended trading contacts throughout the Near East and conquered the desert lands of Nubia south of the First Cataract (see Figure 16.1). The pharaohs became somewhat less despotic and considered themselves more like shepherds of the people, who had some concern for the common welfare. It was during the Middle Kingdom that the city of Thebes came into prominence, especially as a center for the worship of the sun god Amun.

Middle Kingdom 2040 to 1640 B.C.

THE SECOND INTERMEDIATE PERIOD: 1640 TO 1530 B.C.

● ● ●

The Middle Kingdom lasted until approximately 1640 B.C., when another period of political instability and economic disorder ensued. Disputes over the royal succes-

Second Intermediate period 1640 to 1530 B.C.

sion at Thebes led to procession of pharaohs who reigned for short periods. Pharaonic control of the Nile Valley as a whole weakened. Desert herders from the east known as Hyksos, "Princes of Desert Uplands," moved into the fertile lands of the delta. They formed two dynasties that ruled over much of Egypt between 1640 and 1530 B.C., bringing the horse and chariot to Egypt for the first time.

The Hyksos had little control over Upper Egypt, where the pharaohs of Thebes quarreled among themselves. But they brought new ideas to a conservative civilization that was stagnating away from the mainstream of the Near Eastern world. From this point on, the Egyptian pharaohs took an active interest in their Asian neighbors, and there was a constant flow of people and ideas with other nations.

THE NEW KINGDOM: 1530 TO 1070 B.C.

● ● ●

New Kingdom
1530 to 1070 B.C.

The New Kingdom began when a series of Theban pharaohs fought and won a war of independence from the Hyksos. It was Ahmose the Liberator who finally overcame the foreigners and established a firm hold on Egypt from the delta to Nubia. He was the first of a series of great rulers whose names have become symbolic of the power of ancient Egypt: Tutmosis, Amenophis, Seti, and Rameses II. Rameses II, the greatest of Egypt's pharaohs, extended the Egyptian Empire far beyond the narrow confines of the Nile Valley, deep into Nubia and into the Levant. By this time, political events in the Near East involved a delicate balance of diplomatic and military power between the Hittites in Anatolia to the north (Chapter 19) and the Mesopotamians to the east (Chapter 15). All three powers sought to control the lucrative trade and trade routes of the eastern Mediterranean (Chapter 19), and the famous Amarna archives chronicle some of the complex diplomatic maneuvering that went on. In the end, it was Egypt that lost out in the balance of power; its influence steadily declined and was eventually confined to the southern Levant.

Egypt may have been a major player on the world stage during the New Kingdom, but the spiritual center of the empire was at Thebes, where the priests of the great temples of Luxor and Karnak were a potent political force in the affairs of state.

Karl Butzer (1981) argues that episodes of rapid growth in ancient Egyptian civilization were made possible by a series of important innovations. One was improved irrigation organization in the Old Kingdom, after 2800 B.C. This allowed the development of the delta regions of Lower Egypt, once the bureaucratic structure to organize the work was in place. During the Middle Kingdom, the pharaohs responded to several centuries of repeated low floods by placing closer government controls over food distribution and moving large numbers of people out of the valley into such areas as the Fayyum Depression, where they organized huge drainage and irrigation works. The New Kingdom saw the introduction of the *shaduf,* a bucket-and-lever lifting device that raised water a yard or so from wells or ditches to gardens and estates. One result of this innovation was a shift of population from the narrow valley to the broad delta. The culmination of agricultural productivity came in the last few centuries B.C., when the last pharaohs undertook the complete drainage of the Fayyum, introduced summer crops such as sorghum, and encouraged the development of the animal-drawn waterwheel, known as the *saqiya.* The impact of all these innovations was to increase both the productivity of the state and the size of the labor force. It is probable that the population of ancient Egypt rose from less than a million 5000 years ago to approximately 5 million by 1500 B.C.

These innovations were to continue to support Egyptian agriculture right up to the building of the High Dam at Aswan in the twentieth century A.D.

The New Kingdom pharaohs adopted new burial customs and abandoned conspicuous sepulchers. Their mummies were buried in the desolate Valley of Kings on the west bank of the Nile at Thebes (El Mahdy, 1989; Romer, 1981). An entire community of workers did nothing but prepare the rock-cut tombs of the pharaohs, their queens, and privileged nobles. To date, only one undisturbed royal tomb has come to light in the Valley of Kings, that of the pharaoh Tutankhamun, who died in 1323 B.C. (Reeves, 1990). The world was astounded when Howard Carter and Lord Carnarvon discovered and cleared the tomb of the young pharaoh in the 1920s (Figure 16.5). It gives us an impression of the incredible wealth of the New Kingdom pharaohs' courts.

Tutankhamun died in his late teens but was responsible for restoring the religious order after a curious interlude of chaos during the reign of Akhenaten (1353–1335 B.C.) (Aldred, 1986). Like many pharaohs before him, Akhenaten had been worried about the overriding power of the priests of Amun at Thebes, so he espoused the worship of the god Aten, the life-giving disk of the sun. Akhenaten took up the new religion with fanatical zeal and even founded a new capital downstream of Thebes called Akhetaten, near the modern village of el-Amarna. After his death in 1335 B.C., the regents for Tutankhamun worked hard to restore the power and prestige of Amun, a move apparently supported by the mass of the people, for

FIGURE 16.5 The antechamber of Tutankhamun's tomb, stacked with priceless royal possessions. Tutankhamun's chariots lie against the left wall; two animal-headed funerary beds, stools, storage chests filled with possessions, and other items are to the right.

Akhenaten had produced no viable alternatives to the established political and religious institutions he had abolished.

THE LATE PERIOD: 1070 TO 332 B.C.

● ● ●

Late Period
1070 to 332 B.C.

With the death of Rameses III in 1070 B.C., Egypt entered a period of political weakness, when local rulers exercised varying control over the Nile. The pharaohs were threatened by Nubian rulers, who actually ruled over Egypt for a short time in the eighth century B.C. The Assyrians were a constant hazard after 725 B.C. and occupied parts of the country and looted Thebes in 665. After the eclipse of Assyria, the Egyptians enjoyed a few centuries of independence before being conquered by the Persians in 343 B.C. and Alexander the Great in 332 B.C. He in turn was succeeded by the Ptolemies, pharaohs of Greek ancestry, who ruled Egypt until Roman times. It was they who brought much of Egyptian lore and learning into the mainstream of emerging Greek civilization and ensured that the Land of the Pharaohs made a critical contribution to Western civilization.

Ptolemies
332 to 30 B.C.

EGYPT AND AFRICA

● ● ●

The ancient Greeks and Romans believed that Egypt was the fountain of all civilization, the place where all civilized knowledge began. While archaeological discoveries have shown that urban civilization developed in both Egypt and Mesopotamia at much the same time, scholars still argue over the contribution of the ancient Egyptians to the roots of Western civilization. Most Egyptologists argue that civilization developed quite independently along the Nile, in a fertile, if unpredictable, river valley that was a world unto its own. They believe it became an integral part of a cosmopolitan eastern Mediterranean world, especially during the New Kingdom, when Egypt vied with Assyria and the Hittite kings for control of eastern Mediterranean trade routes. Some African-American historians of the so-called Afro-centrism school, disagree, for they believe that the institutions of urban civilization, of the West, were born in tropical Africa, and that ancient Egypt was a black African civilization. And it was from the Nile, they argue, that the institutions of Western civilization were derived. These arguments, which first surfaced in the 1950s, have reached a high level of complexity in Martin Bernal's so-called "Black Athena" theory (1987), in which he presents historical, linguistic, and even archaeological evidence to place ancient Egypt at the core of western civilization. Bernal's researches have been severely criticized by Egyptologists, who have effectively demolished his arguments on the basis that they do not stand against scientific data. For example, Afrocentrists claim that the ancient Egyptians were black-skinned tropical Africans. In fact, both tomb paintings and biological data point to a generally Mediterranean population, but one that became increasingly cosmopolitan in later centuries as Egypt enjoyed closer contacts with other lands, including tropical Africa (Wenke, 1991).

NUBIA, LAND OF KUSH

• • •

If ancient Egypt was indeed a civilization unto itself, what connections did it enjoy with the people of the Nile Valley living south of the First Cataract at Aswan? The arid country that lay upstream was Nubia, the Land of Kush, famous to the ancient Egyptians for its gold, ivory, and slaves. As Nubian expert William Adams remarks (1977): "For millennia Egypt treated [Nubia] as a kind of private game reserve for human and animal game." Nubia straddled the Middle Nile, a narrow strip of fertile land that extended far upstream into modern-day Sudan as far as the borders of highland Ethiopia. The most fertile valley lands lie along the Dongola Reach between the Third and Fourth Cataracts. It was here that some of the earliest complex Nubian societies developed, among groups who had been herders and farmers since before 4000 B.C. Even as early as 3500 B.C., what Adams calls the "shadow of Egypt" was falling across Nubia. Her raw materials attracted a civilization where wealth and divine kingship went together.

Old Kingdom pharaohs sent their armies to subdue Nubia and boasted of lucrative cattle raids. Egyptian prospectors journeyed far into the desert in search of fine rocks and semiprecious stones. The Middle Kingdom kings were more ambitious, for they discovered attractions of Nubian gold. In 1900 B.C. pharaoh Amenemhet fortified strategic reaches with ten strongholds, most of them at strategic points where trade routes intersected with the river. This trade lay in the hands of the Nubian chieftains of Kerma in the heart of the Dongola Reach, a small town with palaces and temples, fortified with elaborate defenses and four gates. Kerma's rulers enjoyed great wealth and were buried under large burial mounds surrounded with as many as 400 sacrificial victims. All this wealth came from trade connections with people living in the desert and farther upstream, and with the Egyptians far downstream. But the New Kingdom pharaohs wanted this wealth for themselves, marched on Kush in 1500 B.C., and made it a colony. Nubia now changed from a country of village farmers and chiefdoms into something resembling a vast plantation state, worked for the benefit of absentee landlords to provide commodities of all types at the cheapest possible cost.

Kingdom of Kush
1900 to 1500 B.C.

The economic and political shock waves that rolled over the eastern Mediterranean after 1200 B.C. not only overthrew the Hittites and weakened Egypt (Chapter 19) but also loosened the pharaohs' hold on Nubia. After four centuries of confusion, Nubian civilization achieved new heights. The rulers of the new Kush espoused ancient Egyptian religious beliefs and assumed the powers and ideology of the pharaohs. Their wealth came from the Egyptian export trade, from gold, ivory, and many other commodities. They were buried under royal pyramids in large cemeteries, not only in Kush, but later far upstream at Meroe. The list of Nubian kings begins in about 806 B.C. and ends in A.D. 320, 1200 years later.

Kingdom of Kush
806 to 593 B.C.

Between 730 and 350 B.C. Nubian monarchs not only ruled over Kush, they presided over Egypt itself. It was Piye, who marched north in 730, honored the sun god Amun at Thebes, then subdued rebellious rulers in the delta far downstream. Piye was content to rule Egypt from Kush, but his successors transferred their court to Thebes, as the servant became the master, the conquered the conquerors. The Nubian pharaohs did much to restore art and religion, but they were inexperienced in foreign affairs, which led to their downfall. In 663 B.C., King Assurbanipal of

Assyria sacked Thebes and the ruler of the day fled to the safety of Kush. In 591, an Egyptian army marched upstream and "waded in Kushite blood." King Aspelta fled far upstream to Meroe, some 300 miles (482 km) upstream, where Nubian monarchs ruled in peace for more than 800 years.

MEROE AND AKSUM

• • •

Meroe
591 B.C. to A.D. 325

The move to Meroe came at a time when the focus of Nubian trade was shifting away from the eastern Mediterranean to the Red Sea and Indian Ocean. This new commercial world linked the Red Sea, the Persian Gulf states, India, and ultimately Southeast Asia and China into a vast web of interconnectedness (Table 16.1). India, for example, had an insatiable demand for African ivory, favored over Indian elephants for making bridal ornaments. Cotton cloth, porcelain and china vessels, silk, and glass items came from India and farther east. Gold, spices, even mangrove poles, all were staples of a trade that flowed down overland caravan routes and on the wings of the monsoon winds of the Indian Ocean. These predictable winds allowed sailing vessels to voyage from India to the Red Sea and East Africa and back in the course of a year.

The island of Socotra off northeast Africa and the mysterious Land of Punt on the coast of the southern Red Sea were spice-rich lands where Africans rubbed shoulders with Arabians, Indians with Egyptians. Well-traveled trade routes linked Red Sea coasts with the Nile and the Levant, traversed by laden asses, and, increasingly, by the camel, aptly named the "ship of the desert" by the Arabians who first domesticated them as early as 2500 B.C. Centuries passed before desert nomads developed fighting saddles for their beasts, turning them from mere beasts of burden into a potent military weapon. By the third century B.C., camel breeders dominated the overland caravan trade and brought prosperity to Meroe.

Meroe lies on the east bank of the Nile, some 124 miles (200 km) south of Khartoum (Shinnie, 1967). Her rulers administered a string of villages and towns along the river from Lower Nubia to Sennar on the Blue Nile, controlling the gold, ivory, and slave trade with Egypt. The city also lay astride bustling caravan routes that linked the river with the Red Sea and extended far to the west, along the southern margins of the Sahara. Today, Meroe lies in a desert landscape, but in Classical times large herds of cattle, goats, and sheep grazed nearby (Figure 16.6). Centuries of overgrazing, combined with voracious charcoal burning to fuel iron smelting furnaces helped chronic drought turn the environment into an arid wilderness.

Some 24 kings and queens ruled over Meroe between 593 and 220 B.C. These black-skinned rulers were the descendants of the great pharaoh Piye and his successors. They preserved many of the conservative standards of ancient Egyptian civilization, but with a distinctive African slant. For centuries, they administered a complex, exploitative economic enterprise for their own benefit, controlling trade through a network of carefully policed trade routes and by force. Most people lived at the subsistence level, for the international trade benefitted but a minority.

Ironworking was big business at Meroe, for iron ore was plentiful nearby. Huge slag heaps overlook the temples and palaces of the city, accumulated over centuries of manufacture that began as early as the seventh century B.C. Iron-tipped tools and weapons gave Meroitic armies strategic advantages over their desert neighbors.

FIGURE 16.6 Royal pyramids and iron slag heaps at Meroe, Sudan.

Early scholars believed that Meroe's ironsmiths introduced the new technology to tropical Africa, but we now know that iron was introduced into the central Sahara and West Africa at about the same time as it was to Meroe itself.

Meroe reached the height of its prosperity during the first century A.D., when it maintained regular trading contacts with the Roman Empire. A century later, the city was in decline, finally overthrown by the armies of King Ezana of the kingdom of Aksum in the nearby Ethiopian highlands between A.D. 325 and 350.

Aksum itself had prospered off the Red Sea trade, an African kingdom, whose rulers adopted many ideas from south Arabia in the five centuries before Christ (Connah, 1987). Its highland homeland was a fertile, if unpredictable environment, where irrigated cereal crops, among them a native grass called teff, flourished, proving large food surpluses in good years. By the first century A.D., Aksum was a powerful kingdom, in regular contact with Rome, handling all manner of exotic luxuries and commodities through its port at Adulis on the Red Sea. An eight-day journey took one inland to Aksum itself, while another caravan route reached Aswan in Egypt in 30 days. Adulis became so important that Aksum soon overshadowed Meroe, as the Nile trade declined. The archaeology of Aksum is still little known, but its rulers lived in imposing multistory palaces and were buried under tall columns up to 108 feet (33 m) high, carved to represent such buildings (Figure

Kingdom of Aksum
?200 B.C. to A.D. 700

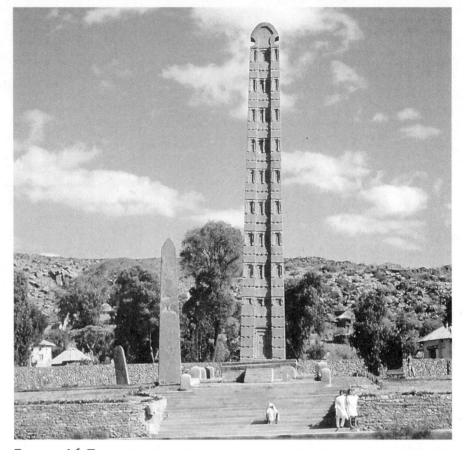

FIGURE 16.7   Royal stela at Aksum, Ethiopia, carved to depict a multistory building.

16.7). At about the time he overthrew Meroe, King Ezana abandoned the religion of his forefathers and adopted Christianity, which had reached his domains through Aksum's widespread trading connections. Christianity flourishes in Ethiopia to this day, but Aksum itself faltered as Islam acquired increasing influence over the Red Sea trade in the seventh century A.D. At the height of its powers, Aksum was a potent symbol of a new, much more international world, which sprang from the ruins of the Roman empire and linked Asia and Africa with lasting ties.

NORTH AFRICA

● ● ●

The North African coast had long been a staging post for maritime traders from the eastern Mediterranean. During the first millennium B.C., the Phoenicians set up port-colonies (N. K. Sanders, 1977), among them the great city of Carthage, but their main concern was with the coastal zone. Carthage became a dominant power by 400 B.C., but a series of devastating wars led to its destruction at the hands of Rome. The Romans realized the agricultural potential of the North African hinterland and turned their new colony into a vast grain combine. It was said that North African granaries fed Rome's masses for nine months, Egypt's for four.

The Romans had little interest in the desert, although there were some indirect contacts with peoples living deep in the Sahara. It was the camel that opened up the desert, once camel breeders had developed a saddle for load carrying and riding over long distances. Soon after the time of Christ, camel routes linked the Nile with the central highlands of the desert and the same mountains with North Africa. There, the Romans used the camel for agriculture and for some cavalry operations. The real expansion of the Saharan caravan trade came in later centuries, especially after Islamic armies swept across North Africa in the seventh century A.D.

Gold and salt—these were the commodities that fueled the Saharan caravan trade. Salt deposits were plentiful in parts of the desert, easily mined and carried on camelback to farmers south of the Sahara, who lacked this vital substance in their homeland. They craved salt but had gold dust to offer in exchange. So eager were some West Africans for salt that they would trade it for its equivalent weight in gold. Gold and salt were the staples of the Saharan trade, but it soon grew into an elaborate network of local and long-distance trade connections that linked North Africa with the West African savanna and forest regions far to the south (Figure 16.8). Tropical foodstuffs and stimulants like the kola nut were in constant demand, as were woollen garments and leather goods from the north, also copper, slaves, and glassware. By the time Christopher Columbus landed in the Bahamas in 1492, two-thirds of Europe's gold came from West African sources.

JENNE-JENO AND THE RISE OF WEST AFRICAN STATES

● ● ●

By 1000 B.C., small farming communities flourished throughout the West African savanna and in the forest regions of the south. Iron technology reached some of these villages by the sixth century B.C., at about the same time as it arrived at distant Meroe. Iron axes and adzes improved the efficiency of forest clearance and agriculture, but it was the Saharan trade that offered new opportunities for ambitious African leaders. For example, Jenne-jeno in Mali's Niger Delta began as a small village of mixed farmers in the third century B.C. (Macintosh and Macintosh, 1980). The settlement was no more than a few acres in extent, but even at this early date, the inhabitants were obtaining iron ore, grindstones, and stone beads from outside their delta homeland. Most likely, they were bartering surplus grain, fish, and animal products in exchange.

Jenne-jeno
c. 200 B.C. to A.D. 1000

During the next five centuries, Jenne-jeno grew rapidly, covering 62 acres (25 ha) by A.D. 300, a prosperous farming and fishing community of brush and mud houses (Figure 16.9). Two centuries later, Jenne-jeno's trading contacts had expanded considerably. Copper from Saharan sources appears by A.D. 400, savanna or forest gold between 600 and 800, by which time the town covered 82 acres (33 ha) and boasted of a mud fortification wall 1.2 miles (2 km) in circumference and 11.8 feet (3.6 m) wide. Ten centuries after its founding, Jenne-jeno was a mature town, with numerous round houses up to 13 feet (3.9 m) in diameter constructed of cylindrical bricks. This growth to maturity coincided with a gradual buildup in local and long-distance trade, as Jenne-jeno became an important exchange point for Saharan copper and salt. Lying as it did at the extreme southwestern end of the Niger Delta, it was ideally placed to barter savanna gold, iron, and agricultural produce. Judging from the hierarchy of lesser, contemporary settlements found nearby, the rulers of Jenne-jeno presided over a considerable area of the floodplain, a

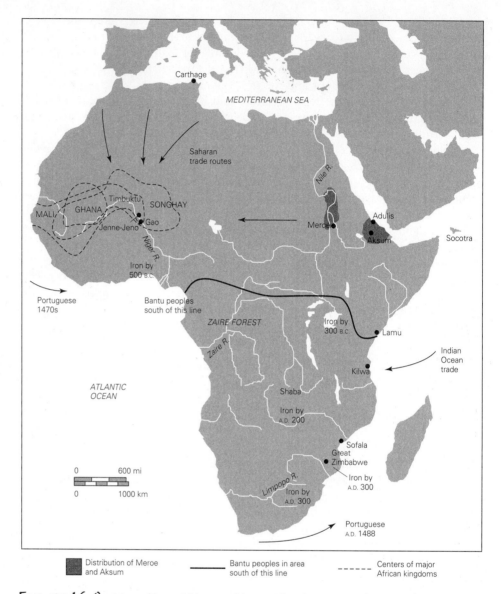

FIGURE 16.8   Map of later African prehistory, showing extent of Bantu Africa and indigenous states mentioned in the text.

territory that may have extended at least 60 miles (100 km) downstream of the town. Their government provided a stable environment for a growing volume of trade with the Sahara.

Jenne-jeno was but one of many such growing communities and states south of the desert (Connah, 1987), all of them basing their prosperity on the gold trade with North Africa. The Saharan trade passed into Islamic hands at the ends of the first millennium A.D. Arab authors began describing the remarkable African kingdoms flourishing south of the desert. The geographer al-Bakri drew a vivid picture of the kingdom of Ghana, whose gold was well known in northern latitudes by the

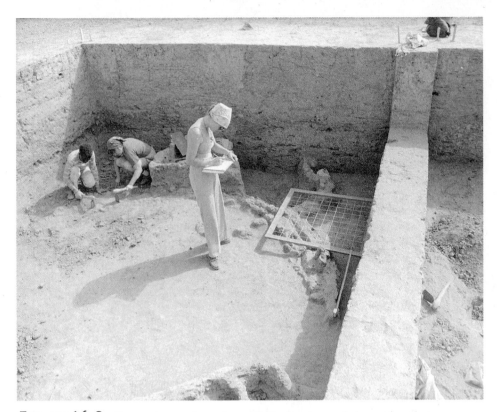

FIGURE 16.9   Excavations at Jenne-jeno, Mali, showing early house foundations.

eleventh century. "It is said," he wrote, "that the king owns a nugget as large as a big stone."

Ghana

The Kingdom of Ghana straddled the northern borders of the gold-bearing river valleys of the upper Niger and Senegal (Levetzion, 1973). No one knows when it first came into being, but the kingdom was described by Arab writers in the eighth century A.D. The Ghanians' prosperity depended on the gold trade and the constant demand for ivory in the north. Kola nuts, slaves, and swords also crossed the desert, but gold, ivory, and salt were the foundations of their power. Islam was brought to Ghana sometime in the late first millennium and linked the kingdom more closely to the desert trade. The king of Ghana was a powerful ruler, who, wrote al-Bakri, "can put 200,000 men in the field, more than 40,000 of whom were bowmen."

Ghana was a prime target for Islamic reform movements, whose desert leaders longingly eyed the power and wealth of their southern neighbor. One such group, the Almoravids, attacked Ghana in approximately A.D. 1062, but it was 14 years before the invaders captured the Ghanaian capital. The power of Ghana was fatally weakened, and the kingdom disintegrated into a series of minor chiefdoms, somewhat, perhaps, as many early Egyptian polities had done in the centuries preceding unification in 3250 B.C.

A.D. 1062

Mali

A.D. 1230

The kingdom of Mali appeared two centuries later, after many tribal squabbles (Levetzion, 1973). A group of Kangaba people under the leadership of Sundiata came into prominence in approximately A.D. 1230 and annexed their neighbors' lands. Sundiata built his new capital at Mali on the Niger River. He founded a vast empire that a century later extended over most of sub-Saharan West Africa. The fame of the Mali kings spread all over the Muslim world. Timbuktu became a widely known center of Islamic scholarship. Malian gold was valued everywhere. When the king of Mali went on a pilgrimage to Mecca in A.D. 1324, the price of gold in Egypt was reduced sharply by the king's liberal spending. Mali appeared on the earliest European maps of West Africa as the outside frontier of the literate world. It provided most of Europe's gold reserves and royal wealth.

The key to Mali's prosperity and political stability was the unifying effect of Islam, which overcame much factionalism and tribal rivalries. Mali's Islamic rulers governed with supreme powers granted by Allah and ruled their conquered provinces with carefully selected religious appointees, or even with politically astute slaves, chosen for their loyalty and political acumen. Islam provided a reservoir of thoroughly trained, literate administrators, who believed that political stability resulted from efficient governance and sound trading practices.

Songhay

A.D. 1325

A.D. 1464 to 1492

A.D. 1550

In approximately A.D. 1325, the greatest of the kings of Mali, Mansa Musa, brought the important trading center of Gao on the Niger under his sway (Hunwick, 1971). Gao was the capital of the Dia kings, who shook off Mali's yoke in approximately A.D. 1340 and founded the kingdom of Songhay. Their state prospered increasingly as Mali's power weakened. The great chieftain Sonni Ali led the Songhay to new conquests between A.D. 1464 and 1492, expanding the frontiers of his empire deep into Mali country and far north into the Sahara. He monopolized much of the Saharan trade, seeking to impose law and order with his vast armies to increase the volume of trade that passed through Songhay hands. Sonni Ali was followed by other competent rulers who further expanded Songhay. Its collapse came in the sixteenth century.

FARMERS AND TRADERS IN EASTERN AND SOUTHERN AFRICA

• • •

Spread of farming
500 B.C. to A.D. 400

While cattle herders had settled in the East African highlands as early as 1000 B.C. (Chapter 11), the great savannas of eastern and southern Africa were still home to Stone Age hunter-gatherer groups. The spread of farming economies into the savanna coincided in part with the spread of iron technology, and with the dispersal of Bantu languages over much of east, central, and southern Africa from a homeland in eastern West Africa. This complex series of local population movements is still little understood, but we know that iron-using farmers had settled in the East African lakes region by 300 B.C., and that they lived by the banks of the Zambezi

Valley soon after the time of Christ, moving across the Limpopo River into South Africa soon afterward. These savanna farmers used shifting agriculture and careful soil selection to produce a diet of sorghum, millet, and other cereal crops. They kept cattle and small stock, relying on hunting and foraging for much of their diet. Their architectural styles and pottery have a clear but indirect relationship with those of many present-day African groups.

Towns and Trade on the East African Coast

● ● ●

The same monsoon winds that linked the Red Sea with India also linked the East African coast between Somalia and Mozambique with a much wider commercial world. As early as the first century A.D., traders from Arabia were coasting southward in search of gold, ivory, and other commodities, trading with small farming communities near the shore. By the end of the first millennium, the coastal trade was under Islamic control, centered on small towns and strategic bays. Lamu in northern Kenya was one such port. So was Kilwa Island off the Tanzanian coast, an important transhipment point, where ocean going dhows (sailing ships) loaded gold dust and ivory obtained from Sofala in southeast Africa. For more than 1000 years, a distinctive coastal civilization flourished along the East African Coast, a cosmopolitan blend of African and Islamic culture based on "stone towns," compact trading settlements of rock and coral controlled by prominent merchant families.

Coastal towns
A.D. 800 to modern times

Until the early nineteenth century, most contacts between the coast and the far interior were indirect, through local middlemen. But the volume of gold, ivory, and copper that flowed to the coast was impressive, commodities in high demand overseas that were bartered for cheap baubles like glass beads and cotton cloth that were worth a fraction of the price. Another popular item was Indian Ocean seashells, worn as ornaments that assumed great prestige in the interior. When explorer David Livingstone passed through western Zambia in 1855, the going price for one circular *Conus* shell was a slave, for five a tusk of elephant ivory. They could be picked up by the dozen on coastal reefs. Just as in West Africa, a series of powerful African states took advantage of the coastal trade.

Great Zimbabwe

● ● ●

Trading states first appear to the south of the Zaire forest in central Africa as early as the ninth century A.D., and especially south of the Zambezi River, where Shona-speaking peoples had settled at about the same time. The Shona were cattle-herding people living in a highland environment, where political power was measured by wealth on the hoof. Both agriculture and herding were high-risk enterprises in a landscape where rainfall was unpredictable, so Shona chiefs were quick to realize the potential of long-distance trade with the coast. They mined gold and hunted elephants, using their exports to acquire exotic commodities like cloth and glass beads, which they then used to acquire more grain and cattle.

By A.D. 1200, plateau society was acquiring some complexity, perhaps a mosaic of small chiefdoms, each with their own territories with sufficient range to graze cattle not only through the rainy season but through the dry months as well. One of them, Zimbabwe on the southern plateau, rose to prominence. Its rulers were able to maintain and raise armies and to intervene in the politics of their neighbors. For many generations, they exacted tribute not only from their own "core" area but also from surrounding chiefdoms. The size of the state fluctuated constantly, for vassal chiefs often acted with remarkable independence.

The gold trade with the Indian Ocean coast flourished because the Shona encouraged it. From the region known as Sofala, the tentacles of the gold and ivory trade extended far inland, up the Limpopo, Sabi, and Zambezi Rivers to the plateau. For centuries, this trade was at best sporadic and on a small scale. It was a long-distance trade that merged imperceptibly with the myriad bush paths that carried essential commodities and luxuries from one village to the next. The change came after the tenth century A.D. on the coast, some time later in the interior, when the international demand for gold and ivory skyrocketed. It can be no coincidence that the Sofala trade picked up dramatically as the East African coastal towns enjoyed their greatest prosperity. The chiefs of Great Zimbabwe managed to dominate the trade between the southwestern goldfields and the coast.

Great Zimbabwe
A.D. 1000 to 1450

The word "Zimbabwe" is either a contraction of the Shona words *dzimba dza mabwe,* "houses of stone," or, more likely, of *dzimba hoye,* "venerated houses," an expression used to describe chiefs' houses or graves. Judging from archaeological data, Great Zimbabwe served both these roles (Garlake, 1973; Beach, 1993). In about A.D. 1000, Shona groups settled near Zimbabwe, probably direct ancestors of the present-day inhabitants of the area. One village lay on the western end of the low hill that now dominates the site, its cattle enclosures and millet gardens spread out over the valley below. These people and their neighbors lived in good farming and cattle country, where they were able to maintain large grain surpluses and develop great wealth on the hoof, but theirs was not an important gold-producing area.

At first, only a few families farmed and grazed their herds at the site. They built circular mud and stick thatched huts both on the hill and in the valley below. As time went on, they erected stone cattle enclosures, then more and more walls. They reinforced the walls of larger huts and joined the large boulders atop the hill to form small enclosures, creating the first stages of a complex known to archaeologists as the Acropolis or Hill Ruin. By 1250, like their neighbors, the Zimbabwe chiefs presided over a sizable territory and measured their wealth in large herds. Perhaps it was the uncertainty of cereal agriculture and cattle herding that made trading with foreigners an attractive risk management strategy—a way of cushioning themselves against the depredations of cattle disease, drought, even of marauding neighbors. Within a few generations, Great Zimbabwe became a sizable town, perhaps with as many as 18,000 people living nearby. Zimbabwe was in part a military state, capable of raising armies from its herding population that could enforce tribute assessments and toll collections. At the same time, the chiefs could manipulate their cattle as a means of acquiring wives and, eventually, relatives and supporters.

Great Zimbabwe's stone buildings, built of easily quarried granite slabs, sprawl over about 3 square miles. The Hill Ruin, often called the Acropolis, overlooks the valley, the summit a mass of weathered granite boulders linked by freestanding stone walls. These form a maze of large and small enclosures, accessible by a narrow stepped entrance on the north side or via a secretive defile that squeezes between large boulders on its way up to the western enclosure on the summit.

FIGURE 16.10 The Elliptical Building at Great Zimbabwe, an important trading and religious center of Shona peoples in the early to mid-second millennium A.D. Most of the Elliptical Building was built by A.D. 1500.

The Hill Ruin looks down on the celebrated "Elliptical Building" or "Great Enclosure" that dominates the valley (Figure 16.10). Its oval-shaped, freestanding outer wall is more than 800 feet (244 m) long and rises 32 feet (9.7 m) at its highest point. The Elliptical Building is a secluded place, divided by low stone walls into several enclosures. Substantially built mud huts once stood within them, for this was the residence of the chief. The valley between the Hill Ruin and the Elliptical Building is a jumble of stone-walled enclosures and large occupation middens, for it was in some of these that the chief's many wives may have resided.

By the fifteenth century, Great Zimbabwe was the most powerful of some ten chiefdoms that flourished on the plateau. Each controlled a territory about 100 miles (161 km) across, sufficient land to allow not only shifting cultivation, but large-scale seasonal grazing of sizable cattle herds. Eventually, overgrazing, exhausted soils, and denuded woodland may have caused much of the population to move elsewhere. Great Zimbabwe was abandoned as the center of political power shifted northward, closer to the Zambezi River, a major trade route to the coast.

EUROPE AND AFRICA

• • •

Even as Columbus landed in the Bahamas, Portuguese ships were coasting southward, seeking to outflank Islam by reaching the West African gold mines from the sea. By 1470 they had rounded the bulge of Africa. In 1488 Bartholomeu Dias rounded the Cape of Good Hope. Nine years later, Vasco da Gama sailed up the East African coast and used the monsoon route to reach India. During the next four centuries, Africans were drawn increasingly into a much wider economic world, fueled by insatiable demands for raw materials and, above all, slaves to man the sugar plantations of the New World. These years of increasing economic dependence were ones when Africans were aggressive in seizing new opportunities, in acquiring wealth and political prestige. It was they who controlled the sources of slaves, who mined for gold, and organized the hunting of elephants. Increasingly, the destiny of Africa became intertwined with the unfolding economic and political fortunes of a wider, and ever more international and industrialized world.

CHAPTER SUMMARY

Ancient Egyptian civilization arose as a result of complex processes of forced and voluntary integration along the Nile Valley. This process was accelerated by increasing trade contacts with other parts of the Near East, culminating in the emergence of the ancient Egyptian state in about 2900 B.C. Egyptologists conventionally subdivide ancient Egyptian civilization into four main periods: the Old, Middle, New, and Late Kingdoms, the first three of which were separated by brief intermediate periods of political chaos. The Old Kingdom is notable for its despotic pharaohs and the frenzy of pyramid construction, an activity that may be connected with pragmatic notions of fostering national unity. The Middle Kingdom saw a shift of political and religious power to Thebes and Upper Egypt. New Kingdom pharaohs made Egypt an imperial power with strong interests in Asia and Nubia. Ancient Egyptian civilization began to decline after 1000 B.C., passing under Roman rule in 30 B.C.

Nubia, upstream of the First Cataract, was exploited by the Egyptians for centuries, but it came into its own as the pharaohs' power declined. Nubian kings from the land of Kush actually ruled over Egypt in the eighth century B.C., but they were forced to retreat to Meroe far upstream two centuries later. Meroe became an important center for the Red Sea and Indian Ocean trade, ruled by kings and queens who preserved Egyptian customs. It prospered until the fourth century A.D., when it was conquered and finally eclipsed by the kingdom of Aksum on the Ethiopian highlands.

The camel opened up the Sahara to regular gold and salt trade, fostering the development of powerful West African states such as Ghana, Mali, and Songhay. At the same time, expanding Indian Ocean trade nurtured a network of trading towns on the East African Coast. During the fourteenth and fifteenth centuries A.D., Great Zimbabwe in southern Africa controlled much of the gold and ivory trade in southeastern Africa.

GUIDE TO FURTHER READING

Aldred, Cyril. 1986. *The Egyptians*, 2d ed. New York: Thames and Hudson.
A superb short essay on ancient Egyptian civilization that is especially good on daily life and society. Exceptional illustrations.

Adams, William. 1977. *Nubia: Corridor to Africa*. London: Alan Lane.
   The definitive account of the archaeology of Nubia. Somewhat outdated, but authoritative and well written.

Connah, Graham. 1987. *African Civilizations*. Cambridge, Eng.: Cambridge University Press.
   A general account of early sub-Saharan African states for the beginning reader.

Kemp, Barry. 1989. *Ancient Egypt: The Anatomy of a Civilization*. London: Routledge.
   Quite simply, the best book on ancient Egyptian civilization ever written. Destined to become a classic for its elegant exposition and beautiful line drawings.

Romer, John. 1981. *The Valley of Kings*. New York: Morrow.
   A description in exhaustive detail of centuries of excavations in the royal burial grounds near Thebes. Shows vividly how modern Egyptology is as much detective work as it is excavation.

CHAPTER 17

EARLY STATES IN SOUTH AND SOUTHEAST ASIA

• • •

In 1950, the famed excavator Sir Mortimer Wheeler assembled a team of young archaeologists, students, and local laborers to work on a confusion of mud bricks that projected out of a weathered citadel mound at Mohenjo-daro on the banks of the Indus River, in Pakistan. The laborers removed foot after foot of sand, the few bricks grew into many, "until the stark walls of a huge platform began to emerge from the hillside. The aspect was of a fortress, towering grim and forbidding above the plain. . . ."

Wheeler puzzled over the mass of brickwork. A grid of narrow passages, signs of a timber superstructure, a carefully designed platform with an approach way. The enormous structure looked less and less like a fortress, but what was it? "We took another village upon our strength and fairly hurled ourselves into the task . . . " wrote Wheeler, "drawing, planning, recording." Suddenly a light went off in his brain. The narrow passages were air ducts to dry the floor of the timber barn that once housed the city's grain, accessible only from the site away from the teeming streets. The "fortress" was the municipal granary (Wheeler, 1955).

More recent excavations have thrown Wheeler's bold interpretation into doubt, but many details of the Harappan civilization, one of the world's least known (Table 15.1), came from his classic investigations of a half century ago. Like so many other aspects of Indian life, much of this remarkable society revolved around water. Water has always played an important role in Indian society and thought, for India's great rivers are the perennial gift of the snow-clad Himalayas. The Indus River, on the banks of which Indian civilization began, rises in southern Tibet and then descends 1000 miles (1609 km) through Kashmir before debouching onto the Pakistani plains (Figure 17.1). The Indus floodplain landscape now is almost entirely humanly made, a network of irrigation canals and flood embankments used to control the inundation that reaches the plains between June and September of each year. The people plant their wheat and barley on the fertile alluvial plains as the floods recede, then harvest them the following spring. They use the flood-borne silts as a natural fertilizer. The soils are soft enough to be cultivated without the aid

FIGURE 17.1   The Harappan civilization, showing sites mentioned in this chapter.

of metal artifacts. By 3000 B.C., the Indus farmers were making use of the same flood cycle to irrigate their fields.

THE ROOTS OF SOUTH ASIAN CIVILIZATION

● ● ●

As in other parts of the world, it seems that the roots of south Asian farming and later civilization were almost entirely indigenous. Most authorities on south Asian archaeology agree that humped cattle, buffalo, and pig were domesticated there from local wild populations (Sharma et al., 1980). Perhaps sheep and goats were also. The earliest dates for domesticated animals are in the period of 4500 to 4000 B.C., from sites near Quetta in Baluchistan and Rajastan in northwest India. However, it seems likely that farmers and herders have lived in these areas for much longer, for palynologists have found evidence for recurrent fires in the desert savanna of Rajastan starting in about 8000 B.C. (Jacobson, 1979). These may signal repeated clearance of sour grass to allow lush grazing for cattle, a practice followed in the area to this day. The farmers eventually domesticated not only indigenous

Indian cultigens such as rice and dwarf wheat but also peas, barley, lentils, and other west Asian species, but the dates of early domestication are still unknown. In the millennia before the emergence of urban civilization in India, dozens of regional variations of farming culture flourished throughout India and Pakistan; these peasant cultures still are little understood (Allchin and Allchin, 1983; Possehl, 1993).

Mehrgarh 6000 to 3000 B.C.

French and Pakistani archaeologists are excavating a series of agricultural settlements at Mehrgarh south of Quetta, 125 miles (201 km) west of the Indus River (Jarrige, 1993). They have found traces of farmers who had settled in the area before 6000 B.C. By 5000 B.C., the Mehrgarh people lived in sizable, permanent houses of mud brick, a building material used not only by the Harappan civilization in later times but also by Indus people to this day. They possessed copper tools and imported turquoise from Iran and shells from the Arabian coast. Living as they did on a direct trade route from the Indus Valley to the Iranian Highlands, the Mehrgarh people learned of the unique qualities of a new Indian-domesticated crop: cotton. This white, fluffy flower turned out to be a priceless asset, for it could be woven into fine cloth not only for convenient domestic use in a hot climate but also for export to people looking for a light, hard-wearing textile. Cotton was to become a staple of Indian trade for the rest of recorded history.

Kot Diji

The Mehrgarh sites include the Nausharo mound, which dates from about 3000 to 500 B.C., about the time when the mature Harappan civilization developed in the lowlands of the Indus Valley. The alluvial plains themselves were settled as early as the fourth millennium B.C. Scattered across a vast area of the plains are hundreds of pre-Harappan settlements, many of them boasting fortifications, metallurgy, and planned streets. There are clear signs that many villages and small towns practiced intensive agriculture and were built above the highest flood level but as close to the river as possible. Typical of these settlements is Kot Diji on the left bank of the Indus approximately 20 miles (33.3 km) from the river (Jacobson, 1979; Mughal, 1974). In the early third millennium B.C., the inhabitants were forced to pile boulders to protect themselves against the inundation. They ended up erecting a massive defensive wall that served as both a flood dike and a fortress. The stone and mud-brick houses of the village were clustered inside the wall. Nevertheless, Kot Diji was attacked and burned at least twice. The same fate must have awaited many other settlements that became involved in quarrels between ambitious local chieftains vying for control of smaller communities and prime agricultural lands. The increased competition is hardly surprising, for between 3000 and 1500 B.C., farming had changed the natural ecology of the Indus Valley beyond all recognition (Kenoyer, 1991).

Botanists have chronicled these ecological changes by using the minute pollen grains embedded in the Indus Valley soils. They found that the natural tree and grass cover on the floodplain increased between 2400 and 1000 B.C., perhaps as a result of a period of higher rainfall that lasted at least 2000 years. This thicker tree cover became established just as the farming population was taking advantage of good rains and expanding agricultural production. The pollen counts show not only more trees but also dramatic rises in the proportions of cereal grains and cultivated weeds at the expense of the natural vegetation. A complex multiplier effect then linked rapidly rising village populations with corresponding increases in agricultural production, leading to drastic consequences for the plains environment. As the valley population rose, so did pressure on the land. The farmers cleared and burned off more and more riverine forest and grazed ever-growing herds of goats and sheep on watershed meadows. Acres of forest were burned to bake bricks for the houses of growing villages and newly founded cities. Mile after mile of the plains were denuded of natural vegetation, with disastrous consequences for erosion control and the floodplain environment. Deprived of natural controls, the rising floodwaters swept over the plains, carrying everything with them. Confronted with what may have seemed like the wrath of the gods, the people had only one defense—cooperative flood-works and irrigation agriculture that fed more mouths and provided at least a degree of security from the vagaries of the elements. The obvious leaders of these new communal efforts were the chieftains, priests, and kin leaders, who acted as intermediaries between the people and the gods. The religious philosophy and motivation that provided the catalyst for these efforts was a simple one, a pervasive belief that humans are part of an ordered cosmos that can be maintained only by unremitting toil and a subordination of individual ambition to the common good.

HIGHLANDS AND LOWLANDS: THE KULLI COMPLEX

● ● ●

This scenario fits the few archaeological facts available from the lowlands. In archaeological terms, the early stages of the Harappan civilization date to between 3200 and 2600 B.C. The people lived in small villages covering only a few acres, and there are no signs of social ranking (Possehl, 1980; Kenoyer, 1991). Their environment was like that of Mesopotamia, low-lying, hot, and with fertile soils but no metals. Thus, its inhabitants could not flourish in isolation. Long before the rise of Harappan civilization in the valley, the peoples of the lowlands interacted constantly with their neighbors to the north and west, especially in the highlands of southern Baluchistan in western Pakistan. Metals, semiprecious stones, and timber came from the highlands, where people depended for their subsistence on dry agriculture and sheep herding. Over the millennia, the relationship between lowlands and highlands was fostered not only by regular exchange of foods and other commodities but also by seasonal population movements that brought enormous herds of goats and sheep down from mountain summer pastures in Baluchistan to the lowlands during the harsh winters in the west. In a real sense, economic and social development in both regions developed along parallel if somewhat diverse tracks, every region dependent on its neighbors.

In Baluchistan, a complex of large and small centers subsumed under the *Kulli Complex* evolved during the third millennium B.C. The largest of these settlements was Nindowari, a major center dominated by a sizable monumental structure and massive public buildings. Nindowari was occupied between about 2600 and 2200 B.C., contemporary with that of mature Harappan civilization in the Indus lowlands. Harappan seals and other artifacts occur at Nindowari, and there are signs that Kulli communities were heavily involved in regular exchange with the lowlands to the east. Kulli, too, lay on the borders of eastern Iran, with its intricate exchange networks that reached far to the west toward Mesopotamia (Chapter 15), but it is uncertain how many of its products flowed to the east. For centuries, the Kulli communities of the highlands were specialized partners of the Harappan civilization of the lowlands. This symbiosis between these two regions, among others, may have been a major catalyst in the rise of complex societies in both areas, a symbiosis that was of vital importance not only in the Indus Valley but in distant Mesopotamia as well.

A RAPID TRANSITION

• • •

Early Harappan society was in sharp contrast to the complex, sometimes urban society that developed in the lowlands after about 2600 B.C. The transition from egalitarian to ranked society was an indigenous one, which took place with what Gregory Possehl (1986) calls "a veritable paroxysm of change." There was a short period of explosive growth over a period of one or two centuries ending about 2500 B.C. This contrasts dramatically with the long period of increasing social, political, and economic complexity in Egypt and Mesopotamia.

Gregory Possehl (1993) believes that this growth may have coincided with a major shift in Sumerian trade patterns. As we saw in Chapter 15, the Sumerians obtained many exotic objects and basic raw materials from the Iranian Plateau before 2600 B.C. Judging from historical records, they experienced considerable frustration in their transactions with these exchange networks. After 2600 B.C., they reorganized their trade in luxuries and raw materials and then obtained many of their needs by sea from three foreign states—Dilmun, known to be located on the island of Bahrein in the Persian Gulf; Magan, a port further east; and Meluhha, even farther away, a place where ivory, oils, furniture, gold, silver, and carnelian, among other commodities, were to be obtained (Rice, 1993). The Mesopotamians exchanged these goods for wool, cloth, leather, oil, cereals, and cedarwood. The location of Meluhha is unknown, but Possehl (1993) believes it to be the Indus Valley region. In about 2350 B.C., King Sargon of Agade boasted that ships from all these locations were moored at his city. There are even records of villages of Meluhhans near Lagash and elsewhere in Mesopotamia. This was a highly organized mercantile trade conducted by specialized merchants, a trade quite different than that of the exchange networks on the highlands far inland.

The sea trade increased the volume of Sumerian imports and exports dramatically. One shipment of 13,000 pounds (5900 kg) of copper is recorded, and the entire enterprise was very different from the basically noncommercial exchange systems of the Iranian Plateau. The trade was under Mesopotamian control, much of it conducted through Dilmun and, in Possehl's (1986) view, it had a major impact on the growth of Harappan civilization. Interestingly, its beginnings coincide with the growth of urban centers in the Indus Valley (Edens, 1993).

A dramatic increase in long-distance trade may well have been the context in which Harappan civilization developed. It is clear that the lowlands were not the source of many of the products shipped to Sumer. Metals, semiprecious stones, and timber came from the highlands to the north and west. It was here that the long-term symbiosis between the highlands and lowlands came into play, for it was this long-term relationship between two separately developing but contiguous regions that made the Harappans' trade with Mesopotamia a practical reality.

THE HARAPPAN CIVILIZATION

• • •

2600 B.C.   By 2600 B.C., the Indus people had mastered the basic problems of irrigation and flood control, partly by using millions of fired bricks made of river alluvium, baked with firewood cut from the riverine forests. Like the Sumerians, they adopted the city as a means of organizing and controlling their civilization. We know of at least five major Harappan cities: Harappa, after which the civilization is known, Mohenjo-daro, Kalibangan, Chanhu-daro, and Dhoraji in Gujerat (Allchin and Allchin, 1983; Possehl, 1982). Harappa and Mohenjo-daro were built on artificial mounds above the floods at the cost of Herculean efforts. Mohenjo-daro was rebuilt at least nine times, sometimes as a result of disastrous inundations. Yet on each occasion the builders followed an irregular, netlike plan that evolved over many generations. Sir Mortimer Wheeler (1962, 1968) characterized both cities as giving an impression of "middle-class prosperity with zealous municipal supervision." The two cities are so similar that they might have been designed by the same architect.

A high citadel lies at the west end of each city, dominating the streets below. Here lived the rulers, protected by great fortifications and flood-works. Harappa's citadel is 460 yards (414 m) long and 215 yards (194 m) wide, surrounded by a forbidding brick wall at least 45 feet (13.5 m) high (Figure 17.2). Mohenjo-daro's towering citadel rises 40 feet (12 m) above the plain and is protected by massive flood embankments and a vast perimeter wall with towers. The public buildings on the summit include a pillared hall almost 90 feet (27 m) square, perhaps the precinct where the rulers gave audience to petitioners and visiting officials. Everything is utilitarian, efficient, and unostentatious, for there are no spectacular temples or richly adorned shrines. Religious life was centered on a great lustral bath made of bitumen-sealed brickwork and fed by a well. An imposing colonnade surrounded the pool, which was approached by sets of steps at both ends. We cannot be sure of the exact use of the great bath, but perhaps it was where the devout carried out their ceremonial bathing rituals.

The rulers of each city looked down on a complex network of at least partially planned streets. The widest thoroughfares at Mohenjo-daro were only 30 feet (9 m)

FIGURE 17.2   Mortimer Wheeler's trench exposed the massive walls of Harappa's citadel.

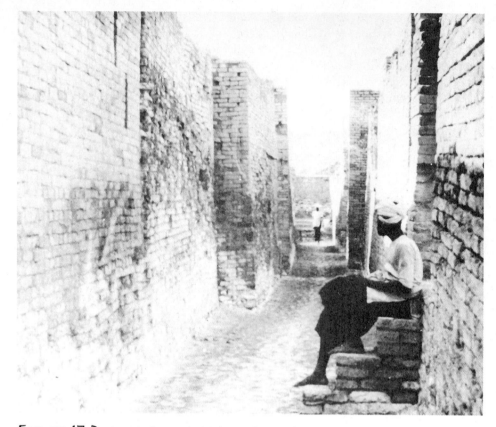

FIGURE 17.3   A typical street in Mohenjo-daro, Pakistan.

wide, the cross streets only half as wide and unpaved (Figure 17.3). Hundreds of drab, standardized houses presented a blind brick façade to the streets and alleys they lined. The more spacious dwellings, perhaps those of the nobility and merchants, were laid out around a central courtyard where guests may have been received, where food was prepared, and where servants probably lounged. Staircases and thick ground walls indicate that some houses had two or even three stories, with wooden balconies overlooking the courtyard rather than the street, as was the case at Sumerian Ur. The larger residences owned a well and had bathrooms and toilets that may have been joined to an elaborate system of public drains.

Some areas of Harappa and Mohenjo-daro were designated as bazaars, complete with shops. Archaeologists have inventoried the finds from artisans' quarters where bead makers, coppersmiths, cotton weavers, and other specialists manufactured and sold their wares. The potters' workshops were filled with painted pots decorated with animal figures and everyday plain, wheel-made vessels manufactured not only in the cities but also in villages for hundreds of miles around. There were water jars and cooking bowls, storage pots, and drinking vessels. Metalworkers cast simple axes in open molds and manufactured chisels, knives, razors, spears, and fish hooks. Only a few expert artisans made more elaborate objects, such as small figurines or a piece as complicated as a canopied cart. They would make a wax model of the cart and encase it in clay, which was fired to melt the wax. Then molten copper or bronze was poured into the mold. This "lost-wax" method is still employed by Indian artists.

The technologies used in Harappan cities were developed centuries earlier in small villages and transferred to the cities without change. One of the most developed manufactures was the seal, made from steatite and other soft rocks. Seal workshops have yielded not only finished specimens, hardened in a furnace, but also the blocks of steatite from which square seals were cut as intaglios. For hours, the seal makers would crouch over the tiny squares, expertly cutting representations of animals in profile. They reserved some of their best efforts for religious scenes. Indian archaeologists working at the Harappan town of Chanhu-daro south of Mohenjo-daro found a complete bead maker's shop that gave some idea of the labor needed to produce small ornaments. The bead makers prepared bars of agate and carnelian approximately 3 inches (7.6 cm) long that were then ground and polished into shorter, perforated cylinders and strung in necklaces. To experience the bead-making process, the archaeologists took a Harappan stone-tipped drill and some abrasive powder from the workshop and attempted to drill through one of the bead blanks. It took them 20 minutes to drill a small pit in the end of the bead. At that rate, it would have taken 24 hours to drill a single bead!

Some Harappan crafts were organized on the basis of kin networks. Others, involving more exotic materials such as metals or semiprecious stones, revolved around long-distance trade and may have required some degree of centralized control.

Who Were the Harappans?

Three-quarters of a century of excavations has revealed a highly varied, state-organized society that archaeologists have named the *Harappan* simply because they do not know what the Harappans called themselves. We do not even know the names of the rulers who controlled the major cities, like Harappa and Mohenjo-daro, nor do we have insights into the intricate ties that linked city with town and major centers with minor hamlets. This civilization was different from that of the predominantly urban Sumerians in Mesopotamia. There were only two major cities the size of Uruk in an area of more than 300,000 square miles (Possehl, 1980). It seems unlikely that there was the cultural and social uniformity that one finds in Sumer. Gregory Possehl makes an analogy with ancient Egypt. The Upper and Lower Nile were part of the same civilization, with many common institutions, but there were always administrative, cultural, and social differences between the two regions. The same may be true with the Harappan, with Mohenjo-daro in Sind and Harappa in the Punjab.

The Indus Valley may have been a cultural focus of the Harappan civilization, but it was only one part of a much larger, very varied civilization, whose influences and ties extended not only over the lowlands of the Punjab and Sind but also from the highlands of Baluchistan to the deserts of Rajastan and from the Himalayan foothills to near Bombay. There was constant interaction throughout this vast area, with abundant evidence that contemporary, relatively complex societies were developing elsewhere at the same time, developments known from sites like Kulli in Baluchistan (Possehl, 1993). The relationships between highland areas like Baluchistan, with their cold winters, and the lowlands led to complicated seasonal population shifts that brought highlanders and their herds to the Indus lowlands. This classic transhumance pattern may have placed the Harappans and their highland neighbors within the same larger cultural system. A similar kind of relationship may have operated between the Indus Valley and Gujerat to the south. Possehl (1980) considers the Harappan civilization an "experiment in sociocultural organization which failed." It was a large system, but one that did not fully mature. Another expert, Walter Fairservis (1976), called it "more village-like than city-like in the western sense." He compared it to the latest stages of the 'Ubaid in Mesopotamia, just before the profound changes of the Uruk period: "For all its sophistication, it lacked the dynamism that led to the innovation that was historical Sumeria."

The Harappan civilization was an important part of a vast network of regional interactions that functioned through trade routes that extended along the Arabian coast, into northern Afghanistan and Turkmenia, and onto the Iranian Plateau, through thousands of square miles of mountainous terrain rich in minerals and other natural resources. There were regular caravan routes that linked lowlands and highlands. These carried grain and textiles, carnelian beads, pearls, and sweet-smelling rosewood, luxuries exchanged for minerals and other raw materials. Much long-distance trade was conducted by deep-sea vessels cruising the shores of the Indian Ocean into the Persian Gulf (Edens, 1993). During the 1950s and 1960s, archaeologists uncovered a Harappan-style coastal town on the Gulf of Cambay. This settlement may have served as a river port, perhaps one of several elsewhere on the Pakistani coast.

The anonymity of the Harappan leaders extends even to their appearance. These were no bombastic rulers, boasting of their achievements on grandiose palace walls. They left almost no portraits. One exception is a limestone figure from Mohenjo-daro that depicts a thick-lipped, bearded man staring at the world through slitted eyes. He seems to be withdrawn in meditation, perhaps detached from worldly affairs. The man wears an embroidered robe that was once inlaid with metal. The only clue to his status is that one shoulder is uncovered, a sign of reverence during the Buddha's lifetime more than 1000 years later. Could it be that the same convention applied in Harappan times and the portrait is that of a priest or a priest-king? Thus far, the evidence of archaeology reveals leadership by rulers, perhaps merchants, ritual specialists, or people who controlled key resources or large areas of land. They seem to have led unostentatious lives marked by a complete lack of priestly pomp or lavish public display. There is nothing of the ardent militarism of the Assyrian kings nor of the slavish glorification of the pharaohs.

The focus of Harappan civilization may have been on the irrigated lands of the Indus, where barley and wheat were cultivated in irrigated fields that lapped the city's suburbs, but most people were still village farmers practicing dry agriculture in and away from the valley. The lowland Harappans relied on rice, a crop first cultivated somewhere between India and Southeast Asia before 5000 B.C. They cultivated cotton and dates and kept cattle and water buffalo. Every farmer turned over a substantial portion of the annual harvest to the state, and indeed the authorities may have controlled the ownership of much of the land. The entire agricultural enterprise was a much larger-scale version of the communal village farming that originally had made colonization of the Indus Valley possible.

Both Harappa and Mohenjo-daro housed a comfortable and unpretentious middle class of merchants and petty officials who lived in stolid and standardized brick houses along the city streets. They wore finely woven, decorated cotton robes. Judging from clay figurines, the women wore short skirts and headdresses and perhaps longer robes (Figure 17.4). Dozens of shops sold wire neck bangles, necklaces, and pendants, but there is nothing of the elaboration found in Egyptian or Mycenaean palaces. The more prosperous city dwellers sometimes owned some ornate carved rosewood furniture, but the lifestyle was far from lavish.

The artisans—metalsmiths, potters, weavers, bead makers, seal carvers—formed a distinct class, as did the many petty bureaucrats and priests needed to run

FIGURE 17.4   Bronze figurine of a dancing girl from Mohenjo-daro, Pakistan, 4.3
inches (11 cm) high.

the multifarious affairs of government, each with his designated quarters. However, such people were a tiny minority compared with the vast mass of the populace: farmers, laborers, seafarers, and menial workers of every type. They lived in small urban dwellings or, more often, in the countryside and wore the simplest cotton loincloths or robes. To judge from modern Indian life, they had an extended family of several generations, which provided a network of kinship ties and other benefits such as communal ownership of property. Perhaps, too, the Harappan people were organized in a hierarchy of castes that restricted upward mobility and provided a wider identity outside the confines of the family.

Harappan Beliefs

Like the Sumerians, the Harappans lived in an environment that they modified for their own protection, one in which the annual floods meant a renewal of life and food for the coming year. Like the Mesopotamians, they seem to have believed that they lived in the valley to serve the gods, who caused crops to grow and soils to be fertile. The primeval roots of Indian religion may have been age-old fertility cults that served the same function as Inanna among the Sumerians and the mother goddess in many other Near Eastern civilizations—an assurance that life would continue. The only clues we have to the origins of Indian religion come from minute seal impressions and small clay figurines from Harappan villages and cities that depict a female deity with conspicuous breasts and sexual organs. We do not know her name, but she probably embodied earth and life-giving nature for the Indus people.

A seal from Mohenjo-daro bears a three-headed figure who sits in the yogic posture and wears a horned headdress. He is surrounded by a tiger, elephant, rhinoceros, water buffalo, and deer. Some archaeologists believe that the seal represents a forerunner of the great god Shiva in his role of Lord of the Beasts. Many Harappan seals depict cattle, which may be symbols of Shiva, who was worshiped in several forms. To judge from later beliefs, he may have had a dual role, serving as a fertility god as well as a tamer or destroyer of wild beasts (Miller, 1985). Shiva gave life by planting the seed but also could destroy any creature, including human beings, at a flick of the finger. In part he may symbolize the unpredictable dangers of flood and famine that could threaten a village or a city. Harappa and Mohenjo-daro have yielded dozens of carved phallic symbols and circular stones with round holes, which represent Shiva's consort Devi's teeming womb. Perhaps these are simple prototypes of the Hindu *lingam* and *yoni* symbols that are found in the temples of Shiva and Devi to this day. If the evidence of figurines and seals is to be believed, the symbolism of early Indus religion bears remarkable similarities to that of modern Hinduism. This similarity highlights the deeply ingrained conservatism of Indian society from the very earliest moments of Harappan civilization.

Writing and Weights

One reason we know so little about the Harappans is that their script still has not been deciphered (Parpola, 1994). Almost 400 different pictographic symbols have been identified from their seals. Linguists do not even agree on the language in the script, let alone the ultimate identity of the Harappans. Some authorities believe the seals served not only as religious symbols but also as tags or labels written in Sumerian on bundles of merchandise sent to distant Sumer. Some success has been attained with computer-aided deciphering techniques, which have established the script as logo-syllabic; that is, it is a mixture of sounds and words, just like Egyptian hieroglyphs.

Enough of the Indus script has been deciphered to show how many of the short seal inscriptions designate the names of individuals and their ranks. It seems, too, that some describe major figures of the Harappan cosmos and name the chiefs, as well as identifying scribes and artisan leaders in society. There are certainly close links between the Harappan script and later writings. Many of the Indus symbols are similar to those on Brahmi documents from the Ganges Valley centuries later. Both were written in what is called the *boustrophedon* style. This writing alternates lines going from right to left and left to right. This style contrasts with English, which progresses from left to right, and Arabic, which runs in the opposite direction. Many signs and symbols used on Harappan seals are found on pottery and other objects made as late as the ninth century B.C.

Even more striking evidence for cultural continuity comes from the humble half-ounce weight. No government monopoly can survive without weights and measures, so the Harappan authorities developed a standard weight that was close to one-half of a modern ounce. Later, Indian societies used a unit known as the *karsa* for the same purpose. This weighed the equivalent of 32 *rattis,* seeds of the Gunja creeper, a measure that could fluctuate slightly from year to year. Four karsas weighed almost exactly the same as the basic Harappan unit of a half ounce. Similar devices could be found in nineteenth-century bazaars.

DECENTRALIZATION AND LOCALIZATION

• • •

The Harappan civilization reached its peak in about 2000 B.C. Mohenjo-daro housed at least 40,000 people at the time and was at the apogee of its prosperity. By 1700 B.C., Harappa and Mohenjo-daro were in decline and soon abandoned. The population dispersed into smaller settlements over an enormous area, as the volume

FIGURE 17.5   Rojdi, Pakistan, a Harappan town dating to the period immediately following the abandonment of cities. (a) Excavation of house walls; (b) artist's reconstruction of the same dwellings.

of long–distance trade declined dramatically, except perhaps in metals (Figure 17.5a and b). The reasons for this change are still little understood, but may be due to a variety of factors, among them possible flooding along the Indus, shifts in patterns of Mesopotamian trade, and changes in subsistence farming (Ghosh, 1993). It may be, for example, that the shift from irrigation farming to dry agriculture, from major urban centers to a more rural settlement pattern, may be the result of major shifts in trading activities throughout northwestern Pakistan and neighboring areas. Some fundamental questions remain. How did the various regions affected by the Harappan civilization form a single, integrated system? What were the links between the Indus Valley core and the periphery? At present, we do not know (Possehl and Raval, 1989).

The rural components of Harappan culture continued to flourish in Gujerat and other areas for two centuries or more, until Aryan nomads swept down on the Indus Valley and the lowlands. By that time, the Harappans had passed on a priceless legacy of beliefs and philosophies that formed one of the mainstreams of all subsequent Indian history.

From the archaeological point of view, the period between the breakdown of the Harappan cities and the beginning of ironworking is the most obscure in India's later prehistory. Despite the abandonment of the cities, there were no major disruptions in economy or material culture. Iron tools appeared in India by 1100 B.C. and

Ironworking
Painted gray wares
1100 B.C.

are associated with painted gray wares, made on a wheel and adorned with simple, black-painted designs. The advent of iron tools enabled farmers to break up the hard, calcareous soils of the Ganges Plain, an area that was to become the heartland of later empires.

516 B.C.

Meanwhile, King Darius of Persia invaded the subcontinent in 516 B.C. and incorporated part of India into the Persian Empire. Two centuries later, Alexander the Great ventured to the Indus River and brought Greek culture to the area. His

316 B.C.

incursion also provided a stimulus for cultural developments in the Ganges, which culminated in a nationalistic revolt headed by the priest Chandragupta. This leader founded an empire that linked the Indus and the Ganges in a single administrative unit that traded as far afield as Malaya and the Near East. The period between approximately 200 B.C. and A.D. 300 saw India linked with lands far to the east and west by regular trading routes that persisted more or less independently of political developments. By this time, the influence of Indian religion in the form of Buddhism and Hinduism was being felt over enormous areas of Asia.

SOUTHEAST ASIAN CIVILIZATIONS

• • •

The emergence of complex states in Southeast Asia (Figure 17.6) probably is closely connected with the spread of rice cultivation and bronze metallurgy. As we saw in Chapter 12, the early history of rice cultivation is inadequately documented, but we do know that the spread of rice agriculture throughout Southeast Asia may prove to be connected with farmers originating in what is now southern China. Pottery that shows the influence of their widespread traditions has been found in Thailand and possibly Malaya. Bronze technology appears in northeast Thailand between 2000 and 1500 B.C. (Higham, 1989) (Figure 17.7, p. 422). Recent excavations at the Non Pa Wai site in that region dissected a large mound of copper smelting debris, dating the earliest levels of metal smelting activity there to about 1500 B.C.

1500 B.C.

Charles Higham's shorter chronology receives important support from excavations in Vietnam's lower Red River Valley. There, bronze appeared by about 1500 B.C. in sites of the late Phung Nguyen culture (Huyen, 1984). Unfortunately, only isolated radiocarbon dates are available, so the chronology is still loosely anchored. Bronze metallurgy was also well established on the Vietnamese coast during the late second millennium B.C. One site near Ho Chi Minh City has yielded sandstone molds and bronze artifacts identical to those found in northeast Thailand (Higham, 1989).

**Dong Son culture
300 B.C.**

Vietnam's Dong Son culture represents the culmination of early bronze and ironworking in prehistoric times. Co Loa, near Hanoi, comprises three sets of ramparts, with moats supplied with water by a tributary of the Red River. At Co Loa's greatest extent, the fortifications enclosed about 1482 acres (600 ha). By this time, rice cultivation was sufficiently productive to support a considerable population density, combined as it was with plow cultivation, double cropping, and water control. According to Chinese records, local chieftains named Lac Lords, keepers of the drums, controlled the rights to rice land. The area was incorporated as a Chinese protectorate in 111 B.C., by which time the Dong Son rulers were in regular contact with Han China (Wheatley, 1979). From this point on, as in earlier times, much social change concerned the states and role of individuals rather than wider communities.

FIGURE 17.6   Southeast Asia.

Foreign Influences

Although archaeological evidence is still largely lacking, it seems likely that state forms of society were evolving in Southeast Asia as early as A.D. 150 (Higham, 1989). What is uncertain is the extent to which foreign influences played a part in the dissemination of more complex state organizations. Much of our information on early Southeast Asian states comes from Chinese and Indian sources (Hall, 1985).

Trading Systems Established

For centuries Southeast Asia was dominated, at least tangentially, by two foreign presences. To the north the Chinese imposed their political will on the Lac peoples

FIGURE 17.7   Excavations at Ban Chiang, a cemetery site in northeast Thailand that yielded evidence of bronze working before 1500 B.C.

on the Bac Bo lowlands and extended their tribute systems into the Red River Valley. This was an arbitrary imposition of an entirely different economic system onto trading systems based on reciprocity. It was quite different from the cultural changes going on in the southerly parts of Southeast Asia.

A.D. 1   By about A.D. 1, the busy sea-trading networks of Southeast Asia were being incorporated into the vast oceanic trade routes stretching from China in the east to the shores of the Red Sea and the east coast of Africa in the west (Table 16.1). No one people controlled the whole of this vast trade. Most of the Indian Ocean commerce was in the hands of traders, who used monsoon winds to traverse the long sea-lanes from India to Africa and from Arabia to both continents. The trade carried raw materials and luxury goods such as glass beads and cloth. During the heyday of the Roman Empire, the Greeks and Egyptians of Alexandria took some interest in the Indian Ocean trade but rarely ventured farther than the Red Sea.

Beyond India, the trade was held by Indian merchants who penetrated deep into the numerous islands and channels of Southeast Asia. The traders themselves were an entirely maritime people, called *Mwani*, or *barbarians*, by the Chinese of the time. They spoke a polyglot of tongues and were of many lands, some Malays, some Indians, true wanderers who ventured as far east as the South China Sea. The Gulf of Tonkin and South China were served by *Jiwet*, Chinese mariners who brought luxuries to the coast, whence they were transported overland to the Chinese capital.

Indian merchants certainly were active on Southeast Asian coasts by the early centuries of the Christian era. They were trading with the tribal societies of both mainland and islands. Voyaging was then accelerated by changing circumstances. First came larger cargo vessels with a more efficient rig that enabled them to sail closer to the wind. No one knows how large these vessels were, but they must have been substantial. The Chinese are known to have transported horses by sea to Indonesia in the third century A.D., and the monk Fa Hsien recorded his sailing trip from Ceylon to China with 200 other passengers in A.D. 414.

Another factor influencing trade was a new demand for gold and other metals. The Emperor Vespasian had prohibited exporting metals from the Roman Empire in approximately A.D. 70, a move that turned Indian merchants' eyes to the southeast, particularly because the Siberian gold mines had been closed to them by nomadic raids on Asian caravans. Metals were not the only attraction; spices could be obtained in abundance. Trade was expanded entirely for commercial profit.

Religions Imported

Buddhism had made great strides in India since it appeared in the fourth century B.C. The older religion, Brahmanism, had placed severe and authoritarian restraints on foreign voyages, but Buddhism and Jainism, a form of Hinduism, rejected the notion of racial purity espoused by the predecessor religion. Travel was encouraged; the merchant became a respected part of Buddhist belief. As voyaging increased, especially from southern India to Southeast Asia, a strong cultural influence came to be felt. The tribal societies of Southeast Asia were introduced to many alien products and some of the foreigners' philosophical, social, and religious beliefs. In a few centuries, kingdoms appeared with governments run according to Hindu or Buddhist ideas of social order.

Chieftains Become Divine Kings

The initial but regular contacts between merchants and tribal societies were seasonal, dictated by the monsoon winds. The chieftains who represented the people of the tribes would have acted as intermediaries between the foreigners and the indigenous people. All exchanges and transactions having to do with the trade were channeled through them. Inevitably, argues Sinologist Paul Wheatley (1975), the chieftains learned a new way of seeing society and the world, perhaps assembling the collection of commodities for trade, acquiring organizational skills alien to their own societies. As principal beneficiaries of the trade, they would gain status, many more possessions, and therefore strong interest in seeing the trade maintained. However, the authority and powers needed to expand and maintain the commerce were not part of the kin-linked society in which the chieftains had lived all their lives. In time, they might come to feel closer sympathy with their visitors, the people who gave them their power and prestige. Philosophically they would come to feel closer to Indian models of authority and leadership. They would become familiar with the Brahman and Buddhist conceptions of divine kingship. There was even a brahmanic rite by which chieftains could be inducted into the ruling class, a group whose authority was vested in an assumption of divine kingship. Wheatley hypothesizes that regular trading contacts, combined with changes in beliefs about the legitimizing of authority, led to the birth of states in Southeast Asia.

Divine kingship was a cultural borrowing from India that revolutionized social and political organization in Southeast Asia. Numerous city-states arose in strategic parts of this huge region. Many were served by Brahman priests, who among other functions consecrated divine kings as they started their reigns. Some of these states became very powerful, with extensive trading connections and large Brahman communities. As early as the third century A.D., Chinese envoys to Southeast Asia reported on a state in the northern part of the Malay Peninsula that enjoyed regular trading contacts with Parthia and India as well as southern China.

Funan
c. A.D. 100 to 546

The Chinese visited many small Southeast Asian kingdoms that modified Indian civilization to their own purposes, but the most famous was Funan, a mercantile empire that extended along the Mekong Delta in Vietnam and some distance inland into Cambodia (Higham, 1989). Funan appears in Chinese histories from approximately the third to seventh centuries A.D. but probably came into being in approximately A.D. 100. Most accounts of Funan extol its "port of a thousand rivers" and its rich trade in gold, silver, bronze, and spices. They tell of the Funan people, who built a drainage and irrigation system that rapidly transformed much of the delta from barren swamps into rich agricultural land. The development of these fields took the communal efforts of hundreds of people living off the fish that teemed in the bayous of the delta. Most Funans lived in large lake cities fortified with great earthworks and moats swarming with crocodiles. Each major settlement was a port connected to the ocean and its neighbors by a network of artificial canals.

Funan prospered greatly from the third to sixth centuries. The ports handled goods from all over the East, even horses brought by sea from central Asia. Large numbers of Chinese merchants and Indian artisans settled in the cities and worked with bronze, ivory, silver, gold, and even coral. They brought new skills with them that the local people copied. In the sixth century many more Indian Brahmans arrived in Funan. They brought the cult of the god Shiva. He appeared in the temples in the form of a *linga,* a phallic emblem of masculine creative power. Where rulers were worshippers of Shiva, the royal linga stood in a temple on the hill that symbolized the center of the capital.

The Rise of the God-Kings

• • •

Chenla
A.D. 611 to 802

Funan was succeeded by Chenla, a patchwork of competing centers and rulers which lay along the central Mekong River (Briggs, 1951; Higham, 1989).This region provided such favorable opportunities for rice cultivation and fishing that it supported a far higher population density than even the irrigated Mekong delta downstream. Competing Chenla rulers acquired sufficient food surpluses to embark on ambitious conquests and, eventually, to develop a new political concept of divine kingship that united their far-flung domains in a common purpose—the glorification of the god-king on earth.

Khmer
A.D. 802 to 1218

The earlier Khmer kings were unable to hold the kingdom together until a dynamic monarch named Jayavarman II was crowned in A.D. 802. The focus of settlement now shifted to the central basin of Cambodia. Most of the year the basin is a shallow series of muddy pools some 40 miles (66.6 km) long, drained by the Tonle Sap River that runs into the Mekong. However, so much water floods into the Mekong Delta from July to January that the Tonle Sap's course is reversed and the pools become a vast lake, 80 to 100 miles (133 to 167 km) long, 15 to 30 miles (25 to 50 km) wide, and up to 50 feet (15.5 m) deep. Late in October the water starts receding, trapping millions of fish in the muddy bayous. The environment was so bountiful that it supported dense urban populations and generated large food surpluses, sufficient to support a glittering, wealthy civilization.

Jayavarman II had spent some years in Java, where he had studied a new cult, the worship of the god-king. This *Devaraja* cult taught that the king did not rule by divine authority alone but that he was a god himself to be worshiped and obeyed without question. Jayavarman II adopted the teachings of this powerful cult to consolidate his vast kingdom. His subjects were taught to worship him as a god. All resources were devoted to the preservation of the cult of the god-king. Everyone, whether noble, high priest, or commoner, was expected to subordinate his or her ambitions to the need to perpetuate the existence of the king on earth and his identity with the god in this life and the next. The symbol of the king's authority was the royal linga (Briggs, 1951). Jayavarman II's new strategy was brilliantly successful. He reigned for 45 years, founded a dynasty that prospered for 600 years, and united the Khmer kingdoms into a colorful, spectacular empire that reached the height of its prosperity between A.D. 900 and 1200, shortly after his death.

Previous monarchs had encouraged the worship of Shiva in the form of this phallic image, but now Jayavarman II presented himself as the reincarnation of Shiva on earth. He was the *varman*, the protector, and his priests were the instruments of practical political power. The high priests were invariably energetic, imposing nobles, who presided over a highly disciplined hierarchy of religious functionaries. They supervised every aspect of Khmer life, from agriculture to warfare and the rituals of the state religion. The custom of building a new majestic and holy temple to house the royal linga of each king was the most important of all the religious rituals. As a result, most of the 30 monarchs who followed Jayavarman II left massive religious edifices to commemorate their reigns. These they built on temple mountains or artificial mounds in the center of their capitals, the hub of the Khmer universe.

Successive Khmer kings presided over a civilization whose religious institutions functioned on the basis of consensus. Their society was one founded on the notions of conformity, on the belief that by giving to the temple, and therefore to the royal elite, people made merit for themselves. Individual welfare as well as that of the kingdom depended on conformity and consensus. For the next three centuries, each Buddhist king ruled as "great master, king of kings." When the people were admitted, they prostrated themselves not before the gods but before the god-king. The Khmer's unique form of kingship produced, instead of an austere civilization like that of the Indus, a society which carried the cult of wealth, luxury, and divine monarchy to amazing lengths.

ANGKOR WAT

● ● ●

The Khmer kings who followed Jayavarman II indulged two passions: warfare and temple building. They surrounded themselves with artists, poets, and sculptors whose sole task was to embellish and adorn their magnificent capitals. Most of these capitals were built in a fertile area teeming with fish near the Tonle Sap, an area known as *Angkor*. Of all the edifices there, the most famous is the Bayon, the temple mausoleum of King Suryavarman II. This extraordinary shrine is a spectacle of beauty, wonder, and magnificence, the largest religious building in the world, greater even than Vatican City, 5000 feet (1500 m) by 4000 feet (1200 m) across. The central block measures 717 feet (215 m) by 620 feet (186 m) and rises more than 200 feet (60 m) above the forest. It dwarfs even the largest Sumerian ziggurat and makes Mohenjo-daro's citadel look like a village shrine. The Bayon took 40 years to build.

Angkor Wat, the mausoleum of Jayavarman VII, is approached through an entrance gallery with a tower by a paved causeway 500 feet (150 m) long that is flanked with balustrades adorned with mythical, multiheaded snakes (Figure 17.8).

FIGURE 17.8   Angkor Wat.

It opens onto a cruciform terrace in front of a rectangular temple that rises in three imposing tiers to a central cluster of five towers. Each tower bears a lofty pinnacle that from afar looks like a giant lotus bud. The causeway leads across a huge moat 600 feet (180 m) wide enclosed by masonry walls 4 miles (6.4 km) in circumference. The engineers built the walls with a total error of less than an inch! The moat still is a beautiful sight, with floating water lilies, wild orchids, and other shimmering blooms. Angkor Wat was built in three great rising squares (Riboud, 1992). A central group of chambers and then long open galleries extend all around each square, with a double square of columns on their outer face. Each terrace is surrounded by a gallery interspersed with corner towers, pavilions, stairways, and other structures. On the highest terrace, the central tower is tied to axial pavilions by galleries supported by pillars that divide it into four paved courts. The towers themselves are without interior windows or staircases and are finished with superb lotus-bud cones.

   Every detail of this extraordinary building reproduces part of the heavenly world in a terrestrial mode. The Khmer believed that the world consists of a central continent known as *Jambudvipa,* with the cosmic mountain *Meru* rising from its center. The gods lived at the summit of Meru, represented at Angkor Wat by the highest tower. The remaining four towers depict Meru's lesser peaks; the enclosure wall, the mountain at the edge of the world; and the surrounding moat, the ocean beyond. Angkor Wat was the culminating attempt of the Khmer to reproduce a monument to the Hindu gods: Shiva, the creator; Vishnu, the preserver of the universe; and Brahma, who raised the earth. Everything about Angkor Wat is on a massive and lavish scale, as if expense, time, and labor were of little importance.

The galleries of Angkor Wat are adorned with more than 4000 feet (1212 m) of polished sandstone bas-reliefs, each approximately 8 feet (2.42 m) high (Giteau, 1966). Some 2000 temple dancers wearing ropes of pearls dance in graceful, acrobatic poses along the galleries, walls, and pillars. These lovely, smiling, and often seductive creatures, naked to the waist, soften the dark gray edifice, stretching for hundreds of feet over the walls of the second and third terraces. Most of the bas-reliefs depict religious scenes, popular legends, and wars. Hundreds of soldiers mounted on elephants ride victorious over opposing armies, warriors fight from chariots, and fleets sail to battle. There are even armies of monkeys and men, and victory marches with bands and banners. The sculptures invoke the Hindu Trinity, gods, goddesses, and guardian deities. The god-king rides on a royal elephant surrounded by attendants and soldiers. He is depicted setting forth to fight Angkor's enemies with the blessings of his priests and is seen administering his domains and enjoying the triumphs of his reign.

Angkor Wat taxed the resources of the kingdom severely. Undeterred, the rulers used thousands of corvee laborers working in the dry season to make merit to erect a huge new capital at Angkor Thom nearby. The sheer size of Angkor Thom is overwhelming. A dark and forbidding 8-mile (12.8-km) wall surrounds the capital. The five gateways rise 60 feet (18 m), and the formerly crocodile-filled moat is 540 feet (162 m) across. When visitors walked into the capital, they entered a symbolic Hindu world with the king's funerary temple at the center. Great triple-headed elephants guard the flanks of the gates, and four huge Buddha faces adorn the towers above the massive doorways. The Grand Plaza of Angkor Thom was the scene of ceremonies and contests, of vast military reviews and massed bands. Long bas-reliefs of animals and kings walking in procession above seas of snakes and fish lead to the plaza and look down on its wide spaces.

It is said that a million people once lived in or near Angkor Thom. The architectural and artistic legacy they left is mind-boggling, one so large that a single frieze of marching elephants extends over 1200 feet (360 m) of sculpted wall. The task of building the city beggared the state. The temple of the king's father contained no fewer than 430 images, with more than 20,000 in gold, silver, bronze, and stone in the wider precincts. Another inscription in the same temple records that 306,372 people from 13,500 villages worked for the shrine, consuming 38,000 tons of rice a year. An inscription in the nearby temple of Ta Prohm inventories a staff of 18 senior priests, 2740 minor functionaries, 615 female dancers, and a total of 66,625 "men and women who perform the service of the gods." The same temple owned gold and silver dishes, thousands of pearls, 876 Chinese veils, and 2387 sets of clothing for its statues. The result of the ruler's megalomaniacal orgy was a totally centripetal and macabre religious utopia in which every product, every person's labor, and every thought was directed to embellishing the hub of the universe and the men who enjoyed it (Wheatley, 1975).

After A.D. 1218, the center and economic gravity moved farther east. There were no longer the resources in the Tonle Sap region to support large irrigation works or ambitious temple projects. Angkor Thom fell to alien armies in approximately 1430, and the divine kings and their works were soon just a shadowy memory.

CHAPTER SUMMARY

State-organized societies in the Indian subcontinent developed from indigenous roots in about 2600 B.C. The Harappan civilization of the lowland Indus Valley developed as the result of a major shift in Sumerian long-distance trade patterns and long-term interactions between the Harappan culture of the lowlands and the Kulli Complex of the Baluchistan highlands. Harappan civilization flourished along the Indus for about a thousand years. It was an urban society with many smaller, satellite settlements, carefully planned and ruled by priest-kings, who controlled both religious and economic life. After 1700 B.C., the major cities went into decline, but Harappan society flourished in rural settings for a considerable time. The period between the end of the Harappa culture and Persian King Darius's invasion of the subcontinent in 516 B.C. remains little known, but there was strong cultural continuity in most areas.

Southeast Asian peoples had developed bronze working by at least 1500 B.C. The process of local state formation began around the same time, but the first historical records of complex states date to the third century A.D. Many such developments were centered around the Central Mekong Valley and, later, the central Cambodian basin. There, the flamboyant Khmer civilization flourished after A.D. 802, a society based on divine kingship and strong notions of conformity. Four centuries later, the center of political gravity moved farther east, and the great palaces and temples of the Tonle Sap region were largely abandoned.

GUIDE TO FURTHER READING

Allchin, Bridget, and Allchin, Raymond. 1983. *The Rise of Civilization in India and Pakistan.* Cambridge, Eng.: Cambridge University Press.
> *A summary account of the roots of the Indus civilization that is readable and well argued.*

Possehl, Gregory. 1986. *Kulli: The Exploration of Ancient Civilization in Asia.* Durham: North Carolina University Press.
> *A wide-ranging analysis of the Kulli Complex, with provocative discussion of the Harappan civilization. A specialist monograph.*

Possehl, Gregory (ed.) 1993. *Harappan Civilization: A Recent Perspective,* 2nd ed. New Delhi: Oxford and IBH Publishing.
> *Specialist essays on the Harappan Civilization which place recent surveys and excavations in perspective. Authoritative and detailed.*

Wheeler, Sir Mortimer. 1962. *The Indus Civilization,* 2d ed. Cambridge, Eng.: Cambridge University Press.
> *Wheeler's classic account is based on his Indus Valley excavations in the late 1940s. Somewhat outdated, but it reads well.*

Wolpert, Stanley A. 1977. *A New History of India.* London: Oxford University Press.
> *By far the most lucid account of Indian history for the beginner. A good synthesis of archaeology, legend, and documentary sources.*

Southeast Asia is difficult to study in any depth, for books are few and far between. However, the following are suggested:

Briggs, L. Cabot. 1951. "The Ancient Khmer Empire." *Transactions of the American Philosophical Society*, 41.

> *Perhaps the standard archaeological and historical source for specialists and lay readers alike. Highly technical but crammed with useful information, much of it from very obscure sources.*

Giteau, M. 1966. *Khmer Sculpture and the Angkor Civilization*. London: Thames and Hudson.

> *A wonderful lay reader's guide to the elaborate artistry and architecture of the Khmer. Lavishly illustrated.*

Higham, Charles. 1989. *The Archaeology of Mainland Southeast Asia*. Cambridge, Eng.: Cambridge University Press.

> *A comprehensive account of mainland Southeast Asia that melds archaeological and historical evidence. Up to date and authoritative.*

SHANG CIVILIZATION IN EAST ASIA

• • •

The weathered, inscribed bone came from a curio shop—part of an ox shoulder blade that seemed out of place among precious jade and porcelain bowls. Archaeologist Tung Tso-pin was intrigued and wondered if the bone was connected to the ancient, and still little known Shang civilization of ancient legend. The Shang people had lived on the banks of the Huanghe River, their capital said to be near the town of Anyang. Even as early as the eleventh century, local scholars had collected exotic bronze vessels from the flat farmland where Shang kings once lived. Tung Tso-pin visited Anyang in the late 1920s, just after the river had changed course nearby, eroding rich cultural debris, including more ox shoulder blades, from the bank. He dug several deep pits that contained carefully packed "archives" of oracle bones, ox shin bones and scapulae, also tortoise shells, marked with inscriptions that gave historians a list of the Shang kings until their capital was destroyed by catastrophic floods. Excavations at Shang capitals have continued sporadically ever since, revealing a civilization known hitherto only from ancient legend (Table 18.1).

THE EMERGENCE OF CHINESE CIVILIZATION

• • •

2500 B.C.   By 2500 B.C., agriculture had taken such hold in China that population densities rose throughout the country (Barnes, 1993; Chang, 1986). The farmers took more and more land into cultivation until there was little new acreage available for planting. Some pollen analyses from northern villages show how the trees that once surrounded many settlements were felled as the fields lapped right up to the houses (Chang, 1986). This population growth also coincided with an expansion of wet rice farming in lowland areas, on moist floodplains, and in lush water meadows where irrigation was easy (Figure 18.1 p.432). Those villages fortunate enough to possess lands that could be irrigated, especially in the Huanghe and Yangtze valleys, soon turned into much more permanent settlements, often protected with earthen walls to guard against floods and marauding neighbors. Even these larger communi-

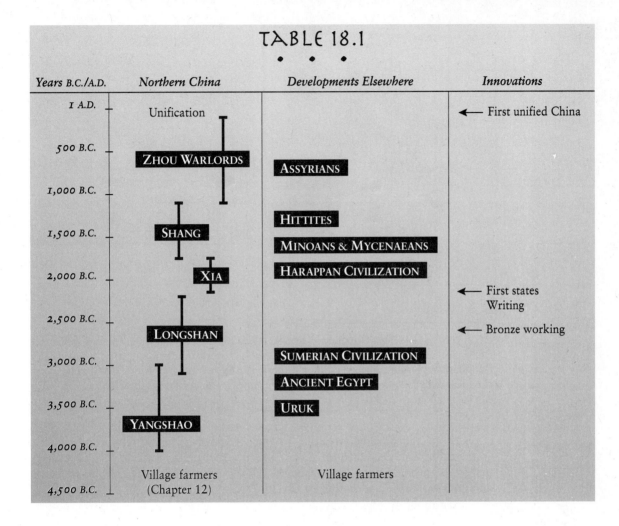

TABLE 18.1
• • •

Years B.C./A.D.	Northern China	Developments Elsewhere	Innovations
1 A.D.	Unification		← First unified China
500 B.C.	ZHOU WARLORDS	ASSYRIANS	
1,000 B.C.			
1,500 B.C.	SHANG	HITTITES MINOANS & MYCENAEANS	
2,000 B.C.	XIA	HARAPPAN CIVILIZATION	← First states Writing
2,500 B.C.	LONGSHAN		← Bronze working
3,000 B.C.		SUMERIAN CIVILIZATION	
3,500 B.C.		ANCIENT EGYPT URUK	
4,000 B.C.	YANGSHAO		
4,500 B.C.	Village farmers (Chapter 12)	Village farmers	

ties were part of a self-regulating folk society in which kinship loyalties and the extended family were all-important and age was deeply revered. The family ancestors were the conduit to the gods who controlled the harmony of the world.

However, there are signs that a new order existed, for some settlements of 3000 B.C. contain elaborate burials adorned with jade ornaments and ceremonial weapons. Village artisans created fine clay vessels exclusively for the use of these privileged people. These were important leaders who are known to have raided their neighbors, for the corpses of their enemies have been found deposited in village wells. In both the north and south, a few peasant villages became important centers ruled by new generations of kin leaders who became the nobles of more sophisticated societies. They probably were expert warriors and certainly were people of great spiritual authority, experts at predicting the future and communicating with the ancestors.

These developments would never have been possible without the unswerving conservatism of the country farmer. The village crops might change from cereals to rice, the fertility of the soils depend on radically different rainfall patterns, and building materials alter from brick and tile to bamboo, but what never varied was the unquestioning acceptance by the peasants of an emerging social order that

FIGURE 18.1   (*Left*) Distribution of farming cultures that immediately preceded Shang civilization in China (sometimes grouped under the generic, but inaccurate, term Longshan). Each outlined area represents a different regional culture (not described in detail in the text). Compare with the second map (*right*), which shows the approximate distribution of Shang culture in about 1400 B.C. (Xiao-tun and other royal sites are close to Anyang).

imposed an almost alien, wealthy, privileged society. The viability of this aristocratic civilization depended on simple loyalties that persisted from the earliest centuries of farming life into modern times. Every Chinese noble, however unimportant, cashed in on this loyalty.

Longshan
?4000 B.C.

After about 4000 B.C., the several regional Longshan farming cultures of north and south China became interlinked in what Chang (1986) calls an "interaction sphere," trading raw materials, luxury goods, and other commodities over long distances. This interdependence spurred similar developments in more complex social organization as well as technological changes that spilled over from narrow territorial boundaries to affect much of China. These innovations included copper metallurgy, construction of stamped-earth town walls, and the first widespread use of earthen fortifications. There is far more evidence for warfare and violence, including the decapitation of prisoners. New, powerful rituals emerged, among them a cosmology based on animals and birds and the use of divination to communicate with the ancestors.

On the east coast, the Liangzhu culture of the Shanghai Delta region had developed by 3250 B.C., a society known largely from its prestigious burials. Liangzhu's expert potters were specialist artisans, some of the first in east Asia. Many of their finely made, black polished wares were made not by hand, but on a potter's wheel. The wealthiest members of society were buried in special burial precincts, their graves adorned with finely made jade ornaments. Some of the elite graves are surrounded by the bodies of sacrificial victims. Liangzhu was a highly stratified society, one of the earliest in China where extreme wealth and an enormous social distance separated rulers from the ruled.

These many changes were the result of constant interaction among many different farming societies, a kind of relationship among complex chiefdoms that inevitably drew them into a larger system (H. T. Wright, 1977). This interaction developed after 4000 B.C., culminating in the emergence of Chinese civilization in about 2000 B.C. (Chang, 1986).

SHOULDER BLADES AND ORACLES

• • •

When archaeologists dug into a walled site named Chengziyai on the Huanghe River in Shandong province in 1930 to 1931, they found not only the remains of a farming village but also dozens of cracked ox shoulder blades that they identified as oracle bones used in divination ceremonies (Figure 18.2) (Keightley, 1978). The cracks

Chengziyai
?2700 B.C.

FIGURE 18.2   Shang oracle bones.

were made by applying hot metal to the bone and then were interpreted as messages from the ancestors. None of the Longshan bones bore written inscriptions, but the hundreds of shoulder blades found in pits near Anyang farther upstream are a mine of information about the origins of Chinese civilization, a unique written archive of official deliberations by the very first kings of northern China. One scholar has suggested that Chinese writing may have originated from the need to interpret the cracks on the bones, with the new writing symbols resembling persistent crack patterns. Clearly some Chinese ideographs originated as pictograms, such as that for the hill, originally shown with three humps and now written as a horizontal line with three vertical strokes (Fitzgerald, 1978).

Perhaps as early as 2500 B.C., divination rituals were a vital part of village government. All official divinations were addressed to the royal ancestors, who acted as intermediaries between the living and the ultimate ancestor and supreme being, the ruler of heaven and the creator, Shang Di. This deity served as the ancestor not only of the royal line but also of the "multitude of the people." The king was the head of all family lines that radiated from his person to the nobility and then to the common people. These actual and imputed kinship ties were the core of early Chinese civilization, for they obligated the peasants to provide food and labor for their rulers.

In addition to shoulder blades from oxen and water buffalo, the diviners used tortoiseshell for their ceremonies. The term *scapulimancy,* meaning "shoulder blade divination," refers to the bones used most frequently in the ceremonies. The bones and shells were smoothed and cleaned and perhaps soaked in liquid to soften them. Rows of hollows were then produced on the underside to make the substance thinner and the surface more susceptible to being cracked. When a question was posed, the diviner would apply a metal point to the base of the hollow, causing the surface to crack. The response of the ancestors was "read" from the fissures. A skillful diviner could control the extent and direction of the cracks. Thus, divination provided an authoritative leader with a useful and highly effective way of giving advice; a leader could regard disagreement as treason.

XIA AND SHANG: ?2700 TO 1100 B.C.

• • •

The obvious starting point in the study of Chinese civilization is Chinese legends, which tell us that the celebrated Huanghe Emperor Huang Di founded civilization in the north in about 2698 B.C. This great legendary warlord set the tone for centuries of the repressive harsh government that was the hallmark of early Chinese civilization. About 2200 B.C., a Xia ruler named Yu the Great gained power through his military prowess and his knowledge of flood control, by which he could protect the valley people from catastrophic inundations.

Xia and Shang dynasties ?2700 to 1100 B.C.

What exactly do these legends mean? Who were the Xia and the Shang? In all probability they were dynasties of local rulers who achieved lasting prominence among their many neighbors after generations of bitter strife (Chang, 1980, 1986). Every chieftain lived in a walled town and enjoyed much the same level of material prosperity, but each ruler came from a different lineage and was related to his competitors by intricate and closely woven allegiances and kin ties. Each dynasty assumed political dominance in the north in turn, but for all these political changes, Shang civilization itself continued more or less untouched, a loosely unified confederacy of competing small kingdoms that quarreled and warred incessantly.

The archaeological record reveals that Shang-type remains are stratified on top of Longshan occupation levels at many places in northern China, and they represent a dramatic increase in the complexity of material culture and social organization (Chang, 1986). The same trends toward increasing complexity are thought to have occurred elsewhere in China at approximately the same time, for literate states may have emerged from a Longshan base in the south and east as well. In form they probably resembled the Shang closely, but few details of the others are known. It seems likely that the Shang dynasty was dominant from approximately 1766 to 1122 B.C. but that other states continued to grow at the same time. The larger area of Chinese civilization ultimately extended from the north into the middle and lower courses of the Huanghe and Yangtze rivers. In this account, we concentrate on northern Chinese civilization simply because more is known about the archaeology of the Shang than about any other early Chinese state.

Shang
1766 to 1122 B.C.

Capitals and Sepulchers

The oracle bones and other historical sources provide only a sketchy outline of the early dynasties and the ways the Shang kings went about their business. The bones inform us that they lived in at least seven capitals, situated near the middle reaches of the Huanghe River in the modern provinces of Henan, Shandong, and Anhui (Keightley, 1978). The sites of all these towns are still uncertain, but in approximately 1557 B.C. the Shang kings moved their capital to a place named Ao, which archaeologists have found under the modern industrial city of Zhengzhou, some 95 miles (153 km) south of Anyang close to the Huanghe River (Wheatley, 1971). Unfortunately, the royal compound lies underneath the modern downtown area, so only limited excavations have been possible. However, the diggers have found traces of a vast precinct surrounded by an earthen wall more than 33 feet (9.9 m) high, enclosing an area of 2 square miles (5.18 sq. km). It would have taken 10,000 workers laboring 330 days a year for no fewer than 18 years to erect the fortifications alone. This walled compound housed the rulers, the temples, and the nobles. Some foundations of their large houses and ancestral altars have come from excavations inside the compound. The residential quarters and craft workshops lay outside the Shang walls. These include two bronze factories, one of them covering more than an acre. The metalworkers lived in substantial houses near their furnaces. There were bone workshops, too, places where animal and human bones were fashioned into arrowheads, pins, and awls. Zhengzhou's potters lived in a satellite village close to the kilns, where they fired hundreds of fine vessels. The excavations revealed dozens of unfired and incomplete vessels.

Early Shang
?1750 to 1650 B.C.

Zhengzhou

Middle Shang
1650 to 1400 B.C.

The capital moved to the Anyang area in approximately 1400 B.C. (the beginning of the Late Shang phase), where it remained until the fall of the Shang more than 250 years later. This new royal domain was known as *Yin* and may in fact have encompassed a network of compounds, palaces, villages, and cemeteries extending over an area some 120 square miles (310 sq. km) on the northern bank of the Huanghe River. The core of this "capital" was near the hamlet of Xiao-tun, 1.5 miles (2.4 km) northwest of the modern city of Anyang. Years of excavations at Xiao-tun have revealed 53 rectangular foundations of stamped earth up to 120 feet (36 m) long, 65 feet (19.5 m) wide, and as much as 5 feet (1.5 m) high, many of them associated with sacrificial burials of both animals and humans (Chang, 1980, 1986). One group of 15 foundations on the north side of the excavated area supported timber houses with mud and stick walls, devoid of sacrificial victims. These

Late Shang
1400 to 1100 B.C.

FIGURE 18.3   Reconstruction of a structure from the ceremonial area at Xiao-tun, Anyang, in Henan Province.

are believed to be the royal residences that housed extended families of nobles living in large halls and smaller rooms closed off with doors (Figure 18.3). Twenty-one massive foundations on an elevated area in the center of the excavations formed two rows of temples associated with a series of five ceremonial gates. The builders buried animals, humans, and even chariots in this vicinity, perhaps to dedicate the temples. Nearby lay semisubterranean houses, where the royal servants and artisans lived. The service areas included bronze foundries, workshops, and pottery kilns.

The Shang Royal Burials

The Shang rulers at first buried their dead in a cemetery just more than a mile northeast of Anyang. Eleven royal graves from this cemetery were excavated during the 1930s (Chang, 1986). They were furnished on a lavish scale and date to between 1500 and 1200 B.C. The best-known grave is in the shape of a crosslike pit approximately 33 feet (9.9 m) deep with slightly sloping walls. Four ramps lead from the surface to each side of the pit (Chang, 1960). The coffin of the ruler, which was placed inside a wooden chamber erected in the burial pit, was accompanied by superb bronze vessels and shell, bone, and stone ornaments. One ceremonial halberd has an engraved jade blade set in a bronze shaft adorned with dragons and inlaid with malachite. The rulers were accompanied in death by slaves and sacrificial victims buried both in the chamber itself and on the approach ramps. Many were decapitated, so their bodies were found in one place and their heads in another.

The Shang kings surrounded their sepulchers with hundreds of lesser burials. No fewer than 1221 small graves have been dug up nearby, many of them burials of between 2 and 11 people in a single tomb. Some of the skeletons are associated with pottery, weapons, or bronze vessels, but most are devoid of all adornment. In 1976 archaeologists uncovered nearly 200 of these graves. Most of them contained decapitated, dismembered, or mutilated bodies. Some of the victims had been bound before death. These can only have been sacrificial offerings consecrated when the kings and their relatives died.

The Bronze Smiths

The Shang people are justly famous for their bronze work, best known to us from ceremonial artifacts found in royal tombs. The prestigious metal was not gold, which was in short supply, but bronze. Most Shang bronzes are food or drinking vessels, some are weapons, a few are musical instruments, and many are chariot and

FIGURE 18.4   Shang ceremonial bronze vessels, from approximately 1300 B.C.

horse fittings. Bronze working was the guarded monopoly of the rulers, a complex art that the Chinese developed quite independently from the West before 2000 B.C. Their smiths produced some of the most sophisticated and elegant bronze objects ever crafted (Figure 18.4).

The Shang people discovered bronze working on their own, perhaps as a result of their long experience with kiln-fired pottery baked at high temperatures (Barnard, 1961). The smaller objects, such as spearheads, arrowheads, and halberds, were made by pouring a mixture of copper and tin into a single- or two-piece mold. Much more complex procedures had to be employed to manufacture large ceremonial vessels. These elaborate display pieces were copies of clay prototypes carefully sculpted around a baked clay core and encased in a segmented mold. Once the clay version was completed, the baked outer mold was removed, the model broken away from the core, and the two parts reassembled to receive the molten bronze. This complex technique remained in use for at least five centuries. An alternative would have been the lost-wax method, in which a single-piece mold encases a wax mold that is heated and then poured out to be replaced with metal.

THE WARLORDS: 1122 TO 221 B.C.

● ● ●

Every early Chinese ruler stayed in power by virtue of a strong army. Shang society was organized on what might be called military lines, so that the royal standing army could be supplemented with thousands of conscripts on very short notice. The kings frequently were at war, protecting their frontiers, suppressing rebellious rivals, or raiding for as many as 30,000 sacrificial victims at one time. In a sense, every early Chinese state was an armed garrison that could call on armies of more than 10,000 men. The secret was a sophisticated, permanent military establishment and a kin organization through which people were obligated to serve the king when called upon. The same basic organization persisted long after the fall of the Shang dynasty in 1100 B.C.

The Anyang graves reveal that every foot soldier carried a set of weapons: a bow and arrows, halberd, shield, small knife, and sharpening stone. The bows were made of horn and ox sinew and were approximately a man's height. They propelled stone-, bone-, or bronze-tipped arrows equipped with feathers. The Shang soldiers used a small leather or basketry shield for chariot warfare and a longer one on foot, both painted with tiger designs. Most surviving Shang weapons come from sacrificial chariot burials, such as the one excavated near Anyang in 1973. The archaeologists did not uncover the wooden chariot itself but a cast of the wooden parts preserved in the soil (Figure 18.5). They brushed away the surrounding soil with great care until they reached the hardened particles of fine sand that had replaced the wooden structure of the buried chariot. They were able to photograph not only the "ghost" of the chariot but also the skeletons of the two horses. The charioteer had been killed at the funeral and his body placed behind the vehicle. The yokes of

FIGURE 18.5   Chariot burial from the royal Shang tombs near Anyang. The wooden parts of the chariot were excavated by following discolorations made by the decaying wood in the ground.

the chariot rested on the horses' necks. Even the reins were marked by lines of bronze roundels in the grave. The charioteer rode on a wicker and leather car measuring between 3 and 4 feet (0.9 and 1.2 m) across and borne on a stout axle and two spoked wheels with large hubs adorned with bronze caps. In all probability, the nailless chariot was held together with sinew lashings, adorned with bronze and turquoise ornaments, and perhaps painted in bright colors.

The Shang dynasty fell in about 1100 B.C. at the hands of the neighboring Zhou. The conquerors did not create a new civilization; rather, they took over the existing network of towns and officials and incorporated them into their own state organization, thus shifting the focus of political and economic power to the south and west, away from Anyang into the fertile Wei Valley near the modern city of S'ian. By this time, the influence of what may loosely be called Shang civilization extended far beyond the north, into the rice-growing areas of the south and along the eastern coasts. The Zhou divided their domains into various almost independent provinces, which warred with one another for centuries (Fitzgerald, 1978). It was not until 221 B.C. that the great emperor Xuang Ti unified China into a single empire. By Roman times, Chinese civilization had been flourishing for more than 2000 years, a distinctive and highly nationalistic culture that differed sharply from its Western contemporaries in its ability to assimilate conquerors and the conquered into its own traditions. In contrast, the Roman Empire was built on the groaning backs of slaves and collapsed into the Dark Ages when attacked by barbarian nomads. The ability of the Chinese people simply to assimilate these same nomadic conquerors explains why the essential fabric of their civilization survives to this day.

CHAPTER SUMMARY

Early Chinese civilization emerged independently of state-organized societies in the West. By 2500 B.C., population densities were rising in farming communities throughout China, and there are signs of social differentiation in village cemeteries. Exchange networks already linked thousands of small communities by 4000 B.C., spurring social and technological changes that included copper metallurgy and the widespread use of earthen fortifications. A new cosmology based on animals and the use of divination to communicate with the dead came into widespread use. The Shang civilization of the Huanghe Valley is the best-known early Chinese state, flourishing from approximately 1766 to 1122 B.C. It probably was the dominant state among several throughout northern China. There were at least three stages of Shang civilization, associated with distinctive writing and bronze metallurgy. Shang society was organized along class lines, with the rulers and nobles living in segregated precincts whereas the mass of the people were scattered in townships and villages in the surrounding countryside. Shang civilization ended with the overthrow of the Shang dynasty by Zhou rulers, who reigned over a wide area of northern China from 1122 to 221 B.C.

GUIDE TO FURTHER READING

Barnes, Gina L. 1993. *China, Korea, and Japan.* London and New York: Thames and Hudson.

A summary of the archaeology of three crucial regions of Asia for the general reader. Lavishly illustrated.

Chang Kwang-Chih. 1980. *The Shang Civilization*. New Haven, CT: Yale University Press.

> *A detailed reconstruction of Shang civilization derived not only from archaeological data but also from a complicated palimpsest of legends, oracle bone inscriptions, and documentary records. An impressive, meticulous book that is an ultimate source on this remarkable society.*

Chang Kwang-Chih. 1986. *The Archaeology of Ancient China*, 4th ed. New Haven, CT: Yale University Press.

> *The fundamental account of prehistoric China for all serious students, with the priceless advantage that it is regularly updated. Lavishly illustrated. Major emphasis on chronology and artifacts.*

Fitzgerald, Patrick. 1978. *Ancient China*. Oxford, Eng.: Elsevier Phaidon.

> *A well-illustrated history (and prehistory) of China for the lay reader that concentrates on the period after the Shang dynasty. Clearly written and a good starting point.*

Wheatley, Paul. 1971. *The Pivot of the Four Quarters*. Chicago: Aldine.

> *A learned book that will daunt many casual readers but is a crucial source for understanding early Chinese civilization. Concentrates on the early Chinese city.*

CHAPTER 19

ANATOLIA, GREECE, AND ITALY

• • •

I have found the graves which, according to tradition, are those of Agamemnon, Cassandra, Eurymedon, and their companions." With this dramatic telegram to the King of Greece, archaeologist Heinrich Schliemann announced the discovery of the gold-smothered graves of Mycenae to an astounded world in 1876. Fresh from his triumphs at Troy, Schliemann had descended on Mycenae like a whirlwind, excavating in a circular area inside the main gate of what he thought was the Homeric hero Agamemnon's fortress. Within a few weeks, he and his wife uncovered fifteen skeletons lying in five gold-smothered graves, a spectacular discovery that prompted his royal telegram. One of the bodies was so well preserved that some of the nonskeletal parts still remained, the gold ornaments in perfect condition. Schliemann commissioned an oil painting of the grave while a local druggist mixed alcohol and gum arabic in a frantic effort to preserve the grave. So much gold came from the excavations that Schliemann lit great watch fires to prevent looting. It was the first watch fire, he said, to shine out at Mycenae since Agamemnon's time.

Later researches have shown that Schliemann was wrong in attributing the Mycenaean graves to Agamemnon and his family, but they are eloquent testimony to the riches and power of the earliest mainland Greek civilization. We must now explore the developments that led to Mycenae and its predecessors. This chapter covers an enormous area of the ancient world. It is concerned not only with the humble beginnings of state formation and complex societies in areas like Anatolia but also with the rapid growth of what we called a nascent world system over the mainland Near East and the entire eastern Mediterranean after about 2000 B.C. (Table 15.1). The societies described in this chapter cannot be considered in isolation, for they all played important parts in a much larger development—the growth of a truly international economic system that extended from Spain in the west to the distant Indus Valley in the east and lasted in various forms into historical times (Figure 19.1).

FIGURE 19.1   Sites and cultures mentioned in this chapter.

EARLY TOWNS IN ANATOLIA

● ● ●

Anatolia, with its rich obsidian and copper outcrops, was an early player in the great regional exchange networks that developed in the Near East as early as 7000 B.C. (Chapter 9). At first, there were few large communities, but those that did flourish controlled trade over a large area around them. Çatal Hüyük in central Anatolia was one such community (Mellaart, 1967). This complex settlement was organized by creating ritual and other mechanisms that attempted to retain the close kinship ties of village life while adapting to the new complexities of long-distance trading and growing population. Unlike Mesopotamia, where new mechanisms and organizations evolved to handle social change, the system at Çatal Hüyük broke down. Anatolia's first and largest town was abandoned, and people went back to living in small villages.

The entire plateau of Anatolia seems to have experienced a subsequent gradual population increase after 3000 B.C., as long-distance trading with Mesopotamia in minerals and other materials increased. The evidence for the concentration of power and wealth in major Anatolian settlements is found after 3000 B.C. in the walled fortresses of Hissarlik (Troy) and Kultepe (ancient Kanesh) (Blegen, 1971).

Troy I (Hissarlik) 3500 B.C.

Hissarlik was first occupied in about 3500 B.C., when a small fortress was built on bedrock. Its foundations show that it contained a rectangular hall of a basic design that had been in use for centuries. The structure was to become the standard palace design of later centuries and perhaps a prototype for the classical Greek temple. In about 2300 B.C., a new settlement known to archaeologists as Troy II flourished at Hissarlik. This fortified town boasted more elaborate buildings and yielded valuable hoards of gold and bronze ornaments—a clear sign that the rulers of the settlement were supporting skilled craftspeople who designed and executed fine ornaments of rank.

Troy II 2300 B.C.

Alaça Hüyük 2000 B.C.

Thirteen royal tombs were found at the site of the town of Alaça Hüyük in central Anatolia, dating to about 2000 B.C. The tombs contain the bodies of men and their wives accompanied by domestic vessels, weapons, and many metal items (Piggott, 1965). The ornaments include copper figurines with gold breasts and finely wrought cast bronze stags inlaid with silver, which were perhaps mounted on the ends of poles (Figure 19.2).

Both the Alaça Hüyük and Hissarlik finds testify to the far-flung exchange networks that crisscrossed Anatolia by 2000 B.C. They were an important and emerging **2000 B.C.** component in the nascent world system that brought copper, tin, and other raw materials from the highlands to the lowlands of Mesopotamia and textiles and other lowland products back in return. The coastal Levant and the island of Cyprus now emerged as major elements in the new trade networks, for maritime trade, using simple coastal vessels, was assuming considerable importance along the Turkish coast and among the Aegean Islands, where a trade in obsidian, timber, pottery, wine, and olive oil had begun centuries earlier. Toward the end of the third millennium B.C., Indo-European-speaking peoples seem to have infiltrated Anatolia from the northwest, causing considerable political unrest. Despite these upheavals, the volume of trade between Anatolia and Mesopotamia reached new heights, as the two areas were becoming part of an ever-more closely meshed economic system. By 1900 B.C., for example, there was a sizable Assyrian merchant colony outside the city of Kanesh, one of several important trading centers *(karums)* that were staging **Kanesh** posts for long-distance commerce in minerals and other commodities. The karums **1900 B.C.** served as marketplaces and caravan termini, natural entrepots where prices for goods were carefully regulated. Local rulers levied taxes on the caravans, which brought important Assyrian ideas to Anatolia and reinforced the economic and political power of the elite at both ends of the trade routes.

FIGURE 19.2   Bronze stag from Alaça Hüyük, Anatolia, inlaid with silver, and a figurine of a ruler.

BALANCE OF POWER: THE HITTITES

• • •

All these developments were symptomatic of ever-closer economic ties between different regions of the Near East. These ties were a symbol of an economic interdependency that persisted regardless of political change or war. The desert caravans of black asses and the ships that plied Mediterranean waters were symptomatic of this interdependency, of a more durable world system that transcended the boundaries of local societies and even entire civilizations. At the center of this world system lay the strategic Levant, a coastline with few natural harbors but with important trade routes to Mesopotamia, Anatolia, and the Nile.

During the second millennium B.C. the eastern Mediterranean coastlands were divided up among a network of small and prosperous states. They lived in the shadow of the great kingdoms that lay inland: Egypt to the south, Mitanni to the east of the Euphrates, and Hatti (the kingdom of the Hittites in Anatolia). Each controlled a large area of territory surrounded by a hinterland that lay more or less under their influence (Figure 19.3). The three states competed directly in the Levant, and they had complex dealings on all frontiers. Mitanni, for example, tried to prevent the city-state of Assur in northern Mesopotamia from going its own way, and the famous Amarna tablets, an archive of Egyptian diplomatic correspondence, tell of shifting allegiances among the city-states of the Levant. By this time, the Levant was a land of many cities, a regular military and diplomatic battlefield for its powerful neighbors.

FIGURE 19.3   The balance of power in the Near East in the second millennium B.C.: Egypt, Mitanni, and the Hittite Empire.

The Hittites were the newest, and perhaps the most able, diplomatic players. Originally the rulers of Kanesh, they expanded their domains and seized control of the rest of Anatolia just before 1650 B.C. (MacQueen, 1987). A foreign minority, the Hittites rose to political power by judiciously melding conquest and astute political maneuvering, quickly becoming acculturated into their new milieu, while preserving their traditional values and outlook on life. They were not intellectuals, but religion was important to them. The king was not deified until after his death, if then. His duties were well defined: to ensure the state's welfare, wage war, and act as high priest under clearly defined circumstances. A hierarchy of officials supported the king, ruling an empire based on a rigid feudal system of land ownership and governance.

Hittite kings exercised enormous political influence in the Near East from their capital at Boghazkoy, with its 4 miles (6.4 km) of city walls. In the fifteenth century B.C., Syria had been a province of the Egyptian empire. The Hittites pressed hard on the Egyptians on both diplomatic and military fronts, until the Great King of Hatti, Suppiluliumas I (1375–1335 B.C.), could claim Lebanon as his frontier. The conflict culminated in the indecisive Battle of Kadesh between the forces of pharaoh Rameses II and the Hittite ruler Muwatallis in 1286. Egypt was exhausted by this effort, and diplomatic archives in Akkadian cuneiform contain records of the peace treaty of about 1269 between the Hittite and Egyptian kings, which confined Egyptian interests to southern Palestine. The same treaty is also recorded on the walls of the temple of Karnak at Thebes. The grandiloquent public architecture of the period commonly depicted Egyptians and Hittites locked in battle with state-of-the-art weaponry. This included light, two-wheeled chariots manned by archers and new siege machinery for use against the many walled cities in the disputed areas.

All of this diplomatic and military activity on the part of the great kingdoms was aimed at control of the lucrative gold, copper, and pottery trade of the eastern Mediterranean, a trade in the hands of Levant and Mycenaean traders vividly illustrated by investigations of Bronze Age shipwrecks off the southern Turkish coast.

The advantage of shipwrecks from the archaeological point of view is that they provide sealed capsules of maritime trade frozen at a moment in time. The famous Uluburun ship, excavated by Çernel Pulak from the waters near Kas off southern Turkey, was shipwrecked in the fourteenth century B.C. The ship carried over 350 copper ingots, each weighing about 60 pounds (27 kg), a load of 10 tons, enough to equip a small army with weapons and armor (Figure 19.4). A ton of resin traveled in two-handled jars made by people living in the Levant; it was used, so Egyptian records tell us, as incense for Egyptian rituals. There were dozens of blue glass disks, ingots being sent to Egypt from Tyre. The cargo also included hardwood, Baltic amber, tortoise shells, elephant tusks and hippopotamus teeth, ostrich eggs, jars of olives, and even large jars holding stacked Canaanite and Mycenaean pottery. Judging from a gold scarab found on board, at least one of the crew members was Egyptian. The Kas ship's cargo contains items from Africa, Egypt, the Levant, the Greek mainland and the Aegean, Cyprus, and even copper from Sardinia. It is a dramatic reflection of the truly international nature of eastern Mediterranean trade in the second millennium B.C., when the Hittites were at the height of their power. It is hardly surprising that the great powers of the day competed savagely for control of the Levant, for it lay at the very center of an interlocking maze of trade routes that spanned the entire civilized world.

FIGURE 19.4　Excavations on the Bronze Age wreck at Uluburun, southern Turkey, with copper ingot in the foreground.

This maritime trade was still expanding in Hittite times. It played a major role in the diffusion of iron tools and weapons over the eastern Mediterranean. Iron is thought to have been first smelted in the middle of the first millennium B.C., perhaps in the highlands immediately south of the Black Sea. The new metal had many advantages, for its tough, sharp edges were invaluable for military tasks and for farming and carpentry. Iron was plentiful, unlike the tin used to alloy bronze. Iron tools soon became commonplace over a wide area of Europe and the Near East, although it was some time before domestic artifacts such as axes and hoes were invariably made with the new technology (Wertime and Muhly, 1980).

1200 B.C.　　By 1200 B.C., Hatti was in trouble. The Hittites had prospered by virtue of their well-organized, professional army, long a stabilizing influence in the eastern Mediterranean. They were expert diplomats, who controlled what is now northern Syria through their rule over two great cities—Carchemish on the Euphrates and Alalakh of Mukish in the west. There were also important treaty relationships with other powerful neighbors, including Ugarit (Ras Shamra) on the northern Levant

Ugarit　　coast. Ugarit was a cosmopolitan city ruled by a monarch who was almost like a merchant-prince. He controlled vast supplies of gold and a fleet of more than 150 ships, some of considerable size. These ventured as far afield as Cyprus and the Nile, the former being an important center of exchange with the Aegean. Ugarit was vital to the Hittites, for they depended on its ships and never became a maritime power.

　　Both the lack of maritime power and a rigid feudal system contributed to

1200 B.C.　　Hatti's undoing. About 1200 B.C., repeated migrations of foreigners flowed into Anatolia from the northwest, whence the Hittites had come only four centuries earlier. These population movements came to a head when the Phrygian peoples from Thrace ravaged the plateau as far south as the Taurus Mountains. The central Hittite government collapsed, partly because of attacks from outside but also because powerful vassals threw off their allegiance to the king. The rulers appealed to Ugarit and other maritime neighbors for assistance, but it was not forthcoming. Anatolia dissolved into the homeland of dozens of small city-states, each striving to maintain its independence. Only a few Hittite communities survived in small states in northern Syria that lasted until they were engulfed in the vast Persian Empire of the first millennium B.C.

THE SEA PEOPLES AND THE RISE OF ISRAEL

● ● ●

The situation in the Levant was explosive, for the withdrawal of the great powers left a political vacuum that could not be filled by local rulers, who depended heavily on mercenary armies. With the collapse of the Mycenaean trade at about the same time, there was a general weakening of authority. The imperial powers and petty kingships that made up the world system of 1200 B.C. were governed by highly centralized palace bureaucracies. The systems they controlled were very specialized, allowing for significant economies of operation and dense population concentrations. This very specialization made the entire system vulnerable to the effects of local upheavals, for a collapse in one area, say, the Hittite Empire, reverberated through the entire system. The exact causes of the almost dominolike collapse of Hittite and Mycenaean civilization, and the weakening of the Egyptian, are still a mystery. The abrupt collapse of the trade weakened urban elites and the foundations of their power (Coote and Whitelam, 1987).

The same interdependencies also affected the nomads and peasants who lived in the hinterlands of Levantine cities, both on the coast and on the mainland. The cuneiform tablets from the city of Mari, at the head of a powerful state on the Euphrates centuries earlier, provide compelling evidence of the intricate relationships between the cities and those who herded their flocks on the outskirts. These groups were also dependent on the international trade, but as the trade declined, they became increasingly politically independent during the period of destruction, a "Dark Age" that lasted more than 300 years. This was a time of piracy and widespread suffering, much of it at the hands of warlike bands, known to archaeologists as "The Sea Peoples."

In the Levant, many rural groups moved to the highlands inland during these centuries, relying more heavily on pastoralism and agriculture as their dependence on trading centers diminished. Village communities, nomadic herders, and even bandits lived in close proximity outside the reach of state power. It was in this milieu that a loose federation of highland villages, small towns, pastoral nomad groups, and former bandits formed to preserve and defend their sovereignty in the face of outside states. This federation became the state of Israel, which acquired its own monarchy after 1000 B.C. and protected itself with a network of walled cities. By this time, eastern Mediterranean trade was recovering and the hillside federation expanded into lowland territory, circumscribed by the sea and the desert and by the still powerful Egyptian and Mesopotamian civilizations on either side.

Israel
1000 B.C.

THE PHOENICIANS

● ● ●

800 B.C.

The general economic recovery of the first millennium B.C. was in large part attributable to the Phoenicians. They had first come into prominence in the Levant by acting as middlemen in a growing trade in raw materials and manufactured goods (Harden, 1962; N. K. Sanders, 1978). Their ships were soon carrying Lebanese cedarwood to Cyprus and the Nile. North of Israel, powerful Phoenician cities like Tyre, Sidon, and Byblos now expanded this trade. Their ships took over the copper and iron ore trade of the Mediterranean. Their trading networks later extended as far as the copper and tin mines of Spain, and Phoenician merchants made enormous profits from purple dye extracted from seashells and much used for expensive fabrics. By 800 B.C., Phoenician merchants were everywhere in the Mediterranean. A century later, the great Phoenician cities were forced to acknowledge Assyrian rule and to pay tribute to foreign masters. Magnificent Phoenician ivories come from the royal palaces at Nimrud on the Tigris, perhaps tribute or plunder from military campaigns. As for Israel, it, too, was absorbed into the Assyrian Empire in the eighth century B.C., as the Levant came under the sway of alien empires for many centuries, right into modern times.

THE AEGEAN AND GREECE

● ● ●

10,000 B.C.

4000 B.C.

Even as early as 10,000 B.C., seagoing ships were plying the waters of the Aegean, trading obsidian from the islands to mainland Greece. Seagoing trade got under way in earnest after 4000 B.C., as long-distance exchange networks expanded rapidly. In a real sense, the history of Aegean and Greek early civilizations is the story of the growth of international trade in eastern Mediterranean waters.

Olives, Vines, and Seagoing Trade

6500 B.C.

Sesklo
5000 B.C.

2500 B.C.

Farming settlements had devloped in parts of mainland Greece and the Aegean as early as 6500 B.C., but more intensive settlement of western Greece, the islands, and Crete did not occur until much later.

The Sesklo village in Thessaly was occupied by about 5000 B.C. and is typical of northern Greek sites of the time (Warren, 1975). The people lived in stone and mud houses connected by courtyards and passages. Their mixed farming economy depended heavily on cereal cultivation. Somewhat similar villages are found on Crete, where farming settlement dates back to at least 5500 B.C.

There were radical changes in the settlement pattern after 2500 B.C., when villages were established in the Cyclades, throughout Crete, and on the Ionian islands of the west. In contrast, northern Greece seems to have lagged behind. The reason may have been agriculture, for southern Greece and the islands are ideal environments for the cultivation of olives and vines, with cereal crops interspersed between them (C. Renfrew, 1972). There was a veritable explosion in village crafts as well, in the manufacture of fine painted pottery, marble vessels, and magnificent stone axes (Figure 19.5). Stone vases and fine seals were made by Cretan workers; the seals were used to mark ownership of prized possessions or pots full of oil or other commodities. By 2500 B.C., the peoples of the Aegean and Greece were smelting copper

FIGURE 19.5   Harper in marble, executed by an artisan on the island of Keros in the Aegean.

and making bronze artifacts as well as ornaments in gold and silver. These included exquisite gold and silver drinking cups and the elaborate ornaments found at Troy II, which included more than 8700 gold beads, wire ornaments, chain links, and objects of fine gold sheet. The achievements of the Aegean metallurgists in part resulted from the rapid expansion of trading throughout the Aegean, far into Anatolia, and to Cyprus, with its rich copper outcrops (see Renfrew and Wagstaff, 1982).

The Aegean is well endowed with comfortable ports and alternative trading routes that provided easy communication from island to island for most of the year. Even relatively primitive vessels could coast from one end of the Aegean to the other in easy stages. Sailing vessels are depicted on Cretan seals dating to approximately 2000 B.C. The Aegean trade flourished on olive oil and wine, metal tools and ores, marble vessels and figurines, and pottery. The success of the trade led to a constant infusion of new products and ideas to Greece and the Aegean. By 2500 B.C., numerous small towns housed farmers, traders, and skilled craftsworkers on the mainland and the islands.

2500 B.C.

The beginnings of town life created considerable cultural diversity in the Aegean, a diversity fostered by constant trading connections and increased complexity in social and political organization. Nowhere is this better documented than on Crete, where a brilliant civilization flourished in towns and palaces throughout the island. In contrast, mainland Greece lagged somewhat behind, its many small towns having only occasional contact with the Aegean islands and Crete.

The Minoans

The development of the Minoan civilization of Crete was almost certainly the result of many local factors, among them the intensive cultivation of the olive and the vine. Its development is best documented at the famous Palace of Knossos near Heraklion in northern Crete (Figure 19.6) (Castleden, 1993; Warren, 1975).

FIGURE 19.6   General view of the Palace of Minos at Knossos.

Knossos
6100 to 1400 B.C.

The first prehistoric inhabitants of Knossos settled there in about 6100 B.C. No fewer than 23 feet (7 m) of early farming occupation underlie the Minoan civilization. The first Knossos settlement was founded at approximately the same time that Çatal Hüyük was first occupied in Anatolia. The Knossos farmers lived in sun-dried mud and brick huts of a rectangular ground plan that provided for storage bins and sleeping platforms. By 3730 B.C., signs of long-distance trading increase in the form of exotic imports such as stone bowls. The first palace at Knossos was built by about 1930 B.C.; it is a large building with many rooms grouped around a rectangular central court.

3730 B.C.

Minoan civilization
c. 2000 to 1400 B.C.

At least nine periods of Minoan civilization have been distinguished by pottery styles found in the later levels of the Knossos site. Even during the earlier periods of the civilization, the Minoans were trading regularly with Egypt, for their pottery and metal objects have been found in burials there. About 1700 B.C., the earlier palaces were destroyed by an earthquake.

1700 B.C.

The high point of Minoan civilization followed that destruction, occurring between 1700 and 1450 B.C., when the Palace of Knossos reached its greatest size. This remarkable structure was made mainly of mud-brick and timber beams with occasional limestone blocks and wood columns. Some buildings had two stories; the plaster walls and floors were decorated initially with geometric designs and, after 1700 B.C., with vivid scenes or individual pictures of varying size. Sometimes the decorations were executed in relief; in other cases, colors were applied to the damp plaster (Figure 19.7).

Artistic themes included formal landscapes, dolphins and other sea creatures, and scenes of Minoan life. The most remarkable art depicted dances and religious ceremonies, including acrobats leaping vigorously along the backs of bulls (Figure 19.8, p. 452). Writer Mary Renault (1963) has vividly reconstructed Cretan life at Knossos in novels that bring Minoan culture to life.

FIGURE 19.7   Reconstruction of the throne room at Knossos, Crete. The wall paintings are modern reconstructions from fragments found at the site; details may be inaccurate.

At the height of its prosperity, Crete was self-supporting in food and basic raw materials, exporting foodstuffs, cloth, and painted pottery all over the eastern Mediterranean. The Cretans were renowned mariners. Their large ships transported gold, silver, obsidian, ivory, and ornaments from central Europe, the Aegean, and the Near East, and ostrich eggs probably were traded from North Africa.

We know very little of Minoan religious beliefs, except for some chilling finds made by Peter Warren (1984) in a house on the north side of Knossos. This fine building had collapsed in the great earthquake of 1450 B.C. The first-floor ceiling fell into the basement, taking a magnificent set of ritual vessels with it. The basement fill also contained the scattered bones of two children in perfect health. A microscopic examination of the limb bones showed that knives had been used to remove flesh from the bone. Warren believes that this may be evidence not only of human sacrifice but, perhaps, of ritual cannibalism as well, possibly related to a fertility rite associated with the Cretan Zeus and the Earth Mother.

A major event during the later stages of the Minoan civilization was the massive volcanic explosion on the island of Thera, a Minoan outpost 70 miles (113 km) from Crete, probably during the late seventeenth century B.C. (Manning, 1988). The eruption probably caused destruction on the north coast of the Minoan kingdom, but Knossos continued to flourish long afterward. This event is equated by some people with the eternal legend of Atlantis, the mysterious continent said to have sunk to the ocean bottom after a holocaust thousands of years ago (Luce, 1973). The Thera eruption may have accelerated the decline of Minoan civilization, which was already showing signs of weakness. In about 1400 B.C., many Minoan sites

FIGURE 19.8   A Minoan bull and dancers, as painted on the walls of the Palace of Knossos. The bull, a domesticated form, has a piebald coat. This very fragmentary scene has been reconstructed from inadequate original pieces and is somewhat controversial. (After Evans, 1921.)

1375 to 1350 B.C.

were destroyed and abandoned. Warrior farmers, perhaps from mainland Greece, established sway over the empire and decorated the walls of Knossos with military scenes. Seventy-five years later the palace finally was destroyed by fire, thought to have been the work of Mycenaeans who razed it. By this time the center of the Aegean world had shifted to the Greek mainland, where Mycenae reached the height of its power.

The dramatic flowering of Minoan civilization stemmed from the intensified trading contacts and the impact of olive and vine cultivation on hundreds of Greek and Aegean villages. As agricultural economies became more diversified and goods and commodities could be exchanged both locally and over longer distances, a far-reaching economic interdependence resulted. Eventually this led to redistribution systems that were organized and controlled by the inhabitants of Minoan palaces and elsewhere in the Aegean where there were major centers of olive production.

The redistribution networks carried metal objects and other luxury products the length and breadth of the Aegean. Interest in long-distance trading brought about some cultural homogeneity from trade, gift exchange, and perhaps piracy. The skills of craftsworkers were highly valued in village and palace alike. Specialized artisans practiced their crafts in the major palaces; they lived well, in stone buildings with well-designed drainage systems, and had wooden furniture.

Colin Renfrew (1973) describes both Minoan society and that of its successors, the Mycenaeans of the Greek mainland, as civilizations. He points to their sophisticated art and metalwork, to the complex palaces organized around specialized craftsworkers, and to their developed redistribution networks for foods. The Minoans and Mycenaeans did not build vast temples like those at Tikal in Guatemala (Chapter 21) or those in Egypt. They also did not live in cities. Palaces and elaborate tombs were the major monuments. Renfrew looks for the origins of Minoan and Mycenaean civilization within Greece and the Aegean and considers them to be the result of local social change and material progress.

The Mycenaeans

**Mycenaeans
1600 to 1200 B.C.**

The Mycenaean civilization, centered on the fertile plain of Argos on the Greek mainland, began to flourish about 1600 B.C. (Taylour, 1990). The chieftains who ruled over the walled fortress of Mycenae (Figure 19.9) were buried in spectacular

FIGURE 19.9   The Lion Gate at Mycenae.

shaft graves that contained weapons adorned with copper and gold as well as fine gold face masks modeled in the likeness of their owners (Figure 19.10). Their wealth and economic power came from far-flung trading contacts and from their warrior skills (Figure 19.11, p. 455). The kings were skilled charioteers and horsemen, whose material culture and lifeway are immortalized in the Homeric epics. These epics, however, were written many centuries after the Mycenaeans themselves had become folk memories (Fagles, 1990).

Mycenaean commerce took over where Minoan left off, although many Greek cargos were carried in ships of other nations. Much of the rulers' prestige was based on their contacts in the metal trade. As the Uluburun ship shows, minerals were in constant demand in the central and eastern Mediterranean, especially tin for alloying copper to make bronze. Both copper and tin were abundant in central Cyprus and Anatolia, and the Mycenaeans developed the necessary contacts to obtain regular supplies.

The Mycenaeans also prized Baltic amber, a yellow-brown fossil resin that when rubbed seems to be "electric." Occasional pieces of this precious substance reached Mycenae, and amber is found in the royal graves there (Piggott, 1965). Just how extensive the Mycenaeans' European trading activities were has been much debated. They may well have been minimal (for a discussion, see Harding, 1984).

So complex did their trading transactions become that the Mycenaeans found it necessary to establish a writing system. They refined one that had been developed by the Minoans. The Mycenaeans used a form of script written in the Greek language, known now as Linear B (Chadwick, 1958; Diringer, 1962). Eighty-nine characters

FIGURE 19.10   Gold mask of a bearded man, from Shaft Grave V at Mycenae, 1600 B.C.

make up Linear B, 48 of which can be traced back to Minoan writing, Linear A. Linear A probably originated in the simple pictographic script of the earliest Minoans (Figure 19.12). The terms *Linear A* and *Linear B* were coined by Sir Arthur Evans when he first studied Minoan writing. Linear B was in more widespread use than A, partly because the Mycenaeans exerted greater political and economic power than their Cretan neighbors.

1150 B.C.   Mycenae was a major partner in eastern Mediterranean trade until about 1150 B.C., when a combination of internal bickering and decline in agricultural yields led to its collapse. In the same century, the Phrygians of the northeast overthrew the Hittite kingdom in Anatolia. This incursion into the Mediterranean world was

FIGURE 19.11   Impression of a warrior fighting an enemy with a dagger, from an engraved gold ring, shaft graves, Mycenae.

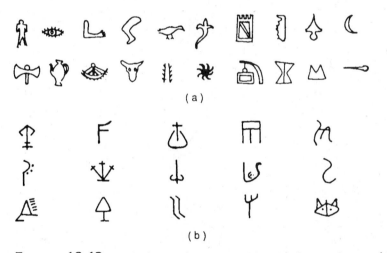

(a)

(b)

FIGURE 19.12   Early forms of Minoan writing: (a) Cretan pictographic script; (b) Minoan Linear A signs.

caused by unsettled political conditions in Europe, at least partly the result of population pressures and tribal warfare (Chapter 20).

GREECE AFTER MYCENAE

After Mycenae fell in 1200 B.C., small-town merchants on the Greek mainland continued to trade, monopolizing commerce in the Aegean and Black seas. By the eighth and seventh centuries B.C., small colonies of Greek settlers lived on the northern and

1200 B.C.

700 to 600 B.C.

western shores of the Black Sea and along the north coast of Anatolia and developed trade in gold, copper, iron, salt, and other commodities (Bonzek, 1985). Other Greeks voyaged westward and settled in southern France; they soon had a brisk trade in wine and other commodities with central Europe (Ridgeway, 1992).

The Greek City-States

In Greece many fertile agricultural areas are separated by ranges of mountains. Traders and seafarers of the Aegean islands and the Greek mainland therefore formed a network of small city-states that competed with one another for trade and political power. Athens was one of the larger and more prosperous states. The island of Sifnos in the Aegean was another, famous for its gold and silver. Paros marble was known all over the eastern Mediterranean, and Milos provided obsidian for many centuries.

490 B.C.

Athens

Greek states unified only in times of grave political stress, as when Persian kings sought to add Greece to their possessions. Darius's defeat at Marathon (490 B.C.) and Xerxes' ten years later in a naval battle at Salamis ensured the security of Greece and made classical Greek civilization possible. Athens was foremost among the Greek states (Morris, 1989), becoming head of a league of maritime cities, which was soon turned into an empire. This was the Athens that attracted wealthy immigrants; built the Parthenon; and boasted of Aeschylus, Sophocles, and other mighty playwrights. Classical Greek civilization flourished for 50 glorious years.

450 B.C.

However, throughout the brilliant decades of Athenian supremacy, bickering with Sparta in Peloponnesus never abated. A deep animosity between the two cities had its roots in radically different social systems. Sparta's government was based on military discipline and a rigid class structure. Athenians enjoyed a more mobile society and democratic government.

431 B.C.

359 B.C.

323 B.C.

The long rivalry culminated in the disastrous Peloponnesian War, from 431 to 404 B.C., which left Sparta a dominant political force on the mainland. The contemporary historian Thucydides documented the war, which was followed by disarray (Livingston, 1943). Greece soon fell under the sway of Philip of Macedon, whose rule between 359 and 336 B.C. began to develop political unity. His son Alexander the Great then embarked on a campaign of imperial conquest that took him from Macedon into Persia and then to Mesopotamia. Alexander was welcomed as a hero and a god in Egypt, where he paused long enough to sacrifice to local deities and have himself proclaimed pharaoh. His continued quests took him as far east as the Indus Valley and back to Babylon, where he died of fever in 323 B.C. By the time of his death, Alexander had united an enormous area of the ancient world under at least nominal Greek rule. His extraordinary empire fell apart within a generation, but his conquests paved the way for the uniform government of Imperial Rome.

THE ETRUSCANS AND ROMANS

● ● ●

During the first millennium B.C., the Mediterranean world was linked from one end to the other by highly intricate mercantile ties. Phoenicians and Greeks controlled much of this trade in metals and other essentials as well as exotic luxuries. The trade extended into temperate Europe and throughout the Italian peninsula, helping set the stage for large-scale Etruscan and Roman urban civilization in later centuries.

The Etruscans

By approximately 1000 B.C., some Urnfield people (named after their habit of bury- ing cremated ashes in clay urns) from central Europe (Chapter 20) had settled south of the Alps in the Po Valley (Wells, 1981). They developed a skilled bronze-working tradition, in which products were traded far into central Europe and throughout Italy. This people evolved into the Villanovan culture, which appeared in the ninth century B.C. and was soon in touch with Greek colonies in southern Italy and per- haps with the Phoenicians (Spivey and Stoddart, 1990). Ironworking was intro- duced to the Villanovans in approximately the ninth century B.C. Iron tools and extensive trading contacts won the Villanovans political control over much of northern and western Italy. They established colonies on the islands of Elba and Corsica. Several centuries of trade and other contacts culminated in a literate Etr- uscan civilization.

Like classical Greece, Etruscan civilization was more a unity of cultural tradi- tion and trade than a political reality. The Etruscans traded widely in the central Mediterranean and with warrior peoples in central Europe. Etruscan culture was derived from the Villanovan, but it owed much to eastern immigrants and trading contacts that brought Oriental influence to Italian towns.

Etruscan territory was settled by city-states with much independence, each with substantial public buildings and fortifications. Their decentralized political organi- zation made them vulnerable to foreign raiders. Warrior bands from central Europe overran some Etruscan cities in the centuries after 450 B.C., at which time Etruscan prosperity began to crumble.

By the time of Etruscan decline, however, the Mediterranean was a civilized lake. Phoenician colonists had founded Carthage and other cities in North Africa and Spain and controlled the western Mediterranean. The rulers of Greece and Egypt and later Philip of Macedonia controlled the east, and the Etruscans were in control of most of Italy and many central European trade routes.

1000 B.C.

Villanovan culture 850 B.C.

Etruscans 650 to 450 B.C.

450 B.C.

The Romans

The Etruscans had been the first people to fortify the seven famed hills of Rome. In 509 B.C., a foreign dynasty of rulers was evicted by these native Romans, who began to develop their own distinctive city-state. The next few centuries saw the emergence of Rome from a cluster of simple villages by the Tiber River to the leadership of the Mediterranean and far beyond. The Romans inherited the mantle of classical Greece and added their own distinctive culture to this foundation. They then carried Greco- Roman civilization to many parts of the world that were still inhabited by preliter- ate peasant societies. Roman legions campaigned not only in Egypt and Mesopotamia and South Arabia but also in central and western Europe and in Britain. If it were not for the Romans, the administrative and linguistic face of Europe would be very different today (Grant, 1960; Vickers, 1977).

By 295 B.C., the power of Rome dominated the whole of Italy. At this time Rome was a form of democracy, governed by a delicate balance of aristocratic and popular authority. This type of governance was appropriate for a large city-state but was hopelessly inadequate for the complexities of a huge empire. Eventually, civil strife led to autocratic rule of the empire under the emperors, the first of whom was

Romans 509 B.C.

295 B.C.

Julius Caesar, familiar to every student of Roman history for his epic conquest of Gaul (France). (His great-nephew Augustus was the first ruler actually to claim the title of emperor.)

200 to 50 B.C.   After two vicious wars with their rich rival, Carthage, the Romans achieved mastery over the western Mediterranean by 200 B.C., and by 50 B.C. much of Asia was under uneasy Roman domination. Unfortunately, the Romans lacked the mechanisms to administer their empire successfully until the Emperor Augustus reorganized the civil service and established the Pax Romana over his vast domains. There ensued a period of great material prosperity and political stability, at the price of political freedom of speech.

The stresses that led to the collapse of the Roman Empire first began to appear on the European frontiers in the second and third centuries A.D. Roman power began to decline as ambition and sophistication grew among the Iron Age tribes living on the edges of Roman territory. The "barbarians" on the fringes of the empire were mainly peasant farmers who had obtained iron by trading and intermarriage with La Tène peoples (Chapter 20). Many served as mercenaries in the Roman armies, acquiring wealth and sophistication and, perhaps most important of all, an insight into Roman military tactics.

A.D. 395   Shortage of farming land and increasing disrespect for Rome caused many Germanic tribes to raid Rome's European provinces. The raids were so successful that the imperial armies were constantly campaigning in the north. In A.D. 395, after **A.D. 410** Emperor Theodosius died, the Roman Empire was split into eastern and western divisions. Large barbarian invasions from northern Europe ensued. Fifteen years later, a horde of Germanic tribesmen from central Europe sacked Rome itself; then the European provinces were completely overrun by warrior peoples. Other Germanic hordes disturbed North Africa and crossed much of Asia Minor but left little lasting mark on history there.

What was the legacy of Rome? Its material legacy can be seen in the road system, which still provides a basis for many of Europe's and the Near East's communications, and in the towns, like London, which are still flourishing modern cities. In cultural terms, its principal legacy was the legal system, which lies at the core of most Western law codes. Roman literature and art dominated European culture for centuries after the Renaissance. Their spoken and written language, Latin, survived for centuries as the language of the educated person and as the principal means of business communication between nations. Latin lies at the base of many modern European languages and was only recently abandoned as the liturgical language of the Roman Catholic Church. The Romans and their culture lie at the foundations of our Western civilization.

CHAPTER SUMMARY

Small towns became important economic centers in parts of Anatolia as early as 3600 B.C. Communities like Çatal Hüyük failed to develop the necessary administrative and social mechanisms to cope with the increased complexity of the settlement and its trading activities. The town failed, and Anatolians of the fifth millennium B.C. reverted to village life. Small fortified villages flourished in the fourth millennium B.C. One of them, Troy I, dates to just after 2500 B.C. Troy II, founded in about 2600 B.C., was a fortified town with more elaborate architecture and fine gold and bronze metallurgy. By this time the Anatolians were trading widely over the highlands and into the Aegean, and chieftaincies were scattered over mineral-rich areas. About 1900 B.C., the Assyrians set up a trading colony at Kanesh in central Anatolia.

The Hittites assumed power in Anatolia in about 1650 B.C. They held a vital place in contemporary history, for they played the Assyrians off against the Egyptians. Hittite power was based on diplomatic and trading skills until about 1200 B.C. when international trade in the eastern Mediterranean collapsed, and a period of confusion, partly the work of the Sea Peoples, ensued. The state of Israel was born during this interregnum, among agricultural and herding peoples in the Levant highlands.

Farming settlements developed in Greece and the Aegean Islands well before 5000 B.C. There were radical changes in the late second millennium B.C., when the cultivation of the olive and the vine became widespread and trading of minerals, stonewares, and other products expanded rapidly. Numerous small towns were flourishing throughout the Aegean and eastern Greece by 2500 B.C., linked by regular trading routes. The Minoan civilization of Crete developed in about 2000 B.C. and lasted until approximately 1400 B.C. Minoan power apparently was weakened by the great explosion of its satellite island, Thera, in the seventeenth century B.C. The center of civilization passed to the mainland after 1400 B.C., where the Mycenaeans flourished until 1150 B.C. Mycenaean civilization collapsed as a result of internal dissention and possibly the exhaustion of agricultural land. Trading activities continued to expand in the Aegean after the decline of Mycenae. Small city-states flourished, unifying only in the face of a common danger such as the Persian invasions of the fifth century B.C. The Athenians enjoyed a long period of supremacy among city-states, the period of classical Greek civilization in the fifth century B.C. Alexander the Great built an enormous empire across the Near East, of which Greece was part, in the late fourth century B.C. The Roman Empire, which followed, marks the entry of the entire Mediterranean area into historic times. Developed from Villanovan and Etruscan roots in Italy, Imperial Roman power was based on the ruins of Alexander's empire.

GUIDE TO FURTHER READING

Castleton, Rodney. 1993. *Minoans: Life in Bronze Age Crete*. London: Routledge.
   A complex, often contradictory image of Minoan civilization written in clear prose.

Coote, Robert B., and Whitelam, Keith W. 1987. *The Emergence of Early Israel.* Sheffield, Eng.: Almond Press.
   A closely argued account of the rise of Israel, based on prehistoric archaeology and ecology. Provocative and convincing.

Hood, Sinclair. 1973. *The Minoans*. London: Thames and Hudson.
   A superb summary of the origins, history, and decline of the Minoan civilization for the informed layperson. Excellent illustrations.

MacQueen, J. G. 1987. *The Hittites*. London: Thames and Hudson.
   A general account of Hittite civilization. Lavishly illustrated.

Spivey, N. and Stoddart, S. 1990. *The Etruscans*. London: Batsford.
   An excellent summary of Etruscan civilization for general readers.

Taylour, Lord William. 1990. *The Mycenaeans*, rev. ed. London: Thames and Hudson.
   Mycenaean civilization described by a leading authority; a companion volume to Hood on the Minoans. *Lavishly illustrated.*

CHAPTER 20 ᴛᴇᴍᴘᴇʀᴀᴛᴇ Eᴜʀᴏᴘᴇ Bᴇꜰᴏʀᴇ ᴛʜᴇ Rᴏᴍᴀɴꜱ

. . .

I n the year 1667, a country squire named John Aubrey galloped into the village of Avebury in southern England during a fox hunt. He was "wonderfully sur- prized" to find it surrounded by a large ditch and bank and circles of massive stones. Aubrey had visited the mysterious stone circles at Stonehenge when he was eight and had long been a casual antiquary. None other than King Charles II encouraged him to survey the ancient earthworks and circles, a task that took Aubrey many years. His great work *Monumenta Britannica* with his survey maps was unfinished at the time of his death in 1697 and was not published until 1980. But archaeologists have long known what he thought of the people who built these ancient shrines: "The inhabitants were almost as savage as the Beasts, whose skins were their only rayment. . . . They were two or three degrees I suppose less savage than the Americans. . . . The Romans subdued and civilized them."

No modern day archaeologist would agree with Aubrey's characterization, for science has shown that both the native Americans and the late prehistoric Europeans were much more sophisticated than Julius Caesar and other Roman authors would have us believe. By the time Roman legions campaigned north of the Alps, temper- ate European society enjoyed a level of complexity that has fascinated archaeolo- gists for generations. How, then, did such complexity arise? Did it develop as a result of indigenous cultural evolution or because of diffusion of people and ideas from the Near East (Table 15.1)?

For years, V. Gordon Childe (1956) and others have argued that the constant demands by Near Eastern societies for copper, tin, and other metals led to cultural development in the backwater that was temperate Europe. However, this traditional viewpoint has been challenged by the calibrated radiocarbon chronologies that place the appearance of copper working in the Balkans earlier than in Greece or the Aegean. Many people now believe that Europeans were just as innovative as their eastern neighbors (Champion et al., 1984).

EARLY COPPER WORKING

● ● ●

Colin Renfrew (1978) and Ruth Tringham (1971) have argued that the farmers of southeast Europe developed copper smelting independently, partly because they already used improved pottery-firing techniques that were very suitable for copper smelting (Figure 20.1), witness the finds at the Varna Cemetery near the Black Sea in Bulgaria.

The Varna Cemetery

Varna
4600 to 4200 B.C.

At the Varna Cemetery, more than 130 richly decorated graves have yielded dozens of fine copper and gold tools and ornaments. Colin Renfrew (1978) has described the Varna finds as "the earliest major assemblage of gold artifacts to be unearthed anywhere in the world," for they date to approximately 4600 to 4200 B.C. Both the copper and the gold are of Balkan origin; indeed both metals were being worked here earlier than they were in the Near East. (Such a statement reflects findings thus far; it does not preclude future discoveries of earlier metals in the Near East.) The Balkan copper industry was quite sophisticated and was organized to serve trading networks over a wide area. At Rudna Glava in Yugoslavia, fissures mark the places where early miners followed ore veins deep into the ground. One mine in Bulgaria has ancient shafts more than 32 feet (10 m) deep. These copper mines are the earliest so far discovered in the world and show that metallurgy developed rapidly into a

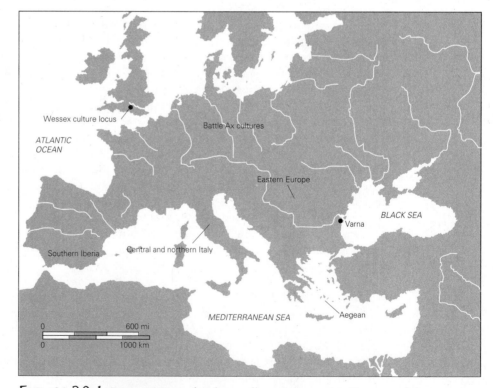

FIGURE 20.1   Major centers of early metallurgy in temperate Europe and the distribution of Battle Ax cultures.

considerable industry in the Balkans during the fifth millennium B.C. (Jovanovic, 1980).

The Varna burials provide striking evidence for differential wealth; some of the graves are richly decorated with gold ornaments whereas others contain few artifacts. Unfortunately, the settlement associated with the Varna Cemetery has yet to be found, but Renfrew (1978) has suggested that the users of the burial ground were part of a chiefdom in which the leaders used gold and copper ornaments to fulfill the social need for conspicuous display. As he points out, the problem with explaining the rise of metallurgy is not a technical but a social one—defining the social conditions under which metal objects first came into widespread use. The earliest copper artifacts had few practical advantages over stone axes. Both copper and gold were used mainly for ornamental purposes (Figure 20.2). Perhaps it was no coincidence that the first metallurgists in temperate Europe developed a wide range of ornaments, luxury items traded through exchange networks that accelerated the spread of copper working to other parts of temperate Europe.

BATTLE AXES AND BEAKERS

● ● ●

The technology of copper working is really an outgrowth of that used for pottery manufacture and probably arose after many experiments with fire, clay, and stone. The beginnings of copper metallurgy in temperate Europe were probably almost imperceptible since a handful of simple, hammered copper artifacts date to as early as 4000 B.C. At least two possible areas of indigenous copper working have been identified in southern Europe, both near copper outcrops. One is in southern Spain (Iberia) and the other in northern Italy. In both regions, the copper workers started smelting by about 3000 B.C. Britain is also rich in copper ores, and the metal was exploited early there, too. Wherever it developed, coppersmithing was probably a seasonal or at best a part-time occupation, and it was not until much later that tougher bronze artifacts came into daily use in the field and the chase.

4000 B.C.

A remarkable archaeological discovery tells us people may have covered long distances in search of minerals. A combination of dry winds and extreme cold dried

FIGURE 20.2 Copper ax heads from the Czech Republic (one-third actual size).

out and preserved a 20-year-old Bronze Age man, who perished high on the Simi-laun glacier in the European Alps in about 3300 B.C. The man lay in a crouched position, as if he had taken shelter in bad weather, while lost. Experts believe the man was either hunting or looking for minerals like copper, which are plentiful in the Alps. He carried a copper ax with a wooden shaft, a leather quiver with 14 bone- and wood-painted arrows and replacement heads, and a puttylike substance for mounting them. He wore leather boots lined with hay for warmth, a stone neck-lace, and leather and fur garments. His knees and back bore small tattoos (Barfield, 1994).

The archaeological record of the period between 3500 and 2000 B.C. is incredi-bly complicated, but we can discern two broad groupings of societies, the so-called Battle Ax and Beaker peoples, who ultimately mingled.

In east Europe, settled farming societies had lived on the edge of the huge Russ-ian steppe for hundreds of years. Like the peoples of Anatolia and Greece, they had sporadic contacts with the nomads who roamed the plains to the east; about these we know little. In the southern Russian region, a widespread population of copper-using agriculturalists lived in rectangular, thatched huts, cultivated many crops, and also tamed domestic animals, possibly including the horse. This loosely defined Kur-gan culture was remarkable for its burial customs, depositing each corpse under a small mound. The Kurgans used wheeled vehicles and made the copper or stone bat-tle ax a very important part of their armory. The wheeled cart and the battle ax had spread widely over central and parts of northern Europe by 3000 B.C. (Piggott, 1992). The globular pots associated with these characteristic artifacts, many of them bearing characteristic cord-impressed decorations, have been found at hundreds of sites. The same artifacts have often been found in megalithic tombs. These new cul-tural traits were absorbed into the millennia-old European cultural tradition, and many experts feel that the Indo-European language spread into Europe at about this time. (Indo-European speech is thought to have originated in the region between the Carpathian and Caucasus mountains. The entire Indo-European controversy is complex and outside the scope of this book, but interested readers should consult Mallory, 1988; C. Renfrew, 1987.)

Kurgan culture
3000 B.C.

It was at about this time that new house forms appeared in temperate zones. Smaller timber dwellings, just large enough to house a single family, replaced the Danubian longhouse. Warriors were buried with their battle axes under small mounds, a reflection of new cultural traditions that were to persist in Europe for thousands of years. The warrior leaders who descended from Bronze Age chieftains were the German tribesmen that the Romans encountered on the frontiers of their European empire.

Beakers
2700 to 2000 B.C.

Between 2700 and 2000 B.C., a series of highly characteristic artifacts came into fashion over a large region of Europe: coastal Spain, southern France, Sardinia, northern Italy, east and central Europe, the Low Countries, and Britain (Figure 20.3) (Harrison, 1980). These include finely made bell-shaped beakers found in hundreds of graves and burial mounds. Archaeologists such as V. Gordon Childe thought in terms of tribes of "Beaker Folk," who spread the length and breadth of Europe, bringing a new culture and copper working with them. It seems more likely that these vessels spread widely not as a result of itinerant merchants or great popu-lation movements but simply because beakers, as well as other trinkets such as metal brooches, became prized status symbols throughout Europe. They may also have been traded for what they contained—perhaps beer or mead. Perhaps they became valued heirlooms, priceless grave furniture, and artifacts exchanged as bride wealth or displayed at tribal gatherings. Beakers were only one of several innovations that

FIGURE 20.3   Beaker vessels and other artifacts, including arrowheads, from various localities in south central Britain.

were changing the face of European society. Another was the plow, which came into widespread use about 2200 B.C., opening the way for the cultivation of heavier soils and much larger acreages.

THE BRONZE AGE

● ● ●

In the Aegean, there was steady development from this early threshold of metal-working toward complex state organizations, but Europe remained settled by small village societies. The temperate zones were densely occupied and exploited, and vast acreages of forest had been cleared and brought under cultivation by 2000 B.C. The villagers managed woodland carefully, engaged in hunting to supplement their diet, and mined both hard ax stone and soft copper ore. They also panned for gold. If ambitious community works were needed, the basic metal technologies were known, and both boats and wheeled transport were available, as well as the human-power and resources. European village society was stable and self-sufficient, with thousands of communities connected by ties of kin and family and by long-established paths that led from valley to valley along well-drained ridges. Above all, European society enjoyed assured and reliable food supplies that helped bind the communities together.

The European Bronze Age began not as a result of dramatic events and military conquest nor because of some startling invention (Coles, 1982; Coles and Harding, 1979). It was merely a gradual and inevitable quickening of responses to a number of new opportunities. Many of these changes were in material culture and settlement patterns. A series of landscape surveys in southern Britain, for example, has revealed vast networks of fields and land boundaries joining river valleys, ridges, and watersheds into a managed landscape, in which different communities owned closely defined agricultural land. One Dorsetshire, England, Bronze Age agricultural system encompassed 494 acres (200 ha), with settlements of four to five huts linked to enclosures with sunken herd paths. There were fields, hoe plots, stock corrals, and homesteads, all joined in single managed agricultural units. By 900 B.C., Bronze Age food production was sophisticated. It relied heavily on plow agriculture and field fallowing as well as manuring, and it was based on the rotation of many different cereal and root crops.

From about 2000 B.C., metallurgy was a growth industry throughout temperate Europe. A series of local bronze industries developed in different parts of Europe, bringing with them a whole range of related activities: trading of ores and finished artifacts from major mining centers and the barter of both prosaic and prestigious artifacts and ornaments over considerable distances. For the first time, a major European industry was practiced in areas where supplies of raw materials were scarce. For instance, Bronze Age communities in Scandinavia, which had no metals, went to considerable trouble to acquire metal ore and finished tools both from tribes in Britain and from central European sources. European smiths produced some of the finest bronze artifacts ever made in the ancient world: axes and adzes, battle axes, daggers, swords, spearheads, shields, and an enormous range of brooches, pins, and other ornaments. They also made delicate, prestigious gold ornaments that were highly prized and buried with important chieftains.

For all these metallurgical innovations, the basic tenor of agricultural life remained unchanged, except for gradual evolution in the structure of European society—the emergence of social ranking. Just what form this ranking took is a matter of lively controversy (Coles, 1982) since it is reflected only in a differentiation of grave goods between a few individuals and the rest of society. In Denmark, for example, excavations on the island of Fyn have revealed rich Bronze Age burials and a nearby settlement with a wealth of gold and bronze. This is clear evidence that there was a powerful community there, having extensive trading connections with metal-rich regions to the south. The evidence from Bronze Age graves across Europe shows that the rich and the poor were buried side by side, the former with substantial quantities of valuable metal artifacts that were thus lost to the people burying them. This can only mean that some members of society, perhaps important traders, more probably influential kin leaders, were aggrandized at the expense of others and became a new elite in European society (Coles and Harding, 1979).

Although the first occurrence of bronze may one day be shown to date to about 4000 B.C. in southeast Europe, the earliest widespread use of tin-copper alloys was approximately 2500 B.C. in what is now Czech Republic (Coles and Harding, 1979). The new bronze implements with tougher working edges (Figure 20.4) were initially in short supply, but their use spread gradually as new trade routes were opened across central and west Europe. The earliest bronze working was centered in Unetice, an industry manufacturing axes, knife blades, halberds, and many types of ornaments (Piggott, 1965). The bronze workers themselves obviously belonged to cultural traditions long established in the area, for their burial customs are identical to those of earlier centuries. Some believe that the art of alloying tin with copper, as well as casting techniques, came to Europe from Syria. Most people now argue, however, that bronze working developed independently in Europe in that the calibrated C14 dates from the Unetice industry are earlier than those for the Near Eastern prototypes from which the other school of thought assumes Unetice to have evolved.

Unetice culture
2500 B.C.

FIGURE 20.4 Copper and bronze implements from Britain: simple flat axes and flanged and socketed axes (*left,* one-third actual size); a dagger and sword blades (*right,* one-fourth actual size).

Bronze working soon appeared in southern Germany and Switzerland as well, where deposits of copper and tin were to be found. Other places with copper outcrops were soon using the new methods, including Brittany, the British Isles, and northern Italy, all more remote from the initial centers of bronze working. The period between approximately 1700 and 1300 B.C. was one of rapid technological progress and considerable social change, generated in large part by the reinforcing effects on the local centers of bronze working of persistent demand for critical raw materials and finished tools.

    1700 to 1300 B.C.

By this time, European trading networks carried far more than bronze artifacts and metal ores. The amber trade went from the shores of the Baltic to the Mediterranean, following well-established routes (Figure 20.5) (P. Phillips, 1980). Seashells, perhaps faience (glass) beads, and other exotic luxuries were dispersed northward into the temperate zones in exchange for raw materials. Some centers of bronze production became major places for redistributing other goods as well. The salt miners of Austria also were very active in the long-distance trade.

By 1300 B.C., even societies remote from metal outcrops were engaged in metallurgy; the archaeological record tells little of increased specialization, although many richly adorned burials testify that the trade was concentrated among wealthy chieftains. The surplus food and energy were not devoted to generating additional

    1300 B.C.

FIGURE 20.5   Amber trade routes in Europe and to Mycenae. The northern coastlines were the primary sources of Baltic amber. Amber was being passed southward to the Mediterranean by the time the Mycenaeans came to power.

surpluses and extra production but, in some societies, were channeled into erecting majestic religious monuments, of which Stonehenge in southern Britain is probably the most celebrated (Figure 20.6).

Stonehenge

Shrouded in fantasy and speculation, associated by many people with the ancient Druids' cult, Stonehenge is in fact a fantastically old religious temple (Chippindale, 1994). It began as a simple circle of ritual pits in about 2700 B.C. and went through vigorous reconstructions, reaching the zenith of its expansion in the late third millennium B.C. That Stonehenge was associated with some form of astronomical activity seems unquestionable, although the details are much debated. Doubtless special priests were needed to maintain this and other major shrines and to perform the rituals in their precincts. Religious activity was supported by the food surplus, not the increased productivity that generated spectacular social evolution in the Near East. Thus, during the third and part of the second millennia B.C., little social evolution went on in Europe; political power and wealth belonged to the chieftains and warriors rather than to divine kings and a hierarchic society.

BRONZE AGE WARRIORS

● ● ●

European societies became more socially ranked as time went on. As trade intensified, local monopolies over salt and other supplies became concentrated in the hands of comparatively few individuals. Population growth and perhaps some climatic deterioration put new pressure on agricultural land (P. Phillips, 1980) (Figure 20.7).

FIGURE 20.6   Stonehenge. View of stone circle looking southwest along axis; midwinter sunset with snow.

All of this may have led to considerable political instability in Europe and to alliances of small tribes under the rule of powerful and ambitious chieftains, themselves once minor village leaders. Some warrior groups even began to strike at the edge of the Mediterranean world, destroying Mycenae and the Hittite Empire.

As time went on, many more copper and bronze artifacts became available for domestic consumption. Some new tool forms were introduced by central European smiths, including socketed axes and varied woodworking tools. More farmers used the *ard* (a scraping plow drawn by oxen) that had been in use since at least 2500 B.C. The ard was a particularly important innovation, for it allowed deeper plowing, more advanced agricultural methods, and higher productivity. More intensive farming techniques were vital to feed the many new mouths, and prime farming land was harder to find than ever before.

Between 1800 and 1200 B.C., the population movements associated with central European peoples introduced a more consolidated system of agriculture to much of Europe, which allowed exploitation of much heavier soils as well as stock breeding (Dennell, 1983). For the first time, stock were fully integrated into the food-producing economy, and cattle were used for meat, milk, and draft work, though sheep were bred as much for wool as for their flesh. Improved technology for new implements of tillage was fully exploited to achieve a truly effective economic symbiosis between flora and fauna, carefully balancing forest clearance with cultivation and pasturage (Figure 20.7).

One powerful group of warrior peoples in west Hungary is known to archaeologists as the Urnfield people because of their burial customs: Their dead were cremated and their ashes deposited in urns; huge cemeteries of urn burials are associated with fortified villages, sometimes built near lakes. Urnfield people began to make full use of horse-drawn vehicles and new weaponry. Skilled bronze smiths produced sheet-metal helmets, shields, and bronze body armor for a warrior elite. These fighters used the slashing sword, a devastating weapon far more effective than the cutting swords of earlier times.

Urnfield culture
1250 B.C.

FIGURE 20.7   Late Bronze Age lakeside settlement at Wasserburg-Buchau, Federsee, Germany. The village was set on marshy ground and first occupied in about 1100 B.C. The village was oval, surrounded with a wooden palisade, with 38 log cabin-like structures inside. Somewhat later, the village was rebuilt with large rectangular dwellings, some joined to make H-shaped or L-shaped houses. All had internal rooms. The settlement was eventually destroyed by fire.

The emergence of warrior elites was accompanied by a quickening of trade, reflected in a remarkable standardization of weapons and burial customs throughout much of central and western Europe. Within a couple of centuries, characteristic slashing swords and other central European tools had been deposited in cemeteries in Italy, the Balkans, and the Aegean. Exploitation of copper mines such as those in Austria's Tyrol was intensified. There, bands of miners used bronze-tipped picks to dig deep into the ground for copper ore. Their efforts increased the supplies of copper and tin available to central Europe (J. G. D. Clark, 1952; Coles and Harding, 1979). Urnfield weaponry and burial rites spread from Hungary throughout central and parts of western Europe.

THE SCYTHIANS AND OTHER STEPPE PEOPLES

◆ ◆ ◆

The vast rolling grasslands and steppes from China to the Ukraine were not settled by farming peoples until they had a culture enabling them to survive in an environment with extreme contrasts of climate and relatively infertile soils. The carrying capacity of the land is such that only a vast territory can support herds of domestic stock. The prehistory of this huge area is obscure until the first millennium B.C., when the Scythians (from Scythia, an area in southeast Europe) and other steppe peoples first appeared in the historical record. No one should doubt, however, the importance of nomads in the prehistory of Europe in earlier millennia (E. D. Phillips, 1972). The Kurgan people and other possible Indo-European speakers were familiar with the vast open spaces of the steppes (Figure 20.8).

Scythians
c. 500 B.C.

As early as 4000 B.C., people living at the Dereivka site on the Ukraine's Dnieper River were riding horses with rope bits. Their successors roamed the steppes for centuries before the Scythians came out of history's shadows, living in stout felt tents and subsisting mostly on horse's milk and cheese as well as on food from hunting and fishing. The nomadic life, though, leaves few traces in the archaeological record, except when permafrost has preserved burials in a refrigerated state.

We are fortunate in having extensive data about the vigorous society of nomad peoples from the spectacular frozen tombs of Siberia. Russian archaeologist Sergei Rudenko (1970) has excavated several nomad burial mounds erected in 400 B.C. at

400 B.C.

FIGURE 20.8 Approximate distribution of Urnfield cultures in Europe.

Pazyryk in northeast Siberia. The chiefs of Pazyryk were elaborately tattooed, wore woollen and leather clothes, and employed skillful artists to adorn their horse trappings and harnesses with exuberant, elaborate, stylized animal art. A powerful chief was accompanied to the next world by his wife and servants, horses and chariots, and many of his smaller possessions. The Pazyryk burials contain fragments of woven rugs, the earliest examples of such art in the world.

The steppe peoples lived to the north of the well-traveled trade routes of Greek merchants, but their territory was constantly being explored and sometimes colonized by farmers whose lands were becoming overpopulated or overgrazed. Enormous areas of steppe were needed to support even a small band of horse riders, for just a slight increase in population could drastically affect the food supplies of the original inhabitants. The result was constant displacement of populations as the nomads sought to expand their shrinking territory to accommodate their own population pressures. The nomads menaced the northern frontiers of the Mediterranean world throughout classical and more recent times.

The Eurasian nomad population flourished during the closing millennia of prehistory. The Pazyryk finds let us glimpse a prehistoric way of life that in some areas survived unchanged into historic times.

THE EMERGENCE OF IRONWORKING

● ● ●

Late Bronze Age Europeans were effective farmers as well as traders and metallurgists capable of exploiting Europe's forested environment far more efficiently than their predecessors could. They lived amid a complicated network of trade that carried not only metals but also salt, grain, gold, pottery, and many other commodities. Their economic organization probably included community smiths, specialists supported by the village, but still no centralized state system of the Near Eastern type.

Ironworking c. 1000 B.C.

These exchange networks facilitated the spread of ironworking techniques across Europe with considerable rapidity after 1000 B.C. In widespread use for both weapons and utilitarian objects by 700 B.C., ironworking is much more difficult than bronze working, for the technology is harder to acquire and takes much longer; however, once it is learned, the advantages of the new metal are obvious. Because the ore is found in many more places, the metal is much cheaper and can be used for weapons and utilitarian artifacts as well. These would, of course, include axes, hoes, and plowshares, all of which contributed much to agricultural efficiency, higher crop yields, and greater food surpluses. The population increases and intensified trading activities of the centuries immediately preceding the Roman Empire are partly attributed to the success of iron technology in changing European agriculture and craftsmanship (Collis, 1984).

As iron technology spread into the country north of the Alps, new societies arose whose leaders exploited the metal's artistic and economic potentials. The tribal chieftaincy was the structure of government; the most coherent broader political unit was a loose confederacy of tribes formed in time of war or temporarily under the aegis of a charismatic chieftain. Despite the onslaught of Roman colonization and exploitation, culture beyond the frontiers retained its essentially European cast, an indigenous slant to cultural traditions that began when farming did (Wells, 1981).

Hascherkeller 1000 to 800 B.C.

For all the technological changes, farming life continued much as before. Peter Wells (1984) has excavated an Iron Age farming community near Hascherkeller in lower Bavaria, Germany, where he found three enclosed farmsteads. The farmstead complexes included dwellings, barns, sheds, and workshops, with between 15 and 30 people living in each settlement. Occupied between 1000 and 800 B.C., they were self-sufficient communities without iron tools that traded foodstuffs for such items as imported bronze scraps, beads, and graphite, the latter used for pottery decoration. Hascherkeller was apparently without iron, which was still a new metal.

The Hallstatt Culture

One strong culture was the Hallstatt, named after a site near Salzburg, Austria (Rowlett, 1967; Wells, 1981). Hallstatt culture began in the eighth and seventh centuries B.C. and owed much to Urnfield practices; the skillful bronze working of earlier times was still practiced, although some immigrants from the east may have achieved political dominance over earlier inhabitants. Bronze, however, was still the dominant metal for horse trappings, weapons, and ornaments. Chiefs were buried in large mounds within wooden chambers, some in wagons (Figure 20.9).

Hallstatt
730 B.C.

FIGURE 20.9 Bronze ritual cart from a Hallstatt grave in Austria, approximately 1 foot (0.3 m) long.

FIGURE 20.10   Distribution of Hallstatt Iron Age cultures (shaded area) in Europe during the eighth to fifth centuries B.C.

The Hallstatt people and their culture spread through former Urnfield territories as far north as Belgium and the Netherlands and into France and parts of Spain (Figure 20.10). Many Hallstatt sites are particularly notable for their fortifications. The Hallstatt people traded with the Mediterraneans along well-traveled routes up the Rhone River and through the Alps into central Europe. A significant import was the serving vessel for wine; containers of Mediterranean wine were carried far into central Europe as Hallstatt chieftains discovered wine drinking.

The La Tène Culture

La Tène
450 B.C.

By the last quarter of the fifth century B.C., a new and highly distinctive technology, La Tène, had developed in the Rhine and Danube valleys (Megaw and Megaw, 1989; James, 1992). An aristocratic clique of chieftains in the Danube Valley enjoyed implements and weapons elaborately worked in bronze and gold. Much of their sophisticated art had roots in classical Greek and Mediterranean traditions, for La Tène craftsworkers were quick to adopt new motifs and ideas from the centers of higher civilization to the south (Figure 20.11). The La Tène people spoke Celtic, a language that spread widely through Europe from perhaps as early as the ninth century B.C. Greek and Roman writers referred to these people as Celts, a term that has survived in their linguistic label.

350 B.C.

La Tène technology was a specific adaptation of ironworking to woodland Europe. The culture extended north into the Low Countries and Britain in the fourth century B.C. La Tène art is deservedly famous, and the hill forts and defensive

FIGURE 20.11   Iron Age helmet from the bed of the River Thames in London, 8.07 inches (205 cm) at the base.

settlements of this Iron Age culture are widespread in west Europe. The superior military tactics of the La Tène people introduced the Romans to the short sword, for Celts sacked Rome in about 390 B.C. The last three centuries before Christ saw considerable change in Europe, with the appearance of coinage, the development of small autonomous states, and the foundation of large settlements known to archaeologists and historians as *oppida,* the Latin word for "towns." Many were fortified and somewhat similar to later towns in medieval Europe. La Tène peoples survived long after France and southern Britain had been conquered by Rome in 55 B.C. (Cunliffe, 1974). Much territory in the temperate zones came under Roman domination, an uneasy frontier province that eventually crumbled before the inexorable pressure of the warlike tribes on its boundaries. The illiterate peoples who eventually sacked Rome and ravaged its provinces were the descendants of prehistoric Europeans whose cultural traditions had been evolving ever since the first farming cultures developed north of the Mediterranean Basin.

Roman conquest
55 B.C.

CHAPTER SUMMARY

Copper working developed in southeast Europe by about 4800 B.C., and soon afterward in Spain and northern Italy. The new technology flourished because of a demand for the fine metal ornaments. It was a logical outgrowth of earlier stone and ceramic technologies. Its more widespread use coincides with the spread of Beaker and Battle Ax artifacts throughout much of Europe. Bronze working began at an unknown date but was widespread in what is now the Czech Republic by 2000 B.C., as part of the Unetice culture. The trading networks of earlier times expanded to meet increased indigenous demand for metal artifacts during a period of rapid technological change after 1700 B.C. Some rich chieftaincies developed in the temperate zones.

About 1400 B.C., new "Urnfield" burial customs and more advanced bronze-working techniques spread over much of central and western Europe. These were associated with an intensification of trading activity and greater social ranking: an elite warrior class. After 1000 B.C., ironworking techniques spread into temperate Europe and diffused through the Hallstatt and La Tène cultural traditions during the first millennium B.C.

GUIDE TO FURTHER READING

Champion, Timothy G., ed. 1984. *Prehistoric Europe.* New York: Academic Press.
  A textbook on European prehistory from the earliest times to the expansion of the Roman Empire. Major emphasis on subsistence, trade, and social organization.

Coles, J. M., and Harding, A. F. 1979. *The Bronze Age in Europe.* London: Methuen.
  An authoritative account of the complexities of the European Bronze Age that covers the topic far more fully than we can in this book.

Collis, John. 1984. *The European Iron Age.* London: Batsford.
  A useful introduction to European ironmaking cultures.

Dennell, Robin. 1983. *European Economic Prehistory: A New Approach.* New York: Academic Press.
  A provocative, readable summary of European prehistory that focuses on major issues, mostly economic.

Piggott, Stuart. 1965. *Ancient Europe.* Chicago: Aldine.
  Somewhat outdated, an account of prehistoric Europe that is closer to Childe than to current evolutionary thinking but is still authoritative, with excellent illustrations.

STATE-ORGANIZED SOCIETIES IN THE AMERICAS

(2000 B.C. TO A.D. 1532)

What, then, must have been the emotions of the Spaniards, when, after working their toilsome way into the open air, the cloudy tabernacle parted before their eyes, and they beheld these fair scenes in all their pristine magnificence and beauty. It was like the spectacle which greeted the eyes of Moses from the summit of Pisgah, and, in the warm glow of their feelings, they cried out, "It is the promised land!"

W. H. PRESCOTT, THE CONQUEST OF MEXICO, 1843

P art VI contains descriptions of the great and complex states of the New World. The theoretical literature surrounding the emergence of states in Mesoamerica and Peru is enormous, and interested readers are referred to Chapter 14 for some of the principal arguments surrounding the subject.

MESOAMERICAN CIVILIZATIONS

21

• • •

By any standards, New York lawyer turned traveler John Lloyd Stephens was a remarkable man. In 1839, he and Scottish artist Frederick Catherwood journeyed deep into the Mesoamerican rain forest, following rumors of vanished civilizations and great ruins masked by primordial jungle. They came first to the tiny village of Copán, where "around them lay the dark outlines of ruins shrouded by the brooding forest. The only sound that disturbed the quiet of this buried city was the noise of monkeys moving around among the tops of the trees." While Catherwood drew the intricate hieroglyphs on the Maya stelae, Stephens tried to buy Copán for $50, so he could transport it block by block to New York. The deal fell through when he found he could not float the antiquities downstream.

Stephens and Catherwood visited Palenque, Uxmal, Chichén Itzá, and other sites. They were the first to recognize the Maya as the builders of these great sites: "These cities . . . are not the works of people who have passed away . . . but of the same great race . . . which still clings around their ruins," Stephens wrote (Stephens, 1841). All subsequent research into the Maya and into ancient Mesoamerican civilization has been based on his work. Today, Maya civilization with its intricate, recently deciphered glyphs and spectacular cities ranks among the most fascinating in the world. As we shall see in this chapter (Table 21.1), its origins lie deep in prehistory.

AGRICULTURAL TECHNIQUES

• • •

Slash and burn

Early Mesoamerican farming communities lived in dispersed villages and used only slash-and-burn agriculture, which as we have seen cannot support high population densities. In fact, there are many highly diverse agricultural environments in both highlands and lowlands, which were exploited in many different ways, probably long before more complex societies appeared.

Some fascinating experiments have involved scanning the Maya lowlands with side-scanning radar. They revealed that areas of wet-season swamp near known

TABLE 21.1
• • •

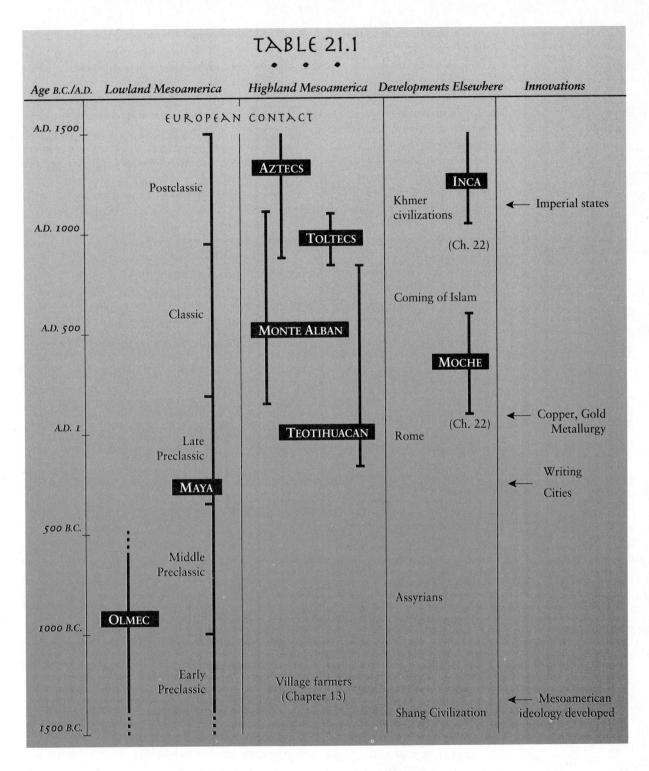

Age B.C./A.D.	Lowland Mesoamerica	Highland Mesoamerica	Developments Elsewhere	Innovations

EUROPEAN CONTACT

A.D. 1500

Postclassic — AZTECS — INCA — Khmer civilizations — ← Imperial states

A.D. 1000 — TOLTECS — (Ch. 22)

Classic — Coming of Islam

A.D. 500 — MONTE ALBAN — MOCHE

A.D. 1 — TEOTIHUACAN — Rome — (Ch. 22) — ← Copper, Gold Metallurgy

Late Preclassic

MAYA — ← Writing   Cities

500 B.C.

Middle Preclassic

Assyrians

1000 B.C. — OLMEC

Early Preclassic — Village farmers (Chapter 13)

Shang Civilization — ← Mesoamerican ideology developed

1500 B.C.

Raised fields   Maya sites often have many irregular grids of gray lines in ladder, lattice, and curvilinear patterns. These are thought to represent long-forgotten raised field systems built in swamps (Adams, Brown, and Culbert, 1981). The Maya and, perhaps to a lesser extent, their predecessors drained and canalized swamps for agricultural and communication purposes, so the swamps became assets rather than liabilities, artificial environments where substantial food surpluses of maize and beans could be grown and then transported readily by canoe. The preparation and maintenance of raised fields were well within the capabilities of individual households and small hamlets (Culbert, 1981b). Most lowland agricultural techniques did not require large numbers of people until there was *intensification* of agricultural production as population densities rose in late Preclassic times. It is significant that some of the largest areas of raised fields are close to major Classic Maya centers like Tikal.

The Mesoamerican highlands are highly diverse agricultural environments, as we have seen in the Tehuacán Valley (Chapter 13). The earliest farming villages in Oaxaca are concentrated in the valley floors, where water is within easy reach of the surface. Modern farmers choose similar villages for simple "pot" irrigation, where they plant their maize and other crops near small shallow wells. They simply dip pots into the wells and water surrounding plants from the shallow water table. Flannery (1968b) has argued that the Oaxacans used the same technique in prehistoric times, for it does not require large numbers of people. In time, as population densities rose, the Oaxacans were able to build on their simple and highly effective farming techniques, expanding onto slopes and into more arid lands with great success. Eventually, the economic power generated by these rising populations gave highland areas like this a decided edge in cultural evolution.

Pot irrigation

Chinampas

Similar diversity of agricultural techniques is found in the Valley of Mexico, where slash-and-burn methods, dry farming, and irrigation agriculture all were in use. The farmers used both floodwaters and canals to bring water to dry gardens. The most famous of all raised field techniques, however, is the *chinampa*, or floating garden technique, a highly intensive and productive agricultural system based on the reclaiming of swamps. The farmers piled up natural vegetation and lake mud to form huge grids of naturally irrigated gardens. The chinampas were used very systematically to grow a variety of crops, so timed that different crops came into harvest throughout the year (Sanders et al., 1970). This system is amazingly productive and is estimated to have supported approximately 100,000 people from 25,000 acres (10,117 ha) in 1519, the time of Spanish contact. Each chinampa produced large food surpluses that could be used to feed thousands of nonagricultural workers and specialists. William Sanders has argued that these 25,000 acres (10,117 ha) of chinampas actually could have supported approximately 180,000 people. That this highly effective agricultural system was the basis of early civilization and urban life in the Valley of Mexico is beyond question.

Market economy   The agricultural system of the Valley of Mexico may seem complicated, but it supported and was part of a far more elaborate system of food marketing, which provided not only tribute for taxes but also opportunities for the trading of special foodstuffs from one area of the highlands to another. The highland peoples relied on elaborate markets that were strictly regulated by the state and conducted on a barter system. The Valley of Mexico was an economic unit before Teotihuacán made it a political one as well. It was the great agricultural productivity of the valley and the sophisticated market economy of the emerging city that made the prodigious social and religious as well as material developments of later centuries possible. This economic system fostered the development of specialist crafts that were sold in the city markets and exported over wide areas.

PRECLASSIC PEOPLES IN MESOAMERICA

● ● ●

By 2000 B.C., sedentary farming villages were common in most of Mesoamerica (Sanders and Price, 1968; Weaver, 1991). In their agriculture, people relied on many plant species, and slash-and-burn farming methods were in wide use in the lowlands. With such methods people could clear small gardens in the forest by cutting tree trunks and brush and carefully burning branches to fertilize the soil with a layer of wood ash. Using pointed digging sticks, they planted maize and other crops. A few seasons later they abandoned the land, planting less important crops on older plots or leaving them to the forest. The search for new lands was constant, even when slash-and-burn was combined with irrigation or riverside agriculture.

Preclassic
c. 2000 B.C. to A.D. 250

Early Preclassic

Many centuries elapsed between the beginnings of village life and that of Mesoamerican civilization. The first signs of political and social complexity appear in many regions of Mesoamerica between about 2000 and 1000 B.C., during the early part of an era named the *Preclassic* or *Formative* by archaeologists, a period that lasted as late as A.D. 250. In many regions, small but often powerful chiefdoms headed by a chief and an elite appeared. The elite dominated economic, political, and religious life and ruled over large nonelite populations. A similar pattern of emerging social and political complexity has been documented in Mesopotamia, Egypt, China, and other areas where early state-organized societies evolved. In Mesoamerica, as elsewhere, the new chiefdoms can be identified by differences in house designs, by the appearance of small shrines, by social rankings detectable through grave goods, and from prestigious as opposed to more utilitarian artifacts. This process is well documented at Cuello in lowland northern Belize, which is radiocarbon dated to between c. 1000 B.C. and A.D. 300 (Figure 21.1) (N. Hammond, 1980, 1982). The inhabitants of this site were maize farmers, who also relied heavily on wild plant foods for their diet.

Cuello
c. 1000 B.C. to A.D. 300

There was no one region where this emerging sociopolitical complexity occurred first. Rather, it was a development that took place more or less simultaneously in many regions of Mesoamerica, not in isolation but with each region interacting with others (Sharer and Grove, 1989). The most famous of these societies is that of the Olmec.

Middle Preclassic: The Olmec and Theories of a Mother Culture

The Olmec people lived on the Mexican south Gulf Coast from about 1500 to 500 B.C. (Figure 21.1) (Bernal, 1969; Coe and Diehl, 1980). Their homeland is low-lying, tropical, and humid with fertile soils. The swamps, lakes, and rivers are rich in fish, birds, and other animals. It was in this region that the Olmec created a highly distinctive art style. Olmec art was executed in sculpture and in relief. The artists concentrated on natural and supernatural beings, the dominant motif being the "were-jaguar," or humanlike jaguar. Many jaguars were given infantile faces; drooping lips; and large, swollen eyes, a style also applied to human figures, some of whom resemble snarling demons. Olmec contributions to Mesoamerican art and religion were enormously significant. For years, scholars have believed that elements of their art style and imagery were diffused southward to Guatemala and San

Olmec
1500 to 500 B.C.

FIGURE 21.1   Mesoamerican archaeological sites mentioned in this chapter. Approximate distributions of various traditions are shown.

Salvador and northward into the Valley of Mexico. In short, the Olmec was the "mother culture" of Mesoamerican civilization (Sharer, 1989). Increasingly, this theory is being questioned (Sharer and Grove, 1989).

The origins of the Olmec are a complete mystery, but the culture probably has strong local roots. The earliest traces of Olmec occupation are best documented at **San Lorenzo 1250 B.C.** San Lorenzo, where Olmec people lived on a platform in the midst of frequently inundated woodland plains. They erected ridges and mounds around their platform, upon which they built pyramids and possibly ball courts and placed elaborate monumental carvings overlooking the site. The earliest occupation of San Lorenzo shows few Olmec features, but by 1250 B.C. the inhabitants were beginning to build some raised fields, a task that required organized labor forces. By that time, too, distinctive Olmec sculpture began to appear. A century later, magnificent monumental carvings adorned San Lorenzo (Figure 21.2), distinctive and often mutilated by the Olmec themselves, perhaps when rulers died (Coe and Diehl, 1980).

One archaeologist has estimated the population of San Lorenzo at 2500 (Coe and Diehl, 1980). The inhabitants enjoyed extensive trade, especially in obsidian and other semiprecious materials obtained from many parts of Mesoamerica. San Lorenzo fell into decline after 900 B.C. and was surpassed by La Venta, the most famous Olmec site, nearer the Gulf of Mexico.

La Venta

La Venta 800 to 400 B.C. The La Venta ceremonial center was built on a small island in the middle of a swamp (Drucker, 1959). A rectangular earth mound, 393 feet long by 229 feet wide and 105 feet high (120 m by 70 m by 32 m), dominates the island. Long, low mounds surround a rectangular plaza in front of the large mound, faced by walls

FIGURE 21.2   Giant stone head from San Lorenzo made from basalt, approximately 8 feet (2.4 m) high. These heads may be portraits of rulers. David Grove (1973) has identified what he thinks may be name glyphs on the "helmets."

and terraced mounds at the other end of the plaza (Figure 21.3). Vast monumental stone sculptures litter the site, including some Olmec heads bearing expressions of contempt and savagery. Caches of jade objects, figurines, and a dull green rock (serpentine) are common, too (Figure 21.4). Every stone for sculptures and temples had to be brought from at least 60 miles (96 km) away, a vast undertaking, for some sculptured blocks weigh more than 40 tons. The people traded ceremonial jade and serpentine from as far away as Costa Rica. La Venta flourished for approximately 400 years from 800 B.C. After approximately 400 B.C., the site probably was destroyed; we deduce this occurrence from signs that many of its finest monuments were intentionally defaced.

San Lorenzo and La Venta, with their relatively small populations, are manifestations of a much more complex social and political order, not in the fashion of a state-organized society, as earlier scholars suggested, but a series of chiefdoms with powerful leaders who maintained contacts with other such societies in the lowlands and perhaps farther afield (Diehl, 1989). This is very different from characterizing

FIGURE 21.3   La Venta, site 4: layout of the major structures.

FIGURE 21.4   An Olmec altar or throne sculpture from La Venta. The sculpture is approximately 6 feet (2 m) high. At least one of these thrones shows the ruler in front connected to his parents on the side by umbilical cords.

the Olmec as the mother culture of all Mesoamerican civilization or as a great imperial empire whose tentacles reached as far as the Mexican highlands. Arthur Demarest (1989) points out that Olmec society changed over the centuries. At first, during the early Preclassic, it was a set of chiefdoms along the Gulf Coast of Veracruz and Tabasco, which may have exercised some influence over adjacent areas of Chiapas and Central Mexico. Later, during the middle Preclassic, Olmec society flourished during a period when art motifs, religious symbols, and ritual beliefs were shared between developing chiefdoms in many regions through the regular contacts between elites and day-to-day trade from region to region (for ancient Mexican religion, see Miller and Taube, 1993). It was what Demarest calls a "lattice of Middle Formative interaction" over many centuries that produced the complex and sophis-

ticated traditions of Mesoamerican civilization that were to follow. Another archaeologist, Kent Reilly (1991), has coined the term "Formative Ceremonial Complex"
to describe the Olmec phenomenon. He believes that Olmec kingship was
antecedent to, and basically similar to that of the lowland Maya. (For discussions of
Mesoamerican ideology, see Demarest and Conrad, 1993.)

Late Preclassic

The trajectory of rapid cultural change continued in many regions during the late
Preclassic (300 B.C. to A.D. 250). This was the period when a common religious system and ideology began to unify large areas of Mesoamerica. The leaders of the new
orders validated their rule with elaborate public ceremonies in spectacular ceremonial centers, commemorating potent and widely recognized deities. Distinctive art
and architecture went with the new religion, the practice of which required precise
measurements of calendar years and of longer cycles of time. Writing and mathematical calculations were developed to affirm religious practices, a unifying political
force in the sense that they welded scattered village communities into larger political
units. By the time the classic Mesoamerican civilizations arose, dynasties of elites
had been ruling parts of Mesoamerica along well-established lines for nearly 1000
years (Sabloff, 1989).

Late Preclassic
300 B.C. to A.D. 250

THE RISE OF A COMPLEX SOCIETY IN OAXACA

● ● ●

The Preclassic cultures of the Valley of Oaxaca have been studied intensively by
Kent Flannery and his students, using highly sophisticated systems approaches to
document changing settlement patterns and economic and demographic trends
(Flannery, 1976; Flannery and Marcus, 1983). Something like 90 percent of the Preclassic Oaxaca villages were little more than hamlets of 50 to 60 people, and the
remainder were much larger settlements of 1000 to 1200, with populations of
priests and craftspeople.

The evolution of larger settlements in Oaxaca and elsewhere was closely connected with the development of long-distance trade in obsidian and other luxuries
such as seashells and stingray spines from the Gulf of Mexico. The simple barter
networks for obsidian of earlier times evolved into sophisticated regional trading
organizations in which village leaders controlled monopolies over sources of obsidian and its distribution. Magnetite mirrors, seashells, feathers, and ceramics were all
traded on the highlands, and from the highlands to the lowlands as well. Olmec pottery and other ritual objects began to appear in highland settlements between 1150
and 650 B.C., many of them bearing the distinctive were-jaguar motif of the lowlands, which had an important place in Olmec cosmology.

Public buildings began to appear in villages such as San José Mogote between
1400 and 1150 B.C. Many of them were oriented 8° west of north; they were built
on adobe and earth platforms. Conch shell trumpets and turtle shell drums from the
Gulf of Mexico are associated with these buildings, as are clay figurines of dancers
wearing costumes and masks (Figure 21.5). There were marine fish spines, too,
probably used in personal bloodletting ceremonies that were still practiced even in
Aztec times. The Spanish described how Aztec nobles would gash themselves with
knives or with the spines of fish or stingray in acts of mutilation before the gods,

San José Mogote
1400 to 1150 B.C

FIGURE 21.5   Four clay figurines shaped and posed deliberately to form a scene, buried beneath an early Preclassic house at San José Mogote, Oaxaca.

penances required of the devout (Saunders, 1989). The diffusion of common art styles throughout Mesoamerica may have resulted both from an increased need for religious rituals to bring the various elements of society together and because the Oaxacan elite, aspiring to the status of their chiefly neighbors, took to the new beliefs in slavish conformity (Flannery, 1976; Flannery and Marcus, 1983). This diffusion took place after long-distance trading had been in existence for centuries and probably signaled an increase in larger villages such as San José Mogote.

Monte Albán

Monte Albán
400 B.C.

By 400 B.C., there were at least seven small polities in the Valley of Oaxaca, of which the one centered at Monte Albán soon became dominant. Although massive population growth and increased economic power were among the interacting factors that aided in the rise of Monte Albán, its special terrain may have been of vital importance in its ascendancy (Blanton, 1978, 1983). Richard Blanton has surveyed more than 2000 terraces on the slopes of Monte Albán, terraces used for agriculture and housing areas. Monte Albán commanded the best terrain in the valley, sloping land that was organized for agriculture and dense settlement by a population of several thousand people, far larger than that of most major settlements in Mesoamerica at the time. Even as early as 400 B.C., some of the terraces were in use by a highly organized population whose leaders resided in a ceremonial and civic center built on the summit of the Monte Albán ridge. Although the large-scale buildings of later times have contoured the summit beyond recognition, it is clear that the first leaders to live there undertook major public works, many of them wood and thatch buildings that had incised sculptures of what may be dead and tortured enemies set into the walls.

Monte Albán went on to develop into a vast ceremonial center with splendid public architecture; its settlement area included public buildings, terraces, and housing zones that extended over approximately 15 square miles (40 sq. km) (Figure 21.6). The more than 2000 terraces all held one or two houses, and small ravines were dammed to pond valuable water supplies. Blanton suggests that between 30,000 and 50,000 people lived at Monte Albán between A.D. 200 and 700. Many very large villages and smaller hamlets lay within easy distance of the city. The enormous platforms on the ridge of Monte Albán supported complex layouts of temples and pyramid-temples, palaces, patios, and tombs. A hereditary elite seems to have ruled Monte Albán, the leaders of a state that had emerged in the Valley of Oaxaca by A.D. 200. Their religious power was based on ancestor worship, a pantheon of at least 39 gods, grouped around major themes of ritual life. The rain god and lightning were associated with the jaguar motif; another group of deities was linked with the maize god, Pitao Cozabi. Nearly all these gods were still worshiped at the time of Spanish contact, although Monte Albán itself was abandoned after A.D. 700, at approximately the same time as another great ceremonial center, Teotihuacán, in the Valley of Mexico, began to decline.

FIGURE 21.6   Monte Albán, Valley of Oaxaca.

TEOTIHUACÁN

• • •

We have already referred to the Valley of Mexico as an economic unit, a network of markets that probably flourished long before large states came into being in the highlands. Perhaps the sequence of events that led to the founding of such polities, especially Teotihuacán, began with the buildup of agricultural populations in diverse environments such as the Valley of Oaxaca in the first and second millennia B.C. This population growth led to the development of more intensive agricultural methods, including both irrigation and chinampa systems. At the same time, different areas were linked by increasingly sophisticated trading networks and by an emerging market economy, perhaps with some specialized merchants.

Religious activity was stimulated by the introduction of beliefs and sacred objects from the lowlands. Trade in exotic luxuries increased as ceremonial centers and stratified societies were founded. By 200 B.C., the effects of increased religious activity, intensified trading, and the production of huge food surpluses from the diverse environment had led to the founding of at least two major cities in the Valley of Mexico. One of these, Teotihuacán, reached an enormous size and enjoyed vast political, economic, and religious power in the centuries that followed. In the Valley of Oaxaca, Monte Albán achieved a similar dominance. The two great states probably enjoyed an uneasy alliance.

Teotihuacán
200 B.C. to A.D. 700

Teotihuacán lies northeast of Mexico City and is now one of the great archaeological tourist attractions of the world. It was one of the dominant political and cultural centers of all Mesoamerica in approximately A.D. 500, the culmination of centuries of vigorous cultural development in the Valley of Mexico (Millon, Drewitt, and Cowgill, 1974; Berto, 1992; Berrin and Pasztory, 1994; Storey, 1992).

The first buildings appeared at Teotihuacán in approximately 200 B.C., making up a handful of villages, at least one of which may have specialized in obsidian manufacture. By 100 B.C., Teotihuacán had begun to expand rapidly, and the scattered villages became a settlement covering more than 3.5 square miles (9.06 sq. km). Much of this early settlement is covered by the vast structures of later times. It is estimated that 600 people inhabited this early town. There were several public buildings.

René Millon, who carried out a systematic survey of Teotihuacán, found that by A.D. 150 the city extended over 5 square miles (12.9 sq. km) and housed more than 20,000 people. Obsidian trade and manufacture were expanding fast (Parsons and Price, 1971). There were two major religious complexes for which, among other structures, the Pyramids of the Sun and Moon were first built at this time.

City layout

Between A.D. 150 and 750, Teotihuacán exploded in size. Anyone traversing the Valley of Mexico had to pass through the city with its diverse population of priests, merchants, craftspeople, and other specialists. The rulers of the city erected hundreds of standardized apartment complexes and continued a master plan that laid out the city on a north-south axis, centered on the Avenue of the Dead (Figure 21.7), with another great avenue oriented east-west. The 8 square miles (20.7 sq. km) of Teotihuacán consisted of avenues and plazas, markets, temples, palaces, apartment buildings, and complex drainage and agricultural works (Figure 21.8). The entire city was dominated by the Pyramid of the Sun (an Aztec name), a vast structure of earth, adobe, and piled rubble. The pyramid, faced with stone, is 210 feet (64 m) high and 650 feet (198 m) square. A wooden temple probably sat on the summit of the terraced pyramid. The long Avenue of the Dead passes the west face of the

FIGURE 21.7   Aerial view of the ceremonial precincts at Teotihuacán, with the Pyramid of the Moon in the foreground. At left in the background (to the left of the Avenue of the Dead) is the Pyramid of the Sun.

FIGURE 21.8   Plan of the major public buildings at Teotihuacán.

pyramid, leading to the Pyramid of the Moon, the second largest structure at the site (Figure 21.7). The avenue is lined with civic, palace, and religious buildings, and the side streets lead to residential areas. A large palace and temple complex dedicated to the Plumed Serpent (Quetzalcóatl), with platform and stairways around the central court, lies south of the middle of Teotihuacán, across from a central marketplace. Mass graves lie close by, probably those of sacrificial victims (Figure 21.8).

The Avenue of the Dead and the pyramids lie amid a sprawling mass of small houses. Priests and craftsworkers lived in dwellings around small courtyards; the less privileged lived in large compounds of rooms connected by narrow alleyways and patios. By any standard, Teotihuacán was a city, and it once housed up to 120,000 people. Although some farmers probably lived within the city, we know that rural villages flourished nearby. These were compact, expertly planned, and administered by city rulers.

The comprehensive settlement pattern data from the Millon survey enable us to say something about the structure of Teotihuacán society. The food surpluses to support the city were produced by farmers who lived both in the city and in satellite villages nearby. Tribute from neighboring states also helped feed the city, and control of large areas of the plateau ensured that adequate food supplies came to Teotihuacán's huge market. Most of the people lived in the city. It is not known how

Agriculture   important chinampa agriculture was for Teotihuacán, but irrigation farming was a key element in subsistence. Craftspeople accounted for perhaps 25 percent of the urban population; they lived in compounds of apartments near the more than 500 workshops that produced everything from obsidian tools to clay vessels. Merchants probably were an important class in the city, as were civil servants, who carried out the routine administration of Teotihuacán. There were even foreign quarters, one of which housed Oaxacans. The elite included priests, warriors, and secular leaders, who controlled the vast city and its many dealings through a strictly class society. Religious beliefs continued the rituals of earlier times, but it appears that cannibalism and human sacrifice became increasingly important in later centuries as the leaders of the city became more and more militaristic, a trend that was to continue into Aztec times.

Teotihuacán ruled the Valley of Mexico and parts of Puebla, but its influence through alliance, tribute, and warfare, as well as trading, extended over a far larger area of Mesoamerica. As in later times, the rulers of Teotihuacán probably controlled some highly strategic and economically important zones, but there were large areas where their influence was minimal. In the final analysis, Teotihuacán probably was a huge city-state bound to other city-states by uneasy alliances and tribute exchanges.

By A.D. 600, Teotihuacán probably was governed by a secular ruler who was looked upon as a divine king of some kind. A class of nobles controlled the kinship groups that organized the bulk of the city's huge population. In approximately A.D. 650, Teotihuacán was deliberately burned down. Only 50 years later its population was scattered in a few villages. Much of the former urban population settled in neighboring regions, which thereby reaped the benefit of Teotihuacán's misfortunes. No one knows exactly why this great city collapsed so suddenly. Its rapid development may have resulted in serious internal weaknesses that made Teotihuacán vulnerable to easy overthrow. A drought may also have weakened the city and provided an opportunity for jealous rivals to attempt an attack.

The very success of Teotihuacán may have accelerated its downfall. The new orders of society and politics spawned by the city may have been copied by other leaders, perhaps more aggressive and less tradition-bound than those of the mother city. Teotihuacán was not the only sophisticated city-state in the highlands between A.D. 500 and 700. William Sanders (1965) has argued that Teotihuacán was overthrown by a coalition of city-states that included Xochicalco in the southwest and Cholula to the southeast. All these expanded after the downfall of Teotihuacán, and all had been powerful regional states at the time of the former's collapse.

Whatever the cause of Teotihuacán's collapse, its heyday marks the moment when one can begin to think of the Mesoamerican world in more than purely local, and even regional, terms. Teotihuacán's political and social influence was considerate, and its traders ventured to many parts of the highlands and lowlands. For example, the ways in which Maya kings went to war were profoundly affected by the military practices and war-making rituals of Teotihuacán. The greatest legacy of Teotihuacán was not merely its cosmology, ideology, and trade networks but a new interconnectedness between the many societies of prehistoric Mesoamerica. In the centuries that followed the fall of Teotihuacán, this interconnectedness was an important factor in the development of more imperial civilizations in the Valley of Mexico. Before examining these civilizations, however, we must go back in time and describe the Maya civilization, whose roots and inspiration came from Preclassic societies elsewhere in Mesoamerica.

MAYA CIVILIZATION

• • •

The Maya civilization is probably the best known of all early American civilizations, one that has excited the imagination of scholars for more than a century. It took shape in lowland rain-forest areas that provided a highly varied environment in which people grew maize and other crops and harvested trees such as the ramon.

Maya Origins

Although the ultimate roots of Maya culture go back far into the Preclassic period, considerable debate surrounds the origins of Maya civilization, partly because until recently virtually nothing was known about Maya subsistence patterns (Coe, 1993; N. Hammond, 1982). Perhaps the initial Maya settlement was dispersed, with villages scattered through the rain forest, in situations that seemed to militate against political or economic unity. The people flourished in a fundamentally empty landscape, where there was plenty of room for slash-and-burn agriculture and little incentive for cooperation. Their predecessors were hunter-gathers, small groups occupying tiny campsites who made no pottery. One such Archaic camp is known from the Coha site in Belize, in a level overlain by farming occupation that dates to later than 1,000 B.C. (Schele and Freidel, 1990). This farming settlement is well documented at the Cuello site, where it dates to the early first millennium B.C. or perhaps a little earlier (Andrews and Hammond, 1990). It is not known whether the Colha and Cuello sites date the changeover from hunting and gathering to farming in this part of the lowlands, but a date of around 1000 B.C. would not be unexpected.

    The earliest certain Maya communities come from the middle Preclassic (1000 to 400 B.C.). Some experts believe that large numbers of farmers moved into the lowlands during this period, bringing with them settled village life, the use of fine

Colha
1000 B.C.

Cuello

Middle Preclassic
1000 to 400 B.C.

clay vessels, and domesticated plants. Migrations from the highlands into the low-lands were commonplace in later times, so it is entirely possible that such migrations took place during the middle Preclassic. What is known is that the lowland Maya experienced a very rapid in-migration of farmers and then a fast population buildup over a wide area during this period. The Maya were well established at Komchen in the Yucatán by 800 B.C., and they were constructing massive pyramids at several sites in the central Petén by 600 B.C. No one has yet accounted for this rapid buildup, but there are reasons to suspect that it was connected with a growing demand for such lowland products as animal pelts and brightly colored bird feath-ers by elites elsewhere. A growing volume of long-distance exchange contributed, then, to an efflorescence of indigenous lowland civilization within a few centuries.

At the same time, ancestral burial within platforms and the cores of other struc-tures took hold as a persistent pattern of interment, as opposed to merely burying people under their houses. Patricia McAnany (1994), who has excavated at K'axob in Belize, believes that this changeover represented the santification of an ancestral place, where ancestors were venerated, as a basis for reckoning genealogy and claiming ownership of places. In other words, ancestor veneration was a way of structuring the inheritance of property and resources from one generation to the next. This was to assume great importance in later Classic Maya civilization.

Nakbe
600 to 400 B.C.

Between 600 and 400 B.C., the middle Preclassic inhabitants of Nakbe were con-structing elaborate complexes of finely finished stone buildings that stood on huge platforms (Coe, 1993). Within a few centuries, they began erecting carved stelae that are thought to depict the center's rulers. Certainly by late Preclassic times the lords of Nakbe were commissioning beautiful masonry and plaster masks of the gods and ancestors on their pyramids. These façades seem to relate directly to the emerging notion of divine kingship, Ch'ul Ahau, in Maya civilization, a form of

Divine kingship

kingship that developed rapidly out of some earlier form of central authority between 600 and 100 B.C. (Freidel and Schele, 1988a, b). Another site of the same general antiquity that has yielded images of kings with deity masks wearing the Jester God crown of kingship is Uaxactún.

El Mirador
150 B.C. to A.D. 50

By far the largest Preclassic Maya center is El Mirador, which was built between about 150 B.C. and A.D. 50. El Mirador covered about 6 square miles (16 sq. km), lying on low, undulating land; parts of the area flooded during the rainy season. The scale of El Mirador is vast, but it bears all the complicated iconography associated with Maya kingship. Archaeologists from Brigham Young University have uncov-ered more than 200 buildings; among them are great complexes of pyramids, plazas, causeways, and buildings (Matheny, 1986; Sabloff, 1990).

The Danta pyramid at the east end of the site dominates El Mirador. It rises from a natural hill more than 210 feet (70 m) high. The western face of the hill is sculpted into large platforms that are surmounted by buildings and temples. A little over a mile (2 km) west rises the Tigre complex, a pyramid 182 feet (55 m) high sur-rounded by a plaza, a small temple, and several smaller buildings (Figure 21.9). The Tigre complex covers about 58,000 square meters—an area a little larger than the base of Teotihuacán's Pyramid of the Sun. Three buildings, with the largest in the center, are on a truncated landing on the pyramid. This "triad" theme is also found at later sites such as Tikal.

El Mirador is unique because it was not altered in any significant way after the Preclassic. As excavations proceed, it should be possible to compare Preclassic with Classic occupation and to study the evolution of Maya architecture, city planning, and social and political organization. El Mirador is yielding some of the earliest

FIGURE 21.9 Archaeologists at work on the east stucco mask on the Tigre Temple, El Mirador. The building and mask date to the late Preclassic. *Inset*: El Mirador, Petén: reconstruction of the Tigre complex of buildings and platforms. The entire complex dates to the late Preclassic period, c. 100 B.C. to A.D. 50.

examples of Maya writing. They appear on an inscribed potsherd, and some symbols are inscribed on the Tigre sculpture. El Mirador itself was an elaborate city and was probably controlled by a highly organized elite. They used artisans, priests, architects, and engineers, as well as traders and thousands of unskilled villagers. This stupendous city flourished successfully for centuries before it suddenly collapsed in the early Christian era. The dynamics of this collapse are little understood but are mirrored at other Preclassic Maya communities, where the institution of kingship arose and was then apparently abandoned. The volatility of many centers may be connected to endemic warfare, but despite this constant change, many centers, among them Tikal and Uaxactún, developed continuously into Classic times.

In 50 B.C. the small late Preclassic town of Cerros near the eastern coast of the Yucatán housed fisherfolk and traders. Within two generations, this tiny community transformed itself into a large center. The village disappeared under plazas and temples, deliberately abandoned in favor of houses erected around the new sacred center. The unknown leaders of Cerros built their new temple according to pyramid designs that had developed among earlier peoples like the Olmec, designs that invoked a symbolic landscape in which religious activity took place (Schele and

Cerros
50 B.C.

Freidel, 1990). Everyone in the community shared in the communal labor of building the sacred mountain, a gateway to the Otherworld that was so important in Maya religion. It was a symbolic act that acknowledged the arrival of kingship in the community. The first temple at Cerros was followed by later shrines, the settings for the ritual bloodlettings and sacrifices that served to legitimize the roles of the emerging nobility and of the leader. Kingship flourished at Cerros for a short time, then collapsed, for reasons that are still a mystery. Perhaps there were problems in transferring power from one generation to the next, or the experiment simply failed, as it did in other Maya communities of the day. In any event, the great temples went into disuse, but people still lived around the ruined structures, living off fishing and trade.

Kingship: Sacred Space and Time

The leaders of Cerros and other Preclassic Maya communities are anonymous. They left no record of their names or personal histories. Their only heritage to their successors was a distinctive architectural heritage that stressed social ranking and the use of the large-scale architecture as a means of perpetuating royal dynasties. The rituals performed by these shaman-lords were performed on pyramids and in plazas of the great Maya centers, which were symbolic replicas of the sacred landscape created by the gods at the beginning. The architecture of the great ritual structures replicated forests, mountains, and caves as stelae, pyramids, and temple openings. These were powerful rituals, so powerful that the places where they were conducted became more and more sacred as successive rulers built new temples on the same spots. Generations of rulers replicated the iconography and sculpture of earlier buildings, elaborating on them to produce the sacred settings within which the strategies of political competition between neighbors were carried out (Miller and Taube, 1993).

Maya civilization was also embedded in a matrix of unfolding, cyclical time. Maya priests used the movements of planets and stars to mark the passage of time. They tried to understand the cycles of the cosmos, deciding which days were propitious for ritual, trade, royal marriages, war, and so on. Religious events were regulated according to a sacred year *(tzolkin)* with 13 months of 20 days each. The 260 days of the sacred year were unrelated to any astronomical phenomenon, being closely tied to ritual and divination. The length of this year was arbitrary and probably established by long tradition. Tzolkins were, however, closely intermeshed with a secular year *(haab)* of 365 days, an astronomical calendar based on the solar cycle. The *haab* was used to regulate state affairs, but the connections between sacred and secular years were of great importance in Maya life. Every 52 years a complete cycle of all the variations of the day and month names of the two calendars occurred, an occasion for intense religious activity.

The calendar was vital to Maya life, for the complex geography of sacred time was just as important as that of space for determining political strategies and social moves. Each day had a character, a distinctive identity in the tzolkin and haab, and a position in all the permutations of cyclical time. The records kept by Maya scribes in hieroglyphic codices (books) were incredibly intricate records of divine actions on each day of the cyclical calendar (Figure 21.10). Each Maya king developed a relationship to this constantly moving time scale. Some events, like planting and harvest, were regular events on the calendar. Others, like dates of accession, important victories, and royal deaths and births, left their marks on the calendar, sometimes as

FIGURE 21.10   Only three certain, and perhaps one doubtful, Maya codices (books of picture writing) are known to have survived destruction by the Spanish. Here is a page from the so-called Dresden Codex, which records astronomical calculations, ritual detail, and tables of eclipses.

days that assumed great significance to the history of an individual dynasty. Maya rulers linked their actions to those of the gods and the ancestors, sometimes legitimizing their descent by claiming that it reenacted mythical events. In a real sense, Maya history was linked to the present and the Otherworld, to the legendary Olmec civilization of the past. Society was embedded in a matrix of sacred space and time (Schele and Freidel, 1990; Schele, Freidel, and Parker, 1993).

The Maya developed a hieroglyphic script used for calculating calendars and regulating religious observances (Coe, 1992). The script was also much used for recording genealogies, king lists, conquests, and dynastic histories. The symbols are fantastically grotesque, consisting mostly of humans, monsters, or god's heads (Figure 21.10). After more than a decade of intensive research, about half the extant Classic descriptions have been read. In its emphasis on religious and cosmological matters, Maya writing is closest to ancient Egyptian script in terms of its role in society (N. Hammond, 1991).

These hieroglyphic records were of cardinal importance in Maya life, for the institution of kingship was based on the principle that the royal crown passed from father to son, or brother to brother to son, in a line that led back to a founding ancestor. From there, families and clans were carefully ranked by their distance from the central royal descent line. This system of family ranking and allegiance was the basis of political power, a system that worked well but that depended on careful documentation of genealogies. Social status was highly prized in Maya society, as we can see at the great center of Copán, a major frontier capital of the Maya world at the edge of the Central American chiefdoms. Its pyramids, temples, and stelae are a remarkable record of Maya kings exercising political and social power. Although cosmology was a feature of Copán's building designs, the main function of the civic structures there, as elsewhere, was to commemorate major events in the lives of kings and the political histories of kingdoms. Each building was dedicated by the king who built it in the context of a specific event, everything from a royal accession to an important victory or a new alliance. Among its many buildings, Copán features a ball court, a stadium used for an elaborate ceremonial contest in which sacrificial victims and kings descended through a symbolic "abyss" into the Otherworld. The players wore protective padding and used a rubber ball, which perhaps they aimed at markers—sometimes stone rings or macaw heads high on the side walls. We do not know the rules of the ball game, but the games were associated with human sacrifice and much pomp and circumstance.

By combining archaeological excavation at Copán with historical art interpretation and text translations, scholars have been able to trace a lineage of nobles who specialized in hieroglyphic writing, a skill that gave them special prestige (Fash, 1991). Members of another noble rank, the *sahalob* ("vassals"), served as expert administrators and received many privileges for their skill. Status was inherited and was one way in which the legitimacy of society as a whole was maintained.

Copán is just one of many sites where archaeologists have documented the complicated political and social history of Maya civilization. The public monuments erected by the Classic Maya emphasize not only the king's role as shaman, as the intermediary with the Otherworld, but also his position as family patriarch. Genealogical texts on stelae legitimize his descent, his close relationship to his often long-deceased parents. Maya kings used both the awesome regalia of their office and elaborate rituals to stress their close identity with mythical ancestral gods. This was a way in which they asserted their kin relationship and political authority over subordinate leaders and every member of society.

The king believed himself to have a divine covenant with the gods and ancestors, a covenant that was reinforced again and again in elaborate private and public rituals. The king was often depicted as the World Tree, the conduit by which humans communicated with the Otherworld. Trees were the living environment of Maya life and a metaphor for human power. So the kings of the Maya were a forest of symbolic human World Trees within a natural, forested landscape. The Maya calendar ensured a constant round of ceremonies and rituals at the great ceremonial centers erected by the labors of hundreds of people, farmers who also fed kings, priests, and artisans. Yet the Maya world view created serious and binding obligations among the king and his nobility and all the people, reflected in the king's responsibilities in gathering and redistributing commodities of all kinds and in implementing agricultural schemes that turned swamps into organized, productive landscapes. The lives of Maya rulers and all their subjects were interconnected in vital, dynamic ways. The king was state shaman, the individual who enriched everyone's life in spiritual and ceremonial ways. His success at organizing trade and agriculture gave all levels of society access to goods and commodities. The great ceremonial centers built by Maya leaders created a setting in which elaborate rituals and ceremonies took on intense significance. The "histories written and pictured by the kings on the tree stones standing before human-made mountains gave form to time and space in both the material and spiritual worlds" (Schele and Freidel, 1990).

Political Organization

Maya civilization was far from uniform, as recent advances in glyph decipherment have shown. It appears to have been a mosaic of political units, large and small, and it is difficult to be specific about the political relationships between Maya settlements, divided as the people were into a myriad of small and multicenter polities. One possible approach is through the identification of "emblem glyphs," titles that were carried by kings and their highest nobility in the major kingdoms. The emblem glyph of Palenque is *Ch'ul Bac Ahaw* ("Holy Bone Lord"), and that of Tikal is *Ch'ul Bal(am) Ahaw* ("Holy Jaguar Lord"). The emblem glyphs can operate as statements of political affiliation with particular kingdoms, for subordinate centers would sometimes use their overlord's glyph. They would identify political control over a territory by stating that events occurred *u cab* ("in the land of"). There appears to have been some form of hierarchical political organization within Maya domains, even if most of the details elude us (Culbert, 1991).

There were many elements common to all Maya polities, among them the calendar and hieroglyphic script, essential to the regulation of religious life and the worship of the gods. Architectural and artistic styles in ceramics and small artifacts varied from center to center as each developed its own characteristics and cultural traditions (Coe, 1993). The Maya were unified more by religion than by political or economic interests, in much the same way, perhaps, as the spread of Islam unified diverse cultures.

The political mechanisms used by the Maya included warfare, which had strong ritual overtones and was probably very destructive in its consequences. It is questionable how important it was in territorial expansion and may have been aimed more at economic hegemony. Much art and many inscriptions concentrate on the ceremonial and ideological aspects of war—the capture and sacrifice of prisoners as a way of validating political authority (Schele and Miller, 1986). Whether this was the primary purpose of going to war is uncertain. However, judging from emblem glyphs, most wars were between immediate neighbors, with the capture and sacrifice of a ruler sometimes leading to dominance of one center by another for generations, at others apparently having little effect. Intermarriage between ruling families of neighboring sites was also a significant political device among the Maya. The marriage of women into other dynasties even allowed some sites to acquire lasting political control over others. The inscriptions tell us that visits by rulers or their representatives to other centers were important occurrences, usually commemorating significant political events such as an accession or occasions when a ruler designated his heir (Culbert, 1991; Danien and Sharer, 1992; Schele and Freidel, 1990; Schele and Miller, 1992).

CLASSIC AND LATE CLASSIC POLITICAL HISTORY

• • •

Cerros and El Mirador were important centers during the late Preclassic, but even as they prospered, important new centers were emerging a short distance away. Tikal and Uaxactún were growing in importance during the late Preclassic and stepped into the political vacuum left by the decline of El Mirador. The two centers were less

Tikal
Uaxactún

than 12 miles (20 km) apart, too close for bitter rivals to coexist. Tikal had expanded greatly during the first century B.C., as large public buildings rose on the foundations of earlier, more humble structures. Clearly, the intent was to rival, and outdo, El Mirador's splendor. During this century, an elite emerged at Tikal, people represented by the burial of a noblewoman under a shrine and tomb paintings of richly decorated nobles. One burial contained a headless and thighless corpse tied up in a bundle, with a green fucsite portrait head that was once the chest pectoral of the deceased. The human face on the pectoral wears the Jester God headdress that kings wore for centuries afterward. Uaxactún just to the north underwent a similar transition during the same century. Here, Preclassic temples bear stucco masks and façades that depict the Maya world and the king who built the structures. At both Tikal and Uaxactún, Maya kings memorialized themselves on their temples, but the two centers were political and economic equals during this century.

A.D. 219

Tikal's inscriptions are the chronicle of a remarkable dynasty that ruled its kingdom from the early Classic until the ninth century A.D. The earliest recorded monarch is Yax-Moch-Xoc, who is thought to have reigned between A.D. 219 and 238. He was not the earliest king but was the one who served as founding ancestor for the great royal clan of Tikal that ruled in coming centuries. Uaxactún also fostered a powerful royal dynasty, whose monuments, like those of the Tikal kings, soon depict rulers with sacrificial victims cowering at their feet, noble victims taken in hand-to-hand combat for later sacrifice in public rituals. These portraits signal a crucial development in Maya history—the increasing role of warfare and campaigns of deliberate conquest.

A.D. 320

A.D. 378

Between A.D. 320 and 376, Great-Jaguar-Paw, the ninth successor of Yax-Moch-Xoc, came to the throne of Tikal. Great-Jaguar-Paw was not only long lived but also a formidable warrior. It was he who defeated the armies of Uaxactún on January 16, A.D. 378, in a conquest war under the generalship of one Smoking Frog that subjugated Tikal's long-term rival. His army ignored long-established rules of combat and sacked Uaxactún, setting up Smoking Frog as the founder of a new dynasty. The war was associated with new rituals first developed at Teotihuacán on the highlands, and it linked the god Tlaloc and the planet Venus. This was a period of regular trading contacts between Teotihuacán and many Maya centers, as evidenced by many finds of the distinctive green obsidian mined by the great city. The same contacts may have brought new philosophies of war and conquest and the rituals associated with them. These rituals were to become part of the Mesoamerican religious tradition for many centuries.

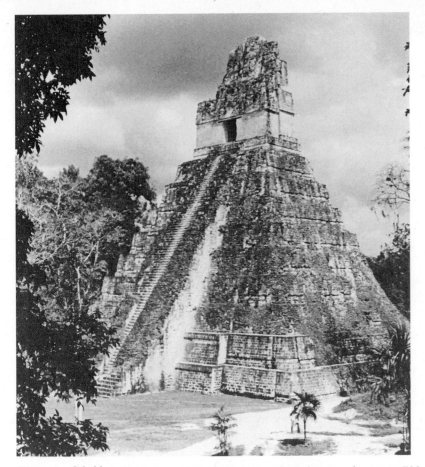

FIGURE 21.11   Temple I at Tikal, Guatemala, which dates to about A.D. 700.

Tikal's royal dynasty prospered in coming centuries. They eventually headed a multicenter polity, extending their influence by conquest and long-distance trade and by judicious political marriages that gave neighboring rulers maternal kin ties to the center. At the height of its powers, Tikal's territory covered 965 square miles (2500 sq. km), with an estimated population of more than 360,000 people. After a period of apparent political trouble between A.D. 534 and 593, Tikal continued to prosper into the late Classic (Figure 21.11).

A.D. 593

The city of Palenque also played a major role in Maya history and is remarkable not only for its fine buildings but also for its rulers' obsession with their ancestry. Two Palenque rulers, Pacal ("shield") and his oldest son, Chan-Bahlum ("Snake-Jaguar"), who ruled in the seventh century A.D., stand out for their vision and wisdom. Palenque's dynastic history began on March 11, A.D. 431, when Bahlum-Kuk ("Jaguar-Quetzal") became ruler, and lasted until sometime after A.D. 799. The experts have used the rich inscriptions left by Pacal and others to reconstruct a dynasty of no fewer than 12 kings, with, however, what Schele and Freidel (1990) call some "minor sidesteps." These sidesteps accounted for the obsession with history that was so remarkable in Pacal and Chan-Bahlum's day. Succession was through the male line, yet Pacal inherited the throne from his mother, Lady Zac-Kuk, who served for a time as ruler (Figure 21.12). She must have been a remarkable woman, although we know nothing of her. Pacal claimed the throne as her son,

Palenque
A.D. 431 to 799

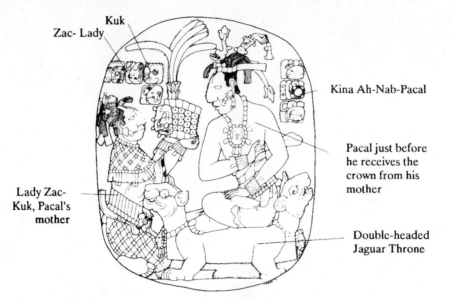

FIGURE 21.12   Pacal the Great (A.D. 603 to 683), ruler of Palenque, reigned for 67 years. This oval tablet commemorates his receipt of the crown from his mother, Lady Zac-Kuk. By using the name of a Maya goddess to refer to his mother, Pacal declared her to be the equivalent of a mother of the gods, making him divine offspring. (After Schele and Freidel, 1990.)

and in so doing had to change the genealogical rules so that he could override the age-old rule of descent through the father and claim succession. In short, he and his son orchestrated orthodox belief with clever fictions. First, they declared Lady Zac-Kuk to be equivalent to the first mother of gods and kings at the beginning of the present creation. This mother deity was the mother of the three major gods of Maya religion. Next, Pacal and Chan-Bahlum claimed that Pacal was born on the very day of the calendar that coincided with that of the goddess's birth. Thus, both Pacal and the goddess were of the same divine substance. Pacal inherited the throne from his mother because this was what had happened at the beginning of creation—authority had been transmitted through both males and females. It may have helped that Pacal ascended to the throne at the age of 12, while his mother was still alive, and that she lived for another 25 years. The real power may have been in her hands for all those years, for it is only after her death in 640 that Pacal commissioned major inscriptions that justified his own rule. Toward the end of his long reign, which lasted 67 years, Pacal built the Temple of the Inscriptions, a masterpiece of Maya architecture under which his tomb lies. His artists carved the images of his direct ancestors around his coffin deep under the temple, on which his strategy of dynastic legitimization was recorded (Schele and Freidel, 1990). Chan-Bahlum continued his father's preoccupation with dynastic succession. Both rulers made Palenque a major power during their lifetimes, between A.D. 603 and 702, but the dynasty survived for only another century or so after Chan-Bahlum's death.

The late Classic period of Maya civilization, after A.D. 600, has been described as a period of warring states. It was a period of profound change in the lowlands, which started when Lord Water of Caracol attacked his mighty neighbor, Tikal, in A.D. 556. Five years later, another war ended the domination of Tikal, which

Caracol
A.D. 556

became a shadow of its former self. In the years that followed, successive lords of Caracol surrounded both Tikal and a neighboring state to the east, named Naranjo, with a circle of allies that were enemies of both states. Repeated attacks reduced Naranjo to a political shadow. With no standing armies, Maya kings could not garrison defeated towns. Not that this was necessary, for if the nobility were removed, there was no one to attract wealth and precious commodities or political influence. There was no way to recruit populations to support the center.

Caracol and its close ally to the north, Calakmul, never succeeded in forging an empire out of the ruins of their conquests and their many alliances. Tikal at the height of its power named its ruler Chac-Te ("Great Tree"), and his subordinate king was named Y'Ahaw ("His King"). The title Chac-Te reappears many times, but there is no evidence that the Maya developed any effective imperial form of government. In the three centuries that followed, the balance of power shifted many times, to Dos Pilas and back to Tikal, in the hands of the famous and vigorous ruler Ah-Cacaw (Figure 21.13). The diplomatic and military landscape was constantly changing, as alliances were formed and just as rapidly collapsed again. During the very late Classic, after A.D. 771, a new political pattern emerged, indicative of changed conditions and stressful times. Carved inscriptions began to appear in the houses of local nobles at Copán and other sites, as if the rulers were now granting the privilege of using inscriptions to important individuals, perhaps as a way of gaining their continued support in times of trouble. This proliferation of inscriptions in the Petén and elsewhere may also reflect minor nobles taking advantage of confused times and a disintegrating political authority to claim their own brief independence. The confusion accelerated. By A.D. 800, Maya populations were declining sharply, and both monument carving and major construction soon came to an end. **A.D. 771**

Most Maya polities were small-scale, independent units that rarely interfered with their neighbors. The lowlands were never unified politically during the classic period. What the elite did share was a set of highly complex traditions and a network of contacts between rulers that transcended the local interests of individual polities and considerable local cultural diversity. Maya civilization was a local phenomenon. Only when a few aggressive, successful leaders emerged at places like Tikal did larger, multicenter polities emerge. These tended to disintegrate within a few generations.

As Norman Yoffee (1991) points out, there are some parallels between the Classic Maya and early Mesopotamian civilizations. The Sumerians were governed by independent rulers with strong ritual powers, presiding over independent polities that were in a constant state of change and interaction. The city-state remained the practical political unit long after Sargon created a theoretically unified Mesopotamia in about 2400 B.C. (Chapter 15). Just as in the Maya lowlands, larger political units forged by leaders of exceptional ability soon fragmented back into their city-state parts. Maya civilization was a local phenomenon in the sense that its constituent states were relatively small, short-lived, and stable kingdoms. Regional ties were crucial, probably far more so than in Mesopotamia. These ties were forged through common religious beliefs, alliances, and marriage ties. For example, the mother of a ruler of Copán named Yax-Pac was a royal princess of Palenque, 1000 miles (1600 km) away. Despite these ties, however, the realities of social and economic instability militated against the long-term stability of any of the multicenter states that rose and fell with such bewildering rapidity during the late Classic.

The central institution of Maya civilization was the kingship, for it was the concept that unified society as a whole. Maya kings lived and carried out their deeds in the context of a history they recorded in building projects at Tikal, Palenque, and

9.15.15.0.0 (June 4, 746), a tree-stone planting by the dead Shield-Jaguar in the land of Bird-Jaguar

Shield-Jaguar

Bird-Jaguar

sky register with the dead parents

Lady Eveningstar, Bird-Jaguar's mother

The dead Shield-Jaguar observing his son

The flapstaff event between Shield-Jaguar and Bird-Jaguar on June 26, 741

Bird-Jaguar's accession as king on May 3, 752 (the unmarked texts on the sides record the date of accession)

Bird-Jaguar as Chac-Xib-Chac, standing before sacrificial victims on June 4, 750

FIGURE 21.13   The aged ruler of Yaxchilan, Shield-Jaguar, conducts a flapstaff ritual with his son Bird-Jaguar on June 26, A.D. 741 (*left*). The flapstaff was a long wooden staff with a cloth tied down its middle. The nature of the ritual is unknown. *Right,* on June 4, 750, Bird-Jaguar wears the mask of the god Chac-Xib-Chac as he presents three unarmed victims for sacrifice. The stela on which these inscriptions were made was erected by Bird-Jaguar as part of a successful campaign to legitimize his claims to the throne of Yaxchilan. (After Schele and Freidel, 1990.)

elsewhere. Maya elites lived out their lives in the context of the kings that ruled them, and in turn, thousands of commoners lived their lives with respect to the nobility (Figure 21.14).

FIGURE 21.14 A portion of the famous Bonampak mural, Chiapas, Mexico. This segment is in Room 4, showing a Maya ruler, warriors, and war captives.

THE COLLAPSE OF CLASSIC MAYA CIVILIZATION
● ● ●

The Maya civilization flourished in the southern states until about A.D. 900, when it suddenly and inexplicably collapsed. Maya civilization reached its peak after A.D. 600. Then, at the end of the eighth century, the great ceremonial centers of the Petén and the southern lowlands were abandoned, the long court calendar was discontinued, and the structure of religious life and the state decayed. No one has been able to explain this sudden and dramatic collapse of Maya civilization, which is the subject of a prolonged debate in American archaeology (Culbert, 1973; 1988).

The Classic Maya collapse has fostered varied traditional explanations, most of them unilinear and monocausal. They have included catastrophes, such as earthquakes, hurricanes, and disease. Ecological theories mention exhausted soils, water loss, and erosion. Internal social revolt might have led the peasants to rebel against cruel rule by their elitist overlords. Each of these hypotheses has been rejected because either the evidence is insufficient or the explanation is oversimplified. Another popular hypothesis is that there was a disruptive invasion of Maya territory by peoples from the highlands. Certainly evidence reports Toltec intrusions into the

A.D. 900
Collapse hypotheses

lowlands, although it is hard to say how broad the effects of the invasions were or what damage they did to the fabric of Maya society.

The late Classic was a period of great activity and rapid population growth at almost all major sites in the Maya lowlands. The collapse began at some sites early in the ninth century. Major centers were abandoned, monumental inscriptions and major public building ceased, and populations declined rapidly. The effects were most strongly felt in the south. Within a century, huge sections of the southern lowlands were abandoned, never to be reoccupied (Culbert, 1988a). At Tikal, perhaps the greatest Maya center, the elite vanished and the population declined to a third of its earlier level. The nonelite survivors clustered in the remains of great masonry structures and tried to retain a semblance of earlier life. Within a century, even they were gone. All this is not to say that Maya civilization vanished completely, for new centers may have emerged in neighboring areas, taking in some of the displaced population. Maya civilization continued to flourish in the northern Yucatán (Sabloff and Freidel, 1984).

Multiple factors

Everyone studying the Maya collapse agrees that a multiplicity of factors led to catastrophe in the southern lowlands (Culbert, 1973). The theories of the 1970s argued that the collapse of Teotihuacán gave the Maya a chance to enlarge their managerial functions in Mesoamerican trade. The elite became increasingly involved in warfare and competition between regions. The late Classic saw a frenzy of public building and increased pressure on the people, the source of both food and labor for prestige projects. Agricultural productivity fell, disease may have reached epidemic proportions, and population densities plummeted, making recovery impossible.

Warfare at Dos Pilas

Endemic warfare may have been a powerful factor in the collapse. At Dos Pilas in northern Guatemala, 65 miles (105 km) from Tikal, Arthur Demarest (1993) has uncovered evidence for civil war and prolonged conflict. Founded by a renegade noble from Tikal in A.D. 645, Dos Pilas' later rulers embarked on campaigns of expansion, which enlarged their territory to more than 1500 square miles by the mid-eighth century. Dos Pilas now controlled major jade and obsidian routes. Its lords lavished wealth on ornate palaces and a pyramid topped by three temples. Demarest and Juan Antonio Valdés dug deep under a small temple behind a stela that commemorated "Ruler 2," who reigned between A.D. 698 and 726. They uncovered the ruler's burial chamber. He wore a shell mosaic headdress adorned with monster faces, a heavy jade necklace, and jade bracelets. At his waist hung a stingray spine, once used for genital bloodletting. Hieroglyphs associated with the grave tell of the lord's carefully contrived diplomatic marriages with neighbors and of his delicate political marriages and military campaigns.

Dos Pilas flourished until A.D. 761. By then, its rulers had overextended themselves, despite frantic efforts to maintain their domains. In that year, nearby Tamrindo attacked its former sovereign, killed "Ruler 4," despite desperate resistance from the Dos Pilas inhabitants. The invaders tore down the royal palace and robbed temple façades to build rough defensive walls with wooden palisades to surround the central precinct. Here, the people clustered in a small village of crude huts, while the nobles fled and built a new center at Aguateca. The new center lay atop a steep cliff above a deep chasm, protected on three sides by natural features, apart from massive defense walls. The Aguatecans held out for another half century, despite repeated attacks. In the early ninth century A.D., Demarest believes, intensive warfare drove the survivors of Dos Pilas into fortified towns and villages, where they even erected defensive walls around large tracts of agricultural land. Local conditions may have become so insecure that farmers were limited to defended acreage, which may have affected crop yields dramatically. In a last desperate stand, they dug three moats, one 460 feet (140.2 m) long, across a peninsula in Lake Petexbatun, creating an island fortress. The bedrock from the canals became defensive walls and a walled wharf for a canoe landing. The outpost did not last long, for the inhabitants abandoned it in the 800s.

These theories have been subjected to exhaustive analysis in recent years by researches that involve both simulation studies and examination of trading patterns and demographic and ecological stresses that could have affected population densities. Patrick Culbert (1988) has examined population densities and the potential for agricultural production in the southern lowlands. He shows that population densities rose as high as 518 persons per square mile (200 per sq. km) during the late Classic over an area so large that it was impossible for people to adapt to bad times by moving to new land or emigrating. He believes that the magnitude of the population loss during the two centuries after A.D. 800 was such that social malfunction alone cannot account for it. Failure of the agricultural base must have been an important component in the collapse equation.

Maya agriculture became increasingly intense as populations rose, with both terrace and raised-field systems covering large areas in many parts of the lowlands. At some of the larger sites like Tikal, the people may have been transporting great quantities of foodstuffs from distances of between 31 and 62 miles (50 and 100 km) away. In the short term, the intensification strategies worked, but they carried the seeds of collapse. The risks of climatic change, plant disease, erosion, and long-term declines in soil fertility were always present in such enterprises. To continue functioning efficiently, the newly intensified systems would have to be managed constantly. Just the repair of field systems after floods and rains would have required watchful effort on a large scale. There are no signs that the Maya made any social changes that enabled them to achieve such a level of management, especially when so many people were engaged in public construction projects and, apparently, in military activity (perhaps the Maya were under pressure from the north).

Agricultural collapse

There are so few data that we can reconstruct almost any scenario of agricultural collapse. Culbert (1988) believes that long-term environmental degradation was an important element in the scenario, where short-term gains in productivity were followed by catastrophic declines. For example, as populations rose, fallow cycles may have been shortened, leading to increased competition between crop plants and weeds; this is a problem that can be solved only by constant weeding, a very labor-intensive activity. Shortened fallow cycles also lead to lower levels of plant nutrients and declining crop yields. We do not know if the Maya counteracted these trends by systematic mulching or by planting soil-restoring crops. The problem of erosion may have been even more acute. There are signs that the people lost much soil to runoff in the lowlands, for they did not build the terraces needed in time to retain the soil. Some of this erosion may have resulted from extensive deforestation.

Culbert makes a convincing case for a major demographic and subsistence disaster. He draws an interesting parallel with Mesopotamia, where at Ur an abundance of water from an expanded canal system led to overirrigation, shortened fallow cycles, and high levels of salt in the soil (R. M. Adams, 1981). To quote Robert Adams, "Long-term agricultural decline was in some ways a direct consequence of its earlier apparent success." The expanding Maya population was dependent on an agricultural system that made no allowance for long-term problems.

Eventually the system could produce no further riches, could not expand, and could only decline—with catastrophic results.

THE TOLTECS

• • •

Although by A.D. 900 the Classic period had ended, Maya religious and social orders continued in northern Yucatán (Figure 21.15). The continuity of the ancient Mesoamerican tradition survived unscathed. Basic economic patterns and technological traditions were retained, although religious and ideological patterns and priorities were disarranged. New ceremonial centers were built, but war and violence became primary as militaristic rulers achieved dominance in Mesoamerica (Davies, 1977, 1980).

Postclassic
a.d. 900 to 1521

We have mentioned the unsettled Postclassic political conditions caused by population movements and tribal warfare. Many groups of invaders vied for political power in central Mexico until the Toltecs achieved dominance in the tenth century.

Toltecs

The oral legends of the Aztec rulers, who followed the Toltecs, describe how the Toltecs came into Mesoamerica from the northwest frontiers beyond the civilized

Tula
A.D. 900

world. They settled at Tula, 37 miles (57 km) north of the Valley of Mexico, where they built a ceremonial center dedicated to their serpent god, Quetzalcóatl (Figure 21.16) (Diehl, 1984; Hanson, 1989). Tula is notable for its animal sculpture and

A.D. 1160

pottery styles, but it did not have a long life, for in approximately A.D. 1160 some newcomers with a less developed religious organization arrived from the north and destroyed the temples.

Chichén Itzá

Chichén Itzá in northern Yucatán was an important Maya ceremonial center in Postclassic times (Figure 21.17) In the ninth century A.D., Chichén Itzá came under

FIGURE 21.15   Distribution of Classic Maya, Toltec, and Aztec civilizations.

FIGURE 21.16 Tula. The summit of its pyramid bears statues of richly adorned warriors with elaborate breastplates. These once supported the roof of the temple of the feathered serpent god Quetzalcóatl.

FIGURE 21.17A Chichén Itzá: Reconstructed view of the site and the Sacred Cenote.

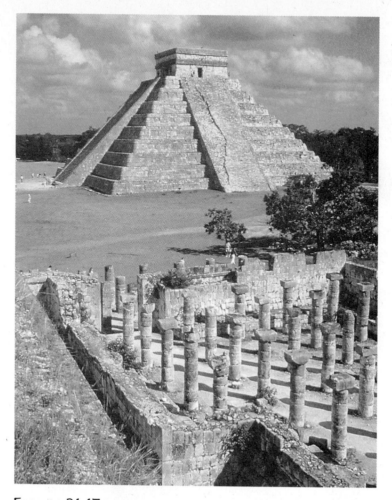

FIGURE 21.17B   Chichén Itzá: The Castillo, the largest building at the site.

Toltec influence (Coggins, 1985; Weaver, 1992). The extent of this influence is much debated, but it probably represented a new political order, a complex mixing of Mexican and Maya factions among the elite. They developed new artistic and political styles that separated political functions from the personality of an individual ruler. The Chichén Toltecs developed a flexibility and a resilience that enabled them to be far more adaptive to changing political conditions than their southern neighbors had been. The leaders of Chichén Itzá developed a truly regional state. They controlled the two great resources of the northern Yucatán: a talented, well-organized population and massive salt fields along the coast. The site was aban-doned in the thirteenth century, but the city of Mayapán, a walled settlement *Mayapán* clustered around a ceremonial center, rose to prominence elsewhere in northern Yucatán. At least 12,000 people lived in this Maya city, which was ruled by the Cocom family. Maya civilization enjoyed a resurgence in this area, although Mayapán declined during the civil wars of the fifteenth century. A century later, the Spanish found Yucatán ruled by numerous petty chiefs.

The militaristic Toltecs were the leading military and political force in Mesoamerica for such a short time that their influence evaporated rapidly when

Tula was destroyed. Another period of political chaos in the Valley of Mexico ensued, as more barbarians from the north (Chichimecs) maneuvered for political power (Davies, 1980).

THE AZTECS AND THE SPANISH CONQUEST

• • •

When the first Spanish conquistadores arrived in highland Mexico in 1519, they were astounded by the rich civilization they found. The capital city of Tenochtitlán was the headquarters of a series of militaristic Aztec kings, who ruled over a wide area by religious decree, constant human sacrifice, and bloodthirsty campaigning. Within a few years of Spanish contact, Aztec civilization literally ceased to exist. Tenochtitlán was reduced to rubble after a siege that lasted 91 days.

The Aztecs were one of several nomadic, semicivilized Chichimeca groups who settled in the Valley of Mexico after the fall of Tula (Clendinnen, 1991; Townsend, 1992). They arrived during the early twelfth century, a politically weak but aggressive group who barely retained their own identity. After years of military harassment, the Aztecs fled into the swamps of Lake Texcoco in about 1325. There they founded a small hamlet named Tenochtitlán (now Mexico City). Less than two centuries later, this village had become the largest city in pre-Columbian America (Conrad and Demarest, 1984).

At first the Aztecs lived peaceably with their neighbors, and Tenochtitlán flourished as an important market center. By judicious diplomacy, discreet military alliance, and well-timed royal marriages, the Aztecs quietly advanced their cause until they were a force to be reckoned with in local politics. Then, in the early fifteenth century, they changed their foreign policy abruptly and embarked on a ruthless campaign of long-term military and economic conquest. Soon they controlled a loosely connected network of minor states and cities that extended across Mesoamerica. The real leader behind this change was a counselor and general named Tlacaelel, who was adviser to a series of aggressive Aztec rulers. It was he who encouraged the use of terror and human sacrifice as a means of controlling conquered territory. The rich tribute from conquered states and cities made Tenochtitlán the center of the Mesoamerican world, the hub of a political and economic confederacy that extended from near the Pacific Ocean to the Gulf of Mexico and from northern Mexico as far south as Guatemala.

Tenochtitlán, a city of more than 200,000 people, was a spectacular sight in the sixteenth century, with markets where more than 60,000 people are said to have assembled every day (Diaz, 1963; J. B. Morris, 1962). The market sold every form of foodstuff and provided every luxury and service. The principal streets of Tenochtitlán were of beaten earth, and there were at least 40 pyramids adorned with fine, decorated stonework (Moctezuma, 1988). Tenochtitlán certainly was larger, and probably cleaner, than many European cities of the time (Figure 21.18).

Large residential areas surrounded the central precincts, and houses with chinampa gardens lay on the outskirts of the city. Six major canals ran through Tenochtitlán, and there were three causeways that connected the city with the mainland. At least 200,000 canoes provided convenient transport for the people of the city, which was divided into 60 or 70 well-organized wards. Tenochtitlán was a magnificent city set in a green swath of country near a clear lake, with a superb backdrop of snow-capped volcanoes.

FIGURE 21.18   Reconstruction drawing of the central precincts at Tenochtitlán, with the Temple of Huitzilopochtli and Tlaloc at the left.

Aztec society was moving closer and closer to a rigid, highly stratified class system at the time of Spanish contact. No ordinary person was allowed to enter a waiting room in the palace used by nobles. The king was revered as a semigod and had virtually despotic powers. He was elected from a limited class group of *pipiltin*, or nobles. There were full-time professional merchants, called *pochteca*, and also a class of warriors whose ranks were determined by the number of people they had killed in battle. Groups of lineages called *calpulli* (big house) were the most significant factor in most people's religious, social, and political life. Many of them coincided with wards in the city. The great mass of the people were free people, or *macehualtin*, and serfs, landless peasants, and slaves made up the bottom strata of society.

Much of Aztec society's efforts went toward placating the formidable war and rain gods, Huitzilopochtli and Tlaloc, whose benevolence was assured by constant human sacrifices. These sacrifices reached their peak at the end of each 52-year cycle, like those of the Maya, when the continuity of the world would be secured by bloodthirsty rites (Figure 21.19).

By the time of the Spanish conquest in 1519, Aztec society seems to have been functioning in a state of frenetic and bloody terrorism that flourished at the behest of arrogant, imperial rulers. The Aztecs had learned the fine art of terror as a political instrument and regularly staged elaborate public displays in Tenochtitlán to which subject leaders were invited. The Spaniards estimated that at least 20,000 people were sacrificed to the gods throughout the Aztec empire each year. This figure may be an exaggeration, but there is no doubt that a considerable number of prisoners of war and slaves perished by having their hearts ripped out in the presence of the gods. There was also a steady flow of sacrificial victims from the Aztecs'

FIGURE 21.19   Aztec human sacrifice. Priests ripped out the still-beating hearts of sacrificial victims and rolled their corpses down the temple steps.

constant military campaigns. Indeed, the finest death for an Aztec warrior was to perish under the sacrificial knife after honorable capture in battle. Such a fate was known as the "flowery death."

The Aztecs have acquired a formidable reputation from historians—and, it must be confessed, from some archaeologists—because of their penchant for human sacrifice and cannibalism. That they were addicted to human sacrifice is certain, the cannibalism less so. Some believe that the Aztec nobles ate human flesh to compensate for a lack of meat in their diet, but the beans they ate as a staple were more than sufficient as a source of protein. It seems more likely that the Aztec nobles and priests engaged in occasional ritual cannibalism as part of their intensely symbolic religious beliefs (Townsend, 1992).

By the time the Spaniards landed on the Mexican lowlands, Aztec civilization was in danger of being torn apart. The society was becoming top-heavy with nobles because they were allowed to marry from the people and their children automatically became aristocrats. The demands for tribute both from subject states and from the free people of the city became ever larger and more exacting. There may well have been intense philosophical disagreements between the militant priests and warriors, who increasingly encouraged conquest and human sacrifice, and those more sophisticated and educated Aztecs who believed in a gentler, less aggressive world. It is fascinating to speculate what would have happened had Cortés not landed in Mexico. Given the past history of Mexico, it seems likely that Aztec civilization would have collapsed suddenly, to be replaced in due time by another society much like it. In truth, Aztec civilization had reached a point of complexity that was beyond the capacity of its rulers to control and administer, a complexity that Old World civilizations had brought under control, and we can be certain that the Aztecs' successors would have eventually done so as well.

The Aztecs were one of the most important groups in Mesoamerica when the Spaniards first explored the New World. From coastal villagers in the lowlands they heard stories of the fabled rich kingdoms in the high interior. Soon the *conquistadores* pressed inland. Hernán Cortés was the first Spaniard to come into contact with the Aztecs, now ruled by Moctezuma II, a despotic ruler who assassinated most of his predecessor's counselors and had himself deified. Moctezuma's reign was disturbed by constant omens of impending doom and predictions that the god Quetzalcóatl would return to reclaim his homeland (Dibble and Anderson, 1978). The king was deeply alarmed by the reports of Spanish ships on the coast. There were, then, considerable internal psychological stresses on Moctezuma and his followers before the Spaniards arrived.(Clendinnen, 1991).

It took Cortés two tough years to reduce the Aztecs to slaves and their marvelous capital to rubble. A handful of explorers on imported horses, armed with a few muskets, were able to overthrow one of the most powerful tribute states in the history of America. Without question, Cortés's task was made easier by both rebellious subjects of the Aztecs and the extraordinary stresses the Aztecs had placed on themselves.

By 1680, the Indian population of the Aztec heartland was reduced from approximately 1.2 million to some 70,000—a decimation resulting from war, slavery, disease, overwork and exploitation, famine, and malnutrition. Mesoamerica as a whole lost between 85 and 95 percent of its indigenous population during that 160-year period. Only a few fragments of the fabulous Mesoamerican cultural tradition survived into modern times, and the Indian population faced a new and uncertain chapter in their long history (Gibson, 1964).

CHAPTER SUMMARY

The Preclassic period of Mesoamerican prehistory lasted from approximately 2000 B.C. to A.D. 250, a period of major cultural change in both lowlands and highlands. Sedentary villages traded with each other in raw materials and exotic objects. These exchange networks became increasingly complex and eventually came under the monopolistic control of larger villages. Increasing social complexity went hand in hand with the appearance of the first public buildings and evidence of social stratification. These developments are well chronicled in the Valley of Oaxaca and in the Olmec culture of the lowlands, which flourished from approximately 1500 to 500 B.C. Olmec art styles and religious beliefs were among those that spread widely over lowlands and highlands during the late Preclassic period. Preclassic cultural developments culminated in the highlands in a number of great cities, among them Monte Albán and Teotihuacán. Teotihuacán collapsed in approximately A.D. 700, probably as a result of warfare with other rival states in the highlands.

Religious ideologies, ritual organization, and extensive trading networks were key factors in the development of Maya society in the lowlands after 1000 B.C. Classic Maya civilization flourished from A.D. 250 to 900 and consisted of an ever-changing patchwork of competing states. Maya glyphs show that Maya civilization was far from uniform. The Maya were unified more by religious beliefs than by political or economic interests. Until about A.D. 600, the largest states were in northeast Petén, with a multicenter polity headed by the "Sky" rulers of Tikal. Maya civilization reached its height in the southern lowlands after the seventh century, collapsing suddenly in the Yucatán after A.D. 900. The reasons for the collapse are still uncertain, but pressure on the labor force and food shortages doubtless were among them.

Teotihuacán's collapse in the highlands resulted in a political vacuum for some centuries, which eventually was filled by the Toltecs and then the Aztecs, whose bloodthirsty civilization was dominant in the Valley of Mexico at the time of the Spanish conquest in A.D. 1519.

GUIDE TO FURTHER READING

Clendinnen, Inga. 1991. *The Aztecs: An Interpretation.* Cambridge, Eng.: Cambridge University Press.
> *A wonderfully articulate and sophisticated analysis of Aztec civilization and its institutions. Truly engrossing.*

Coe, Michael. 1993. *The Maya,* 5th ed. London and New York: Thames and Hudson.
> *A well-established synthesis of Maya civilization that is both readable and authoritative.*

Marcus, Joyce. 1993. *Mesoamerican Writing Systems: Propoganda, Myth, and History in Four Ancient Civilizations.* Princeton, NJ: Princeton University Press.
> *A discussion of Mesoamerican writing from an anthropological perspective. Controversial, but essential reading for the serious student.*

Sabloff, Jeremy A. 1989. *The Cities of Ancient Mexico.* New York: Thames and Hudson.
> *A straightforward account of major Mesoamerican centers and cities for a general audience.*

Schele, Linda, and Freidel, David. 1990. *A Forest of Kings.* New York: Morrow.
> *A superb popular account of Maya history as known from glyphs. Entertaining, provocative, and challenging.*

Schele, Linda, and Miller, E. 1986. *The Blood of Kings.* Austin: University of Texas Press.
> *A brilliant, definitive account of Maya civilization and political history based on inscriptions and glyphs. An exemplary piece of long-term research.*

Townsend, Richard F. 1992. *The Aztecs.* London and New York: Thames and Hudson.
> *A straightforward description of Aztec civilization for the general reader. Richly illustrated and authoritative.*

CHAPTER

22

ANDEAN STATES

· · ·

The year was 1911. American explorer Hiram Bingham was high in the Andes, struggling along precipitous, densely forested paths, slipping ankle deep in mud at every corner. He and his men climbed in places on all fours, high above the tumbling Urubamba River. Suddenly, he emerged into the open high atop a mountain ridge. Bingham climbed a granite stairway leading to a plaza with two temples. He wandered through "a maze of beautiful granite houses . . . covered with trees and moss and the growth of centuries." He wandered for hours among "walls of white granite . . . carefully cut and exquisitely fitted together." This was Machu Picchu, an Inca settlement in such a remote, inaccessible setting that Bingham claimed it was the "lost city of the Incas." For three years, Bingham worked at Machu Picchu, clearing, excavating, and mapping houses and temples.

Machu Picchu is one of the most spectacular archaeological sites in the world, but never a lost city, for the local Inca were well aware of its existence. What makes it so dramatic is its mountain setting, its testimony to the incredible skill of the Andeans at mastering climatic extremes (Table 22.1).

In its late fifteenth-century heyday, the vast Inca empire, known as Tawantinsuyu ("The Land of the Four Quarters"), extended from high-altitude mountain valleys in the Andes through dry highland plains to foothills to tropical rain forests and to coastal deserts, some of the driest landscape on earth (Figure 22.1. Each environment of the highlands and lowlands posed different environmental challenges, that is, confronted the Andeans with radically different climatic conditions and entirely disparate food resources. Thus, Andean civilization pursued many different evolutionary pathways, which came together in a remarkable mosaic of states and empires, in large part as a result of widely held spiritual beliefs and by constant interchange between the coast and the highlands and between neighboring valleys and large population centers. Tawantinsuyu itself was a unique political synthesis sewn together by the Inca lords of the Andes in the centuries just before European contact. It was the culmination of centuries of increasing social complexity throughout the Andean area. How did such complex states arise in this landscape of extraordinary contrasts? Recent archaeological researches have generated some sophisticated hypotheses to account for them (Keatinge, 1988).

TABLE 22.1
• • •

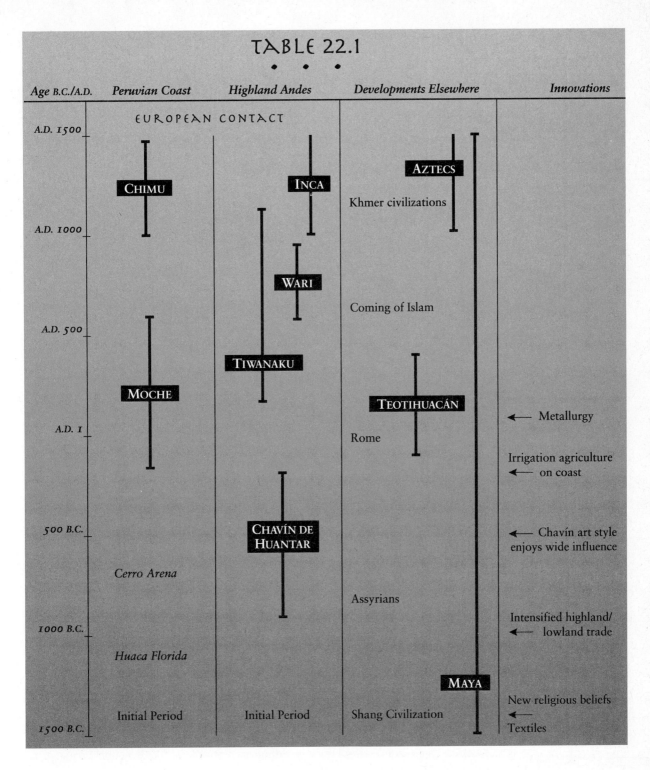

Age B.C./A.D.	Peruvian Coast	Highland Andes	Developments Elsewhere	Innovations
	EUROPEAN CONTACT			
A.D. 1500	CHIMU	INCA	AZTECS	
			Khmer civilizations	
A.D. 1000		WARI		
			Coming of Islam	
A.D. 500		TIWANAKU		
	MOCHE		TEOTIHUACÁN	
A.D. 1			Rome	← Metallurgy
				Irrigation agriculture ← on coast
500 B.C.		CHAVÍN DE HUANTAR		← Chavín art style enjoys wide influence
	Cerro Arena		Assyrians	
1000 B.C.				Intensified highland/ ← lowland trade
	Huaca Florida			
			MAYA	New religious beliefs
1500 B.C.	Initial Period	Initial Period	Shang Civilization	← Textiles

FIGURE 22.1   Archaeological sites mentioned in this chapter. Approximate distributions of various traditions are also shown.

THE MARITIME FOUNDATIONS OF ANDEAN CIVILIZATION

◆ ◆ ◆

The rugged central Andean mountains are second only to the Himalayas in height, but only 10 percent of their rainfall descends the Pacific watershed. The foothill slopes and plains at the western foot of the mountains are mantled by one of the world's driest deserts, which extends virtually from the equator to 30° south, much of it along the Peruvian coast. At the opposite extreme, the richest fishery in the Americas hugs the Pacific shore, yielding millions of small schooling fish such as anchovies. These easily netted shoals support millions of people today, and they supported dense prehistoric populations. In contrast, the cultivation of this dry landscape requires controlling the runoff from the Andes with large irrigation systems that use long canals built by the coordinated labors of hundreds of people.

Only 10 percent of this desert can be farmed, so its inhabitants rely heavily on the incredible bounty of the Pacific. Surprisingly, perhaps, this apparently inhospitable desert was a major center of complex early states, which traded with neighbors in the highlands and built large ceremonial centers.

The mechanisms by which complex states arose on the Peruvian coast are still little understood, partly because research has tended to concentrate on larger, more spectacular sites (Haas et al., 1987; Moseley, 1975b, 1986; D. J. Wilson, 1983). Such researches tell us little about the relative size of different communities or about population densities, which are critical measures of an evolving state society. It is only recently that larger-scale river valley surveys have collected such data, researches like Gordon Willey's (1963) classic work on the Virú and Donald Proulx's (1985) fieldwork in the Nepeña Valley. These investigations have shown that there were major changes in site clustering through time, especially after the introduction of maize agriculture and irrigation to the coast after 2500 B.C.

In the 1970s, archaeologist Michael Moseley (1975b) proposed what he called the "maritime foundations of Andean civilization" hypothesis. He argued that the unique maritime resources of the Pacific coast provided sufficient calories to support rapidly growing, sedentary populations, which clustered in large communities. In addition, the same food source produced sufficient surplus to free up time and people to erect large public monuments and temples, work organized by the leaders of newly complex coastal societies. This scenario runs contrary to conventional archaeological thinking, which regards agriculture as the economic basis for state-organized societies. In the Andes, argued Moseley, it was fishing. For thousands of years, coastal populations rose, and their rise preadapted them to later circumstances, under which they would adopt large-scale irrigation and maize agriculture.

Maritime foundations theory

Moseley (1975b) implies that mollusks and large fish were vital resources on the coast, but marine biologists drew his attention to the incredible potential of anchoveta and other small schooling fish. Anchoveta can be easily netted throughout the year from small canoes. The fish offer predictable food supplies that can be dried or ground into fine meal. Such harvests would provide an abundance of protein. Judging from modern yields, if prehistoric coastal populations had lived at 60 percent of the carrying capacity of the fisheries and eaten nothing but small fish, the coast could have supported more than 6.5 million people. That is not to say that it did, but the figures make the point that the exploitation of small fish would have provided a more than adequate economic base for the emergence of complex societies on the coast. It is interesting that small mesh nets and floats have come from earlier coastal sites such as Paloma (Chapter 13).

Several critiques of the maritime foundations hypothesis have appeared, all of them based on the assumption that large coastal settlements could not have been supported by maritime resources alone (see, for example, D. J. Wilson, 1981, 1983). Most of these critiques have tended to ignore the potential of anchovetas. Another argument revolves around the famous El Niño phenomenon, the periodic changes in Pacific currents that reduce the fisheries to a shadow of their normal selves for several years at a time. In fact, as Moseley (1986) points out, El Niño brings unfamiliar fish species to the coast as well as violent rainfall that has the potential to disrupt irrigation systems with catastrophic results, some of which are now being identified in the archaeological record. Overall, the maritime foundations hypothesis has stood the test of time well, provided it is seen as a component in a much broader evolutionary process, which also took place inland, in the highlands, and in areas where the width of the coastal shelf precluded extensive anchoveta fishing.

Critiques of maritime foundations

Richard Burger (1985) argues that changing dietary patterns in the highlands, where agriculture became increasingly important, would have created a demand among farmers for lowland products—salt, fish, and seaweed. Seaweed is rich in marine iodine and could have been an important medicine in the highlands, used to combat endemic goiter and other conditions. By the same token, carbohydrate foods like oca, ullucu, and white potatoes that could not be grown on the coast have been found in preceramic sites in the Ancón-Chillón area of the Pacific lowlands. Thus, the formation of states in both lowlands and highlands may have been fostered by continuous, often highly localized interchange between coast and interior.

Michael Moseley believes that this reliance on maritime resources led to a preadaptation in the form of large, densely concentrated populations, whose leaders were able to organize the labor forces needed not only for building large ceremonial centers but also for transforming river valleys with sizable irrigation schemes. Under this scenario, irrigation farming was in the hands of a well-defined group of authority figures, who took advantage of existing simple technology and local populations to create new economies. This transformation, based as it was on trade, maize agriculture, and a maritime diet, acted as a "kick" for radical changes in Andean society (Moseley, 1986). But the transformation was based on ancient fishing traditions, which can be documented thousands of years earlier at early coastal villages.

Moseley's key point is that Andean civilization evolved in many ways, in a wide variety of ecological zones, from highland, tropical rain-forest, and lowland strategies that were all of great antiquity, some dating to the earliest millennia of human settlement. Thus, the maritime foundations hypothesis may help explain the development of states on the Peruvian coast, but it cannot account for parallel developments elsewhere in South America.

COASTAL FOUNDATIONS: THE INITIAL PERIOD

● ● ●

Sometime between 2500 and 1800 B.C., maize agriculture came to the Peruvian coast, and many villages moved inland. By this time the coastal fishing villages were much larger communities with highly organized social structures, as reflected in the first signs of communal structures, such as an 80-foot-high (24-m) temple mount at Salinas de Chao. The people may have cooperated in fishing and food gathering, but the cooperative effort in erecting large earthen platforms for temples or other public buildings satisfied entirely different needs and requires explanation.

**Initial Period
1900 to 900 B.C.**

This Initial Period of Andean civilization was an important millennium, for new concerns both with the cosmos and with religion permeated the Andes (Demarest and Conrad, 1993). The new beliefs manifested themselves in a wave of monumental construction in both lowlands and highlands. By 400 B.C., the inhabitants of the Casma Valley on the coast were building the huge stone-faced 130-foot-high (40-m) platform of Sechin Alto. This mound, nearly 1000 feet (300 m) long and over 800 feet (250 m) wide, formed the base of a huge U-shaped ceremonial center with sunken courts, plazas, and flanking mounds. A vast sprawl of houses and platforms lies around this largest of all early ceremonial structures on the coast. Only small parts of the site have been excavated, including a small building, erected in about 1300 B.C., surrounded by a mosaic of carved monoliths depicting a procession of armed men and dismembered human remains.

The shrines at Sechin Alto employ one of the persistent themes of ceremonial architecture in the Andes and on the coast, that of artificially raising or lowering sacred spaces relative to one another in what Michael Moseley (1985) calls "complementary opposition arranged linearly along a horizontal axis." On the coast, early ceremonial sites feature rectangular platform mounds fronting on a circular, sunken court that is usually housed in a rectangular forecourt (Donnan, 1985). This form of architecture appeared by at least 2000 B.C. It had people enter the forecourt of the sacred complex at ground level, descend into the sunken court, and then climb the temple platform.

After 2000 B.C., coastal ceremonial buildings were greatly elaborated, with new architectural devices being adopted, among them a distinctive U-shaped platform, often associated with elaborate adobe friezes. This arrangement is found in the great Río Rímac complex of Huaca Florida, built in about 1700 B.C.

Huaca Florida, 1700 B.C.

El Paraíso, close to the mouth of the Chillón River near Lima, is the oldest of these U-shaped ceremonial complexes and the closest one to the Pacific (Figure 22.2) (Engel, 1957; Quilter, 1985). This vast site consists of at least six huge square buildings constructed of roughly shaped stone blocks cemented with unfired clay. The people painted the polished clay-faced outer walls in brilliant hues. Each complex consisted of a square building surrounded by tiers of platforms reached by stone and clay staircases. The largest is more than 830 feet (250 m) long and 166 feet (50 m) wide, standing more than 30 feet (10 m) above the plain. The rooms apparently were covered with matting roofs supported by willow posts. Perhaps as many as 100,000 tons of rock excavated from the nearby hills were needed to build the El Paraíso buildings. There are few signs of occupation around them, though, as if they

FIGURE 22.2   El Paraíso.

were shrines and public precincts rather than residential quarters. The two largest mounds of collapsed masonry lie parallel to one another, defining a vast, elongated patio covering more than 6 acres (2.5 ha). This U-shaped layout is thought to be the precursor of this intrusive architectural style on the coast after 2000 B.C.

What is most surprising is that these huge structures were erected by people from dozens of scattered villages. For reasons not yet understood, they united in a building project that channeled most of their surplus energies into a vast monumental center, a place where few people lived but where everyone apparently congregated for major public ceremonies. The people themselves lived a life of seeming simplicity. They owned only simple stone and wooden artifacts and wore cotton clothing decorated with basic geometric patterns and stylized animal-like motifs. They buried their dead in several layers of garments, nets, or looped sacks. Why should such a village society build such enormous structures, and who were the leaders who organized these massive public works?

El Paraíso is thought to have been built by people who subsisted off a fish-meal diet from the incredibly rich fisheries close offshore and who traded extensively with communities inland. Its U-shaped layout coincides with the florescence of similarly shaped ceremonial centers in the interior, at a time when coastal people began to consume much larger amounts of root crops, to make pottery, and to shift their settlements inland to river valleys. Some scholars believe that this move coincided with the introduction of large-scale canal irrigation (for discussion, see Moseley, 1985). Perhaps the spread of U-shaped ceremonial centers reflects a radical restructuring of society that coincided with major economic change. Moseley argues that the introduction of irrigation technology required a major reorganization of labor, which coincided with the appearance of new artistic traditions and architectural devices.

What does this mean in ritual terms? In many parts of the Americas the ritual manipulation of smoke and water served as a way of bridging stratified layers of air, earth, and bodies of water in the cosmos (Lathrap, 1985). Thus, it is argued, the early ceremonial centers of the coast and highlands reflect an ancient tradition of using these substances to maintain communication with the cosmos. Burnt offerings are found at some Andean sites, among them Kotosh. Water flowed through masonry channels and cut stone ways at many highland sites and also at the famous ritual center at Chavín de Huántar. There, galleries and ritual waterways flowed through the ceremonial platform and beneath a circular, sunken court, connections that allowed the water to resonate under the ground so that the temple "roared." The vast, open courts of coastal U-shaped ceremonial complexes may have housed sacred orchards and gardens irrigated with specially manipulated water supplies. These ritual waterways were to reach their greatest elaboration with the Chimu state of the coast and the great imperial Inca capital at Cuzco thousands of years later (Donnan, 1985).

In social and political terms, the Initial Period remains somewhat of a mystery. There are few signs in burial rituals of any social ranking or of personal wealth. It seems that decision making and leadership probably were not inherited and may have been rotated from one person to the next on a regular basis. The many ceremonial centers suggest that different kin groups commemorated their identities by erecting their own shrines, perhaps on a competitive basis. There were probably some larger polities extending over several river valleys, one centered on the Casma Valley, three others along nearby parts of the coast ; but who held sway over each of these political units is unknown (Pozorski and Pozorski, 1987).

THE EARLY HORIZON, CHAVÍN, AND THE INITIAL PERIOD

• • •

In 1943, archaeologist Julio Tello identified a distinctive art style in stone, ceramics, and precious metals over a wide area of highland Peru, a style he named Chavín after a famous prehistoric ceremonial center at Chavín de Huántar in central Peru. Tello's research led to a long-held belief among Peruvianists that the widespread Chavín art style was a "mother culture" for all later Andean civilizations, somewhat equivalent to the Olmec phenomenon in Mesoamerican prehistory (Pozorski and Pozorski, 1987). This became a distinctive "Early Horizon" in Peruvian prehistory, dating to about 900 B.C., a period when there was a great expansion of indigenous religious belief by conquest, trade, and colonization—the time when civilization began.

There is no doubt that Chavín de Huántar is testimony to an elaborate, well-developed iconography. The temple area is terraced with an impressive truncated pyramid on the uppermost level. The 32-foot-high (10-m) pyramid appears solid but is in fact hollow, a honeycomb of stone passages and rooms. The galleries are ventilated by special rectangular tubes. The temple housed a remarkable carving of a jaguarlike human with hair in the form of serpents (Figure 22.3) (Burger, 1992). Chavín art, like this carving, is dominated by animal and human forms: Jaguar motifs predominate; humans, gods, and animals have jaguarlike fangs or limbs; snakes flow from the bodies of many figures. The art has a grace that is grotesque and slightly sinister. Many figures were carved in stone, others in clay or bone (Benson, 1971).

With its tangled animal and human motifs, Chavín art has all the flamboyance and exotic touches of the tropical forest. The animals depicted—cayman, jaguar, and snake—are all forest animals. The art may have originated in the tropical forests to the east of the Andes, but the Early Horizon Chavín temple has a U shape with a sunken central plaza, an architectural design documented centuries earlier at other coastal and highland sites (Burger, 1985; Pozorski and Pozorski, 1987).

Chavín de Huántar is far more than just a temple. Richard Burger (1992) has excavated areas outside the well-known ceremonial precincts and established that the site was occupied between about 850 and 200 B.C. At first the population was small, perhaps few more than 100 people. It seems to have expanded considerably by the fourth century B.C., at which point as many as 2000 to 3000 people may have been living near the temple precincts. Chavín de Huántar was certainly a large center, probably an influential place within its local area, and one of the largest settlements in Peru at the time of its occupation. It failed to expand into a fully developed urban center, however, and the nascent civilization that worshiped there collapsed, leaving nothing more than a small town and a persistent art style and iconography.

The Chavín style may have influenced artistic traditions over a wide area of Peru, and it may also be that the religious beliefs behind the motifs were more important than the art itself. Settlements like Chavín de Huántar were important ceremonial centers that unified surrounding farming villages with a common religious belief, but Chavín de Huántar was not unique. There were many other, often much earlier centers with the same general architectural and iconographic style.

For example, from about 2000 to 200 B.C., the small ceremonial center at Huaricoto in the highlands, only 34 miles (55 km) from Chavín de Huántar, was the

Chavín de Huántar
900 B.C.

Huaricoto
2000 to 200 B.C.

FIGURE 22.3 (*Below*) A Chavín wall insert, approximately 7.8 inches (20 cm) high, showing feline features, from Chavín de Huántar and (*right*) a Chavín carving on a pillar in the temple interior at Chavín de Huántar. Stone insets such as these are common on the walls of the Chavín ceremonial buildings.

home of a religious ideology (Burger and Salazar-Burger, 1985). This "Kotosh Religious Tradition" is known to us by sacrificial hearths in which ceremonial offerings were burnt. These included animal bones and grain. The ritual hearth was sunk into the floor with a ventilator leading to the outside. Once the sacrifice was complete, the hearth was filled in. At first the rituals were performed in the open, but by the late Initial Period the hearths were surrounded by larger superstructures. The rituals may have been performed sporadically at certain times of the year, with the audience watching in the open. The Kotosh religious tradition appears to have flourished over an area of at least 155 miles (250 km) north to south in the highlands in the region where the Chavín cult, with its wild and extravagant animal motifs, was to gain strength.

The so-called Early Horizon associated with Chavín has often been assumed to have been a period of unification and coalescence of early Peruvian culture under the rubric of a single theology. The Initial Period saw a set of interacting polities emerge along the north and central parts of the coast after 1800 B.C. Political units centered on the Moche, Casma, Chillón, and other river valleys where irrigation agriculture developed. Centuries before, when pottery was unknown on the coast but cotton was already widely cultivated, communication networks had arisen that linked not only neighboring coastal river valleys but lowlands and highlands as well. These trade routes, which straddled all manner of environmental zones, helped spread technology, ideology, pottery making, and architectural styles over large areas, giving a superficial sense of unity that was reflected in the widespread use of common art motifs.

Initial Period sites are known from many coastal river valleys (see Haas et al., 1987, for details). For example, Huaca Florida is an imposing mound of boulders and adobe lying approximately 8 miles (12.8 km) inland of El Paraíso (Patterson, 1985). Built somewhat later, in about 1700 B.C., and on an even larger scale, the great platform is more than 840 feet (252 m) long, 180 feet (54 m) wide, and towers 100 feet (30 m) above the valley. A rectangular court lies close to the north side of the platform, but here the landscape is revealing, for Huaca Florida lies in the midst of an artificial environment created by irrigation. The focus of human settlement had moved inland, and the subsistence base changed from fishing to large-scale irrigation agriculture.

This was by no means the earliest irrigation in Peru, for even the first farmers probably made some limited use of canals to water their riverside gardens. However, the new works were on a far larger scale, spurred by the availability of an army of workers fed by abundant Pacific fish; by the presence of gentle, cultivable slopes inland; and by the expertise of the local people in farming cotton, gourds, and many lesser crops such as squashes and beans. Huaca Florida's leaders organized the reclamation of the desert by building canals along the steeper areas of the coastal valleys, in places where the gradients made the diversion of river water an easy task. This earliest of irrigation works may seem straightforward, but considerable organization was required to coordinate and develop it, and many people were needed to supervise the digging, to mediate land ownership disputes, and to maintain canals.

At first, each family may have worked together to irrigate its own sloping gardens, but gradually each community grew so much that essential irrigation works could be handled only by cooperative effort. Organized irrigation perhaps began as many minor cooperative works between individual families and neighboring villages. These simple projects eventually evolved into elaborate public works that embraced entire inland valleys, controlled by a corporate authority who held a monopoly over both the water and the land it irrigated. The process of organization, which may have taken centuries, was the result of many complex interacting factors, among them population growth and the emergence of increasing numbers of non-farming society members such as priests and artisans, whose food needs had to be met by other people. By the time El Paraíso and Huaca Florida were built, it is possible that public works such as irrigation canals and temples were constructed through a form of taxation by labor. Perhaps the rulers devised a forerunner of the *mita* tax employed 2000 years later by the Inca, by which people worked a certain number of days per year for the state, as either construction laborer or farmers. When one worked for the state, pay was given in food and shelter, sometimes in the form of a share of the yield from the land allocated to the state (Donnan, 1985).

As for Chavín itself, it is a late manifestation of a primeval Andean architectural style, a coalescence of traits and ideas from both the coast and the forest that formed a flamboyant cultural manifestation over a local area of the highlands. The Early Horizon itself, rather than being a catalytic time of unification, may well have been a long period of disruption of age-old communication networks and well-established small polities on the coast. For instance, the Casma polity was invaded by foreigners from the highlands, who forged the coastal valley and neighboring highlands into a single political unit for the first time in prehistory. This development was the precursor of far larger states. Perhaps it is better to refer to the Early Horizon as the Early Period, a prolonged time of cultural change and political adjustment.

Textiles and Coastal Prehistory

Initial and Early Period sites are remarkable for their fine textiles. Few prehistoric societies rivaled the textile artistry of the coastal Peruvians. They lived in an environment in which both animal and plant (especially cotton) fibers were plentiful, and they were able to create fine and complex fabrics adorned with colorful, intricate patterns (Figure 22.4). The textiles have survived remarkably well in the dry coastal environment, in huge cemeteries where the dead were wrapped in fabric burial shrouds. The most spectacular textile finds come from huge cemeteries of mummified Indians on the sandy, desolate Paracas Peninsula south of the modern town of Pisco. The (Early Horizon) Paracas bodies lie in bottle-shaped chambers or stone-lined subterranean vaults with wooden roofs approximately 16 ft (4.87 m) high and 13 ft (3.90 m) across cut through sand into soft rock. The sepulchers were divided into small chambers, where dozens of mummy bundles were placed. The Indians did not practice mummification in the formal ancient Egyptian sense. They simply took advantage of the exceptionally dry climate. Each corpse was disemboweled and then allowed to dry out in the hot sand in a fetal position with the knees at the chin. Eventually, the bodies were wrapped in brightly colored cotton, wool, or both. Sometimes the dead wore decorated mantles, shirts, turbans, or loincloths tailored

FIGURE 22.4   A border motif from a Paracas mantle showing an anthropomorphic figure wearing a tunic and skirt similar to those found on Paracas mummy bundles.

FIGURE 22.5 Archaeologist excavating an effigy pot of a kneeling warrior at a burial site at the Pyramid of the Sun and Moon, Chan Chan, Peru.

to the size of the mummy bundle rather than the living person. Occasionally, the mourners attached small ornaments to the mummies or buried tools, food, or even pet monkeys or parrots with the deceased (Figure 22.5).

It is from these mummies that we learn the most minute details of Peruvian textiles, for the wrapping cloths are often almost perfectly preserved. The earliest textiles preserved on the coast date to approximately 4500 B.C., soon after cotton was first cultivated. The weavers were expert dyers and used more than 190 hues from plant dyes. The earliest dye in common use was blue, followed by red and then a multitude of bright colors. Decorative motifs included simple checkerboards; filled squares; and stylized depictions of birds, felines, and other animals. The oldest textiles had rather coarse and uneven yarns produced by twisting untreated yarn. After 2000 B.C., however, the weavers began to use delicate wood and thorn spindles mounted in a special pottery, gourd, or wooden cup that minimized vibration. Thus they could produce much finer cloth. Most of the textiles found in coastal tombs were made on backstrap looms just like those still in use in Peru today (Figure 22.6). Two sticks carry the lengthwise threads, the upper one suspended from a post and the lower tied to a belt around the weaver's back. As the work proceeds, the fabric is unrolled from the upper bar and the finished cloth is rolled onto the lower stick. The yarn is wound with a figure-eight motion between the two stakes and is laced fast to the loom sticks so that the edges of the fabric are uniformly finished off. The disadvantage of this type of loom is that the width of the cloth is limited by the span of the weaver's arms. The Indians sometimes combined several backstrap looms to create wider cloths.

FIGURE 22.6   Backstrap loom in use.

From the Initial Period onward, the Andean region witnessed an extraordinary array of state-organized societies that displayed a remarkable diversity of culture, art, organization, and religious belief. At the same time, there were broad similarities in cosmology and culture that distinguish these societies from states elsewhere in the prehistoric world. As Michael Moseley and many others have pointed out, we are only now beginning to understand just how diverse and complicated the evolution of state-organized societies was in this region (see Haas et al., 1987).

THE EARLY INTERMEDIATE PERIOD

• • •

By 200 B.C., irrigation agriculture had developed on a very large scale on the coast, so much so that some settlements, such as Cerro Arena in the Moche Valley, covered more than a square mile. Excavations during the 1970s revealed more than 2000 separate structures, some with as many as 20 rooms. A small group of 25 finely finished houses may have formed the administrative and residential quarters of Cerro Arena. There were considerable variations between these quarters and the humbler dwellings that surrounded them, as if Cerro Arena society was more complex than that of earlier settlements. This and other large settlements were supported by irrigation systems that required organized labor to construct and maintain them as well as strict water controls. Most of the cultivated land lay along the terraced edges of the valleys, where the soils were better drained and easily planted with simple wooden digging sticks, just as they are to this day. Even today the local people divert the seasonal river water into side canals by building dams of stakes and boulders into the streams. There is no reason to suppose that the same simple but effective technique was not used in antiquity. The ancient irrigation canals wound along the sides of the valleys, a series of narrow channels approximately 4 ft (1.2 m) wide, set in loops and S-shaped curves, watering plots approximately 70 ft (21.3 m) square. The surplus flowed off into the Pacific.

Moche

By 200 B.C., the Moche state had begun in northern coastal Peru, flourishing for 800 years. Its origins lay in the Chicama and Moche valleys, with great ceremonial centers and huge irrigation works (Donnan and McClelland, 1979). Information about the Moche peoples of 2000 years ago comes not only from irrigation systems and spectacular monuments but also from hundreds of finely modeled clay pots and human burials preserved in the dry desert sand of their cemeteries. Unfortunately, these burials are a prime target of commercial grave robbers. Many Moche cemeteries look like battlefields after heavy bombardment, for their pots fetch astronomical prices on the international art market.

Moche
200 B.C. to A.D. 600

The spectacular discovery of undisturbed Moche tombs near the village of Sipán about 420 miles (680 km) northwest of Lima has revolutionized our knowledge of Moche's elite (Alva and Donnan, 1993). Peruvian archaeologist Walter Alva has excavated three unlooted royal burials. The first contained a plank coffin that held the extended skeleton of a man in his thirties lying on his back with his arms along his sides. He wore gold nose and ear ornaments, gold and turquoise bead bracelets, and copper sandals. A ceremonial rattle, crescent-shaped knives, scepters, spears, and exotic seashells surrounded the body. Three young women, each about 18 years old, lay at the head and foot of the coffin, and two males in their mid-thirties on either side. A dog, two sacrificial llamas, and hundreds of clay vessels lay in the grave. Comparing the objects found in the tomb with people depicted in Moche art, Christopher Donnan (1989) has identified the man as a warrior-priest. Such individuals are depicted on Moche pots presiding over sacrifices of prisoners of war. Apparently, Moche warriors went to war specifically to take captives. They would strip them of their armor and weapons, then lead them in front of the Warrior-Priest. Then the prisoner's throat was cut, the Warrior-Priest and others drinking the blood of the slain victim, while the corpse was dismembered. On pot after pot, the Warrior-Priest wears a crescent-shaped headdress atop a conical helmet, exactly the regalia found in the Sipán tombs. Such men were a priesthood of nobles living in different parts of the kingdom, who enacted the Sacrifice Ceremony at prescribed times. When they died, they were buried at the place where they had performed the ritual, wearing the formal regalia and objects they used in the ceremony. Their successors assumed their roles, wearing new sets of the same costumes and artifacts, perpetuating not only the official religion, but assuring work for the dozens of skilled artisans who manufactured precious artifacts for the nobility. Alva has unearthed two earlier burials, one of them an older man with a gold funerary mask, a magnificent necklace of golden spiders atop their webs, and a gilded copper crab effigy of a deity more than 2 feet (0.6 m) tall that was once mounted on a fabric banner (Donnan, 1990).

What little we know about Moche folk comes from undisturbed burials and from museum studies of looted pots. They show that Moche society consisted of farmers and fisherfolk as well as skilled artisans and priests, who are depicted on pots with felinelike fangs set in their mouths and wearing puma-skin headdresses.

A few expert craft potters created superb modeled vessels with striking portraits of arrogant, handsome men who can only have been the leaders of Moche society (Figure 22.7a). The potters modeled warriors, too, complete with shields and war clubs, well-padded helmets, and colorful cotton uniforms. Moche burials show that some members of society were much richer than others, lying in graves filled with as many as 50 vessels or with weapons or staffs of rank. We do not know exactly how Moche society was organized, but we can assume that the ruler wielded authority over a hierarchical state of warriors, priest-doctors, artisans, and the mass of the agricultural population. For instance, there was at least one Moche-style settlement in each subject valley.

Fortunately, the Moche artists and artisans gave us some more intimate glances at their society than do many civilizations (Figure 22.7b). Their paintings show the ruler with a fine feather headdress seated on a pyramid, while a line of naked prisoners parades before him. A decapitated sacrifice at the base of one painting reminds us that human sacrifice may have been the fate of some prisoners of war. We see Moche soldiers in battle, charging their opponents with raised clubs. The defenders raise their feather-decked shields in defiance as the battle is fought to the death. The potters modeled maize-beer-befuddled drunks being supported by their solicitous friends, women giving birth with the midwife in attendance, and wives carrying babies on their backs in shawls and in wooden cradles suspended by nets. The women carried out all domestic activities, and the men served as warriors, farmers, and fishermen. We see them on a seal hunt, clubbing young seals on the rocky coast as their prey scurries in every direction. A clay llama strains reluctantly under its load, and a mouse eats a maize cob.

FIGURE 22.7 Mo vessels. (a) Portrait vess approximately 11.4 inc (29 cm) high. (b) A dep tion of an owl-woman healer.

a

b

The pots also depict vividly what the Moche people wore. The men worked in short loincloths or cotton breeches and short sleeveless shirts underneath tunics that ended above the knee, fastened around the waist with colorful woven belts. More important people wore large mantles and headdresses made from puma heads or feathers from highland jungles. Nearly everyone donned some form of headgear: Brightly decorated cotton turbans wound around small caps and held in place with fabric chin straps were in common use. A small cloth protected the back of the neck from the burning sun. Moche women dressed in loose tunics that reached the knee and went bareheaded or draped a piece of cloth around their heads. Many men painted their lower legs and feet in bright colors and tattooed or daubed their faces with lines and other motifs. They often wore disk or crescent nose ornaments and cylindrical bar earrings, sometimes modeled in gold. Their necks bore large collars of stone beads or precious metal, and bracelets covered their arms and legs. Many people wore fiber sandals to protect their feet from the hot sand.

By this time the coastal people were expert metalworkers (Benson, 1979). They had discovered the properties of gold ore and extracted it by panning in streambeds rather than by mining. Soon they had developed ways of hammering it into fine sheets and had learned how to emboss it to make raised designs (Figure 22.8). They also had worked out the technique of annealing, making it possible to soften the metal and then hammer it into more elaborate forms, and they joined sheets with fine solder. The smiths used gold as a setting for turquoise and shell ornaments, crafted crowns, circlets, necklaces, pins, and tweezers. Gold was in such short supply in prehistoric times that the metalworkers became expert at depletion gilding, an annealing technique that oxidizes the metal in an alloy of copper and gold to give the finished product a goldlike appearance even when the gold content is as low as

FIGURE 22.8   Moche hammered gold breastplate.

12 percent by weight. Many of the large gold objects such as animals and plate decorations seized from the Inca by Pizarro's soldiers were in fact made of an elaborate alloy of some gold, silver, and copper.

The greatest efforts of the Moche people were devoted not to irrigation systems or elaborate burials but to the erection of vast monumental platforms and temples on the southern edge of the cultivated land in the Moche Valley, approximately 4 miles (6.4 km) southeast of the modern city of Trujillo. They used tax labor to build a huge adobe temple platform rising 76 feet (23 m) above the plain at the foot of a conical hill named Cerro Blanco. The Spaniards called this complex *Huaca de la Luna,* the Temple of the Moon. *Huaca del Sol* (Temple of the Sun) stands close to the west, a confused mass of mud brick that once consisted of a ramp that gave access to five temple platforms, the highest, to the south, towering 135 feet (41 m) above the ground. The sides of the pyramid were steeply terraced and have been badly damaged by erosion and looters. Both platforms once supported courts, corridors, and room complexes, perhaps roofed with matting. Huaca del Sol may have been a palace, for there are deep rubbish heaps on the summit of the platform. In contrast, Huaca de la Luna is spotlessly clean, its temple buildings painted with brightly colored murals.

The Moche was a multivalley state that may have consisted of a series of satellite centers that ruled over individual valleys but owed allegiance to the great centers of the Moche Valley. At one time the Moche Valley presided over the coast as far south as the Nepeña Valley. Where possible, the Moche extended their ambitious irrigation systems to link several neighboring river valleys and then constructed lesser copies of their capital as a basis for secure administration of their new domains. Their traders were in contact with the north and with the Nasca people on the south coast as well (Proulx, 1983a). In approximately A.D. 600, the Moche people moved their center of administrative activity north to the Pampa Grande in the Lambayeque Valley. By this time the southern centers were abandoned, as the political and economic influence of the southern highlands and coast began to rise. The agricultural system of the southern valleys may have collapsed, perhaps as a result of major droughts, so the people moved north to an area where there was more water. They may also have been under pressure from people inland.

THE MIDDLE HORIZON: THE FIRST EMPIRES

• • •

A series of brilliant states had flourished on the coast and in the highlands during the Early Intermediate Period—Moche on the north coast, Nasca in the south, and Recuay and Pucara in the highlands, to mention only a few. The same period also saw the beginnings of monumental building at a highland site that would influence much of the Peruvian world—Tiwanaku (Kolata, 1993).

Middle Horizon
A.D. 600 to 1000

Between A.D. 600 and 1000 (the so-called Middle Horizon), the wealthiest highland districts lay at the southern end of the central Andes, in the high flat country surrounding Lake Titicaca. This was fine llama country. The local people maintained enormous herds of these beasts of burden and were also expert irrigation farmers. The *altiplano* supported the densest population in the highlands, and almost inevitably, the Titicaca region became an economic and demographic pole to the prosperous northern coast. By A.D. 200 Tiwanaku, on the eastern side of the

Tiwanaku
?A.D. 200 to c. 1200

lake, was becoming a major population center as well as an important economic and religious focus for the region (Kolata, 1986, 1993). The arid lands on which the site lies were irrigated and supported a population of perhaps 20,000 around the monumental structures near the center of the site. By A.D. 600 Tiwanaku was acquiring much of its prosperity from trade around the lake's southern shores. Copper working was especially important and probably developed independently of the well-established copper technology on the northern coast.

Tiwanaku was not only an economic force; it was a very important religious one as well. The great enclosure of Kalasasaya is dominated by a large earth platform faced with stones. Nearby, a rectangular enclosure is bounded with a row of upright stones and there is a doorway carved with an anthropomorphic god, believed to be the staff god, sometimes called Viracocha (Figure 22.9). Smaller buildings, enclosures, and huge statues are also near the ceremonial structures. One recently excavated temple contained the skeleton of a young warrior, perhaps a captive, sacrificed in A.D. 600.

It is the Tiwanaku art style that is most striking, a style which is related to earlier iconography found at Pucara. Like Chavín, this tradition probably represents a powerful iconography. Tiwanaku's art motifs include pumas and condors as well as

FIGURE 22.9   Gateway of the Sun at Tiwanaku, Bolivia, made from one block of lava. The central figure is known as the Gateway God; notice its jaguar mouth and serpent-ray headdress. The running figures flanking the god often are called messengers.

anthropomorphic gods being attended to by lesser deities or messengers. They occur over much of southern Peru as well as in Bolivia, the southern Andes, and perhaps as far afield as northwest Argentina. So powerful was the iconography and, presumably, the political and economic forces behind Tiwanaku that there was a serious political vacuum in the south after A.D. 1200, when Tiwanaku inexplicably collapsed into obscurity.

Tiwanaku obtained much of its food from large, community-based raised field systems developed on the lowlying pampa and surrounded with irrigation canals. The water in the canals provided excellent protection for potatoes and other growing plants against harsh winter frosts, which decimated crops on higher ground. The same fields were highly fertile, the soils enriched with muck from the surrounding canals. In recent years, archaeologists have worked closely with development agencies to reintroduce the ancient agricultural expertise to local villages, with marked success (Erickson, 1992; Kolata, 1993).

The influence of Tiwanaku can be seen at Wari in the Mantaro Valley, an important lowland ceremonial center that stands on a hill (Isbell and Schreiber, 1978). It is associated with huge stone walls and many dwellings that cover several square miles. The Wari art styles show also some Pukara influence, especially in anthropomorphic, feline, eagle, and serpent beings depicted on ceramic vessels. Like their southern neighbors, the Wari people seem to have revered a Viracocha-like being. By A.D. 800, their domains extended from Moche country in the Lambayeque Valley on the northern coast to south of Nasca territory and into the highlands south of Cuzco. They were expert traders, who probably expanded their domain through conquest, commercial enterprise, and perhaps religious conversion. Storehouses and roads probably were maintained by the state. As with the Inca of later centuries, the state controlled food supplies and labor (Schreiber, 1987).

Wari
?A.D. 600 to 900

Wari itself was abandoned in the ninth century A.D., but its art styles persisted on the coast for at least two more centuries. Both Wari and Tiwanaku were a turning point in Peruvian prehistory, a stage when small regional states became integrated into much larger political units. This unification may have been achieved by conquest and other coercive means, but the iconography shared by many coastal and highland Peruvians at the time must have been a powerful catalyst for closer political unity. There was constant and often intensive interaction between two poles of Andean civilization in the highlands and lowlands, each with quite different food resources and products. This interaction, long a feature of Andean life, was to intensify in the centuries that lay ahead.

These two great polities collapsed toward the end of the first millennium, leaving a vast political vacuum of small, competing states that was filled by the Inca after a period of conflict and warfare.

THE LATE INTERMEDIATE PERIOD: LATE COASTAL STATES

• • •

Chimu

Chimu
?A.D. 1000 to 1476

The highland states traded regularly with several emerging polities on the coast, each of them founded on extensive irrigation systems. Of these, the most famous is the Chimu kingdom, centered on the Moche Valley of the northern coast, the same area inhabited 400 years earlier by the Moche people. The Moche Valley had long been densely cultivated, but the Chimu people now embarked on much more ambitious irrigation schemes; they built large storage reservoirs and terraced hundreds of miles of hillside to control the flow of water down steep slopes. One channel extended nearly 20 miles (32 km) from the Chicama Valley to the capital, Chan Chan, designed to supplement the relatively limited water supplies that came from the nearby Moche Valley (Figure 22.10). Even in periods of extreme drought these canals carried water from the deep-cut riverbed to terraces long distances away. Thus, the Chimu created thousands of acres of new fields and used water from great distances to harvest two or three crops a year from plots where only one crop had been possible before, and that at the time of the annual flood. So effective were these irrigation techniques that the Chimu controlled more than 12 river valleys with at least 125,000 cultivable acres, all of it farmed with hoes or digging sticks. Today, the local Indians water their maize crops approximately every ten days, and this probably was the practice in Chimu times as well.

According to seventeenth-century Spanish chroniclers, the Chimu always maintained that their domains were originally ruled over by petty chiefs, but when the Inca conquered them between 1462 and 1470 they were led by a ruler named Michancamán, who governed through a network of hereditary local nobility. His courtiers held specific ranks, such as "Blower of the Shell Trumpet"; "Master of the Litter and Thrones"; and "Preparer of the Way," the official who scattered powdered shell dust wherever the ruler was about to walk. An archaeologist working at Chan Chan in 1969–1970 found a layer of powdered shell dust on a bench in a forecourt, perhaps evidence that the Preparer of the Way had been at work. The various provinces of the kingdom were ruled by loyal local leaders. They enjoyed not only tribute privileges but also rights to crops and land and to agricultural labor by commoners. Perhaps the most privileged members of society were the *Oquetlupec,* herb curers paid by the state to look after the sick. This was a hierarchical, highly organized society with strict social classes of nobles and commoners. Perhaps to enforce the social hierarchy, the legal system was very strict (Rowe, 1946).

The focus of the Chimu state was Chan Chan, a huge complex of walled compounds lying near the Pacific at the mouth of the Moche Valley. Chan Chan covers

FIGURE 22.10   Chan Chan. Oblique air photograph of a walled enclosure or compound.

nearly 4 square miles (10.3 sq. km), the central part consisting of nine large enclosures laid out in a sort of broken rectangle. Each enclosure probably functioned as the palace for the current ruler of Chan Chan, who probably built himself a new headquarters near those of his predecessors (Moseley, 1975a; Moseley and Day, 1982). The adobe walls of these compounds once stood as high as 33 feet (9.9 m) and covered areas as large as 670 by 2000 feet (201 by 600 m). The walls were not constructed to defend the rulers but to provide privacy and some shelter from the ocean winds. Each enclosure had its own water supply, a burial platform, and lavishly decorated residential rooms roofed with cane frames covered with earth and grass. The same enclosure that served as a palace during life became the ruler's burial place in death. The common people lived in tracts of small adobe and reed-mat houses on the western side of the city. Similar dwellings can be seen on the coast to this day.

Oral traditions tell us that the Chimu rulers practiced the institution of split inheritance, whereby each ruler inherited no material possessions to finance his reign. Split inheritance was to play a major role in Inca civilization, described below. Chimu rulers had access to and control of a huge labor pool. They employed laborers to expand and maintain irrigation works, and they served as military levies to acquire new lands and expand the tax base (Pozorski, 1987). Rulers soon learned the value of efficient communications, of officially maintained roadways that enabled them to move their armies from one place to the next with rapid dispatch. They constructed roads that connected each valley in their domain with the capital. The rural routes were little more than tracks between low adobe walls or widely spaced posts, mostly following centuries-old paths through the fields. In the densely populated valleys, Chimu roads were between 15 and 25 feet (4.5 and 7.5 m) across. In some places the roadway widened dramatically to 80 feet (24 m) or more. These were the roads that carried gold ornaments and fine hammered vessels to Chan Chan and textiles and fine, black-painted vessels throughout the empire. The traveler occasionally would encounter heavily laden llamas carrying goods to market, but most loads were carried on people's backs, for the Chimu never developed the wheeled cart. All revenues and tribute passed along the official roadways, as did newly conquered peoples being resettled in some area far from their original homeland. This draconian resettlement tactic was so successful that the Inca adopted it. The ruler then would install his own appointee in the new lands, in a compound palace that was a smaller version of Chan Chan itself.

The Chimu Empire extended far south, at least to Casma and perhaps reaching to the vicinity of modern Lima, for the main focus of civilization lay on the northern Peruvian littoral, where the soils were fertile and large-scale irrigation was a practical reality. Chimu armies fought with powerful neighbors to the south, among them the chief of Pachácamac, who controlled some narrow valleys south of Lima. Pachácamac had long been a venerated shrine and already boasted a terraced temple covering two-thirds of an acre (0.3 ha). Pachácamac has been a grave robbers' paradise for centuries. Later, the Inca built a vast Temple of the Sun at Pachácamac, an irregular trapezoid in a commanding position on a rocky hill.

For all its wide-ranging military activities and material wealth, the Chimu Empire was very vulnerable to attack from outside. The massive irrigation works of the northern river valleys were easily disrupted by an aggressive conqueror, for no leader, however powerful, could hope to fortify the entire frontier of the empire. We know little of the defenses, except for Paramonga in the Fortaleza Valley, a massive terraced structure built of rectangular adobes that overlooks the probable southern limits of Chimu territory. The Chimu were vulnerable to prolonged drought, too, for the storage capacity of their great irrigation works was only sufficient to carry them over one or two lean seasons. Perhaps, too, the irrigated desert soils became too saline for agriculture, so that crop yields fell drastically at a time when population densities were rising sharply. Since the Chimu depended on a highly specialized agricultural system, once that system was disrupted—whether by natural or artificial causes—military conquest and control of the irrigation network was easy, especially for aggressive and skillful conquerors such as the Inca, who conquered the Chimu in the 1460s.

THE LATE HORIZON: THE INCA STATE

• • •

The Late Horizon of Peruvian archaeology was also the shortest, dating from A.D. 1476 to 1534. It is the period of the Inca Empire, when those mighty Andean rulers held sway over an enormous area of highland and lowland country (Rowe, 1946).

Late Horizon
A.D. 1476 to 1534

The Inca were born into an intensely competitive world, their homeland lying to the northwest of the Titicaca basin in the area around Cuzco (Conrad and Demarest, 1984). They were a small-scale farming society living in small villages, organized in kin groups known as *ayllu,* groups claiming a common ancestry and also owning land in common (Hastorf, 1992). The Inca were a self-sufficient people, and their ayllu leaders contributed labor to one another as a means of organizing and distributing labor on a reciprocal basis. The ayllu was legitimized in its land ownership and protected by the ancestors. It was small wonder that the Inca always took good care of their ancestral mummies. The bodies of the dead, their tombs, and their fetishes, as well as numerous other sacred places and phenomena, were known as *huaca.*

The later Inca rulers clothed their origins in a glorious panoply of heroic deeds. It is likely, however, that the Inca were a fractious, constantly quarreling petty chiefdom. The chronicles of early conquest reflect the constant bickering of village headmen, and the earliest Inca rulers were probably petty war leaders *(sinchi),* elected officials whose success was measured by their victories and booty. To stay in office, they had to be politically and militarily adept so that they could both defeat and appease their many potential rivals. The official Inca histories spoke of at least eight Inca rulers between 1200 and 1438, but these genealogies are hardly reliable (Rowe, 1946). They probably depict little more than legendary figures. During the fourteenth century, a number of small tribal groups in the southern highlands began to develop a more powerful military confederacy, but the Inca flourished in this competitive atmosphere because their leaders were expert politicians as well as warriors. A leader named Viracocha Inca rose to power at the beginning of the fifteenth century. Unlike his raiding predecessors, however, he turned to permanent conquest and soon presided over a small kingdom centered in Cuzco. Viracocha Inca became the living god, the first in a series of constant religious changes that kept the new kingdom under tight control. At about the same time a new religious cult emerged, that of Inti, a celestial divine ancestor who was part of the sky god. (We say *part* because Inti was more of a cluster of solar aspects than the sun god.)

Inca
A.D. 1200 to 1534

Around 1438, a brilliant warrior named Cusi Inca Yupanqui was crowned Inca after a memorable victory over the neighboring Chanca tribe. He immediately took the name Pachakuti ("He Who Remakes the World") and set about transforming the Inca state. In particular, he and his henchmen developed a form of royal ancestor cult. This in itself was not especially significant since Pachakuti simply reworked an age-old Andean tradition, but the law of split inheritance that went along with it had a lasting and profound significance. A dead ruler was mummified. His palace, servants, and possessions were still considered his property and were maintained by all his male descendants *except* his successor, normally one of his sons. The deceased was not considered dead, however. His mummy attended great ceremonies and would even visit the houses of the living. Those entrusted to look after the king ate and talked with him, just as if his life were still going on. This element of continuity was extremely important because it made the royal mummies some of the holiest artifacts in the empire. Dead rulers were living sons of Inti, visible links with the gods, the very embodiment of the Inca state and of the fertility of nature. Meanwhile the ascending ruler was rich in prestige but poor in possessions. The new king had to acquire wealth so he could both live in royal splendor and provide for his mummy in the future—and the only wealth in the highland kingdom was taxable labor.

Therefore, every adult in Inca country had to render a certain amount of labor to the state each year after providing for the basic subsistence needs of his own ayllu. This *mita* system repaired bridges and roads, cultivated state-owned lands, manned the armies, and carried out public works. It was a reciprocal system. The state, or those benefiting from the work, had to feed and entertain those doing it. The split inheritance of the Inca rulers meant that their predecessors' estates remained the property of the dead ruler and not of the newcomer. He had to develop his own estate and could do so in only two ways: by levying more labor from existing taxpayers or by conquering new lands. Since the Inca rulers needed land to provide food for those who worked for them and the earlier kings owned most of the land near Cuzco, the only way a new ruler could obtain his own royal estates was by expansion into new territory. This expansion could not take the form of temporary raids. The conquest had to be permanent, the conquered territory had to be controlled and taxed, and the ruler's subjects had to be convinced of the value of a policy of long-term conquest.

The Inca rulers turned into brilliant propagandists, reminding everyone that they were gods and that the welfare of all depended on the prosperity of all rulers, past and present, and on constant military conquest. There were initial economic advantages, too, in the form of better protection against famine. Also, the rulers were careful to reward prowess in battle. Nobles were promoted to new posts and awarded insignia that brought their lifestyle ever closer to that of the king, and even a brave regular warrior could become a member of the secondary nobility. A highly complicated set of benefits, economic incentives, rewards, and justifications fueled and nourished the Inca conquests. Their successful ideology provided them with a crucial advantage over their neighbors, and within a decade of Pachakuti's accession they were masters of the southern highlands. Their army had become an invincible juggernaut, and in less than a century the tiny kingdom taken over by Pachakuti had become a vast empire. Topa Inca (1471–1493) extended the Inca Empire into Ecuador, northern Argentina, parts of Bolivia, and Chile. His armies also conquered the Chimu state, whose water supplies Topa already controlled. The best Chimu craftsworkers were carried off to work for the court of the Incas. Another king, Wayna Capac, ruled for 32 years after Topa Inca and pushed the empire deeper into Ecuador (for a different view of Inca development, see Bauer, 1992).

The Inca rulers developed an efficient administrative system to run their empire, one based firmly on the precedents of earlier societies. *Tawantinsuyu*, "The Land of the Four Quarters," was divided into four large provinces known as *suyu* (quarters),

each subdivided into smaller provinces, some of them coinciding with older, conquered kingdoms (Hyslop, 1990; Patterson, 1992). The conquered peoples in the
Inca Empire were usually ruled by a leading member of a local family, known as a
curaca. These hereditary chiefs were a form of secondary non-Inca nobility who
governed a taxpaying population of 100 people or more, but all the really important
government posts were held by Inca nobles. The Inca rulers realized, however, that
the essence of efficient government in such varied topography was efficient communications, so the road builders commandeered a vast network of age-old Indian
highways from the states they conquered. They linked them in a coordinated system
with regular rest houses so that they could move armies, trade goods, and messengers from one end of the kingdom to the other in short order (Hyslop, 1984).

The Incas' passion for organization impinged on everyone's life. Their society
was organized into 12 age divisions for the purposes of census and tax assessment,
divisions based on both physical changes like puberty and major social events like
marriage. The most important stage was adulthood, which lasted as long as one
could do a day's work. All the census and other data of the empire were recorded
not on tablets but on knotted strings. The *quipu* were a complex and sophisticated
record-keeping system that seems to have been so efficient that it more than made
up for the lack of writing (Ascher and Ascher, 1981). They also were a powerful
instrument for codifying laws, and providing data for the inspectors, who regularly
visited each household to check that everyone was engaged in productive work and
living in sanitary conditions. For all its political controls, Inca society at the local
level was very diverse (D'Altroy, 1993).

At the time of the Spanish conquest, the Inca controlled the lives of as many as
6 million people, most of them living in small villages dispersed around religious
and political centers. It was here that Inca artisans labored, producing major works
of art in gold and silver. Brightly painted Inca pottery is found throughout the
empire; it is decorated with black, white, and red geometric designs. Despite the
widespread distribution of Inca pots and artifacts, however, regional pottery styles
flourished because the village potters, many of whom were conquered subjects, continued the cultural traditions of earlier centuries.

Inca political and religious power was centered on important centers like Cuzco
in the Andes, where the ceremonial center was built of carefully fitted stones (Figure
22.11) (Protzen, 1986). Such locations as Machu Picchu, high in the Andes (Figure
22.12, p. 539), are famous for their fine masonry structures (Gasparini and Margolies, 1980). The Inca ruler held court in Cuzco, surrounded by plotting factions
and ever-changing political tides. One villain was the very institution of split inheritance that fueled Inca military conquest. Every ruler faced increasingly complex governance problems as a result. The need for more and more conquests caused great
military, economic, and administrative stress. The logistics of long-distance military
campaigns were horrendous, and the soldiers had to be fed from state-owned land,
not royal estates. Moreover, although their tactics were well adapted to open country, where their armies were invincible, the rulers eventually had to start fighting in
forest country, where they fared badly. Meanwhile the empire had grown so large
that communication became a lengthier and lengthier process, compounded by the
great diversity of people living within the Inca domain. Also, the increasing number
of high-ranking nobles devoted to the interests of dead rulers led to chronic factionalism in Cuzco. Under its glittering façade, *Tawantinsuyu* was becoming a rotten
apple. In the end, the Inca Empire was overthrown not by Peruvians but by a tiny
band of foreigners with firearms who could exploit the inherent vulnerability of
such a hierarchical, conforming society.

Cuzco

Machu Picchu

FIGURE 22.11   Inca masonry from the fortress of Sacsahuaman, near Cuzco.

THE SPANISH CONQUEST: 1532–1534

• • •

This vulnerability came home to roost in 1532, when a small party of rapacious Spanish conquistadores landed in northern Peru. When Francisco Pizarro arrived, the Inca state was in some political chaos, its people already decimated by smallpox and other diseases introduced by the first conquistadores. Inca Wayna Capac had died in an epidemic in A.D. 1525. The empire was plunged into a civil war between his son Huascar and another son, Atahuallpa, half brother to Huascar. Atahuallpa eventually prevailed, but as he moved south from Ecuador to consolidate his territory, he learned that Pizarro had landed in Peru.

A.D. 1533
A.D. 1536

The Spaniards had vowed to make Peru part of Spain and were bent on plunder and conquest. Pizarro arrived in the guise of a diplomat, captured Atahuallpa by treachery, ransomed him for a huge quantity of gold, and then brutally murdered him. A year later the Spaniards captured the Inca capital with a tiny army. They took over the state bureaucracy and appointed Manco Inca as puppet ruler. Three years later, Manco Inca turned on his masters in a bloody revolt. Its suppression finally destroyed the greatest of the Peruvian empires.

The Spanish conquest of Mexico and Peru saw the first major confrontation between the forces of an expanding Europe that was emerging from centuries of feudalism and complex non-Western societies that were still living with the full legacy of prehistoric times. The four and a half centuries since the Spanish conquests of Mexico and Peru have seen European settlement in all corners of the globe, the emergence of the industrial state, and the acting out of the last, tragic chapter of

FIGURE 22.12   Machu Picchu. Forgotten for 400 years after the Spanish Conquest, it was rediscovered by the American explorer Hiram Bingham in 1911.

human prehistory: the clash between the Western and non-Western worlds (Wolf, 1984).

CHAPTER SUMMARY

The earliest complex societies of coastal Peru may have developed as a result of intensive exploitation of maritime resources, especially small fish easily netted from canoes. In time, abundant food surpluses, growing population densities, and larger settlements may have preadapted coastal people for adopting intensive irrigation agriculture. These societies were organized in increasingly complex ways. During the so-called Initial Period of Peruvian prehistory, large monumental structures appeared, many of them U-shaped, just before and during the transition toward greater dependence on maize agriculture. This was also a period of continuous inter-action and extensive trade between coast and highlands.

This florescence of social complexity, new art traditions, and monumental architecture coincided with the emergence of several small polities in river valleys on the coast. The culmination of this trend is seen in various local traditions, among them the famous Chavín style. This central Peruvian style, once thought to have been the source of Peruvian civilization, is now known to be a late manifestation of cultural trends that began as early as 2000 B.C. After the Early Period ended in about 200 B.C., a series of coastal kingdoms developed, the political and economic influ-ence of which spread beyond their immediate valley homelands. These states included Moche and Nasca, remarkable for their fine pottery styles and expert alloy and gold metallurgy. They flourished in the first millennium A.D. This Middle Horizon lasted from A.D. 600 to 1000 and saw the rise of numerous small states that traded with one another and depended heavily on irrigation agriculture.

In approximately A.D. 1000, Chimu, with its great capital at Chan Chan on the northern coast, dominated a wide area of the coast. Its compounds reflect a stratified state, with many expert craftspeople and a complex material culture. During the Late Horizon of Peruvian prehistory, there was unification of highlands and lowlands under the Inca Empire, which may have emerged as early as A.D. 1200 and lasted until the Spanish conquest in A.D. 1534. The Inca rulers were masters of bureaucracy and military organization and governed a highly structured state—one, however, that was so weakened by civil war and disease that it fell easily to the conquistador Francisco Pizarro and his small army of adventurers.

GUIDE TO FURTHER READING

Alva, Walter, and Donnan, Christopher. 1993. *Royal Tombs of Sipán*. Los Angeles, CA: Fowler Museum of Cultural History, UCLA.
  A magnificently illustrated and definitive account of one of the most important archaeological discoveries of the twentieth century.

Conrad, Geoffrey W., and Demarest, Arthur A. 1984. *Religion and Empire: The Dynamics of Aztec and Inca Expansionism*. Cambridge, Eng.: Cambridge University Press.
  A clear and succinct analysis of two imperial, preindustrial civilizations. A sophisticated, well-argued book. Strongly recommended.

Haas, Jonathan, Pozorski, S., and Pozorski, T., eds. 1987. *The Origins and Development of the Andean State*. Cambridge, Eng.: Cambridge University Press.
  A useful series of essays on the complex processes of state formation in the Andean region. Not for beginners.

Moseley, Michael E. 1975. *The Maritime Foundations of Andean Civilization*. Menlo Park, CA: Cummings.
  A short essay that argues that the foundations of Peruvian civilization lay on the coast in subsistence patterns that relied heavily on maritime resources. Controversial but convincing for the most part.

―――. 1992. *The Incas and Their Ancestors*. London and New York: Thames and Hudson.
  A definitive account of Andean prehistory and complex societies for the general reader. Lavishly illustrated.

Rowe, John H. 1946. *Inca Culture at the Time of the Spanish Conquest*. Vol. 2, *Handbook of South American Indians*. Washington, DC: Smithsonian Institution.
  The classic account of Inca culture reconstructed from historical documents and limited archaeological investigations.

BIBLIOGRAPHY OF WORLD PREHISTORY
· · ·

The literature of world prehistory proliferates more and more every year, to the point that it is now beyond the ability of any one scholar to keep abreast of it. This bibliography is not intended as a comprehensive reference guide to world prehistory. Rather it is a compilation of both the majority of sources used to write this book and a cross section of the most important monographs and papers relating to all parts of the world. Readers interested in probing more deeply into the literature should pursue the references given in the publications listed here or consult a specialist.

Adams, R. E. W., Brown, W. E., and Culbert, T. Patrick. 1981. "Radar Mapping, Archeology, and Ancient Maya Land Use." *Science* 213 (4515):1457–1462.

Adams, Robert M. 1966. *The Evolution of Urban Society*. Chicago: Aldine.

———. 1981. *Heartland of Cities*. Chicago: University of Chicago Press.

Adams, Robert M., and Nissen, Hans J. 1972. *The Uruk Landscape*. Chicago: University of Chicago Press.

Adovasio, J. M. 1993. "The Ones that Will Not Go Away: A Biased View of Pre-Clovis Occupations in the New World." In Olga Soffer and N. D. Praslov, eds., *From Kostenki to Clovis: Upper Paleolithic Paleo-Indian Adaptations*, pp. 199–218. New York: Plenum Press.

Adovasio, James M., et al. 1981. *Meadowcroft Rockshelter and the Archaeology of the Cross Creek Drainage*. Pittsburgh: University of Pittsburgh Press.

Adovasio, J. M., Donahue, J., and Stuckenrath, R. 1990. "The Meadowcroft Rockshelter Radiocarbon Chronology, 1975–1990." *American Antiquity* 55 (2): 348–354.

Aigner, Jean S. 1970. "The Unifacial, Core, and Blade Site on Anagula Island, Aleutians." *Arctic Anthropology* 7 (2):59–88.

Aikens, C. Melvin. 1970. *Hogup Cave*. Salt Lake City: University of Utah Press.

Aikens, C. Melvin, and Higuchi, Takayasu. 1981. *Prehistory of Japan*. New York: Academic Press.

Aitken, M. J. 1985. *Thermoluminescence Dating*. Orlando, FL: Academic Press.

———. 1990. *Science-Based Dating in Archaeology*. Reading, MA: Addison Wesley.

Akazawa, Takeru. 1982. "Cultural Change in Prehistoric Japan." *Advances in World Archaeology* 1:151–212.

Aldred, Cyril. 1968. *Akhenaten*. London: Thames and Hudson.

———. 1986. *The Egyptians*, 2d ed. New York: Thames and Hudson.

Algaze, Guillermo. 1989. "The Uruk Expansion." *Current Anthropology* 30 (5):571–608.

———. 1993. "Expansionary Dynamics of Some Early Pristine States," *American Anthropologist* 95 (2):304–337.

Allan, William. 1965. *The African Husbandman*. Edinburgh: Oliver and Boyd.

Allchin, Bridget, and Allchin, Raymond. 1983. *The Rise of Civilization in India and Pakistan*. Cambridge, Eng.: Cambridge University Press.

Allen, J. 1969. "The Hunting Neolithic: Adaptations to the Food Quest in Prehistoric Papua, New Guinea." In J. V. S. Megaw, ed., *Hunters, Gatherers, and First Farmers Beyond Europe*, pp. 167–188. Atlantic Highlands, NJ: Humanities.

———. 1989. "When Did Humans First Colonize Australia?" *Search* 20 (5):149–154.

Allen, J., Golson, J., and Jones, Rhys, eds. 1977. *Sunda and Sahel: Prehistoric Studies in Southeast Asia, Melanesia, and Australia.* New York: Academic Press.

Allen, J., Gosden, C., and White, J. P. 1989. "Pleistocene New Ireland." *Antiquity* 63 (240):548–561.

Allen, J., and White, J. P. 1989. "The Lapita Homeland: Some New Data and an Interpretation." *Journal of the Polynesian Society* 93:129–146.

Alva, Walter, and Donnan, Christopher. 1993. *Royal Tombs of Sipán.* Los Angeles, CA: Fowler Museum of Cultural History, UCLA.

Ambrose, Stanley H. 1984. "The Introduction of Pastoral Adaptations to the Highlands of East Africa." In J. Desmond Clark and Steven A. Brandt, eds., *From Hunters to Farmers,* pp. 212–239. Berkeley and Los Angeles: University of California Press.

Anderson, Douglas. 1990. *Lang Rongrien.* Philadelphia: University of Pennsylvania Museum.

Ammerman, A., and Cavalli-Sforza, L. 1984. *The Neolithic Transition and the Genetics of Populations in Europe.* Princeton: Princeton University Press.

Anderson, Arthur O., and Dibble, Charles, eds. 1978. *The Florentine Codex.* Salt Lake City: University of Utah Press.

Anderson, Atholl. 1987. "Recent Developments in Japanese Prehistory: A Review." *American Antiquity* 61 (232):270–281.

———. 1991. "The Chronology of Colonization in New Zealand." *Antiquity* 65:767–795.

Anderson, Atholl, and McGlone, M. 1991. "Living on the Edge: Prehistoric Land and People in New Zealand." In J. Dodson, ed., *The Native Lands: Prehistory and Environmental Change in Australia and the Southwest Pacific,* pp. 199–241. Sydney: Longman Cheshire.

Anderson, D. G., and Hanson, Glen T. 1988. "Early Archaic Settlement in the Southeastern United States: A Case Study from the Savannah River Valley." *American Antiquity* 53 (2):262–286.

Anderson, Douglas. 1970. "Akmak." *Acta Arctica* 15:1–25.

———. 1979. "Archaeology and the Evidence for the Prehistoric Development of Eskimo Culture." *Arctic Anthropologist* 16 (1):16–26.

Andrews, E. W., and Hammond, Norman. 1990. "Redefinition of the Swasey Phase at Cuello, Belize." *American Antiquity* 55 (3):570–584.

Arsuaga, Juan-Luis, and others. 1993. "Three new human skulls from the Sima de los Huevos Middle Pleistocene site in Sierra de Atapuerca, Spain." *Nature* 362:534–539.

Ascher, Marcia, and Ascher, Robert. 1981. *The Code of the Quipu.* Ann Arbor: University of Michigan Press.

Bahn, P., and Vertut, Jan. 1988. *Images of the Ice Age.* New York: Viking Press.

Baillie, M. G. L. 1982. *Tree Ring Dating and Archaeology.* New York: Columbia University Press.

Barfield, Lawrence. 1994. "The Iceman Reviewed," *Antiquity* 68 (258):10–26.

Barker, Graeme. 1985. *Prehistoric Farming in Europe.* Cambridge, Eng.: Cambridge University Press.

Barker, Phillip. 1983. *Techniques of Archaeological Excavation,* 2d ed. London: Batsford.

Barnard, Alan. 1992. *Hunters and Herders of Southern Africa.* Cambridge, Eng.: Cambridge University Press.

Barnard, Noel. 1961. *Bronze Casting and Bronze Alloys in Ancient China.* Canberra: Australian National University.

Barnes, Gina L. 1990. *Bibliographic Reviews of Far Eastern Archaeology 1990: Hoabhinian, Jomon, Yayoi.* Oxford, Eng: Oxbow Books.

———. 1993. *China, Korea, and Japan.* London and New York: Thames and Hudson.

Barry, John C., et al. 1985. "Neogene Mammalian Faunal Change in Southern Asia: Correlations with Climatic, Tectonic, and Eustatic Events." *Geology* 13:637–640.

Bar-Yosef, O. 1975. "Archaeological Occurrences in the Middle Pleistocene of Israel." In Karl Butzer and Glynn Ll. Isaac, eds., *After the Australopithecines,* pp. 571–604. Chicago: Aldine.

———. 1986. "The Walls of Jericho." *Current Anthropology* 27 (2):157–162.

———. 1987. "Late Pleistocene Adaptations in the Levant." In Olga Soffer, ed., *The Pleistocene Old World: Regional Perspectives,* pp. 219–236. New York: Plenum.

Bar-Yosef, O., and Belfer-Cohen, A. 1989. "The Origins of Sedentism and Farming Communities in the Levant." *Journal of World Prehistory* 3 (4):447–498.

Bauer, Brian S. 1992. *The Development of the Inca State.* Norman, OK: University of Oklahoma Press.

Bayard, Donn T. 1970. "Excavations at Non Nok Tha, Northeast Thailand, 1968: An Interim Report." *Asian Perspectives* 13:109–144.

———. 1972. "Early Thai Bronze: Analysis and New Dates." *Science* 176:1411–1421.

———. 1977. "Phu Wiang Pottery and the Prehistory of Northeastern Thailand." In G. Bartstra et al., eds., *Modern Quaternary Research in Southeast Asia,* pp. 57–102. Rotterdam: Balkema.

———. 1986. "Agriculture, Metallurgy, and State Formation in Southeast Asia." *Current Anthropology* 25 (1):103–105.

Beach, David. 1993. *The Shona.* Oxford: Blackwell.

Beadle, George. 1981. "The Ancestor of Corn." *Scientific American* 242 (1):96–103.

Bellwood, Peter. 1970. "Fortifications and Economy in Prehistoric New Zealand." *Proceedings of the Prehistoric Society* 37 (1):56–95.

———. 1979. *Man's Conquest of the Pacific.* Oxford, Eng.: Oxford University Press.

———. 1985. *The Prehistory of the Indo-Malaysian Archipelago.* North Ryde, NSW: Academic Press.

———. 1987a. *The Polynesians.* London: Thames and Hudson.

———. 1987b. "The Prehistory of Island Southeast Asia: A Multidisciplinary Review of Recent Research." *Advances in World Archaeology* 1 (2):171–224.

Bellwood, Peter, and Koon, J. 1989. "Lapita Colonists Leave Boats Unburned." *Antiquity* 63 (240):613–622.

Bender, Barbara. 1985. "Emergent Tribal Formations in the American Midcontinent." *American Antiquity* 50 (1):52–62.

Benfer, Robert. 1982. "The Lomas Site of Paloma (5000 to 7500 B.P.), Chilca Valley, Peru." In Ramerio Matos, ed., *Andean Archaeology,* pp. 27–54. New York: Academic Press.

Benson, Elizabeth, ed. 1971. *Dumbarton Oaks Conference on Chavín.* Washington, DC: Dumbarton Oaks.

———. 1979. *Pre-Columbian Metallurgy of South America.* Washington, DC: Dumbarton Oaks.

Berlo, Janet C. (ed.) 1992. *Art, ideology, and the city of Teotihuacán: a symposium at Dumbarton Oaks 8th and 9th October 1988.* Washington DC: Dumbarton Oaks Research Library.

Bernal, Ignacio. 1969. *The Olmec World.* Berkeley and Los Angeles: University of California Press.

Bernal, Martin. 1987. *The Afroasiatic Roots of Classical Civilization.* New Brunswick, NJ: Rutgers University Press.

Berrin, Kathleen, and Pasztory, R. (eds.). 1994. *Teotihuacán.* London: Thames and Hudson.

Bettinger, R. L. 1987. "Archaeological Approaches to Hunter-Gatherers." *Annual Review of Anthropology* 16:121–142.

Binford, Lewis R. 1964. "A Consideration of Archaeological Research Design." *American Antiquity* 29:425–441.

———. 1979. "Organization and Formation Processes: Looking at Curated Technologies." *Journal of Anthropological Research* 35 (3):225–273.

———. 1983. *In Pursuit of the Past.* New York: Thames and Hudson.

———. 1984. *Faunal Remains from Klasies River Mouth.* New York: Academic Press.

Binford, Lewis R., and Binford, Sally. 1966. "A Preliminary Analysis of Functional Variability in the Mousterian of Levallois Facies." *American Anthropologist* 68 (2):238–295.

Birdsell, J. 1977. "The Recalibration of a Paradigm for the First Peopling of Greater Australia." In J. Allen, J. Golson, and R. Jones, eds., *Sunda and Sahul,* pp. 113–167. Orlando, FL: Academic Press.

Blanc, Alberto C. 1961. "Some Evidence for the Ideologies of Early Man." In S. L. Washburn, ed., *The Social Life of Early Man,* pp. 119–136. New York: Viking Fund.

Blanton, Richard E. 1978. *Monte Albán: Settlement Patterns at the Ancient Zapotec Capital.* New York: Academic Press.

———. 1983. "Advances in the Study of Cultural Evolution in Prehispanic Highland Mesoamerica." *Advances in World Archaeology* 2:245–288.

Blegen, Carl. 1971. *Troy.* London: Thames and Hudson.

Blumenschine, Robert, and Cavallo, John. 1992. "Scavenging and Human Evolution," *Scientific American* 257 (10):90–96.

Boguchi, Peter. (ed.) 1993. *Case Studies in European Prehistory.* Boca Raton, FL: CRC Press.

Bogucki, Peter, and Grygiel, Ryszard. 1983. "Early Farmers of the North European Plain." *Scientific American* 248 (4):105–115.

Bonsell, Clive. ed. 1989. *The Mesolithic in Europe.* Edinburgh: Edinburgh University Press.

Bonzek, Jan, ed. 1985. *The Aegean, Anatolia, and Europe in the 2nd Millenium* B.C. New York: Academic Press.

———. 1988. *Forest Farmers and Stockherders.* Cambridge, Eng.: Cambridge University Press.

Bordes, François. 1968. *The Old Stone Age.* New York: McGraw-Hill.

Boserup, Ester. 1965. *The Conditions of Agricultural Growth: The Economics of Agrarian Change Under Population Pressure.* Chicago: Aldine.

Boule, Marcellin, and Vallois, H. 1957. *Fossil Men.* London: Thames and Hudson.

Bovill, E. W. 1968. *The Golden Trade of the Moors.* London: Heinemann.

Bowdler, J. M., Jones, R., and Thorne, A. G. 1970. "Pleistocene Human Remains from Australia: A Living Site and Human Cremation from Lake Mungo, Western New South Wales." *World Archaeology* 2:39–60.

Bower, John R. F. 1984. "Settlement Behavior of Pastoral Cultures in East Africa." In J. Desmond Clark and Steven A. Brandt, eds., *From Hunters to Farmers,* pp. 252–259. Berkeley and Los Angeles: University of California Press.

Braidwood, L. S., ed. 1982. *Prehistoric Village Archaeology in South-eastern Turkey.* Oxford, Eng.: British Archaeological Reports, International Series, no. 138.

Braidwood, R. J., and Braidwood, L. S., eds. 1983. *Prehistoric Archaeology Along the Zagros Flanks.* Chicago: Oriental Institute.

Braidwood, R. J., and Cambel, H. 1980. *Prehistoric Research in Southeastern Anatolia.* Istanbul: Edebiyat Facultesi Basimevi.

Brauer, Günter. 1992. "Africa's place in the evolution of *Homo sapiens.*" In Günter Brauer and F. H. Smith, eds., *Continuity or Replacement: Controversies in* Homo sapiens *Evolution,* pp. 83–98. Rotterdam: Balkema.

Breuil, Henri. 1908. *La Caverne d'Altamira.* Paris: Payot.

———. 1952. *Four Hundred Centuries of Cave Art.* Montignac, France: Centre d'Etudes et de Documentation.

Briggs, L. Cabot. 1951. "The Ancient Khmer Empire." *Transactions of the American Philosophical Society,* no. 41.

Brose, David C. 1979. "A Speculative Model of the Role of Exchange in the Prehistory of the Eastern Woodlands." In David C. Brose and N'omi Greber, eds., *Hopewellian Archaeology,* pp. 3–8. Kent, OH: Kent State University Press.

Brose, David C., and Greber, N'omi. 1979. *Hopewellian Archaeology.* Kent, OH: Kent State University Press.

Brothwell, Don R. 1985. *Digging Up Bones*. London: British Museum.

Browman, David L. 1978. "Toward the Development of the Tiahuanaco (Tiwanaku) State." In David L. Browman, ed., *Advances in Andean Archaeology*, pp. 327–349. The Hague: Mouton.

Brown J., and Phillips, J., eds. 1983. *Late Archaic Hunter-Gatherers in the Midwest*. New York: Academic Press.

Brumfiel, Elizabeth. 1983. "Aztec State Making: Ecology, Structure, and the Origin of the State." *American Anthropologist* 85 (2):261–284.

———. 1992. "Distinguished Lecture in Archaeology: Breaking and Entering the Ecosystem," *American Anthropologist* 94 (3):551–567.

Bunn, Henry, and Kroll, J. 1986. "Systematic Butchery by Plio/Pleistocene Hominids at Olduvai Gorge, Tanzania." *Current Anthropology* 27 (5):431–451.

Bunn, Henry, et al. 1980. "FxJj50: An Early Pleistocene Site in Northern Kenya." *World Archaeology* 12 (2):109–136.

Burger, Richard L. 1985. "Prehistoric Stylistic Change and Cultural Development at Huaricoto, Peru." *National Geographic Research* 1 (4):505–534.

———. 1992. *Chavín and the Origins of Andean Civilization*. London and New York: Thames and Hudson.

Burger, Richard L., and Salazar-Burger, Lucy. 1985. "The Early Ceremonial Center of Huaricoto." In Christopher Donnan, ed., *Early Ceremonial Architecture in the Andes*, pp. 111–138. Washington, DC: Dumbarton Oaks.

Butzer, Karl. 1971. *Environment and Archaeology*. Chicago: Aldine.

———. 1974. *Environment and Archaeology*, 3d ed. Chicago: Aldine.

———. 1976. *Early Hydraulic Civilization in Egypt*. Chicago: University of Chicago Press.

Butzer, Karl, and Isaac, Glynn Ll., eds. 1975. *After the Australopithecines*. Chicago: Aldine.

Byrd, B. F. 1989. "The Natufian: Settlement Variability and Economic Adaptation in the Levant at the End of the Pleistocene." *Journal of World Prehistory* 3 (2): 159–198.

Cahen, David, and Van Noten, Francis. 1981. *The Hunter-Gatherers of Meer*. Tervuren: Musée Royal de L'Afrique Centrale.

Canby, Thomas. 1979. "The Search for the First Americans." *National Geographic Magazine*, September, 1979, pp. 330–363.

Caneva, I., Frangipane, M., and Palmiere, A. 1987. "Predynastic Egypt: New Data from Maadi." *African Archaeological Review* 5:105–114.

Cann, R. L., et al. 1987. "Mitochondrial DNA and Human Evolution." *Nature* 325:31–36.

Carneiro, Robert L. 1970. "A Theory of the Origin of the State." *Science* 169:733–738.

Carter, Howard. 1923. *The Tomb of Tut-ankh-Amun*. London: Macmillan.

Caton-Thompson, G., and Gardner, E. W. 1934. *The Desert Fayum*, 2 vols. London: Royal Anthropological Institute.

Ceram, C. W. 1953. *Gods, Graves and Scholars*. New York: Knopf.

Chadwick, John. 1958. *The Decipherment of Linear B*. Cambridge, Eng.: Cambridge University Press.

Chagnon, Napoleon, and Irons, J., eds. 1979. *Evolutionary Biology and Social Behavior*. North Scituate, MA: Duxbury.

Champion, Timothy G., et al. 1984. *Prehistoric Europe*. New York: Academic Press.

Chang Kwang-Chih. 1980. *Shang Civilization*. New Haven, CT: Yale University Press.

———. 1981. "In Search of China's Beginnings: New Light on an Old Civilization." *American Scientist* 60:148–160.

———. 1986. *The Archaeology of Ancient China*, 4th ed. New Haven, CT: Yale University Press.

Chapman, Jefferson, et al. 1982. "Man-Land Interaction: 10,000 Years of American Indian Impact on Native Ecosystems in the Lower Little Tennessee Valley, Eastern Tennessee." *Southeastern Archaeology* 1:115–121.

Childe, V. G. 1936. *Man Makes Himself*. London: Watts.

———. 1952. *New Light on the Most Ancient East*. London: Routledge & Kegan Paul.

———. 1956. *Piecing Together the Past*. London: Routledge & Kegan Paul.

Chippindale, Christopher. 1994. *Stonehenge Complete,* 2nd ed. London: Thames and Hudson.

Chung Tang and Pei Gai. 1986. "Upper Palaeolithic Cultural Traditions in North China." *Advances in World Archaeology* 5:339–364.

Cinq-Mars, Jacques. 1979. "Bluefish Cave I: A Late Pleistocene Eastern Beringian Cave Deposit in the Northern Yukon." *Canadian Journal of Anthropology* 3:1–32.

Claessen, H.J.M., and Skalník, P. eds. 1979. *The Early State.* The Hague, Netherlands: Mouton.

Clark, J. Desmond. 1959. *The Prehistory of Southern Africa.* Baltimore: Pelican.

——. 1967. "The Problem of Neolithic Culture in Sub-Saharan Africa." In W. W. Bishop and J. Desmond Clark, eds., *Background to Evolution in Africa,* pp. 601–628. Chicago: University of Chicago Press.

——. 1971. "A Re-examination of the Evidence for Agricultural Origins in the Nile Valley." *Proceedings of the Prehistoric Society* 37 (2):34–79.

——. 1983. "The Significance of Culture Change in the Early Later Pleistocene in Northern and Southern Africa." In Erik Trinkaus, ed., *The Mousterian Legacy,* pp. 1–12. Oxford, Eng.: British Archaeological Reports, International Series, No. 151.

——. 1984. "Prehistoric Cultural Continuity and Economic Change in the Central Sudan in the Early Holocene." In J. Desmond Clark and Steven A. Brandt, eds., *From Hunters to Farmers,* pp. 113–126. Berkeley and Los Angeles: University of California Press.

—— (ed.). 1991. *Cultural Beginnings: Approaches to Understanding Early Hominids' Life-Ways in the African Savanna.* Bonn, Germany: Rudolf Habelt.

Clark, J. D., and Brandt, Steven A., eds. 1984. *From Hunters to Farmers.* Berkeley: University of California Press.

Clark, J. Desmond, and Harris, J. W. K. 1985. "Fire and Its Roles in Early Hominid Lifeways." *African Archaeological Review* 3:3–28.

Clark, J. G. D. 1952. *Prehistoric Europe: The Economic Basis.* Palo Alto, CA: Stanford University Press.

——. 1954. *Star Carr.* Cambridge, Eng.: Cambridge University Press.

——. 1958. "Blade and Trapeze Industries of the European Stone Age." *Proceedings of the Prehistoric Society* 24:24–42.

——. 1965. *Archaeology and Society.* New York: Barnes and Noble.

——. 1975. *The Earlier Stone Age Settlement of Scandinavia.* Cambridge, Eng.: Cambridge University Press.

——. 1979. *Mesolithic Prelude.* Edinburgh: Edinburgh University Press.

Clendinnen, Inga. 1991. *The Aztecs: An Interpretation.* Cambridge, Eng.: Cambridge University Press.

Clutton-Brock, Juliet. 1981. *Domesticated Animals from Early Times.* Austin: University of Texas Press.

Coe, M. D. 1968. *America's First Civilization: Discovering the Olmec.* New York: American Heritage.

——. 1992. *Breaking the Maya Code.* London and New York: Thames and Hudson.

——. 1993. *The Maya,* 5th ed. London and New York: Thames and Hudson.

——. 1994. *Mexico,* 4th ed. London and New York: Thames and Hudson.

Coe, Michael D., and Diehl, Richard. 1980. *In the Land of the Olmec.* 2 vols. Austin: University of Texas Press.

Coe, William, and Haviland, William A. 1982. *Introduction to the Archaeology of Tikal, Guatemala.* Philadelphia: University Museum, University of Pennsylvania. (The first of a projected 39 reports on Tikal.)

Coggins, Clemency. 1985. *The Sacred Cenote of Sacrifice.* Austin: University of Texas Press.

Cohen, Mark, 1977. *The Food Crisis in Prehistory.* New Haven, CT: Yale University Press.

——. 1988. *Health and the Rise of Civilization.* New Haven, CT: Yale University Press.

Coles, B., and Coles, J. M. 1989. *People of the Wetlands.* London and New York: Thames and Hudson.

Coles, J. M. 1982. "The Bronze Age in North West Europe: Problems and Advances." *Advances in World Archaeology* 1:266–321.

Coles, J. M., and Harding, A. F. 1979. *The Bronze Age in Europe*. London: Methuen.

Collis, John. 1984. *The European Iron Age*. London: Batsford.

Colwell, R. N., ed. 1983. *Manual of Remote Sensing*, 2d ed. Falls Church, VA: American Society of Photogrammetry.

Connah, Graham. 1987. *African Civilizations*. Cambridge, Eng.: Cambridge University Press.

Conrad, Geoffrey W., and Demarest, Arthur A. 1984. *Religion and Empire: The Dynamics of Aztec and Inca Expansionism*. Cambridge, Eng.: Cambridge University Press.

Cooper, J. S. 1983. *Reconstructing History from Ancient Inscriptions: The Lagash-Umma Border Dispute*. Malibu, CA: Undena Publications.

Cordell, Linda. 1984a. *Prehistory of the Southwest*. New York: Academic Press.

———. 1984b. "Southwestern Archaeology." *Annual Review of Anthropology* 13:130–132.

Cosgrove, R., Allen, J., and Marshall, B. 1990. "Pleistocene Occupation of Tasmania." *Antiquity* 64 (242):59–78.

Courand, Claude. 1985. *L'Art Azilien*. Paris: Gallia Prehistoire.

Covey, Curt. 1984. "The Earth's Orbit and the Ice Ages." *Scientific American* 280 (2):58–77.

Cowan, Wesley, and Watson, Patty Jo, eds. 1992. *The Origins of Agriculture*. Washington DC: Smithsonain Institution Press.

Crawford, Gary. 1992. "Prehistoric Plant Manipulation in East Asia: The Japanese perspective." In Wesley Cowan and Patty Jo Watson, eds., *The Origins of Agriculture*, pp. 7–38. Washington DC: Smithsonain Institution Press.

Crawford, Harriett. 1991. *Sumer and the Sumerians*. Cambridge, Eng.: Cambridge University Press.

Croes, Dale, and Hackenberger, S. 1988. "Hoko River Archaeological Complex: Modelling Prehistoric Northwest Coast Economic Evolution." *Research in Economic Anthropology* Supplement 3: 19–85.

Crown, Patrica L. 1990. "The Hohokam of the American Southwest." *Journal of World Prehistory* 4 (2):223-255.

Crown, Patricia L., and Judge, W. James, eds. 1991. *Chaco and Hohokam: Regional Systems in the American Southwest*. Santa Fe, NM: School of American Research Press.

Culbert, T. Patrick, ed. 1973. *The Classic Maya Collapse*. Albuquerque: University of New Mexico Press.

———. 1988. "The Collapse of Classic Maya Civilization." In Norman Yoffee and George Cowgill, eds., *The Collapse of Ancient States and Civilizations*. Tucson: University of Arizona Press.

———, ed. 1991. *Classic Maya Political History*. Cambridge, Eng., and Santa Fe, NM: Cambridge University Press and School of American Research.

Cunliffe, Barry. 1974. *Iron Age Communities in Britain*. London: Routledge & Kegan Paul.

D'Acevedo, Warren. 1986. *The Great Basin*. Vol. 5, *Handbook of North American Indians*. Washington, DC: Smithsonian Institution.

D'Altroy, B. 1993. *Provincial Power in the Inka Empire*. Washington, DC: Smithsonian Institution Press.

Daniel, Glyn E. 1973. *Megaliths in History*. London: Thames and Hudson.

Danien, Elin C., and Sharer, Robert J., eds. 1992. *New Theories on the Ancient Maya*. Philadelphia: University Museum Symposium Series no. 3.

Dart, Raymond A. 1925. "*Australopithecus africanus*: The Man-Ape of Southern Africa." *Nature* 115:195.

Davidson, Janet. 1985. "New Zealand Prehistory." *Advances in World Archaeology* 4:239–292.

Davies, Nigel. 1977. *The Toltecs*. Norman: University of Oklahoma Press.

———. 1980. *The Toltec Heritage*. Norman: University of Oklahoma Press.

Davis, Richard S. 1987. "Regional Perspectives on the Soviet Central Asian Paleolithic." In Olga Soffer, ed., *The Pleistocene Old World: Regional Perspectives,* pp. 121–134. New York: Plenum.

Davis, S. J. M. 1987. *The Archaeology of Animals.* London: Batsford.

Deacon, Hilary. 1979. "Excavations at Boomplas Cave: A Sequence Through the Upper Pleistocene and Holocene in South Africa." *World Archaeology* 10:241–257.

———. 1992. "Southern Africa and Modern Human Origins." *Philosophical Transactions of the Royal Society,* Series B, 337:177–183.

Deetz, James. 1967. *Invitation to Archaeology.* Garden City, NY: Natural History Press.

Delson, Eric. 1986. "Human Phylogeny Revised Again." *Nature* 322:496–497.

Demarest, Arthur. 1989. "The Olmec and the Rise of Civilization in Eastern Mesoamerica." In Robert Sharer and David Grove, eds., *Regional Perspectives on the Olmec,* pp. 303–344. Cambridge, Eng.: Cambridge University Press.

Demarest, Arthur A., and Conrad, Geoffrey W. 1993. *Ideology and Pre-Columbian Civilizations.* Santa Fe, NM: School of American Research.

Dennell, Robin C. 1983. *European Economic Prehistory: A New Approach.* New York: Academic Press.

Diaz, Bernal. 1963. *The True History of the Conquest of New Spain.* Translated by J. M. Cohen. Baltimore: Pelican.

Dibble, Charles E., and Anderson, Arthur J. O. 1978. *Florentine Codex,* vol. 14. Salt Lake City: University of Utah Press.

Dibble, Harold. 1987. "Reduction Sequences in the Manufacture of Mousterian Implements of France." In Olga Soffer, ed., *The Pleistocene Old World: Regional Perspectives,* pp. 33–46. New York: Plenum.

Diehl, Richard. 1989. "Olmec Archaeology: What We Know and What We Wish We Knew." In Robert Sharer and David Grove, eds., *Regional Perspectives on the Olmec,* pp. 17–32. Cambridge, Eng.: Cambridge University Press.

———. 1984. *Tula.* London: Thames and Hudson.

Dillehay, Tom. 1984. "A Late Ice Age Settlement in Southern Chile." *Scientific American* 254 (4):100–109.

———. 1989. *Monte Verde: A Late Pleistocene Settlement in Chile.* Blue Ridge Summit, PA: Smithsonian Institution Press.

———and Meltzer, David J., eds. 1991. *The First Americans: Search and Research.* Boca Raton, FL: CRC Press.

Di Peso, C. C., et al. 1974. *Casas Grandes: A Fallen Trading Center of the Gran Chichimeca.* Flagstaff, AZ: AmerInd Foundation.

Diringer, David. 1962. *Writing.* New York: Praeger.

Dolukhanov, Paul H. 1982. "Upper Pleistocene and Holocene Cultures of the Russian Plain and Caucasus." *Advances in World Archaeology* 1:323–358.

Donnan, Christopher B., ed. 1985. *Early Ceremonial Architecture in the Andes.* Washington, DC: Dumbarton Oaks.

———. 1989. "Unraveling the Mystery of the Warrior Priest." *National Geographic Magazine* 174 (4):550–555.

———. 1990. "Master Works Reveal a Pre-Inca World." *National Geographic Magazine* 177 (6):34–49.

Donnan, Christopher B., and McClelland, Donna. 1979. *The Burial Theme in Moche Iconography.* Washington, DC: Dumbarton Oaks.

Dorn, R. I., Nobbs, M., Cahill, T. A. 1988. "Cation-ratio Dating of Rock Engravings." *Antiquity* 62 (237):681–689.

Dortch, Charles, and Merrilees, Duncan. 1973. "Human Occupation of Devil's Lair, Western Australia, During the Pleistocene." *Archaeology and Physical Anthropology in Oceania* 8:89–115.

Dragoo, Don W. 1976. "Some Aspects of Eastern North American Prehistory: A Review 1975." *American Antiquity* 41 (1):3–27.

Drucker, Phillip. 1959. *La Venta, Tabasco: A Study of Olmec Ceramics and Art.* Washington, DC: Smithsonian Institution.

Dumond, Don. 1987a. *The Eskimos and Aleuts.* London: Thames and Hudson.

———. 1987b. "A Reexamination of Eskimo-Aleut Prehistory." *American Anthropologist* 89 (1):32–56.

Earle, Timothy. 1978. *Economic and Social Organization of a Complex Chiefdom: The Halelea District, Kaua'i, Hawaii.* Ann Arbor: Museum of Anthropology, University of Michigan.

Edens, Christopher. 1992. "Dynamics of Trade in the Ancient Mesopotamian World System." *American Anthropologist* 94 (1):118–139.

———. 1993. "Indus-Arabian Interaction during the Bronze Age: A Review of Evidence." In Gregory Possehl (ed.), *Harappan Civilization,* 2nd ed., pp. 335–363 New Delhi. Oxford and IBH Publishing.

Eisenberg, J. F. 1981. *The Mammalian Radiation.* London: Athlone.

Eliade, Mircea. 1959. *The Sacred and the Profane.* New York: Harcourt, Brace.

El Mahdy, Christine. 1989. *Mummies, Myth, and Magic in Ancient Egypt.* New York: Thames and Hudson.

Elphick, Richard. 1977. *Kraal and Castle.* New Haven, CT: Yale University Press.

Erickson, Clark L. 1992. "Applied Archaeology and Rural Development: Archaeology's Potential Contribution to the Future." *Journal of the Steward Anthropological Society* 20 (1 and 2):1–16.

Ericson, J. E., and Baugh, T. G., eds. 1993. *The American Southwest and Mesoamerica.* New York: Plenum Press.

Evans, Sir Arthur J. 1921. *The Palace of Minos at Knossos,* 4 vols. Oxford, Eng.: Clarendon.

Fagan, Brian M. 1979. *Return to Babylon.* Boston: Little, Brown.

———. 1985. *The Adventure of Archaeology.* Washington, DC: National Geographic Society.

———. 1987. *The Great Journey.* London: Thames and Hudson.

———. 1990. *The Journey from Eden.* New York: Thames and Hudson.

———. 1992. *The Rape of the Nile.* Providence, RI: Moyer-Bell.

———. 1994a. *In the Beginning,* 8th ed. New York: HarperCollins.

———. 1994b. *Archaeology: A Brief Introduction,* 5th ed. New York: HarperCollins.

———. 1995. *Ancient North America,* 2nd ed. New York: Thames and Hudson.

Fagan, Brian M., and van Noten, F. 1971. *The Hunter-Gatherers of Gwisho.* Tervuren. Belgium: Musée Royal de l'Afrique Centrale.

Fagles, Robert. 1990. *The Iliad.* New York: Viking.

Fairbanks, Richard G. 1989. "A 17,000-year Glacio-Eustatic Sea Level Record: Influence of Glacial Melting Rates on the Younger Dryas Event and Deep Sea Circulation." *Nature* 342:637–642.

Fairservis, Walter A. 1976. *The Roots of Ancient India,* 2d ed. New York: Macmillan.

———. 1983. "The Script of the Indus Valley Civilization." *Scientific American* 243 (3):58–77.

Falk, Dean. 1984. "The Petrified Brain." *Natural History* 93 (9):36–39.

Farnsworth, Paul, et al. 1985. "A Re-evaluation of the Isotopic and Archaeological Reconstruction of Diet in the Tehuacán Valley." *American Antiquity* 50 (1):102–116.

Fash, William. 1991. *Scribes, Warriors, and Kings.* London and New York: Thames and Hudson.

Feder, Kenneth L. 1990. *Frauds, Myths, and Mysteries.* Mountain View, CA: Mayfield.

Fiedel, Suart J. 1992. *Prehistory of the Americas,* 2nd ed. Cambridge, Eng.: Cambridge University Press.

Finley, M. I. 1963. *The Ancient Greeks.* London: Chatto & Windus.

Finney, Ben R. 1967. "New Perspectives on Pacific Voyaging." In Genevieve Highland et al., eds., *Polynesian Culture History,* pp. 141–166. Honolulu: Bishop Museum.

Fitzgerald, Patrick. 1978. *Ancient China.* Oxford, Eng.: Elsevier Phaidon.

Flannery, Kent V. 1965. "The Ecology of Early Food Production in Mesopotamia." *Science* 147:1247–1256.

————. 1968a. "Archaeological Systems Theory and Early Mesoamerica." In Betty Meggers, ed., *Anthropological Archaeology in the Americas,* pp. 67–87. Washington, DC: Anthropological Society of Washington.

————. 1968b. "The Olmec and the Valley of Oaxaca: A Model for Interregional Interaction in Formative Times." In Elizabeth Benson, ed., *Dumbarton Oaks Conference on the Olmec,* pp. 79–110. Washington, DC: Dumbarton Oaks.

————. 1969. "Origins and Ecological Effects of Early Domestication in Animals." In Peter J. Ucko and G. W. Dimbleby, eds., *The Domestication and Exploitation of Plants and Animals,* pp. 207–218. London: Duckworth.

————. 1972. "The Cultural Evolution of Civilizations." *Annual Review of Ecology and Systematics* 4:399–426.

————. 1973. "The Origins of Agriculture." *Annual Review of Anthropology* 2:271–310.

————. ed. 1976. *The Early Mesoamerican Village.* New York: Academic Press.

————. ed. 1982. *Maya Subsistence.* New York: Academic Press.

————. 1983. "Settlement, Subsistence, and Social Organization of the Proto-Otomangueans." In Kent V. Flannery and Joyce Marcus, eds., *The Cloud People,* pp. 32–36. New York: Academic Press.

Flannery, Kent V., and Marcus, Joyce, eds. 1983. *The Cloud People.* New York: Academic Press.

Flannery, Kent V., et al. 1981. "The Preceramic and Formative of the Valley of Oaxaca." In Jeremy A. Sabloff, ed., *Archeology.* Vol. 1, *Supplement to the Handbook of American Indians,* pp. 48–93. Austin: University of Texas Press.

Flannery, Kent V., et al. 1986. *Guilá Naquitz.* Orlando, FL: Academic Press.

Fleischer, Robert L. 1975. "Advances in Fission Track Dating." *World Archaeology* 7 (2):136–150.

Flint, R. F. 1971. *Glacial and Quaternary Geology.* New York: Wiley.

Folan, William J., et al. 1983. *Coba: A Classic Maya Metropolis.* New York: Academic Press.

Foley, Robert. 1984a. "Early Man and the Red Queen." In Robert Foley, ed., *Hominid Evolution and Community Ecology,* pp. 85–110. London: Academic Press.

————. ed. 1984b. *Hominid Evolution and Community Ecology: Prehistoric Human Adaptation in Biological Perspective.* London: Academic Press.

————. 1984c. "Putting People into Perspective." In Robert Foley, ed., *Hominid Evolution and Community Ecology,* pp. 1–24. London: Academic Press.

————. 1987a. *Another unique species: Patterns in human evolutionary ecology.* London: Longman.

————. 1987b. "Hominid Species and Stone-Tool Assemblages: How Are They Related?'" *Antiquity* 61:380–392.

————. Foley, R. A. 1989. "The evolution of hominid social behavior." In V. Standen and R.A. Foley (eds.), *Comparative Socioecology: The Behavioral Ecology of Humans and Other Mammals,* pp. 473–494. Oxford, England: Blackwell Scientific Publications.

Ford, Richard I., ed. 1985. *Prehistoric Food Production in North America.* Ann Arbor: University of Michigan Museum of Anthropology.

Forest, J. D. 1986. "Tell el-Oueili: Preliminary Report on the 4th Season." *Iraq* 44 (1–2):55–60.

Fowler, Melvin L. 1958. *Modoc Rockshelter.* Springfield: Illinois State Museum.

————. 1978. "Cahokia and the American Bottom: Settlement Archaeology." In Bruce D. Smith, ed., *Mississippian Settlement Patterns,* pp. 455–478. New York: Academic Press.

Freeman, Leslie, and Echegaray, Jesús. 1981. "El Juyo: A 14,000-Year-Old Sanctuary from Northern Spain." *History of Religions* 21:1–19.

Freidel, David, and Schele, Linda. 1988a. "Kingship in the Late Preclassic Lowlands." *American Anthropologist* 90 (3):547–567.

————. 1988b. "Symbol and Power: A History of the Lowland Maya Cosmogram." In Elizabeth Benson and Gillett Griffin, eds., *Maya Iconography.* Princeton, NJ: Princeton University Press.

Frison, George C. 1992. *Prehistoric Hunters of the High Plains,* 2nd ed. New York: Academic Press.

Galinat, Walter C. 1985. "Domestication and Diffusion of Maize." In Richard I. Ford, ed., *Prehistoric Food Production in North America,* pp. 245–278. Ann Arbor: University of Michigan Museum of Anthropology.

Galloway, P., ed. 1989. *The Southeastern Ceremonial Complex.* Lincoln: University of Nebraska Press.

Gamble, Clive. 1986a. "The Mesolithic Sandwich." In Marek Zvelebil, ed., *Hunters in Transition,* pp. 33–42. Cambridge, Eng.: Cambridge University Press.

———. 1986b. *The Palaeolithic Settlement of Europe.* Cambridge, Eng.: Cambridge University Press.

Gardner, R. Allen, and Gardner, Beatrice A. 1969. "Teaching Sign Language to a Chimpanzee." *Science* 163:664–672.

Garlake, Peter. 1973. *Great Zimbabwe.* New York: McGraw-Hill.

Garrod, D. A. E., and Bate, Dorothea. 1937. *The Stone Age of Mount Carmel.* Cambridge, Eng.: Cambridge University Press.

Gasparini, Graziano, and Margolies, Luise. 1980. *Inca Architecture.* Bloomington: Indiana University Press.

Gebauer, A., and Price, T.D. 1992. "Introduction." In A. Gebauer and T.D. Price, eds., *Transitions to Agriculture in Prehistory,* pp. i–xx. Madison, WI: Prehistory Press.

Ghosh, A. 1993. "Deurbanization of the Harappan Civilization." In Gregory Possehl, ed. *Harappan Civilization,* 2nd ed., pp. 381–383. New Delhi: Oxford and IBH Publishing.

Gingerich, Phillip D. 1985. "Nonlinear Molecular Clocks and Ape-Human Divergence Times." In Philip V. Tobias, ed., *Hominid Evolution: Past, Present, and Future,* pp. 441–466. New York: Liss.

Golson, Jack. 1977. "No Room at the Top: Agricultural Intensification in the New Guinea Highlands." In J. Allen, J. Golson, and Rhys Jones, eds., *Sunda and Sahel,* pp. 602–638. New York: Academic Press.

———. 1986. *The Chimpanzees of Gombe.* Cambridge, MA: Harvard University Press.

Gorman, Chester A. 1969. "Hoabhinian: A Pebble-Tool Complex with Early Plant Associations in Southeast Asia." *Science* 163:671–673.

———. 1971. "Hoabhinian and After: Subsistence Patterns in Southeast Asia During the Late Pleistocene and Early Recent Periods." *World Archaeology* 2 (3):300–320.

Gosden, C., Allen, J., et al. 1989. "Lapita Sites of the Bismarck Archipelago." *Antiquity* 63 (240):561–586.

Goudie, Andrew. 1983. *Environmental Change,* 2d ed. Oxford, Eng.: Clarendon Press.

Gould, Richard A. 1977. *Puntutjarpa Rockshelter and Australian Desert Culture.* New York: American Museum of Natural History.

———, ed. 1978. *Explorations in Ethnoarchaeology.* Albuquerque: University of New Mexico Press.

———. 1980. *Living Archaeology.* Cambridge, Eng.: Cambridge University Press.

Gowlett, John. 1978. "Culture and Conceptualization: The Oldowan-Acheulian Gradient." In G. N. Bailey and P. Callow, eds., *Stone Age Prehistory,* pp. 243–260. Cambridge, Eng.: Cambridge University Press.

———. 1987. "The Archaeology of Radiocarbon Accelerator Dating." *Journal of World Prehistory* 1 (2):127–170.

Grant, Michael. 1960. *The Romans.* London: Weidenfeld and Nicholson.

Grayson, Donald K. 1991. "Late Pleistocene Mammalian Extinctions in North America: Taxonomy, Chronology, and Explanations." *Journal of World Prehistory,* 5 (3):193–232.

Greenberg, Joseph. 1987. *Language in the Americas.* Palo Alto, CA: Stanford University Press.

Griffin, J. B. 1967. "Eastern North American Prehistory: A Summary." *Science* 156:175–191.

Groube, L., et al. 1986. "40,000-Year-Old Human Occupation Site at Huon Peninsula, Papua, New Guinea." *Nature* 324:453–455.

Grove, David. 1973. "Olmec Altars and Myths." *Archaeology* 26:128–135.

Groves, Colin P. 1989. "A Regional Approach to the Problem of Modern Humans in Australasia." In Paul Mellars and Christopher Stringer, eds., *The Human Revolution,* pp. 274–285. Edinburgh: Edinburgh University Press.

Grygiel, Ryszard, and Bogucki, P. 1986. "Early Neolithic Sites at Brzesc Kujawski, Poland." *Journal of Field Archaeology* 13 (2):121–138.

Guidon, Niede, and Delibrias, G. 1986. "Carbon 14 Dates Point to Man in the Americas 32,000 Years Ago." *Nature* 321:769–771.

Haas, Jonathan, et al., eds. 1987. *The Origins and Development of the Andean State.* Cambridge, Eng.: Cambridge University Press.

Haland, Randi, and Shinnie, Peter. 1985. *African Iron Working—Ancient and Traditional.* Bergen: Norwegian University Press.

Hall, Kenneth R. 1985. *Maritime Trade and State Development in Early Southeast Asia.* Honolulu: University of Hawaii Press.

Hallam, Sylvia. 1975. *Fire and Hearth.* Canberra: Australian Institute of Aboriginal Studies.

Hammond, F. 1981. "The Colonization of Europe: The Analysis of Settlement Process." In Ian Hodder et al., eds., *Pattern of the Past,* pp. 211–248. Cambridge, Eng.: Cambridge University Press.

Hammond, N. 1980. "Early Maya Ceremonial at Cuello, Belize." *Antiquity* 54:176–190.

———. 1982. *Ancient Maya Civilization.* New Brunswick, NJ: Rutgers University Press.

———. 1986. "New Light on the Most Ancient Maya." *Man* 21:299–413.

———. 1991. "Introduction." In Patrick T. Culbert, ed., *Classic Maya Political History,* pp. 1–18. Cambridge, Eng., and Santa Fe, NM: Cambridge University Press and School of American Research.

Hanson, D., ed. 1989. *Tula of the Toltecs.* Iowa City: University of Iowa Press.

Hapgood, Phillip J. 1989. "The Origin of Anatomically Modern Humans in Australasia." In Paul Mellars and Christopher Stringer, eds., *The Human Revolution,* pp. 245–273. Edinburgh: Edinburgh University Press.

Harding, A. F. 1983. "The Bronze Age in Central and Eastern Europe: Advances and Prospects." *Advances in World Prehistory* 2:1–50.

———. 1984. *The Mycenaeans and Europe.* New York: Academic Press.

Harlan, J. R. 1967. "A Wild Wheat Harvest in Turkey." *Archaeology* 19 (3):197–201.

Harlan, J. R. et al., eds. 1976. *Origins of African Plant Domestication.* The Hague: Mouton.

Harris, David R., ed. 1980. *Human Ecology in Savanna Environments.* New York: Academic Press.

Harris, D., and Hillman, G., eds. 1989. *Foraging and Farming.* London: Unwin Hyman.

Harris, Marvin. 1968. *The Rise of Anthropological Theory.* New York: Crowell.

Harrison, Richard J. 1980. *The Beaker Folk.* London: Thames and Hudson.

Hasegawa, T. et al. 1983. "New Evidence of Scavenging Behavior in Wild Chimpanzees." *Current Anthropology* 24:231–232.

Hassan, Fekri. 1981. *Demographic Archaeology.* Orlando, FL: Academic Press.

———. 1986. "Desert Environment and Origins of Agriculture in Egypt." *Norwegian Archaeological Review* 19 (2):63–76.

———. 1987. "High Precision Radiocarbon Chronology of Ancient Egypt, and Comparisons with Nubia, Palestine, and Mesopotamia." *Antiquity* 61 (231):119–135.

———. 1988. "The Pre-Dynastic of Egypt." *Journal of World Prehistory* 2 (2):135–186.

Hastorf, Christine A. 1992. *Agriculture and the Onset of Political Inequality Before the Inka.* Cambridge, Eng.: Cambridge University Press.

Hather, Jon, and Kirch, P. V. 1991. "Prehistoric sweet potato (*Ipomoea batatas*) from Mangaia Island, Central Polynesia." *Antiquity* 65:887–893.

Haury, Emil. 1936. *The Mogollon Culture of Southwestern New Mexico.* Globe, AZ: Gila Pueblo.

———. 1976. *Hohokam, Desert Farmers and Craftsmen: Excavations at Snaketown.* Tucson: University of Arizona Press.

Hayden, Brian. 1981. "Research and Development in the Stone Age: Technological Transitions Among Hunter-Gatherers." *Current Anthropology* 22 (5):519–548.

Hayden, Brian. 1990. "Nimrods, piscators, pluckers, and planters: The emergence of food production." *Journal of Anthropological Archaeology* 9:31–69.

Haynes, C. Vance. 1982. "Were Clovis Progenitors in Beringia?" In David M. Hopkins et al., eds., *Paleoecology of Beringia*, pp. 383–398. New York: Academic Press.

Hays, T. R. 1984. "A Reappraisal of the Egyptian Predynastic." In J. Desmond Clark and Steven A. Brandt, eds., *From Hunters to Farmers*, pp. 65–73. Berkeley and Los Angeles: University of California Press.

Heizer, R. F., and Berger, Rainer. 1970. "Radiocarbon Age of the Gypsum Cave." *Contributions of the University of California Archaeological Research Facility* 7:1–12.

Henry, Donald O. 1989. *From Foraging to Agriculture*. Philadelphia: University of Pennsylvania Press.

Higham, Charles F. W. 1989. *The Archaeology of Mainland Southeast Asia*. Cambridge, Eng.: Cambridge University Press.

———. 1993. "The Transition to Rice Cultivation in Southeast Asia." In Douglas Price and Birgitte Gebauer, eds. *Transitions to Agriculture in Prehistory*, pp. 210–231. Madison, WI: Prehistory Press.

Hill, Andrew. 1984. "Hyaenas and Hominids." In Robert Foley, ed., *Hominid Evolution and Community Ecology*, pp. 111–128. London: Academic Press.

Hillman, G. C. and Davis, M. S. 1990. "Measured Domestication Rates in Wild Wheats and Barley Under Primitive Cultivation, and Their Archaeological Implications." *Journal of World Prehistory* 4 (2):157–222.

Ho Ping-Ti. 1969. "Loess and the Origins of Chinese Agriculture." *American Historical Review* 75:1–36.

Hodder, Ian, ed. 1982. *Symbolic and Structural Archaeology*. Cambridge, Eng.: Cambridge University Press.

———. 1990. *The Domestication of Europe*. Oxford: Blackwell.

Hoffecker, John F. and others. 1993. "The Colonization of Beringia and the Peopling of the New World." *Science* 259:46–53.

Hoffecker, John F. and C. A. Wolf, eds. 1988. *The Early Upper Palaeolithic*. Oxford: British Archaeological Reports, International Series, No. 437.

Hoffman, Michael A. 1979. *Egypt Before the Pharaohs*. New York: Knopf.

Hoffman, Michael A., et al. 1982. *The Predynastic of Hierakonpolis*. Cairo: Egyptian Studies Association.

Hole, Frank, Flannery, Kent V., and Neely, J. A. 1969. *The Prehistory and Human Ecology of the Deh Luran Plain*. Ann Arbor: University of Michigan Museum of Anthropology.

Hood, Sinclair. 1973. *The Minoans*. London: Thames and Hudson.

Hopkins, David M., et al., eds. 1982. *Paleoecology of Beringia*. New York: Academic Press.

Howell, F. Clark. 1966. "Observations on the Earlier Phases of the European Lower Palaeolithic." *American Anthropologist* 68 (2):111–140.

———. 1974. *Early Man*. Chicago: Time-Life.

Howell, F. Clark, and Clark, J. Desmond. 1963. "Acheulian Hunter-Gatherers of Sub-Saharan Africa." *Viking Fund Publications in Anthropology* 36:458–533.

Howell, John M. 1987. "Early Farming in Northwestern Europe." *Scientific American* 237 (11): 118–126.

Hunwick, John D. 1971. "Songhay, Bornu and Hausaland in the Sixteenth Century." In Jacob F. Ajayi and Michael Crowder, eds., *History of West Africa*, vol. 1, pp. 120–157. London: Longmans.

Huot, Jean-Louis. 1989. "'Ubaidian villages of lower Mesopotamia." In E. F. Henrickson and I. Thueson, eds., *Upon these Foundations: The 'Ubaid Period*. Copenhagen: National Museum of Denmark.

Huyen Pham Minh. 1984. "Various Phases of the Development of Primitive Metallurgy in Viet Nam." In Donn T. Bayard, ed., *The Origins of Agriculture, Metallurgy, and the State in Mainland Southeast Asia*, pp. 173–182. Dunedin, New Zealand: University of Otago Press.

Hyslop, John. 1984. *The Inca Road System*. New York: Academic Press.

———. 1990. *Inka Settlement Patterns*. Austin: University of Texas Press.

Hyslop, John, et al. 1987. *Huaca Prieta.* New York: American Museum of Natural History.

Irwin, G. 1992. *The Prehistoric Exploration and Colonisation of the Pacific.* Cambridge, Eng.: Cambridge University Press.

Irwin, G., Brickler, S., and Quirke, P. 1990. "Pacific Voyaging by Canoe and Computer." *Antiquity* 64 (242):34–50.

Irwin, H. T., and Wormington, H. M. 1970. "Paleo-Indian Tool Types in the Great Plains." *American Antiquity* 325:24–34.

Irwin-Williams, C. 1973. "The Oshara Tradition: Origins of Anasazi Culture." *University of New Mexico Contributions in Anthropology,* No. 4.

Isaac, Glynn. 1981. "Emergence of Human Behavior Patterns." *Philosophical Transactions of the Royal Society of London* 292:177–188.

———. 1984. "The Archaeology of Human Origins: Studies of the Lower Palaeolithic in East Africa, 1971–1981." *Advances in World Archaeology* 3:1–89.

Isaac, Glynn Ll., and Harris, J. W. K. 1978. "Archaeology." In M. D. Leakey and Richard E. Leakey, eds., *The Fossil Hominids and an Introduction to Their Context, 1968–1974.* Vol. 1, *Koobi Fora Research Project,* pp. 47–76. Oxford, Eng.: Clarendon.

Isbell, William, and Schreiber, Katharina J. 1978. "Was Huari a State?" *American Antiquity* 43:372–389.

Jacobsen, Thomas W. 1981. "Franchthi Cave and the Beginning of Village Settled Life in Greece." *Hesperia* 50:303–319.

——— and Farrand, W. R. 1987. *Franchthi Cave and Paralia.* Bloomington: Indiana University Press.

Jacobson, Jerome. 1979. "Recent Developments in South Asian Prehistory and Protohistory." *Annual Review of Anthropology* 8:467–502.

James, Simon. 1992. *The World of the Celts.* London and New York: Thames and Hudson.

Jarrige, Jean-François. 1993. "Excavations at Mehrgarh: Their Significance for Understanding the Background of the Harappan Civilization." In Gregory Possehl (ed.), *Harappan Civilization,* 2nd ed., pp. 79–84. New Delhi: Oxford and IBH Publishing.

Jeffries, R. W. 1987. *The Archaeology of Carrier Mills.* Carbondale: Southern Illinois University Press.

Jennings, Jesse D. 1957. *Danger Cave.* Salt Lake City: University of Utah Press.

———, ed. 1983. *Ancient Native Americans,* 2nd ed., 2 vols. New York: Freeman.

Jochim, Michael. 1981. *Strategies for Survival: Cultural Behavior in Ecological Context.* New York: Academic Press.

———. 1983. "Paleolithic Cave Art in Ecological Perspective." In G. N. Bailey, ed., *Hunter-Gatherer Economy in Prehistory,* pp. 212–219. Cambridge, Eng.: Cambridge University Press.

Johanson, Donald C., and Edey, Maitland A. 1981. *Lucy: The Beginnings of Humankind.* New York: Simon & Schuster.

Johanson, Donald C., and White, Tim. 1979. "A Systematic Assessment of Early African Hominids." *Science* 202:321–330.

Johanson, Donald C., et al. 1987. "New Partial Skeleton of *Homo habilis* from Olduvai Gorge, Tanzania." *Nature* 327:205–211.

Jones, Rhys. 1989. "East of Wallace's Line: Issues and Problems in the Colonization of the Australian Continent." In Paul Mellars and Christopher Stringer, eds., *The Human Revolution,* pp. 743–782. Edinburgh: Edinburgh University Press.

Joukowsky, Martha. 1981. *A Complete Manual of Field Archaeology.* Englewood Cliffs, NJ: Prentice Hall.

Jovanovic, Borislav. 1980. "The Origins of Copper Mining in Europe." *Scientific American* 242 (5):152–168.

Keatinge, Richard, ed. 1988. *Peruvian Prehistory.* Cambridge, Eng.: Cambridge University Press.

Keeley, Lawrence H., and Cahen, Daniel. 1989. "Early Neolithic Forts and Villages in NE Belgium: A Preliminary Report." *Journal of Field Archaeology* 16 (2):157–176.

Keeley, Lawrence H. and Toth, Nicholas. 1981. "Microwear Polishes on Early Stone Tools from Koobi Fora, Kenya." *Nature* 293:464–465.

Keightley, David N. 1978. *Sources of Shang History: The Oracle Bone Inscriptions of Bronze Age China.* Berkeley and Los Angeles: University of California Press.

Kemp, Barry. 1989. *Ancient Egypt: The Anatomy of a Civilization.* London: Routledge.

Kennedy, David. 1987. *Rise and Fall of the Great Powers.* New York: Vintage Books.

Kennett, Douglas J., and Kennett, James P. 1994. "Influence of Early Holocene Marine Transgression and Climatic Change on Human Cultural Evolution in Southern Mesopotamia." In Press.

Kenoyer, J. M. 1991. "The Indus Valley Tradition of Pakistan and Western India." *Journal of World Prehistory* 5(4): 331–386.

Kenyon, Kathleen. 1981. *Excavations at Jericho,* vol. 3. Jerusalem: British School of Archaeology.

Kidder, A. V. 1927. *An Introduction to the Study of Southwestern Archaeology, with a Preliminary Account of the Excavations at Pecos.* New Haven, CT: Yale University Press.

Killion, Thomas W. ed. 1992. *Gardens of Prehistory.* Birmingham: University of Alabama Press.

Kimball, William H., Johanson, Donald C., and Rak, Yoel. 1994. "The First Skull and Other New Discoveries of *Australopithecus afarensis* at Hadar, Ethiopia." *Nature* 368: 449–451.

Kinnes, Ian. 1982. "Les Fouaillages and Megalithic Origins." *Antiquity* 56:24–30.

Kirch, Patrick V. 1982. "Advances in Polynesian Prehistory: Three Decades in Review." *Advances in World Archaeology* 2:52–102.

———. 1984. *The Evolution of the Polynesian Chiefdoms.* Cambridge, Eng.: Cambridge University Press.

———. 1985. *Feathered Gods and Fishhooks.* Honolulu: University of Hawaii Press.

———, ed. 1986. *Island Societies.* Cambridge, Eng.: Cambridge University Press.

———. 1988. "The Talepakemalai Lapita Site and Oceanic Prehistory." *National Geographic Research* 4 (3):328–342.

Kirk, Ruth. 1975. *Hunters of the Whale.* New York: Morrow.

Kirkby, Anne V. T. 1973. *The Use of Land and Water Resources in the Past and Present Valley of Oaxaca.* Ann Arbor: University of Michigan Museum of Anthropology.

Klein, Jeffrey, et al. 1982. "Calibration of Radiocarbon Dates." *Radiocarbon* 24 (2):103–150.

Klein, Richard G. 1979. "Stone Age Exploitation of Animals in Southern Africa." *American Scientist* 67:23–32.

———. 1984. "The Prehistory of Stone Age Herders in South Africa." In J. Desmond Clark and Steven A. Brandt, eds., *From Hunters to Farmers,* pp. 281–289. Berkeley and Los Angeles: University of California Press.

———. 1989. *The Human Career.* Chicago: University of Chicago Press.

Knecht, Heidi, and others. 1992. *Before Lascaux.* Boca Raton, FL: CRC Press.

Kohl, P. 1975. "Carved Chlorite Vessels: A Trade in Finished Commodities in the Mid-Third Millennium." *Expedition* (Fall): 18–31.

———. 1978. "The Balance of Trade in Southwestern Asia in the Mid-Third Millennium B.C." *Current Anthropology* 19:463–492.

Kolata, Alan L. 1986. "The Agricultural Foundations of the Tiwanaku State: A View from the Heartland." *American Antiquity* 51 (4):748–762.

———. 1993. *Tiwanaku.* Oxford, Eng: Blackwell.

Kramer, Samuel. 1963. *The Sumerians.* Chicago: University of Chicago Press.

Kurtén, Björn. 1968. *Pleistocene Mammals in Europe.* Chicago: Aldine.

Kurtén, Björn, and Anderson, E. 1980. *Pleistocene Mammals of North America.* New York: Columbia University Press.

Laitman, Jeffrey T. 1984. "The Anatomy of Human Speech." *Natural History* 93 (9):20–27.

Lamberg-Karlovsky, C. C. 1973. "Urban Interactions on the Iranian Plateau: Excavations at Tepe Yahya, 1967–1973." *Proceedings of the British Academy* 59:5–43.

———. 1978. "The Proto-Elamites and the Iranian Plateau." *Antiquity* 52:114–120.

Lancaster, Jane, and Whitten, Phillip. 1980. "Family Matters." *The Sciences* 1:10–15.

Larichev, Vitaliy, et al. 1987. "Lower and Middle Paleolithic of Northern Asia: Achievements, Problems, and Perspectives." *Journal of World Prehistory* 1 (4):415–464.

———. 1988. "The Upper Paleolithic of Northern Asia." *Journal of World Prehistory* 2 (4):359–396.

———. 1993. "The Upper Paleolithic of Northern Asia: Achievements, Problems, and Perspectives III: Northeastern Siberia and the Russian Far East." *Journal of World Prehistory* 6 (4):441–476.

Lathrap, Donald W. 1985. "Jaws: The Control of Power in the Early Nuclear American Ceremonial Center." In Christopher Donnan, ed., *Early Ceremonial Architecture in the Andes,* pp. 241–268. Washington, DC: Dumbarton Oaks.

Laughlin, William S. 1980. *Aleuts, Survivors of the Bering Land Bridge.* New York: Holt, Rinehart & Winston.

Laughlin, William S., Marsh, G. H., and Harper, A. B., eds. 1979. *The First Americans: Origins, Affinities and Adaptations.* New York: Fisher.

Laville, Henri, Rigaud, Jean-Philippe, and Sackett, James. 1980. *Rock Shelters of the Perigord.* New York: Academic Press.

Leakey, L. S. B. 1951. *Olduvai Gorge, 1931–1951.* Cambridge, Eng.: Cambridge University Press.

Leakey, M. D. 1971. *Olduvai Gorge,* vol. 3. Cambridge, Eng.: Cambridge University Press.

———. 1978. "Pliocene Footprints at Laetoli, Tanzania." *Antiquity* 52:133.

Leakey, M. D., and Harris, J. D. 1990. *Laetoli: A Pliocene Site in Northern Tanzania.* Oxford, Eng.: Oxford University Press.

Leakey, Richard, and Lewin, Roger. 1977. *Origins.* New York: Dutton.

Lee, Richard B. 1979. *The !Kung San.* Cambridge, Eng.: Cambridge University Press.

Lee, Richard B., and DeVore, Irven, eds. 1976. *Kalahari Hunter-Gatherers.* Cambridge, Eng.: Cambridge University Press.

Legge, A. J., and Rowley-Conwy, Peter. 1987. "Gazelle Hunting in Stone Age Syria." *Scientific American* 238 (8):88–95.

Lehner, Mark. 1994. *The Pyramids.* London and New York: Thames and Hudson.

Leroi-Gourhan, Andre. 1965. *Treasures of Palaeolithic Art.* New York: Abrams.

———. 1984. *The Dawn of European Art: An Introduction to Palaeolithic Cave Painting.* Cambridge, Eng.: Cambridge University Press.

Leveque, François, and Vandermeersch, Bernard. 1982. "Les découvertes de restes humains dans un horizon Castelperronien de Saint-Césaire (Charente-Maritime)." *Bulletin de la Société Prehistorique Française* 77:35.

Levetzion, Nehemiah. 1973. *Ancient Ghana and Mali.* London: Methuen.

Lewin, Roger, 1987. *Bones of Contention.* New York: Simon & Schuster.

———. 1988a. *Human Evolution,* 2d ed. Oxford, Eng.: Blackwell.

———. 1988b. "A Revolution of Ideas in Agricultural Origins." *Science* 240:984–986.

Lewis, David. 1972. *We the Navigators.* Honolulu: University of Hawaii Press.

Lewis-Williams, David. 1981. *Believing and Seeing: Symbolic Meanings in Southern San Rock Art.* New York: Academic Press.

Lhote, Henri. 1959. *The Search for the Tassili Frescoes.* London: Hutchinson University Library.

Lieberman, Philip. 1991. *Uniquely Human: The Evolution of Speech, Thought, and Selfless Behavior.* Cambridge, MA: Harvard University Press.

Livingstone, Sir R., trans. 1943. *Thucydides' History of the Peloponnesian War.* Cambridge, Eng.: Oxford University Press.

Lloyd, Seton. 1983. *The Archaeology of Mesopotamia,* 2d ed. London: Thames and Hudson.

Lourandos, Henry. 1987. "Pleistocene Australia: Peopling a Continent." In Olga Soffer, ed., *The Pleistocene Old World: Regional Perspectives,* pp. 147–166. New York: Plenum.

Luce, J. V. 1973. *Atlantis.* New York: McGraw-Hill.

Lumley, Henry de. 1969. "A Paleolithic Camp near Nice." *Scientific American* 87:23–32.

Lynch, Thomas F. 1980. *Guitarrero Cave.* New York: Academic Press.

———. 1989. "Glacial-Age Man in South America? A Critical Review." *American Antiquity* 55 (1):12–36.

McAnany, Patricia. 1994. *Living with the Ancestors: Kinship and Kingship in Ancient Maya Society.* Austin: University of Texas Press.

McCorriston, Joy, and Hole, Frank. 1991. "The Ecology of Seasonal Stress and the Origins of Agriculture in the Near East." *American Anthropologist* 93:46–69.

McGhee, Robert. 1984. "Contact Between Native North Americans and the Medieval Norse: A Review of Evidence." *American Antiquity* 49 (2):4–26.

McIntosh, S. K., and McIntosh, R. J. 1980. *Prehistoric Investigations at Jenne-jeno, Mali.* Oxford: British Archaeological Reports.

——— 1988. "From Stone to Metal: New Perspectives on the Later Prehistory of West Africa." *Journal of World Prehistory* 2 (1):89–131.

MacNeish, Richard, ed. 1970. *The Prehistory of the Tehuacán Valley.* Austin: University of Texas Press.

———. 1971. "Early Man in the Andes." *Scientific American,* no. 4, pp. 36–46.

———. 1978. *The Science of Archaeology.* North Scituate, MA: Duxbury.

———. 1983. "Mesoamerica." In Richard Shutler, Jr., ed., *Early Man in the New World,* pp. 125–136. Beverly Hills, CA: Sage.

MacQueen, J. G. 1987. *The Hittites.* London: Thames and Hudson.

Maisels, Charles. 1993. *The Near East: Archaeology in the "Cradle of Civilization."* London: Routledge.

Malinowski, Bronislaw. 1922. *Argonauts of the Western Pacific.* London: Routledge & Kegan Paul.

Mallory, J. P. 1988. *In Search of the Indo-Europeans.* New York: Thames and Hudson.

Manning, Stuart. 1988. "The Bronze Age Eruption of Thera." *Journal of Mediterranean Archaeology* 1 (1):17–82.

Marcus, Joyce. 1993. *Mesoamerican Writing Systems: Propoganda, Myth, and History in Four Ancient Civilizations.* Princeton, NJ: Princeton University Press.

Marks, Anthony E. 1983. "The Middle to Upper Palaeolithic Transition in the Levant." *Advances in World Prehistory* 2:51–98.

Marquardt, William H. 1978. "Advances in Archaeological Seriation." *Advances in Archaeological Method and Theory* 1:1–26.

Marshack, Alexander. 1972. *The Roots of Civilization.* New York: McGraw-Hill.

———. 1975. "Exploring the Mind of Ice Age Man." *National Geographic* 154:62–89.

Martin, Paul, and Klein, Richard, eds. 1984. *A Pleistocene Revolution.* Tucson: University of Arizona Press.

Matheny, Ray. 1986. "Early States of the Maya Lowlands during the Late Preclassic Period." In Elizabeth P. Benson, ed., *City-States of the Maya: Art and Architecture,* pp. 1–44. Denver: Rocky Mountain Institute of Pre-Columbian Studies.

Maxwell, Moreau S. 1985. *Prehistory of the Eastern Arctic.* New York: Academic Press.

Mayr, Ernst. 1982. *The Growth of Biological Thought.* Cambridge, MA: Harvard University Press.

Megaw, R., and Megaw, J. V. S. 1989. *Celtic Art from its beginnings to the Book of Kells.* London and New York: Thames and Hudson.

Mellaart, James. 1967. *Çatal Hüyük.* New York: McGraw-Hill.

———. 1975. *The Neolithic of the Near East.* London: Thames and Hudson.

Mellars, Paul. 1985. "The Ecological Basis of Social Complexity in the Upper Palaeolithic of Southwestern France." In T. Douglas Price and James Brown, eds., *Prehistoric Hunter-Gatherers: The Emergence of Cultural Complexity,* pp. 271–297. Orlando, FL: Academic Press.

Meltzer, David. 1988. "Late Pleistocene Adaptations in Eastern North America." *Journal of World Prehistory* 2 (1):1–52.

Mendelssohn, Kurt. 1974. *The Riddle of the Pyramids.* New York: Praeger.

Menzel, Dorothy, et al. 1964. "The Paracas Pottery of Ica." *University of California Bulletins in American Archaeology and Ethnology,* vol. 50.

Michels, Joseph W. 1973. *Dating Methods in Archaeology.* New York: Seminar.

Milanich, Jerald, et al., eds. 1984. *McKeithen Weeden Island: The Culture of Northern Florida, A.D. 200–900.* Orlando, FL: Academic Press.

Milisauskas, S., and Kruk, J. 1989. "Neolithic Economy in Central Europe." *Journal of World Prehistory* 2 (3):403–446.

Miller, Daniel. 1985. "Ideology and the Harappan Civilization." *Journal of Anthropological Archaeology* 4:1–38.

Miller, Mary, and Taube, Karl. 1993. *The Gods and Symbols of Ancient Mexico and the Maya.* London and New York: Thames and Hudson.

Millon, R., Drewitt, R. Bruce, and Cowgill, George. 1974. *Urbanization at Teotihuacán, Mexico.* Austin: University of Texas Press.

Mithen, Stephen. 1989. "Evolutionary Theory and Postprocessual Archaeology." *Antiquity* 63 (240):483–495.

Mochanov, Yuri A. 1978. "Stratigraphy and Chronology of the Paleolithic of Northeast Asia." In Alan L. Bryan, ed., *Early Man in America from a Circum-Pacific Perspective,* pp. 67–68. Edmonton: University of Alberta.

Moctezuma, Eduardo Matos. 1988. *The Great Temple of the Aztecs.* New York: Thames and Hudson.

Molleson, Theya. 1989. "Seed Preparation in the Neolithic: the osteological evidence." *Antiquity* 63 (239):356–362.

Moore, Andrew, T. 1979. "A Pre-Neolithic Farming Village on the Euphrates." *Scientific American* 241 (2):62–70.

———. 1985. "The Development of Neolithic Societies in the Near East." *Advances in World Archaeology* 4:1–70.

———. 1989. "The Transition from Foraging to Farming in South West Asia." In D. Harris and G. Hillman, eds., *Foraging and Farming,* pp. 620–631. London: Unwin Hyman.

Moorey, P. R. S. 1982. "The Archaeological Evidence for Metallurgy and Related Technologies in Mesopotamia, c. 5500–1200 B.C." *Iraq* 44:13–38.

Moratto, Michael. 1985. *California Archaeology.* New York: Academic Press.

Morgan, Lewis. 1877. *Ancient Society.* New York: Holt, Rinehart, and Winston.

Morlan, Richard E. 1983. "Pre-Clovis Occupation North of the Ice Sheets." In Richard Shutler, Jr., ed., *Early Man in the New World,* pp. 47–66. Beverly Hills, CA: Sage.

Morlan, Richard E., and Cinq-Mars, Jacques. 1982. "Ancient Beringians: Human Occupation in the Late Pleistocene of Alaska and the Yukon Territory." In David M. Hopkins et al., eds., *Paleoecology of Beringia,* pp. 353–382. New York: Academic Press.

Morris, J. Bayard, ed. 1962. *Five Letters of Cortés to the Emperor, 1519–26.* New York: W.W. Norton.

Morse, Dan, and Morse, P. A. 1983. *Archaeology of the Central Mississippi Valley.* New York: Academic Press.

Moseley, Michael. 1975a. "Chan Chan: Andean Alternative to the Preindustrial City." *Science* 187:219–225.

———. 1975b. *The Maritime Foundations of Andean Civilization.* Menlo Park, CA: Cummings.

———. 1985. "The Exploration and Explanation of Early Monumental Architecture in the Andes." In Christopher Donnan, ed., *Early Ceremonial Architecture in the Andes,* pp. 28–58. Washington, DC: Dumbarton Oaks.

———. 1992. *The Incas and their Ancestors.* London and New York: Thames and Hudson.

Moseley, Michael, and Day, Kent C., eds. 1982. *Chan Chan: Andean Desert City.* Albuquerque: University of New Mexico Press.

Movius, Hallam L. 1944. "Early Man and Pleistocene Stratigraphy in South and East Asia." *Papers of the Peabody Museum* 19:3.

———. 1977. *Excavation of the Abri Pataud, Les Eyziés (Dordogne).* Cambridge, MA: Peabody Museum.

Mueller, James A., ed. 1975. *Sampling in Archaeology.* Tucson: University of Arizona Press.

Mughal, R. M. 1974. "New Evidence of the Early Harappan Culture from Jalipur, Pakistan." *Archaeology* 27 (2):106–113.

Muller, Jon D. 1983. "The Southeast." In Jesse D. Jennings, ed., *Ancient Native Americans,* 2d ed, pp. 222–326. San Francisco: Freeman.

———. 1989. "The Southern Cult." In Patricia Galloway, ed., *The Southeastern Ceremonial Complex: Artifacts and Analysis,* pp. 11–26. Lincoln: University of Nebraska Press.

Müller-Beck, Hans-Jurgen. 1982. "Late Pleistocene Man in Northern Eurasia and the Mammoth-Steppe Biome." In David M. Hopkins et al., eds., *Paleoecology of Beringia,* pp. 329–352. New York: Academic Press.

Nelson, Sarah. 1993. *The Archaeology of Korea.* Cambridge, Eng.: Cambridge University Press.

Nilsson, Tage. 1983. *The Pleistocene.* Stuttgart: Enke Verlag.

Nissen, Hans J. 1988. *The Early History of the Near East 9000–2000 B.C.* Chicago: University of Chicago Press.

Nitecki, Matthew H., and Nitecki, Doris V, eds. 1994. *Origins of Anatomically Modern Humans.* New York: Plenum.

Oates, Joan. 1973. "The Background and Development of Early Farming Communities in Mesopotamia and the Zagros." *Proceedings of the Prehistoric Society* 39:147–181.

Oliver, Douglas. 1977. *Ancient Tahitian Society.* Honolulu: University of Hawaii Press.

Olsen, S. J. 1987. "The Practice of Archaeology in China Today." *Antiquity* 61 (232):282–290.

Otto, Martha Potter. 1979. "Hopewell Antecedents in the Adena Heartland." In David C. Brose and N'omi Greber, eds., *Hopewellian Archaeology,* pp. 9–14. Kent, OH: Kent State University Press.

Ovey, C. D., ed. 1964. *The Swanscombe Skull: A Survey of Research on a Pleistocene Site.* London: Royal Anthropological Institute.

Parkington, John. 1987. "Prehistory and Paleoenvironments at the Pleistocene-Holocene Boundary in the Western Cape." In Olga Soffer, ed., *The Pleistocene Old World: Regional Perspectives,* pp. 349–364. New York: Plenum.

Parpola, Asko. 1994. *Deciphering the Indus Script.* Cambridge: Cambridge University Press.

Pearsall, D. 1989. *Paleoethnobotany: A Handbook of Procedures.* Orlando, FL: Academic Press.

Parsons, Lee, and Price, Barbara. 1971. "Mesoamerican Trade and Its Role in the Emergence of Civilization." *Contributions of the University of California Archaeological Research Facility* 11:169–195.

Patterson, Thomas C. 1985. "The Huaca La Florida, Rímac Valley, Peru." In Christopher Donnan, ed., *Early Ceremonial Architecture in the Andes,* pp. 59–70. Washington, DC: Dumbarton Oaks.

Patterson, Thomas. 1992. *The Inca Empire.* London: Berg.

Pearson, Richard J., et al., eds. 1986. *Windows on the Japanese Past: Studies in Archaeology and Prehistory.* Ann Arbor: Center for Japanese Studies, University of Michigan.

Penck, Albrecht, and Brückner, Edward. 1909. *Die Alpen im Eiszeitalter.* Leipzig: Tauchnitz.

Perigrine, Peter N. 1992. *Mississippian Evolution: A World-System Perspective.* Madison, WI: Prehistory Press.

Pfeiffer, John E. 1982. *The Creative Explosion.* New York: Harper & Row.

Phillips, E. D. 1972. "The Scythian Domination in Western Asia." *World Archaeology* 4:129–138.

Phillips, J., and Brown, J. A. eds. 1983. *Archaic Hunter-Gatherers in the Midwest.* Orlando, FL: Academic Press.

Phillips, Patricia. 1980. *The Prehistory of Europe.* Bloomington: Indiana University Press.

Piggott, Stuart. 1965. *Ancient Europe.* Chicago: Aldine.

———. 1992. *Wagon, Chariot, and Carriage.* London and New York: Thames and Hudson.

Pilbeam, David. 1986. "Distinguished Lecture: Hominoid Evolution and Hominoid Origins." *American Anthropologist* 88 (2):295–312.

Plog, Fred T., and Upham, Steadman. 1983. "Analysis of Prehistoric Political Organization." In Elizabeth Tooker, ed., *The Development of Political Organization in Native North America,* pp. 199–213. Washington, DC: American Ethnological Society.

Plomley, N. J. B. 1969. *An Annotated Bibliography of the Tasmanian Aborigines.* London: Royal Anthropological Institute.

Pope, Geoffrey G. 1984. "The Antiquity and Paleoenvironment of the Asian Hominidae." In R. O. I. Whyte, ed., *The Evolution of the East Asian Environment,* pp. 922–947. Hong Kong: Center of Asian Studies, University of Hong Kong.

———. 1989. "Bamboo and Human Evolution." *Natural History* 10 (89):49–56.

Pope, Geoffrey G., et al. 1986. "Earliest Radiometrically Dated Artifacts from Southeast Asia." *Current Anthropology* 27 (3):275–279.

Pope, Michael. 1973. *Decipherment.* London: Thames and Hudson.

Possehl, Gregory L., ed. 1979. *Ancient Cities of the Indus.* Durham: University of North Carolina Press.

———. 1980. *Indus Civilization in Saurashta.* Delhi: B. R. Publishing.

———. 1986. *Kulli.* Durham: University of North Carolina Press.

———. 1993. *Harappan Civilization,* 2nd ed. New Delhi: Oxford and IBH Publishing.

———. and Raval, M. H. 1989. *Harappan Civilization and Rojdi.* New Delhi, India: Oxford and IBH Publishing.

Postgate, Nicholas. 1993. *Early Mesopotamia: Economy and Society at the Dawn of History.* London: Kegan Paul.

Potts, Richard. 1984a. "Home Bases and Early Hominids." *American Scientist* 72:338–347.

———. 1984b. "Hominid Hunters? Problems of Identifying the Earliest Hunter-Gatherers." In Robert Foley, ed., *Hominid Evolution and Community Ecology,* pp. 129–166. London: Academic Press.

Powers, William R., and Hamilton, Thomas D. 1978. "Dry Creek: A Late Pleistocene Human Occupation in Central Alaska." In Alan L. Bryan, ed., *Early Man in America from a Circum-Pacific Perspective,* pp. 72–78. Edmonton: University of Alberta.

Pozorski, Thomas. 1987. "Changing Priorities Within the Chimu State: The Role of Irrigation Agriculture." In Jonathan Haas et al., eds., *The Origins and Development of the Andean State,* pp. 111–120. Cambridge, Eng.: Cambridge University Press.

Pozorski, Thomas, and Pozorski, Sheila. 1987. "Chavín, the Early Horizon, and the Initial Period." In Jonathan Haas et al., eds., *The Origins and Development of the Andean State,* pp. 36–46. Cambridge, Eng.: Cambridge University Press.

Premack, Ann James, and Premack, David. 1972. "Teaching Language to an Ape." *Scientific American* 241 (1):92–99.

Price, T. Douglas. 1983. "The European Mesolithic." *American Antiquity* 48:761–778.

———. 1985. "Foragers of Southern Scandinavia." In T. Douglas Price and James Brown, eds., *Prehistoric Hunter-Gatherers: The Emergence of Cultural Complexity,* pp. 212–236. New York: Academic Press.

———. 1987. "The Mesolithic of Western Europe." *Journal of World Prehistory* 1 (3):225–305.

Price, T. Douglas, and Brown, James, eds. 1985. *Prehistoric Hunter-Gatherers.* New York: Academic Press.

Price, T. Douglas, et al. 1982. "Thermal Alteration in Mesolithic Assemblages." *Proceedings of the Prehistoric Society* 48:467–485.

Protzen, Jean-Pierre. 1986. "Inca Stonemasonry." *Scientific American* 254 (2):94–105.

Proulx, Donald. 1985. "An Analysis of the Early Cultural Sequence in the Nepeña Valley, Peru." *Research Report of Department of Anthropology, University of Massachusetts, Amherst,* no. 25.

Prufer, Olaf. 1964. "The Hopewell Complex of Ohio." In R. Caldwell and R. L. Hall (eds.), *Hopewellian Studies,* pp. 35–84. Springfield, IL: Illinois State Museum.

Quilter, Jeffrey. 1985. "Architecture and Chronology at El Paraíso, Peru." *Journal of Field Archaeology* 12 (3):274–298.

Raab, Mark L., and Goodyear, Albert C. 1984. "Middle Range Theory in Archaeology: A Critical Review of Origins and Applications." *American Antiquity* 49:255–268.

Radiocarbon. 1993. Calibration Issue, 35:215–230.

Raikes, Robert. 1967. *Water, Weather, and Prehistory*. London: Baker.

Rak, Yoel. 1983. *The Australopithecine Face*. New York: Academic Press.

Ramenovsky, Ann. 1987. *Vectors of Death*. Albuquerque: University of New Mexico Press.

Ravensloot, J. C. 1988. *Mortuary Practices and Social Differentiation at Casas Grandes, Chihuahua, Mexico*. Tucson: University of Arizona Press.

Raymond, J. Scott. 1981. "The Maritime Foundations of Andean Civilization: A Reconsideration of the Evidence." *American Antiquity* 46:806–820.

Redman, Charles L. 1978. *The Rise of Civilization: From Early Farmers to Urban Society in the Ancient Near East*. San Francisco: Freeman.

Reeves, Nicholas. 1990. *The Complete Tutankhamun*. New York: Thames and Hudson.

Reilly, Kent. 1991. "Olmec Iconographic Influences on the Symbols of Maya Rulership: An Examination of Possible Sources." In Virginia M. Fields. ed., *Sixth Palenque Round Table, 1986*, pp. 151–174. Norman: University of Oklahoma Press.

Renault, Mary. 1963. *The King Must Die*. New York: Random House.

Renfrew, Colin. 1970. "The Tree-Ring Calibration of Radiocarbon: An Archaeological Evaluation." *Proceedings of the Prehistoric Society* 36:280–311.

———. 1972. *The Emergence of Civilization*. London: Methuen.

———. 1973. *Before Civilization*. New York: Knopf.

———. 1978. "Varna and the Social Context of Early Metallurgy." *Antiquity* 52:199–203.

———. 1983. "The Social Archaeology of Megaliths." *Scientific American* 249:152–163.

———, ed. 1984. *The Megalithic Monuments of Western Europe*. London: Thames and Hudson.

———. 1987. *The Archaeology of Language*. London: Cape.

Renfrew, Colin, and Bahn, Paul. 1991. *Archaeology: A Handbook of Ideas and Methods*. New York: Thames and Hudson.

Renfrew, Colin, Dixon, J. E., and Cann, J. R. 1966. "Obsidian and Early Cultural Contact in the Near East." *Proceedings of the Prehistoric Society* 32:1–29.

Renfrew, Colin, and Shennan, S. J. eds. 1982. *Ranking, Resource and Exchange: Aspects of the Archaeology of Early European Society*. Cambridge, Eng.: Cambridge University Press.

Renfrew, Colin, and Wagstaff, J. M., eds. 1982. *An Island Polity: The Archaeology of Exploitation in Melos*. Cambridge, Eng.: Cambridge University Press.

Reynolds, Robert. 1986. "Computer Simulation." In Kent Flannery, ed., *Guilá Naquitz*, pp. 263–289. Orlando, FL: Academic Press.

Reynolds, T. E. G., and Barnes, G. L. 1984. "The Japanese Palaeolithic: A Review." *Proceedings of the Prehistoric Society* 50:49–62.

Riboud, Marc. 1992. *Angkor*. London and New York: Thames and Hudson.

Rice, Michael. 1993. *The Archaeology of the Arabian Gulf*. London: Routledge.

Rick, John. 1980. *Prehistoric Hunters of the High Andes*. New York: Academic Press.

Ridgeway, David. 1992. *The First Western Greeks*. Cambridge, Eng.: Cambridge University Press.

Rightmire, Philip. 1990. *The Evolution of* Homo erectus. Cambridge, Eng.: Cambridge University Press.

Rindos, David. 1984. *The Origins of Agriculture: An Evolutionary Perspective*. New York: Academic Press.

Rizkana, I., and Seeher, J. 1984. "New Light on the Relation of Maadi to the Upper Egyptian Cultural Sequence." *Mitteilungen des Deutchen Archaologischen Instituts Abteilung Kairo* 40:237–252.

Roberts, M. B., Stringer, C. B., and Parfitt, S. A. 1994. "A Hominid Tibia from Middle Pleistocene Sediments at Boxgrove, UK." *Nature* 369:311–312.

Roberts, Neil. 1989. *The Holocene: An Environmental History*. Oxford: Blackwell.

Roberts, R. G., et al. 1990. "Thermoluminescence Dating of a 50,000-year-old Human Occupation Site in Northern Australia." *Nature* 345:153–156.

Roe, Derek, 1981. *The Lower and Middle Palaeolithic Periods in Britain.* London: Routledge & Kegan Paul.

Rognon, Pierre. 1981. "Interprétation paleoclimatique des changements d'environments en Afrique du Nord et au Moyen Orient durant les 20 derniers millénaires." *Palaeoecology of Africa* 13:21–44.

Rose, M. D. 1984. "Food Acquisition and the Evolution of Primate Behavior: The Case of Bipedalism." In D. J. Chivers et al., eds., *Food Acquisition and Processing in Primates,* pp. 509–524. New York: Plenum.

Rosenberg, Michael, and Davis, Michael K. 1992. "Hallan Çemi Tepesi, An Early Aceramic Neolithic Site in Eastern Anatolia." *Anatolica,* VXIII:1–18.

Rowe, John H. 1946. *Inca Culture at the Time of the Spanish Conquest.* Vol. 2, *Handbook of South American Indians.* Washington, DC: Smithsonian Institution.

———. 1948. "The Kingdom of Chimor." *Acta Americana* 6:26–59.

Rowlett, Ralph. 1967. "The Iron Age North of the Alps." *Science* 161:123–134.

Rowley-Conwy, Peter. 1986. "Between Cave Painters and Crop Planters: Aspects of the Temperate European Mesolithic." In Marek Zvelebil, ed., *Hunters in Transition,* pp. 17–32. Cambridge, Eng.: Cambridge University Press.

Rudenko, Sergei. 1970. *The Frozen Tombs of Siberia: The Pazyryk Burials of Iron Age Horsemen.* Translated by M. W. Thompson. Berkeley and Los Angeles: University of California Press.

Ruffle, John. 1977. *Heritage of the Pharaohs.* Oxford, Eng.: Phaidon.

Sabloff, Jeremy A. 1989. *The Cities of Ancient Mexico.* New York: Thames and Hudson.

———. 1990. *The New Archaeology and the Ancient Maya.* New York: Scientific American Library.

Sabloff, Jeremy A., and Freidel, David A. 1984. *Cozumel: Late Maya Settlement Patterns.* New York: Academic Press.

Sabloff, Jeremy A., and Lamberg-Karlovsky, C. C., eds. 1975. *Ancient Civilization and Trade.* Albuquerque: University of New Mexico Press.

Sahlins, Marshall, and Service, Elman, eds. 1960. *Evolution and Culture.* Ann Arbor: University of Michigan Press.

Sanders, N. K. 1977. *The Sea People.* London: Thames and Hudson.

Sanders, William T. 1965. *The Cultural Ecology of the Tehuacán Valley.* University Park: Pennsylvania State University Press.

Sanders, William T., Parsons, Jeffrey R., and Santley, Robert S. 1979. *The Basin of Mexico: Ecological Processes in the Evolution of a Civilization.* New York: Academic Press.

Sanders, William T., and Price, Barbara J. 1968. *Mesoamerica: The Evolution of a Civilization.* New York: Random House.

Sanders, William T., and Webster, David. 1978. "Unilinealism, Multilinealism, and the Evolution of Complex Societies." In Charles L. Redman et al., eds., *Social Archaeology,* pp. 249–302. New York: Academic Press.

Sanders, William T., et al. 1970. *The Natural Environment: Contemporary Occupation and Sixteenth Century Population of the Valley: Teotihuacán Valley Project Final Report.* University Park: Pennsylvania State University Press.

Sanlaville, Pierre. 1989. "Considérations sur l'évolution de la Basse Mésopotamie au cours des derniers millénaires." *Paleorient* 15 (2):5–27.

Sarich, Vincent. 1983. "Retrospective on Hominoid Macromolecular Systematics." In R. L. Ciochon and R. S. Corrucini, eds., *New Interpretations of Ape and Human Ancestry,* pp. 137–150. New York: Plenum.

Saunders, Nicholas. 1989. *People of the Jaguar.* London: Souvenir Press.

Schele, Linda, and Freidel, D. 1990. *A Forest of Kings.* New York: Morrow.

Schele, Linda, Freidel, David, and Parker, Joy. 1993. *Maya Cosmos.* New York: Morrow.

Schele, Linda, and Miller, E. 1992. *The Blood of Kings.* London and New York: Thames and Hudson.

Schick, Kathy D. 1994. "The Movius Line Reconsidered: Perspectives on the Earlier Paleolithic of Eastern Asia." In Robert S. Corruccini and Russel L. Ciochon, eds., *Integrative Paths to the Past: Paleoanthropological Advances in Honor of F. Clark Howell.* Englewood Cliffs, NJ: Prentice Hall.

Schiffer, M. B. 1983. "Towards the Identification of Site Formation Processes." *American Antiquity* 48:675–706.

———. 1987. *Site Formation Processes of the Archaeological Record.* Orlando, FL: Academic Press.

Schiffer, M. B., and House, John. 1977. *The Cache River Archaeological Project.* Fayetteville: Arkansas Archaeological Survey.

Schledermann, Peter. 1990. *Crossroads to Greenland.* Calgary, Alta.: Arctic Institute of North America.

Schmandt-Besserat, D. 1992. *Before Writing,* 2 vols. Austin: University of Texas Press.

Schreiber, Katharina J. 1987. "Conquest and Consolidation: A Comparison of the Wari and Inka Occupation of a Highland Peruvian Valley." *American Antiquity* 52 (2):266–284.

Scudder, Thayer. 1962. *The Ecology of the Gwembe Tonga.* Manchester, Eng.: Manchester University Press.

———. 1971. *Gathering Among African Woodland Savannah Cultivators.* Lusaka: University of Zambia.

Sebastian, Lynn. 1992. *The Chaco Anasazi: Sociopolitical evolution in the prehistoric Southwest.* Cambridge, Eng.: Cambridge University Press.

Serge, Aldo, and Asconzi, Antonio. 1984. "Italy's Earliest Middle Pleistocene Hominid Site." *Current Anthropology* 25 (2):230–235.

Service, Elman. 1962. *Primitive Social Organization.* New York: Random House.

———. 1975. *The Origins of the State and Civilization.* New York: W. W. Norton.

Shackleton, N. J., and Opdyke, N. D. 1973. "Oxygen Isotope and Paleomagnetic Stratigraphy of Equatorial Pacific Ocean Core V28–238." *Quarternary Research* 3:38–55.

Sharer, Robert. 1989. "Olmec Studies: A Status Report." In Robert Sharer and David Grove, eds., *Regional Perspectives on the Olmec,* pp. 3–7. Cambridge, Eng.: Cambridge University Press.

Sharer, Robert, and Grove, David, eds. 1989. *Regional Perspectives on the Olmec.* Cambridge, Eng.: Cambridge University Press.

Sharer, Robert J., and Ashmore, Wendy. 1992. *Archaeology: Discovering Our Past,* 2nd ed. Mountain View, CA: Mayfield.

Sharman, G. R., et al. 1980. *Beginning of Agriculture.* Allahabad, India: University of Allahabad.

Shawcross, Kathleen. 1967. "Fern Root and Eighteenth-Century Maori Food Production in Agricultural Areas." *Journal of the Polynesian Society* 76:330–352.

Shennan, Stephen J. 1993. "Settlement and Social Change in Central Europe." *Journal of World Prehistory* 7 (2):121–162.

Sherratt, Andrew G. 1981. "Plough and Pasture." In Ian Hodder et al., eds., *Patterns of the Past,* pp. 344–361. Cambridge, Eng.: Cambridge University Press.

Shinnie, Peter. 1967. *Meroe.* London: Thames and Hudson.

Shipman, Pat. 1984. "Scavenger Hunt." *Natural History* 93 (4):20–28.

Shipman, Pat, and Rose, J. 1983. "Evidence of Butchery and Hominid Activities at Torralba and Ambrona." *Journal of Archaeological Studies* 10 (5):475–482.

Silverberg, Robert. 1968. *The Mound Builders of Ancient America.* New York: New York Graphic Society.

Simons, Elwyn. 1984. "Dawn Ape of the Fayum." *Natural History* 93 (5):18–20.

Singer, Ronald, et al. 1973. "Clacton-on-Sea, Essex: Report on Excavations 1969–1970." *Proceedings of the Prehistoric Society* 39:6–74.

Smith, Andrew B. 1992. *Pastoralism in Africa.* Johannesburg: Witwatersrand University Press.

Smith, Bruce D. ed. 1978a. *Mississippian Settlement Patterns.* New York: Academic Press.

———. 1978b. "Variations in Mississippian Settlement Patterns." In Bruce D. Smith, ed., *Mississippian Settlement Patterns,* pp. 479–503. New York: Academic Press.

———. 1986. "The Archaeology of the Southeastern United States: From Dalton to De Soto, 10,500–500 B.P." *Advances in World Archaeology* 5:1–92.

———. 1992. *Rivers of Change.* Washington DC: Smithsonian Institution Press.

———. 1994. *The Emergence of Agriculture.* New York: Scientific American Library.

Smith, M. T. 1987. *Archaeology of Aboriginal Culture Change in the Interior Southeast.* Gainesville, FL: University of Florida Presses.

Smith, P. E. L. 1978. "An Interim Report on Ganj Dareh Tepe, Iran." *American Journal of Archaeology* 82:538–540.

Snow, Dean. 1980. *Archaeology of New England.* New York: Academic Press.

Soffer, Olga. 1985. *The Upper Palaeolithic of the Central Russian Plains.* New York: Academic Press.

———. 1987. "Upper Palaeolithic Connubia, Refugia, and the Archaeological Record from Eastern Europe." In Olga Soffer, ed., *The Pleistocene Old World,* pp. 333–348. New York: Plenum Press.

———. 1993. "Upper Paleolithic Adaptations in Central and Eastern Europe and Man-Mammoth Interactions." In Olga Soffer and N.D. Praslov eds., *From Kostenki to Clovis,* pp. 31–47. New York: Plenum Press.

Soffer, Olga, and Gamble, Clive, eds. 1990. *The World in 18,000 B.P.* Edinburgh: Edinburgh University Press.

Spivey, N., and Stoddart, S. 1990. *The Etruscans.* London: Batsford.

Spooner, Brian, ed. 1972. *Population Growth: An Anthropological Perspective.* Cambridge, MA: MIT Press.

Spriggs, Matthew. 1989. "Dating the Island Southeast Asian Neolithic." *Antiquity* 63 (240):587–613.

Spriggs, Matthew, and Anderson, Atholl. 1993. "Late Colonization of Eastern Polynesia." *Antiquity* 67:200–217.

Stahl, Ann Bower. 1984. "Hominid Dietary Selection Before Fire." *Current Anthropology* 25 (2):151–168.

Stark, Barbara. 1986. "Origins of Food Production in the New World." In David Meltzer et al., eds., *American Archaeology Past and Future,* pp. 277–322. Washington, DC: Smithsonian Institution.

Starling, N. J. 1985. "Colonization and Success: The Earlier Neolithic of Central Europe." *Proceedings of the Prehistoric Society* 51:41–57.

Steinkeller, P. 1989. *Sales Documents of the Ur III Period.* Stuttgart, Germany: Steiner Verlag.

Stephens, John Lloyd. 1841. *Incidents of Travel in Central America, Chiapas, and Yucatan.* New York: Harpers.

Steponaitis, V. 1986. "Prehistoric Archaeology in the Southeastern United States 1970–1985." *Annual Review of Anthropology* 15:363–404.

Steward, Julian. 1970. *A Theory of Culture Change.* Urbana: University of Illinois Press.

Steward, Julian, et al. 1955. *Irrigation Civilizations: A Comparative Study.* Washington, DC: Pan American Union.

Stoltman, J. B. ed. 1992. *New Perspectives on Cahokia: Views from the Periphery.* Madison, WI: Prehistory Press.

Stoltman, J. B., and Barreis, D. A. 1983. "The Evolution of Human Ecosystems in the Eastern and Central United States." In H. E. Wright, ed., *The Holocene.* Vol. 2, *Late Quaternary Environments of the United States,* pp. 252–268. Minneapolis: University of Minnesota Press.

Storey, Rebecca. 1992. *Life and Death in the Ancient City of Teotihuacán.* Birmingham: University of Alabama Press.

Stringer, C. B. 1984. "Human Evolution and Biological Adaptation in the Pleistocene." In Robert Foley, ed., *Human Evolution and Community Ecology,* pp. 55–84. London: Academic Press.

Stringer, C. B., et al. 1979. "The Significance of the Fossil Hominid from Petralona, Greece." *Journal of Archaeological Science* 6:235–253.

———. 1984. "The Origin of Anatomically Modern Humans in Western Europe." In Fred Smith and Frank Spencer, eds., *The Origins of Modern Humans,* pp. 51–136. New York: Liss.

Stringer, Christopher, and Gamble, Clive. 1993. *The Search for the Neanderthals*. London: Thames and Hudson.

Struever, Stuart, and Holton, Felicia Antonelli. 1979. *Koster: Americans in Search of Their Past*. New York: Anchor Press/Doubleday.

Suess, Hans. 1965. "Secular Variations of the Cosmic-Ray-Produced Carbon 14 in the Atmosphere." *Journal of Geophysical Research* 70:23–31.

Swisher, Carl, and others. 1994. "Age of the Earliest Known Hominids in Java, Indonesia." *Science* 263:1118–1121.

Tainter, Joseph. 1988. *The Collapse of Civilizations*. Cambridge, Eng.: Cambridge University Press.

Taylour, Lord William. 1990. *The Mycenaeans*, 2d ed. London: Thames and Hudson.

Telegin, D. J. 1987. "Neolithic Cultures of the Ukraine and Adjacent Areas and Their Chronology." *Journal of World Prehistory* 1 (3):307–331.

Terrace, H., Petitto, L., Sanders, R., and Bever, T. 1979. "Can an Ape Create a Sentence?" *Science* 206:891–902.

Terrell, John. 1988. *Prehistory in the Pacific Islands*. Cambridge, Eng.: Cambridge University Press.

Thomas, David. 1989. *Archaeology*, 2nd ed. New York: Holt, Rinehart & Winston.

Thomas, David, and Bettinger, Robert. 1983. *The Archaeology of the Monitor Valley*. New York: American Museum of Natural History.

Thomas, Julian. 1987. "Relations of Production and Social Change in the Neolithic of Northwestern Europe." *Man* 22 (3):405–430.

Tobias, P.V. 1991. *Olduvai Gorge, volume 4: Homo habilis*. Cambridge, Eng.: Cambridge University Press.

Torrance, Robin. 1986. *Production and Exchange*. Cambridge, Eng.: Cambridge University Press.

Tosi, Maurizo, ed. 1983. *Prehistoric Sistan I*. Rome: ISMEO.

Toth, Nicholas. 1985. "The Oldowan Reconsidered: A Close Look at Early Stone Artifacts." *Journal of Archaeological Science* 12:101–120.

Toth, Nicholas, and Schick, K. D. 1986. "The First Million Years: The Archeology of Protohuman Culture." *Advances in Archeological Method and Theory* 9:1–96.

——— 1993. *Making Silent Stones Speak: Human Evolution and the Dawn of Technology*. New York: Simon and Schuster.

Townsend, Richard F. 1992. *The Aztecs*. London and New York: Thames and Hudson.

Toynbee, Arnold. 1962. *The Study of History*. Oxford, Eng.: Oxford University Press.

Trigger, Bruce G. 1989. *A History of Archaeological Thought*. Cambridge, Eng.: Cambridge University Press.

Trigger, Bruce D. 1991. "Distinguished Lecture in Archaeology: Constraint and Freedom." *American Anthropologist* 93 (3):551–569.

Trigger, Bruce G., et al. 1983. *Ancient Egypt: A Social History*. Cambridge, Eng.: Cambridge University Press.

Tringham, Ruth. 1971. *Hunters, Fishers, and Farmers of Eastern Europe: 6000–3000 B.C.* London: Hutchinson University Library.

Tringham, Ruth, et al. 1980. "The Early Agricultural Site of Selevac, Yugoslavia." *Archaeology* 33 (2):24–32.

Trinkaus, Erik, ed. 1983a. *The Mousterian Legacy*. Oxford, Eng.: British Archaeological Reports, International Series, No. 151.

———. 1983b. *The Shanidar Neanderthals*. New York: Academic Press.

Trinkaus, Erik, and Howells, W. W. 1979. "The Neanderthals." *Scientific American* 241:118–133.

———, and Shipman, Pat. 1992. *The Neanderthals: Changing the Image of Mankind*. New York: Alfred A. Knopf.

Turner, Christy. 1984. "Advances in the Dental Search for Native American Origins." *Acta Anthropogenetica* 8:23–78.

Tuttle, Russell, ed. 1972. *The Functional and Evolutionary Biology of Primates*. Chicago: Aldine-Atherton.

Tylor, Edward. 1871. *Anthropology.* London: Macmillan.

Upham, Steadman, et al. 1987. "Evidence Concerning the Origin of Maize de Ocho." *American Anthropologist* 89 (3):410–419.

Vavilov, N. I. 1951. "Phytogeographic Basis of Plant Breeding." *Chronica Botanica* 13:14–54.

Vickers, Michael. 1977. *The Roman World.* Oxford, Eng.: Elsevier Phaidon.

Villa, Paola. 1983. *Terra Amata and the Middle Pleistocene Archaeological Record of Southern France.* Berkeley and Los Angeles: University of California Press.

Vinnecombe, Patricia. 1976. *People of the Eland.* Pietermaritzburg: Natal University Press.

Walker, Alan. 1981. "Dietary Hypotheses and Human Evolution." *Philosophical Transactions of the Royal Society of London* 292:56–64.

Wallerstein, Immanuel. 1974. *The Modern World System.* New York: Academic Press.

Warren, Peter. 1975. *The Aegean Civilizations.* Oxford, Eng.: Elsevier Phaidon.

———. 1984. "Knossos: New Excavations and Discoveries." *Archaeology* 37 (4):48–57.

Watson, Patty Jo, LeBlanc, Steven, and Redman, Charles L. 1984. *Archeological Explanation: The Scientific Method in Archeology.* New York: Columbia University Press.

Wauchope, Robert. 1962. *Lost Tribes and Sunken Continents.* Chicago: University of Chicago Press.

Weaver, Muriel Porter. 1991. *The Aztecs, Maya, and Their Predecessors,* 3d ed. New York: Academic Press.

Webb, Clarence H. 1968. "The Extent and Content of Poverty Point Culture." *American Antiquity* 33:297–331.

Webb, W. S. 1974. *Indian Knoll,* new ed. Knoxville: University of Tennessee Press.

Weiss, Harvey, ed. 1986. *The Origins of Cities in Dry-Farming Syria and Mesopotamia in the Third Millennium B.C.* Guildford, CT: Four Quarters Publishers.

Weiss, Mark L., and Mann, Alan E. 1988. *Human Biology and Behavior,* 5th ed. Boston: Scott, Foresman/Little, Brown.

Wells, Peter. 1981. *Culture Contact and Culture Change.* Cambridge, Eng.: Cambridge University Press.

———. 1984. "Early Iron Age Community in Central Europe." *Scientific American* 249 (6):68–93.

Wendorf, Fred, ed. 1968. *The Prehistory of Nubia.* Dallas, TX: Southern Methodist University Press.

Wendorf, Fred, and Schild, Romuald. 1980. *Prehistory of the Eastern Sahara.* New York: Academic Press.

Wendorf, Fred, Schild, Romuald, and Close, Angela E. 1980 *Loaves and Fishes: The Prehistory of Wadi Kubbaniya.* Dallas: Department of Anthropology, Southern Methodist University.

Wendorf, Fred, et al., eds. 1984. *Cattle Keepers of the Eastern Sahara: The Neolithic of Bir Kiseiba.* Dallas, TX: Southern Methodist University Press.

Wenke, R. J. 1991a. *Patterns in Prehistory.* New York: Oxford University Press.

———. 1991b. "The Evolution of Early Egyptian Civilization: Issues and Evidence," *Journal of World Prehistory* 5(3): 279–329.

Wenke, R. J., Long, J. E., and Buck, Paul E. 1988. "Epipaleolithic and Neolithic Settlement in the Fayyum Oasis of Egypt." *Journal of Field Archaeology* 15 (1):29–51.

Wertime, Theodore A., and Muhly, James D., eds. 1980. *The Coming of the Age of Iron.* New Haven, CT: Yale University Press.

Wheat, Joe Ben. 1972. *The Olsen-Chubbock Site.* Washington, DC: Society for American Archaeology.

Wheatley, Paul. 1971. *The Pivot of the Four Quarters.* Chicago: Aldine.

———. 1975. "Satyarta in Suvarnadvípa: From Reciprocity to Redistribution in Ancient Southeast Asia." In Jeremy A. Sabloff and C. C. Lamberg-Karlovsky, eds., *Ancient Civilization and Trade,* pp. 227–284. Albuquerque: University of New Mexico Press.

———. 1979. "Urban Genesis in Mainland Southeast Asia." In R. B. Smith and W. Watson, eds., *Early Southeast Asia.* pp. 288–303. Oxford, Eng.: Oxford University Press.

———. 1980. *Kings of the Mountain.* Kuala Lumpur: University of Malaysia Press.

Wheeler, Sir Mortimer. 1954. *Archaeology from the Earth*. Oxford, Eng.: Clarendon Press.
———. 1955. *Still Digging*. London: Michael Joseph.
———. 1962. *The Indus Civilization,* 2d ed. Cambridge, Eng.: Cambridge University Press.
White, Joyce C. 1982. *Ban Chiang: The Discovery of a Lost Bronze Age Civilization*. Philadelphia: University of Pennsylvania Press.
White, J. P., Allen, J., and Specht, J. 1988. "The Lapita Homeland Project." *Australian Natural History* 22 (9):410–416.
White, J. Peter, and O'Connell, James. 1982. *A Prehistory of Australia, New Guinea, and Sahul*. Sydney: Academic Press.
White, Leslie. 1949. *The Science of Culture*. New York: Grove.
White, Randall. 1982. "Rethinking the Middle/Upper Paleolithic Transition." *Current Anthropology* 23 (2):169–191.
———. 1986. *Dark Caves and Bright Visions*. New York: American Museum of Natural History.
Whitelaw, K. W., and Coote, R. B. 1987. *The Emergence of Israel in Historical Perspective*. Sheffield, Eng.: Almond Press.
Whittle, Alasdair. 1985. *Neolithic Europe: A Survey*. Cambridge, Eng.: Cambridge University Press.
Wickler, Stephen, and Spriggs, Matthew. 1988. "Pleistocene Occupation of the Solomons." *Antiquity* 62 (237):703–707.
Wilk, R. R., and Ashmore, Wendy, eds. 1987. *House and Household in the Mesoamerican Past*. Albuquerque: University of New Mexico Press.
Willey, Gordon R. 1953. *Prehistoric Settlement in the Virú Valley, Peru*. Washington, DC: Smithsonian Institution.
———. 1963. *The Archaeology of the Virú Valley, Peru*. Cambridge, Eng.: Peabody Museum.
———. 1966. *North and Middle America*. Vol. 1, *An Introduction to American Archaeology*. Englewood Cliffs, NJ: Prentice Hall.
———. 1971. *South America*. Vol. 2, *An Introduction to American Archaeology*. Englewood Cliffs, NJ: Prentice Hall.
Wills, S. H. 1989. *Early Prehistoric Agriculture in the American Southwest*. Santa Fe, NM: School of American Research.
Wilson, David J. 1981. "Of Maize and Men: A Critique of the Maritime Hypothesis of State Origins on the Coast of Peru." *American Anthropologist* 83:931–940.
———. 1983. "The Origins and Development of Complex Prehispanic Society in the Lower Santa Valley, Peru: Implications for Theories of State Origins." *Journal of Anthropological Archaeology* 2:209–276.
Wilson, Edward O. 1980. *Sociobiology: The Abridged Edition*. Cambridge, MA: Harvard University Press.
Windels, Ferdinand. 1965. *The Lascaux Cave Paintings*. London: Faber & Faber.
Winters, Howard. 1967. *The Riverton Culture*. Springfield: Illinois State Museum.
Wittfogel, Karl W. 1957. *Oriental Despotism: A Comparative Study of Total Power*. New Haven, CT: Yale University Press.
Wolf, Eric. 1984. *Europe and the People Without History*. Berkeley: University of California Press.
Wolpert, Stanley A. 1977. *A New History of India*. London: Oxford University Press.
Wolpoff, Milford H. 1984. "Multiregional evolution: the fossil alternative to Eden." In P. Mellars and C. Stringer, eds., *The Human Revolution,* vol. 1, pp. 62–108. Edinburgh: Edinburgh University Press.
Woolley, Sir Leonard. 1934. *The Royal Cemetery*. Vol. 2, *Ur Excavations*. London: British Museum.
Wright, Gary. 1971. "Origins of Food Production in Southwestern Asia: A Survey of Ideas." *Current Anthropology* 12:447–478.
Wright, H. T. 1993. "Environmental Determinism in Near Eastern Prehistory." *Current Anthropology* 34:458–469.

Wright H. T., and Pollock, Susan. 1986. "Regional Socio-Economic Organization in Southern Mesopotamia: The Middle and Late 5th Millennium." *Prehistoire de la Mesopotamie,* pp. 317–329.

Wright, R. V. S. 1977. *Stone Tools as Cultural Markers.* Canberra: Australian Institute of Aboriginal Studies.

Wylie, Alison. 1985. "The Reaction Against Analogy." *Advances in Archaeological Method and Theory* 8:63–111.

Wynn, T., and McGrew, W. C. 1989. "An Ape's View of the Oldowan." *Man* 24 (3):383–398.

Yellen, John E. 1977. *Archaeological Approaches to the Present.* New York: Academic Press.

Yerkes, Richard. 1988. "The Woodland and Mississippian Traditions in the Prehistory of Midwestern North America." *Journal of World Prehistory* 2 (3):307–358.

Yoffee, Norman. 1991. "Maya Elite Interaction: Through a Glass Sideways." In Patrick T. Culbert, ed., *Classic Maya Political History,* pp. 285–310.

Zohary, D., and Hopf, Marie. 1988. *Domestication of Plants in the Old World.* Oxford, Eng.: Clarendon Press.

Zvelebil, Marek, ed. 1986. *Hunters in Transition.* Cambridge, Eng.: Cambridge University Press.

Zvelebil, Marek, and Dolukhanov, Paul M. 1991. "The Transition to Farming in Eastern and Northern Europe." *Journal of World Prehistory* 5 (3):233–278.

Zvelebil, Marek, and Rowley-Conwy, Peter, eds. 1984. "Transition to Farming in Northern Europe: A Hunter-Gatherer Perspective." *Norwegian Archaeological Records* 17:104–128.

CREDITS

• • •

page ii: Granger.

CHAPTER 1

Figure 1.1: Photography by Egyptian Expedition. The Metropolitan Museum of Art. **page 4 top left:** © Georgia, Photo Researchers. **page 4 top right:** © Tortoli, Photo Researchers. **page 4 bottom left:** Reprinted courtesy of The Colonial Williamsburg Foundation. **page 4 bottom right:** © Rakoczy, Photo Researchers. **page 5 top left:** Reprinted courtesy of The University of California/W. Swalling photographer. **page 5 top right:** Reprinted courtesy of The University Museum, University of Pennsylvania/Nick Hartman photographer. **page 5 bottom left:** © Wolfgang Kaehler. **page 5 bottom right:** Photo by D. C. Ochsner, © UCLA Institute of Archaeology and JoAnne Van Tilburg, Director Moai Documentation Project, Easter Island 1984. **Figure 1.2:** © British Museum. **Figure 1.3:** Barkley, Union County Advocate/Kentucky Heritage Council. **Figure 1.6:** From *Invitation to Archaeology* by James Deetz. Copyright © 1967 by James Deetz. Reprinted by permission of Doubleday, a division of Bantam, Doubleday, Dell Publishing Group, Inc. **Figure 1.7 left:** Vida Freeman/Earthwatch. **Figure 1.7 right:** Courtesy of the Society of Antiquaries of London. **Figure 1.8:** From *Invitation to Archaeology* by James Deetz. Copyright © 1967 by James Deetz. Reprinted by permission of Doubleday, a division of Bantam, Doubleday, Dell Publishing Group, Inc. **Figure 1.9:** Shostak, Anthro-Photo. **Figure 1.11:** Museum of Anthropology, University of Michigan. **Figure 1.12:** Reproduced with permission from Colin Renfrew and Paul Bahn, *Archaeology: Theories, Methods, and Practice,* Thames and Hudson, London and New York 1991.

CHAPTER 2

Figure 2.2: From Alison Jolly. 1985. *The Evolution of Primate Behavior.* New York: Macmillan. Used by permission of the author. **Figure 2.3:** Redrawn with permission of Macmillan Publishing Co., Inc. from *The Ascent of Man* by David Pilbeam. Copyright © 1972 by David Pilbeam. **Figure 2.4c:** Redrawn with permission Bantam Books, Inc. from *Monkeys and Apes* by Prudence Napier, copyright © 1972. All rights reserved. **Figure 2.5:** Photograph by courtesy of the Transvaal Museum, South Africa. **Figure 2.6:** Courtesy of Alan R. Hughes, University of Witwatersrand. **Figure 2.7:** Institute of Human Origins. **Figure 2.8:** Photograph by John Reader, courtesy of Mary Leakey. **Figure 2.9:** © Copyright held by The National Museums of Kenya, P.O. Box 40658, Nairobi, Kenya. **Figure 2.10:** Institute of Human Origins. **Figure 2.12:** Robert Foley/Antiquity Publications Ltd. **Figure 2.13:** Henry T. Bunn. **Figure 2.14:** Photographed by Hugo van Lawick © National Geographic Society. **Figure 2.15:** From *Life Nature Library/Early Man.* Redrawn from Lowell Hess © 1980

Time-Life Books Inc. **Figure 2.16 top:** From *Life Nature Library/Early Man.* Redrawn from Lowell Hess © 1980 Time-Life Books Inc. **Figure 2.16 bottom:** Adapted by permission from *Olduvai Gorge: Excavations in Beds I and II* by M. D. Leakey, © 1971, Cambridge University Press. **Figure 2.17:** From John Gowlett in Robert Foley, ed., *Hominid Evolution and Community Ecology* (New York: Academic Press), 1984, p. 176.

CHAPTER 3

Figure 3.1a: From N. J. Shackleton and N. D. Opdyke, "Oxygen Isotope and Paleomagnetic Stratigraphy of Equatorial Pacific Ocean Core V28-238," in *Quaternary Research* 3:38–55. Reprinted by permission. **Figure 3.1b:** After Flint. 1971. *Glacial and Quaternary Geology.* New York: Wiley. Adapted by permission of John Wiley & Sons. **Figure 3.2:** S. Mutara, National Museum of Kenya. **Figure 3.3:** Cambridge Museum of Archaeology and Anthropology. **Figure 3.4:** From John Gowlett in Robert Foley, ed., *Hominid Evolution and Community Ecology* (New York: Academic Press), 1984, p. 176. **Figure 3.5a:** AP/Wide World. **Figure 3.5b:** From H. L. Movius, Jr., "The Lower Paleolithic Structures of Southern and Eastern Asia," *Transactions of the American Philosophical Society,* Vol. 38, Pt. 4 (1948). Reprinted by permission of the Society and the author. **Figure 3.6:** © Brake, Photo Researchers. **Figure 3.7 top:** From Grahame Clark, *Aspects of Prehistory.* Copyright © 1970 by the Regents of the University of California. Reprinted by permission of the University of California Press. **Figure 3.7 bottom:** Redrawn by permission from Ronald Singer et al., "Excavation of the Clactonian Industry," *Proceedings of the Prehistoric Society,* by permission of the Society. **Figure 3.8 top:** From John Gowlett in Robert Foley, ed., *Hominid Evolution and Community Ecology* (New York: Academic Press), 1984, Figs. 7.3, 7.5, and 7.6. **Figure 3.10a:** Acheulian hand ax from Figure 26 *The Swanscombe Skull: A Survey of Research on Pleistocene Site* (Occasional Paper No. 20, Royal Anthropological Institute of Great Britain and Ireland), by permission of the Society. **Figure 3.10b:** From *The Distribution of Prehistoric Culture in Angola* by J. D. Clark, Companhia de Diamantes de Angola, Africa, 1966. **Figure 3.11:** Courtesy of F. Clark Howell. **Figure 3.12:** Karl Butzer, *Environment and Archaeo-logy,* Cambridge University Press, 1982. Reprinted with permission of Cambridge University Press. **Figure 3.13:** By permission of Henry de Lumley, Laboratoire de Paléontologie Humaine et de Préhistoire, Marseilles. **Figure 3.15:** Drawings by Janis Cirulis from *Mankind in the Making* by William Howells. Copyright © 1959, 1967 by William Howells. Reprinted by permission of Doubleday, a division of Bantam, Doubleday, Dell Publishing Group, Inc. **Figure 3.16:** From John Gowlett in Robert Foley, ed., *Hominid Evolution and Community Ecology* (New York: Academic Press), 1984, p. 176. **Figure 3.17:** Drawings by Janis Cirulis from *Mankind in the Making* by William Howells. Copyright © 1959, 1967 by William Howells. Reprint-ed by permission of Doubleday, a division of Bantam, Doubleday, Dell Publishing Group, Inc. **Figure 3.20:** From Jacques Bordaz, *Tools of the Old and New Stone Age,* copyright 1970 by Jacques Bordaz. Copyright © 1958 by the American Museum of Natural History. Reprinted by permission of the author. **Figure 3.21 bottom left:** Adapted from *Prehistory of Africa* by J. D. Clark, Thames and Hudson Ltd., London. **Figure 3.21 bottom right:** Redrawn from J. M. Coles and E. S. Higgs, *The Archaeology of Early Man* by permission of Faber and Faber Ltd.

CHAPTER 4

Figure 4.2: From Karl W. Butzer, *Environment and Archaeology,* 2nd edition (Hawthorne, NY: Aldine Publishing Company), 1971. Reprinted by permission of the author. **Figure 4.3:** Chris Stinger, The Natural History Museum. **Figure 4.4:** Nationalmuseet, Denmark. **Figure 4.5:** Topham/The Image Works. **Figure 4.6:** Adapted by permission from the following sources: H. Breuil; *Le Paléolithique* *supérieur en Périgord* by Denise de Sonneville-Bordes, Directeur de recherches au Centre national de la Recherche scientifique, Institut du Quaternaire, Université de Bordeaux; Lowell Hess, *Early Man,* Life Nature Library, © 1965 Time Inc. by permission of the publisher, Time-Life Books Inc.; *The Old Stone Age* by F. Bordes. Copyright © 1968 by McGraw-Hill, Inc. Used with permission of McGraw-Hill Book Company and Weidenfeld & Nicolson Ltd; and Jacques Bordaz, *Tools of the Old and New Stone Age,* Copyright 1970 by Jacques Bordaz. Reprinted by permission. **Figure 4.7:** Ulmer Museum. **Figure 4.8:** Collection Musée de l'Homme. **Figure 4.9:** Collection Musée de l'Homme. **Figure 4.10:** Coxe, American Museum of Natural History. **Figure 4.11:** Collection Musée de l'Homme. **Figure 4.12:** © Alexander Marshack, 1972. **Figure 4.13:** Stringer, Christopher, and Gambe, *The Search for the Neanderthals,* Thames and Hudson Ltd., 1993. **Figure 4.14:** From O. Soffer, *The Upper Paleolithic of the Central Russian Plain,* Academic Press, 1985, Fig. 2.67. Reprinted with permission of Academic Press and the author. **Figure 4.15:** Reprinted with permission of Faber and Faber Ltd. From J. M. Coles and E. S. Higgs, *The Archaeology of Early Man.* **Figure 4.16:** From C. B. M. McBurney, *Early Man in the Soviet Union,* Fig. 6, p. 44. Published by Oxford University Press for The British Academy; from the Proceedings of the British Academy, Volume LXI, 1975.

CHAPTER 5
Figure 5.1: Adapted from Fekri Hassan. 1981. *Demographic Archaeology.* Orlando. Academic Press. Adapted by permission. **Figure 5.2:** From Jacques Bordaz, *Tools of the Old and New Stone Age.* Copyright 1970 by Jacques Bordaz. Reprinted by permission. **Figure 5.3:** Stark Museum of Art, Orange, Texas. **Figure 5.4:** Courtesy of the Smithsonian Institution. Photo No. T13301. **Figure 5.5:** South African Archeological Bulletin and Professor V. Riet Lowe. **Figure 5.7:** WSU Hoko River Archaeological Project. **Figure 5.9:** Nationalmuseet, Denmark. **Figure 5.10:** From O. Bar-Yosef and A. Belfar-Cohen. 1989. "The Origins of Sedentism and Farming Communities in the Levant." *Journal of World Prehistory* 3(4):460. Used by permission of Plenum Publishing Corporation. **Figure 5.11:** From Donald O. Henry. 1989. From *Foraging to Agriculture: The Levant at the End of the Ice Age.* Philadelphia: University of Pennsylvania Press. Used by permission. **Figure 5.12 left:** Redrawn from D. A. E. Garrod and D. M. A. Bate, *The Stone Age of M. Carmel* by permission of Oxford University Press. **Figure 5.12 right:** From James Mellaart, *The Earliest Civilizations of the Near East.* Reprinted by permission of Thames and Hudson Ltd., London.

CHAPTER 6
Figure 6.2: Redrawn with permission of the Glencoe Press from *Foundations of Archeology* by Jason W. Smith. Copyright © 1976 by Jason W. Smith. **Figure 6.3:** From Brian M. Fagan, *The Great Journey* (London: Thames and Hudson), 1987, p. 93. **Figure 6.4:** Tom D. Dillehay. **Figure 6.5:** University of Arizona Museum. **Figure 6.6:** Courtesy of University of Colorado Museum, Joe Ben Wheat photo. **Figure 6.7:** Redrawn by permission of McGraw-Hill Book Company from *PreHistory of North America* by Jesse D. Jennings. **Figure 6.8:** Drawing by Thomas R. Whyte. Courtesy of The Frank H. McClung Museum, The University of Tennessee, Knoxville. **Figure 6.9:** From Brian M. Fagan, *The Great Journey* (London: Thames and Hudson), 1987, p. 162. **Figure 6.10:** Field Museum of Natural History (Neg. #953.5.73.6), Chicago. **Figure 6.11:** University of Alaska Museum.

CHAPTER 7
Figure 7.2: *South African Archaeological Bulletin* and Murray Schoonraal. **Figure 7.3:** Paul den Hoed and Thomas A. Dowson, Rozk Art Research Unit, University of Witwatersrand. **Figure 7.4:** Marshall/!Kung San Foundation. **Figure 7.5:** F. Peron. **Figure 7.6:** Reproduced with permission of the publishers from Bellwood, P.,

Prehistory of the Indo-Malaysian Archipelago, Academic Press, Sydney, Australia, 1985. **Figure 7.8:** Reprinted by permission from *Nature,* Vol. 324, pp. 453–455. Copyright © 1986 Macmillan Magazines Limited. **Figure 7.9:** Stephen Wickler. **Figure 7.11:** Australian Information Service. **Figure 7.13:** Rudy Frank, Courtesy R. F. Cosgrove. **Figure 7.14:** Redrawn by permission from Richard A. Gould, "The Archaeologist as Ethnographer," *World Archeology* 3,2 (1971), 143–177, Fig. 18.

CHAPTER 8

Figure 8.1: A. I. Richards, Royal Anthropological Institute © 1935. **Figure 8.2:** Adapted by permission from *The Material Culture of the People of the Gwembe Valley* by Dr. Barrie Reynolds, published by Manchester University Press for the Livingstone Museum, Zambia. **Figure 8.3:** From Roger Lewin, *Human Evolution,* Blackwell Scientific Publications Ltd., 1984. Reprinted by permission. **Figure 8.4:** S. von Herbenstain. **Figure 8.5:** Used by permission of Dr. Gordon Hillman. **Figure 8.6:** Used by permission of Dr. Gordon Hillman. **Figure 8.7 top:** Wyatt Davis, Courtesy of Museum of New Mexico (Neg. 44191). **Figure 8.7 bottom left:** Tyler Dingee, Courtesy of Museum of New Mexico (Neg. 73453). **Figure 8.7 bottom right:** Tyler Dingee, Courtesy of Museum of New Mexico (Neg. 73449). **Figure 8.8:** Reproduced courtesy of the Trustees of The British Museum.

CHAPTER 9

Figure 9.2: Courtesy of Tell Abu Hureyra excavation. **Figure 9.4:** British School of Archaeology in Jerusalem. **Figure 9.5:** Peter Dorrell & Stuart Laidlaw, Institute of Archaeology, University of London. **Figure 9.6:** Redrawn from James Mellaart, *Çatal Hüyük* by permission of Thames and Hudson Ltd., London. **Figure 9.7:** Redrawn from James Mellaart, *Çatal Hüyük* by permission of Thames and Hudson Ltd., London.

CHAPTER 10

Figure 10.1: From *Proceedings of the Prehistoric Society* by permission of the Society. **Figure 10.3:** From *Prehistory* by Derek Roe, with permission of the Biologisch-Archaeologisch Institut der Rijksuniveristeit Groningen, the Netherlands. **Figure 10.4:** From Grahame Clark, *World Prehistory,* 3rd ed., p. 140: © 1977 Cambridge University Press. **Figure 10.5:** The China Friendship Society: from Grahame Clark, *World Prehistory,* 3rd edition, © 1977 Cambridge University Press. **Figure 10.6:** From *Prehistory* by Derek Roe, with permission of Presses Universitaires de France. **Figure 10.7:** Neg. #39604, Courtesy Department of Library Services, American Museum of Natural History. **Figure 10.8:** Redrawn from *Ancient Europe* by Stuart Piggott, with permission of Edinburgh University Press. Copyright © Stuart Piggott, 1965.

CHAPTER 11

Figure 11.1: Chris Scarre, The McDonald Institute for Archaeological Research.

CHAPTER 12

Figure 12.2: C. F. W. Higham. **Figure 12.4:** Reprinted by permission from *The Archaeology of Ancient China,* 3rd ed. by Kwang-chih Chang (New Haven: Yale University Press, 1977). **Figure 12.5:** Reprinted by permission from *The Archaeology of Ancient China,* 3rd ed. by Kwang-chih Chang (New Haven: Yale University Press, 1977). **Figure 12.6:** Reprinted by permission from *The Archaeology of Ancient China,* 3rd ed. by Kwang-chih Chang (New Haven: Yale University Press, 1977). **Figure 12.8:** Scala/Art Resource, N.Y. **Figure 12.10:** Courtesy of Professor R. C. Green. **Figure 12.11:** Field Museum of Natural History (Neg. #100629), Chicago. **Figure 12.12:** Courtesy of The British Library.

CHAPTER 13

Figure 13.1: Reprinted by permission from *Prehistoric Food Production in North America,* ed. by Richard Ford, University of Michigan Museum of Anthropology. **Figure 13.3:** Courtesy R. S. Peabody Foundation for Archaeology, Andover, Mass. **Figure 13.4:** Photo by Thomas F. Lynch. **Figure 13.5:** From Gordon R. Willey, *An Introduction to American Archaeology Vol. II: South America,* © 1971. Reprinted by permission of Prentice Hall Inc., Englewood Cliffs, N.J. **Figure 13.6:** Drawing by Junius Bird. Courtesy of The American Museum of Natural History. **Figure 13.7:** Teiwes, Arizona State Museum. **Figure 13.9:** Rawlings, Robert Harding. **Figure 13.10:** Courtesy of the Louisiana Office of State Parks. **Figure 13.11:** The Smithsonian Museum of the American Indian. **Figure 13.12a:** Courtesy of the Werner Forman Archive Limited. **Figure 13.12b:** Field Museum of Natural History (Neg. #90925), Chicago. **Figure 13.12c:** Courtesy of the Werner Forman Archive Limited. **Figure 13.13a:** Artist's reconstruction by William Iseminger. Photograph courtesy of Cahokia Mounds State Historic Site. **Figure 13.13b:** Courtesy of Cahokia Mounds State Historic Site.

CHAPTER 14

Figure 14.2: Adapted from *Physical Anthropology and Archaeology* by Clifford J. Jolly and Fred Plog. Copyright © 1976 by Alfred A. Knopf, Inc. Reprinted by permission of Alfred A. Knopf, Inc. **Figure 14.3:** From *The Rise of Civilization: From Early Farmers to Urban Society in the Ancient Near East* by Charles Redman. W. H. Freeman and Company. Copyright © 1978. Reprinted by permission.

CHAPTER 15

Figure 15.2: Courtesy of the Oriental Institute, University of Chicago. **Figure 15.3:** Fotoarchiv Hirmer Verlag München. **Figure 15.4 top:** From *Early Mesopotamia and Iran* by Max E. Mallowan. Thames and Hudson Ltd., London. **Figure 15.4 bottom:** Fotoarchiv Hirmer Verlag München. **Figure 15.5:** From Samuel Noah Kramer, "The Sumerians," *Scientific American,* October 1957. Reprinted with permission of W. H. Freeman and Company. Copyright © 1957 by Scientific American, Inc. All rights reserved. **Figure 15.6:** Courtesy of The University Museum, University of Pennsylvania.

CHAPTER 16

Figure 16.3: © George Holton, Photo Researchers. **Figure 16.4:** Michael Holford, London. **Figure 16.5:** All rights reserved, The Metropolitan Museum of Art. **Figure 16.6:** © 1981 Bernheim, Woodfin Camp. **Figure 16.7:** Werner Forman Archive, Art Resource. **Figure 16.9:** © 1981, Roderick J. McIntosh. **Figure 16.10:** Courtesy of the Rhodesian National Tourist Board.

CHAPTER 17

Figure 17.2: Courtesy of the Winchester Excavations Committee, Winchester, England. **Figure 17.3:** Roger-Viollet Documentation Generale Photographique, Paris. **Figure 17.5:** G. Possehl, The University Museum, University of Pennsylvania. **Figure 17.7:** Courtesy of the University Museum, The University of Pennsylvania. **Figure 17.8:** Robert Harding.

CHAPTER 18

Figure 18.2: Peabody Museum, Harvard University, © President & Fellows of Harvard College. Photo by Hillel Burger #N28172 © 1978. **Figure 18.4:** Courtesy of Smithsonian Institution. **Figure 18.5:** The China Friendship Society: from Grahame Clark, *World Prehistory,* 3rd edition, © 1977 Cambridge University Press.

CHAPTER 19

Figure 19.2 left: From *Ancient Europe* by Stuart Piggott, with permission of Edinburgh University Press. Copyright © Stuart Piggott, 1965. **Figure 19.2 right:** Reproduced by Courtesy of the Trustees of The British Museum. **Figure 19.4:** Donald A. Frey, Institute of Nautical Archaeology. **Figure 19.5:** Ekdotike Anthenon S. A. Athens. **Figure 19.6:** Fotoarchiv Hirmer Verlag München. **Figure 19.11:** From *Ancient Europe* by Stuart Piggott, with permission of Edinburgh University Press. Copyright © Stuart Piggott, 1965. **Figure 19.12:** Adapted from *Writing* by David Diringer, with permission of Thames and Hudson Ltd., London © David Diringer, 1962.

CHAPTER 20

Figure 20.1: From *Ancient Europe* by Stuart Piggott, with permission of Edinburgh University Press. Copyright © Stuart Piggott, 1965. **Figure 20.2:** From *Ancient Europe* by Stuart Piggott, with permission of Edinburgh University Press. Copyright © Stuart Piggott, 1965. **Figure 20.3:** Courtesy of the Ashmolean Museum. **Figure 20.4:** From R. F. Tylecote in *The Prehistory of Metallurgy in the British Isles,* 1986. Reprinted by permission of R. F. Tylecote. **Figure 20.6:** Henle, Monkmeyer Press Photo. **Figure 20.7:** Coles, Byron, and Coles, John, *People of the Wetlands,* Thames and Hudson Ltd., 1989. **Figure 20.8:** From *Ancient Europe* by Stuart Piggott, with permission of Edinburgh University Press. Copyright © Stuart Piggott, 1965. **Figure 20.11:** Reprinted courtesy of the Trustees of The British Museum. **Figure 21.2:** Courtesy of Franklin Graham. **Figure 21.3:** From Gordon Willey, *An Introduction to American Archeology, Vol. I: North and Middle America.* © 1966. Reprinted by permission of the author and Prentice Hall, Inc., Englewood Cliffs, N.J.

CHAPTER 21

Figure 21.4: From Gordon Willey, *An Introduction to American Archeology, Vol. I: North and Middle America.* © 1966. Reprinted by permission of the author and Prentice Hall, Inc., Englewood Cliffs, N.J. **Figure 21.5:** From Robert D. Drennan, "Contextual Analysis of Ritual Paraphernalia from Formative Oaxaca," in Kent V. Flannery (ed.), *The Early Mesoamerican Village* (Orlando, Fla.: Academic Press, 1976). Reprinted by permission of the author and the publisher. **Figure 21.6:** Robert Harding. **Figure 21.7:** © Muller, Woodfin Camp. **Figure 21.8:** Sabloff, Jeremy A., *The Cities of Ancient Mexico,* Thames and Hudson Ltd., 1989. **Figure 21.9 photo:** Copyright © Project El Mirador. **Figure 21.9 drawing:** Copyright © Richard Hansen. **Figure 21.10:** Courtesy of Smithsonian Institution, National Anthropological Archives. **Figure 21.11:** Photo Researchers/Carl Frank. **Figure 21.12:** From Linda Schele and David Freidel, *A Forest of Kings.* New York: William Morrow, Fig. 6.7. Copyright © 1990 by Linda Schele and David Freidel. Used by permission of William Morrow and Company, Inc./Publishers, New York. **Figure 21.13:** From Linda Schele and David Freidel, *A Forest of Kings.* New York: William Morrow, Fig. 7.8. Copyright © 1990 by Linda Schele and David Freidel. Used by permission of William Morrow and Company, Inc./Publishers, New York. **Figure 21.14:** Peabody Museum, Harvard University © President and Fellows of Harvard College. Neg. #21622 F. P. Orchard © 1953. **Figure 21.15:** Courtesy of Smithsonian Institution. **Figure 21.16:** Lesley Newhart. **Figure 21.17a:** Sabloff, Jeremy A., *The Cities of Ancient Mexico,* Thames and Hudson Ltd., 1989. **Figure 21.17b:** Rennie, Robert Harding. **Figure 21.18:** The American Museum of Natural History. **Figure 21.19:** Codex Magliabecchi, Photo by John Freeman, © British Museum.

CHAPTER 22

Figure 22.2: Photo by Jeffery Quilter. **Figure 22.3 left:** Courtesy Gordon Willey. **Figure 22.3 right:** Courtesy of Franklin Graham. **Figure 22.4:** Anne Paul/Earthwatch.

INDEX

• • •

Note: An italicized page number indicates a page on which an illustration appears.